RÉSUMÉS IN CYBERSPACE

Your Complete Guide to a Computerized Job Search

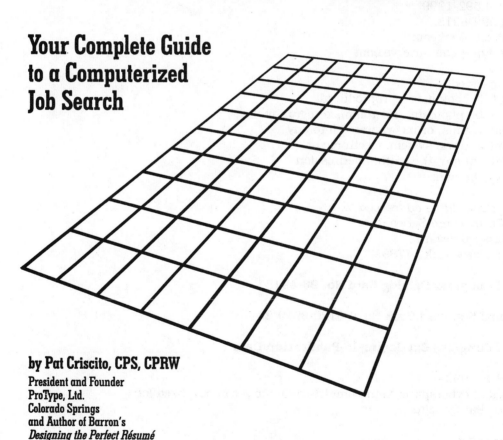

by Pat Criscito, CPS, CPRW

President and Founder
ProType, Ltd.
Colorado Springs
and Author of Barron's
Designing the Perfect Résumé

BARRON'S

© Copyright 1997 by Pat Criscito
ProType, Ltd.
Post Office Box 49552
Colorado Springs, Colorado 80949
Phone: (719) 592-1999
Fax: (719) 598-8918
E-mail: criscito@aol.com
E-mail: protype@compuserve.com

All inquiries should be addressed to:
Barron's Educational Series, Inc.
250 Wireless Boulevard
Hauppauge, New York 11788

Library of Congress Catalog Card No. 96-49151

International Standard Book No. 0-8120-9919-2

Library of Congress Cataloging-in-Publication Data

Criscito, Pat. 1953–
    Résumés in cyberspace: Your complete guide to a computerized job search / by Pat Criscito.
        p. cm.
    Includes index.
    ISBN 0-8120-9919-2
    1. Résumés (Employment)—Data processing. 2. Job hunting—Data processing. 3. Internet (Computer network) I. Title
HF5383.C744 1997
650.14'0285—dc21   96-49151
                                       CIP

PRINTED IN THE UNITED STATES OF AMERICA
9 8 7 6 5 4 3 2 1

Dedicated

To Mike

Contents

Page

Preface vii

Acknowledgements ix

1   *What Is an Electronic Résumé?* 1

    The Scannable Résumé 2
    The E-mailable Résumé 3
    The Multimedia Résumé for Your Home Page 4
    The Paper Résumé Is NOT Dead! 4
    Sample Résumés 6
    Some Options 10

2   *How to Write the Perfect Electronic Résumé* 11

    Step-by-Step Writing Process 11
    Creating an ASCII Text File 20
    Some Don'ts 22
    Sample Résumés 23
    Power Verbs 28
    Keywords 31

3   *The Journey of the Scannable Résumé* 37

    Optical Character Recognition (OCR) 37
    Faxed Résumés That Never See Paper 39
    Applicant Tracking Systems 40
    Which Companies Scan Résumés? 42

4   *Designing the Perfect Scannable Résumé* 49

    The Complete Guide to Style, Fonts, Paper, and so on ... 49
    Sample Scannable Résumés 56

5   *Designing the Perfect E-mailable Résumé* 73

    What Is E-mail? 73
    A Word About Confidentiality 78
    The Equipment and Software You Need 79
    How to Find E-mail Addresses 81
    Steps for Creating an ASCII Text File of Your Résumé ... 82
    Sample E-mailable Résumés 85
    Sending a Binary File 97
    How to E-mail Your Résumé Directly to a Company's Recruiter .. 98

6 **Using the Internet in Your Job Search** 99

What Is the Internet? 99

What Is the World Wide Web? 101

What Is Telnet? 103

What Are Newsgroups (Usenet)? 104

What Is a Mailing List? 114

How to Post Your Résumé to the Internet 119

Posting Your Résumé Directly to a Company's Home Page 121

Résumé Databases and Job Banks 151

Career-related Internet Sites 156

7 **Online Services and Your Job Search** 229

America Online 230

CompuServe 231

Delphi 232

GEnie 232

Microsoft Network 233

Prodigy 234

8 **Using a BBS in Your Job Search** 235

What Is a Bulletin Board Service? 235

How to Find a BBS That Meets Your Needs 235

How to Access a BBS 236

Career-related Bulletin Board Services 237

9 **Creating a Home Page for Your Résumé** 251

Why Create a Home Page for Your Résumé? 251

How to Create a Home Page 251

Adding Multimedia to Your Résumé 258

Where and How to Upload Your Home Page 260

Getting the Word Out 263

10 **Into the Future** 265

The Electronic Revolution Isn't Over Yet 265

How to Keep Up with the Times 265

Strategies for Finding New Online Resources 266

Using Search Engines to Research Potential Employers 273

Colleges and Your Electronic Job Search 274

Glossary: The Terms You Need to Know 281

Appendix: Alphabetical Listing of URLs 287

Index 317

Preface

The purpose of this book is to give you the skills you need to add an electronic dimension to your résumé and to help you step boldly into the computerized world of today's new job search. It is devoted to teaching you, in easy-to-understand language, how to write and design your résumé for use in cyberspace.

It will walk you through the basics of understanding the technology and then give you the resources you need to take full advantage of the Internet. You will learn not just how to write and design the perfect electronic résumé but also how and where to post it on the Internet, newsgroups, bulletin board services, and online services. This book lists thousands of Internet addresses where employers post job openings and accept résumés online. Each chapter gives you ideas for using the Internet and commercial online services to make networking contacts and to research potential employers.

You will also learn how to design a paper résumé that will make it through the scanning process without becoming a jumble of incomprehensible words, increasing your chances of popping to the top in a keyword search. The listing of companies that scan résumés will help you decide whether creating a scannable résumé is a necessity for you, and the insights into how companies use these applicant tracking systems will forever change the way you search for a job.

When you are finished with this book, you will have an advantage over your competition in today's tight job market.

■ Overview

Résumés in Cyberspace is logically organized to take you step by step through the process of writing, designing, and then using the perfect electronic résumé. The first four chapters help you create a scannable paper résumé that can then be turned into an electronic version for e-mail or posting on the Internet.

Once you have written and designed both your paper and electronic résumés, the book walks you through the process of understanding the technology of the Internet, e-mail, newsgroups, bulletin board services, and commercial online services. In chapters 5 through 8, there are extensive listings of online resources where you can place your résumé or search for job openings. These resources are categorized by industry and type so you don't waste time wading through hundreds of addresses that would be useless in your own personal job search. All of the online addresses (Universal Resource Locators) have been researched to ensure they are relevant and as current as the evolving nature of the Internet will allow.

In Chapter 9, you will discover whether a home page is a good place for your résumé online and if you could benefit from a multimedia résumé. Then you will learn how to create a home page résumé, how to make it multimedia, where to place it on the Internet, and how to get the word out to potential employers that you are there.

Finally, you will learn how to keep up with the times by using search engines and gophers to find new online resources and potential employers. Chapter 10 also shows you how colleges and universities can help you in your job search and lists Internet addresses for hundreds of career service centers around the world.

The Glossary makes the technical terms discussed in the book easier to understand and the Appendix lists alphabetically all of the URLs mentioned in the book. The Index will help you locate all the key concepts discussed and every job title covered in the sample résumés.

This comprehensive resource is the most user-friendly guide to job hunting in cyberspace today. All you need is a computer, a modem, and this essential guide to:

- Learn the basics of the Internet and e-mail.
- Use the power of the Internet to find your next job.
- Search the most current job banks and tap into thousands of job openings around the world.
- Access listings of thousands of current Internet resources with their addresses.
- Discover which career-related services are available from commercial online services like CompuServe, America Online, Prodigy, Delphi, GEnie, and others.
- Design an attention-getting electronic résumé and then post it on the Internet, online services, and bulletin board services.
- Create your own home page and multimedia résumé on the World Wide Web.
- Use online resources to network and find job leads.
- Research potential employers before the interview.
- Utilize strategies for keeping up with the times.

■ *About the Author*

Pat Criscito is a Certified Professional Résumé Writer with more than 25 years of experience and résumé clients in 42 different countries. Pat is also the author of Barron's *Designing the Perfect Résumé* (a comprehensive idea book for designing your paper résumé) and guest journalist for newspapers and magazines nation-wide. As the president and founder of ProType, Ltd., in Colorado Springs, she writes more than 1,000 résumés a year and speaks nationally on the subject, appearing regularly at universities and on television and radio.

Acknowledgments

My undying gratitude to Don Desjardins, Recruiting Manager for MCI Telecommunications Corporation and the person responsible for integrating MCI's Internet home page, e-mail, scanned résumé database, and applicant tracking system into a single database of more than 200,000 résumés. His insights into the world of large companies, and experience as a private recruiter before MCI, were invaluable to the research of this book.

Thank you to Michael Forrest, former Executive Director of the National Association of Colleges and Employers, for his research into how college placement offices and human resource managers use cyberspace to place and recruit workers. Michael is now the Chief Executive Officer of *careerpath.com*, one of the hottest career-related sites on the Internet.

I am very grateful to Resumix, Inc., and Restrac, Inc., the manufacturers of two of the most popular software programs for scanning résumés and tracking applicants. Their public relations and marketing staff were exceptionally helpful in the research of this book. They spent hours answering my questions and sent screen shots of their software to help my readers visualize the technology of computerized applicant tracking systems. Resumix set up interviews with their software engineers and arranged for me to visit with their clients to get hands-on experience with the scanning process, for which I am more than appreciative.

To all those human resource managers, recruiters, and directors of university career centers who willingly gave their time to complete the surveys and interviews that served as the basis for much of the data and conclusions in this book, thank you.

A special thank you to Jefferson Wood for lending his illustrative talents to the book. A graduate of the Savannah College of Art and Design, Jeff did a great job of adding a warm, almost Norman Rockwell, feel to the often cold subject of computer technology.

Thank you to Linda Turner, my editor at Barron's, for her patience and insights, which made this book even better.

And last, but not least, to Dana Pipkins, my right hand since 1989. I couldn't have done it without her.

1 What Is An Electronic Résumé?

Millions of paper résumés are distributed every day by anxious job seekers looking for the perfect job to fulfill their lives. These résumés serve one purpose—to entice potential employers to open their doors for an interview. Résumés are marketing tools designed to give job seekers an opportunity to sell themselves in person. Electronic résumés serve the same purpose as printed résumés but using a different medium—computers. They are a reflection of our changing times. Just a few years ago, finding your dream job depended on who you knew, how good your résumé was, and how many newspapers you were willing to thumb through. Today, however, the rules are different.

Dick Knowdell, President of Career Research and Testing, draws some interesting word pictures of how job hunting has changed in the last 40 years. In the 1950s, your career was like a train. You got on the, let's say, "Accounting Train" right out of school and stayed on it until you reached your destination. Someone else was driving and there was little opportunity to change trains. At the end of the track, you simply stepped off the train with your gold watch and retired. In the 1960s and 1970s, your career became more like a bus. It became acceptable to get on the "Accounting Bus" and then transfer to the "Sales Bus" somewhere down the road. However, someone else was still driving. Today, your career is more like an ATV (all-terrain vehicle). You are definitely the driver but you often don't know your destination at the beginning. Your career path can change rapidly as you careen from one obstacle to another—downsizing, subcontracting, re-engineering, and so on. Your career choice is now up to you, and it is an ongoing process of change and adaptation.

David Lynch and Del Jones, in an article in *USA Today* stated, "If the job markets of the 21st century are going to be in constant flux, employers and employees are going to need better ways to find each other than the local help-wanted ads. As good jobs become more technical and more specialized, companies increasingly will recruit nationally—or even globally—not locally." Lynch and Jones suggest that the Internet is creating a nationwide job network that will require a new set of job hunting skills in the 21st century.

In order to manage your career today, you need a wide variety of tools, and one of those tools is your résumé. Just a few short years ago, that meant a simple paper document that listed your work experience, accomplishments, education, and a few other details. Today, it means a paper résumé plus an electronic version that can be left in cyberspace to work for you 24 hours a day, just in case.

So, just what is an electronic résumé? There are actually three kinds of electronic résumés. The first kind of electronic résumé is a paper résumé that becomes an electronic version against your will when it is scanned into a computer. Second is a generic computer file that you create especially to send through cyberspace without ever printing it onto paper—an e-mailable version. And the third is a multimedia résumé that is given a home page at a fixed location on the Internet for anyone to visit at will. Let's look at each kind in turn.

■ *The Scannable Résumé*

With this first kind of electronic résumé, you innocently create a handsome paper résumé and mail it to a potential employer. Without your knowing it, that employer has implemented a computerized system for scanning résumés as they arrive in the human resource department. Instead of a human being reading your résumé and deciding how best to forward it along or file it, a clerk sets your résumé on the glass of a scanner bed and the black dots of ink are turned into words in a computer. The paper is then either filed or thrown away.

Also falling into this class is your paper résumé when it is faxed to a potential employer. Instead of receiving a printout of your résumé, a potential employer allows your fax to sit in a computer's queue until such time as a clerk can verify and summarize the information into the same computerized database where the scanned paper résumés have been stored.

According to *U.S. News & World Report*, more than 1,000 unsolicited résumés arrive every week at most Fortune 500 companies, and before the days of applicant tracking systems and résumé scanning, 80 percent were thrown out after a quick review. It was simply impossible to keep track of that much paper. Today, as companies downsize and human resource departments become smaller, it is even more important to manage the job application and screening processes in an efficient manner.

Recent sources indicate that nearly half of all mid-sized companies and almost all large companies are scanning résumés and using computerized applicant tracking systems. Smaller companies turn to service bureaus—such as kiNexus, SkillSearch, Job Bank USA, and Career Placement Registry—and recruiters to find potential employees for them, and these same service bureaus and recruiters scan résumés.

In the future, as more and more companies establish a presence on the Internet and open up their computer databases to e-mailed résumés, the scanability of your résumé will become less of an issue. When you e-mail your résumé directly to a company, you have total control over whether or not your information is correct. You are not at the whim of a scanner's ability to read your font or formatting. However, companies that scan résumés will continue to use their investment in this technology as long as they receive enough paper résumés to make the process worthwhile, so making your paper résumé scanner friendly will continue to be important.

■ *The E-mailable Résumé*

When you type words onto a computer screen in a word processing program, you are creating what is called a *file* or *document*. When you save that file, it is saved with special formatting codes like fonts, margins, tab settings, and so on, even if you didn't add these codes. Each word processing software (WordPerfect, Microsoft Word, etc.) saves its files in its own native format, making the file readable by anyone else with the same software or with some other software that can convert that file to its own native format.

Only by choosing to save the document as a generic ASCII text file can your document be read by anyone, regardless of the word processing software he or she is using. This is the type of file you must create in order to send your résumé via e-mail, and you will find complete instructions for creating this file in Chapter 5. An ASCII text file is simply words—no pictures, no fonts, no graphics—just plain words. If you print this text, it looks very boring, but all the words are there that describe your life history, just like in the handsome paper résumé you created to mail to a potential employer. This computer file can be sent to a potential employer in one of two ways.

First, you can send the file directly to a company's recruiters via an e-mail address, if you can get that address. Second, you can use this file to post your résumé onto the Internet (to the home page of a company, to a job bank in answer to an online job posting, or to a newsgroup), an online service (like CompuServe or America Online), or a bulletin board service. In any case, the file ends up in the same type of computerized database where the scanned paper résumés have been stored.

There are many advantages to e-mailed résumés. First, they save you money over conventional mailing of a paper copy of your résumé with a cover letter, envelope, and postage. Second, they are faster, getting to a potential employer in only seconds instead of days. You also make a powerful first impression when you understand the technology enough to e-mail your résumé. And, lastly, your résumé will be accessible every time the hiring manager searches the résumé database using keywords. Your résumé will never again be relegated to languishing in a dusty filing cabinet.

■ *The Multimedia Résumé for Your Home Page*

If you are a computer programmer, home page developer, graphics designer, artist, sculptor, actor, model, animator, cartoonist, or anyone who would benefit by the photographs, graphics, animation, sound, color, or movement inherent in a multimedia résumé, then this résumé is for you. Chapter 9 will give you everything you need to know to take full advantage of this medium to sell your special abilities.

For most people, however, a multimedia résumé and home page on the Internet can be an expensive luxury. In today's harried world, most recruiters and hiring managers have so little time to read résumés that they are turning to scanned résumés and applicant tracking systems to lighten their load. They don't have the time to search for and then spend 15 minutes clicking their way through a multimedia presentation of someone's qualifications, either online at your home page or on a disk you might mail to them, so I wouldn't recommend spending much money having a home page developed or paying for server space to keep it online. However . . . if it's free, it never hurts to add this networking tool to your job search. You might be that one in a million that gets directly to the decision maker when he or she is at home playing on the Internet and happens to make direct contact with your résumé!

Most Internet service providers and online services provide some space on their computers for subscribers' own home pages at no extra charge. For instance, America Online allows its subscribers two megabytes of space in *My Place* to establish a personal home page. Your URL (Universal Resource Locator—pronounced "earl") is your home page address and would look something like this: *http://members.aol.com/criscito*. Granted, you don't have your own domain name *(http://pat@criscito.com)*, but it's FREE!

A word of caution about photographs and video, which are usually a part of the multimedia résumé. Human resource professionals try very hard not to discriminate, and a photograph that discloses your sex, race, or age makes it very difficult for them not to be biased. Hiring managers today would just as soon avoid even the hint of discrimination, so they may not view a multimedia résumé mailed to them on a disk for that very reason. Unless your appearance is a bona fide occupational qualification for a job (modeling, television, acting, etc.), then avoid using your photograph on any résumé.

■ *The Paper Résumé Is NOT Dead!*

This brave new world of computers and the Internet will coexist with the more traditional world of paper and human networking contacts forever. Therefore, you should think about having two résumés, one for human eyes and one for computer eyes.

Your paper résumé for human eyes should be one page (no more than two, unless you are in the medical or academic fields and need a curriculum vitae— *course of one's life*) and designed in such a way that it is appealing to a human reader, both in words and in appearance (see the sample on page 6, which is not scannable because of its reverse box and unusual typeface). This is the résumé you will carry to an interview or mail to a small- or medium-sized company, since only large companies have the need and budget (the software and hardware can cost anywhere from $20,000 to $1 million) to process large volumes of résumés with a scanner. My companion book from Barron's, *Designing the Perfect Résumé*, can help you create the perfect paper résumé, so I won't go into a lot of detail here (available in bookstores across the country or by calling 1-800-446-2408).

If you are in a more creative industry where the chances of your résumé being scanned are extremely low, then you have some license to design your paper résumé with some imagination and you can *almost* forget about a résumé for computer eyes. You are not limited in font selection, margins, graphics, or style. For instance, if you are a cartoonist, you can scan cartoons onto your résumé. If you are an artist, use one of your paintings as a watermark in the background of your text (see the sample on page 7). Get creative. The chances that an art gallery will scan your résumé are nonexistent and it is your individuality that is your strongest selling point. This visual selling component of your résumé is really the determinant for choosing to create a multimedia résumé for your home page on the Internet instead of worrying about whether your paper résumé will scan (see Chapter 9).

On the other hand, if you are a computer programmer and will be sending your résumé to both small companies and to a Fortune 500 company like MCI, then you had better be certain your paper résumé will not only look good but also scan perfectly. Chapter 4 will cover all the basics of how to design a paper résumé that does just that. The résumé on page 8 is a good example of a handsome, yet scannable, résumé.

1234 Westminster Boulevard #123
Arvada, Colorado 80003
Phone: (303) 555-1234

OBJECTIVE

A challenging opportunity in corporate or industrial training.

SUMMARY OF QUALIFICATIONS

- Five years of experience as an instructor in both the corporate and public sectors.
- Strong background in developing company training programs and computer-based instruction.
- Skilled in organization, leadership, management, and problem solving.
- Effective team player with proven interpersonal, communication, and presentation skills.
- Comfortable with IBM PCs, Windows, MS Word, Excel, PowerPoint, and telecommunications software.
- Certifications: Indiana Teaching Certificate.

PROFESSIONAL EXPERIENCE

CONFERTECH INTERNATIONAL, Westminster, Colorado   1993 – Present
Corporate Instructor (1994 – Present)
- Administer professional development, supervisory, and software training programs in three locations.
- Conduct on-site visits to monitor operations and compliance with policies and procedures.
- Act as liaison between managers, instructors, supervisors, and trainees.
- Develop learning objectives for in-house computer training programs and devise instructional materials.
- Make presentations, including lectures, seminars, and orientations for groups of six to ten employees.
- Devise evaluation instruments to analyze performance; institute program changes to meet training goals.
- Wrote and designed computer-based training manuals, user materials, and training publications.

Operations Manager (1993 – 1994)
- Managed the operations of a 300-employee department.
- Administered all policy and procedure documentation and ensured consistency with corporate objectives and training efforts.
- Created, implemented, and monitored personnel training programs.
- Developed new guidelines for the call center.

DICKINSON MIDDLE SCHOOL, South Bend, Indiana   1992
Teacher
- Instructed 25 junior high school students in after-school programs.

PROJECT HEAD START, Bloomington, Indiana   1991
Teacher
- Taught basic skills to preschool children.

EDUCATION

BACHELOR OF SCIENCE, Indiana University, Bloomington, Indiana   1992
- Major in Education

CONTINUING EDUCATION, University of Colorado, Denver, Colorado   1996 – Present
- Studies toward a Master of Arts in Instructional Technology

AFFILIATIONS

- International Society of Performance Improvement
- American Society of Training Development

Not Scannable

12345 Northface Court
Colorado Springs, Colorado 80919
Phone: (719) 555-1234

Education

BACHELOR OF ARTS (1994–1996)
Whittier College, Whittier, California
- Studio arts major
- Emphasis in oil painting

DENMARK INTERNATIONAL STUDIES (1995)
Copenhagen, Denmark
- Studied abroad for a semester

UNIVERSITY OF NORTHERN COLORADO (1992–1994)
Greeley, Colorado

SAVANNAH COLLEGE OF ART AND DESIGN (1990–1991)
Savannah, Georgia

Exhibitions

- Two paintings chosen for the Whittier College "Literary Review" (1996)
- Two works selected for display at the Whittier College "Senior Art Exhibit" (1996)
- Abstract oil painting exhibited for two months at Whittier College Library (1996)
- Hired to paint a mural for a Whittier College dormitory (1994)
- Designed a t-shirt print for a fraternity fund raiser (1995)
- Selected to paint a homecoming parade float for the University of Northern Colorado radio station (1992)

Other Experience

RECEPTIONIST (1996), Whittier College Computer Center, Whittier, California
- Provided customer service and answered telephones.

COOK (Summers 1993–1995), Old Chicago's Pizza, Colorado Springs, Colorado
- Prepared food (pizza, pasta, dough).
- Opened and closed the pizza line and pasta bar.

CUSTOMER SERVICE (1993), Pudge Brothers', Greeley, Colorado
- Managed the cash register and assisted customers in a newly opened pizza delivery restaurant.

Portfolio

Available upon request

SCANS PERFECTLY

QUALIFICATIONS

- Demonstrated success in management positions for more than 22 years.
- Definitive abilities in leadership, planning, organization, and decision making.
- Well organized, efficient administrator capable of shouldering responsibility and using initiative to successfully bring a project to conclusion within budget.
- Skilled in discovering resourceful and enterprising solutions to problems.
- Steady, focused team player committed to professionalism and integrity.

EXPERIENCE
Management

- Managed the daily operations of a land development company and its 1600-acre master planned community, including contract negotiation and administration, transaction closings, architectural review of plans, and construction management.
- Created a management and financial partnership with the city for infrastructure development.
- Coordinated with legal counsel, co-brokers, builder sales teams, title insurance firms, and appraisers.
- Served as liaison with lenders, city government, and engineering and land planning firms.

Marketing

- Conceptualized land use and marketed major land assets to builders, developers, and individuals.
- Organized and marketed two of the most successful parades of homes ever conducted in the region.

Supervision

- Supervised both office and field personnel and administered insurance and employee benefit programs.
- Provided direction to subcontractors for planning, zoning, engineering, and infrastucture construction.

Financial

- Generated budgets and forecasts for partners and other senior management.
- Developed market data files and statistical tracking strategies that supported the internal financing requirements of the development together with the marketing strategies of the firm.
- Ensured compliance with governmental regulations and property tax obligations.

Consulting

- Provided management guidance and support for a bankrupt wholesale floral enterprise; directed the filing of Chapter 11 petition for the company.
- Initiated administrative cost reduction measures, inventory control, and product purchasing disciplines.
- Sold unprofitable operations and property; instituted effective management and accounting systems.
- Reduced accounts receivable, restaffed key positions, restructured the financial obligations, and provided the basis for a reorganization plan acceptable to the bankruptcy court.

WORK HISTORY

Business Manager, Hausman Management Corporation, Colorado Springs, Colorado, 1992 – Present
Real Estate Consultant, Independent Broker, Colorado Springs, Colorado, 1991 – 1992
Management Consultant, RF Wholesale, Las Vegas, Nevada, 1990 – 1991
Business Manager, Hausman Management Corporation, Colorado Springs, Colorado, 1983 – 1990
Office Manager, Jones-Healy, Inc., Pueblo, Colorado, 1969 – 1983

EDUCATION

BACHELOR OF SCIENCE, 1966
California State Polytechnic College, San Luis Obispo, California
Colorado State University, Fort Collins, Colorado

LICENSES

Colorado Real Estate Broker, 1973 – present

AFFILIATIONS

- Land Developer Representative on Joint City/County Drainage Board (appointed by City Council of Colorado Springs and El Paso County Board of Commissioners), 1986 – 1990
- Colorado Springs Board of Realtors and Home Builders Association, 1983
- Director, Pueblo Association of Home Builders, 1981
- Advisory Board Member, University of Southern Colorado College for Community Services, 1976
- Officer and Director, Pueblo Board of Realtors, 1975
- Instructor, University of Colorado Real Estate Certificate Program, 1974

ADDRESS

1234 Del Oro Circle, Colorado Springs, Colorado 80919   (719) 555-1234

SCANS PERFECTLY
1234 Del Oro Circle, Colorado Springs, Colorado 80919
(719) 555-1234

QUALIFICATIONS

Demonstrated success in management positions for more than 22 years. Definitive abilities in leadership, planning, organization, and decision making. Well organized, efficient administrator capable of shouldering responsibility and using initiative to successfully bring a project to conclusion within budget. Skilled in discovering resourceful and enterprising solutions to problems. Steady, focused team player committed to professionalism and integrity.

EXPERIENCE

Management: Managed the daily operations of a land development company and its 1600-acre master planned community, including contract negotiation and administration, transaction closings, architectural review of plans, and construction management. Created a management and financial partnership with the city for infrastructure development. Coordinated with legal counsel, co-brokers, builder sales teams, title insurance firms, and appraisers. Served as liaison with lenders, city government, and engineering and land planning firms.

Marketing: Conceptualized land use and marketed major land assets to builders, developers, and individuals. Organized and marketed two of the most successful parade of homes ever conducted in the region.

Supervision: Supervised both office and field personnel and administered insurance and employee benefit programs. Provided direction to subcontractors for planning, zoning, engineering, and infrastucture construction.

Financial: Generated budgets and forecasts for partners and other senior management. Developed market data files and statistical tracking strategies that supported the internal financing requirements of the development together with the marketing strategies of the firm. Ensured compliance with governmental regulations and property tax obligations.

Consulting: Provided management guidance and support for a bankrupt wholesale floral enterprise; directed the filing of Chapter 11 petition for the company. Initiated administrative cost reduction measures, inventory control, and product purchasing disciplines. Sold unprofitable operations and property; instituted effective management and accounting systems. Reduced accounts receivable, restaffed key positions, restructured the financial obligations, and provided the basis for a reorganization plan acceptable to the bankruptcy court.

WORK HISTORY
Business Manager, Hausman Management Corporation, Colorado Springs, CO, 1992 - Present
Real Estate Consultant, Independent Broker, Colorado Springs, CO, 1991 - 1992
Management Consultant, RF Wholesale, Las Vegas, NV, 1990 - 1991
Business Manager, Hausman Management Corporation, Colorado Springs, CO, 1983 - 1990
Office Manager, Jones-Healy, Inc., Pueblo, CO, 1969 - 1983

EDUCATION
Bachelor of Science, 1966
California State Polytechnic College, San Luis Obispo, California
Colorado State University, Fort Collins, Colorado

LICENSES
Colorado Real Estate Broker, 1973 - present

AFFILIATIONS
Land Developer Representative on Joint City/County Drainage Board (appointed by City Council of Colorado Springs and El Paso County Board of Commissioners), 1986 - 1990
Colorado Springs Board of Realtors and Home Builders Association, 1983
Director, Pueblo Association of Home Builders, 1981
Advisory Board Member, University of Southern Colorado Community Services, 1976
Officer and Director, Pueblo Board of Realtors, 1975
Instructor, University of Colorado Real Estate Certificate Program, 1974

■ Some Options

What if you are uncertain whether your résumé will scan well and you have learned from Chapter 3 of this book that the company to which you are sending your résumé does, in fact, scan every paper résumé it receives? What do you do? Well, you can always take the computer file of your paper résumé, strip it of all its fancy formatting codes, add some white space to help define the sections, print it on a nice white bond paper (see the sample on page 9), and send it along with your handsome résumé. That way the company can decide which résumé will suit its purposes best and you haven't lost anything. This version of your résumé is now almost ready to save as an ASCII text file from your word processor (see Chapter 5 for the details of creating this ASCII file) for transmission directly through cyberspace via e-mail or the Internet.

Once your résumé has entered the electronic world, you immediately have an advantage over the paper résumé that is stored in a wall of filing cabinets waiting for a recruiter or clerk to remember it is there. Recruiters or hiring managers can now search through an entire database of computerized résumés in a matter of seconds, using keywords to narrow the search to those potential candidates who are the most qualified. It is those keywords that are the major difference between your paper résumé and your electronic version.

Let's talk now about writing the perfect résumé and how to use those keywords to your advantage. The next chapter will walk you through a step-by-step process for getting those keywords down on paper. When you are finished, you will have the perfect résumé for both cyberspace and the paper world.

2 How to Write the Perfect Electronic Résumé

Writing your résumé is one of the most difficult things you will ever do! You must turn your life history into a one-page, glittering advertisement that highlights all of your best attributes, and that's hard for most people. This chapter will develop a résumé for an experienced electrical engineer with a background in the support of complex computer networks. The finished résumé can be found on page 23.

■ Step-by-Step Writing Process

Using a twelve-step process to write your résumé will help you clarify your experience, accomplishments, skills, education, and other background information and make the job of condensing your life onto a sheet of paper a little easier.

❑ Step One—Focus

Decide what type of job you will be applying for and then write it at the top of a piece of paper. In the past, this objective did not have to become an actual part of your paper résumé. The cover letter was the best place to personalize your objective for each job opening.

However, electronic résumés are a little different. If your résumé is scanned into a computerized database, you have a 50-50 chance that your cover letter will be scanned, too. Without an objective on the résumé, you are at the whim of the scanner operator who must choose words to categorize your information in the applicant tracking software. Therefore, it is a good idea to put an objective statement at the top of an electronic résumé either as a separate objective section or as the first line of your profile section, which you will see in step twelve. After you have created your master résumé, it is possible to alter individual résumés with personalized objectives that reflect the actual job title for which you are applying. Just make sure that the rest of your information is still relevant to the new objective.

Never write an objective statement that is not precise. You should name the position you want so specifically that, if a janitor came by and knocked over all the stacks of sorted résumés on a hiring manager's desk, he could put yours back in its right stack without even thinking about it. That means saying, "A marketing management position with an aggressive international advertising agency" instead of "A position which utilizes my education and experience to mutual benefit."

❑ Step Two—Education

Under this objective, list any education or training that might relate. If you are a recent college graduate and have little relevant experience, then your education section will be placed at the top of your résumé. As you gain more experience, your education almost always gravitates to the bottom.

If you participated in college activities or received any honors or completed any notable projects that relate directly to your target job, this is the place to list them.

Listing high school education and activities on a résumé is only appropriate when you are under 20 and have no education or training beyond high school. Once you have completed either college courses or specialized technical training, drop your high school information.

Continuing education shows that you care about life-long learn-

Objective: An electrical engineering position utilizing an extensive background in the design and support of complex, large computer networks.

Objective: An electrical engineering position utilizing an extensive background in the design and support of complex, large computer networks.

Education:

1. Master of Science, Electrical Engineering (1989-90)
Air Force Institute of Technology,
Wright-Patterson AFB, Ohio
Concentration in Electro-Optics
2. Bachelor of Science, Electrical Engineering (1981-85)
United States Air Force Academy, Colorado
Concentration in Communications
3. Continuing Professional Education (1985-89)
Air Force Institute of Technology
Wright-Patterson AFB, Ohio
Digital Signal Processing, Fiber Optic Communications,
Local Area Networks, Electrical Power Distribution,
Spread Spectrum Communications, Optimizing . . . .

ing and self-development, so think about any relevant training since your formal education was completed. *Relevant* is the key word here. Always look at your résumé from the perspective of a potential employer. Don't waste space by listing training that is not directly or indirectly related to your target job.

❏ *Step Three—Job Descriptions*

Get your hands on a written description of the job you wish to obtain and any jobs you have held in the past. If you are presently employed, your human resource department is the first place to look. If not, then go to your local library and ask for a copy of *The Dictionary of Occupational Titles*. This industry standard reference guide offers two volumes of occupational titles and job descriptions for everything from Abalone Divers to Zoo Veterinarians (and thousands in between). Another resource available at your local library or college career center is *Job Scribe*, a computer software program with more than 3,000 job descriptions. Other places to look for job descriptions include your local government job service agencies, professional and technical organizations, head hunters (i.e., recruiters), and associates who work in the same field.

Make a copy of the applicable descriptions and then highlight the sentences that describe anything you have done in your past or present jobs. These job descriptions are important sources of keywords, so pay particular attention to nouns and phrases that you can incorporate into your own résumé.

❏ *Step Four—Your Jobs*

Starting with your present position, list the title of every job you have held on a separate sheet of paper, along with the name of the company, the city and state, and the years you worked there. You don't need to list addresses and zip codes, although you will need to know that information when it comes time to fill out an application.

You can list years only (1996 – present) or months and years (May 1996 – present), depending on your personality. People who are more detail oriented are usually more comfortable with a full accounting of their time. Listing years alone covers some gaps if you have worked in a position for less than a full year while the time period spans more than one calendar year. For instance, if you worked from September 1996 through May 1997, saying 1996 – 1997 certainly looks better.

From the perspective of recruiters and hiring managers, most don't care whether you list the months and years or list the years only. However, regardless of which method you choose, be consistent throughout your résumé. Don't use months some of the time and years alone somewhere else. Consistency of style is important on a résumé, since it is that consistency that makes your résumé neat, clean, and easy to read.

❏ *Step Five—Duties*

Under each job, make a list of your duties, incorporating phrases from the job description wherever they apply. You don't have to worry about making great sentences yet or narrowing down your list.

❏ *Step Six—Accomplishments*

When you are finished, go back to each job and think about what you might have done above and beyond the call of duty. Did you exceed sales quotas by 150 percent each month? Did you save the company $100,000 by developing a new procedure? Did you generate new product publicity in trade press? Write down any accomplishments that show potential employers what you can do for them. Quantify whenever possible. Numbers are always impressive.

United States Air Force (1985–Present)

Chief, Network Control Center, USAF Academy, CO

Managed an eight-person help desk to assist more than 9,000 customers with trouble shooting their own software problems or to assign technicians to correct the problems on site. Programmed hubs and routers; ran unshielded twisted pair and fiber optic cabling. Diagnosed client software and hardware problems. Used HP OpenView, Cabletron's LanView, for SNMP management of local area networks. Selected, trained, and supervised 27 civilian and military personnel with a wide range of responsibilities, including client configuration, network connectivity, and file server availability. Developed infrastructures for Banyan networks, VINES, TCP-IP to include remote, dial-in access via LanExpress. Maintained microcomputers, printers, and more than 90 file servers. Limited project costs to $250,000, while an alternative proposal was provided for $2,500,000.

❏ *Step Seven—Delete*

Now that you have the words on paper, go back to each list and think about which items are relevant to your target job. Cross out those things that don't relate, including entire jobs (like flipping hamburgers back in high school if you are now an electrical engineer with ten years of experience). Remember, your résumé is just an enticer, a way to get your foot in the door. It isn't intended to be all-inclusive. You can choose to go back only as far as your jobs relate to your present objective.

❏ *Step Eight—Sentences*

Make sentences of the duties you have listed under each job, combining related items to avoid short, choppy phrases. Never use personal pronouns in your résumé (I, my, me). Instead of saying, *"I planned, organized, and directed the timely and accurate production of code products with estimated annual revenues of $1 million,"* say, *"Planned, organized, and directed. . . ."* Using third person makes your sentences more powerful and attention grabbing.

Make your sentences positive, brief, and accurate. Since your ultimate goal is to get a human being to read your résumé, remember to structure the sentences so they are interesting to read. Use verbs at the beginning of each sentence (designed, supervised, managed, developed, formulated, and so on) to make them more powerful (see the list at the end of this chapter). Make certain each word means something and contributes to the quality of the sentence. If you find it difficult to write clear, concise sentences, take the information you have just written to a professional writer who can help you turn it into a winning résumé (preferably someone who is a Certified Professional Résumé Writer—CPRW).

❑ *Step Nine—Keywords*

In today's world of e-mailed and scannable résumés, make sure your sentences contain keywords. Keywords are the nouns or short phrases that describe your experience and education that might be used to find your résumé in a keyword search of a résumé database. They are the essential knowledge, abilities, and skills required to do your job. They are concrete descriptions like: C++, UNIX, fiber optic cable, network, project management, etc. Even well-known company names (AT&T, IBM, Hewlett-Packard, MCI) and universities (Harvard, Yale, SMU, SUNY, USC, Stanford, Tulane, Thunderbird) are sometimes used as keywords, especially when it is necessary to narrow down an initial search that calls up hundreds of résumés from a résumé database.

Acronyms and abbreviations here can either hurt you or help you, depending on how you use them. One example given to me by an engineer at Resumix was the abbreviation "IN." Think about it. "IN" could stand for *intelligent networks, Indiana,* or the word *in.* It is better to spell out the abbreviation if there could be any possible confusion. However, if a series of initials is so well known that it would be recognized by nearly everyone in your industry and would not likely be confused with a real word, then the keyword search will probably use those initials (i.e., IBM, CPA, UNIX). When in doubt, always spell it out at least one time on your résumé. A computer only needs to see the combination one time for it to be considered a "hit" in a keyword search.

Soft skills are often not included in search criteria, especially for very technical positions, although I have interviewed some companies that use them extensively for the initial selection of résumés for management positions. For instance, "communicate effectively," "self-motivated," "team player," and so on, are great for describing your abilities and are fine to include in your profile, but concentrate more on your hard skills, especially if you are in a high-tech field.

At the end of the chapter, you will find more examples of keywords for specific industries, although there is no such thing as a comprehensive listing of keywords for any single job. The computerized applicant tracking programs used by many companies allow the recruiter or hiring manager to personalize his or her list for each job opening, so it is an evolving process. You will never know whether you have listed absolutely every keyword possible, so focus instead on getting on paper as many related skills as possible, remembering to be absolutely honest and accurate.

The job description you found in step three is one of the most important sources for keywords. You can also be certain that nearly every noun and some adjectives in a job posting or advertisement will be keywords, so make sure you use those words somewhere in your résumé, using synonyms wherever you can. Make a list of the keywords you have determined are important for your particular job search and then list synonyms for those words. As you incorporate these words into the sentences of your résumé, check them off.

One caution. Always tell the truth. The minute a hiring manager speaks with you on the telephone or begins an interview, any exaggeration of the truth will become immediately apparent. It is a bad idea to say, "I don't have experience with WordPerfect computer software" just to get the words *WordPerfect* or *computer software* on paper so your résumé will pop up in a keyword search. In a cover letter, it might be appropriate to say that you "don't have five years of experience in marketing but can add two years of university training in the subject to three years of in-depth experience as a marketing assistant with Hewlett-Packard." That is legitimate reasoning, but anything more manipulative can be hazardous to your job search.

❏ *Step Ten—Rearrange*

You are almost done! Now, go back to the sentences you have written and think about their order of presentation. Put a number 1 by the most important description of what you did for each job. Then place a number 2 by the next most important duty or accomplishment, and so on until you have numbered each sentence. Again, think logically and from the perspective of a potential employer. Keep related items together so the reader doesn't jump from one concept to another. Make the thoughts flow smoothly.

United States Air Force (1985-Present)

Chief, Network Control Center, USAF Academy, CO

2) Managed an eight-person help desk to assist more than 9,000 customers with trouble shooting their own software problems or to assign technicians to correct the problems on site. 3) Programmed hubs and routers; ran unshielded twisted pair and fiber optic cabling. 7) Diagnosed client software and hardware problems. 6) Used HP OpenView, Cabletron's LanView, for SNMP management of local area networks. 1) Selected, trained, and supervised 27 civilian and military personnel with a wide range of responsibilities, including client configuration, network connectivity, and file server availability. 4) Developed infrastructures for Banyan networks, VINES, TCP-IP to include remote, dial-in access via LanExpress.

8) Maintained microcomputers, printers, and more than 90 file servers. 5) Limited project costs to $250,000, while an alternative proposal was provided for $2,500,000.

❏ *Step Eleven—Related Qualifications*

At the bottom of your résumé, think about anything else that might qualify you for your job objective. This includes licenses, certifications, affiliations, and sometimes even interests if they truly relate. For instance, if you want a job in sports marketing, stating on your résumé that you play tennis or are a triathlete would be an asset. In the case of the certified Banyan engineer on page 24, it is relevant that he has served as president of the board of directors of the Association of Banyan Users International and as vice president of the local Banyan Users Group in Colorado.

❑ Step Twelve—Profile

Last but not least, write four or five sentences that give an overview of your qualifications. This profile or qualifications summary should be placed at the beginning of your résumé. You can include some of your personal traits or special skills that might have been difficult to get across in your job descriptions.

Here is a sample profile section for the electrical engineering résumé we have been developing to this point. It is also acceptable to use a keyword summary that gives a "quick and dirty" look at your qualifications (like the sample on page 24). Although this type of "laundry list" isn't very interesting for a human being to read, some recruiters in high-tech industries like this list of terms

Qualifications:

Experienced electrical engineer with an extensive background in the design and support of complex, large computer networks with primary responsibility for an 8,000-user network.

Strong communication, leadership, management, and problem solving skills.

Dedicated professional who enjoys the challenge of solving computer problems.

Able to work with minimal supervision and as a cooperative team member.

Knowledge of DOS, Windows, MS Office Suite, FormFlow, C/C++ languages, among others.

because it gives them a quick overview of an applicant's skills. An experienced trial attorney with less technical skills might use something like the profile section on page 26.

Busy recruiters spend as little as ten seconds deciding whether to read a résumé from top to bottom. You will be lucky if the first third of your résumé gets read, whether it is an electronic résumé or a paper one, so make sure the information at the top entices the reader to read it all.

This profile section must be relevant to the type of job for which you are applying. It might be true that you are "compassionate," but will it help you get a job as a high-pressure salesperson? Write this profile from the perspective of a potential employer. What will convince this person to call you instead of someone else?

Another important reason for adding this profile section to your résumé is to ensure that the clerk who classifies your résumé into a category and summarizes your information into the applicant tracking software doesn't have to read your entire résumé and guess what words are important. Even companies that don't scan résumés or receive them through cyberspace (which includes most small and mid-sized companies) still have computerized systems for tracking résumés, so these words of advice apply to all résumés, not just the electronic kind.

❏ *You're Done—Well, Almost*

Now you must typeset your information in a style that reflects your personality for your paper résumé, which is an entirely different subject. There is a science behind laying out a paper résumé just like there is a science behind designing advertisements, and you need to feel comfortable with your word processing software before you even start. If you are not, then you should call in a professional for this part. You have just finished the hardest part of a résumé, though, so you may be able to save some money by shopping around when getting it typeset. Make sure the designer knows you need a résumé that will scan perfectly and that you need a copy of the file on a computer disk so you can create your e-mailable version.

An experienced résumé writer and designer can take the work you have done and enhance it with a wealth of seasoned knowledge, turning it into a finely tuned marketing instrument that truly reflects who you are. The finished résumé will attract a reader to learn more about you in an interview, which is the whole purpose of your résumé anyway.

Following are some résumé services that have a presence on the Internet, which means they are probably comfortable with writing and designing electronic résumés. I haven't personally seen the quality of their work, except for my own company, of course, so buyer beware. You might also check your local Yellow Pages for companies that mention the Internet or electronic résumés in their advertising. Always look for the *CPRW* after someone's name in an advertisement. That way you can be assured that the person has passed the strictest test of résumé writing and design in the country, which is administered by the Professional Association of Résumé Writers (PARW).

- 1st Impressions Résumés & Career Strategies
  http://www.1st-Imp.com

- A+ On-Line Résumés
  http://ol-resume.com

- AAA Résumé
  http://www.infi.net/~resume/upload.html

- Acorn Career Counseling and Résumé Writing
  acorn@mhv.net

- Affordable Résumé and Interview Skills Service
  http://www.aaow.com/john_schwartz

- Bakos Résumé Service
  http://www.branch.com/

- Canadian Résumé Centre
  http://netaccess.on.ca/~resume/

- Career and Résumé Management for the 21st Century!
  http://crm21.com

- Career Marketing-Résumé Service
  http://www.careermarketing.com

- Career Transitions
  http://www.bfservs.com:80/bfserv.html

- CareerPath
  careerhelp@aol.com

- CareerPro
  http://www.catalog.com/tsw/geturjob/index.htm

- CareerPro
  http://www.career-pro.com/

- Cole Employment Services
  http://www.shopperusa.com/employment.html

- eRésumés & Resources
  http://www.resumelink.com

- Get to Work
  http://global.net.au/~sasman/

- JobSmart: Résumé Help
  http://jobsmart.org/tools/resume/

- K&F Résumés and Professional Services
  http://wyp.net/us/20003740

- Keyword Résumé and Fax Service
  http://ourworld.compuserve.com/homepages/DeckerServices

- Market Yourself Services
  http://www.webcom.com/nccareer/market/mymain.html

- Myth Breakers Résumé Service
  http://www.mythbreakers.com/resumes.htm

- North American Business Concepts
  http://www.digimark.net/NoAm/

- One-Way Résumé
  http://www2.connectnet.com/users/blorincz

- OWL—Online Writing Lab, Purdue University
  http:/owl.trc.purdue.edu/

- Paper Works
  http://www.websrus.com/theworks/index.html

- Professional Association of Résumé Writers Membership List
  http://PARW.com

- ProType, Ltd.
  http://members.aol.com/criscito

- R&R Associates
  http://pages.prodigy.com/proposal/resume.htm

- The Résumé Maker
  http://www.iguide.com/work_mny/resume/rmaker.htm

- Résumé Management—21st Century
  http://amsquare.com/america/amerway/res21ndx.html

- Résumé Publishing Company
  http://www.csn.net

- Résumé Solution
  http://tribeca.ios.com/~Dave2

- Résumé'Net
  http://www.resumenet.com/main.html

- RésuméPosters
  http://wons.com/resumeposters/index.shtml

- Résumés in a Flash
  http://www.northcoast.com/unlimited/services_listing/resflash/resflash.html

- Résumés on the Web
  http://www.resweb.com

- RésuméXPRESS!
  http://ResumeXPRESS.com

- Sunrise Press
  http://www.garlic.com/vplex/sunrise

- Superior Résumés
  http://www.mindtrust.com

- Winning Résumés
  http://pages.prodigy.com/FL/mike3/mike5.html

Whether you typeset your résumé yourself or hire someone else to do it for you, the ultimate responsibility for the accuracy of your résumé is *yours*. Make sure every word is spelled correctly and that your grammar is perfect. Double proofread your dates, address, phone number, and any other numbers that might appear in your résumé. Make sure punctuation is consistent and that you haven't used the ampersand (& sign) in place of the word *and* (except in the case of a company name when the company uses it that way). When you are absolutely certain it is perfect, then have someone else read it again just to make sure!

■ *Creating an ASCII Text File*

After you have saved your résumé to a computer disk, the next step is to take the computer file you have just created for your paper résumé and strip it of all the formatting codes in order to save the file again (under a new name) as an ASCII text file ready for e-mailing or posting online. Chapter 5 will walk you through the process in complete detail, but the following screens will give you a general idea of how it works.

Every word processing software accomplishes this in a different way, but most of them have an option to convert a file to ASCII, MS-DOS text, or some other type of generic text file. For instance, in WordPerfect for Windows (see the sample below), you choose the "Save As" option from the "File" menu and select "ASCII (DOS) Text." In WordPerfect for DOS, you choose "ASCII Text (Standard)."

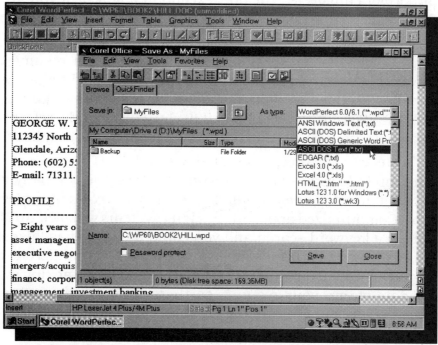

Screen shot of WordPerfect reprinted with permission from Corel Corporation.

In Microsoft Word (below), you also choose the "Save As" option from the "File" menu, but you will select "MS-DOS Text with Line Breaks" instead.

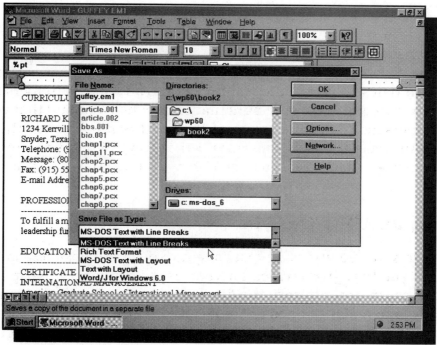

Screen shot of Microsoft Word reprinted with permission from Microsoft Corporation.

■ *Some Don'ts*

There is no need to list references on any résumé; however, it is even more important not to list references on an electronic résumé since so many people have access to it. This will avoid the possibility of invading the privacy of friends, associates, or former employers. The only exception might be if you are responding to an advertisement that requests references, but in that case, it is better to send the résumé via regular mail.

By the way, avoid that needless line at the bottom of a résumé that says, "References available upon request." It takes up valuable white space that you need to help define sections on your résumé in order to draw the reader's eyes logically down the page. It is assumed that you will provide references when requested, which is usually at the time you complete an application or are interviewed.

Don't send multiple copies of your résumé to the same company within any six-month period if they are *significantly different* in their content, unless they are simply updates. Computerized applicant tracking systems will pick up all versions of your résumé in a keyword search and you could be labeled as false if multiple versions of your résumé pop up in the search that are very different from each other. If you send an updated résumé, most of the applicant tracking systems will automatically date stamp your résumé, so there is no need to type "updated 9/1/97" on your résumé to indicate the most recent version.

Mark A. Phillips

PROFILE
- Experienced electrical engineer with an extensive background in the design and support of complex, large computer networks with primary responsibility for an 8,000-user network.
- Strong communication, leadership, management, and problem solving skills.
- Dedicated professional who enjoys the challenge of solving computer problems.
- Able to work with minimal supervision and as a cooperative team member.
- Knowledge of DOS, Windows, MS Office Suite, FormFlow, C/C++ languages, among others.

EXPERIENCE

UNITED STATES AIR FORCE   1985 – Present

CHIEF, NETWORK CONTROL CENTER
United States Air Force Academy, Colorado (1994 – Present)
- Selected, trained, and supervised 27 civilian and military personnel with a wide range of responsibilities, including client configuration, network connectivity, and file server availability for an 8,000-user local area network valued at over $35 million.
- Managed an 8-person help desk to assist more than 9,000 customers with trouble shooting their own software problems or to assign technicians to correct the problems on site.
- Programmed hubs and routers, and ran unshielded twisted pair and fiber optic cabling.
- Developed infrastructures for Banyan networks, VINES, TCP-IP to include remote, dial-in access via LanExpress.
- Limited project costs to $250,000, while an alternate proposal was provided for $2,500,000.
- Used HP OpenView, Cabletron's LanView, for SNMP management of local area networks.
- Diagnosed client software and hardware problems.
- Maintained microcomputers, printers, and more than 90 file servers; monitored more than $1 million in annual computer maintenance contracts.

ATMOSPHERIC PROPAGATION ENGINEER
USAF/Phillips Laboratory, Hanscom AFB, Massachusetts (1991 – 1994)
- Developed computer models and conducted field experiments to quantify the atmospheric propagation of light for infrared sensors.
- Defined the parameters for an airborne laser program intended to shoot down missiles.
- Managed a $1.4 million analysis contract supporting electro-optical sensing projects.
- Designed a unique interface software to improve wind sensing accuracy by 50 percent.
- Gained extensive experience with UNIX workstations and PCs.

CHIEF ENGINEER, ELECTRICAL POWER AND COMMUNICATIONS SYSTEM
Utah Test and Training Range, Layton, Utah (1985 – 1989)
- Responsible for the daily operation and maintenance of $70 million of power distribution and microwave communication systems for a 20,000 square mile land/airspace test and training range.
- Installed and maintained power protection equipment, uninterruptible power systems, and automatic transfer switches to protect data processing equipment.
- Wrote specifications for contractor engineering projects to improve system performance.

EDUCATION

MASTER OF SCIENCE, ELECTRICAL ENGINEERING (1989 – 1990)
Air Force Institute of Technology, Wright-Patterson AFB, Ohio
- Concentration in electro-optics

BACHELOR OF SCIENCE, ELECTRICAL ENGINEERING (1981 – 1985)
United States Air Force Academy, Colorado
- Concentration in communications

CONTINUING PROFESSIONAL EDUCATION (1985 – 1989)
Air Force Institute of Technology, Wright-Patterson AFB, Ohio
- Digital Signal Processing, Fiber Optic Communications, Local Area Networks, Electrical Power Distribution, Spread Spectrum Communications, Optimizing Network Server Performance, Acquisition Professional Development Series (4 courses)

ADDRESS   123 East Antelope Drive, USAF Academy, Colorado 80840   (719) 555-1234

Michael L. Patterson, CBI, CBE

12 Parkview, Suite 123
Fort Worth, Texas 76102

Telephone: (817) 555-1234
Voice Mail: (214) 555-1234

Objective   A position as a computer network engineer and instructor for a network and integration company.

Keywords   Banyan VINES network, UNIX, DOS, VAX cluster, gateways, servers, clients, SMTP, DNS, firewall, Internet, dual broadband system, VAX cluster, WAN connections, DMSP ground system, 10base2 wiring, 10baseT wiring, virus scanning, Lotus Notes, ground radar systems, Certified Banyan Engineer, Instructor, and Specialist

Experience

Independent Systems Consultant, Fort Worth, Texas . . . . 1996 to Present
 ◆ Develop training and update courses for VINES administrators and conduct classes.
 ◆ Provide client support in resolving network problems either directly on-site or via the telephone.

Meridian Oil, Incorporated, Fort Worth, Texas . . . . 1994 to 1996
SENIOR STAFF INFORMATION SYSTEMS & TECHNOLOGY ANALYST
 ◆ Set up and managed the Internet connection using SMTP, DNS, and a firewall.
 ◆ Supported outlying offices with either direct on-site or phone support for resolving network problems.
 ◆ Set up and maintained a company-wide virus scanning software on both servers and clients.
 ◆ Assisted in a Coopers & Lybrand audit to ensure security on the Internet connection.
 ◆ Developed and conducted training and update classes for VINES administrators company-wide.
 ◆ Used Lotus Notes 3.2 and performed limited development with canned applications.

United States Air Force . . . . 1973 to 1994
Twenty-one years of progressively more responsible service and training positions that included contact with manufacturers, service contractors, and major computer suppliers. Extensive specialized training at both Department of the Air Force and manufacturers' schools.

CHIEF, HARDWARE SERVICES DIVISION, ACADEMIC COMPUTING SERVICES
Department of the Air Force, Dean of Faculty, USAF Academy, Colorado (1993 to 1994)
 ◆ Supervised an office of 10 technicians, with a wide range of responsibilities including the installation of a 65-server Banyan VINES network with 6,000+ clients.
 ◆ Prepared and conducted training for group and building VINES administrators for the USAF Academy.
 ◆ Worked with the dual broadband system for distribution of VAX cluster output and connections.
 ◆ Engineered design and trade-off studies; assembled and distributed systems to operational users.
 ◆ Supported base-level contracting with technical information needed to complete purchase requests.
 ◆ Improved process methods, reducing expenditures and minimizing total man-hours for all projects.

PROGRAM MANAGER FOR COMPUTER INFORMATION SYSTEMS
Training System Program Office, Wright-Patterson AFB, Ohio (1990 to 1993)
 ◆ Managed and provided engineering support for a 12-server Banyan VINES network with 400+ clients.
 ◆ Completed an upgrade of the network from 10base2 client wiring to 10baseT wiring, which included WAN connections to an off-site work location during the upgrade with no loss of work time.
 ◆ Designed and deployed an extension of the network to a division located in Utah, using Internet for connectivity.
 ◆ Engineered design and trade-off studies; supported base-level contracting with technical information.

ASSISTANT TO THE PROGRAM MANAGER
Training Systems Program Office (SPO), Wright-Patterson AFB, Ohio (1987 to 1990)
 ◆ Assisted in leading a team of 13 functional experts in defining, acquiring, and fielding maintenance training devices.
 ◆ Managed the Support Equipment Requirement Development list for the C-17 Maintenance Training Devices program in coordination with HQ Air Mobility Command, HQ Air Training Command, C-17 Airlifter SPO, and the contractor.

Experience (continued)

FIELD ENGINEER, DEFENSE METEOROLOGICAL SATELLITE PROGRAM (DMSP) GROUND SYSTEM
1000 Satellite Operations Group, Offutt AFB, Nebraska (1983 to 1986)
- Evaluated proposals for any changes to the Satellite Ground Control Facility.
- Lead Engineer on embedded microcomputer applications for controlling the DMSP Ground System links and equipment.
- Test Engineer for installation of new electronic systems.
- Controlled equipment failures and coordinated with DMSP SPO, three contractors, and two detachments when failure trend analysis indicated needed action.

Education

College Degrees
- Master of Science, Systems Management, Air Force Institute of Technology
- Bachelor of Science, Electrical Engineering, Texas A&M University
- Applied Associate of Science, Instructor of Technology, CCAF
- Applied Associate of Science, Electronics Engineering Technology, CCAF
- Applied Associate of Science, Ground Radar Systems Technology, CCAF

Certifications
- Certified Banyan Instructor, 1994 (Basic/Advanced VINES Administration and 6.0 Update Courses)
- Certified Banyan Engineer, 1993 (Recertified 1994, 1995, 1996)
- Certified Banyan Specialist, 1993 (Recertified 1994, 1995, 1996)

Banyan Courses
- Train-the-Trainer Update for VINES Administration (VINES 6.0), Banyan, 1996
- VINES 6.00 Engineering Update, ABUI Training Institute, 1995
- Train-the-Trainer for VINES Administration (VINES 5.5), Banyan, 1994
- Advanced VINES Administration & Planning (VINES 5.5), Banyan, 1994
- Basic VINES Administration (VINES 5.5), Banyan, 1994
- VINES 5.5 Engineering Update (VINES 5.5), Banyan, 1993
- Technical Tools II (VINES 5.0), Banyan, 1993
- Technical Tools I (VINES 5.0), Banyan, 1992
- VINES Gateways, Banyan, 1992

Other Courses
- Systems Engineering Course, Systems Management & Development Corp, DSMC, 1992
- Computer Resources Acquisition Course, AFMC SAS, 1992
- Advanced Systems Acquisition Management Course, AFSC SAS, 1989

Activities

Association of Banyan Users International (ABUI) .... 1990 to Present
President, Board of Directors, with responsibility for overseeing corporate operations as CEO (1995 to Present). Secretary, Board of Directors, with responsibility for overseeing minutes and corporate records (1994 to 1995). Chairman for Asynchronous Technical Wizards Interface Group (TWIG) with the responsibilities of overseeing session content at the semiannual conferences, conducting sessions, and coordinating the tracking of member requirements with a Banyan representative as related to asynchronous and WAN issues (1990 to 1994).

Banyan Users In Colorado (BUIC) .... 1993 to 1994
Vice President of the Regional Banyan user group; assisted in the development of the BUIC.

DAVID H. PARKER

ADDRESS   12 Parkview Boulevard, Colorado Springs, Colorado 80906   (719) 555-1234

PROFILE

- Licensed attorney in private practice since 1969 (Colorado and New Mexico).
- Board Certified Civil Trial Specialist with extensive litigation experience.
- Recognized specialist in workers' compensation law by the New Mexico Legal Specialization Board.
- Admitted to practice before the U.S. Court of Appeals, 10th Circuit; U.S. District Court for the District of New Mexico; U.S. District Court for the Western District of Texas; District Courts of the State Colorado; and all courts in the State of New Mexico.
- Extensive experience in the preparation and trial of injury claims resulting from both workers' compensation and off-the-job injuries.
- Exceptional knowledge of administrative procedures, rules of evidence, and trial practices.

EXPERIENCE

- Member of a three-attorney panel appointed by the New Mexico Court of Appeals to issue advisory decisions in pending civil appeals.
- Wrote the advisory decision in the appeal of *Miller v. NM Dept. of Transportation,* the essence of which was adopted by the New Mexico Supreme Court.
- Selected twice in fifteen months as an arbitrator for the New Mexico trial-level court to arbitrate cases with damage claims less than $15,000, using procedures similar to those governing American Arbitration Association proceedings.

Personal Injury

- Lead counsel or sole counsel for the injured plaintiff/worker in at least 30 jury trials with a minimum trial length of three days, plus another 50 non-jury trials of at least two days.
- Since 1983, have prepared and prosecuted to conclusion, either by trial or settlement, over 650 workers' compensation cases involving both physical and economic injuries.
- Interviewed witnesses, propounded and responded to interrogatories, requested productions and admissions, took and defended depositions, briefed interlocutory motions, filed requested findings and conclusions in non-jury cases, and prepared and argued requested instructions in jury trials.
- Developed considerable experience in determining when the record should be closed or supplemented.

Expert Witnesses

- Defined case issues and facts, then determined what type of expert witnesses would be needed.
- Located highly competent and persuasive experts in the required field.
- Consulted with and prepared the experts based on the definition of the issues and facts.
- Examined and cross-examined all types of fact witnesses and expert witnesses from nearly all areas of medicine and many scientific fields.

Management

- Managed a private law practice for more than 20 years, including all aspects of administration, accountability for profit and loss, controlling costs, and achieving revenue objectives.
- Recruited, supervised, motivated, and evaluated employees, including clerical staff and paralegals.
- Met deadlines for pretrial procedures, trials, and appellate briefings by effectively utilizing attorney associates and support staff.
- Designed a complete set of recurring forms to manage a typical workers' compensation claim from initial client interview through requested findings and conclusions.
- Competent in IBM, Windows, and WordPerfect computer software.

EDUCATION

JURIS DOCTOR   1969
University of New Mexico School of Law, Albuquerque, New Mexico

GRADUATE SCHOOL   1966 – 1967
University of New Mexico, Albuquerque, New Mexico
- 18 hours of Modern European History

BACHELOR OF ARTS   1965
University of Minnesota, St. Paul, Minnesota
- Major in English

SIGNIFICANT CASES

- *Nick Andler v. City of Gallup and NM Self-Insurer's Fund,* NM Dept. of Labor, Workers' Compensation Administration No. WCA 92-03246.
- *Greene v. Proto/Stanley-Proto,* San Juan County, N.M. District Court No. CV-88-540-3, 1993 (jury verdict, products liability case, eight-day trial, $282,000 plus costs)
- *Vickaryous v. City of Albuquerque,* Bernalillo County, N.M. District Court No. CV-91-02098, 1992 (alleged police negligence in failing to take keys from DWI driver resulting in paralysis)
- *Chevron Resources ex rel. Blatnik v. New Mexico Superintendent of Ins.,* 838 P.2d 988, 114 N.M. 371 (Ct. App. 1992)
- *Johnson v. Sears, Roebuck & Co.,* 832 P.2d 797, 113 N.M. 736 (Ct. App. 1992)
- *Richardson v. Farmers Ins. Co.,* 811 P.2d 571, 112 N.M. 73 (S. Ct. 1991)
- *Roybal v. Mutual of Omaha,* USDC, DCNM No. CIV 88-01195 SC, 1991 ($300,000 settlement on appeal breach of insurance contract claims for nonpayment of benefits health/major medical policy)
- *Cano v. Smith's Food King,* 781 P.2d 322, 109 N.M. 50 (Ct. App. 1989)
- *Strong v. Sysco Corp./Nobel Sysco,* 776 P.2d 1258, 108 N.M. 639 (Ct. App. 1989)
- *Rodriguez v. X-Pert Well Serv., Inc.,* 759 P.2d 1010, 107 N.M. 428 (Ct. App. 1988)
- *Jimmy Davis, et al. v. Aztec Drilling, et al.,* San Juan County, N.M. District Court, 1988 (seven-day jury trial, natural gas field explosion, bifurcated liability and damages trials; settled for $500,000 for Jimmy Davis following jury verdict on liability)
- *Thompson v. Ruidoso-Sunland, Inc.,* 734 P.2d 267, 105 N.M. 487 (Ct. App. 1987)
- *Robert Shattuck v. Lovelace Medical Center,* Bernalillo County, N.M. District Court No. CIV 85-03953, (medical/hospital malpractice case settled after two days of trial for $800,000, Nov. 1987)
- *John Sauters v. Jack B. Kelley: American Western Securities, Inc., et al.,* USDC, DCNM No. CV 84-0826 HB, 1986 (bench decision for $180,000 minority shareholders dilution action against broker-dealer and principal broker)
- *Bledsoe v. Garcia,* 742 F.2d 1237 (10th Cir. 1984)
- *Garrison v. Safeway Stores,* 692 P.2d 1328, 102 N.M. 179 (Ct. App. 1984)
- *Moreno v. Marrs Mud Co.,* 695 P.2d 1322, 102 N.M. 373 (Ct. App. 1984) (exception to "firemen's rule" absolute assumption of risk defense to tort claim by policeman/fireman recognized)
- *Kathy Penley v. Buena Suerta Ranch, Inc., et al.,* USDC, DCNM No. CIV 82-0878, JB, 1984 ($60,000 jury verdict in breach of bailment contract by horse owner v. horse ranch and trainer)
- *Patterson v. City of Albuquerque,* 661 P.2d 1331, 99 N.M. 632 (Ct. App. 1983)

AFFILIATIONS

- American Bar Association
- Colorado Bar Association
- New Mexico Bar Association
- Association of Trial Lawyers of America
- New Mexico Trial Lawyers Association (Board of Directors, 1987 – 1988)
- Colorado Trial Lawyers Association
- Albuquerque Lawyers Society

PRESENTATIONS

- "Workers' Compensation: Calculation of Disability Benefits Under the New Grid Systems," New Mexico Trial Lawyers Association, 1994.
- "Direct Examination of a Cardiologist in Heart Attack Cases" and "Establishing Disability with the Dictionary of Occupational Titles," New Mexico Trial Lawyers Association, 1993.

WORK HISTORY

STAFF ATTORNEY, McDivitt Law Firm, Colorado Springs, Colorado	1995 – Present
PRESIDENT, David H. Parker, P.A., Albuquerque, New Mexico	1980 – 1995
PARTNER, Parker & Diamond, Albuquerque, New Mexico	1979 – 1980
PRESIDENT, David H. Parker, P.A., Albuquerque, New Mexico	1976 – 1979
PARTNER, Parker & Shoobridge, Albuquerque, New Mexico	1975 – 1976
PARTNER, Aldridge, Baron, Parker & Campbell, Albuquerque, New Mexico	1973 – 1975
PARTNER, Aldridge & Parker, Albuquerque, New Mexico	1971 – 1973
PRESIDENT, David H. Parker, P.A., Albuquerque, New Mexico	1969 – 1971

■ *Power Verbs*

Just because a computer will screen your résumé in the beginning and look for keywords is no excuse for poor writing. Your ultimate goal is to entice a human being to read your résumé, so keep the sentences interesting by using positive power verbs. Here are some great power verbs to use at the beginning of your sentences:

A

abridged
absolved
accelerated
accomplished
accounted for
achieved
acquired
acted
adapted
added
addressed
adjusted
administered
advanced
advertised
advised
aided
allocated
altered
analyzed
answered
applied
appointed
appraised
approved
arbitrated
arranged
articulated
assembled
assessed
assigned
assimilated
assisted
attained
attended
audited
augmented
authored
authorized
automated

B

balanced
began
bid
blended
broadened
budgeted
built

C

calculated
calibrated
cared for
carved
categorized
catalogued
chaired
changed
charted
chose
clarified
classified
coached
coded
collaborated
collated
collected
combined
communicated
compared
compiled
completed
composed
compounded
computed
conceived
conceptualized
condensed
conducted
conferred

confirmed
confronted
conserved
considered
consolidated
contracted
constructed
consulted
contacted
contracted
contributed
controlled
converted
conveyed
convinced
cooperated
coordinated
copied
corrected
corresponded
counseled
created
critiqued
customized
cut

D

debated
debugged
decided
decreased
defined
delegated
delineated
delivered
demonstrated
derived
described
designated
designed
detected

determined
developed
devised
diagnosed
differentiated
directed
disbursed
discovered
dispatched
dispensed
displayed
disproved
distinguished
distributed
diversified
doubled
drafted
dramatized
drew up

E

earned
edited
educated
effected
elaborated
elicited
eliminated
enabled
encouraged
enforced
engineered
enhanced
enlisted
ensured
entertained
established
estimated
evaluated
examined
exceeded

executed
exhibited
expanded
expedited
experimented
explained
explored
expressed
extended
extracted

F

fabricated
facilitated
familiarized
fashioned
filed
fixed
focused
followed
forecasted
formulated
fortified
found
founded
framed
functioned as
furnished
furthered

G

gained
gathered
generated
governed
greeted
guaranteed
guided

H

halted
halved
handled
headed
helped
hired
hosted

I

identified
illustrated
implemented
improved
incorporated
increased
individualized
indoctrinated
influenced
informed
initiated
innovated
inspected
installed
instilled
instituted
instructed
insured
integrated
interacted
interpreted
intervened
interviewed
introduced
invented
invested
investigated
involved
isolated
itemized

J

joined
judged
justified

L

launched
lectured
led
lessened
listened
litigated
limited
located
logged

M

made
maintained
managed
manipulated
manufactured
marketed
mastered
measured
mediated
memorized
merged
met
modeled
moderated
modified
molded
monitored
motivated

N

named
narrated
navigated
negotiated
netted
neutralized
nominated
normalized
notified
nurtured

O

observed
obtained
offered
offset
opened
operated
orchestrated
ordered
organized
originated
outlined
overhauled
oversaw
owned

P

participated
perceived
performed
persuaded
photographed
pinpointed
pioneered
planned
predicted
prepared
prescribed
presented
presided
prevented
printed
prioritized
processed
produced
programmed
projected
promoted
proposed
protected
proved
provided
publicized
purchased

Q

qualified
quantified
quoted

R

raised
realized
rearranged
received
recommended
reconciled
recorded
recruited
rectified
redesigned
reduced
referred

registered
regulated
rehabilitated
reinforced
related
remodeled
rendered
reorganized
repaired
replaced
replicated
reported
represented
reproduced
researched
reserved
resolved
responded
restored
restructured
retrieved
revamped
reversed
reviewed
revised
revitalized
routed

saved
scheduled
screened

sculptured
searched
secured
selected
served
serviced
set up
shaped
shortened
signed
simplified
simulated
sketched
smoothed
solicited
sold
solidified
solved
sparked
spearheaded
specialized
specified
speculated
spoke
sponsored
staffed
standardized
started
stimulated
streamlined
strengthened
stretched
structured

studied
submitted
succeeded
suggested
summarized
supervised
supplied
supported
surpassed
surveyed
synthesized
systemized

T

tabulated
tallied
tasted
taught
tempered
terminated
tested
testified
traced
tracked
trained
transformed
translated
transmitted
traveled
trimmed
troubleshot
turned
tutored

U

uncovered
underlined
underscored
undertook
underwrote
unearthed
unified
united
updated
upgraded
used
utilized

V

validated
vaulted
verified
visualized
volunteered

W

widened
won
worked
wrote

■ *Keywords*

As discussed in step nine on page 15, using the right keywords for your particular experience and education is critical to the success of your electronic résumé. Without the right keywords, your résumé will float in cyberspace forever waiting for a hiring manager to find it. If your résumé contains all of the right keywords, then you will be among the first candidates whose résumés are reviewed. If you lack only one of the keywords, then your résumé will be next in line after résumés that have them all, and so on.

Remember, your keywords are the experience and skills that come from the specific terminology used in your job. For instance, *operating room* and *ICU* immediately classify the experience of a nurse, but *pediatric ICU* narrows it down even further. Don't try to limit your résumé by using fewer words. If your information is longer than one page, a reader looking at a computer screen won't be able to tell, but the computer doing a keyword search will know if a word is not there. Recall, however, that you only need to use a word one time for it to be considered a "hit" in a keyword search. Try to use synonyms wherever possible to broaden your chances of being selected.

You should also understand the difference between a simple keyword search and a "concept" search. When a recruiter brings up an e-mailed résumé onto the screen and sends the computer on a search for a single word like *market-ing*—which you can do in any word processing program with a few clicks of a mouse or function key—he or she is performing a keyword search. You are also performing a keyword search when you type a word or combination of words into the command line of a search engine like Yahoo or Excite. In that case, sometimes the computer searches entire documents for matches and other times it looks only at headers or extracts from the files.

A concept search, on the other hand, can bridge the gap between words by reading entire phrases and then using sophisticated artificial intelligence to interpret what is being said, translating the phrase into a single word, like *network*, or a combination of words, like *project management.*

The software that allows scanners to read your paper résumé and turn it into an electronic résumé is able to do just that. Resumix, one of the most widely used applicant tracking systems, reads the grammar of noun, verb, and adjective combinations and extracts the information for placement on the form that will become your entry in a résumé database. Its expert system extraction engine uses a knowledge base of more than 120,000 rules and over ten million résumé terms. It even knows the difference between *Harvard Graphics* (a computer software program) and *Harvard* (the university) by its placement on the page and its relationship to the header that precedes it *(Computer Skills* or *Education).* Aren't computers amazing. For a more detailed explanation of how your résumé looks once it has been scanned, see the next chapter, "The Journey of the Scannable Résumé."

Because of this complicated logic, and because each company and each hiring manager has the ability to personalize the search criteria for each job opening, it is impossible to give you a concrete list of the thousands of possible keywords that could be used to search for any one job. For instance, in one high-tech company I interviewed, a keyword search included the following criteria from two different hiring managers for the same job title:

Financial Analyst/Senior Accountant:

REQUIRED:
- BS in finance or accounting with 4 years of experience or
- MBA in related field with 2 years of relevant experience
- certified public accountant
- forecasting

DESIRED:
- accounting
- financial
- trend analysis
- financial statement
- results analysis
- trends
- strategic planning
- develop trends
- financial modeling
- personal computer
- microcomputers
- DCF
- presentation skills
- team player

REQUIRED:
- BS in finance or accounting with 4 years of experience or
- MBA in related field with 2 years of relevant experience
- accounting
- financial reporting
- financial statement
- Excel

DESIRED:
- ability
- customer
- new business
- financial analysis
- financial
- forecasting
- process improvement
- policy development
- business policies
- PowerPoint
- Microsoft Word
- analytical ability

You can see why it is so difficult to give definitive lists of keywords and concepts. However, it is possible to give you samples of actual keyword searches used by recruiters I have interviewed to give you some ideas. Let me emphasize again that you should list only experience you actually have gained. Do not include these keywords in your résumé just because they are listed here.

Business Manager (Central Archive Management):

REQUIRED:
- BS in engineering or computer science
- 10 years of related engineering and/or manufacturing experience
- strategic planning
- network
- product management
- program management

DESIRED:
- business plan
- line management
- pricing
- team player
- CAM
- marketing
- product strategy
- vendor
- general management
- OEM
- profit and loss

Business Operations Specialist:

REQUIRED:
- bachelor's degree
- 4 years of directly related experience
- production schedule
- project planning

DESIRED:
- ability to implement
- CList
- data analysis
- off-shift
- team player
- automation
- ability to plan
- customer interaction
- VM
- CMS
- JCL
- REXX
- MVS
- UNIX
- analytical ability
- customer interface
- network
- skills analysis
- automatic tools

Project Manager Human Resources:

REQUIRED:
- bachelor's degree in human resources, business, or related field
- 6 years broad experience

DESIRED:
- communications
- project management
- milestone development
- time management
- credibility
- recruiting
- long-range planning
- sourcing

Secretary III:

REQUIRED:
- high school education or equivalent
- 5 years of experience
- typing skill of 55-60 wpm
- interpersonal skills
- oral communication

DESIRED:
- administrative assistance
- clerical
- data analysis
- file maintenance
- material repair
- PowerPoint
- project planning
- reports
- screen calls
- troubleshoot
- answer phones
- communication skills
- document distribution
- mail sorting
- Microsoft Word
- presentation
- publication
- schedule calendar
- secretarial
- appointments
- confidential
- edit
- material
- policies and procedures
- problem solving
- records management
- schedule conference
- telephone interview

Senior Software Engineer:

REQUIRED:
- BS/MS in engineering, computer science or closely related field
- 8 to 9 years of experience

DESIRED:
- C
- customer
- hiring/firing
- prototype
- structured design
- code development
- DASD
- methodology
- real time
- supervision
- communication skills
- experiment design
- problem solving
- software design
- testing

Perhaps it would help to visualize what a hiring manager would see using the Restrac software. In this first step, the general category of skills is selected.

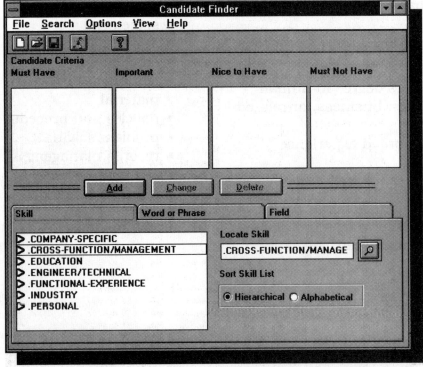

Screen shot of Candidate Finder reprinted with permission from Restrac.

Then specific criteria is chosen, depending on whether the skill is a "must," "important," "nice to have," or "must not have."

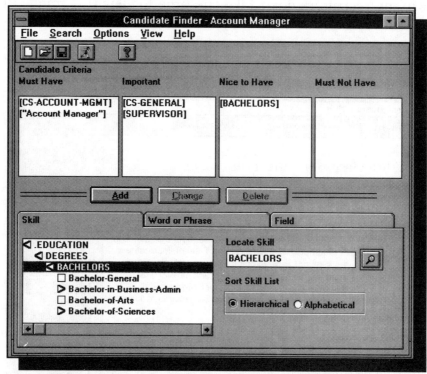

Screen shot of Candidate Finder reprinted with permission from Restrac.

The results of the search are ranked according to how many "hits" were found in each résumé.

ST	SCORE	FIRST_NAME	LAST_NAME	CITY	STATE	DATE_
✓	1.00	Cynthia	Kandar	Newton	MA	31-Aug
	0.97	Robert	Richtarek			29-Jul-S
✓	0.92	Robert	Miller	Weymouth	MA	29-Jun-S
✓	0.89	Pegi	Davis	Medford	MA	29-Jul-S
✓	0.89	Thaddeus	Florczak	Londonderry	NH	29-Jul-S
	0.87	Christopher	Ischay			22-Jul-S
✓	0.79	Brian	Day-Lewis	Tyngsboro	MA	31-Aug-S
	0.71	Gary	Lea	Martinez	CA	29-Jul-S
	0.71	Ernest	Strange	Framingham	MA	30-May
	0.66	Mary	Clupper	Tewksbury	MA	29-Jul-S
	0.66	Joseph	Matthews	Hudson	NH	31-Aug
✓	0.66	Robert	Bagley	Grafton	MA	31-Aug
	0.66	Brian	Morgan	Billerica	MA	29-Jun-
	0.61	Edward	Rappoli	Stoughton	MA	31-Aug
	0.47	Kevin	Mcgonigle	Exton	PA	29-Jul-S
	0.47	Edmund	Rucels	Brampton	ON	19-Sep
	0.37	William	Byam	Bedford	MA	14-Jul-S
	0.32	Mario	Sarabia	San Jose	CA	29-Jul-S
	0.21	Scott	Ellyn	Marina Del R	CA	20-Jun-
	0.21	Michael	Tizio	Taunton	MA	29-Jul-S
	0.03	Robert	Moniz	Leominster	MA	28-Jul-S
	0.03	Julia	Muszynski	Burlington	MA	31-Aug-
	0.03	Charles	Stockler	Westford	MA	31-Aug-

Results: 23 Match of 492 Documents, 23 Retrieved, 23 shown

Status
Show Text
Show Image
Show Record
Print
Close
☐ Show All

Screen shot of Candidate Finder reprinted with permission from Restrac.

And finally, a résumé is selected and the text viewed on the screen. This is not an actual snapshot of the original résumé but is instead the result of the optical character recognition process. It is possible to bring up a picture of the paper résumé, but many recruiters don't take the time to view this image unless there is something confusing about the OCR version of the résumé that they see in this screen.

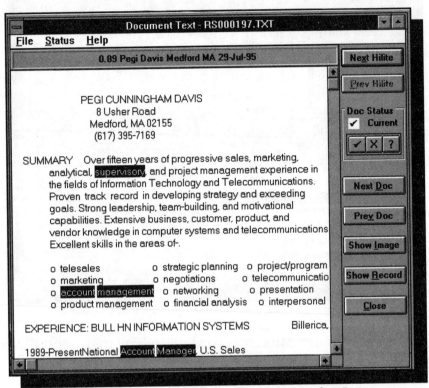

Screen shot of Candidate Finder reprinted with permission from Restrac.

Now that you have a basic understanding of the concept of keywords and know how to get the words of your résumé written on paper, the next chapter will walk you through the more technical aspects of what happens to your résumé once it is received in a human resource department and begins the journey to becoming a résumé in cyberspace.

3 | The Journey of the Scannable Résumé

As mentioned in the introduction to the concept of scannable résumés in Chapter 1, employers are being flooded with résumés from very qualified applicants, sometimes receiving as many as 50,000 unsolicited résumés a year. As companies continue to downsize and human resource departments become smaller, they can no longer afford to hand sort résumés. In order to manage this deluge of paper, these same companies have turned to computers and scanners.

In order to give you some insight into this technology, this chapter will be devoted to walking you through the journey your paper résumé takes from the moment it is received in a human resource department until you are hired. At the end of this chapter you will find a list of some of the companies that use the three most popular résumé scanning and applicant tracking systems (Resumix, Restrac, and SmartSearch2), which will help you determine whether creating a scannable résumé is really a necessity for you. Don't be hesitant to call a company's human resource department to ask if they scan résumés. It is the only way to be absolutely certain that your résumé needs to be scannable.

■ Optical Character Recognition (OCR)

When your paper résumé is received by a human resource department that uses a computerized applicant tracking system, your résumé must first be transferred into binary information that a computer can read before it can be stored in the résumé database. This is accomplished with a scanner that is connected to a computer running a special kind of software that can examine the dots of ink on your printed page and determine by their shapes which letters they represent. This is called optical character recognition, or OCR for short.

This software matches patterns with sets of characters stored in its memory, which is one of the reasons why it is important to choose a type style (or font) for your résumé that conforms to normal letter shapes. If you use a highly decorative type style, the OCR software will have difficulty making matches and will misinterpret letters. This means your words won't be spelled correctly, which of course means that a keyword search for the word *bookkeeping* will never turn up your résumé if the OCR thought you typed *bmkkeepmg*. The next chapter will guide you through designing your résumé with this in mind.

For now, let's assume that you have designed a résumé that the scanner can read. First, depending on the company's procedures, your résumé will be received directly by the recruiter assigned to fill a certain position (if the job was advertised) or by the human resource department in general (if you have sent your résumé unsolicited).

When the recruiter has finished reviewing your information, your résumé is added to the stacks of résumés to be processed by the computer that day. A staffing professional will then put your cover letter and résumé into the feeder bin of a flatbed scanner, separating your résumé from the one above and below it with a blank piece of paper. Some companies scan only the résumés, but those that do scan the cover letters generally do not extract information from them for their résumé databases. Why? Because people generally go into detail about what they want in their cover letters and not just what they have done. This confuses the applicant tracking systems and adds qualifications that you don't have.

Within seconds, the scanner has passed its light over your pieces of paper and the computer begins extracting information to fill in its electronic form, which will become part of your résumé in cyberspace. There are actually three versions of your résumé created in this step. One is a snapshot of your paper résumé so the hiring manager can actually view your résumé in the format in which it arrived. The second is a generic text version of your résumé. This is the result of the optical character recognition. The pretty formatting is deleted and all that is left is your text. This one looks fairly messy, but the words are all there. The third is an electronic form that the applicant tracking software extracts from the information it finds in your résumé. In Resumix, this summary form would look something like the screen shot on the right.

This electronic form contains much

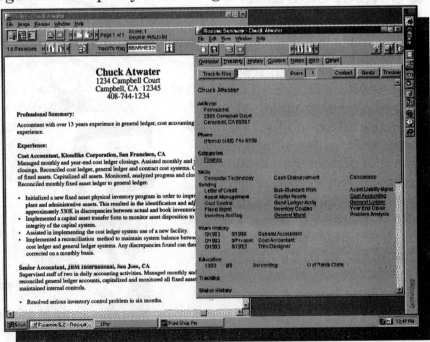

Screen shot of Resumix reprinted with permission from Ceridian Corporation.

information that can be used to keep track of you from the moment you are called for an interview to years after you are hired. There are spaces to record the date your résumé was received, where you heard about the job, test results, interview dates, correspondence, comments, contact tracking, and much more.

After the computer has finished creating your electronic résumé, a clerk will verify some of the information. This person usually spends only about five minutes checking your name, phone number, and address and making sure that important information isn't missing. Seldom will the verifier spend much more time reviewing your summary form, skills, or résumé.

The computer can automatically generate a letter acknowledging that your résumé was received and let you know how long it will be retained in the résumé database. As already mentioned, this can vary from 90 days to a year to forever if you have skills that are in short supply. Resumix software will even allow a company to use a voice response system where applicants can call a special telephone number to verify that their résumé was received and provide the date of receipt. The letter you receive will tell you if this option is available.

Now your résumé is sitting in cyberspace waiting for a hiring manager to find it in a search. Before addressing what happens to your résumé from this point on, you should know that there is another way for your résumé to enter this database.

■ Faxed Résumés That Never See Paper

When a classified advertisement publishes a fax number and you send your résumé via a facsimile machine, you have bypassed the U.S. Postal Service and the job of the scanner. A fax machine is simply a specialized computer, scanner, and printer combined into one device. The scanner part of the fax machine translates your text into binary data that is then transferred over the phone lines to a machine at the other end of the connection. If the machine at the other end is a computer instead of a fax machine, your data is stored on a hard drive until someone chooses to print it on paper.

Companies using computerized applicant tracking systems to store résumés in a database rarely print the résumés received via fax. Instead, they leave your résumé in a queue until a clerk can process your file and extract the information for the same electronic form used to summarize the paper résumés. The quality of the optical character recognition is often not as good as a scanned paper résumé, so I usually advise my clients to mail a hard copy of their résumés and cover letters in addition to faxing them whenever possible. This gives your résumé double exposure and helps to ensure that a more accurate version of your résumé ends up in the résumé database. Actually, e-mailing your ASCII text file or entering your résumé directly at an Internet site (or at a kiosk in a company's human resource department) are your best choices since you have total control over what ends up in your file. Chapters 5 and 6 will talk more about these options.

■ *Applicant Tracking Systems*

What happens next? Your résumé has been successfully scanned, faxed, or e-mailed into a company's résumé database. The data is floating in cyberspace just waiting for someone to discover it. Now it is time for a hiring manager to write a "job requisition" for an open position. This document contains the absolute requirements for the job, including the level of education and experience required, necessary and

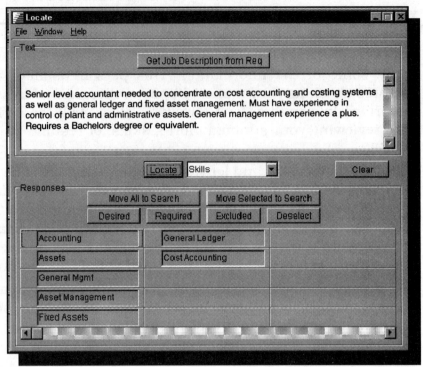

Screen shot of Resumix reprinted with permission from Ceridian Corporation.

optional skills, and a written job description. This job description contains the keywords that will be used by the computer software to find your résumé (see the screen shot from Resumix above).

Staffing professionals can weight these keywords by how much importance they want the words to have. For instance, if knowledge of WordPerfect is more critical to a job than knowledge of PowerPoint, then WordPerfect can be assigned more weight.

Once the criteria for the search have been set, the computer searches the database and chooses the candidates whose résumés contain the chosen keywords (see the screen shot from Resumix on the right). The résumés are ranked on the screen by how many matches the computer found. Résumés that match the criteria with 100 percent accuracy—

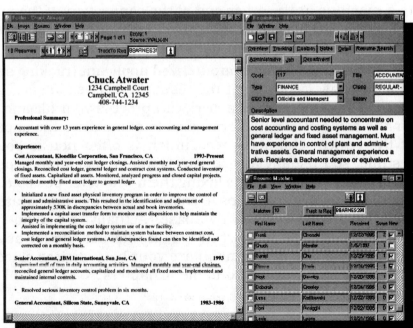

Screen shot of Resumix reprinted with permission from Ceridian Corporation.

which is rare, by the way—will be listed first, with résumés ranked in descending order.

Once a set of résumés has been selected using the initial keywords, it is often necessary to shorten the list. The first keyword search can turn up 500 résumés, depending on the size of the database, so the hiring manager must decide whether to make some of the "desired" keywords "required" and try again or to narrow the search by adding criteria. This can be accomplished by searching for a job title in your past experience or by the name of a well-known company for whom you might have worked or by the particular university you attended. Which criteria is the most important to the hiring manager depends a great deal on his or her industry. For instance, a research facility or university would be more interested in the name of the school where you studied. A company that develops software, on the other hand, would want to know the skills of the programmer instead. An accounting firm might be more interested in whether you worked for Arthur Andersen at some time in your past.

The selected résumés can be viewed on screen, printed, faxed, or e-mailed as required. This sometimes includes a snapshot of your résumé exactly as you presented it, although this usually depends on whether the recruiter wishes to wait the couple of minutes it can sometimes take for the image to appear on the screen (see the screen shot from Resumix below).

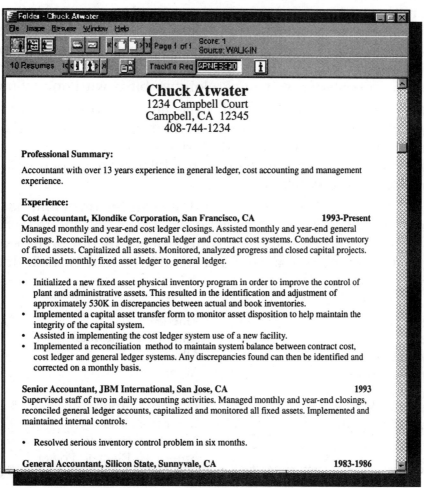

Screen shot of Resumix reprinted with permission from Ceridian Corporation.

■ *Which Companies Scan Résumés?*

If you are sending your résumé to a Fortune 1000 company, you can almost be 100 percent certain that the company is using some type of computerized applicant tracking system. These companies are accepting electronic résumés from their Internet sites and via e-mail, then integrating the pure electronic versions with the paper résumés they receive via the Postal Service and fax. Once the paper résumés are scanned, all of the résumés are then stored in one massive computer database. This process is expensive and generally not cost effective for smaller companies—"smaller" meaning companies with fewer than 1,000 employees.

There are some exceptions to this rule, however. High-tech companies usually have the infrastructure in place to make implementing programs such as this less expensive, and they tend to have higher turnover, which means more advertised job openings and more résumés to process.

Some companies use the outsourcing services offered by the manufacturers of the applicant tracking software, which means they pay someone else to scan the résumés and then they simply use the applicant tracking software to perform keyword searches on a database already set up for them.

Recruiters are another exception to the rule of 1,000 employees or more. Recruiting firms might have small staffs themselves, but they process incredible numbers of résumés. Assume that your résumé will be scanned into a computerized database if you are sending it to a recruiter. It never hurts to pick up the telephone and call the recruiting firm just to be certain. You will probably be calling them anyway to get the name of the person to whom you will be addressing your cover letter, so you can kill two birds with one stone.

Even federal, state, county, and large city governments are turning to applicant tracking systems in order to make their hiring processes more efficient. For instance, the State of Arizona and Maricopa County (Phoenix metropolitan area) use Resumix to manage applicants. They fill 95 percent of their job openings from their computerized database.

Here are just some of the companies that scan résumés and use computerized applicant tracking systems. This list doesn't even pretend to be all inclusive, so I encourage you to call human resource departments or recruiters before submitting your résumé, or just send a scannable résumé by default to any mid-sized or large company.

Abbott Laboratories	AlliedSignal
Ace Hardware	Allmerica Financial
Advanced Micro Devices	Allstate
Aetna Life & Casualty	Alltel
AFLAC	Alumax
Aid Association for Lutherans	Amdahl Corporation
Air Products & Chemicals	Amerada Hess
Albertson's	American Brands
Alco Standard	American Electric Power
Alcoa	American Express
Allegheny Power System	American Financial Group

American General
American Home Products
American International Group
American President
American Standard
American Stores
Amerisource Health
Ameritech
Amoco
AMP
AMR
Amway
Anheuser-Busch
AON
Apple Computer
Applied Materials
Arizona State Government
Aramark
Archer Daniels Midland
Armstrong World Ind.
Arrow Electronics
Asarco
Ashland
Associated Insurance
AST Research
AT&T
Atlantic Richfield
Automatic Data Processing
Avery Dennison
Avnet
Avon Products
Baker Hughes
Ball
Baltimore Gas & Electric
Banc One Corporation
Bank of America
Bank of New York Company
Bank of Boston Corporation
Bankamerica Corporation
Bankers Trust N.Y. Corporation
Barnett Banks
Baxter International
Bear Stearns
Becton Dickinson
Bell Atlantic
Bell Helicopter
Bellsouth
Bergen Brunswig
Berkshire Hathaway
Best Buy
Bethlehem Steel
Beverly Enterprises

Bindley Western
Black & Decker
Boatmen's Bancshares
Boeing
Boise Cascade
Bristol-Myers Squibb
Browning-Ferris Industries
Bruno's
Brunswick
Burlington Northern Santa Fe
Caldor
Caliber Systems
Campbell Soup
Canadian Tire Corporation
Cardinal Health
Carolina Power & Light
Case
Caterpillar
Centerior Energy
Centex
Central & South West
Champion International
Chase Manhattan Corporation
Chemical Banking Corporation
Chevron
Chiquita Brands International
Chrysler
Chubb
CIGNA
Cinergy
Circle K
Circuit City Stores
Cisco Systems
Citicorp
Clorox Company
CMS Energy
Coastal
Coca-Cola
Coca-Cola Enterprises
Colgate-Palmolive
College Ret. Equities Fund
Columbia Gas System
Columbia/HCA Healthcare
Comcast
Comerica
Compaq Computer Corporation
CompUSA
Computer Associates International
Computer Sciences
ConAgra
Conrail
Conseco

Consolidated Edison of N.Y.
Consolidated Freightways
Consolidated Natural Gas
Continental Airlines
Cooper Industries
Corestates Financial Corporation
Cornell University
Corning
Cotter
CPC International
Crown Cork & Seal
CSX
Cummins Engine
Cyprus Amax Minerals
Dana
Dayton Hudson
Dean Foods
Dean Witter Discover
Deere
Dell Computer
Delta Air Lines
Dial
Diamond Shamrock
Digital Equipment
Dillard Department Stores
DMR Group, Inc.
Dole Food
Dominion Resources
Dover
Dow Chemical
Dresser Industries
DTE Energy
Duke Power
Dun & Bradstreet
E.I. DuPont de Nemours
Eastman Chemical
Eastman Kodak
Eaton
Echlin
Eckerd
Edison International
Electronic Data Systems
Eli Lilly
Emerson Electric
Engelhard
Enron
Entergy
Estée Lauder
Exxon
Farmland Industries
Federal Express
Federal Home Loan Mtg.

Federal National Mortgage Association
Federated Department Stores
FHP International
Fidelity Investments
First Bank System
First Chicago NDB Corporation
First Data
First Interstate Bancorp
First Union Corporation
Flagstar
Fleet Financial Group
Fleetwood Enterprises
Fleming
Florida Progress
Fluor
FMC
Food 4 Less Holdings
Ford Motor Company
Foster Wheeler
Foundation Health
Foxmeyer Health
FPL Group
Fred Meyer
Gannett
Gap
Gateway 2000
Geico
General Dynamics
General Electric
General Instrument
General Mills
General Motors
General Public Utilities
General RE
Genuine Parts
Georgia-Pacific
Giant Food
Gillette
Glaxo, Inc.
Golden West Financial Corporation
Goodyear Tire & Rubber
Graybar Electric
Great Western Financial Corporation
GTE
Guardian Life of America
H. F. Ahmanson
H. J. Heinz
Halliburton
Hannaford Bros.
Harcourt General
Harris
Hasbro

Health Systems International
Hershey Foods
Hewlett-Packard
Home Depot
Honeywell
Hormel Foods
Household International
Houston Industries
Humana
IBP
Illinois Tool Works
Ingersoll-Rand
Inland Steel Industries
Intel
Intelligent Electronics
International Business Machines
International Paper
ITT
ITT Hartford Group
ITT Industries
J.C. Penney
J.P. Morgan & Co.
James River Corporation of Virginia
Jefferson Smurfit
John Hancock Mutual Life Insurance
Johnson & Johnson
Johnson Controls
K-Mart
Kaiser Permanente
Kellogg
Kelly Services
Kerr-McGee
Keycorp
Kimberly-Clark
Knight-Ridder
Kroger
Lear Seating
Lehman Brothers Holdings
Levi Strauss Associates
Liberty Mutual Insurance Group
Limited
Lincoln National
Litton Industries
Lockheed Martin
Loews
Logica
Long Island Lighting
Longs Drug Stores
Loral
Louisiana-Pacific
Lowe's
LTV

Lyondell Petrochemical
Manpower
Manville
Mapco
Maricopa County, Arizona
Marriott International
Marsh & McLennan
Masco
Massachusetts Mutual Life Insurance
Mattel
Maxxam
May Department Stores
Maytag
MBNA
McDonald's
McDonnell Douglas
McGraw-Hill
MCI Communications
McKesson
Mead
Mellon Bank Corporation
Melville
Memorial Sloan-Kettering Cancer Center
Mercantile Stores
Merck
Merisel
Merrill Lynch
Metropolitan Life Insurance
Microage
Micron Technology
Microsoft
Minnesota Mining & Mfg.
Mobil
Monsanto
Morgan Stanley Group
Morrison Knudsen
Morton International
Motorola
Mutual of Omaha Insurance
Nash Finch
National City Corporation
Nationsbank Corporation
Nationwide Insurance Enterprise
Navistar International
New York Life Insurance
Newell
NGC
Niagara Mohawk Power
Nike
Noram Energy
Nordstrom
Norfolk Southern

Northeast Utilities
Northern States Power
Northrop Grumman
Northwest Airlines
Northwestern Mutual Life
Norwest Corporation
Nucor
NYNEX
Occidental Petroleum
Office Depot
OfficeMax
Ohio Edison
Olin
Olsten
Oracle
Overnite Transportation Company
Owens & Minor
Owens-Corning
Owens-Illinois
Paccar
Pacific Gas & Electric
Pacific Mutual Life Insurance
Pacific Telesis Group
Pacificare Health Systems
Pacificorp
Paine Webber Group
Panenergy
Parker Hannifin
Payless Cashways
Peco Energy
Penn Traffic
Pennzoil
PeopleSoft
Pepsico
Peter Kiewit Sons
Pfizer
Pharmacia & Upjohn
Phelps Dodge
Philip Morris
Phillips Petroleum
Pitney Bowes
Pittston
PNC Bank Corporation
PP&L Resources
PPG Industries
Praxair
Premark International
Price Costco
Principal Mutual Life Insurance
Procter & Gamble
Progressive
Provident Cos.

Providian
Prudential Insurance of America
Public Service Entr. Group
Publix Super Markets
Quaker Oats
Quantum
R.R. Donnelley & Sons
Ralston Purina
Raytheon
Reader's Digest Association
Reebok International
Reliance Group Holdings
Republic New York Corporation
Revco D.S.
Reynolds Metals
Rite Aid
RJR Nabisco Holdings
Rockwell International
Rohm & Haas
Roundy's
Ryder System
Safeco
Safeway
Salomon
Sara Lee
SBC Communications
Schering-Plough
SCI Systems
Seagate Technology
Sears Roebuck
Service Merchandise
ServiceMaster
Sharp HealthCare
Shaw Industries
Sherwin-Williams
Smith's Food & Drug Centers
Sonoco Products
Southern
Southern Pacific Rail
Southwest Airlines
Spartan Stores
Sprint
St. Paul Cos.
Stanley Works
Staples
State Farm Group
State Street Boston Corporation
Stone Container
Stop & Shop
StorageTek
Student Loan Marketing Association
Sun

Sun Microsystems
Suntrust Banks
Supermarkets General Holdings
Supervalu
Sysco
Tandy
Teachers Ins. & Annuity
Tech Data
Tele-Communications
Teledyne
Temple-Inland
Tenet Healthcare
Tenneco
Texaco
Texas Instruments
Texas Utilities
Textron
Thrifty Payless Holdings
Time Warner
Times Mirror
TJX
Tosco
Toys 'R Us
Trans World Airlines
Transamerica
Travelers Group
Tribune
TRW
Turner Broadcasting
Turner Corporation
Tyco International
Tyson Foods
U.S. Bancorp
U.S. Healthcare
U.S. Industries
UAL
Ultramar
Unicom
Union Camp
Union Carbide
Union Pacific
Unisys

United Healthcare
United Parcel Service
United Services Auto. Assn.
United Technologies
Universal
Unocal
Unum
U S WEST
USAIR Group
USF&G
USG
USX
Utilicorp United
Valero Energy
VF
Viacom
Vons
W. R. Grace
W. W. Grainger
Waban
Wachovia Corporation
Wal-Mart Stores
Walgreen
Walt Disney, Inc.
Warner-Lambert
Wellpoint Health Networks
Wells Fargo & Co.
Westinghouse Electric
Westvaco
Weyerhaeuser
Whirlpool
Whitman
Willamette Industries
Williams
Winn-Dixie Stores
WMX Technologies
Woolworth
Worldcom
Xerox
Yellow
York International

4 Designing the Perfect Scannable Résumé

In all of my interviews with companies that scan résumés into computerized databases, the staffing professionals emphasized the importance of a résumé designed with scannability in mind. Your paper résumé must be formatted in such a way that a scanner can read it or the words won't be spelled right. And, if the words aren't spelled right, a keyword search will never turn up your résumé.

This chapter is devoted to helping you avoid the pitfalls that commonly cause a résumé to scan poorly. This includes choosing the right fonts, laying out the text of your résumé in such a way that it is scanner friendly, selecting the right paper color, etc. At the end of the chapter are some samples of résumés that made it through the scanning process with flying colors. With these guidelines, your résumé will be ripe picking for the hiring manager's computerized keyword search.

■ *The Complete Guide to Style, Fonts, Paper, and so on*

Let's start at the top of your résumé and work our way down. Since your résumé is basically an advertisement for you and your skills, you should think about the design of your résumé from a marketing standpoint. When you see a well-designed ad, what is the first thing you notice (besides a picture of the product)? The product name, of course. Since you *are* the product, your name should be the first thing a reader sees and remembers.

❑ *Your Name*

The size and boldness of the type of your name should be larger than the largest font used in your text, but for a scannable résumé it should be no larger than 20-point type. You may use either all capital letters or a combination of upper and lower case for your name but avoid using a combination of capitals with small capitals (LIKE THIS). This is an example of a Times Roman Bold font in a few good point sizes for the name on a scannable résumé:

- **14 POINT NAME**
- **16 POINT NAME**
- **18 POINT NAME**
- **20 POINT NAME**

Avoid using decorative fonts like these for either your name or your text:

- **Bodini**
- **BROADWAY ENGRAVED**
- Bullwinkle
- *Commercial Script*
- COTTONWOOD

- Crazed
- *Freestyle Script*
- Kashmir
- *Kaufmann*
- Linotext

Using reverse boxes to print white type on a black (or gray shaded) background is another mistake. Scanners can't read them and your name will be missing from your résumé! Here is a sample of a reverse boxed name:

PAT CRISCITO

Lastly, make certain your name is at the top of each page of your résumé. The clerks who scan résumés are often dealing with hundreds of pieces of paper a week—if not every day. It is very easy for the pages of your résumé to become separated from each other, especially since it is not a good idea to staple a scannable résumé.

❑ *Address*

Next comes your contact information. It isn't always necessary to put your address at the top of your scannable résumé. Today's sophisticated applicant tracking systems know by more than position on the résumé whether the text is an address or phone number. It is six of one, half a dozen of another whether you put your contact information at the top or bottom of your résumé. Choose based on your personal preference. However, always list your e-mail address in addition to your phone/fax numbers and postal mailing information. It shows you are comfortable with today's technology.

❏ *Fonts*

Use popular fonts that are not overly decorative in order to ensure optimum scannability.

This sentence is typeset in a decorative font that is known to cause problems with résumé scannability (Sanvito).

So is this sentence (AGaramond Italic).

Following are some samples of good fonts for a scannable résumé:

Serif Fonts *(traditional fonts with little "feet" on the edges of the letters)*

Bookman . . . . The quick brown fox jumps over a lazy dog
THE QUICK BROWN FOX JUMPS OVER A LAZY DOG

Clearface . . . . The quick brown fox jumps over a lazy dog
THE QUICK BROWN FOX JUMPS OVER A LAZY DOG

Garamond . . . . The quick brown fox jumps over a lazy dog
THE QUICK BROWN FOX JUMPS OVER A LAZY DOG

Minion Condensed . . . . The quick brown fox jumps over a lazy dog
THE QUICK BROWN FOX JUMPS OVER A LAZY DOG

New Century Schoolbook . . . . The quick brown fox jumps over a lazy dog
THE QUICK BROWN FOX JUMPS OVER A LAZY DOG

Palatino . . . . The quick brown fox jumps over a lazy dog
THE QUICK BROWN FOX JUMPS OVER A LAZY DOG

Times Roman . . . . The quick brown fox jumps over a lazy dog
THE QUICK BROWN FOX JUMPS OVER A LAZY DOG

Utopia . . . . The quick brown fox jumps over a lazy dog
THE QUICK BROWN FOX JUMPS OVER A LAZY DOG

Sans Serif *(contemporary fonts with no decorative "feet")*

Avant Garde . . . . The quick brown fox jumps over a lazy dog
THE QUICK BROWN FOX JUMPS OVER A LAZY DOG

Eurostile . . . . The quick brown fox jumps over a lazy dog
THE QUICK BROWN FOX JUMPS OVER A LAZY DOG

Helvetica	The quick brown fox jumps over a lazy dog
	THE QUICK BROWN FOX JUMPS OVER A LAZY DOG
Helvetica Condensed	The quick brown fox jumps over a lazy dog
	THE QUICK BROWN FOX JUMPS OVER A LAZY DOG
Helvetica Narrow	The quick brown fox jumps over a lazy dog
	THE QUICK BROWN FOX JUMPS OVER A LAZY DOG
Myriad	The quick brown fox jumps over a lazy dog
	THE QUICK BROWN FOX JUMPS OVER A LAZY DOG
Optima	The quick brown fox jumps over a lazy dog
	THE QUICK BROWN FOX JUMPS OVER A LAZY DOG

It doesn't make any difference whether you choose a serif or a sans serif font, but the font size should be no smaller than 9 points and no larger than 12 points for the text. Having said that, you will notice that the fonts in the examples above are all slightly different in size even though they are exactly the same point size. Every font has its own designer and its own personality, which means that no two typefaces are exactly the same. Look at the difference between the 9 point Avant Garde and the 9 point Times Roman fonts below:

- Times Roman—9 point

- Avant Garde—9 point

You will notice that the Times Roman appears considerably smaller and could potentially cause problems with a scanner, while the 9 point Lucinda Sans (and the other sans serif fonts above) scanned fine in all of our tests.

The key to choosing a font for a scannable résumé is that none of the letters touch one another at any time. This can be caused by poor font design, by adjusting the kerning (the spacing between letters) in your word processor, or by printing your résumé with a low-quality printer (i.e., some dot matrix printers). Even ink jet printers can cause the ink to run together between letters with the wrong kind of paper.

Any time one letter touches another, a scanner will have a difficult time distinguishing the shapes of the letters and you will end up with misspellings on your résumé. A keyword search looks for words that are spelled correctly, so a misspelled word is as good as no word.

This is the same reason you don't want to use underlining on your résumé. Underlines touch the descenders on letters like g, j, p, q, and y and make it difficult for an OCR program to interpret their shapes. Take a look at these words and see if you can tell where a scanner would have trouble:

- The quick brown fox jumps over a lazy dog

- The quick brown fox jumps over a lazy dog

- **The quick brown fox jumps over a lazy dog**

- The quick brown fox jumps over a lazy dog

Related to fonts are bullets—special characters used at the beginning of indented short sentences to call attention to individual items on a résumé. These characters should be round and solid (•) for a scannable résumé. Scanners interpret hollow bullets (○) as the letter "o." Don't use unusually shaped bullets (▫, ❖, ✛) because the scanner will either eliminate them altogether or try to interpret them as letters.

While we are on the topic of special characters, the % and & signs cause problems for some OCR software, so always spell out the words *percent* and *and*. Foreign accents and letters that are not part of the English alphabet will also be misinterpreted by optical character recognition.

Even though you have probably heard that italics are a no-no on a scannable résumé, today's more sophisticated optical character recognition software can usually read italics without difficulty. The experts at Resumix, Restrac, and SmartSearch2 all state that their software has no problem reading italics, and my staff has confirmed that with tests. We have even scanned résumés typeset in all italics without a problem, although I don't recommend that simply from a readability standpoint. The key is to choose a font that is easy to read and not overly decorative. The italic typefaces of any of the samples in this chapter would be fine to use as accents on your résumé.

❏ *Format*

Rely on white space to define sections. Scanners like white space. They use it to determine when one section has ended and the next has begun. Horizontal lines can also be used to define sections since they are usually ignored by more sophisticated scanning software, provided they do not touch any of the letters on the page. However, avoid the use of short, vertical lines or boxes since scanners try to interpret these as letters.

Don't use columns (like a newspaper) on your résumé. Scanners read from left to right and often have difficulty determining how to arrange text that was originally set in columns. Although the keywords will be intact, your résumé may end up looking like garbage in the ASCII text version created during the OCR process.

Dot leaders (like this . . . .) can cause major headaches for the scanner, so avoid them.

One nice thing about electronic résumés is that they don't have to be limited to one page. The more keywords and synonyms you are able to use, the better your chances of being selected in a keyword search. Therefore, it is better to have a two-page résumé with all of your skills and qualifications listed than to have a one-page résumé with information missing because you tried to conserve space. The general rule for an electronic résumé today is:

- New graduates—one page
- Most people—one or two pages
- Senior executives—two or three pages

One caution, however. The reader sees only one screen at a time and may decide to stop reading after the first screen if something doesn't entice him or her to read on. Therefore, you should make certain that the meat of your résumé is on the first half of the first page. This can be accomplished with a profile or keyword summary, followed by a list of your achievements (see the screen shot below for a good example).

Remember to keep your sentences powerful and interesting to read. Cyberspace doesn't negate the need for good writing. You still want a human being to read your résumé sooner or later!

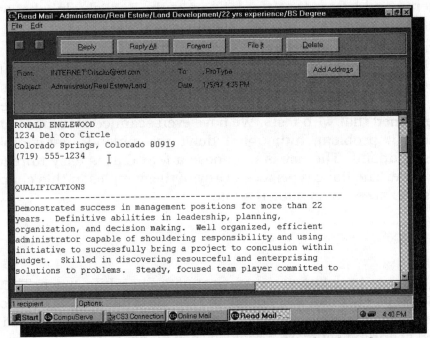

Screen shot of CompuServe E-mail reprinted with permission from CompuServe.

❑ *Paper*

Print your résumé on a high-quality, light-colored paper (white, off-white, or *very* light gray). Never use papers with a background (pictures, marble shades, or speckles). The scanner tries to interpret the patterns and dots as letters. This is a good rule to follow even for paper résumés that will never be scanned. Often companies will photocopy your résumé to hand to a hiring manager, and dark colors or patterns will simply turn into dark masses that make your résumé difficult to read. If a company has multiple locations, the original résumé may even get faxed from one site to another and the same thing happens.

Avoid using photocopies of your résumé. Original laser printed masters are best, although a high-quality ink-jet printer is acceptable. Do not use a dot matrix printer since the letters sometimes touch each other or are not solid.

Print on only one side of the page and use standard-size, 8½ × 11 paper. The scanner cannot turn your page over, so the reverse side might be missed when the clerk puts your résumé into the automatic document feeder. That same process is the reason why you should not use 11 × 17 size paper. The pages would have to be cut into 8½ × 11 sheets and the printing on the reverse side would not get scanned.

Don't fold your résumé since the creases make it harder to scan. It is much better to invest in flat, 9 × 12 envelopes and an extra two bits of postage to make a good first impression. Laser print and copier toner tend to crack off the page when creased, making the letters on the fold line less than solid, which a scanner could easily misinterpret. Staple holes cause the same problem, so never put a staple in a résumé you know will be scanned.

Now that you know all the secrets for designing a résumé that will pass the scannability test, let's look at some sample résumés that scanned well.

KEVIN BERRIE

| Address | 123 Sand Road, Woodland Park, Colorado 80863 | (719) 555-1234 |

PROFILE

- Ambitious sales professional with more than ten years of proven sales experience.
- Strong background in building territories and using creative marketing approaches.
- Respected for powerful negotiating and closing abilities.
- Self-motivated and focused; comfortable working independently with little supervision.
- Computer literate in Windows, MS Word, MS Office, and the Internet.

EXPERIENCE

SALES REPRESENTATIVE (1996 – Present)
Russ Berrie Company, Colorado Springs, Colorado
- Sold giftware to wholesale accounts for the largest distributor in the United States
- Consistently exceeded sales goals; increased new accounts by 20 percent and sales volume by 35 percent in first three months.
- Gained extensive experience in cold calling and getting to the decision maker.
- Made courtesy calls to existing customers to ensure satisfaction and customer retention.

OWNER/MANAGER (1986 – 1996)
Sierra Distributing, Colorado Springs, Colorado
- Owned and operated a company that manufactured and distributed leather goods, jewelry, and other items to major clients in the motorcycle industry, including Harley-Davidson and the Motorcycle Warehouse.
- Developed new customers through trade shows and effective sales and marketing campaigns.
- Managed all aspects of administration, purchasing, inventory management, manufacturing, quality control, cost controls, importing, and achieving revenue objectives.

ACCOUNT EXECUTIVE (1993 – 1995)
Western Distributing, Colorado Springs, Colorado
- Opened new accounts for the area's largest beverage distributor.
- Achieved a minimum of 30 percent monthly growth in an established territory.
- Awarded salesman of the month within the first three months.
- Earned a bonus every month for exceptional sales volume.
- Written up in corporate newsletters for sales achievements.

PLANT MANAGER/PRODUCTION MANAGER (1982 – 1985)
Coulson of Texas, Dale Electronics, and *Hyer Boot Company*, El Paso, Texas
- Coordinated and supervised all phases of production, including plant engineering and layout, research and development, quality control, shipping and receiving, inventory control, warehousing, security, maintenance, and budgeting.
- Directed as many as 250 plant personnel, including 14 supervisors.
- Increased production by 30 percent, substantially upgraded product quality, cut production costs by 10 percent, and reduced overtime.

EDUCATION

BACHELOR OF SCIENCE IN BIOLOGY (1974)
University of Texas, El Paso, Texas
- Minor in Geology.

CONTINUING EDUCATION
- Extensive sales training through corporate seminars and independent study.

Ken E. Kearney

1234 Traverse Court • Colorado Springs, Colorado 80916 • (719) 555-1234

QUALIFICATIONS

- Skilled assembler with 15 years of diverse experience
- Background in quality control and new product startup
- Results-oriented professional who gets the job done
- Effective team player with strong communication and facilitation skills

EXPERIENCE

Technical

- Developed "Saturn" disk drives for Quantum and supported engineering in two locations with process development.
- Established manufacturing production of new 2- and 4-gigabyte disk drives in a state-of-the-art 100K clean room.
- Served as lead facilitator for the disk drive rework room.
- Set up all work stations and obtained certifications in over 95 percent of them.
- Built 7/8 platter disk drives as an Assembler III; performed failure analysis.
- Traveled to Sequel in San Jose to set up the 8X line purchased from DEC.
- Served as liaison between line workers and management.
- Produced master valves for Eaton within $3/10,000^{th}$ of customer specifications.

Quality Control

- Tested disk drives in an evaluation laboratory to assure compatibility.
- Checked valves—both visually and using a Pentrex booth—for surface metallurgical defects.
- Set tolerances on the production lines, gauges, and dial indicators to assure quality.
- Calibrated micrometers and calipers; tested and maintained various equipment.
- Corrected machine problems on the manufacturing floor and performed parts review following blueprint changes.

Inventory Management

- Implemented a just-in-time manufacturing/pull system.
- Simplified ordering parts by setting up a Kanban system and changing the layout to match the clean room.
- Maintained inventory and ordered parts to match the build schedule.

Training and Supervision

- Supervised up to eighteen workers in clean-room assembly; audited and completed time cards.
- Trained staff in assembly, quality control, and inventory control concepts.

EMPLOYMENT HISTORY

1994–1995	**Assembler III**	Quantum Corporation	Colorado Springs, CO
1992–1994	**Assembler III**	Digital Equipment Corporation	Colorado Springs, CO
1990–1992	**Clean Room Facilitator**	Digital Equipment Corporation	Colorado Springs, CO
1987–1990	**Material Controller**	Digital Equipment Corporation	Colorado Springs, CO
1986–1987	**Material Handler**	Digital Equipment Corporation	Colorado Springs, CO
1985–1987	**Material Handler**	Talent Tree Temporaries	Denver, CO
1981–1985	**Quality Assurance Inspector**	Eaton Corporation	Kearney, NE

EDUCATION

University of South Dakota, Springfield, South Dakota
3 credits short of an Associate Degree in Diesel Technology

U.S. Navy, Memphis, Tennessee
Aviation Hydraulics Class "A"

JEFFREY A. MCENTIRE

PROFILE

- Dynamic public speaker with a strong background in the food, beverage, and travel industries.
- Demonstrated success in a broad range of management positions for more than 11 years.
- Self-motivated and focused; comfortable working independently or as part of an integrated team.
- Adept at communicating effectively with people of diverse interests and levels of authority.

PHILOSOPHY

Guest obsession is the act of taking exceptional customer service to the next level. Inside every conscious being is the simple "Wow!" sensation. It is a universal feeling that crosses language barriers, cultures, and genders. Everyone has it! If you can make customers think, feel, or even say "Wow!" because of something you have done to service them, they will be your customers for life.

EXPERIENCE
Training

- Designed and presented "The Wow Factor" seminar to numerous service-based companies. Part one of the seminar is for managers and supervisors and is designed to help them internalize The Wow Factor, making it a part of their lives and allowing them to train their workers. Part two is for employees. It teaches them how to believe in The Wow Factor and how the concept can put money in their pockets.
- Presented monthly seminars to Macaroni Grill staff members to promote guest obsession and personal development.
- Trained and developed restaurant managers through the management development program.
- Instructed more than 70 Disney bartenders in guest service and flair as part of a mandatory course.
- Created a regular "personal challenge day" for employees, a day dedicated to team building exercises and group events, ending with a personal challenge (bungee jumping or hang gliding).
- Guest speaker for a 125-member luncheon of the Osceola Chamber of Commerce.
- Invited to speak for the graduation ceremonies of the Kissimmee Culinary Institute.

Management

- Successfully opened and managed various high-profile restaurants throughout the Southeast.
- Assumed the management of a large-volume Macaroni Grill restaurant, increasing sales in just under two months to $4.6 million, moving the store from number four to number two in the area.
- Recruited, hired, supervised, and motivated assistant managers, chefs, and up to 250 staff.
- Accountable for budgeting, profit and loss, and full business planning.

Walt Disney

- Assisted in the development of the concept for the Beach Club at Walt Disney World and in implementing the conversion to a $6.2 million operation; stayed on as General Manager.
- Devised and executed profitable promotions never before attempted by Walt Disney World, including the Venus Swimwear Pageant and the Pleasure Island Jet Ski Tournament.
- Coordinated service staff, nightly promotions, and tours for celebrities such as Tom Cruise, Warren Beatty, Michael Jackson, and Steven Spielberg, among others.
- Assisted in the pre-opening development of Pleasure Island and managed the operations of the Comedy Warehouse, Adventurers Club, and Neon Armadillo with a staff of 250 (gained experience in labor union contracts and negotiations).
- Planned and placed the initial $600,000 liquor order for all of Pleasure Island.
- Managed the Steermans Quarters Restaurant on the Empress Lilly Riverboat with full-service breakfast, lunch, and dinner, and two seatings of 500 per day for the Disney character breakfast.

Entrepreneurial

- Created a successful company that was designed to take guest obsession to a new level with high-profile travelers, allowing travelers to maximize their travel time through the use of a personal itinerary specialist who traveled with and coordinated every detail.
- Raised capital through research and development of a detailed business plan.
- Handled clients such as Reba McEntire, Ricky Skaggs, Robin Leech, etc.
- Established detailed network of contacts throughout Florida and the Caribbean, including restaurants, hotels, golf courses, boat charters, and other travel organizations.
- Successfully negotiated a contract for the design and development of a country music nightclub for The Shooters Corporation, including everything from interior design to merchandise sales.
- Owned and operated Success Analysis, a company that sent secret shoppers into restaurants to critique the operation, providing a detailed report to enhance customer service.

ADDRESS

17 Turkey Point Drive, Melbourn, Florida 32932   Pager (800) 555-1234, Phone (407) 555-1234

58

WORK HISTORY	**General Manager**, Romano's Macaroni Grill, Dunwoody, Georgia	1995 – 1996
	General Manager, Romano's Macaroni Grill, Kissimmee, Florida	1995
	Manager, Romano's Macaroni Grill, Altamonte Springs, Florida	1993 – 1994
	Entrepreneur, Travel Itineraries, Inc., and Success Analysis	1991 – 1993
	Walt Disney Management Development Program	1988 – 1991
	Beach Club, Pleasure Island, Empress Lilly Riverboat	
	Associate General Manager, Safari Bar and Restaurant, Houston, Texas	1985 – 1988
	Promoted from various positions, including Assistant Manager, Bar Manager, Head Music Programmer, and Front Door Manager in six different locations	

EDUCATION

WALT DISNEY MANAGEMENT DEVELOPMENT PROGRAM   1988
- Completed six-month program in only four months.
- Learned every facet of the Disney organization, from in-depth culinary skills to financial controls.

UNIVERSITY OF SOUTH ALABAMA   1983 – 1985
- Concentration in business management.

COMMUNITY

SERVICE

- Member of the Osceola Chamber of Commerce Board of Directors, Kissimmee, Florida   1995 – 1996
- Board Member and Counselor for Central Florida Marshall Arts and Boxing Academy (a not-for-profit prison youth release program)   1991 – 1994

COMPUTERS

- Knowledge of both DOS and Macintosh computer environments
- Skilled in Internet communications, Excel, PageMaker, Adobe Photoshop, Filemaker Pro, Daytimer, Quicken, and MacWrite

KENNETH MELBOURNE

123 Potomac Avenue • University Park, Texas 75205 • (214) 555-1234

PROFILE

- Highly motivated, confident, and energetic sales professional with a background in high-tech industries.
- Award-winning history of building new territories and using creative marketing approaches.
- Team player with exceptional communication and presentation skills.
- Experience with international marketing, competitive strategy, strategic business planning, re-engineering, case studies/data driven models, telecommunications, and information technology.
- Proficient in PC, Windows NT, Windows, UNIX, and Macintosh computer environments; extensive experience with Access, PowerPoint, MS Word, Excel, and programming languages.

EDUCATION

SOUTHERN METHODIST UNIVERSITY, Cox School of Business, Dallas, Texas   1995 – 1997
UNIVERSITY OF TEXAS, Arlington, Texas   1993 – 1995
Bachelor of Business Administration, May 1997
- Major in Management Information Services; Minor in International Business
- SMU Scholarship, Who's Who Among Students in American Universities and Colleges
- Financial Management Association National Honor Society, Alpha Chi National Honor Society
- Beta Gamma Sigma National Honor Society for Collegiate Schools of Business, Golden Key Honor Society

EXPERIENCE

Southern Methodist University, Dallas, Texas   *Systems Administrator*   1995 – Present
Improved efficiency by identifying areas requiring change and specifically developing, testing, and implementing new practices and procedures. Streamlined an automated network-based database that maintains records in excess of $1.3 million within the External Relations Office. Analyzed, designed, and supported the faculty information system for the Cox School of Business. Created and maintained HTML web pages for the Dean's Council. Work/study program for 30 hours per week while carrying a full-time academic schedule.

Interstate Battery Systems of America, Dallas, Texas   *National Sales Representative*   1988 – 1991
Performed quantitative analyses and evaluations of distributor business reports at corporate headquarters. Prepared, summarized, and presented findings to senior management. Promoted to National Sales Representative after only six months of employment. Traveled extensively to establish new business opportunities for distributors. Maintained 100+ local client accounts. Managed point-of-sale merchandising systems. Received awards for yearly top sales and most new accounts generated (52 percent cold-call closing ratio).

IDD Products, Irving, Texas   *Sole Proprietor*   1984 – 1988
Developed market entry strategy for home building related consumer goods products for the Dallas/Fort Worth metroplex. Implemented promotional strategy and sold to a 200+ customer base, providing comparative market research of cost savings to customers. Buyer in the World Trade Center and Dallas Trade Mart and Design Center.

Lanier Business Products, Dallas, Texas   *Electronic Technician*   1983 – 1984
Maintained client accounts for 300+ corporations within a 200-mile radius of the Dallas/Fort Worth metroplex. Analyzed and serviced 3M copy machines and sold maintenance contracts for equipment. Recognized by Atlanta headquarters for generating highest yearly sales volume in the Western Region following first six months of employment. Eight-time recipient of top production award for monthly volume.

ADDITIONAL EXPERIENCE

- Gained extensive teamwork experience through membership in university committees, including Presidential, Student Advisory, Missions and Objectives, Marketing Task Force, Appeals, Rules, Recruitment, and Affairs.
- Used strong presentation skills to address North Texas Articulation Council Advisor's Conference.
- President and founding officer of the University Club; negotiated contract with Texas Rangers baseball club and sports food management; raised more than $30,000 within six months.

Molly Fitch

PROFILE
- Experienced advertising account executive with a diverse background.
- Dedicated professional who works until the job is done.
- Well-organized but flexible problem solver who enjoys being challenged.
- Effective team player with strong interpersonal and communication skills.

EXPERIENCE

ACCOUNT EXECUTIVE (1/95 – Present)
RPM Advertising (formerly Graham Advertising), Colorado Springs, Colorado
- Plan, coordinate, and direct advertising campaigns for clients.
- Responsible for more than $2.5 million in total advertising budgets, focusing on the automotive industry.
- Confer with clients to determine advertising requirements and budget limitations, utilizing knowledge of products, media capabilities, and audience characteristics.
- Work with agency artists and other media production specialists to select media type and cost, and to determine media timing.
- Negotiate contracts with newspapers and billboard advertisers.
- Coordinate activities of workers engaged in market research, copy writing, artwork layout, media buys, development of special displays and promotional items, and other production activities as needed to carry out approved campaign.
- Design preliminary newspaper ad layouts and write scripts for television and radio advertising.

MANAGER IN TRAINING (9/94 – 12/94)
Abercrombie and Fitch, Denver, Colorado
- Responsible for opening and closing the store, regulating saleable and damaged merchandise, collecting money for sales, and researching/collecting returned checks.
- Input payroll for more than 50 sales associates and balanced the books.
- Provided customer service in a retail environment and ensured customer satisfaction.

ASSISTANT MANAGER (5/93 – 9/94)
Cook's Nook, Fort Worth, Texas
- Assisted customers with purchases and maintained inventory of merchandise.
- Opened and closed the store each day, and balanced cash register receipts.

MARKETING INTERNSHIP (5/93 – 7/93)
The Marketing Group, Dallas, Texas
- Organized, edited, and distributed mass mailings for promotional campaigns.

RECEPTIONIST (Summers 1990, 1991, 1992)
Vidmar Motor Company, Pueblo, Colorado
- Contacted newspaper and radio stations to schedule advertising, make recommendations, and monitor trafficking.
- Assisted in editing television commercial promotions.
- Regulated telephone calls for 60 associates and maintained mail correspondence.

SALES REPRESENTATIVE (8/91 – 12/91)
Texas Christian University Skiff, Fort Worth, Texas
- Marketed advertisements for TCU's newspaper, *The Skiff*.
- Assisted in the design and layout of advertisements.

EDUCATION

BACHELOR OF ARTS, ADVERTISING/PUBLIC RELATIONS (5/94)
Texas Christian University, Fort Worth, Texas
- Emphasis in Business

ADDRESS

1234 Samuel Point, Colorado Springs, Colorado 80906, Phone (719) 555-1234

ROGER LE BARON

Address	*123 Plainview Place, Manitou Springs, Colorado 80829*	*(719) 555-1234*

PROFILE
- Dedicated fire chief and inspector with more than 20 years of firefighting experience.
- Background includes management, fire inspection, firefighting, and emergency treatment.
- Experienced in the application of the Uniform Fire Code, field supervision, personnel training, community relations, and public education.
- Effective team player with strong interpersonal and communication skills.
- Adept at working under pressure and handling emergency situations.

CERTIFICATION
- Colorado State Certified Firefighter II
- Colorado State Certified Fire Suppression Systems Inspector
- Colorado State Certified Code Enforcement Officer
- Scheduled to take ICBO Fire Inspector exam, November 1996
- Certified Emergency Medical Technician, 1974 – 1994

EXPERIENCE

Fire Chief
- Ensured the preservation of life, property, and safety through direction of proper emergency scene management.
- Supervised fire suppression, emergency medical treatment, and rescue operations.
- Investigated fire origins and wrote fire reports.
- Recruited and screened volunteer firefighters.
- Provided classroom and field training in strategies of fire suppression, ground hose lays, use and maintenance of equipment, safety and first aid, and rural and wildland firefighting.
- Coordinated activities with other fire departments in overlapping jurisdictions, ensuring smooth working relationships.
- Instrumental in the formation of the Northeast Teller County Fire Protection District.

Fire Inspector
- Inspected commercial/residential buildings and fire detection/suppression systems in order to detect hazardous conditions and to ensure compliance with city ordinances and fire codes.
- Consulted with architects, engineers, and contractors to expedite construction; conducted on-site inspections and plans reviews of construction in progress.
- Used long-term planning, conflict resolution, and follow-up skills to ensure that existing facilities were in compliance with code.
- Implemented a successful fire prevention program in the Manitou Springs schools through site visits, open houses, and building inspections.

Firefighting
- More than 20 years of firefighting experience.
- Received alarms, dispatched volunteers, and responded to fire scenes.
- Provided emergency medical care for the sick and injured, and assisted in rescues during fire and nonfire situations.

Zoning Ordinance
- Conducted extensive field investigations of properties, structures, and signs and enforced violations of the city zoning and land use ordinances.
- Evaluated and categorized violations and determined the appropriate course of action.
- Made presentations before the City Council, Planning Commission, and Hearing Officer on variances, appeals, ordinance amendments, and other enforcement-related matters.

Administration
- Responsible for six ambulances and a crew of twelve with Schaefer Ambulance Service.
- Supervised field operations, trained new drivers, and maintained vehicles and equipment.
- Helped the ambulance company grow to Santa Ana's largest ambulance service.
- Managed budgets, inventoried equipment, and ordered supplies.

WORK HISTORY	**Fire Code Inspector**, City of Colorado Springs, Colorado	1995 – Present
	Firefighter (Volunteer), Manitou Springs Fire Department, Colorado	1986 – Present
	Zoning Inspector, City of Colorado Springs, Colorado	1985 – 1994
	Fire Chief, Northeast Teller County Fire Protection District, Colorado	1985 – 1986
	Captain/Firefighter, Northeast Teller County Fire Protection District, Colorado	1982 – 1985
	Fire Inspector, City of Manitou Springs, Colorado	1984 – 1985
	Driver/Engineer, Ivywild/Cheyenne Cañon Fire Protection District, Colorado	1979 – 1984
	Captain (Volunteer), Ivywild/Cheyenne Cañon Fire Protection District, Colorado	1979 – 1984
	Field Supervisor/Crew Chief, Schaefer Ambulance Service, Santa Ana, California	1974 – 1979

TRAINING	**Fire Inspection Principles** (two weeks), National Fire Academy, Emmettsburg, Maryland	1996
	Annual ICBO Conference (one week)	1995, 1996
	Alarm Systems (four days), National Fire Protection Association	1995
	Firefighter Safety and Survival, National Fire Academy, Emmettsburg, Maryland	1986
	Arson Investigation Seminar, EMTAC Conference	1984
	High Rise Firefighting Seminar (two days), International Society of Fire Service Instructors	1982
	Rural Firefighting Tactics Seminar (two days), State of Colorado	1982
	Basic Auto Extrication (three days), Emergency Squad Training Institute	1980
	Various Other Courses with local fire departments throughout career	

HOLLY D. FIDELIO

123 Spring Grove Terrace • Colorado Springs, Colorado 80906 • (719) 555-1234

PROFILE
- Goal-directed hotel professional with a background in sales/marketing, project management, public relations, customer service, training, and supervision.
- Adept at managing multiple, complex tasks simultaneously.
- Respected for effective problem-solving and decision-making skills.
- Articulate and persuasive with strong interpersonal and communication skills.

EXPERIENCE

RADISSON INN NORTH, Colorado Springs, Colorado . . . . 1995 – Present
Director of Sales (May 1996 – Present)

Sales/Marketing
- Maximized customer satisfaction and revenue goals by developing and implementing effective sales and marketing strategies for regional and national sales accounts.
- Increased sales volume and profitability by formulating and executing projects for all markets.
- Maintained and built local corporate accounts by designing programs to meet client needs.
- Established sales goals and coordinated the development of the marketing plan and budget.
- Implemented strategies to improve market penetration and developed alternatives.

Administration
- Controlled the date, availability, and rate of guest rooms and function space.
- Reviewed market analysis to determine client needs, occupancy potential, desired rates, etc.
- Coordinated transient and group room commitments to ensure proper market mix.
- Qualified prospective leads and analyzed sales statistics to maximize profitability.
- Negotiated with clients to achieve maximum profit while ensuring customer satisfaction.

Supervision
- Selected qualified employees, conducted orientations and Radisson's "Yes I Can" training, evaluated performance, and recommended salary increases as appropriate.
- Utilized leadership skills and motivation techniques to optimize employee productivity.

Associate Director of Sales (November 1995 – May 1996)

Sales/Marketing
- Recruited by Radisson to assist the director of sales with department operations, market research, budgeting, sales planning, goal setting, and staff training.
- Achieved budget by identifying and actively soliciting individual and group business from new and existing local, regional, and national sales accounts.
- Aided in the development of group markets for off-season months.
- Assisted in the formation of the hotel marketing plan.
- Coordinated all bookings with other departments to ensure complete customer satisfaction.

LE BARON HOTEL, Colorado Springs, Colorado . . . . 1995 – 1995
Sales Manager

Sales/Marketing
- Negotiated and booked group business to achieve revenue and customer satisfaction goals.
- Achieved budgeted goals by making outside sales calls to solicit new and existing business from social, military, education, religious, fraternal, and association market segments.
- Assisted in the development of annual sales goals and room revenue budget.
- Entertained clients weekly and conducted on-site inspections.
- Serviced in-house customers to foster additional business, repeat bookings, and referrals.

FIGURE SKATING PROFESSIONAL, Colorado Springs, Colorado . . . . 1994 – Present

Instruction
- Taught figure skating, choreographed routines, and evaluated student performance.
- Motivated and assisted students in setting and achieving objectives.

Honors/Awards
- World-class figure skater and former national and international competitor.
- Gold medalist in ice dancing, 1989 World Junior Team Member, Sarajevo, Yugoslavia.
- Participated in USFSA seminar for elite American ice dancers and in the Olympic Training Center's sports science programs.
- National recipient of NutraSweet's "Giving it 100 percent" Award in 1988.
- Guest star on various ice shows throughout the United States.

MEDIA PLAY, Colorado Springs, Colorado . . . . 1993 – 1994
Manager

Management
- Actively involved in the design and start-up of a 50,000 sq. ft. retail outlet store.
- Responsible for merchandising, public relations, advertising, sales promotions, and book signings.
- Implemented human resource, cash control, and customer service procedures.
- Interviewed and hired employees; conducted performance evaluations.
- Managed load balancing and statistics for inventory, ordering, and sales databases.

64

EXPERIENCE (continued)	**PLAZA ICE CHALET**, Colorado Springs, Colorado . . . . 1989 – 1993 **Head Figure Skating Coach** • Served as head coach; supervised and managed coaching staff. • Provided individual and group instruction; implemented off-ice ballet, jazz, conditioning, and strength training programs. • Directed the annual Springspree and Festival of Lights ice shows, including choreography, music selection, publicity, advertising, and scheduling.
EDUCATION	**BACHELOR OF ARTS, PSYCHOLOGY**, *Summa Cum Laude*, GPA 4.0 . . . . 1993 **University of Colorado**, Colorado Springs, Colorado • Recognized as the Outstanding Social Sciences Undergraduate • University of Colorado Regent Scholar • Recipient of Colorado Scholastic Scholarship • Participated in the Psychology Honor Program • Member of the American Psychological Association, Psi Chi National Honor Society, Business Club, and Society for Human Resource Management
COMPUTERS	Experience with WordPerfect, MS Word, Windows, SPSS, Fidelio, Lotus 1-2-3, e-mail, and database management for local and network file systems
VOLUNTEER	• Teach marketing to university business classes as a guest speaker • Research Assistant to University of Colorado psychology professor • Assisted in homeless shelters and soup kitchens • Fund-raising volunteer for the United States Figure Skating Association
AFFILIATIONS	• Southern Colorado Business Travel Association, Board of Directors, 1997 • Society of Government Meeting Planners • United States Figure Skating Association • Professional Skaters Guild of America • National Strength and Conditioning Association • University of Colorado Alumni Association

SANDRA K. FRANCIS

12 Dolphin Circle • Colorado Springs, Colorado 80918 • (719) 555-1234

PROFILE
- Experienced Critical Care Nurse dedicated to providing excellence in patient care
- Detail oriented, thorough, and accurate working under pressure
- Adept at managing multiple and diverse tasks simultaneously
- Outstanding communication and interpersonal skills
- An empathetic, professional caregiver who is able to quickly establish and maintain rapport with patients

PROFESSIONAL EXPERIENCE

STAFF NURSE/CHARGE NURSE (July 1987 – Present)
St. Francis Hospital/Penrose Hospital, Intensive Care Unit, Colorado Springs, Colorado
- Assess, plan, and implement primary care of the critical medical, surgical, pediatric, and trauma patients and perform charge nurse functions.
- Monitor and trouble shoot ventilators, invasive hemodynamic catheters, and intracerebral pressure lines.
- Operate as primary fluid resuscitation nurse for trauma team and perform Code Blue functions according to ACLS protocols.

STAFF NURSE (RN) (October 1982 – July 1987)
Sacred Heart Hospital, Adult and Pediatric Intensive Care Unit, Pensacola, Florida
- Served as staff nurse in Pediatric ICU for the first four years, providing ongoing assessment, analysis, planning, evaluation, and problem solving.
- Provided primary care to critical pediatric patients, including medical, surgical, trauma, acute, and chronic care.
- Responsible for ventilators, intracerebral pressure lines, invasive hemodynamic catheters, and electrocardiograms.
- Rotated between adult and pediatric ICU during the last year.
- Responded to adult and pediatric traumas and Code Blues.

STAFF NURSE (LPN) (October 1979 – May 1982)
Sacred Heart Hospital, Orthopedic Floor, Pensacola, Florida
- Team nurse responsible for half of patients under direct supervision of a Registered Nurse while working toward an undergraduate degree in nursing.
- Gained experienced with total knee surgery, back surgery, back pain, trauma, and general overflow patients from other floors.
- Administered all medications except intravenous ones.
- Performed dressing changes and general care.

EDUCATION/ TRAINING

UNIVERSITY OF COLORADO, Colorado Springs, Colorado (1995)
Completed Pre-Med Requirements: general chemistry, physics, biology, organic chemistry, calculus, genetics, biochemistry

UNIVERSITY OF SOUTH ALABAMA, Mobile, Alabama (1989)
Bachelor of Science in Nursing

PENSACOLA JUNIOR COLLEGE, Pensacola, Florida (1982)
Associate of Science in Registered Nursing

OTHER TRAINING
- 16-week Critical Care Course (October 1985), Florida Hospital, Orlando, Florida
- Certificate of Occupation Proficiency in Practical Nursing (August 1979), Pensacola Junior College, Pensacola, Florida

PROFESSIONAL ACCOMPLISHMENTS
- CCRN certification by American Association of Critical Care Nurses (Since 1990)
- Advanced Cardiac Life Support (ACLS) (Since 1986)
- Trauma Nursing Core Course (TNCC) (November 1994)
- Proposed and implemented pediatric protocols and pediatric trauma cart at St. Francis Hospital ICU (1991)
- St. Elizabeth Ann Seton Nursing Award for Excellence (1990)

Anne K. Ferrer

1234 Camfield Circle • Phoenix, Arizona 80920 • (602) 555-1234

PROFILE

- Eleven years of diverse clinical experience as a speech-language pathologist
- Graduate degree in speech-language pathology with a GPA of 4.6/5.0
- Certified as clinically competent in speech pathology by the American Speech-Language-Hearing Association
- Team player with an infectious positive attitude and strong communication skills
- Highly self-motivated and confident problem solver who continually seeks ways to expand clinical knowledge

EXPERIENCE

Clinical Speech-Language Pathology

- Provided speech-language diagnostics and therapy to neurologically impaired adults in acute care hospital, rehabilitation, nursing home, and home health care settings.
- Interfaced with interdisciplinary team to develop functional outcome goals, returning adults and adolescents to previously held jobs with a 90 percent success rate by providing speech-language diagnostics and therapy in a mild traumatic brain injury rehabilitation program.
- Experienced in working with children (ages birth to three years) in an early intervention community program and with adults with neurogenic disorders and head/neck cancers.
- Experienced in providing therapy for dysphagia, aphasia, dysarthria, verbal apraxia, head trauma, voice disorders, fluency disorders, right hemisphere brain injuries, and articulation/phonology.
- Background in computer-assisted cognitive rehabilitation, diagnosis of swallowing disorders using the modified barium swallow procedure, and feeding groups.

Program Development

- Developed a mild head injury screening tool and informal cognitive evaluation criteria.
- Assisted in developing an Activities of Daily Living questionnaire to assess cognitive functional limitations.
- Met with team members weekly to develop programs for assisting patients in successfully returning to daily living functions.
- Initiated and implemented a sucking/swallowing intervention program for infants in a neonatal intensive care unit.
- Developed and implemented programs in tracheoesophageal puncture (TEP), cognitive retraining using a computer, and evaluation and treatment of swallowing disorders.

Supervision and Training

- Supervised speech-language pathology graduate students in diagnostics and therapy.
- Provided patient and family education to assist patients in achieving functional goals.
- Taught in-service and cross-training classes to peers and other medical staff.
- Served as in-service coordinator for a rehabilitation department for two years.

WORK HISTORY

CLINICAL SPEECH-LANGUAGE PATHOLOGIST

The Penrose-St. Francis Healthcare System, Colorado Springs, Colorado	1992 – present
Patti McGowan-Ferrer, MS, CCC, Colorado Springs, Colorado	1995 – present
Symphony Home Care Services, Colorado Springs, Colorado	1996 – present
Marquette General Hospital, Marquette, Michigan	1990 – 1992
Speech-Language-Hearing Center, Lubbock, Texas	1988 – 1989
Texas Tech University, Lubbock, Texas	Summer 1988
St. Mary's Hospital, Decatur, Illinois	1985 – 1987

EDUCATION

MASTER OF SCIENCE IN SPEECH AND LANGUAGE PATHOLOGY	1985
BACHELOR OF SCIENCE IN SPEECH AND HEARING SCIENCE	1983

University of Illinois, Champaign, Illinois

GARY D. BELLEVUE

Post Office Box 123456 • Peterson, Colorado 80914 • (719) 555-1234

OBJECTIVE   A challenging position in computer electronics.

PROFILE
- **EXPERIENCE** – Three years of in-depth experience as a computer and switching systems specialist.
- **EDUCATION** – Undergraduate degree in computer information systems. Associate degree in electronic systems technology.
- **TRAINING** – Extensive on-site computer training with Lockheed Martin, Digital Equipment Corporation (DEC), IBM, and the United States Air Force (USAF).
- **SKILLS** – Well organized, detail oriented, and analytical problem solver; able to pinpoint problems and initiate creative solutions in a timely and efficient manner.
- **LEADERSHIP** – Outstanding leader with a proven record of accomplishments.
- **TEAMWORK** – Member of the Unit Advisory Council and Work Center Quality Air Force team.
- **COMPUTERS** – Knowledge of IBM PC and mainframe computer systems, DOS, Windows, UNIX, MVS, VMS, Silicon Graphics, DEC hardware, and Netex networks.

EXPERIENCE   **ELECTRONICS SPECIALIST** (1993 – Present)
United States Air Force, NORAD, Cheyenne Mountain, Colorado Springs, Colorado
- Performed troubleshooting and repair on more than 200 printed circuit modules, power supplies, switch panels, keyboards, peripherals, and other repairable components of computer systems.
- Provided support for the logistical transition, troubleshooting, and repair of the new Space Defense Operations Center (SPADOC) computer system.
- Skilled in the use of diagnostic programs, oscilloscopes, I/O prom burners, logic analyzers, Genrad 1792D automatic test equipment, computer test beds, and other precision measuring equipment to diagnose problems.
- Supervised and trained five technicians, ensuring quality and productivity and prioritizing the work load to meet or exceed established milestones.
- Personally developed a simplified training program for the NOVA 1220 test bed, decreasing qualification time by more than 30 percent.
- Created more efficient programs for monitoring benchstock, fire prevention, tools, remote network security, and ground safety by reorganizing guidelines and procedures.
- Personally created a new method of isolating diagnostic subroutine failures by using a complex logic analyzer test set, identifying several undetected failures and increasing test bed reliability 20 percent.
- Was recognized by the Air Force for saving $25 to $75 per integrated circuit by using EPROM programmer expertise to program integrated circuits, allowing re-use of firmware.

EDUCATION   **MASTER OF SCIENCE, COMPUTER INFORMATION SYSTEMS** (1996 – Present)
University of Colorado, Colorado Springs, Colorado

BACHELOR OF SCIENCE, COMPUTER INFORMATION SYSTEMS (1989 – 1993)
Bellevue University, Bellevue, Nebraska
- Minor in Business Administration

ASSOCIATE OF SCIENCE, ELECTRONIC SYSTEMS TECHNOLOGY (1993 – 1996)
Community College of the Air Force, Maxwell Air Force Base, Montgomery, Alabama

TRAINING   **CIVILIAN ON-SITE TRAINING:** Lockheed Martin SPADOC 4C Hardware Maintenance Training (240 hours), 1996 • Digital SPADOC 4C Hardware Maintenance Training (200 hours), 1995 • IBM SPADOC 4C Hardware Maintenance Training (320 hours), 1995 • IBM I/O System Training, 1995 • Digital VAX 4000 Diagnostic and Module Level Repair, DSSI Subsystems, Baseband Ethernet Hardware, and TU80/81 Magtape Maintenance, 1995

U.S. AIR FORCE TRAINING: High Reliability Soldering (40 hours), 1994 • Apprentice Electronic Computer and Switching Systems Specialist (413 hours), 1993 • Computer and Switching Principles (574 hours), 1993 • Benchstock Management (8 hours), 1995 • Fiber Optics (32 hours), 1995 • Quality Awareness (16 hours), 1996

JAN T. CAMFIELD

SUMMARY OF QUALIFICATIONS

- Reliable and committed sales and marketing professional with 15 years of experience in the telecommunications industry.
- Proven track record of success in positions of increasing responsibility.
- Outstanding organizational and management skills; talent for seeing "the big picture."
- Adept at establishing effective working relationships with clients, colleagues, and industry associations.
- Highly motivated with a strong commitment to delivering quality service.
- Skilled in contract negotiations; articulate and persuasive in written and verbal presentations.

PROFESSIONAL EXPERIENCE

Sales/Marketing

Member of the sales team responsible for launching two cable television networks—Cable Health Network and Lifetime Television:

- Established network affiliates in the Central Region through analysis of the marketplace, cold calling, and exceptional after-sale service.
- Positioned niche network, negotiated contracts, and effected ongoing affiliate support with local ad sales, promotions, and community outreach programs.
- Consistently exceeded annual goals by 20 percent; recipient of four "Region of the Year" awards.

As Manager, Special Markets for Lifetime Television:

- Negotiated more than 200 new client agreements, expanding national distribution and revenue.
- Collaborated with marketing department to create targeted marketing campaigns for new distribution outlets, resulting in increased value, awareness, and sales.
- Organized participation in and worked trade shows.
- Developed and conducted product training seminars for client staff.

Management

As Manager, Special Markets for Lifetime Television (a newly created position and division of the company), developed and implemented sales and marketing strategies to increase distribution for the cable television network through alternate technologies, increasing annual revenue stream by $10M:

- Developed strategic plans, competitive analyses, budgets, and a business plan for the division.
- Worked closely with legal department to create form agreements for five distinct distribution outlets and revised agreements based on changing demands of marketplace.
- Acted as internal consultant on government rules and regulations affecting alternate markets.
- Made presentations and participated in panels at industry trade shows, increasing awareness and value of the network in the new marketplace.
- Directed trade association task forces to examine and resolve industry issues.

WORK HISTORY

1988 – 1996	Special Markets Manager	Lifetime Television, Dallas, Texas
1985 – 1988	Regional Account Manager	Lifetime Television, Dallas, Texas
1984 – 1985	Marketing Coordinator	Lifetime Television, Dallas, Texas
1982 – 1984	Marketing Coordinator	Cable Health Network (sold to Lifetime), Dallas, Texas
1980 – 1982	Sales/Marketing Assistant	Frito-Lay, Inc., Dallas, Texas
1978 – 1980	Account Representative	Paramount Pictures, Atlanta, Georgia

1234 Biltmore Court • Aspen, Colorado 80907 • (719) 555-1234

EDWARD L. PETERSON

1234 Arequa Ridge Drive • Colorado Springs, Colorado 80919 • (719) 555-1234

QUALIFICATIONS
- Experienced project manager with a background in military logistics and the private sector
- Profit-oriented, conscientious manager with strong organizational skills
- Exceptional communication skills
- Able to motivate others to function as a successful team

EXPERIENCE

JAMITCH ENTERPRISES, Peterson AFB, Colorado (1992 – Present)
Project Manager, Standard Base Supply System Contract
- Responsible for the overall planning, directing, and resource management of a private-sector contract with the U.S. Air Force ($150 million of inventory and 110,000 transactions per month).
- Realized a profit through efficient utilization of resources, cost controls, safety and quality control, problem resolution, and budget programming.
- Selected and managed a work force of approximately 140 personnel at four locations, ensuring effective staffing and union negotiations.

TECOM, INC., Peterson AFB, Colorado (1983 – 1992)
Project Manager, Standard Base Supply System Contract (1987 – 1992)
Project Manager, Transient Alert Services (1986 – 1987)
Consultant (1983 – 1986)
- Responsible for the same duties as above for five years.
- Managed Transient Alert Services, including the provision of appropriate arrival and departure services for 500–600 transient aircraft per month.
- Supervised, trained, and scheduled a staff of 26.
- Served as a consultant for three years in the preparation of proposals for base supply and aircraft maintenance contracts, including staffing, organization, PWS responses, quality control plans, and safety procedures.

USAF ACADEMY AERO CLUB, Colorado (1983 – 1986)
Contract Flight Instructor
- Taught student pilots to commercial/instrument ratings, accumulating approximately 650 hours.

UNITED STATES AIR FORCE (1958 – 1983)
Assistant to the Deputy Chief of Staff for Logistics, USAF Academy, Colorado (1982 – 1983)
Director of Supply, USAF Academy, Colorado (1977 – 1982)
Deputy Base Commander, RAF Alconbury, England (1976 – 1977)
Supply Squadron Commander, RAF Alconbury, England (1973 – 1976)
Staff Supply Officer, Directorate of Civil Engineering, HQ USAF (1967 – 1973)
- More than 24 years of logistics experience, including materiel management, inventory, supply, budgeting, transportation, fuels, and procurement.
- Assisted the Deputy Chief of Staff with supply, contracting, transportation, logistics plans, and program directorates, including squadron commander responsibilities for more than 325 personnel.
- As Deputy Base Commander, administered the support requirements for 6,000 personnel, including involvement with security police, legal services, personnel, recreation services, civil engineering, and equal opportunity/affirmative action policies.
- Formulated, analyzed, and evaluated policy methods and procedures and implemented directives necessary for facilities management support.
- As Supply Squadron Commander, managed the efforts of more than 250 personnel to provide supply support to three squadrons.
- Gained four years of experience with headquarters staff in the formulating and implementation of policies and procedures.
- Developed a new concept for contracting supply support that was employed by a majority of air force bases.
- Projected and presented annual CE supply budget to the Office of the Secretary of Defense Budget Committee.

EDUCATION

BACHELOR OF SCIENCE, University of Missouri
U.S. AIR FORCE TRAINING: Industrial College of the Armed Forces, Squadron Officers School, Staff Supply Officer Course

70

ALBERT JACKSON III

12 S.E. 115th Avenue • Portland, Oregon 97202 • (503) 555-1234

EXPERIENCE

CONTRACTS MANAGER, DATA SERVICES DIVISION *(1995 – 1996)*
Aerotek, Inc., *Portland, Oregon, and Colorado Springs, Colorado*
- *Recruited and qualified technical consultants for job placements within Fortune 500 clients nationwide.*
- *Negotiated contract parameters on behalf of the consultants to maximize their productivity and suitability for the labor agreement.*
- *Created a sales team whereby recruiters could develop leadership skills and refine sales techniques for a smooth transition into account management.*
- *Marketed services to undeveloped territories with a primary focus on network communications.*
- *Generated $300,000+ in annual net revenues for the company.*

FINANCIAL ADVISOR, RETAIL DIVISION *(1993 – 1994)*
Prudential Securities, Inc., *Atlanta, Georgia*
- *Procured, developed, and managed institutional and private client accounts.*
- *Consulted with client base on government regulations, market conditions, and securities reports.*
- *Refined financial sales efforts through the use of seminars, telemarketing, and direct-mail promotions.*
- *Executed transactions through the New York Stock Exchange, over the counter, and commodity trading desks.*

FLOOR SUPERVISOR *(1992 – 1993)*
J. Crew Group, Inc., *Jackson, Wyoming*
- *Instructed and supervised associates in all sales and operational activities.*
- *Monitored departmental sales figures and created promotional campaigns to enhance merchandise movement.*
- *Maintained customer profiles and ensured that customer service standards were met.*
- *Worked directly with the corporate office to define the needs and goals of the factory outlet.*

ASSISTANT PROJECT MANAGER *(1991 – 1992)*
Central Parking Systems, *Washington, D.C.*
- *Managed the marketing, operation, and maintenance of a 3,000-space parking facility.*
- *Supervised cash handling, accounts payable, accounts receivable, and inventory control procedures.*
- *Coordinated the efforts of 29 hourly employees.*
- *Participated in corporate proposal efforts throughout Maryland, Virginia, and Washington, D.C.*
- *Compiled internal quality control information for upper management.*

RANCH HAND *(Summers 1987 – 1992)*
A Bar A Ranch, *Encampment, Wyoming*
- *Accounted for financial records and large cash deposits.*
- *Directed bartending procedures during convention week.*
- *Greeted and oriented guests to the ranch.*
- *Supervised operations in the absence of the foreman and general manager.*
- *Selected as Top Hand for summer 1989.*

EDUCATION

BACHELOR OF ARTS IN ECONOMICS *(1991)*
University of North Carolina, *Chapel Hill*

INTERESTS

Computers: *Lotus 1-2-3, MS Word, PowerPoint, IBM and Macintosh computers*
Languages: *Working knowledge of French*
International: *Traveled throughout Western Europe (1983)*

ACTIVITIES

Sports: *Colorado Outward Bound School, South San Juans, Colorado (1988); Member of the LaCrosse Club and Soccer Teams (1986 – 1987) and Ski Team (1988 – 1989)*
Community Service: *Volunteer for Big Brother (1986 – 1987); Fund Raiser for American Heart Association (1986); Rush Advisor for Inter-Fraternity Council (1986)*

5 Designing the Perfect E-mailable Résumé

■ What Is E-mail?

E-mail stands for electronic mail. It is an electronic message sent from one computer to another via the Internet or commercial online service. E-mail is a very rapid and cost-effective means of communication, and it makes your information available to potential employers immediately. There is no longer a need to wait for snail mail (the U.S. Postal Service) to get your résumé and cover letter across the country or across the world. With e-mail it will be there within minutes, giving you a competitive advantage over someone who does not yet feel comfortable with the technology of cyberspace.

❑ The Parts of an E-mail Address

Each computer on the Internet is assigned its own address. This address identifies the name and location of the computer, just like your home address tells people who you are and where you live.

The first element of an e-mail address is your user name (criscito). User names are then followed by the @ (at) sign. This @ sign separates your user name from the name of the computer where you established your Internet account.

The second part of the e-mail address is that specific computer system where your account is located (system). Depending on the specific structure of the network, this part may not be present.

Third is the site of the network—the school or the company or the organization (i.e., aol).

The domain is the top-level Internet directory where the site is registered. This domain name can represent a purpose or a country. For instance:

.edu   = educational institution like Arizona State University

.com   = business and commercial organizations

.mil   = military and defense organizations

.org   = usually nonprofit organizations

.net   = computers that help to run the Internet

.gov   = government institutions (nondefense)

.int   = international (NATO)

If an address ends with two letters, then it is a foreign country, such as:

.ad	= Andorra	.cc	= Cocos Island (Keeling)
.ae	= United Arab Emirates	.cf	= Central African Republic
.af	= Afghanistan	.cg	= Congo
.ag	= Antigua and Barbuda	.ch	= Switzerland (Schweiz)
.ai	= Anguilla	.ci	= Ivory Coast
.al	= Albania	.ck	= Cook Islands
.am	= Armenia	.cl	= Chile
.an	= Netherland Antilles	.cm	= Cameroon
.ao	= Angola	.cn	= China
.aq	= Antarctica	.co	= Colombia
.ar	= Argentina	.cr	= Costa Rica
.as	= American Samoa	.cs	= Czechoslovakia
.at	= Austria	.cu	= Cuba
.au	= Australia	.cv	= Cape Verde
.aw	= Aruba	.cx	= Christmas Island
.az	= Azerbaijan	.cy	= Cyprus
.ba	= Bosnia-Herzegovina	.cz	= Czech Republic
.bb	= Barbados	.de	= Germany (Deutschland)
.bd	= Bangladesh	.dj	= Djibouti
.be	= Belgium	.dk	= Denmark
.bf	= Burkina Faso	.dm	= Dominica
.bg	= Bulgaria	.do	= Dominican Republic
.bh	= Bahrain	.dz	= Algeria
.bi	= Burundi	.ec	= Ecuador
.bj	= Benin	.ee	= Estonia
.bm	= Bermuda	.eg	= Egypt
.bn	= Brunei Darussalam	.eh	= Western Sahara
.bo	= Bolivia	.er	= Eritrea
.br	= Brazil	.es	= Spain
.bs	= Bahamas	.et	= Ethiopia
.bt	= Bhutan	.fi	= Finland
.bv	= Bouvet Island	.fj	= Fiji
.bw	= Botswana	.fk	= Falkland Islands
.by	= Belarus	.fm	= Micronesia
.bz	= Belize	.fo	= Faroe Islands
.ca	= Canada	.fr	= France

.ga	= Gabon	.li	= Liechtenstein
.gb	= Great Britain	.lk	= Sri Lanka
.gd	= Grenada	.lr	= Liberia
.ge	= Georgia	.ls	= Lesotho
.gf	= Guyana	.lt	= Lithuania
.gh	= Ghana	.lu	= Luxembourg
.gi	= Gibraltar	.lv	= Latvia
.gl	= Greenland	.ly	= Libya
.gm	= Gambia	.ma	= Morocco
.gn	= Guinea	.mc	= Monaco
.gp	= Guadeloupe	.md	= Moldova
.gq	= Equatorial Guinea	.mg	= Madagascar
.gr	= Greece	.mh	= Marshall Islands
.gs	= South Georgia	.mk	= Macedonia
.gt	= Guatemala	.ml	= Mali
.gu	= Guam	.mm	= Myanmar
.gw	= Guinea Bissau	.mn	= Mongolia
.gy	= Guyana	.mo	= Macau
.hk	= Hong Kong	.mp	= Northern Mariana Island
.hm	= Heard/McDonald Islands	.mq	= Martinique
.hn	= Honduras	.mr	= Mauritania
.hr	= Croatia	.ms	= Montserrat
.ht	= Haiti	.mt	= Malta
.hu	= Hungary	.mu	= Mauritius
.id	= Indonesia	.mv	= Maldives
.ie	= Ireland	.mw	= Malawi
.il	= Israel	.mx	= Mexico
.in	= India	.my	= Malaysia
.iq	= Iraq	.mz	= Mozambique
.ir	= Iran	.na	= Namibia
.is	= Iceland	.nc	= New Caledonia
.it	= Italy	.ne	= Niger
.jm	= Jamaica	.nf	= Norfolk Island
.jo	= Jordan	.ng	= Nigeria
.jp	= Japan	.ni	= Nicaragua
.ke	= Kenya	.nl	= Netherlands
.kg	= Kyrgyz Republic	.no	= Norway
.kh	= Cambodia	.np	= Nepal
.ki	= Kiribati	.nr	= Nauru
.km	= Comoros	.nu	= Niue
.kn	= St. Kitts Nevis Anguilla	.nz	= New Zealand
.kp	= North Korea	.om	= Oman
.kr	= South Korea	.pa	= Panama
.kw	= Kuwait	.pe	= Peru
.ky	= Cayman Islands	.pf	= Polynesia
.kz	= Kazachstan	.pg	= Papua New Guinea
.la	= Laos	.ph	= Philippines
.lb	= Lebanon	.pk	= Pakistan
.lc	= Saint Lucia	.pl	= Poland

.pm	= St. Pierre & Miquelon		.th	= Thailand
.pn	= Pitcairn		.tj	= Tadjikistan
.pr	= Puerto Rico		.tk	= Tokelau
.pt	= Portugal		.tm	= Turkmenistan
.pw	= Palau		.tn	= Tunisia
.py	= Paraguay		.to	= Tonga
.qa	= Qatar		.tp	= East Timor
.re	= Reunion		.tr	= Turkey
.ro	= Romania		.tt	= Trinidad/Tobago
.ru	= Russian Federation		.tv	= Tuvalu
.rw	= Rwanda		.tw	= Taiwan
.sa	= Saudi Arabia		.tz	= Tanzania
.sb	= Solomon Islands		.ua	= Ukraine
.sc	= Seychelles		.ug	= Uganda
.sd	= Sudan		.uk	= United Kingdom
.se	= Sweden		.us	= United States
.sg	= Singapore		.uy	= Uruguay
.sh	= St. Helena		.uz	= Uzbekistan
.si	= Slovenia		.va	= Vatican City
.sj	= Svalbard/Jan Mayen		.vc	= St. Vincent/Grenadines
.sk	= Slovakia		.ve	= Venezuela
.sl	= Sierra Leone		.vg	= British Virgin Islands
.sm	= San Marino		.vi	= U.S. Virgin Islands
.sn	= Senegal		.vn	= Vietnam
.so	= Somalia		.vu	= Vanuatu
.sr	= Surname		.wf	= Wallis/Futuna Islands
.st	= St. Tome and Principe		.ws	= Samoa
.su	= Soviet Union		.ye	= Yemen
.sv	= El Salvador		.yt	= Mayotte
.sy	= Syria		.yu	= Yugoslavia
.sz	= Swaziland		.za	= South Africa
.tc	= Turks/Caicos Islands		.zm	= Zambia
.td	= Chad		.zr	= Zaire
.tf	= French S. Territory		.zw	= Zimbabwe
.tg	= Togo			

At America Online, your Internet address has three parts: Your screen name (*criscito*), followed by *@aol.com* (*criscito@aol.com*).

There are no spaces in an e-mail address, and Internet e-mail is often case sensitive (meaning it makes a difference whether or not something is capitalized). Every online service uses slightly different conventions for creating e-mail addresses. For instance, my America Online address would appear to a GEnie user as: *criscito@aol.com@inet#*. A CompuServe address is a series of numbers with a comma just before the last series of digits. To convert this to an Internet address, you must change the comma to a period. For instance, my CompuServe address is *71331,3077*. If I wanted to give my Internet address to someone, it would be: *71311.3077@compuserve.com*. Always check with your Internet access provider or commercial online service for any idiosyncrasies in converting your e-mail address to an Internet e-mail address.

❏ *The Mailer-Daemon*

Once you have sent an e-mail message, how do you know if your e-mail was received? Well, you will never know for sure. The recipient may be one of those people who only checks her e-mail once a week or once a month. Once you have sent an e-mail message, it is irretrievable. You can't get it back!

Occasionally, however, an e-mail message you have sent will be returned to you like unopened mail. You will receive a rather long, cryptic message from the MAILER-DAEMON telling you that your mail could not be delivered as addressed. There are usually two reasons for this.

First, the site you were mailing to may not exist. When that happens, you get a "host unknown" message from the MAILER-DAEMON. The site part of the e-mail address (after the @ sign) must be a valid Internet site and it must be spelled correctly and in the right case *(CRISCITO@AOL.com* is not the same as *criscito@aol.com)*. If the host you specified in the e-mail address can't be found, your message will be bounced back to you. Double check the address, make any changes, and try it again.

Second, the problem may be that the user name part of the e-mail address (before the @ sign) is either not spelled correctly, is in the wrong case, or the person doesn't exist. The message in this case would be "user unknown." Again, double check the address and try again.

Occasionally, there might be a third reason for returned mail. It is possible that the receiving end is having computer problems. In that case, simply try again later. If you don't get a message from the MAILER-DAEMON, you can assume that your mail reached its destination.

There is a difference between an e-mail address and an URL (Universal Resource Locator—pronounced "earl"). An e-mail address *(criscito@aol.com)* allows you to send a message to someone else's computer. An URL is a physical address where something is located on the Internet; you cannot send a message to an URL. The first part of an URL *(http://, ftp://, gopher://)* tells the computer what type of Internet resource you want to access:

- *http://* is a Web site
- *ftp://* is a file transfer protocol site
- *gopher://* is a Gopher search engine site

The second part of an URL is the specific computer system where your account is located *(www.)*. Depending on the structure of the network, this part may not be present. Third is the site of the network—the school or the company or the organization *(.yahoo)*. The domain is the top-level Internet directory where the site is registered *(.com)*. The complete URL would like something like this: *http://www.yahoo.com*. This would take you to Yahoo's home page. To get more specific, after the *.com*, an URL can direct you to a specific file you would like to access once you reach the computer. For instance, *http://www.yahoo.com/ economy* takes you immediately to the page that focuses on the economy. To read an Internet address out loud to someone, you would say, "http, colon, slash, slash, www, dot, yahoo, dot, com, slash, economy."

■ *A Word About Confidentiality*

First of all, there is no such word as *confidential* in cyberspace. Think of your e-mail as a postcard. Once you transmit your words via any electronic means, they are free for all to see. Your boss can read the trail left behind by your e-mail at work any time he or she wishes. There are even companies that regularly check e-mail messages for fraud, waste, or abuse. In fact, a recent survey indicated that as many as 36.4 percent of managers read their employees' e-mail, and there are 20 million Americans using e-mail at work. What that means is that you shouldn't say anything in your company e-mail that you wouldn't want your boss to read.

By the way, I don't recommend using your work e-mail account to send and receive job hunting information even if you are using it after work hours. Why? First, for the obvious reason that your employer may discover that you are thinking about leaving your current job. Second, your e-mail header shows potential employers that you are using company equipment for personal business, which is a turn-off. Don't put work phone numbers on your résumé or cover letters for the same reason.

In addition to the problem with confidentiality at work, on the Internet your e-mail is accessible by anyone with the knowledge of how to filter data from the various networks of computers through which your e-mail must pass. Anyone with system administration access on any of these computers could potentially read your mail. The chances are slim that this will happen—most people just don't have the time or the inclination to read someone else's mail—but there is always a remote possibility that your e-mail could get into the hands of a dishonest person. Although there are encryption programs, even they can be broken. My best advice is never to say anything in an e-mail message that you wouldn't want published on the front page of *The New York Times* or shouted from the top of a building!

If you are concerned that your résumé will be seen by your current employer, there are some things you can do to ensure confidentiality. Most of the résumé writing services that offer to post your résumé on the Internet can replace your name and address with "Confidential Résumé #1234, for more information on this applicant, please fax a request on your company letterhead to ProType, Ltd., 1-719-598-8918." Your current employer's name will also be eliminated from the résumé for your protection. For a modest fee (usually around $100), these companies will act as your intermediary for a year or more, calling you when a request is received to see if you want to be contacted by the inquiring company.

You can do something similar yourself by removing your current employer's name, replacing your address with an e-mail address that doesn't include your name, and using an alternate contact phone number on your résumé with someone screening calls for you.

■ *The Equipment and Software You Need*

Before you can receive or send e-mail, you need a computer, a modem, a phone line, and computer software that will allow you to connect and communicate with another computer. Don't get nervous about the technical details here. Think of your computer like you would your microwave oven; you don't have to know how it works in order to use it effectively.

❑ *The Computer*

Whether you have a PC or a Macintosh computer doesn't matter. The computer doesn't even have to be lightning fast, but the more powerful your computer, the faster it can process the graphical data coming in from the phone line. If you have an older computer, you can choose to view incoming data as text only, which will speed things up. An 8086 computer with a 2400 bps (bits per second) modem is okay for e-mail to your mother, but you will have time to fix supper while you wait for a home page to download from the Internet.

❑ *The Modem*

The same goes for your modem. The faster, the better. A modem is a piece of computer hardware that connects your computer to a phone line, allowing you to communicate with another computer. *Modem* stands for *modulate–demodulate,* which is the converting of digital signals from your computer to the analog signals of your telephone line and then back into digital signals at the other end of the line. The faster your modem, the faster you can receive and send data through the telephone line. Speeds range from 2,400 bps to 56,000 bps, although you can reach speeds of 128 kbps if you have an ISDN telephone line, which doesn't require a modem at all since the telephone line itself is digital. All you need is a network-style adapter card in your computer.

❑ *The Phone Line*

Speaking of telephone lines, in the future, all telephone lines will be digital (whether they are ISDN, ADSL, or cable), and you will be able to surf the Internet at 128 kpbs and receive an incoming voice call at the same time. For now, however, you will either have to settle for your regular analog telephone line or pay a premium price to have an ISDN line run to your home or office.

If you intend to surf the Net often, it pays to have a dedicated telephone line for your modem. Otherwise, the other members of your family may hate you, especially if you have teenagers who don't appreciate your tying up "their" telephone line. If you have only one telephone line and it has call waiting, you must turn off call waiting before logging onto your Internet service provider or commercial online service.

❏ *The Software*

In order to send or receive e-mail or to access the Internet, you must establish an account with either an Internet service provider (a company dedicated to offering customers direct access to the Internet and a few basic services) or a commercial online service like America Online, CompuServe, Prodigy, or GEnie, among others.

Commercial online services offer broad packages of value-added services that include everything from e-mail, access to the Internet, home page space on their servers, forums for real-time chatting with other members, and an incredible array of information resources. You pay a fixed price (like $9.95) for a certain number of hours per month (usually 5 to 10) and then pay a premium for any hours you use beyond your contract amount, starting at around $2 an hour. Some commercial online services charge a flat rate for unlimited access (AOL's unlimited plan is $19.95 per month). The software is free with a simple phone call to a toll-free number, with a set number of free online hours for newcomers as an enticer. The main advantage of using commercial online services is that they are easy to set up (essentially "plug and play") and easy to use. This is a quick solution to setting up an e-mail account and accessing the Internet, and most people start here.

Besides the wealth of value-added benefits that commercial online services provide, you can access your account from almost anywhere in the country with a local telephone number. If you travel, being able to access your e-mail and the Internet without paying long distance charges from anywhere in the world is a real benefit. See Chapter 7 for more information on contacting these commercial online services and for listings of career-related resources.

If you find yourself using your commercial online service primarily to access the Internet and are using very little of its value-added services, and if you are spending more than $20 a month for your online time, a local Internet Service Provider (ISP) may be the best way to access the Internet. You can find an ISP that offers unlimited hours of online time per month (and sometimes only 40 to 50 hours) for as little as $20, and the software to get you started is usually free.

ISPs that offer free access (no charge) usually offer very limited service. It's like being invited to a free buffet but all they serve is mashed potatoes. It is better to pay $20 a month for a full-service ISP and avoid getting busy signals when you dial in. Simply look for providers in your local telephone book or in the free computer magazines you will find in the racks at your local grocery store or office supply outlet. The *Boardwatch Magazine Internet Service Providers* directory is an excellent source for locating an ISP. You can find it at your local bookstore or newsstand. All of the major long distance telephone companies offer Internet access, and it won't be long before cable television companies get into the act with cable modems. The only things holding them back are the fact that most of our television sets are not yet made to offer both television and Internet access, and the typical coaxial cable that connects your television to the cable company has a tendency to interject noise on the line. This will be solved eventually when cable companies replace these lines with fiber-optic cables.

If you already have access to the Internet, there are sites that list ISPs:

- *http://www.yahoo.com/Business_and_Economy/Companies/Internet_Service_Providers/Internet_Access_Providers/*
- *http://thelist/iworld.com/*

Look for an ISP that will be dependable and offers high-speed access. Make certain it offers technical support at least during normal business hours, preferably 24 hours a day. Most ISPs will meet your needs, but some are often overloaded, which means you may have trouble gaining access to the Internet at certain peak times of the day. Look for an ISP with a user-to-modem ratio of no more than ten to one—five to one is ideal.

Setting up the software for an account with an ISP can be a little daunting for novice computer users, so you should be prepared to spend some time on the telephone with their technical support people to work out the kinks.

One major advantage an ISP has over a commercial online service is the speed of data transfer. When America Online or CompuServe or other commercial online service is experiencing heavy usage, your data transfer is slowed down considerably.

■ *How to Find E-mail Addresses*

Unfortunately, there is no quick and easy method of finding e-mail addresses. There are no "White Pages" listing every e-mail address on the Internet, although there are several sites that list several million. Often the most reliable means of discovering an e-mail address is to call the person and ask. If you can't do that, there are a few sites on the Internet that can help you find someone's e-mail address.

- List of more than one million e-mail addresses (including celebrities!)
  http://www.four11.com/

- List of both e-mail addresses and more than 90 million U.S. residential phone listings and addresses
  http://www.whowhere.com/

- Global white pages
  http://www.bigfoot.com/

- How to find someone's e-mail address
  http://kaml1.csi.uottawa.ca:3000/how-to-email.html

- Frequently asked questions about finding someone's e-mail address
  http://www.cis.ohio-state.edu/hypertext/faq/usenet/finding-addresses/faq.html

- Frequently asked questions about finding college e-mail addresses
  http://www.qucis.queensu.ca/FAQs/email/college.html

- E-mail database of college students
  ftp://ftp.qucis.queensu.ca/pub/dalamb/college-email/college.html

- Newsgroups that list e-mail addresses
  news.answers, soc.net-people, soc.college

Don't neglect to check the member directory of your commercial online service. If you have an AOL, CompuServe, Prodigy, MSN, or other account, you have access to millions of e-mail addresses of fellow subscribers simply by looking in the member directory.

To find e-mail addresses for specific companies, you can use the search engines discussed in Chapter 10 to hunt down their home pages, or you can turn to the online Yellow Pages. Following are some of the resources for finding e-mail addresses for companies:

- US WEST Marketing Resources has put their Yellow Pages on the Internet
  http://yp.uswest.com

- An online Yellow Pages with more than 11 million companies, including their credit ratings, geographic mapping, and company information
  http://www.whowhere.com/

- More than 16 million U.S. businesses, street-level maps for each entry, and third-party reviews of restaurants and hotels
  http://www.bigbook.com/

- 15 million listings for businesses nationwide with location maps
  http://www.onvillage.com/

- An interactive Yellow Pages with information from more than 11 million listings found in excess of 5,000 Yellow Pages directories nationwide, business web site directory, and classified advertising
  http://superpages.gte.net/

■ *Steps for Creating an ASCII Text File of Your Résumé*

First you must understand the difference between a native word processing format and an ASCII text file. ASCII (pronounced "askee") is an abbreviation for American Standard Code for Information Interchange. It is a universal code that nearly all computers understand, and most e-mail messages are sent in this format. ASCII text files are very generic—they have no special fonts, margins, tabs, bold, italic, or other formatting codes added. When you create a file in a word processor (like WordPerfect or Microsoft Word), on the other hand, the program automatically formats and saves its files in a "native" format. This native format includes codes that not all computers or software programs can read.

Don't use any special bells and whistles when you type your electronic résumé in a word processing program. That means don't use boldface, underline, italics, fonts, font size, margins settings, etc. Tabs will disappear when you convert your file, so use your spacebar to move text over instead of tabs. Also be careful of the "smart quotes" that many word processing programs automatically place when you press the " key on your keyboard. These special characters will not translate when you save your file as ASCII text. That includes mathematical symbols, em-dashes, en-dashes, and any character that does not appear on your keyboard. Your choices for bullets are also limited to the characters on your keyboard. Some of the better symbol choices to highlight lines of text are: >, *, +, but I recommend using paragraphs and generous white space on an e-mailable résumé.

Many browsers and e-mail readers are set to 60-character line lengths. If the lines in your e-mail or your résumé are longer, they won't display properly and will look sloppy on the computer screen. Don't let your sentences "wrap" to a new line. Hit the enter key at the end of the line instead. That way, you can be sure the lines will break where you intended and your online résumé will look neat on the screen.

An electronic résumé can be longer than one page, but remember that you have one screenful of space (about 15 lines) to grab your reader's attention and motivate him or her to click down to the next screen. You should start with a summary of your qualifications and achievements at the top of your résumé and then list your chronology of experience.

If you have already created a neat, formatted paper résumé and have saved it on your computer, it is easy to strip it of all the codes to create this generic file that can be saved as an ASCII text file. In most word processing software, you can reveal codes and delete the "bells and whistles" or you can use the program's search and replace feature to do it automatically. Choose whichever method you are most comfortable with and undo all the hard work you did to make a pretty résumé (see the résumés beginning on page 85). When you are finished, remember to save the file under a new name in the next step. You don't want to save over your formatted paper résumé and lose all that hard work!

Now that you have a generic file on your computer screen, you need to save your file a special way or your word processor will still add hidden codes that will make your file unreadable on the Internet. Every word processing software accomplishes this in a different way, but most of them have an option to convert a file to ASCII, MS-DOS text, or

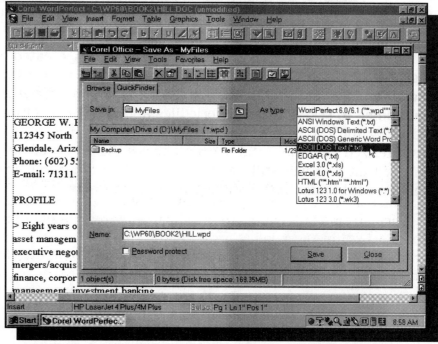

Screen shot of WordPefect reprinted with permission from Corel Corporation.

some other type of generic text file. For instance, in WordPerfect for DOS, you choose "ASCII Text (Standard)" when you press F7 to "Save As." In WordPerfect for Windows, you choose the "Save As" option from the "File" menu and select "ASCII (DOS) Text."

In Microsoft Word, you also choose the "Save As" option from the "File" menu, but you will select "MS-DOS Text with Line Breaks" instead.

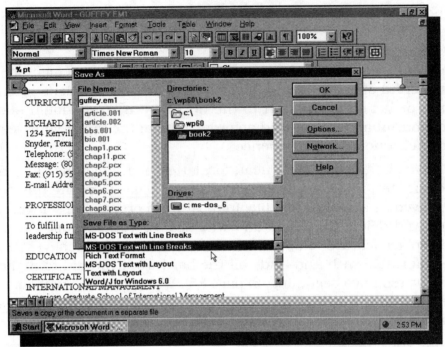

Screen shot of Microsoft Word reprinted with permission from Microsoft Corporation.

On the following pages are sample résumés created in word processing programs but saved as ASCII text files. You will notice that they are nothing special to look at and more than one page long, but hiring managers are accustomed to seeing these generic files and aren't expecting beauty. This "ugly" ASCII résumé serves a specific purpose, and that is to get your words into a computerized résumé database or across the Internet as e-mail. Remember, though, that you will still need a neat, formatted paper résumé to take to an interview and to use with your networking contacts.

GEORGE J. HILL
E-mail: 71311.3077@compuserve.com
123 E. Highland Street
Allentown, Pennsylvania 18103
Phone: (610) 555-1234

PROFILE

> Eight years of extensive, high-level corporate finance and
asset management experience with a background in senior-level
executive negotiations, structured transactions,
privatizations, mergers/acquisitions/divestments, project
finance, international finance, corporate debt restructuring
and reorganizations, project management, investment banking

> Strong analytical, quantitative, entrepreneurial, and
written communication abilities

> Skilled in @Risk, Ibbotson, Excel, WordPerfect, MS Word,
Access, PowerPoint, Paradox, Lotus 1-2-3, and other computer
software

> Multilingual: Fluent in English and Arabic; proficient in
French

> Multicultural: International experience in the Caribbean and
with French companies

PROFESSIONAL EXPERIENCE

RESOLUTION TRUST CORPORATION   (1989 to 1994)
Valley Forge, Pennsylvania

Senior Asset Specialist (1992 to 1994)
Oversight Asset Specialist (1991 to 1992)
Asset Specialist (1989 to 1991)

Independently managed high-value loans involving
infrastructure development and appraisal and valuation
reviews. Full responsibility for evaluating the performance
of 15 management contracts for the restructure/recovery of
$4.6 billion portfolio (5,800 assets), utilizing teams of
15-20 personnel from functional areas. Complete autonomy for
the strategic planning, development, staffing, and operations
of two start-up departments, resulting in dramatic
improvements in organizational productivity, credit quality,
and uniformity of operations. Advised staff and distressed
financial institutions in complex credit workouts as Credit
Policy/Compliance Officer. Full supervisory authority for the
training, technical guidance, and oversight of 20 asset
management personnel in the administration and disposition of
a $685 million commercial real estate portfolio (450 assets).
Managed restructuring, workout, and recovery of 60
nonperforming commercial assets valued at $500 million,

including commercial loans, commercial real estate loans, international loans, tax-exempt bond structured transactions, limited partnerships, subsidiaries, joint ventures, trade financing, and international letters of credit. Directed a staff of 15 consultants, asset managers, and attorneys responsible for the management of complex real estate assets and bankruptcy, litigation, and environmentally related issues. Negotiated with developers, syndicators, and corporate borrowers to restructure assets and mediate settlements. Specialized in complicated loan workouts with national exposure, including environmentally sensitive issues requiring analyzation of remediation and cleanup options. Managed disposition of Hill Financial Capital Corporation (assets of $93 million), recovered $30 million from Clarion Hotel restructuring, liquidated assets and managed an international franchise territorial agreement with a major French corporation, and restructured a $9.6 million loan for a private nursing home and retirement center. Personally negotiated resolution/recovery of an intricate $120 million loan/equity investment project for the development of a high-end shopping mall through a creative debt/equity swap. Appointed Assets Team Leader to coordinate acquisition and privatization of 20 banks for the federal government. Evaluated bids and awarded contracts as a member of the RTC Contracting Award Committee. Created computerized modeling system for monitoring decision processes. Case reviewer on commercial credit decisions with authority to approve strategic recommendations.

HILL FINANCIAL SAVINGS ASSOCIATION (1987 to 1989)
Red Hill, Pennsylvania

Project Specialist

Responsible for restructuring, recovery, and workout of a $400 million portfolio of commercial/real estate financings. Independently managed negotiations with developers, corporate borrowers, and attorneys.

PREVIOUS EXPERIENCE (1983 to 1987)
Includes a series of increasingly responsible positions in international textile manufacturing, telecommunications, hospitality marketing, financial management, and as a general partner in a supermarket franchise.

EDUCATION

MASTER OF INTERNATIONAL MANAGEMENT (1996)
American Graduate School of International Management (Thunderbird), Glendale, Arizona
> Focus: International Finance and European/Eastern European Studies (with honors)

> Appointed to the 1995 and 1996 World Economic Development Congress (Power Project Financing and Water Resources Development Summits)
> Specialized course work in Managing Financial and Political Risk: Emerging Markets, International Securities Investments, Technology Transfer, Foreign Direct Investment, International Banking, International Trade and Finance, Advanced Portfolio Analysis and Management, and Advanced Corporate Finance
> Academic Research Projects: Foreign Direct Investment Policies of Turkey, Asia Third World Strategy (India, Japan) of Morgan Stanley, Inc., Cultural Overview of Doing Business in Saudi Arabia, Evaluation of Russia's Economic Restructuring Policy, Analysis of Investment Opportunities in Mexico: Mexican Banking Crisis, China's Financial System, Financial Models: Country Risk Analysis, Asset/Liability Management

CONTINUING PROFESSIONAL EDUCATION (1990 to 1992)
Temple University, Pennsylvania State University, Bank Administration Institute
> Total of 240 hours, including 15 credits in real estate investments, financing, law, and appraisal
> Real estate law instructor
> Participated in workout and bankruptcy conferences and commercial/corporate credit training

BACHELOR OF SCIENCE, BUSINESS ADMINISTRATION (1983)
Pennsylvania State University, State College, Pennsylvania
> Major: Finance and Computer Science
> Calculus Instructor; Dean's List for two years; PSU Kunkle Academic Scholarship

AFFILIATIONS

> World Affairs Council/Advisory Committee (1988 to 1992)
> Founded chapter of a nonprofit educational organization to educate business and government about U.S. foreign policy and economic development through renowned diplomats, ambassadors, economists, and world trade representatives
> Turnaround Management Association, Education Committee
> American Bankruptcy Institute, Executive Committees (International Insolvency, Banking/Finance)
> Arab Bankers Association of North America (ABANA)
> Urban Land Institute
> Who's Who in the World (1994 to 1995)
> Phi Sigma Iota International Language Honor Society
> International Real Estate Federation (FIABCI)

AWARDS

> FDIC Special Achievement Award for contributions above and beyond regular duty (October 1993)
> FDIC Special Achievement Award for the formation and establishment of two new credit departments (June 1992)

MICHAEL D. NEWTON
123 Clairmont Drive
Pittsburgh, Pennsylvania 15241
Phone: (412) 555-1234
E-mail: 71311.3077@compuserve.com

EDUCATION
===

MASTER OF INTERNATIONAL MANAGEMENT (December 1996)
American Graduate School of International Management
Thunderbird Campus, Glendale, Arizona
* InterAd Japan - Crew Member: Assisted in market research of
Smirnoff, including surveys and focus groups; designed cover
book illustration and advertising storyboards.
* Relevant course work: Advanced Corporate Finance,
International Finance and Trade, International Insurance,
International Marketing Research, International Marketing
Management, Multinational Business Management, Intelligence in
Diplomacy and Commerce.

SEMESTER ABROAD (Summer 1991)
* Institute for International Studies and Training,
Fujinomiya, Japan

BACHELOR OF ARTS (May 1990)
Grove City College, Grove City, Pennsylvania
* Major: Political Science/Pre-Law
* Concentration: Economics

RELEVANT EXPERIENCE
===
MARKET INTELLIGENCE MANAGER (February 1995 - May 1996)
Newton Networks, Seattle, Washington
* Performed competitive intelligence studies of the Seattle
and Vancouver metropolitan markets.
* Assisted in the startup of an international online training
service.
* Trained project managers to develop, manage, and implement
export programs.
* Facilitated information flow between domestic functional
departments and international personnel; managed
implementation of multilingual packaging.
* Assisted in the planning and supervision of all aspects of
production, advertising, media selection, information
dissemination, and publicity.
* Designed a successful direct mail campaign and followed up
with focus groups.

SALES REPRESENTATIVE (January 1994 - February 1995)
Sprint Corporation, Reston, Virginia
* Qualified, sold, and maintained small to medium commercial
accounts for the first four months of customer's life cycle.

* Achieved 100 percent of sales and revenue objectives monthly through cold calling.
* Identified, escalated, and resolved customer activation concerns.
* Prepared billing analyses and proposals.
* Negotiated term agreements and offered approved special pricing promotions.
* Refined ability to manage multiple priorities with a high level of concentration amidst constant distractions.

ASSISTANT MANAGER (April 1993 - January 1994)
Spokes, Etc., Oakton, Virginia
* Marketed, sold, and distributed bicycles and accessories.
* Supervised sales and technical personnel; set daily personnel objectives.

INTERNATIONAL MARKETING SPECIALIST (September 1991 - May 1992)
The Greater Phoenix Economic Council, Phoenix, Arizona
* Reviewed the international investment opportunities in greater Phoenix.
* Made recommendations on targeting strategies (advertising, direct mail, etc.).
* Assisted in targeting potential corporations in Asia interested in direct investments.
* Brainstormed projects needed to carry out a successful international strategy.
* Assisted with trade shows and other international events such as the Japan Week.
* Maintained relations with international organizations.

LANGUAGES
==
Proficient in Korean
Working knowledge of Japanese
Knowledge of German

COMPUTERS
==
WordPerfect, MS Word, Excel, PowerPoint, Access

❏ *How to Compose and Send E-mail*

After creating a résumé and saving it in ASCII format from your word processor, retrieve the ASCII file back into your word processor or attach it to an e-mail message (see page 92) and send it to yourself. Remember, there is usually a short delay between the time you upload a file online and when it is available. Look at it on your computer screen. If the text and spacing didn't translate correctly, this is the time to fix it. Save it again and then look at it one more time.

Now your résumé is ready to send as e-mail. Most commercial online services and Internet service providers make sending e-mail as uncomplicated as possible. You simply pull down a menu that allows you to create a message and fill in the blanks.

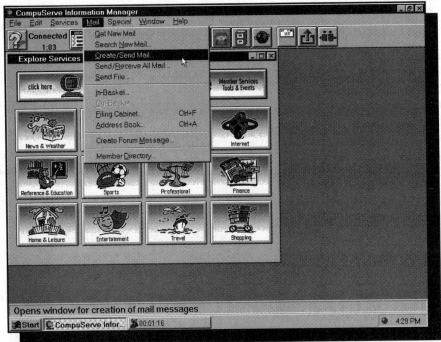

Screen shot of CompuServe E-mail reprinted with permission from CompuServe.

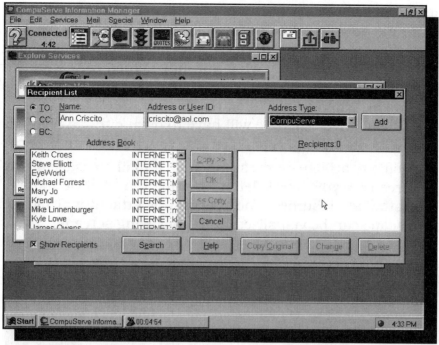

Screen shot of CompuServe E-mail reprinted with permission from CompuServe.

The subject line is a valuable tool for introducing who you are and what you do. Don't neglect this line. You can use it for your objective statement, to reference the job opening for which you are applying, or to show that you are updating a résumé you have sent previously.

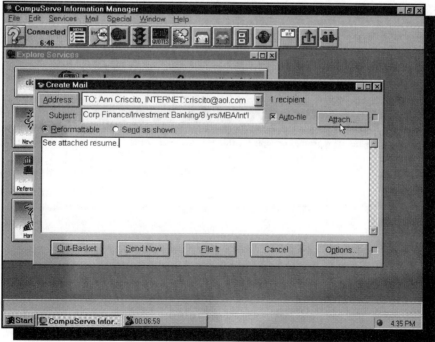

Screen shot of CompuServe E-mail reprinted with permission from CompuServe.

There are actually two different ways you can compose your e-mail. First, you can attach the file you saved to an e-mail message, which means it doesn't become part of the e-mail message box. If you choose to do this, the recipient of your e-mail message will see only what you have typed in the subject line and your brief explanation in the message box that your résumé is attached (like in the previous screen). When he clicks on the icon to "Get Mail," your résumé will be saved on his hard drive. Then he will have to open either a word processor or text editor like Windows Notepad and retrieve your résumé in order to view it.

If you are going to attach your résumé to an e-mail message, it is best to use the message screen for your cover letter or something a little more substantial than just "see attached résumé." The process for attaching a file to an e-mail message in Netscape can be visualized in the following screens:

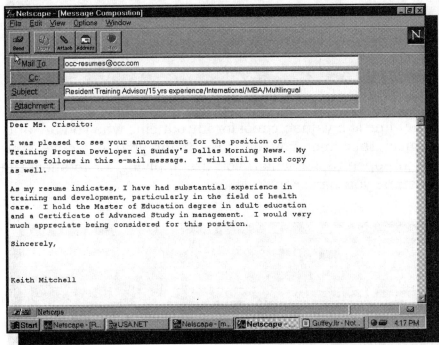

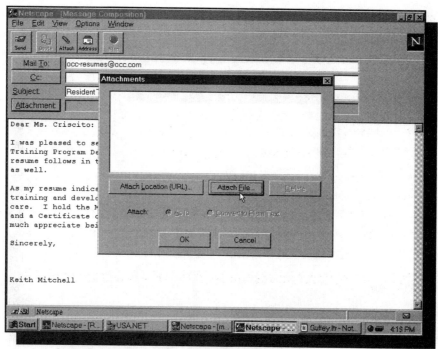

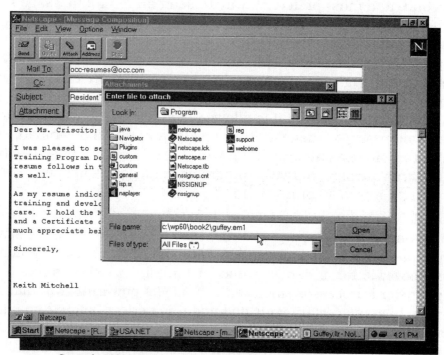

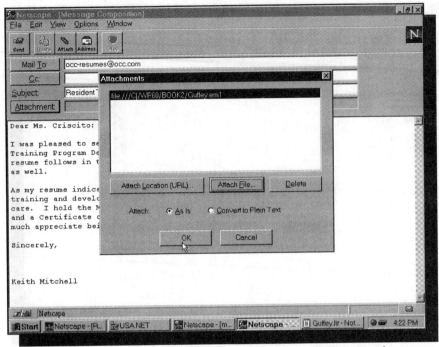

The second, and most preferred, way to send an e-mail message is to make your résumé the text of the e-mail message screen. That way the reader sees your entire message immediately without having to leave his or her e-mail screen. It also gets around the fear some people have of contracting a virus by downloading an attached file, although the chances of that happening are extremely rare. (For the computer novice, a virus is a computer program that is intended to cause damage to your computer files if it is allowed to enter, but viruses are not spread by simple e-mail messages. Instead, they reside in files you download, especially program files that are executed with .EXE or .COM. Even though the chances of contracting a virus are slim, antivirus programs are a good safety measure for any computer with an Internet connection.)

So, how do you get your résumé into that tiny e-mail message screen? Trust me, there is room. You can type your entire résumé into the message screen from scratch, but that's not a good idea since you can't spell check it. When you are composing a cover letter and/or résumé for e-mail, it is always much better to start with your word processor since you can use its powerful grammar and spell check features to make certain your document is perfect before e-mailing it to a potential employer. It is better to learn how to cut and paste the text of your ASCII résumé from the Windows Notepad (or other text editor) into the e-mail message screen so it becomes a part of the e-mail message itself. Here's how you do it:

First, open the Windows Notepad and click on "File." Choose "Open" and type in the file name with the full path for your ASCII text file résumé.

Screen shot of Microsoft Notepad reprinted with permission from Microsoft Corporation.

Second, block the text of your résumé by clicking and holding down your left mouse button at the top of the résumé, dragging the cursor until all of your résumé is highlighted. Lift your finger from the mouse button and click on "Edit." Select copy and then either minimize or close your Notepad window.

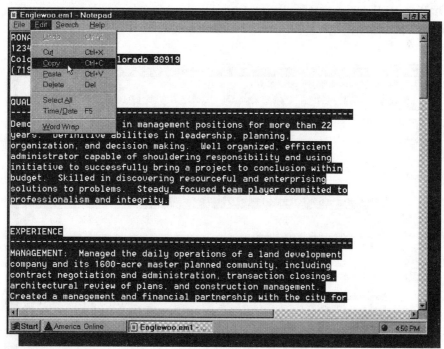

Screen shot of Microsoft Notepad reprinted with permission from Microsoft Corporation.

Third, open your Internet browser or commercial online service software (you don't have to log on yet) and maximize your e-mail screen. After you have typed in the address where you will be sending your message and your subject line, click on the message box so your cursor is active in the large white space. Then click on "Edit" and choose "Paste."

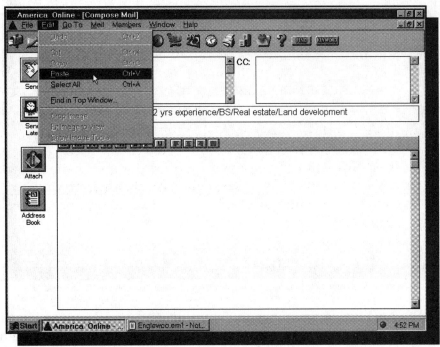

Your text will appear in the message box and you are ready to click on "Send." America Online will automatically log on for you and send your message, or you can schedule it to send later.

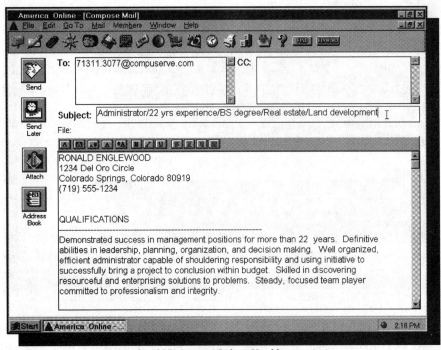

■ Sending a Binary File

Sending ASCII text e-mail across the Internet is relatively painless, but attaching binary files can get complicated. If you create a file in a word processor (like your résumé) and then attempt to attach that binary file to an e-mail message without converting it to ASCII text, you will often get the message "the receiving server does not accept binary files." In order to send files across the network of computers that make up the Internet, binary files must be encoded in a special way before they are sent and then decoded when they are received at the other end.

Most commercial online services (America Online, CompuServe, Prodigy, Delphi, etc.) will automatically encode an attached file, but the person receiving the file on the other end will need a separate decoding program in order to read the file. This is why is it so difficult to send your nicely formatted, word processor file of your résumé to a recruiter and why it is necessary to save the file first in generic ASCII text format.

On the other hand, it is easy to attach a binary file to an e-mail message when you are exchanging files with someone else with the same commercial online service or Internet service provider. For instance, if you and your friend both have CompuServe accounts, you simply attach any file you like and send the message. Because the file does not have to cross the Internet, it is like saving a file on your own computer and then having your friend copy it directly from the same computer.

❏ File Transfer Protocol (ftp)

There is one other option, too. Ftp (File Transfer Protocol) can be used to transfer a binary file that can then be retrieved into a word processing program, like WordPerfect or Microsoft Word (or whatever software was used to create the file in the first place) and viewed or printed as if it were on your own computer.

You will usually find ftp as one of the options on your Internet browser. Simply click on ftp and tell the software where on your hard drive to find the file that you wish to send and where you wish to send it. Viola! You're done. You can retrieve files from a host the same way, but you will need to know the exact Internet address of the site and you must use a logon name and password. The word *anonymous* is the default logon name on many systems and your e-mail address is the password. File names on many ftp archive systems are case sensitive, so you must type the file and directory name exactly as you see them listed.

One caveat, however. It isn't a good idea to send your résumé to a company or recruiter this way, unless someone at the other end has asked you to do so. This binary file (in the native word processor's format) cannot be added to a résumé database unless it is converted to ASCII text, so the only real reason for sending a binary file of your résumé is so that someone at the other end can manipulate it in a word processor or print out a hard copy that looks like your original paper résumé.

■ *How to E-mail Your Résumé Directly to a Company's Recruiter*

The same generic ASCII text file that you created can be used to send your résumé directly to a company's recruiter or human resource department. Many classified advertisements in today's newspapers list e-mail addresses or home page addresses on the Internet. When you access a company's home page and search their database of job openings, there will be a hypertext link (the highlighted text, usually blue, underlined, or made to stand out in some way) that will allow you to send your résumé directly to the company's recruiters or human resource department.

When you see an e-mail address in a newspaper advertisement, simply follow the instructions on page 92 for creating and sending an e-mail message from your online service or Internet service provider. This e-mail message of your résumé is received by a specific person, usually the recruiter assigned to fill the job opening or sometimes directly by the hiring manager. After a certain period of time, usually 30 days or less, the file is uploaded to the company's main résumé database (applicant tracking system) where your résumé becomes accessible to any recruiter or hiring manager in the company who is looking to fill a position. Your résumé will remain there for sometimes as long as a year before it is purged, which means you can be considered for jobs during keyword searches that you hadn't even thought about, which of course is one of the benefits of a computerized résumé database and applicant tracking system.

As human resource personnel and recruiters become comfortable with the technology of accepting résumés through e-mail and the Internet, you will find e-mail addresses published more often. Always send your résumé via e-mail when you see an e-mail address published in a help-wanted advertisement. This shows you are comfortable with today's technology and gives you an advantage over those applicants who choose to mail a paper résumé only. There is nothing wrong with sending an e-mail message and then following up with a cover letter and a paper copy of your résumé mailed to the address shown in the advertisement. This gives your résumé two chances to be seen, and the paper résumé allows you to show more of your personality than the boring ASCII text of an e-mail message.

6 Using the Internet in Your Job Search

The Internet, World Wide Web, the Web, WWW, Information Superhighway, the Net, the I'way—no matter what you call it, millions of employers and potential employees are accessing the Internet every week. As of this writing, more than 12 percent of employers are looking for their employees on the Internet. That may seem like a low number, but it actually equates to one million hits per month on the various career-related Internet sites and the number is growing exponentially every day. In WebCrawler alone (a popular search engine), the word *employment* generates 43,000 hits per week.

To grasp how important computers and the Internet are becoming, think about how your life would be without a telephone. Cyberspace will soon become as important to your daily life as your telephone, if it hasn't already. Today, you can choose to use computers or not, but in the future, your choice will become more like deciding not to have electricity or running water. Tomorrow, cyberspace networking and job searching may make the difference between getting the job you want and settling for anything you can find.

■ *What Is the Internet?*

The Internet evolved from a military research program in the late 1960s (ARPAnet), but the government has almost no role in its operation today. It originally developed out of the tensions of the Cold War when computer networks were considered vulnerable in the event of nuclear war. Using a set of computer protocols called TCP/IP, the original ARPAnet was created as a self-healing network. Data was placed into tiny packets, each sent with complete addressing information, so that if one route to a destination failed, the packets could be routed to another. Each packet was switched by computers along a path that would take it to its final destination, but no two packets needed to follow the same path. At the end of the path, the packets were reassembled by a destination computer. The Internet of today works in much the same way.

In the 1980s, the military component became a separate network and the civilian network grew under the sponsorship of the U.S. National Science Foundation, which created the NSFnet, a network of free, high-speed "backbone" lines and supercomputers. Universities, supercomputer sites, NASA, the Department of Energy, and the National Institutes of Health soon joined their networks to this network. This connection of computer networks was called the "Internet" because it interconnected many networks (try to say that fast!). It was at this time that special computers called "gateways" began to act as traffic cops of the Internet, directing messages between networks and translating protocols.

By 1990, business had entered the picture as companies began using the Internet to exchange e-mail and access files. Today, the Internet is the world's largest computer network. In 1981, there were only about 200 host computers on the Internet. Each host could provide access for one person or an entire organization. Today, the Internet links more than 5 million host computers, 275,600 servers, and thousands of bulletin board systems into one massive, international information system.

❏ Evolution

The Internet is a construction in process, a constantly evolving place, so don't expect perfection. Be prepared for glitches, crashes, and occasional annoyances. Think of it as the Wild West, a frontier with dirt roads and no traffic laws. There will always be potholes. When the Internet works well, it is a fun place to surf, but it is often not as fast or reliable as you would like. Every day there are new ways to access the Internet, better and faster browsers, new technologies, and new ideas for using the medium. This new technology is driving the content of the Internet. The faster modems become, the more complex the data in files can be, so be ready for paved roads in the future.

With progress, however, there comes a sheriff. No one organization owns the Internet, although there are some organizations and companies that help manage different parts of the networks that serve as the backbone that ties everything together. Because many of these networks reside outside of the United States, it may be impossible to ever fully regulate the Internet, but Congress is currently pondering how best to control it, at least within our borders. No one knows what will happen in the future, so enjoy the frontier while it lasts.

The Internet has attracted so much attention that Nielsen, the predominant media research company, has developed programs to analyze and measure Internet traffic. Their August 1996 survey showed that Internet access in the United States and Canada was up by 50 percent in only a seven-month period, and more than half of these users were new to the Internet since the previous study. Even the demographics had changed. The survey found that 22–24 percent of the population of the United States and Canada 16 years of age or older had access to the Internet. The National Association of College and Employers (NACE) conducted a study in 1996 that showed that 71.6 percent of all college students have access to the Internet. David Harkness, senior vice president of business development for Nielsen Media Research, said, "Internet access and use are becoming increasingly mainstream."

What does all this mean to you and your job search? Nearly every kind of business imaginable has established a presence on this fundamental information medium. Like television in the 1940s, the Internet is becoming an important communication, entertainment, educational, and employment medium. Almost any aspect of business conducted in print, in person, or on the telephone can be conducted through the Internet . . . and that includes hiring.

■ *What Is the World Wide Web?*

The World Wide Web (WWW) is the linked information of the Internet, while the Internet is the physical collection of computers and cables by which Web files are transmitted. The World Wide Web was created in 1992 at CERN (the European Laboratory for Particle Physics in Geneva), a huge Swiss research laboratory, as a project to link physicists around the world. Because of its intuitive, easy-to-use hypertext design, the Web quickly spread beyond its original users.

Today, the Web is the commercial part of the Internet. It is usually, although not always, where companies place their home pages and where much of the commerce of the Internet is conducted. According to Digital's AltaVista search engine, there are more than 40 million Web pages and the number is growing exponentially every day. Whenever you see *http://* in a Universal Resource Locator (URL) address, you know that the address points to a Web page.

The Web is graphically oriented, meaning you can see images and hear sounds on your computer screen instead of viewing simple, boring text. Web resources are linked together, so you can click on highlighted words (hypertext) or pictures and go directly to related Web resources, which makes the Web very user friendly. These hypertext links carry you to computer sites that exist all over the Internet. One minute you may find yourself reading a document that resides on a computer in New York, and the next minute you will click on a word that sends you flying off to Australia. Using distributed hypermedia, the Web moves you effortlessly across the Internet with blinding speed. Think of the World Wide Web as a spider's web with all of the strings interconnected. The spider (you) can get to any location on the web by simply traveling along the strings.

❏ *Browsers*

In order to travel on this Web, you must have a browser—a computer software program that resides on your hard drive and allows you to read special files. Some of the better known browsers include Netscape, Internet Explorer, Mosaic, Lynx, and MacWeb. When you subscribe to a commercial online service, a browser is installed automatically on your hard drive when you install the program. Internet

Explorer is preinstalled in Windows 95 and ready for you to simply dial into an account and register. If you use an Internet service provider, you will more than likely be given Netscape with your subscription. All of these programs work in basically the same way. They read the files that come into your computer from other computers via the Internet and translate the HTML codes they see into pictures and words on your computer's monitor.

Most sites on the Web are free, but there are a few that either charge an additional fee for their products and services or are closed to the general public. If you access a private, password-protected Web site, you will need to get access from the Webmaster of that site. Most closed Web pages also have a public area where you can find out how to access the private area.

❑ *Bookmarks*

As you visit various Web sites, you might want to bookmark the locations that you find particularly interesting. Thanks to hyperlinks, as you surf the Net, it is easy to lose track of where you are and how you got there. Although you could keep a log and write down all of the URLs (addresses) that you want to remember, most browsers offer a bookmark feature that allows you to save the address of a Web site for use later. Simply click "Bookmarks" from the menu bar and select "Add Bookmark." Netscape and other browsers will even allow you to organize your bookmarks by category and save them as a file to transfer to another computer. When you want to return to a site, you click "Bookmarks" again and select the site you wish to revisit. This prevents a lot of writer's cramp!

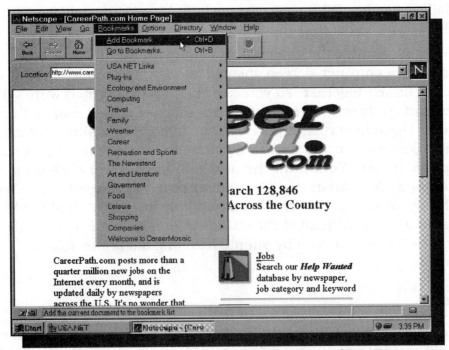

Screen shot of CareerPath home page reprinted with permission of Times Mirror.

■ What Is Telnet?

Telnet is a communications program that is fundamental to the functioning of the Internet. It is a service that allows you to logon to other computers on the Internet in an interactive, command-line mode, meaning you are actually giving the computer commands from your keyboard as if you were sitting at the host computer yourself. Telnet technology is text based and predates e-mail.

With Telnet, you can use your laptop computer to Telnet into a university's mainframe supercomputer and get all of that machine's power and speed. In fact, if you are a student who has gone home for the summer, you can Telnet to your university through a local Internet service provider (ISP) or commercial online service and retrieve your e-mail as if you were sitting in your dorm. When you travel, you can access your CompuServe or AOL account and Telnet to your local ISP without paying long distance charges to logon to your ISP account.

Using Telnet is as simple as clicking on an icon in CompuServe, AOL, or your ISP browser and then typing in the site address. For instance, to reach Rutgers University's information site, you would type in *telnet://info.rutgers.edu*. Some public sites may ask for a logon name and password. Often, the password is "guest." If that doesn't work, you may need to ask the person who gave you the address to provide that information.

Telnet commands are simple, but the program does expect you to know how to use the remote computer before you begin. Type "open" followed by the address and it takes you to the computer you want. Type "close" or "quit" and it takes you back to your prompt or the ISP menu. The "?" key brings up a list of other commands to help you navigate via Telnet.

Telnet can take you straight to public, academic, medical, legal, and other libraries where you can conduct research. You won't be able to actually read the books, but you will discover what resources are available. With Telnet, you can access bulletin board services that cover many areas and explore universities without ever setting a foot on campus. Government sites are great Telnet resources. You can visit the Library of Congress at *locis.loc.gov* or visit FedWorld at *fedworld.gov*. There are lists of Telnet sites on the Internet at:

- *http://www.magna.com.au/bdgtti/bdg_92.html#SEC95*
- *http://www.nova.edu/Inter-Links/start.html*
- *http://galaxy.einet.net/hytelnet/HYTELNET.html*
- *http://library.usask.ca/hytelnet/*
- *gopher://marvel.loc.gov/* (Select: *Internet Resources* and then *HYTELNET*)

❑ Job-related Telnet Sites

- AIPJOBS, American Institute of Physics Employment Opportunities
  telnet://aip.org/:23
  Logon: *aipjobs*
  Password: *aipjobs*
  Enter: *first name and e-mail address*

- Arizona Telecommunication Community (AzTeC)
  telnet://azetc.asu.edu
  Logon: *guest*
  Password: *visitor*

- European Astronomical Society "Situations Vacant" service
  telnet://STARJOBS@rlstar.bnsc.rl.ac.uk

- Hispanic Experts Database
  telnet://hrc.la.asu.edu

- Mobile, Alabama, Area Free-Net
  telnet://ns1.maf.mobile.al.us
  Logon: *visitor*

- New York State Department of Labor's WORKstation
  telnet://WORK@sallib.sals.edu:23

- Southeastern Ohio Regional Freenet
  telnet://seorf.ohiou.edu

- Texas Employment Commission
  telnet://hi-tec.tec.state.tx.us/

■ *What Are Newsgroups (Usenet)?*

Usenet stands for Users Network, which consists of thousands of computers that are organized under a set of groupings known as newsgroups. Each newsgroup is devoted to a particular subject, such as jobs or chemistry or dance. These newsgroups can be serious, fun, work related, or even obscene. There is no regulation of the Internet, so be forewarned.

Kevin Savetz, an Internet consultant with America Online, describes newsgroups as follows: "Usenet is simply the largest, most active, and most varied discussion forum in the world. Imagine a bulletin board on a wall. Imagine that as people pass it, they glance at what's there, and if they have something to add, they stick their note up, too. Now imagine that there are thousands of bulletin boards in this building, and that there are actually tens of thousands of such buildings throughout the world, each with its own identical copy of the bulletin boards. Got it? That's Usenet."

Newsgroups are the Internet equivalent of the live chat rooms and forums of commercial online services. They offer you the opportunity to broadcast articles (i.e., messages) back and forth on a topic thread among a large number of computers. When you reply to an article, you can continue the thread or start a new thread. There are more than 7 million people actively using in excess of 20,000 newsgroups around the world, and it is estimated that the number of newsgroups is growing by 20 to 30 every week.

Some newsgroups are moderated, meaning that your article (message) is sent to a moderator who first reviews it before making it available to the public. This keeps the discussion focused on a given subject and limits the number of inappropriate or irrelevant messages. In unmoderated newsgroups, you simply post an article and it is broadcast to everyone in the newsgroup. Alternative newsgroups tend to be unmoderated and much less structured than traditional newsgroups.

Each newsgroup contains messages from the people who participate in them. At the top of each message is the author's name, subject, date and time, the name of the originating computer system, and the body of the message itself. Some of the messages will be new and others will be responses to previous messages.

To access a newsgroup from your computer, logon to your Internet service provider or commercial online service account and click on the newsgroup (or Usenet) icon under the Internet options. Type in the URL for the site, press the Enter key, and you are there. You can read to your heart's content or add to the message thread with options provided by your news reader software. If you don't like the way your particular news reader works, you can download through ftp a copy of Trumpet for DOS at *oak.oakland.edu* or NewsWatcher for Macintosh at *ftp.acns.nwu.edu (/pub/newswatcher)*.

❏ *Domains*

Newsgroups are organized into a very structured format with periods separating the various topic levels. The first part of a newsgroup name is its general topic. The following are the eight major Usenet domains:

comp	Computer subjects (hardware and software)
sci	Scientific topics (both physical and social sciences)
soc	Social and cultural issues
rec	Recreation, arts, and hobbies
talk	Controversial issues (these groups are more debate oriented)
news	Newsgroup, network, and administration topics
misc	Subjects that are difficult to classify under other categories
alt	Alternative topics (this is where you have to be your own censor)

There are other, more local top-level newsgroup domains (actually more than 300) that generally refer to a specific school, city, state, country, or area of interest. This allows local groups in say, San Francisco, to discuss things of interest to them that would not be of interest to someone in New York. You may not be able to access corporate or school newsgroups, but it never hurts to try. You can find out a lot about a company's culture in its newsgroup. Some examples are:

ab	Alberta, Canada
apple	Apple Computer
atl	Atlanta
aus	Australia
ba	San Francisco Bay area
balt	Baltimore
bc	British Columbia
biz	Business topics, commercial traffic, company press releases
bln	Berlin

brasil	Brazil
br	Britain
ca	California
cam	Cambridge, Massachusetts
dk	Denmark
fr	France
hp	Hewlett-Packard
hsv	Huntsville, Alabama
k12	Teachers and students (K-12th grade)
ne	New England
netcom	Netcom local newsgroups
pnw	Pacific Northwest
purdue	Purdue University
ri	Rhode Island
tamu	Texas A&M University
ucb	University of California at Berkeley

These general areas are then subdivided into other newsgroups that deal with more specific topics within the subject area. For example, the *sci.biology* newsgroup is designed for the discussion of biology. The subnewsgroups of *sci.biology.molecular* and *sci.biology.research* focus on more specific topics within the biology discipline.

❑ Networking

As part of a newsgroup, you can join conversations about issues and trends in your industry and make great networking contacts. Then you can use e-mail to nurture those relationships that might lead to a job. It is usually a good idea to sit back and lurk for a week or two in a newsgroup before you speak. As you get a feel for the topics that are appropriate for discussion in a particular newsgroup, you can ask for feedback on your résumé or talk about the culture or job opportunities within certain companies.

Not all newsgroups appreciate résumé postings, so watch and learn, and then ask before posting. Posting a résumé inappropriately or making rude comments is considered bad manners, which can be disastrous to your job search. You don't want to leave a bad impression on even one potential contact, let alone thousands of people in a newsgroup!

❑ Netiquette

The unwritten rules of the Internet are called netiquette. These rules include being honest, polite, and legal when dealing with others in the virtual community of the Internet. Lurking is considered good manners in newsgroups. Before posting anything, including your résumé, you should lurk for a while until you understand the focus of the newsgroup. Some newsgroups are primarily for announcements or questions and not for discussions. Each newsgroup has its own unique culture. Some are virtual free-for-alls (like "misc," "talk," and "alt"), while others are more civilized. As a general rule, the "sci," "comp," and "news" newsgroups focus on facts and not opinions. "Soc" and "rec" newsgroups are a little more opinionated and are open to new member opinions.

❏ FAQs

Most newsgroups have a list of frequently asked questions (FAQs) that you should always read before posting an article. You will generally find the list of FAQs when you access the Usenet site, but there is a meta-site on the Internet that is a compilation of all the Usenet FAQs posted to newsgroups. It can be found at *http://www.cis.ohio-state.edu/hypertext/faq/usenet/FAQ-List.html.* Also read the articles *news.announce.newusers* and *news.answers* before joining in the discussion on a newsgroup. These sources will help you understand the purpose of the newsgroup and keep you out of hot water—or better yet, keep you from getting flamed (the Internet equivalent to hate mail).

Some other tips for posting articles in newsgroups include:

1. Avoid needless messages (like thank you or other things not of general interest). Send these messages via e-mail instead. Your message could be read by millions of people, so make your words something you will be proud of. Your message reflects on you. You want to make a good impression on possible networking contacts, and you never know who might be reading your message.

2. Make the subject line of your message clear and informative. It is here that people will decide whether to read the rest of your message.

3. Format your article clearly so it is easy to read and uses 60-character lines. Remember that it must be sent as an ASCII text message.

4. It is okay to include additional information about yourself at the end of your article, but avoid a long signature (no more than four lines). Avoid those cutesy pictures created from text characters.

5. Don't advertise on general purpose newsgroups. There are newsgroups that allow commercial postings ("comp" and "biz"), but always check the FAQs for each newsgroup first.

6. If you get an e-mail message with only RTFAQ in it, you know you are in trouble. RTFAQ stands for Read the Frequently Asked Questions. Newsgroup readers get tired of answering the same questions again and again, so they create FAQs. If you are new to newsgroups, read the FAQs before asking questions.

7. Don't send a "This is just a test" message to any newsgroup or you will get some pretty nasty e-mail messages in return. If you must try a test, there is a newsgroup just for that purpose. It is *misc.test.*

8. Avoid submitting your article to multiple newsgroups (spamming). It may be okay to cross-post to a few appropriate newsgroups, but don't do so randomly without some specific purpose.

9. Don't send your article to the same newsgroup twice. It takes a while for your file to end up in the newsgroup, so don't assume it isn't there because you can't find it immediately. Give it some time before reposting your article.

There are dozens of newsgroups devoted to jobs and job hunting, but not all of the messages in them are directly related to employment. Some are solicitations, get-rich-quick schemes, questions about interviewing techniques, or how to write a résumé. Despite this, however, newsgroups can yield connections to jobs. Executive recruiters post most of the real jobs found in newsgroups, and recruiters are valuable contacts for any job hunter. Use these newsgroup job postings to get a feel for a particular recruiter's specialty, and then contact the recruiter whose job postings match your experience. For a list of more than 1,400 recruiters, check the site at *http://www.onramp.net/ron/*.

There are some newsgroups that encourage you to post your résumé, including *atl.jobs.resumes, ba.jobs.resumes, israel.jobs.resumes, misc.jobs. resumes.* Many industry-oriented newsgroups include subtopics that are related to job hunting, so don't search simply for "jobs" or "résumés." A great resource for finding newsgroups that are specifically related to job hunting is the *Career Magazine* Web site *http://www.careermag.com.* Each day, *Career Magazine* downloads all job-related newsgroups and indexes the full text, not just the subject headers. You can search by location, keywords, or job title words. There is also a directory of recruiters, career books and tapes, résumé writing, and relocation services. There are even separate sections for freelance consulting jobs and self-employment opportunities.

One thing to keep in mind when writing a résumé for a newsgroup is that you are generally limited to 20,000 characters. Longer newsgroup messages may be split into two or more parts, and employers won't bother to look for the pieces or to glue them together again. The subject field that is a part of every newsgroup message is a great place to grab an employer's attention. Be specific. Instead of saying, "A career position with a dynamic company," it is better to say, "Sports marketing professional, proven track record, willing to relocate."

❏ *Job-related Newsgroups*

Industry Specific

alt.medical.sales.jobs.offered	Medical Sales
alt.medical.sales.jobs.resumes	Medical Sales
alt.support.telecommute	Telecommuters
bionet.jobs	Biotechnology
bionet.jobs.offered	Biotechnology
bionet.jobs.wanted	Biotechnology
bionet.women-in-bio	Biotechnology
bit.listserv.biojobs	Biotechnology
biz.jobs.offered	Business/Nontechnical
comp.jobs.offered	Computers
dod.jobs	U.S. Department of Defense

```
fnet.fin.jobs . . . . . . . . . . . . . . . . . . . . . . . . . . . . . . . . . . . . Finance
hepnet.jobs . . . . . . . . . . . . . . . . . . . . . . . . . . . . High Energy Physics
hsv.jobs . . . . . . . . . . . . . . . . . . . . . . . . . . . . . . . . . . Health Services
prg.jobs . . . . . . . . . . . . . . . . . . . . . . . . . . . . Computer Programmers
rec.radio.broadcasting . . . . . . . . . . . . . . . . . . . Radio Broadcasting
sci.research.careers . . . . . . . . . . . . . . . . . . . . . . . . Science Research
sci.research.postdoc . . . . . . . . . . . . . . . . . Postdoctoral Science Research
slac.jobs . . . . . . . . . . . . . . . . . . . . . Stanford Linear Accelerator Center
soc.org.nonprofit . . . . . . . . . . . . . . . . . . . . . . . . . . . . . . . . . Nonprofit
su.jobs . . . . . . . . . . . . . . . . . . . . . . . . . . . . . Stanford University
ucb.cs.jobs . . . . . . . . . . . . . . . . . . . . . . . . . . . . Computer Science
vmsnet.jobs . . . . . . . . . . . . . . . . . . . . . Digital Equipment Corporation
```

Alabama
```
hsv.jobs . . . . . . . . . . . . . . . . . . . . . . . . . . . . . . Huntsville, Alabama
```

Arizona
```
az.jobs . . . . . . . . . . . . . . . . . . . . . . . . . . . . . . . . . . . . . Arizona
```

Arkansas
```
uark.jobs . . . . . . . . . . . . . . . . . . . . . . . . . . . University of Arkansas
```

California
```
ba.jobs.contract . . . . . . . . . . . . . . . . . . . . San Francisco, California (Bay Area)
ba.jobs.misc . . . . . . . . . . . . . . . . . . . . . San Francisco, California (Bay Area)
ba.jobs.offered . . . . . . . . . . . . . . . . . . San Francisco, California (Bay Area)
ba.jobs.resumes . . . . . . . . . . . . . . . San Francisco, California (Bay Area)
la.jobs . . . . . . . . . . . . . . . . . . . . . . . . . . . . . Los Angeles, California
la.wanted.jobs . . . . . . . . . . . . . . . . . . . . . . . . Los Angeles, California
sdnet.jobs . . . . . . . . . . . . . . . . . . . . . . . . . . . . . San Diego, California
ucb.jobs . . . . . . . . . . . . . . . . . . . . . . University of California, Berkeley
ucd.cs.jobs . . . . . . . . . . . . . . . . . . . . . University of California, Davis
ucd.kiosk.jobs . . . . . . . . . . . . . . . . . . University of California, Davis
```

Connecticut
```
conn.jobs.offered . . . . . . . . . . . . . . . . . . . . . . . . . . . . . Connecticut
```

Florida
```
fl.jobs . . . . . . . . . . . . . . . . . . . . . . . . . . . . . . . . . . . . . . . Florida
fsu.job . . . . . . . . . . . . . . . . . . . . . . . . . . . . Florida State University
```

Georgia
```
alt.jobs . . . . . . . . . . . . . . . . . . . . . . . . . . . . . . . . Atlanta, Georgia
alt.resumes . . . . . . . . . . . . . . . . . . . . . . . . . . . . . Atlanta, Georgia
git.ohr.jobs.digest . . . . . . . . . . . . . . . Georgia Institute of Technology
```

Illinois
```
chi.jobs . . . . . . . . . . . . . . . . . . . . . . . . . . . . . . . . Chicago, Illinois
```

il.jobs.misc . . . . Illinois
il.jobs.offered . . . . Illinois
il.jobs.resumes . . . . Illinois
uiuc.cs.jobs . . . . University of Illinois
uiuc.misc.jobs . . . . University of Illinois, Urbana-Champaign

Indiana
in.jobs . . . . Indiana

Iowa
ia.jobs . . . . Iowa

Louisiana
lou.lft.jobs . . . . Lafayette, Louisiana

Maryland
balt.jobs . . . . Baltimore, Maryland

Michigan
mi.jobs . . . . Michigan
mi.wanted . . . . Michigan
umich.jobs . . . . University of Michigan

Minnesota
mn.jobs . . . . Minnesota
umn.cs.jobs . . . . University of Minnesota
umn.general.jobs . . . . University of Minnesota
umn.itlab.jobs . . . . University of Minnesota

Missouri
stl.jobs . . . . St. Louis, Missouri

Nebraska
nb.jobs . . . . Nebraska

Nevada
nv.jobs . . . . Nevada

New Mexico
nm.jobs . . . . New Mexico

New York
li.jobs . . . . Long Island, New York
nyc.jobs.contract . . . . New York City
nyc.jobs.misc . . . . New York City
nyc.jobs.offered . . . . New York City
nyc.jobs.wanted . . . . New York City
nyc.jobs . . . . New York City

North Carolina

triangle.jobs . . . . Research Triangle, North Carolina

Ohio

cinci.jobs . . . . Cincinnati, Ohio
cle.jobs . . . . Cleveland, Ohio
cmh.jobs . . . . Columbus, Ohio
oh.jobs . . . . Ohio
osu.jobs . . . . Ohio State University

Oregon

pdaxs.jobs.clerical . . . . Portland, Oregon
pdaxs.jobs.computers . . . . Portland, Oregon
pdaxs.jobs.construction . . . . Portland, Oregon
pdaxs.jobs.delivery . . . . Portland, Oregon
pdaxs.jobs.domestic . . . . Portland, Oregon
pdaxs.jobs.engineering . . . . Portland, Oregon
pdaxs.jobs.management . . . . Portland, Oregon
pdaxs.jobs.misc . . . . Portland, Oregon
pdaxs.jobs.restaurants . . . . Portland, Oregon
pdaxs.jobs.resumes . . . . Portland, Oregon
pdaxs.jobs.retail . . . . Portland, Oregon
pdaxs.jobs.sales . . . . Portland, Oregon
pdaxs.jobs.secretary . . . . Portland, Oregon
pdaxs.jobs.temporary . . . . Portland, Oregon
pdaxs.jobs.volunteers . . . . Portland, Oregon
pdaxs.jobs.wanted . . . . Portland, Oregon

Pennsylvania

pgh.jobs.offered . . . . Pittsburgh, Pennsylvania
pgh.jobs.wanted . . . . Pittsburgh, Pennsylvania
phl.jobs.offered . . . . Philadelphia, Pennsylvania
phl.jobs.wanted . . . . Philadelphia, Pennsylvania

Tennessee

memphis.employment . . . . Memphis, Tennessee
tnn.jobs . . . . Tennessee

Texas

austin.jobs . . . . Austin, Texas
dfw.jobs . . . . Dallas/Fort Worth, Texas
houston.jobs.offered . . . . Houston, Texas
houston.jobs.wanted . . . . Houston, Texas
tx.jobs . . . . Texas
ut.jobs . . . . University of Texas
utcs.jobs . . . . University of Texas, Austin

Utah

utah.jobs . . . . Utah
utah.valley.jobs . . . . Area around Salt Lake City, Utah

Washington

seattle.jobs.offered . . . . Seattle, Washington
seattle.jobs.wanted . . . . Seattle, Washington

Washington, D.C.

dc.jobs . . . . Washington, D.C.

Wisconsin

milw.jobs . . . . Milwaukee, Wisconsin

United States

alt.jobs . . . . All
au.jobs . . . . All
misc.jobs.contract . . . . Contract
misc.jobs.entry . . . . Entry Level
misc.jobs.offered . . . . All
misc.jobs.offered.entry . . . . Entry Level
misc.jobs.misc . . . . All
misc.jobs.resumes . . . . All
misc.jobs.wanted . . . . Wanted
ne.jobs . . . . New England
ne.jobs.contract . . . . New England Contract
pnet.jobs.volunteer . . . . Volunteer
pnet.jobs.wanted . . . . All
relcom.commerce.jobs . . . . All
su.jobs . . . . Stanford
ucb.jobs . . . . All
uiuc.misc.jobs . . . . All
us.jobs.contract . . . . Contract
us.jobs.misc . . . . All
us.jobs.offered . . . . All
us.jobs.resumes . . . . All
vmsnet.employment . . . . All

International

ab.jobs . . . . Alberta, Canada
at.jobs . . . . Austria
aus.jobs . . . . Australia and New Zealand
aus.ads.jobs . . . . Australia
bc.jobs . . . . British Columbia, Canada
bermuda.jobs.offered . . . . Bermuda
bln.jobs . . . . Berlin, Germany
can.jobs . . . . Canada
cl.kontakte . . . . Germany

```
de.markt.jobs . . . . . . . . . . . . . . . . . . . . . . . . . . . . . . . . . . . . . . . . . . . Germany
dk.jobs . . . . . . . . . . . . . . . . . . . . . . . . . . . . . . . . . . . . . . . . . . . . . . . . Denmark
fr.jobs.demandes . . . . . . . . . . . . . . . . . . . . . . . . . . . . . . . . . . . . . . . . . France
fr.jobs.offres . . . . . . . . . . . . . . . . . . . . . . . . . . . . . . . . . . . . . . . . . . . France
fr.jobs.d . . . . . . . . . . . . . . . . . . . . . . . . . . . . . . . . . . . . . . . . . . . . . France
ie.jobs . . . . . . . . . . . . . . . . . . . . . . . . . . . . . . . . . . . . . . . . . . . . . . Ireland
iijnet.jobs . . . . . . . . . . . . . . . . . . . . . . . . . . . . . . . . . . . . . . . . . . . . . Japan
kingston.jobs . . . . . . . . . . . . . . . . . . . . . . . . . . . . . . Kingston, Ontario, Canada
kw.jobs . . . . . . . . . . . . . . . . . . . . . . . Kitchener-Waterloo, Ontario, Canada
ont.jobs . . . . . . . . . . . . . . . . . . . . . . . . . . . . . . . . . . . . . Ontario, Canada
ott.jobs . . . . . . . . . . . . . . . . . . . . . . . . . . . . . . . . . . . . . . Ottawa, Canada
qc.jobs . . . . . . . . . . . . . . . . . . . . . . . . . . . . . . . . . . . . . . Quebec, Canada
relcom.commerce.jobs . . . . . . . . . . . . . . . . . . . Russia, Eastern Europe
sg.jobs.offer . . . . . . . . . . . . . . . . . . . . . . . . . . . . . . . . . . . . . . . Singapore
swnet.jobs . . . . . . . . . . . . . . . . . . . . . . . . . . . . . . . . . . . . . . . . . Sweden
tor.jobs . . . . . . . . . . . . . . . . . . . . . . . . . . Toronto, Ontario, Canada
uk.jobs . . . . . . . . . . . . . . . . . . . . . . . . . . . . . . . . . . United Kingdom
uk.jobs.contract . . . . . . . . . . . . . . . . . . . . . . . . . . . . . . United Kingdom
uk.jobs.d . . . . . . . . . . . . . . . . . . . . . . . . . . . . . . . . . . United Kingdom
uk.jobs.offered . . . . . . . . . . . . . . . . . . . . . . . . . . . . . . United Kingdom
uk.jobs.wanted . . . . . . . . . . . . . . . . . . . . . . . . . . . . . . United Kingdom
za.ads.jobs . . . . . . . . . . . . . . . . . . . . . . . . . . . . . . . . . . South Africa
```

There are several different kinds of resources for finding newsgroups on the Internet. One of the best search engines dedicated to Usenet newsgroups is Deja News. Since its inception in May of 1995, it has had the largest collection of Usenet news available anywhere. While most Usenet search engines will carry at the most one month of news, Deja News typically gives you access to newsgroups that go back to March of 1995 (at this writing, 53 million articles). Their ultimate goal is to index almost all of the Usenet since it began in 1979. Several of the major search engines—AltaVista, Excite, and InfoSeek—also index newsgroups. To find newsgroups that relate to your industry or to your job search, you can use the following resources to look for messages about particular topics or companies discussed in thousands of newsgroups and mailing lists.

- Active Newsgroups List and List of All Newsgroups
  ftp://ftp.uu.net
  Logon: *anonymous*
  Password: *your e-mail address*
  cd usenet/news.answers/active-newsgroups: get *part 1.Z* and *part 2.Z*
  cd networking/news/config: get *newsgroups*

- AltaVista
  http://www.altavista.digital.com

- Awebs Newsgroups Archive
  http://awebs.com/news_archive

- Deja News
  http://www.dejanews.com

- Excite
  http://www.excite.com

- InfoSeek
  http://www.infoseek.com/Home?page=Home.html&sv=N2

- Last Files From the News
  http://www.cnam.fr/Images/Usenet/

- Liszt: Directory of E-mail Discussion Groups
  http://www.liszt.com

- NPAC Oracle 7
  http://asknpac.npac.syr.edu

- Reference.Com
  http://www.reference.com

- SIFT—Stanford Information Filtering Tool
  http://hotpage.stanford.edu/

- The Usenet Newsstand
  http://CriticalMass.com/Concord

■ *What Is a Mailing List?*

A mailing list is an organized form of e-mail. You subscribe to a mailing list that interests you and mail comes to you automatically. You can also send e-mail to many people at the same time using a mailing list. These lists are wonderful sources of information about your chosen profession. You can enhance your general knowledge base, which will make you more employable, or learn something that will make you appear more knowledgeable in an interview. There are some general rules, or netiquette, however, that you should know before participating in mailing lists.

First, as a general rule, mailing lists are noncommercial and participants dislike receiving commercial ads and solicitations. Doing business on the Internet is acceptable; it's just a matter of how it is conducted. Mailing lists are generally not the place to conduct business unless you belong to a mailing list exclusively set up for that purpose. Second, don't waste people's time by sending junk e-mail messages of little value ("spamming").

Now, let's get down to the business of subscribing to a mailing list. There are many kinds of mailing lists (electronic magazines and newsletters, personal information distribution lists, small clubs where people of like mind share information, public debate and discussion lists, and news and information dissemination lists, among others)—an estimated 25,000 of them exist on the Internet. All mailing lists fall into either the interactive or reactive categories. Interactive lists encourage the participation of list members in exchanging ideas and information, either in unrestricted or restricted ways. Reactive lists are more for news/information distribution. Reactive lists will accept submissions of articles or digests from members but rarely encourage member-to-member discussion. In either type, members are expected to relate their information to the topics normally discussed in that particular mailing list.

Before you subscribe to a mailing list, you should do a little research to make sure the list will meet your needs. Commercial online services often have mailing list databases where you can read comprehensive information on any given list. If you are using an ISP to access the Internet, these resources will not be available to you and your best option is to check with the list owner via e-mail for more information and answers to frequently asked questions. Avoid joining a mailing list and then quickly leaving it, since doing so is considered rude.

❏ *To Subscribe*

Once you have determined that a particular mailing list is relevant, you must send an e-mail message to the list owner asking to subscribe. The exact wording of the message differs with each mailing list, but generally a simple command like the following, typed in your e-mail message screen, is all that is needed:

SUBSCRIBE [type the list name here] Yourfirstname Yourlastname

Sometimes, a mailing list will require that you list the reasons why the list owner should admit you to the list. In some cases, you may even need to send a second piece of e-mail to confirm your desire to be added to the list. The resources listed under "Job-related Mailing Lists" will show you the exact messages you need to send in order to subscribe, but here is a sample screen:

Once you subscribe to a mailing list, the actual day-to-day participation is easy. You simply read your e-mail every day. If you don't, your mailbox can quickly over-fill, depending on how many pieces of e-mail your service allows you to have at any one time. You may also exchange e-mail with other list members and sometimes even participate in real-time chats. Look

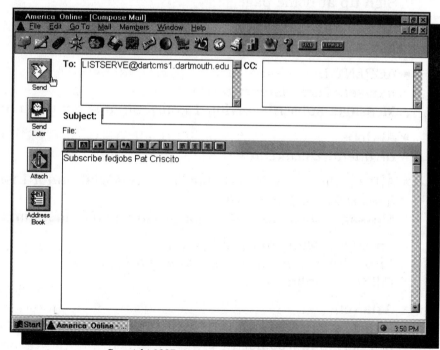

Copyright 1997, America Online. Used by permission.

before you leap, however. It is always a good idea to read a list for several weeks before attempting to post.

❏ *To Unsubscribe*

If you are going to be away from your computer for some time, either unsubscribe from the list or use the NOMAIL or POSTPONE features to temporarily suspend your subscription (not all mailing lists support these features). When you are ready to discontinue your subscription, you simply send a one-word e-mail message to the list owner that says:

UNSUBSCRIBE [type the list name here]

Mail from the list may continue to be delivered for several days after you have actually left the list, but it should stop within a few days. If not, then check the FAQs you read before subscribing to make sure there wasn't some other procedure you needed to follow to unsubscribe. Contact the list owner if the problem continues.

Many mailing lists are echoed at Usenet sites, which means that you can fully participate in the mailing list without having to worry about reading your e-mail everyday. You simply go to the Usenet site and read or download the information you want. This is like driving to the corner store and buying a newspaper instead of reading whatever mail is delivered to your mailbox.

❏ *Job-related Mailing Lists*

- 3DSite
  http://www.lightside.com/~dani/cgi/offers/index.html
  Sign up at home page

- ABLE-JOB
  listserv@sjuvm.stjohns.edu

- ACRLNY-L
  mailserv@acfcluster.nyu.edu
  Message: *subscribe acrlny-1 yourfirstname yourlastname*

- AI-Jobs
  ai+query@cs.cmu.edu

- AIR-L, Electronic Newsletter of the Association for Institutional Research
  listserv@vtvm1.cc.vt.edu
  Message: *subscribe AIR-L yourfirstname yourlastname*

- American Mathematical Society
  http://www.ams.org/committee/profession/
  Fill in an online form

- AsiaNet
  http://www.asia-net.com
  Subscribe to free list

- AV-Jobs
  LISTSERV@rotor.com
  Message: *subscribe AV-Jobs yourname*

- BizOp, Business Opportunities Mailing List
  bizbot@teletron.com
  Message: *subscribe*

- Career Network
  http://sgx.com/hg/
  Instructions on home page ($)

- Career-Quest International
  http://careerquest.com
  Instructions on home page

- CIS-L – Careers in Information Systems
  cis-l@ubs.ubalt.edu
  To Subscribe: *listserv@ube.ubalt.edu*
  Message: *subscribe CIS-L yourfirstname yourlastname*

- CIS-L – Careers in Information Systems
  cis-l@ubs.bitnet
  To Subscribe: *listserv@ubs.bitnet*
  Subject: *new subscription*

- Computist's Communique
  LAWS@ai.sri.com

- Corporate Staffing Center, Inc.
  http://www.corporate-staffing.com/csc/
  Enter your e-mail address

- ELMAR – Researchers in Marketing
  elmar-request@columbia.edu
  Message: *SUBSCRIBE ELMAR-LIST or ELMAR-DIGEST*
  Indicate which subscription you prefer

- ENVENG-L – Environmental Engineering
  enveng-l@pan.cedar.univie.ac.at
  To Subscribe: *listproc@pan.cedar.univie.ac.at*
  Message: *subscribe enveng-1*

- Executive Connection
  listserv@execon.metronet.com

- Federal Government LISTSERV
  LISTSERV@dartcms1.dartmouth.edu
  From: *your address*
  Subject: *leave blank*
  Message: *Subscribe fedjobs firstname lastname*

- FEDJOBS – The Federal Job Bulletin Board
  listserv@dartmouth.edu
  Message: *SUB FEDJOBS yourfirstname yourlastname*

- Fin-jobs
  listproc@financenet.gov
  Message: *SUBSCRIBE fin-jobs yourname*

- FROGJOBS – Scientific Jobs in France
  Listproc@list.cren.net
  Message: *subscribe frogjobs yourname*

- GEOSCI-JOBS
  listserv@netcom.com
  Message: *subscribe GEOSCI-JOBS your e-mail address*

- GIS Jobs Clearinghouse – University of Minnesota, Forestry, Remote Sensing Lab
  gis-jobs-request@MAILBASE.AC.UK

- HPCWire BULLETIN
  Free trial subscription: *trial@hpcwire.ans.net*
  Subject: *667* (to receive job listings)

- ICEN-L—International Career and Employment
  listserv@iubvm.indiana.edu
  Message: *subscribe icen-l yourfirstname yourlastname*

- JapanNet
  Majordomo@lists.mindspring.com
  Message: *subscribe japan-net*

- Job-Link
  Job-Link-Admin@listserv.job-link.com
  Message: *subscribe, Job-Link, yourname*

- JobPlace
  listserv@news.jobweb.org

- JobServe (UK)
  subscribe@jobserve.com

- LIBJOB-L
  listserv@ubvm.cc.buffalo.edu
  Message: *subscribe libjob-1 yourfirstname yourlastname*

- LIS-JOBLIST
  mailserv@ac.dal.ca
  Message: *subscribe LIS-JOBLIST*

- MET-JOBS—Jobs in Meteorology, Climatology, and Atmospheric Sciences
  listserv@netcom.com
  Message: *subscribe MET-JOBS your e-mail address*

- ORCHESTRALIST
  listproc@hubcap.clemson.edu
  Message: *subscribe orchestralist*

- Physics World Jobs Online
  listproc@listerver.ioppublishing.com
  Message: *subscribe PWJOBS yourname*

- Project Connect
  NVickers@Chickasaw.AState.Edu

- SLAJOB (Library)
  listserv@iubvm.ucs.indiana.edu
  Message: *subscribe SLAJOB yourfirstname yourlastname*

- Software AG Community
  listserv@uafsysb.uark.edu
  Message: *SUBSCRIBE SAG-L yourname*

- TESLJB-L, Teaching English As a Foreign Language
  listserv@cunyvm.cuny.edu
  Message: *subscribe TESLBJ-L yourfirstname yourlastname*
  Participants must be members of the TESL-L main list to join this list.

- USNONPROFIT-L
  majordomo@coyote.rain.org
  Message: *subscribe usnonprofit-1*

- VISTA-L, VISTA On-Line
  listserv@american.edu
  Message: *subscribe vista-l yourfirstname yourlastname*

- Young Scientist Network Electronic Newsletter
  ysnadm@crow-t-robot.stanford.edu
  Message: *subscribe yourfirstname yourlastname*

There are sites on the Internet that list mailing lists, although they are not specifically job related, so you will need to sift through them for clues as to their subject.

- Indiana Mailing List Archive
  http://scwww.ucs.indiana.edu/mlarchive/

- Publicly Accessible Mailing Lists (PAML)
  http://www.neosoft.com/internet/paml/

■ *How to Post Your Résumé to the Internet*

The generic ASCII text file of your résumé that you created in your word processor can be used to cut and paste into various fill-in-the-blank electronic forms on the Internet. For instance, when you access a company's home page and search its database of job openings, there will be a hyperlink (highlighted text or picture) that will allow you to send your résumé directly to the company's recruiters or human resource department, or you can send your résumé to job banks (like Online Career Center, E-Span, Monster Board, CareerPath, and so on) where it can be searched by potential employers at any time of the day or night. This 24-hour access to your résumé increases your exposure to potential employers, which increases your chances of finding a job quicker. Think about how many résumés you would mail out in a normal, nonelectronic job search . . . maybe 100. By posting your résumé in a résumé database, you increase your exposure thousands of times over with one simple submission!

There are basically three ways to get your résumé into one of these databases. First is an electronic form that you can complete while you are at the Internet site, like the one at E-Span below.

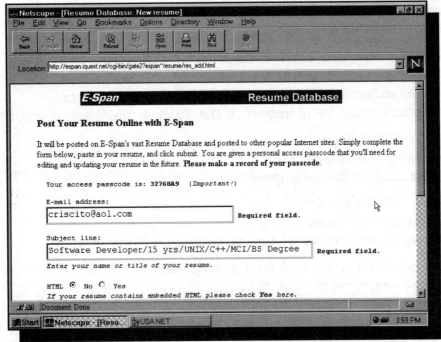

Screen shot of E-Span home page reprinted with permission from E-Span.

The second way to get your résumé into these databases is to send an e-mail message with your résumé as the text of the e-mail message, like in the screen shot below. See Chapter 5 for complete instructions on doing this.

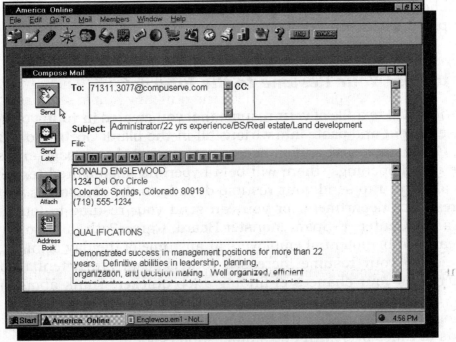

Copyright 1997, America Online. Used by permission.

The third way is to attach the ASCII text file of your résumé to an e-mail message that has a cover letter as the text of the message, like the sample below. Again, see Chapter 5 for complete instructions.

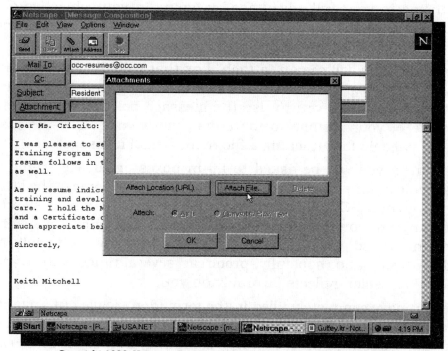

■ *Posting Your Résumé Directly to a Company's Home Page*

One of the best kept secrets of the Internet is that many large companies do not post their job openings in the job banks (E-Span, CareerPath, Monster Board, and so on). Instead, they use the company profile sections of these sites to establish a hyperlink to their own home pages where they only need to update job openings one time. That means you need to check the company profile sections of every one of these sites, or go directly to the company's home page by using the search engines (AltaVista, Excite, Yahoo, WebCrawler, and so on) to find their URLs (home page addresses). You can also check the list of company Internet addresses beginning on page 123. Once there, you will find current press releases, annual reports, company histories, executive profiles, and an incredible wealth of other information to prepare you for an interview or to help you determine whether or not you would really like to work for this company.

If it is well designed, somewhere on the company's home page you will find a hyperlink to job openings or their résumé database. Keep digging. Sometimes these sections are buried on deeper pages, meaning you have to hyperlink to other sections off the main home page before finding them. Once you discover the pot of gold, search the job openings by keyword and then submit your generic ASCII text file résumé in application to positions that interest you.

Each company's site will be designed to accept this information in a slightly different way. Some will simply list a hyperlink e-mail address for a recruiter. When you click on the hyperlink, an e-mail box will appear and you will need to cut and paste (or retype) your résumé into the spaces provided. Don't forget to use the subject line to your full advantage by typing in your objective or strategic keywords. Follow the instructions beginning on page 94 for cutting and pasting your information into the e-mail message box.

Occasionally you will see an "attach" box that will allow you to attach your résumé file to the e-mail message instead of cutting and pasting it into the message box. This allows you to use the message box for a cover letter. Then attach the file of your résumé to the e-mail message. Follow the instructions beginning on page 92 for attaching a file to an e-mail message.

Other times, you will be asked to fill in boxes on an electronic form that requests specific information. You can still cut and paste some of the larger blocks of text from your ASCII file (see page 94 for instructions). Avoid retyping information anytime you can, since it introduces the possibility of spelling errors. When you can cut and paste from the file that has already been spell checked by your word processor and, hopefully, proofread several times, your e-mail will be of higher quality, which reflects favorably on you.

When you have completely filled in the form (don't leave out any information they request), there will be a button or highlighted text that allows you to submit the information directly to the company's computer. In most of these cases, your résumé is e-mailed to a specific person, usually the recruiter assigned to fill the job opening or sometimes directly to the hiring manager. After the recruiter has finished with your résumé (usually when the job is filled—hopefully by you—or you are eliminated from consideration), the file is then forwarded to the company's main résumé database (applicant tracking system) where your résumé becomes accessible to any recruiter or hiring manager in the company who decides to perform a keyword search to fill a position. Your résumé will continue to float in this cyberspace for a specified period of time (usually six months to a year) before being purged.

Set up a system for keeping track of the expiration dates of your résumé. Most résumé databases, job banks, and companies keep your résumé for only a specific length of time. Most will keep your résumé for a year, but there are several, including Online Career Center (OCC), that will only store your résumé for 30 to 90 days. Always check the Web page for the storage policies of each site.

Most companies that use the electronic applicant tracking systems manufactured by Resumix, Restrac, and SmartSearch2 generate automatic letters of acknowledgment that will usually tell you how long they will keep your résumé. For instance, in a recent letter mailed to one of my clients by Hewlett-Packard's automated applicant tracking system, she was informed that her résumé would be kept in the computerized database for six months and checked for a possible match with each job opening that became available. At the end of the six-month period, it was possible for her to call the Employment Response Center and request that her résumé be kept on file for another six months, but it was up to her to call. These options for renewing your résumé without resubmitting it will disappear if you are past the deadline. Make a note of the date your résumé will expire on each database. Back up a week or so to give yourself time to renew or resubmit it and write a reminder on your calendar.

❏ *Companies*

The following companies are just some of the ones that list jobs and accept résumés at their Internet sites. All of the addresses listed here were current at the time this book was published, but sites come and go like the wind. If you find that one address is no longer valid, simply go on to the next one and accept the fact that the site has died, hopefully a painless death. Sometimes you can delete all of the Internet address after the *.com* and try to reach the home page. Then you can hyperlink to the job posting or résumé pages. There are times, however, when a site has simply changed its address entirely. See Chapter 10 for ways to use search engines to see if these sites still exist or to find new resources. For a list of more than 3,000 companies that actively use the Internet for recruiting, check: *http://www.occ.com/occ/occMemberJobs.html.*

For your convenience, this list is reproduced at my home page on the Internet so you can hyperlink to the companies without typing in individual URL addresses. You will find the most up-to-date version of this list through a hyperlink at *http://members.aol.com/criscito.*

@Home Network	*http://www.home.net/*
20/20 Software	*http://www.twenty.com/Pages/CIA.shtml#anchor422422*
2Way Media, Inc.	*http://www.2launch.com/employ.html*
3Com	*http://www.3com.com/*
3Dlabs	*http://www.3dlabs.com/jobs.htm*
3DO Company	*http://www.3do.com/company/job_list.html*
3DSite	*http://www.3dsite.com/3dsite/projects/3dsite/ads/jobad.html*
4-Sight (UK)	*http://www.four-sight.co.uk/4-sight/jobs.html*
7th Level, Inc.	*http://www.7thlevel.com:80/*
7Up	*http://www.7up.com/Index.html*
A&W Computers, Inc. (Canada)	*http://www.awinc.com/custom/jobs.htm*
ABB Atom (Sweden)	*http://www.abb.se/atomweb/posopen.htm*
Abbott Laboratories	*http://www.abbott.com/career/index.htm*
AccelGraphics, Inc.	*http://www.accelgraphics.com/*
Access Health Incorporated	*http://www.access-Health.com/employ/hr2.htm*
ACE*COMM Corporation	*http://www.acec.com/eeo.htm*
Acer America Corporation	*http://www.acer.com/aac/about/jobs.htm*
ACI US, Inc.	*http://www.aci-4d.com/Pages/GUI/ACI_US/ English/About_ACI/Jobs.html*
Acorn Computers Limited (UK)	*http://www.acorn.co.uk/aboutacorn/jobs.html*
ACT Networks, Inc.	*http://www.acti.com/jobs.html*
Actel Corporation	*http://www.actel.com/marcom/topview*
Action Instruments	*http://www.actionio.com/*
Active Voice Corporation	*http://www.activevoice.com/avhome/aboutav/jobop.htm*
Active Window Productions	*http://www.actwin.com/actwin/job.html*
Activision	*http://www.activision.com/HR/*
Adaptec	*http://www.adaptec.com/career/*
Adaptive Solutions, Inc.	*http://www.asi.com/asi/jobs.html*
Adax, Inc.	*http://www.adax.com/*

ADB Matisse	http://www.adb.com/Company/hiring.html
ADC Kentrox	http://www.kentrox.com/jobs/employment.html
ADC Telecommunications, Inc.	http://www.ps-mpls.com:80/CORP_DIR.html
Addison-Wesley	http://www.aw.com/hrd/
Adept Scientific (UK)	http://www.adeptscience.co.uk//as/adept/adept.html
Adobe Systems Incorporated	http://www.adobe.com/JOBS.html
ADP	http://www.careermosaic.com/cm/adp/adp11.html
Adra Systems, Inc.	http://www.adra.com/jobs.shtm
ADTRAN, Inc.	http://www.adtran.com/
Advanced ChemTech	http://www.peptide.com/ac03005.htm
Advanced Computer Communications	http://www.acc.com/stedirectory/Index.html
Advanced Digital Information Corporation (ADIC)	http://www.adic.com/corp/employ.html
Advanced Engineering and Research Associates, Inc.	http://www.aera.com/jobs.htm
Advanced Gravis Computer Technology Ltd. (Canada)	http://www.gravis.com/humanres.htm
Advanced Input Devices	http://www.advanced-input.com/career.htm
Advanced Logic Research, Inc.	http://www.alr.com/corp/employ/employ.htm
Advanced Micro Devices, Inc.	http://www.amd.com/html/employment/employment.html
Advanced Microelectronics	http://www.aue.com/home.html
Advanced Technology Center	http://www.atc.com/atc_job.html
Advanced Technology Laboratories (ATL)	http://www.atl.com/hr/hr_main.html
Advanced Visual Systems, Inc.	http://www.avs.com/about/jobs/index.html
AEON Solutions, Inc.	http://www.aeons.com/aeon/
Aeroquip Corporation	http://www.aeroquip.com/recruit-h.html
AeroSpace Corporation	http://www.careermosaic.com/cm/aerospace/
Aetna, Inc.	http://www.aetna.com/opp.htm
AgentSoft Ltd.	http://www.agentsoft.com/employ.htm
Agile Networks	http://www.agile.com/employment/employment.html
Aid Association for Lutherans	http://www.aal.org/career/
AimNet, Inc.	http://www.aimnet.com/employ.html
Air Products and Chemicals, Inc.	http://www.airproducts.com/employ/emplinfo.html
AirSoft	http://www.airsoft.com/employ.html
Ajilon	http://www.ajilon.com/ajilon/jo/
Aladdin Systems, Inc.	http://www.aladdinsys.com/index.html
Alden Electronics, Inc.	http://www.alden.com/jobs.html
Alfa Laval Automation (Sweden)	http://www.automation.alfalaval.se/homepage.htm
Algor, Inc.	http://www.algor.com/employ.htm
Alias|Wavefront	http://www.alias.com/Corporate/career_opportunities.html
Allen Systems Group	http://allensysgroup.com/gateway/asg_hr.htm
Allergo New Media Incorporated	http://www.allegronm.com/
Alliance Semiconductor	http://www.alsc.com/corporate/ALSCHR.html
Allianz Aktiengesellschaft Holding (Germany)	http://www.allianz.de
Allied Irish Bank (AIB) (Ireland)	http://www.aib.ie/it-place/welcome.html
Allied Telesyn International	http://www.alliedtelesyn.com/employop.htm
AlliedSignal Aerospace	http://www.allied.com/aerospace/employment/index.htm
Alpha Microsystems	http://www.alphamicro.com/compny/jobs.htm
Alpha Software Corporation	http://www.alphasoftware.com/jobs.htm
Alphatronix	http://www.alphatronix.com/html/jobs.html
AltaVista–Digital	http://altavista.digital.com/cgi-bin/query?pg=jobs
Altera Corporation	http://www.altera.com/html/hr/employ.html
Altris Software Inc.	http://www.alpharel.com/Flash/jobline.html
AMAX Engineering Corporation	http://www.amax.com/career.htm
Amdahl Corporation	http://www.amdahl.com/doc/employment/
American Airlines	http://www.americanair.com/aa_home/aa_hr/hr_index.html
American Digital	http://www.helpwanted.com/adjb.htm
American Digital Network	http://www.jobscape.com/job.html

American Management Systems (AMS) . . . . *http://www.amsinc.com/career/career.htm*
American Megatrends, Inc. . . . . *http://www.megatrends.com/*
American Power Conversion Corporation *http://www.apcc.com/english/about/about009.htm*
AmeriData Technologies, Inc. . . . . *http://www.ameridata.com/employment_ops.html*
Amerinex Applied Imaging, Inc. . . . . *http://www.aai.com/AAI/AAI/EmploymentSW.html*
Ameristar Casinos, Inc. . . . . *http://www.ameristars.com/*
Ames Department Stores, Inc. *http://205.161.53.12/hiring.html*
Amgen . . . . *http://www.bio.com/hr/job/amgen_1.html*
Amoco Corporation . . . . *http://www.amoco.com/what_we_do/ss/hr/*
AMP, Inc. . . . . *http://www.amp.com/jobs/jobs.html*
AMS Tech . . . . *http://www.amsnote.com/*
Amulet, Inc. . . . . *http://www.amulet.com/career/career.htm*
Amylin Pharmaceuticals, Inc. . . . . *http://www.amylin.com/jobs/jobpage.html*
ANADIGICS, Inc. . . . . *http://www.anadigics.com/jobs.html*
Analog Devices, Inc. . . . . *http://www.analog.com/about/jobops/jobops.html*
Analysys Limited (UK) . . . . *http://www.analysys.co.uk/recruit/default.htm*
Ancot Corp . . . . *http://www.ancot.com/employ.htm*
AND Communications . . . . *http://www.alantec.com/*
Andataco . . . . *http://www.andataco.com/cgi-bin/SpiffChoice?/otnfs/otn
/genesis/segment1/jobs/index.html+nocolor+text+nologin*
Andersen Consulting . . . . *http://www.ac.com/recruit/welcome.htm*
Andyne Computing Limited . . . . *http://www.andyne.com/cgi/nav.cgi?2careers*
ANSA (UK) . . . . *http://www.ansa.co.uk/APM/job-ad.html*
Ansoft Corporation . . . . *http://www.ansoft.com/Job/*
Anstec, Inc. . . . . *http://www.anstec.com/EmpIndex.htm*
Answer Systems, Inc. . . . . *http://www.answer.com/jobs/jobs.html*
Aon Corporation . . . . *http://www.aon.com/*
Apertus Technologies, Inc. . . . . *http://www.apertus.com/jobs/joblist.htm*
APL Limited . . . . *http://www.apl.com/cgi-bin/hr.pl*
Apple Computer, Inc. *http://www2.apple.com/employment*
Applied Biosystems, Inc. . . . . *http://www.perkin-elmer.com:80/ab/abww0006.htm#career*
Applied Computer Solutions . . . . *http://www.acsacs.com/employ.html?*
Applied Data Resource Management . . . . *http://www.adrm.com/emplopp.htm*
Applied Immune Sciences, Inc. *http://www.ais4cells.com/jobs.html*
Applied Innovation, Inc. . . . . *http://www.aiinet.com/index.html*
Applied Language Technologies . . . . *http://www.altech.com/employ.htm*
Applied Materials, Inc. . . . . *http://www.careermosaic.com/cm/applied_materials/*
Applied Micro Circuits Corp. (AMCC) . . . . *http://www.amcc.com/jobs.html*
Applied Microsystems Corporation . . . . *http://www.amc.com/*
Applied Signal Technology . . . . *http://www.appsig.com/job_postings/job_postings.html*
Applix, Inc. . . . . *http://www.applix.com/stats/jobs.htm*
Architext Software . . . . *http://www.atext.com/Jobs/*
Ariel Corporation . . . . *http://www.ariel.com/*
ARMS, Inc. . . . . *http://ssnet.com/~timperry/wilm_emp.html*
Aromat Corporation . . . . *http://www.mew.com/Aromat/Employ/employ.html*
Array Microsystems, Inc. . . . . *http://www.array.com/jobs.html*
Arrick Robotics . . . . *http://www.robotics.com/employ.html*
ARRIS Pharmaceutical Corp. . . . . *http://www.arris.com/Carreer_Opps/Career_Opportunities*
Arthur Anderson *http://www.arthurandersen.com/firmwide/recruit/cl0.htm*
Arthur D. Little, Inc. . . . . *http://www.adlittle.com/careers.html*
Artisoft, Inc. . . . . *http://www.artisoft.com/*
ARTIST Graphics . . . . *http://www.artgraphics.com/employ.htm*
Asante Technologies, Inc. *http://www.asante.com:80/Jobs/jobs.html*
ASAP Software Express, Inc. . . . . *http://www.asapsoftware.com/career/*
Ascend Communications, Inc. . . . . *http://www.ascend.com/compinfo/joblist.html*

Ascom Timeplex, Inc. . . . . *http://www.timeplex.com/jobs/new.htm*
Aspect Telecommunications . . . . *http://www.aspect.com/hiring.html*
Aspen Technology, Inc. . . . . *http://www.aspentec.com/jobops/*
AST Computer . . . . *http://WWW.ast.com/americas/joboppor.htm*
Astound Incorporated . . . . *http://www.astoundinc.com/jobs/jobs.html*
Astra Pharmaceuticals . . . . *http://www.astra.com/astra/career/career.htm*
AT&T *http://www.careermosaic.com/cm/att/att6.html*
AT&T Paradyne . . . . *http://www.paradyne.att.com/company/recruit.htm*
AT&T Wireless Services . . . . *http://www.mccaw.com/*
ATEL Capital Group *http://www.hooked.net:80/atel/empl.htm*
ATI Technologies, Inc. . . . . *http://www.atitech.ca/hr/hr.html*
Atlantic Financial . . . . *http://www.af.com/Atlantic/employ.html*
Atmel Corporation *http://www.atmel.com/atmel/career/career1.html*
Attachmate Corporation *http://www.atm.com/corpinfo/cooljob/cooljob1.htm*
Aurum Software, Inc. . . . . *http://www.aurum.com/corporate/careers/careers.html*
Auspex Systems . . . . *http://www.auspex.com/Jobs.html*
Austria Mikro Systeme International AG (Austria) . . . . . . *http://www.ams.co.at/jobs/jobs_00.htm*
Autocam Corporation . . . . *http://www.autocam.com/docs/employ.htm*
Autodesk . . . . *http://www.autodesk.com/*
Automata, Inc. *http://indy2.automata.com/*
Automated Concepts, Inc. *http://www.careermosaic.com/cm/aci/*
Automated Graphic Systems . . . . *http://www.ags.com/employment/employment.htm*
Automated Systems Incorporated . . . . *http://www.asieng.com/employ.html*
Automatic Data Processing, Inc. (ADP) . . . . *http://www.adp.com/about/index.html*
Automation Works, Inc. . . . . *http://www.automators.com/jobsf.htm*
Avalan Technology . . . . *http://www.avalan.com/home.html*
Avance Logic, Inc. . . . . *http://www.avance.com/employ.htm*
Avant! Corporation . . . . *http://www.avanticorp.com/*
Avantos Performance Systems, Inc. . . . . *http://www.avantos.com/*
AVEX Electronics, Inc. *http://www.huber.com/Avex/avex95/career.htm*
Axent Technologies, Inc. *http://www.axent.com:80/axent/career/career.html*
Axiom Management Consultants . . . . *http://www.axiom.com/axemploy.htm*
Aztech Labs . . . . *http://www.aztechca.com/empopp.html*
B. H. Blackwell Ltd (UK) . . . . *http://www.blackwell.co.uk/libserv/jobs/jobs.html*
Baan Company <The> . . . . *http://www.baan.com/10_Job/default.htm*
Ball Aerospace & Technologies Corp. . . . . *http://www.ball.com/aerospace/jobhome.html*
Bank of America . . . . *http://www.bankamerica.com/*
Bank of Boston . . . . *http://www.helpwanted.com/company/bkb/bkbhp.htm*
Bank One Corporation . . . . *http://www.careernet-bankone.com/*
BankersTrust . . . . *http://www.bankerstrust.com/hr/hr.html*
Barnett Banks, N.A. . . . . *http://www.barnett.com/jobs.htm*
Barr Engineering Company . . . . *http://www.barr.com/job_opp.html*
BARRA, Inc. . . . . *http://www.barra.com/AboutBARRA/employ.html*
Barrios Technology, Inc. *http://www.barrios.com/JobsS17.html*
Bay Network . . . . *http://www.baynetworks.com/Corporate/Employment/*
Bayer AG *http://www.bayer.com/english/3xxxmita/3300/3300.htm*
BayNet World, Inc. *http://www.baynet.com/employment.html*
BayWare, Inc. . . . . *http://www.bayware.com/jobs.html*
BBN Corporation . . . . *http://www.bbn.com/bbnjobs/jobsrch.htm*
BBN Internet Services Corporation . . . . *http://www.helpwanted.com/bbnhome.html*
BBN Planet . . . . *http://www.bbnplanet.com/doc/jobs.html*
BC Research Inc. (Canada) . . . . *http://www.bcr.bc.ca/jobs/*
BDM International, Inc. *http://www.bdm.com/bdm/l1_car.htm*
Be, Inc. . . . . *http://www.be.com/about_be/jobs/*
Bechtel Corporation . . . . *http://www.bechtel.com/hr/*

Beckman Instruments, Inc. . . . . *http://www.beckman.com/gen-info/careers.htm*
Belcan Services Group . . . . *http://www.belcan.com/infoserv.htm*
Bell Atlantic NYNEX Mobile . . . . . . *http://www.careermosaic.com/cm/bell_nynex/bell_nynex1.html*
Bell Microproducts . . . . *http://www.bellmicro.com/Bell/employment/mainemp.htm*
Bell Sygma . . . . *http://www.careermosaic.com/cm/bell_sygma/*
Bellcore–Bell Communications Research . . . . *http://www.bellcore.com/*
Bellcore–Bell Communications Research (2) *http://www.careermosaic.com/cm/bellcore2/*
BellSouth Corporation *http://www.atglab.bls.com:80/employment/employment-main.html*
BellSouth Telecommunications . . . . *http://www.bellsouth.com/employment/*
Belmont Research, Inc. . . . . *http://www.belmont.com/jobs.html*
Bentley Systems, Inc. *http://www.bentley.com/bentley/jobs/jobs.html*
Berkeley Design Technology, Inc. . . . . *http://www.bdti.com/jobs/jobs.htm*
Berkeley National Laboratory . . . . *http://www.lbl.gov/LBL-Documents/CJOs/*
Berkeley Software Design, Inc. . . . . *http://www.bsdi.com/job-listings/*
Berkeley Systems, Inc. . . . . *http://www.berksys.com/www/aboutbsi/jobs/index.html*
Bernard Hodes Advertising . . . . *http://www.hodes.com/lo_res/hot_jobs.html*
Bertelsmann Fachinformation (Germany) . . . . *http://www.fachinformation.bertelsmann.de/pm/*
                                                                                                      pm_home.htm
Best Programs, Inc. . . . . *http://www.bestprograms.com/website/jobs.html*
BFR Systems, Inc. . . . . *http://www.bfrsys.com/*
BGS Systems, Inc. . . . . *http://www.bgs.com/jobs.htm*
BigBook, Inc. . . . . *http://www.bigbook.com/about/jobs/*
BioData, Inc. . . . . *http://www.biodata.com/biodata/bd_jobs.html*
Biogen, Inc. *http://www.careermosaic.com/cm/biogen/biogen1.html*
Biomet, Inc. . . . . *http://www.biomet.com/job_postings.html*
Biospherics Incorporated . . . . *http://www.biospherics.com/jobline.htm*
Black & Veatch . . . . *http://www.bv.com/bv/service/human_resources.shtml*
Black Sun Interactive, Inc. *http://ww3.blacksun.com/about/employment.html*
Bloomberg L.P. . . . . *http://www.bloomberg.com/*
Blue Sky Software Corporation . . . . *http://www.blue-sky.com/career.htm*
Blue Sky Studios . . . . *http://www.blueskyprod.com/opportunity/index.html*
Blueridge Technologies . . . . *http://www.blueridge.com*
Bluestone . . . . *http://www.bluestone.com/cgi-bin/human_resources/job_list*
Blyth Software . . . . *http://www.blyth.com/Jobs/index.html*
BMC Software, Inc. . . . . *http://www.bmc.com/bmc/FULL-DOC/WORK/employ.html*
Boeing Company <The> . . . . *http://www.boeing.com/Boeing_Employment_Update/*
                                                                                    Pages/0_Boeing_Employment.html
Boffin, Ltd. . . . . *http://www.boffin.com/opp.html*
Bolt Beranek and Newman, Inc. *http://www.bbn.com/working.html*
Books That Work, Inc. . . . . *http://www.btw.com./corporate/jobs.htm*
Boole & Babbage, Inc. . . . . *http://www.boole.com/jobs.html*
Booz, Allen Consulting . . . . *http://www.bah.com/shared/careers.html*
Border Network Technologies, Inc. . . . . *http://www.border.com/jobs.html*
Borland International, Inc. . . . . *http://www.borland.com/CorpInfo/hr/hrhome.html*
BORN Information Services Group . . . . *http://www.born.com/emply.html*
Boston Technology . . . . *http://www.bostontechnology.com/employ.htm*
Bottomline Technologies, Inc. . . . . *http://www.bottomline.com/joblist.html*
Brainstorm Technologies . . . . *http://www.braintech.com/employ.htm*
BrainTree Technology, Inc. . . . . *http://www.bti.com/jobs.html*
Braun Intertec Corporation . . . . *http://www.brauncorp.com/jobs.htm*
Brierley & Partners . . . . *http://www.brierley.com/career.html*
Brightware, Inc. *http://www.brightware.com/openings.html*
Brilliant Media, Inc. . . . . *http://www.brilliantmedia.com/BMIJobs.html*
Bristol Technology . . . . *http://bristol.com/Company/jobs.html*
Bristol-Myers Squibb Pharmaceutical . . . . . . *http://www.bms.com/squibb/employ/employops.html*

Brite Voice Systems, Inc. . . . . *http://www.brite.com/html/netscape/employ.html*
British Airways (UK) . . . . *http://www.british-airways.com/bans/mworld/jobs.htm*
British Broadcasting Corporation (BBC) (UK) . . . . *http://www.bbcnc.org.uk/jobs/*
British Telecom Laboratories (UK) . . . . *http://www.labs.bt.com/*
British Telecommunications plc (Netherlands) . . . . *http://www.tallis.bt.com/recruit.htm*
BroadBand Technologies, Inc. . . . . *http://www.bbt.com/career/index.htm*
BroadVision, Inc. . . . . *http://www.broadvision.com/people/career/*
Broadway & Seymour, Inc. . . . . *http://www.bsis.com/class/clasfied.html*
Broderbund Software, Inc. . . . . *http://www.broder.com/company/jobs.html*
Brookhaven National Laboratory . . . . *http://www.bnl.gov/JOBS/jobs.html*
Brooks Automation . . . . *http://www.brooks.com/hr.htm*
Brooktree Corporation . . . . *http://www.brooktree.com/brooktree/html/job_desc/employ.htm*
Brooktrout Technology . . . . *http://www.brooktrout.com/human/index.htm*
Brown Brothers Harriman & Co. . . . . *http://www.bbh.com/employ/index.htm*
Brown, Todd, & Heyburn PLLC . . . . *http://www.bth-pllc.com/careers/careers.html*
BRUKER Instruments, Inc. . . . . *http://www.helpwanted.com/brujb.htm*
BTG Incorporated . . . . *http://www.btg.com/btg_home/careers/careers.htm*
                                              http://www.btg.com/jobs/jobmenu.html
Btrieve Technologies, Inc. . . . . *http://www.btrieve.com/company/compa_17.htm*
BTU International . . . . *http://www.btu.com/career.htm*
Buckle <The> . . . . *http://www.buckle.com/CareerOps/*
Burlington Coat Factory . . . . *http://www.coat.com/jobs.html*
Burns & McDonnell . . . . *http://www.burnsmcd.com/joblist.htm*
BusLogic, Inc. (Mylex Corp.) . . . . *http://www.buslogic.com/*
C-Cube Microsystems *http://www.c-cube.com:80/*
Cable & Wireless plc . . . . *http://www.cwplc.com/jobs/index.htm*
Cabletron Systems, Inc. . . . . *http://www.ctron.com/jobs/*
Cablevision Systems Corporation . . . . *http://www.cablevision.com*
CACI International . . . . *http://www.caci.com/employment.html*
Cadence Design Systems, Inc. . . . . *http://www.cadence.com/employment.html*
CADmazing Solutions, Inc. . . . . *http://www.cadmazing.com/cadmazing/pages/jobs.html*
Caere Corp. . . . . *http://www.caere.com/live/content/about/jobs/jobs.htm*
Calgene, Inc. . . . . *http://www.calgene.com/humres.htm*
Calgiri Corporation . . . . *http://www.caligari.com/*
Calgon Corporation . . . . *http://www.calgon.com/employ.htm*
Caliber Technology, Inc. . . . . *http://www.calibersys.com/technlgy/employ.htm*
Calico Corners . . . . *http://www.calicocorners.com/employmentfrm.html*
California Software, Inc. . . . . *http://www.calsoft.com/employment/*
CallWare Technologies, Inc. . . . . *http://www.callware.com/about/jobs.html*
Calspan SRL Corporation . . . . *http://www.calspan.com/*
CAM Data Systems, Inc. . . . . *http://www.camdata.com/jobops/jobopps.htm*
Cambridge Technology Partners . . . . *http://www.ctp.com/EmployOpp/*
CambridgeSoft Corporation . . . . *http://www.camsci.com/abouthome.html*
Camp Dresser & McKee . . . . *http://www.cdm.com/humanres/index.html*
Candle Corporation . . . . *http://www.candle.com/about/oppt/index.htm*
Canon Information Systems *http://www.careermosaic.com/cm/canon/canon1.html*
Canon Research Centre Europe (UK) . . . . *http://www.cre.canon.co.uk/jobs.html*
Canon USA, Inc. . . . . *http://www.careermosaic.com/cm/canon-usa/canon_01.html*
Capital Technologies . . . . *http://www.captech.com/jobs/MAC.html*
CapitalNet Ltd. . . . . *http://www.capital.net/hiring.html*
Cardiff Software, Inc. . . . . *http://www.cts.com/~cardiff/html/helpwanted.html*
Caresoft, Inc. . . . . *http://www.caresoft.com/corp/c_jobs.html*
Cargill, Incorporated . . . . *http://www.cargill.com/*
CARL Corporation . . . . *http://www.carl.org/jobs.html*
Carleton Corporation . . . . *http://www.carleton.com/jobopps.html*

Carnegie Group, Inc. . . . . *http://www.cgi.com/FAQ.html*
Carondelet Health Care . . . . *http://www.careermosaic.com/cm/carond/*
Carver Corporation . . . . *http://www.carver.com/employment.html*
Cascade Communications Corp. *http://www.casc.com/*
Catalytica, Inc. . . . . *http://www.catalytica-inc.com/corp/jobs.html*
Catapult Entertainment, Inc. *http://www.xband.com:80/XBAND/catapult/opp/opp.html*
Caterpillar Inc. . . . . *http://www.caterpillar.com/envision/*
Cato Research, Ltd. . . . . *http://www.cato.com/interweb/cato/crl/employ.html*
CATS Software, Inc. . . . . *http://sweb.srmc.com/*
CDI Information Services . . . . *http://www.cdiis.com/docs/usee/jobs.html*
CDW Computer Centers, Inc. . . . . *http://www.cdw.com/cgi-bin/cdwhome.exe*
CE Software . . . . *http://www.cesoft.com/info/deptnews/jobopenings.html*
Cedars-Sinai Medical Center . . . . *http://www.careermosaic.com/cm/cedars-sinai/*
Celeritek, Inc. . . . . *http://www.celeritek.com/jobs.html*
CellNet Data Systems . . . . *http://www.cellnet.com/employment/employment.html*
Center for Applied Large-Scale Computing *http://quasar.poly.edu:80/CALC/jobs.html*
CenterLine Software, Inc. . . . . *http://www.centerline.com/corporate/jobs.html*
Centers for Disease Control . . . . *http://www.cdc.gov/hrmo/hrmo.html*
Centigram Communications Corporation . . . . *http://www.centigram.com/centigram/*
Employment/employment.html
Centocor . . . . *http://www.centocor.com/employ.htm*
Central Design Systems, Inc. . . . . *http://www.cdsi.com/sempl.html*
Centura Software Corporation . . . . *http://www.centurasoft.com/job/doc/jobindex.htm*
CERFnet . . . . *http://www.cerf.net/cerfnet/about/jobs.html*
Cerion Technologies, Inc. . . . . *http://www.cerion.com/employ.html*
Cerner Corporation . . . . *http://www.cerner.com./*
CFD Research Corporation . . . . *http://www.cfdrc.com/datab/Employment/employment.html*
CGSD Corporation . . . . *http://www.cgsd.com/jobs.html*
CH2M HILL *http://www.ch2m.com/ch2mhill*
Chaco Communications, Inc. . . . . *http://www.chaco.com/company/jobs/*
Channel1 . . . . *http://www.channel1.com/channel1/htmls/*
Charles Schwab & Co., Inc. . . . . *http://www.schwab.com/SchwabOnline/*
Charles Stark Draper Laboratory, Inc. <The> . . . *http://www.draper.com/HTML/HR/human_re.htm*
Charter Systems, Inc. . . . . *http://www.nes.com/jobs.html*
Chase Manhattan Corporation <The> . . . . *http://www.chase.com/noframes/careers/index.html*
Chase Research (UK) . . . . *http://www.chaser.co.uk/jobs.htm*
Checkfree Corporation . . . . *http://www.checkfee.com/Jobs.html*
CheckPoint Software Technologies Ltd. . . . . *http://www.checkpoint.com/*
Chemical Bank . . . . *http://www.careermosiac.cm/cm/chemical-bank*
Chemical Industry Institute of Toxicology–CIIT . . . . *http://www.ciit.org/JOBOPPS/jobopps.html*
Cheyenne Software *http://www.cheyenne.com:80/Career/hp-career.html*
Chicago Board of Trade . . . . *http://www.cbot.com/jobopen.htm*
Chip Express Corporation . . . . *http://www.chipexpress.com/corporate/hr.html*
Chipcom Corporation . . . . *http://www.chipcom.com/public/company/*
Chips and Technologies, Inc. . . . . *http://www.chips.com/chipsjob.htm*
Chromatic Research . . . . *http://www.chromatic.com/careers.html*
Chronologic Systems, Inc. (Canada) . . . . *http://www.chronologic.ca/positions.html*
Churchill Insurance (UK) . . . . *http://www.churchill.co.uk/recruit.html*
CIBER, Inc. . . . . *http://www.csn.net/ciber/nrecr.html*
Cincinnati Bell Information Systems . . . . *http://www.cbis.com/employment/*
Cincom Systems, Inc. *http://www.cincom.com/people/*
Cirrus Logic, Inc. . . . . *http://www.cirrus.com/career/*
Cisco Systems, Inc. . . . . *http://cisco.com/Jobs/*
Citibank . . . . *http://www.careermosaic.com/cm/citibank/*
CitySearch, Inc. . . . . *http://www.citysearch.com/company/jobs.html*

CKS *http://www.cks.com/connect/507.html*

CLAM Associates . . . . *http://www.clam.com/clam/clamjobs.html*

CLARiiON Advanced Storage Solutions . . . . *http://www.helpwanted.com/clajb.htm*

ClariNet Communications Corp. . . . . *http://www.clarinet.com/jobs.html*

Claris Corporation . . . . *http://www.claris.com*

Clarity Software, Inc. . . . . *http://www.clarity.com/Corp.html#Jobs*

CLONTECH Laboratories, Inc. *http://www.clontech.com/clontech/Jobs.html*

Clorox Company <The> . . . . *http://www.clorox.com/employ.html*

CMC Magazine . . . . *http://www.december.com/cmc/mag/people/wanted.html*

CMstat Corporation . . . . *http://www.cmstat.com/positions.html*

Coastcom . . . . *http://www.coastcom.com/jobs/jobs.html*

Cognos Incorporated . . . . *http://www.cognos.com/about_cognos/1-4.html*

Coherent Communications Systems Corporation . . . . *http://www.coherent.com/index.html*

Columbia/HCA Healthcare Corporation *http://www.careermosaic.com:80/cm/*
columbia/columbia2.html

Com21, Inc. *http://www.com21.com/posts.html*

CommerceNet . . . . *http://www.commerce.net/*

Commercial Union (UK) . . . . *http://www.commercial-union.co.uk/cu/curecrut.htm*

Communication Technologies . . . . *http://www.getnet.com/~gia/cti/ctiemploy.html*

Community Professional Loudspeakers . . . . *http://www.community.chester.pa.us/employ.html*

Compaq Computer Corporation . . . . *http://www.compaq.com/corporate/employment.html*

COMPASS Design Automation . . . . *http://www.compass-da.com/joblist/index.html*

CompCore Multimedia, Inc. . . . . *http://www.compcore.com/compcore/*

Compression Labs, Inc. *http://www.clix.com/Human_resources/*

CompuCom Systems . . . . *http://www.compucom.com/*

CompuData, Inc. . . . . *http://www.gncs.com/cdi/cdi.html*

CompuServe . . . . *http://www.compuserve.com/cgi-bin/sub?index*

Computer Associates International, Inc. . . . . *http://www.cai.com/*

Computer Language Research, Inc. . . . . *http://www.atg.fasttax.com/hr/*

Computer Literacy Bookshops, Inc. . . . . *http://www.clbooks.com*

Computer Management Sciences, Inc. . . . . *http://www.cmsx.com/*

Computer Sciences Corporation . . . . *http://www.csc.com/career/career.html*
http://www.csc.com/career.html

Computer Task Group, Inc. (CTG) . . . . *http://www.ctg.com/*

Computron Software Inc. . . . . *http://www.ctronsoft.com/*

Compuware Corporation . . . . *http://www.compuware.com/employ/employ.htm*

COMRISE Technology, Inc. . . . . *http://www.comrise.com/employment.html*

Comtrol Corporation . . . . *http://www.comtrol.com/*

Concentric Network Corporation . . . . *http://www.cris.com/*

Connectix Corporation . . . . *http://www.connectix.com/connect/job.html*

ConnectSoft, Inc. . . . . *http://www.connectsoft.com/*

Conner Peripherals, Inc. . . . . *http://www.conner.com/c-human.html*

Connix . . . . *http://www.connix.com/connix/openings.html*

Conseco, Inc. *http://www.conseco.com/cnc04020.htm*

Consilium, Inc. . . . . *http://www.consilium.com/company/jobs/index.html*

Continuus Software Corporation *http://www.continuus.com/w1000819.html*

Convex Computer Corporation . . . . *http://www.convex.com/htbin/jobs/list*

Cool Software Technology, Inc. . . . . *http://www.cooltech.com/cooljobs.html*

Cooper & Chyan Technology, Inc. . . . . *http://www.cctech.com/company/jobs/index.htm*

Coopers & Lybrand L.L.P. . . . . *http://www.colybrand.com/*

Corbis . . . . *http://www.corbis.com/*

Core Technology Corporation . . . . *http://www.ctc-core.com/job.html*

Corel Corporation . . . . *http://www.corel.ca/*

Corollary, Inc. . . . . *http://www.corollary.com/jobs.html*

CorVel Corporation . . . . *http://www.corvel.com/*

CP Clare Corporation . . . . *http://www.helpwanted.com/cpcjb.htm*
Creative Digital Research *http://www.cdr1.com/employ.htm*
Creative Labs, Inc. . . . . *http://www.creaf.com/www/marjob.html*
Creative Technologies . . . . *http://www.creativetech.com/jobs.htm*
Creative-Leadership, Inc. . . . . *http://www.cts.com/~clc/ads.html*
Cree Research, Inc. . . . . *http://www.cree.com/enhanced/employ.htm*
CrossKeys Systems Corporation . . . . *http://www.crosskeys.com/cross/employ/employ.html*
CrossWind Technologies, Inc. . . . . *http://www.crosswind.com/employ.htm*
CWC . . . . *http://www.cwcinc.com/jobs.html*
Cyan *http://206.107.159.125/Online/Cyan/Employment%20Opps*
CyberCash, Inc. . . . . *http://www.cybercash.com/cybercash/jobs/jobs.html*
Cybercom Partners, Inc. . . . . *http://www.cyberparts.com/jobs.htm*
Cybernet Systems . . . . *http://www.cybernet.com/Jobs/Jobs/html*
Cyclades Corporation . . . . *http://www.cyclades.com/employ.html*
Cygnus . . . . *http://www.cygnus.com/jobs*
Cylink Corporation . . . . *http://www.cylink.com/*
Cypress Semiconductor Corporation . . . . *http://www.careermosaic.com/cm/cypress/*
Cyrix Corporation . . . . *http://www.cyrix.com/hr/hrhp.htm*
Dallas Semiconductor Corporation . . . . *http://www.dalsemi.com/info/index.html*
Damar Group . . . . *http://www.dgl.com/jobs.html*
Darex Corporation . . . . *http://www.darex.com/help.htm*
DASAR Incorporated . . . . *http://www.dasar.com/career.html*
Data Exchange Corporation . . . . *http://www.dex.com/hr/*
Data General Corporation . . . . *http://www.dg.com/info/*
Data Life . . . . *http://www.datalife.com/datalife/jobs.htm*
Data Systems Network Corporation . . . . *http://www.datasystems.com/*
DataBeam Corporation . . . . *http://www.databeam.com/Corp/employmt.html*
Dataflex Corporation . . . . *http://www.dataflex.com/*
DataFocus, Inc. . . . . *http://www.datafocus.com/fra_wc_home.htm*
Datalogix International, Inc. *http://www.datalogix.com/career2.html*
DataMind Corp. . . . . *http://www.datamindcorp.com/dmjobs.html*
Dataquest *http://www.dataquest.com/irc/ir-b009.html*
DATASTORM . . . . *http://www.datastorm.com/jobs/*
Datastream Systems, Inc. . . . . *http://www.dstm.com/*
Datatel, Inc. . . . . *http://www.datatel.com/*
DataViews Corporation, Inc. . . . . *http://www.dvcorp.com/*
Dataware Technologies . . . . *http://www.dataware.com/*
DataWorks Corporation . . . . *http://www.dataworks.com/eppopp.htm*
Daugherty Systems . . . . *http://www.daugherty.com/employment.htm*
David Sarnoff Research Center . . . . *http://www.sarnoff.com/Opp/job.shtml*
Davidson and Associates, Inc. *http://www.davd.com:80/jobs/jobs.html*
Davox Corporation . . . . *http://www.davox.com/empl.html*
DayStar Digital, Inc. . . . . *http://www.daystar.com/*
dbINTELLECT Technologies . . . . *http://www.dbintellect.com/careers/career.htm*
Delco Electronics Corporation . . . . *http://www.delco.com/*
Dell Computer Corporation *http://www.us.dell.com:80/*
Dell Computer Corporation (2) . . . . *http://www.careermosaic.com/cm/dell/*
Deloitte & Touche LLP *http://www.dttus.com/dttus/hr/dthr1.htm*
DeLorme Mapping . . . . *http://www.delorme.com/employ/*
DeltaPoint, Inc. *http://www.deltapoint.com/corp/co03000.htm*
Denkart . . . . *http://www.denkart.be/company/jobs.htm*
Design Data Systems Corporation . . . . *http://www.designdatasys.com/JobList.htm*
Deutsche Bank . . . . *http://www.deutsche-bank.de/db/personal/pa_ha_1.htm*
Develcon Electronics Ltd. . . . . *http://www.develcon.com/employ/employ.htm*
Development Bank of Singapore Ltd. <The> . . . . *http://www.technet.sg/DBS/hr.html*

Dialogic Corporation . . . . *http://www.dialogic.com/*

Diamond Multimedia . . . . *http://www.diamondmm.com/whats-new/emp-opp.html*

DIGEX . . . . *http://www.digex.net/news/jobs.html*

Digi International . . . . *http://www.digibd.com/careerops/index.html*

Digital Domain *http://www.d2.com/nw/recruit.html*

Digital Equipment Corporation . . . . *http://www.digital.com/info/careers/*

Digital Equipment Corporation . . . . *http://www.research.*
    (Cambridge Research Laboratory)   *digital.com/CRL/jobs/unix-sysadmin.html*

Digital Evolution . . . . *http://www.digev.com/main/jobs.htm*

Digital Link . . . . *http://www.dl.com/jobs.html*

Digital PC . . . . *http://www.pc.digital.com/employ/employ.htm*

Digital Planet . . . . *http://www.digiplanet.com/community/classifieds.html*

Digital Products, Inc. . . . . *http://www.digprod.com/jobs.html*

Digital Sound Corporation . . . . *http://polaris.dsc.com/careers/*

Dimension X, Inc. *http://www.dimensionx.com/people/Index.html*

Disneyland . . . . *http://www.disney.com/Disneyland/business/casting.html?GL=H*

Diva Communications, Inc. . . . . *http://www.diva.com/employment/intro_jhr.html*

DiviCom . . . . *http://www.divi.com/jobs.htm*

DocuMagix . . . . *http://www.documagix.com/company/employ.htm*

Dodge Group, Inc. <The> . . . . *http://www.dodge.com/*

Dolby Laboratories . . . . *http://www.dolby.com/carops.html*

Donahue and Moore Associates, Inc. . . . . *http://amsquare.com/america/dma.html*

Dow Chemical Company <The> *http://www.dow.com:80/r*

Dow Jones & Company, Inc. . . . . *http://www.dowjones.com/careers/*

Draft Engineering (Netherlands) *http://www.195.108.71.252/*

Dragon Systems, Inc. . . . . *http://www.dragonsys.com/general/jobs.html*

Dreamers Guild, Inc. <The> . . . . *http://www.dreamersguild.com/Jobs.htm*

DSA, Inc. . . . . *http://dsainc.com/position.htm*

Dun & Bradstreet Corporation <The> . . . . *http://www.careermosaic.com/cm/dnb/*

Dun & Bradstreet Software Services *http://www.dbsoftware.com/info-ctr/carops/list2.htm*

DuPont . . . . *http://www.dupont.com/careers/index.html*

DXI Corporation . . . . *http://isotropic.com/dxicorp/dxihome.html*

Dynacs Engineering . . . . *http://www.dynacs.com/*

Dynamic Healthcare Technologies . . . . *http://www.dht.com/fr_5.htm*

DynCorp . . . . *http://www.dyncorp.com/jobs.htm*

e-Commerce, Inc. . . . . *http://www.e-Commerce.com/*

EarthWeb . . . . *http://www.earthweb.com/mainjobs.html*

Eastman Chemical Company . . . . *http://www.eastman.com/hr/index.shtml*

Eastman Kodak . . . . *http://www.kodak.com/aboutKodak/corpInfo/*
    employmentOps/employmentOps.shtml

Edify Corporation . . . . *http://www.edify.com/edify/jobs/jobs.htm*

Edison International . . . . *http://www.edisonx.com/html/news/jobs/jobs.htm*

Edmark Corporation . . . . *http://www.edmark.com/about/jobs.html*

Educational Service District 112 . . . . *http://164.116.2.120/Job_Opp/Jobs.html*

Efficient Networks . . . . *http://www.efficient.com/dox/jobs.html*

Egghead . . . . *http://www.egghead.com/egg/jobs/listing/*

Eikon Group, Inc. *http://www.worldweb.com/Eikon/*

Electromagnetic Sciences, Inc. . . . . *http://www.lxe.com/emsmap.map?378,22*

Electronic Arts, Inc. *http://www.ea.com/topten.html*

Electronic Data Systems Corporation *http://www.eds.com:80/home.html*

Electronics Boutique, Inc. <The> . . . . *http://www.eboutique.com/docs/employ.html*

Electronics for Imaging, Inc. . . . . *http://www.efi.com/employment.html*

Electrotek Concepts, Inc. . . . . *http://www.electrotek.com/jobs/jobs.htm*

Elegant Graphics Corporation . . . . *http://www.correspond.com/jobs.html*

Eli Lilly and Company . . . . *http://www.lilly.com/career/stat.html*

EMASS	http://www.emass.com/Jobs/Jobs_Top.html
EMC	http://www.emc.com/mkt/info/hr/main.htm
Empress Software, Inc.	http://www.empress.com/careers/overview.htm
ENCAD, Inc.	http://www.encad.com/joblist.htm
Encore Computer Corporation	http://www.encore.com/company_info/jobs.html
Enhanced Technologies Inc.	http://www.enhtech.com/jobs.html
ENSCO, Inc.	http://www.ensco.com/Employment/
Ensemble Systems, Inc.	http://www.ansa.com/ensemsys/opportunity.html
Entergy Corporation	http://nola-web.entergy.com/career.htm
Enterprise Integration Technologies	http://www.eit.com/new/new.html
ENTEX	http://www.entex.com/career/index.htm
Environmental Resources Management (ERM)	http://www.erm.com/employment/
Environmental Systems Research Institute, Inc.	http://www.esri.com/
Ericsson International, Sweden	http://www.ericsson.se/Jobs/index.html
Ernst & Young	http://www.ernsty.co.uk/welcome.html
Ernst & Young LLP	http://www.ey.com/us/uscareer.html
Essex Corporation	http://www.essexcorp.com/jobs.htm
Est Software, Netherlands	http://www.euronet.nl/users/estsoft/vacancy.html
Etak, Inc.	http://www.etak.com/Jobs.html
Ethan Allen Inc.	http://www.ethanallen.com/adspecial.html
Evans and Sutherland	http://www.es.com/Career.html
EveryWare Development Corporations	http://www.everyware.com/employment/ employ_R&D.html
eWorld–Apple Computers Online	http://www.eworld.com/
Ex Machina, Inc.	http://exmachina.com/recruit.shtml
Exa Corporation	http://www.exa.com/jobs.html
EXAR Corporation	http://www.exar.com/employ/empmenu.htm
Excalibur Technologies Corporation	http://www.excalib.com/rev2/
Excellon Automation Co.	http://www.excellon.com/jobs/jobs.htm
Executive Software	http://www.execsoft.com/jobad.htm
Executone Information Systems, Inc.	http://www.executone.com/
Executone Telecommunications	http://www.execu.net:8080/employ.html
Exide Electronics	http://www.careermag.com/careermag/ employers/exide/index.html
Expansion Programs International	http://www.thunderstone.com/
Expersoft Corporation	http://www.expersoft.com/corpinfo/employ.htm
Express Scripts, Inc.	http://www.express-scripts.com/corporate/jobs.html
Express Systems	http://www.express-systems.com/
Extended Systems	http://www.extendsys.com/career/index.html
Extensis Corporation	http://www.extensis.com/
FACT Software International Pvt. Ltd	http://www.fact.com.sg/Jobs/
FactSet Research Systems, Inc.	http://www.factset.com/careers/career.htm
Failure Analysis Associates	http://www.fail.com/
Fair, Isaac & Company, Inc.	http://www.careermosaic.com:80/cm/fair_isaac/fi4.html
Falcon System	http://www2.falcons.com/falcon/employment.html
FarPoint Technologies	http://www.fpoint.com/employ-main.htm
FastComm Communications Corporation	http://www.fastcomm.com/jobs.html
FCR Software, Inc.	http://www.fcr.com/jobs.html
FDP Corporation	http://www.shadow.net/~fdp/fdpjb.htm
Federal Government	gopher://dartcms1.dartmouth.edu/11/fedjobs
Fibernet Corporation	http://www.fiber.net/fnemployment.html
Fidelity Investments	http://www.helpwanted.com/fidelhp.html
Fifth Third Bancorp	http://205.243.79.2:80/bancorp/hr/jobs/
FileNet Corporation	http://www.filenet.com/empopps/
Financial Data Planning Corporation	http://www.helpwanted.com/fdpjb.htm

Finlay Fine Jewelry Corporation . . . . *http://helpwanted.com/hwdocs/company/*
finlay/jobs/fffchp.htm
First Floor . . . . *http://www.firstfloor.com/*
First Union Corporation . . . . *http://www.firstunion.com/*
First USA *http://www.careermosaic.com/cm/first-usa/first1.html*
First Virginia Banks, Inc. *http://www.firstvirginia.com/employ.html*
First Virtual Corporation . . . . *http://www.fvc.com/jobopp.ht*
First Virtual Holdings, Inc. *http://www.fv.com:80/info/opportunities.html*
FlexiInternational Software, Inc. *http://www.flexi.com/flxjobs.html*
Floathe Johnson . . . . *http://www.floathe.com/*
Fluent, Inc. . . . . *http://www.fluent.com/jobs/index.html*
FMC Corporation . . . . *http://www.fmc.com/Career/careerHome.html*
FMS, Inc. . . . . *http://www.fmsinc.com/helpwant.htm*
Folio Corporation . . . . *http://www.folio.com/*
Ford Motor Company . . . . *http://www.ford.com/careercenter/*
FORE Systems, Inc. . . . . *http://www.fore.com/html/hr/*
Forrester Research, Inc. . . . . *http://mars.silknet.com/noframes/wh_empl.htm*
http://www.forrester.com/
Forte Software, Inc. . . . . *http://www.forte.com/*
Foundation Center <The> . . . . *http://fdncenter.org/aboutfc/oppt.html*
FourGen Software, Inc. . . . . *http://www.fourgen.com/jobs/jobs.htm*
Fourth Shift Corporation . . . . *http://www.fs.com/*
Fractal Design Corporation . . . . *http://www.fractal.com/about_us/hr/index.html*
Franklin Company <The> *http://www.careermosaic.com/cm/franklin/franklin1.html*
Free Range Media . . . . *http://www.freerange.com/home/jobs/*
Friends of the Earth (UK) . . . . *http://www.foe.co.uk/fap/personnel/index.html*
Fritz Companies, Inc. . . . . *http://www.fritz.com/hr/position/position.htm*
Front Page <The> . . . . *http://www.thefrontpage.com/tfp/emplymnt/welcome.html*
Frontier Technologies Corporation . . . . *http://www.frontiertech.com/*
Frontline Distribution Ltd (UK) . . . . *http://www.frontline.co.uk/CareerInfo/index.htm*
FTP Software, Inc. . . . . *http://www.ftp.com/hr/index.html*
Fuji Xerox Co., Ltd. (Japan) . . . . *http://www.fujixerox.co.jp/pilotE/recruitmentE.html*
Fujitsu America, Inc. . . . . *http://www.fujitsu.com/HR/index.html*
Fujitsu Microelectronics, Inc. . . . . *http://www.fujitsumicro.com/employ/employ.html*
Fulcrum Technologies, Inc. . . . . *http://www.fultech.com/*
Funk Software, Inc. . . . . *http://www.funk.com/jobs.html*
Fusion Systems Corporation . . . . *http://www.fusn.com/*
Fusion Systems Group, Inc. *http://www.fsg.com/careers/index.htm*
FWB, Inc. . . . . *http://www.fwb.com/software/who_we_are/jobs/jobopp.html*
Gallup Organization . . . . *http://www.gallup.com/employment.html*
Gateway 2000 . . . . *http://www.gw2k.com/employ/employ.htm*
Gateway Group, Inc. . . . . *http://www.gatewaygroup.com/ggjobs.html*
General DataComm Industries, Inc. . . . . *http://www.gdc.com/Career.html*
General Electric Company . . . . *http://www.ge.com/*
General Instrument Corporation . . . . *http://www.gi.com/employ/employ.htm*
General Magic . . . . *http://www.genmagic.com/extjob.html*
General Mills, Inc. . . . . *http://jobs.genmills.com/*
General Motors Corporation . . . . *http://www.gm.com/edu_rel/careers/career.htm*
General Public Utilities . . . . *http://www.gpu.com/cgi-bin/jobs_index.pl*
General Signal Networks–Tautron . . . . *http://www.tautron.com/EMPLOY.HTM*
Genome Therapeutics Corporation . . . . *http://www.cric.com/htdocs/corporate/jobs/index.html*
Gensym Corporation . . . . *http://www.gensym.com/companycontacts/contactpeople.html*
GeoWorks . . . . *http://www.geoworks.com/htmpages/jobs.htm*
Geraghty & Miller, Inc. . . . . *http://www.gmgw.com/Employment.html*
GigaLabs, Inc. . . . . *http://www.gigalabs.com/helpwntd/jobs.htm*

Glenayre Technologies, Inc. . . . . *http://www.glenayre.com/jobs.html*
Global Internet . . . . *http://www.gi.net/company/opportunities.html*
Global Management Systems Incorporated . . . . *http://www.gmsi.com/joblistings/newjobs.html*
Global Village Communication, Inc. . . . . *http://www.globalvillage.com/joblist.html*
GNP Computers . . . . *http://www.gnp.com/company/career.htm*
Goldman Sachs Group, L.P. <The> . . . . *http://www.gs.com/recruiting/*
Good Guys, Inc. <The> *http://www.careermosaic.com/cm/goodguys/tgg1.html*
Goodwill Industries . . . . *http://www.spectracom.com/goodwill/*
Government Technology Services, Inc. (GTSI) . . . . . . *http://www.gtsi.com/support/jobs/allpos.htm*
Gradient Technologies . . . . *http://www.gradient.com/about/Employment/jobs.htm*
Grand Heritage Hotels International . . . . *http://grandheritage.com:80/htmlcode/emp_opps.html*
Graphix Zone, Inc. . . . . *http://www.gzone.com/careers.html*
GRC International, Inc. . . . . *http://www.grci.com/jobs/*
Great Lakes Chemical Corporation . . . . *http://www.jobweb.org/employer/great_la.htm*
Greyhound Lines, Inc. . . . . *http://www.greyhound.com/jobs.html*
Grolier Electronic Publishing . . . . *http://www.gi.grolier.com/gi/info/careers/docs/careers.html*
Group Health Cooperative . . . . *http://www.ghc.org/about_gh/employ/emptoc.html*
GROWMARK, Inc. . . . . *http://www.growmark.com/employ/index.html*
GTE Corporation . . . . *http://www.gte.com/Working/working.html*
HaL Computer Systems, Inc. . . . . *http://www.hal.com/jobs/*
Hale and Dorr . . . . *http://www.haledorr.com/employment/Employment.html*
Hamilton Standard . . . . *http://www.hamilton-standard.com/humanres/divers.html*
Harbinger Corporation . . . . *http://www.harbinger.com/hr/index.htm*
Harlequin . . . . *http://webserver.harlequin.com/full/recruitment.html*
Harmonix Corporation . . . . *http://harmonix.hxi.com/*
HarperCollins Publishers . . . . *http://www.harpercollins.com/jobopps.htm*
Harris Computer Systems Corporation . . . . *http://www.csd.harris.com/*
Harris Corporation . . . . *http://www.harris.com/employment/*
Harvard Community Health Plan . . . . *http://www.hchp.org/menus/career/career.htm*
HBO & Company . . . . *http://www.cweb.com/hboc*
Henningson, Durham & Richardson Engineering, Inc. . . . . *http://www.hdrinc.com/hdr_emp.htm*
Herring Communications . . . . *http://www.herring.com/jobs.html*
Hewlett Packard *http://wwwjobs.external.hp.com:80/*
Hewlett Packard–Europe . . . . *http://www-europe.hp.com/JobPosting/*
Hickory Tech Corporation . . . . *http://www.jobweb.org/employer/hickory.htm*
Hitachi Computer Products (America), Inc. . . . . *http://www.hitachi.com/*
Hitachi Data Systems *http://www.hdshq.com/hds/hds110.html*
Hitachi Instruments, Inc. . . . . *http://www.hii.hitachi.com/company/work.htm*
HitCom Corporation . . . . *http://www.hitcom.com/employ.html*
HNC Software, Inc. . . . . *http://www.hnc.com/career.htm*
Hoechst AG . . . . *http://www.hoechst.com/career_e/index_e.htm*
Hollowell Engineering . . . . *http://www.hollowelleng.com/employ.html*
Honeywell Industrial Automation and Control . . . . *http://www.iac.honeywell.com/*
Pub/Jobs/jobopen.html
Hoover Online . . . . *http://www.hoovers.com/job.html*
Horizons Technology, Inc. *http://www.horizons.com/web20/jobs/jobs.htm*
HoTMail, Inc. . . . . *http://www.hotmail.com/jobs.html*
HotWired Ventures LLC . . . . *http://www.hotwired.com/jobs/*
Hughes Electronics Corporation . . . . *http://www.hughes.com/college.html*
Hughes Network Systems, Inc. . . . . *http://www.hns.com/Careers/home.html*
Hughes Space and Communications . . . . *http://www.hughespace.com/hugheshsc/home.html*
Hughes STX Corporation . . . . *http://www.stx.com/career/center.html*
Human Code . . . . *http://www.humancode.com/hchomepage/HelpWanted.html*
Hummer Winblad Venture Partners . . . . *http://www.humwin.com/jobs/jobs.html*
Hummingbird Communications Ltd. *http://www.hummingbird.com:80/jobs/index.html*

Hybrid Networks, Inc. . . . . *http://www.hybrid.com/corp/jobs.html*
HYNET Technologies . . . . *http://www.hynet.com/Fjobs.htm*
Hyundai Electronics America . . . . *http://www.hea.com/emp_center/*
I-3 Telecom *http://www.i3tele.com/careerops.html*
I-Kinetics . . . . *http://www.i-kinetics.com/STAFFING/EMPOPP.HTM*
i-Logix, Inc. . . . . *http://www.ilogix.com/company/jobs/jobs.htm*
IBM . . . . *http://www.empl.ibm.com/*
IBM–Research . . . . *http://www.research.ibm.com/employment/*
ichat, Inc. . . . . *http://www.ichat.com/jobs.htm*
ICL . . . . *http://www.icl.com/services/higher/index.html*
Iconovex Corporation . . . . *http://www.iconovex.com/EMPLOY.HTM*
ICTV, Inc. . . . . *http://www.ictv.com/ictv/jobs.html*
Idaho Power Company . . . . *http://www.idahopower.com/ipjobs.htm*
IgLou . . . . *http://www.iglou.com*
Ikonic, Inc. . . . . *http://www.ikonic.com/ikonia/jobs.htx?name=unknown*
IKOS Systems . . . . *http://www.ikos.com/jobs/*
Illustra Information Technologies . . . . *http://www.illustra.com/cgi-bin/*
Webdriver?MIval=classifieds_list

ILOG, Inc. . . . . *http://www.ilog.com/ilog/career/offers.html*
IMC Networks . . . . *http://www.imcnetworks.com/imcdocs\employ.htm*
IMI Systems, Inc. . . . . *http://www.careermosaic.com/cm/imi/*
IMP, Inc. . . . . *http://www.impweb.com/JOBS.html*
IMPAC Medical Systems . . . . *http://www.impac.com/jobs.htm*
Imperative! . . . . *http://www.imperative.com/cgi-bin/genobject/employindex_*
Inacom Corp. . . . . *http://www.inacom.com/careers.html*
Index Stock Photography, Inc. . . . . *http://www.indexstock.com/pages/jobs.htm*
Individual, Inc. . . . . *http://www.individual.com/company/jobs.htm*
Inference Corporation . . . . *http://www.inference.com/*
InfiNet . . . . *http://www.infi.net/*
InfoAccess, Inc. . . . . *http://www.infoaccess.com/aboutia/jobs.htm*
InFocus Systems . . . . *http://www.infs.com/infsBin/jobs.pl*
Infodata Systems Inc. *http://www.infodata.com/INFDB4.HTM*
Infonautics Corporation . . . . *http://www.infonautics.com/jobs.htm*
Infonet Services Corporation . . . . *http://www.info.net/*
InfoPost . . . . *http://www.infopost.com/career/index.html*
Informatica Corporation . . . . *http://www.informatica.com/emplpage.html*
Information Builders Inc. (IBI) . . . . *http://www.ibi.com/jobs.htm*
Information Dimensions, Inc. . . . . *http://www.idi.oclc.org/html/career.htm*
Information Handling Services . . . . *http://www.ihs.com/cgi-bin/serve?/hr/jobs.current.html*
Information Storage Devices . . . . *http://www.isd.com/*
Infoseek Corporation . . . . *http://info.infoseek.com/doc/Jobs.html*
Inmac Corp . . . . *http://www.inmaconline.com/inmacemp.htm*
Innosoft International, Inc. . . . . *http://www.innosoft.com/iii/company/employment.html*
Innovative Computer Enterprises . . . . *http://www.rio.com/~ice/icejobs.html*
Innovative Interfaces, Inc. . . . . *http://www.iii.com/screens/jobs.html*
Innovative Solutions & Support, Inc. . . . . *http://www.innovative-ss.com/JOBS.html*
Insight Enterprises, Inc. *http://www.insight.com/web/gjobs.html*
Insignia Solutions . . . . *http://www.insignia.com/hr/Jobs.html*
Inso Corporation *http://www.inso.com/frames/corporate/corp4fr.htm*
Intecom, Inc. . . . . *http://www.intecom.com/em.html*
Integral Development Corp. . . . . *http://www.integral.com/opportunities/application/*
Integral Solutions Ltd. (UK) . . . . *http://www.isl.co.uk/job.html*
Integral Technologies, Inc. . . . . *http://www.integralTI.com*
Integrated Computer Solutions . . . . *http://www.ics.com/Jobs/*
Integrated Device Technology, Inc. . . . . *http://www.idt.com/hr/Welcome.html*

Integrated Systems, Inc. . . . . *http://www.isi.com/Latest/JobOpenings.html*
Integrated Telecom Technology, Inc. . . . . *http://www.igt.com/employ.htm*
Intel Corporation *http://web.jf.intel.com:80/intel/oppty/index.htm*
http://www.intel.com/intel/index.htm
Intelligent Instrumentation, Inc. . . . . *http://www.instrument.com/employ.htm*
IntelliQuest Information Group, Inc. . . . . *http://www.intelliquest.com/employ.htm*
Intellon Corporation . . . . *http://www.intellon.com/employment.html*
Intellution, Inc. . . . . *http://www.intellution.com/employ.html*
Interactive Data Corporation . . . . *http://www.intdata.com/employ.htm*
Intergraph Corporation . . . . *http://www.careermosaic.com/cm/intergraph/*
Interleaf, Inc. . . . . *http://www.ileaf.com/jobs/JobOps.html*
Interlink Electronics *http://www.interlinkelec.com/employ/page01.htm*
Intermetrics . . . . *http://www.inmet.com/jobs.html*
International Data Corporation . . . . *http://www.idcresearch.com/employme.htm*
International Data Group . . . . *http://www.idg.com/profile/careers/careersmain.html*
International Microcomputer Software, Inc. . . . . *http://www.imsisoft.com/about/career.html*
International Network Services . . . . *http://199.0.193.16:80/wiz_want/wiz_want.html*
International Rectifier . . . . *http://www.irf.com/~ir/career/*
International Technology Corporation . . . . *http://www.jobweb.org/employer/intltech.htm*
Internet Access Company, Inc. <The> . . . . *http://www.tiac.net/*
Internet Securities . . . . *http://www.securities.com/Public/Employment/employment.html*
Internet Shopper Ltd (UK) . . . . *http://www.net-shopper.co.uk/jobs.htm*
Internic . . . . *http://rs.internic.net/jobs.html*
Interphase Corporation . . . . *http://www.iphase.com/Public/Openings/*
Interplay Productions . . . . *http://www.interplay.com/help.html*
InterSolv, Inc. . . . . *http://www.intersolv.com/hr_req/index.htm*
InterStream, Inc. . . . . *http://www.i-stream.com/*
InterVoice, Inc. . . . . *http://www.intervoice.inter.net/comphr.htm*
InterVU, Inc. . . . . *http://www.intervu.com/meet/jobs.html*
InterZine Productions . . . . *http://www.igolf.com/aboutig/wlisting.htm*
IntuMedia Works . . . . *http://www.intumedia.com/*
Iomega . . . . *http://www.careermosaic.com/cm/iomega/*
Ionics, Inc. *http://204.166.120.7:80/aboution/Employment/*
IOtech, Inc. . . . . *http://www.iotech.com/career.html*
IPC Technologies . . . . *http://www.ipctech.com/Employment.html*
http://www.ipc.tech.com/~jobsjoblist.html
IQ Software Corporation . . . . *http://www.iqsc.com/aboutiq/jobs.htm*
IS Robotics . . . . *http://isr.com/HelpWanted.html*
Isis Pharmaceuticals, Inc. . . . . *http://www.isisph.com/jobs.htm*
ISOTRO Network Management, Inc. . . . . *http://www.isotro.com/ISOTRO/career.html*
ISYS/Odyssey Development, Inc. . . . . *http://www.isysdev.com/employment.html*
IT/Net (Canada) . . . . *http://www.interlog.com/~itnet/itcons.htm*
ITAC Systems, Inc. . . . . *http://www.mousetrak.com/job.htm*
Iterated Systems, Inc. . . . . *http://www.iterated.com/iterated/jobs/j_list.htm*
Itron, Inc. . . . . *http://www.itron.com/career/career.html*
IVAC Medical Systems . . . . *http://www.ivac.com/jobs.html*
J. Sainsbury plc (UK) . . . . *http://www.j-sainsbury.co.uk/jobs/*
J. Sainsbury plc (UK) . . . . *http://protector.j-sainsbury.co.uk/jobs/*
J.D. Edwards . . . . *http://www.jdedwards.com/career/index.htm*
Jackson Hewitt, Inc. *http://www.infi.net/~jhewitt/hire.html*
Jandel Scientific . . . . *http://www.jandel.com/about/jobs/*
Janna Systems, Inc. *http://www.janna.com/jobsatjanna.htm*
JC Penney . . . . *http://www.jcpenney.com/careers/woo/*
Jefferson-Pilot Life Insurance Company . . . . *http://www.jpc.com/jp-g-job.htm*
JetForm Corporation . . . . *http://www.jetform.com/career/career.html*

Jobscope Corporation . . . . *http://web.sunbelt.net/~jobscope/EMP.HTM*

Johnson & Johnson . . . . *http://www.jnj.com/recruit/recruit.htm*

Johnson Controls, Inc. . . . . *http://www.jci.com/bg/employ.htm*

Jones Interactive, Inc. . . . . *http://www.jii.com/*

JP Morgan & Co. Incorporated . . . . *http://careers.jpmorgan.com/*

Jupiter Communications . . . . *http://www.jup.com/*

JYACC, Inc. . . . . *http://www.jyacc.com/*

Katz Media Group, Inc. *http://www.katz-media.com/jobs.htm*

Keane, Inc. *http://www.keane.com:80/careers/index.shtml*

Kenan Systems Corporation . . . . *http://www.kenan.com/employ/emp_home.htm*

KenTera . . . . *http://www.netadventure.com/jobs.htm*

Ki Networks . . . . *http://www.ki.com/*

Kinetix . . . . *http://www.ktx.com/jobs/joblist.htm*

KL Group, Inc. . . . . *http://www.klg.com/jobs/index.html*

KLA Instruments Corporation . . . . *http://hrweb.kla.com/empl/index.htm*

KnightWeb . . . . *http://www.knightweb.com/KnightWeb/employment.html*

Knowledge Adventure, Inc. . . . . *http://www.adventure.com/company/employment/*

Komag . . . . *http://www.komag.com/career/career.html*

Konami (America), Inc. *http://www.wtinet.com:80/wti/helpwant.htm*

KPIX . . . . *http://www.kpix.com/jobs/*

KPMG (Australia) . . . . *http://www.kpmg.com.au/recindex.html*

KPMG (Canada) . . . . *http://www.kpmg.ca/careers/main.html*

KPMG Peat Marwick LLP . . . . *http://www.us.kpmg.com/career/*

KQED, Inc. . . . . *http://www.kqed.org/fromKQED/HR/menu.html*

Kurzweil Applied Intelligence, Inc. . . . . *http://www.kurz-ai.com/jobs/*

L-Soft *http://www.lsoft.com/jobs1.html*

LABTECH . . . . *http://www.labtech.com/career.html*

Lafayette American Bank . . . . *http://www.labk.com/empl.htm*

Lahey Computer Systems, Inc. . . . . *http://www.lahey.com/employ.htm*

Lande Group <The> . . . . *http://www.lande.com/tlgempop.htm*

Lansing Pugh Associates . . . . *http://www.acadlp.com/jobs.htm*

Lante . . . . *http://www.lante.com/*

Larscom . . . . *http://www.larscom.com:80/abt_emp.htm*

LaserMaster Corp. *http://www.lasermaster.com/careers/*

Lattice Semiconductor Corporation . . . . *http://www.lattice.com/*

Lawrence Berkeley Laboratory . . . . *http://www.lbl.gov/*

Lear Corporation . . . . *http://www.lear.com/recruit/*

Learjet, Inc. . . . . *http://www.nationjob.com/learjet*

Learning Company <The> *http://www.softkey.com/html3/hr/index.html*

Legato Systems, Inc. *http://www.legato.com/jobs/lgto.apo.html*

Lehle Seeds . . . . *http://www.arabidopsis.com/!pj.html*

Level Nine, Inc. . . . . *http://genghis.com/homepage/employment.htm*

Level One Communications *http://www.level1.com/jobs.html*

LEXIS-NEXIS . . . . *http://www.lexis-nexis.com/lncc/about/employment/employment.html*

Lexmark International, Inc. . . . . *http://www.lexmark.com/employ/empopp.html*

Library of Congress *gopher://marvel.loc.gov/11/employee/employ*

http://lcweb.loc.gov/

Life Technologies . . . . *http://www.lifetech.com/cgi-bin/WebObjects/JobServer*

Lighthouse Design, Ltd. . . . . *http://www.lighthouse.com/*

Livingston Enterprises, Inc. *http://www.livingston.com:80/Tech/Employ/index.shtml*

Lockheed Martin . . . . *http://juggler.lmsc.lockheed.com/ladc/html/career_op.html*

Lockheed Martin . . . . *http://www.lmco.com/jobs.html*

Lockheed Martin *http://www.careermosaic.com/cm/lockheed/lockheed1.html*

Lockheed Martin Missiles and Space . . . . *http://www.lmsc.lockheed.com/jobs/staffing.htm*

Logica, Inc. *http://www.careermosaic.com:80/cm/logica/logica4.html*

Logicraft .... *http://www.logicraft.com/news/jobs.htm*
LogicVision .... *http://www.lvision.com/career.htm*
Long Island Savings Bank <The> .... *http://www.lisb.com/working/*
Los Alamos National Laboratory .... *http://hrsun.lanl.gov/*
Los Alamos National Laboratory .... *http://www.lanl.gov/Public/Welcome.html*
Lotus .... *http://www.lotus.com/corporate/*
Lower Colorado River Authority (LCRA) <The> .... *http://www.lcra.org/about/apply.html*
Lowe's Companies, Inc. *http://www.lowes.com:80/empopps/*
LSI Logic Corporation *http://www.lsilogic.com/employ/unit7.html*
Lucent Technologies .... *http://www.careermosaic.com/cm/lucent/*
Lynx Real-Time Systems, Inc. .... *http://www.lynx.com/jobs/index.html*
MacDonald Dettwiler and Associates Ltd. (Canada) .... *http://www.mda.ca/*
                                                         EmploymentOpportunities.html
Macintosh Application Environment (Apple) .... *http://www.mae.apple.com/*
Macmillan Publishing .... *http://www.mcp.com/general/jobs/*
MacNeal-Schwendler Corporation <The> .... *http://www.macsch.com/msc/jobs.html*
Macromedia .... *http://www.macromedia.com/Industry/*
                                                         Job/mm.job.openings.html
Madge Networks .... *http://www.madge.com/about/a_03_div.htm*
Magic Software Enterprises .... *http://www.magic-sw.com/pages/intro/joinmtea.htm*
MAI Systems Corporation .... *http://www.maisystems.com/employment.htm*
Mainland Information Systems, Inc. .... *http://mainland.ab.ca/*
Mainsoft Corporation .... *http://www.mainsoft.com/employ.htm*
Malcolm Pirnie, Inc. .... *http://www.Pirnie.com/jobs/*
Manugistics Group, Inc. .... *http://www.statgraphics.com/html/career.html*
MAPCO, Inc. .... *http://www.mapcoinc.com/employ.html*
MapInfo Corporation .... *http://www.mapinfo.com/mapinfo/team/team.html*
Marimba, Inc. .... *http://www.marimba.com/company/jobs.html*
Markel Corporation .... *http://www.markelcorp.com/markel/corp/hr/index.html*
Market Guide, Inc. .... *http://www.marketguide.com/*
Marquette .... *http://www.mei.com/bin/webjoblist.pl*
Marshall Industries .... *http://www.marshall.com/cgi-bin/imagemap/header1?276,40*
Massachusetts Mutual
    Life Insurance Company .... *http://www.massmutual.com/career/career.html*
Mastech Corporation .... *http://www.mastech.com/OPP/Opportunities_F.html*
MathSoft, Inc. .... *http://www.mathsoft.com/jobs.html*
MathWorks, Inc. .... *http://www.mathworks.com/jobs.html*
Matrox Graphics, Inc. .... *http://www.matrox.com/employ.htm*
Mattson Technology .... *http://www.mattson.com/jobs.htm*
Maxis, Inc. .... *http://www.maxis.com/simbusiness/open_jobs/open_jobs.html*
Maxtor Corporation .... *http://www.maxtor.com/mco.html*
May Department Stores Company <The> ...... *http://www.maycompany.com/College/index.html*
Mayo Clinic .... *http://www.mayo.edu/career/career.html*
McCaw Cellular Communications .... *http://www.attws.com/jobs/*
McDonnell Douglas .... *http://pat.mdc.com/LB/JOB.html*
MCI Telecommunications Corporation .... *http://www.mci.com/aboutmci/career/*
McMahan Research Laboratories .... *http://www.mrl.com/job-offering-lists.html*
MDL Information Systems, Inc. .... *http://www.mdli.com/info/jobs.html*
Media Circus .... *http://www.mediacircus.com/mcircus/html/jobs.html*
Media Vision, Inc. .... *http://www.mediavis.com/employment.htm*
Medtronic, Inc. .... *http://www.medtronic.com/public/medtronic/employment/*
Medtronic Micro-Re .... *http://www.careermosaic.com/cm/micro-rel/mrl.html*
Mellon Bank .... *http://www.mellon.com/jobs/*
Melson Technologies .... *http://www.melson.com/quantra/careers.html*
Memorex Telex N.V. .... *http://www.mtc.com/MTCus/MTCus.career.html*

Merac Projects Ltd. . . . . *http://www.merak.com/careers/index.html*

Mercer Management Consulting, Inc. . . . . *http://www.mercermc.com/careers/recruit.html*

Merck & Co., Inc. . . . . *http://www.merck.com/careers/*

Meridian Data, Inc. . . . . *http://www.meridian-data.com/company/jobs.html-ssi*

Mesaba Airlines . . . . *http://www.mesaba.com/employ.htm*

Metamor Technologies Ltd. . . . . *http://www.metamor.com/pages/opportunity.html*

MetaWare Incorporated . . . . *http://www.metaware.com/misc/employmt.html*

Metricom . . . . *http://www.metricom.com/career.html*

Metro Link Incorporated . . . . *http://www.metrolink.com/reference/Employment.html*

Metro Tech . . . . *http://www.metrotech.org/general_info/jobs.html*

Metrowerks . . . . *http://www.metrowerks.com/about/jobs/index.html*

MFS Communications . . . . *http://www.careermosaic.com/cm/mfs*

MICOM Communications Corp. . . . . *http://www.micom.com/human-resources/empopp.html*

MICROCADAM, Inc. . . . . *http://www.microcadam.com/employment/index.html*

Microchip Technology, Inc. *http://www.ultranet.com/jobs/index1.html*

Microcom, Inc. . . . . *http://www.microcom.com/jobs/jobs.htm*

Microelectronics and Computer Technology Corporation *http://www.mcc.com:80/jobs/*

Micron Electronics, Inc. . . . . *http://www.mei.micron.com/employment/employ.htm*

Micron Technology, Inc. . . . . *http://www.micron.com/mti/hr/index.html*

Microplex Systems Ltd. . . . . *http://www.microplex.com/microplex/employment/*

Micropolis Pty. Ltd . . . . *http://www.microp.com/Openings.html*

MicroSim Corporation . . . . *http://www.microsim.com/employment.html*

Microsoft Corporation . . . . *http://www.microsoft.com/jobs/*

MicroStrategy . . . . *http://www.strategy.com/recruit/msi_emp1.htm*

Microtec Research, Inc. *http://www.mri.com/jobs/jobs.html*

MicroWorks: Systems By Design . . . . *http://www.microwrks.com/employ.html*

Miller . . . . *http://www.careermosaic.com/cm/miller/*

Millipore Corporation . . . . *http://www.millipore.com/corporate/hr/index.html*

Mindflight Technology, Inc. . . . . *http://www.mindflight.com/jobs.htm*

MindSource Software, Inc. . . . . *http://www.mindsrc.com/reqs.html*

MindSpring Enterprises, Inc. . . . . *http://www.mindspring.com/aboutms/jobs.html*

Minnesota Mutual Insurance Company . . . . *http://www.minnesotamutual.com/*
career/caropts.html

Mitel Corporation . . . . *http://www.mitel.com/careers.htm*

Mitel Semiconductor *http://studio99.mitel.csemijobs.htm*

Mitre Corporation *http://www.mitre.org:80/jobs*

Mitsubishi Electric Research Laboratories . . . . *http://www.merl.com/*

MOD_2000 . . . . *http://www.mod2000.com/jobs.html*

Modicon . . . . *http://www.modicon.com/careero.html*

Molecular Dynamics . . . . *http://www.mdyn.com/jobs/jobs.htm*

Molecular Simulations, Inc. . . . . *http://www.msi.com/corp/jobs.html*

Molex, Inc. . . . . *http://www.molex.com/jobs.html*

Molloy Group, Inc. <The> . . . . *http://www.molloy.com/employ.html*

Molten Metal Technology *http://www.mmt.com/company/employ/emp1.htm*

Monsanto Company *http://www.monsanto.com:80/MonPub/Careers/index.html*

Morning Star Technologies . . . . *http://www.morningstar.com/MorningStar/Opportunities.html*

Mortice Kern Systems, Inc. . . . . *http://www.mks.com/jobs/*

Mosel Vitelic Corporation . . . . *http://www.moselvitelic.com/employ.htm*

Mott MacDonald (UK) . . . . *http://www.westlake.co.uk/datalake/eng/mottgrad.html*

MPath Interactive, Inc. . . . . *http://www.mpath.com/employment/mpath-employ.html*

MPR Teltech Ltd. . . . . *http://WWW.MPR.CA/employment/*

MTC Telemanagement Corporation . . . . *http://www.fractals.com/mtc/html/mtc_intro.html*

Multi-Tech Systems, Inc. *http://www.multitech.com/jobs.htp*

Mustang Software, Inc. . . . . *http://www.mustang.com/public/jobs/jobs.htm*

Mylex Corporation . . . . *http://www.mylex.com/employment/career.htm*

Myriad Genetics, Inc. . . . . http://www.myriad.com/jobs.html
Nabalco Pty. Ltd. (Australia) . . . . http://www.nabalco.aust.com/
Nabisco, Inc. . . . . http://www.nabisco.com/townhall/jobs/
Nanothinc . . . . http://www.nanothinc.com/Nanothinc/Jobs/Employment.html
Narrative Communications Corp. . . . . http://www.narrative.com/jobs.htm
National Business Group . . . . http://www.nbg.com/jobs.htm
National Computer Systems . . . . http://www.ncs.com/
National Institutes of Health . . . . http://www.nih.gov/employee/
National Instruments . . . . http://www.natinst.com/corp/jobs.htm
National Semiconductor . . . . http://www.nsc.com/careers/index.html
NationWide Building Society (UK)(2) . . . . http://www.nationwide.co.uk/jobs/jobs.htm
Natural Intelligence . . . . http://www.natural.com/pages/jobs/index.html
Navio Communications, Inc. . . . . http://www.navio.com/aboutus/career.html
NCA Computer Products . . . . http://www.NCAcomputers.com/
NCompass Labs, Inc. . . . . http://www.ncompasslabs.com/employment.htm
NCR Corporation http://www.careermosaic.com/cm/ncr/ncr1.html
NEC Corporation . . . . http://www.nec.com/web/company/jobs/index.html
Nellcor Puritan Bennett http://www.nellcorpb.com:80/nellcor/employment/employment1.html
net.Genesis . . . . http://www.netgen.com/corpinfo/jobs/jobs.html
NetCarta Corp . . . . http://www.netcarta.com/html/jobs.htm
NETCOM . . . . http://www.netcom.com/netcom/jobs.html
NetDynamics, Inc. . . . . http://www.netdynamics.com/company/jobs.html
NetEdge Systems, Inc. . . . . http://www.netedge.com/pages/jobs.html
NetFRAME Systems Incorporated . . . . http://www.netframe.com/employ/
NetGravity, Inc. http://www.netgravity.com/company/jobs.html
NetManage . . . . http://www.netmanage.com/company/employment/index.html
NetObjects, Inc. . . . . http://www.netobjects.com/html/jobs.html
Netscape Communication Corporation . . . . http://www.netscape.com/comprod/
                                                          about_netscape/hr/index.html
NetStart, Inc. . . . . http://careers.netstartinc.com/
Network Appliance . . . . http://www.netapp.com/career/index.html
Network Computing Devices . . . . http://www.ncd.com/human_resources/jobreq/
Network Engineering . . . . http://www.neteng.com/jobs.htm
Network Express, Inc. . . . . http://www.nei.com/job/job.htm
Network Peripherals, Inc. . . . . http://www.npix.com/hresource/career.html
Network Systems . . . . http://www.network.com/netcom/career/
Network-1 Software & Technology, Inc. http://www.network-1.com/corporate/jobs/
New Frontier Information Corporation . . . . http://www.nfic.com/Positions.html
Newbridge Networks Corporation . . . . http://www.newbridge.com/Employment/index.html
Newport Corporation . . . . http://www.newport.com/about/employment.html
NeXT Computer http://www.next.com/NeXTanswers/HTMLFiles/1835.htmld/1835.html
                                                http://www.next.com/HumanResources/
Nil Ltd. (Slovenia) . . . . http://www.nil.si/nil/zaposlitve.html
Nokia Telecommunications . . . . http://www.nokia.com/careers/
Nomura Research Institute, Ltd. (Japan) . . . . http://www.nri.co.jp/Personnel-Dept/
Northern Trust Corporation . . . . http://www.ntrs.com/jobs/index.html
Northwest Nexus, Inc. . . . . http://www.nwnexus.com/nexusinfo/jobs.html
Nosh Productions, Inc. . . . . http://www.nosh.com/employ.html
NovaLink Technologies, Inc. . . . . http://www.novatech.com/employment.html
NovaLogic . . . . http://www.novalogic.com/
NovaQuest InfoSystems . . . . http://www.novaquest.com/docs/employment.html
Novell, Inc. . . . . http://www.novell.com/job/
Now Software . . . . http://www.nowsoft.com/jobs/jobs.html
Number Nine Visual Technology, Inc. . . . . http://www.nine.com/jobs.html
NuMega Technologies, Inc. http://www.numega.com/WWW/numega1/jobs.html

NVIDIA . . . . *http://www.nvidia.com/corporate/jobopp.html*
Oak Ridge National Lab *gopher://gopher.ornl.gov/11/Employment*
Oak Technology . . . . *http://www.oaktech.com/employmt.html*
Object Design, Inc. . . . . *http://www.odi.com/AboutObject Design/jobs/index.html*
Object Technology International, Inc. . . . . *http://www.oti.com/corporat/employ.htm*
Objective Systems Integrators . . . . *http://www.osi.com/CompanyInfo/jobs.html*
ObjectSpace, Inc. . . . . *http://www.objectspace.com/Employment/*
OC Technologies, Inc. . . . . *http://www.idsonline.com/online/*
Octel Communications Corporation . . . . *http://www.octel.com/About/job.openings.html*
Office Technology, Inc. . . . . *http://www.officetech.com/employ.html*
Olicom (Denmark) . . . . *http://www.olicom.com/jobs/*
Olsen & Associates (Switzerland) . . . . . . *http://www.olsen.ch/export/employment/employment.html*
Omni Development, Inc. . . . . *http://www.omnigroup.com/Info/Jobs.html*
ONE TOUCH Systems, Inc. . . . . *http://www.onetouch.com/jobs.htm*
OneNet Communications. . . . . *http://www.one.net/employment/*
Online Consultants, Inc. . . . . *http://www.idsonline.com/online/*
Online Environs, Inc. . . . . *http://www.environs.com/environs/jobs.html*
Online Magic . . . . *http://www.onlinemagic.com/online/*
OnLive! Technologies . . . . *http://www.onlive.com/corp/jobs/index.htm*
Ontrack Computer Systems, Inc. . . . . *http://www.ontrack.com/team.html*
ONYX Software . . . . *http://www.onyxcorp.com/*
Open Environment Corporation *http://www.oec.com/em/em1.htm*
Open Market, Inc. . . . . *http://www.openmarket.com/hiring/*
Open Software Foundation . . . . *http://www.osf.org/general/joblist.html*
Open Text Corporation . . . . *http://www.opentext.com/corp/otm-about-career-intro.html*
Open Vision Technologies . . . . *http://www.ov.com/jobs.html*
OPN Systems, Inc. . . . . *http://www.opn.com/openings.html*
OPTi, Inc. . . . . *http://www.opti.com/employmt/index.htm*
Optical Cable Corporation . . . . *http://www.occfiber.com/employment.html*
Optical Data Systems, Inc. . . . . *http://www.ods.com/compinfo/employ/employ.htm*
Optimal Networks, Inc. . . . . *http://www.optimal.com/jobs.htm*
Optimized Computer Solutions . . . . *http://www.ocsny.com/index.html*
Oracle Corporation . . . . *http://www.oracle.com/corporate/hr/html/index/html*
Orbit Semiconductor, Inc. . . . . *http://www.orbitsemi.com/job.html*
Orbital Sciences Corporation . . . . *http://careers.oscsystems.com/*
Organic, Inc. . . . . *http://www.organic.com/jobs/*
Ositech Communication . . . . *http://www.ositech.com/employ.htm*
Otis Elevator Co. . . . . *http://www.otis.com/*
Overseas Union Bank (Singapore) . . . . *http://davinci.technet.sg/*
O'Reilly & Associates . . . . *http://www.ora.com/human-resources/employ/index.html*
Pacific Data Images . . . . *http://www.pdi.com/PDIPage/recruiting/recruiting.html*
Pacific Enterprises . . . . *http://www.pacent.com/class/emplops.html*
Pacific Gas and Electric Company (PG&E) . . . . *http://www.pge.com/about_us/employment/*
Pacific Northwest National Laboratory *http://www.pnl.gov:2080/general/hrpublic/index.html*
PacifiCare Health Systems . . . . *http://www.phs.com/cgi-win/phs_hr.exe/all*
Packard Bell Electronics, Inc. . . . . *http://www.packardbell.com/gfx/hr/index.html*
PairGain Technologies, Inc. . . . . *http://www.pairgain.com/ovr_emp.htm*
PAR Technology Corporation . . . . *http://www.partech.com/ptc/jobs.htm*
Paranet . . . . *http://www.paranet.com/career/index.html*
PAREXEL International Corporation . . . . *http://www.parexel.com/job/default.htm*
Park City Group . . . . *http://www.parkcity.com/employ/index.stm*
Parsons Technology . . . . *http://www.parsonstech.com/infocentral/careers.html*
Patterson Dental Company . . . . *http://www.pdental.com/employ/employ.htm*
Paul-Tittle Associates *http://www.careermosaic.com/cm/pta/pta1.html*
PC DOCS, Inc. . . . . *http://www.pcdocs.com/joblist\default.htm*

PCS Group . . . . *http://www.iglou.com/pcsgroup/opps.htm*
PCSI . . . . *http://www.pcsi.com/dir.shtml*
Peace Corps . . . . *http://www.peacecorps.gov/*
Peachtree Software . . . . *http://www.peachtree.com/hr/employ.htm*
Peapod, Inc. . . . . *http://www.peapod.com/employ.html*
Pegasystems, Inc. . . . . *http://www.pega.com/recruit.html*
Pencom . . . . *http://www.pencomsi.com/planet.html*
PeopleSoft . . . . *http://www.peoplesoft.com/*
Performance Systems International, Inc. . . . . *http://www.psi.com/*
Perkin-Elmer Corporation . . . . *http://www.perkin-elmer.com/ab/about/listing.html*
Perot Systems Corporation . . . . *http://www.psc.careersite.com/cgi/search-jobs*
Persoft, Inc. . . . . *http://www.persoft.com/employ/employ.htm*
Personal Library Software . . . . *http://www.pls.com/sitemap.html*
Peterson's Education Center . . . . *http://www.petersons.com/career/main.html*
Pharos Technologies, Inc. . . . . *http://www.pharos.com/*
Philips Electronics . . . . *http://www.philips.com/employment/*
Philips Semiconductors *http://www.semiconductors.philips.com/philips19.html*
Phoenix Technologies Ltd. . . . . *http://www.ptltd.com/jobs/jobs.html*
PictureWorks Technology, Inc. . . . . *http://www.pixworks.com/jobopps.html*
Pilot Software . . . . *http://www.pilotsw.com/jobs/Welcome.htm*
Pinnacle Micro, Inc. . . . . *http://www.pinnaclemicro.com/jobs.html*
PKWARE, Inc. . . . . *http://www.pkware.com/work.html*
Platform Computing Corporation (Canada) . . . . *http://www.platform.com/company/*
companyinfo.html#Jobs
Platinum Software Corporation . . . . *http://www.platsoft.com/corporate/jobs.htm*
Platinum Solutions, Inc. . . . . *http://www.platsol.com/platsol/jobsopen/index.html*
PLATINUM Technology, Inc. *http://www.platinum.com/employ/emptoc3.htm*
PMC-Sierra, Inc. *http://www.careermosaic.com:80/cm/pmc-sierra/*
PointCast, Inc. . . . . *http://www.pointcast.com/jobs/index.html*
Policy Management Systems Corporation (PMSC) . . . . *http://www.pmsc.com/career.html*
PolyLinks. *http://www.polymers.com/jobbank/wantads/home.html*
Portable Software Corporation . . . . *http://www.quickxpense.com/recruit.htm*
Positive Support Review, Inc. . . . . *http://www.psrinc.com/Career.htm*
Power Computing Corporation . . . . *http://www.powercc.com/Company/employment.html*
Power Store <The> . . . . *http://www.powerstore.com/powerstore/jobs.html*
PowerCerv Corporation *http://pacific.powercerv.com:80/jobs.html*
Powersoft Corporation (a division of Sybase, Inc.) . *http://www.sybase.com/careers/careeropps.html*
Praxis plc. (UK) . . . . *http://www.praxis.co.uk/jobs.htm*
PRC, Inc. . . . . *http://www.prc.com/careers.html*
Precept Software, Inc. . . . . *http://www.precept.com/company/employment.htm*
Premenos Corp. . . . . *http://www.premenos.com/premenos/jobs/*
PREPnet . . . . *http://www.prep.net/ops.html*
Price Waterhouse . . . . *http://www.pw.com/wo/career/htm*
Price Waterhouse LLP Management Consulting Services . . . . *http://www.careermosaic.com/*
cm/pwllp/pwllp2.html
Principal Financial Group <The> . . . . *http://www.principal.com/employ/employ.htm*
PRIOR Data Sciences (Canada) . . . . *http://www.prior.ca/prior/careers/careers.htm*
Prism Technologies, Ltd. (UK) *http://www.prismtech.co.uk/home40.html*
Prism Solutions, Inc. . . . *http://www.prismsolutions.com/news-info/employment/jobs-category.html*
Pro-Log Corporation . . . . *http://www.pro-log.com/employ.htm*
Procom Technology, Inc. . . . . *http://www.procom.com/homepage/wbhyjobs.html*
Procter and Gamble Company <The> . . . . *http://www.pg.com/careers/*
Professional Land Corporation . . . . *http://www.proland.com/employ.htm*
Profound Consulting, Inc. *http://www.indy.net/~profound/career.html*
Progress Software Corporation . . . . *http://www.progress.com/bin/procgi.pl/careers/careers.p*

Progressive Corporation *http://www.auto-insurance.com/employ1.htm*
Progressive Networks .... *http://www.prognet.com/jobs/jobs.html*
Project Software & Development, Inc. .... *http://www.psdi.com/www/jobs.html#scsea*
Promega Corporation .... *http://www.promega.com/hr/careers.html*
Proteon, Inc. .... *http://www.proteon.com/docs/career/hrmainpg.htm*
Proxicom, Inc. *http://xenon.proxima.com:80/career/*
Prudential Insurance Company of America .... *http://www.prudential.com/universal/*
                                            careers/unczz1000.html
PS Computer Services Ltd. .... *http://www.pscomputer.co.uk/*
PSINet .... *http://www.psi.net/employment/*
PSW Technologies .... *http://www.pswtech.com/*
Pure Atria .... *http://www.pureatria.com/career/index.html*
Pure Software, Inc. .... *http://www.pure.com/career/index.html*
Pyramid Technology Corp. .... *http://www.pyramid.com/about/career.html*
QNX Software Systems .... *http://www.qnx.com/hr/jobs.html*
Qosina, Inc. .... *http://www.qosina.com/qosina/overview/jobs/*
Quad Systems Corporation .... *http://www.quad-sys.com/html/employment.htm*
Quadbase Systems, Inc. .... *http://www.quadbase.com/employment.html*
Qualcomm, Inc. .... *http://www.qualcomm.com/HR/*
Quality Semiconductors, Inc. .... *http://www.qualitysemi.com/main/hiring.html*
Qualix Group, Inc. .... *http://www.qualix.com/ref/employ.htmld/*
Qualtos .... *http://www.qualtos.com/about/job.html*
Quantum Corporation .... *http://www.quantum.com/hr/hr.html*
Quarry Communications .... *http://www.quarry.com/People/Job_Openings/*
Quarterdeck Corporation .... *http://www.qdeck.com/jobs/*
Quickturn Design Systems, Inc. .... *http://www.qcktrn.com/corp/emp/employmn.htm*
Quintus Corporation .... *http://www.quintus.com/jobs/*
R/GA Digital Studios *http://www.rga.com/7r/jobs/index.htm*
Racal Avionics (UK) .... *http://www.ravl.co.uk/careers.html*
Racal-Datacom .... *http://www.careermosaic.com/cm/racal/*
RAD Technologies .... *http://www.rad.com/web/personel/person.htm*
Radian International LLC. .... *http://www.radian.com/misc/jobs.htm*
RadioMail Corporation .... *http://www.radiomail.net/corpinfo/careers/*
RadiSys Corporation .... *http://www.radisys.com/employment.html*
Radius, Inc. .... *http://www.radius.com/About/Opps.html*
RadMedia, Inc. .... *http://www.radmedia.com/radsite/company/jobs.html*
Rainbow Technologies, Inc. .... *http://www.rnbo.com/HR.HTM*
Ratelco Electronics .... *http://www.ratelco.com/hr/index.html*
Raymond Karsan Associates .... *http://www.raykarsan.com/employ.html*
Raytheon Company .... *http://www.raytheon.com/jobs.html*
RDI Computer Corporation .... *http://www.rdi.com/career.html*
Read-Rite Corporation .... *http://www.readrite.com/aahtml/hr/htm*
Recruitment On-Line Inc. .... *http://www.helpwanted.com/paramjobs.html*
Red Brick Systems, Inc. .... *http://www.redbrick.com/cgi-bin/nph-jobs/rbs/jobposts.htmf*
Reference Press, Inc. <The> .... *http://www.hoovers.com/job.html*
Remedy Corporation .... *http://www.remedy.com/career/jobslst.shtml*
Rendition, Inc. .... *http://www.rendition.com/rendjobs.html*
Research Engineers, Inc. .... *http://www.reiusa.com/gen/jobs.htm*
Research in Motion Limited .... *http://www.rim.net/careers.htm*
Respironics, Inc. .... *http://www.respironics.com/*
Reuters Information Technology, Inc. ... *http://www.careermosaic.com/cm/reuters/reuters_04.html*
Revco D.S., Inc. .... *http://www.revco.com/emp-op-main.htmld/*
Reynolds Metals Company .... *http://www.rmc.com/employ.html*
ReZ.n8 Studios *http://www.rezn8.com/001/index.html*
Rhythm & Hues Studios .... *http://www.rhythm.com/homepage/help/index.shtml*

RICOH California Research Center . . . . *http://www.crc.ricoh.com/jobs/jobs.html*
River Forest Bancorp, Inc. . . . . *http://www.financial-net.com/usa/riverforest/job-opps.html*
Riverside Technology, Inc. . . . . *http://www.riverside.com/employ/empintro.html*
Rochester City Joblink . . . . *http://isl.net/city/joblink.html*
Rocket Science . . . . *http://www.rocketsci.com/plans.html*
Rocket Scientists . . . . *http://www.rocketsci.com/corporate/jobops.html*
Rockwell International . . . . *http://www.rockwell.com/~careers/jobs.html*
Rockwell Telecommunications . . . . *http://www.nb.rockwell.com/dept/personnel/job_top.html*
Rogers Communications, Inc. . . . . *http://www.rogers.com/RCI/employ.htm*
Rogue Wave Software . . . . *http://www.roguewave.com/company/jobs/jobs.htm*
Ross Systems, Inc. . . . . *http://www.rossinc.com/html/job.htm*
Ross Technology, Inc. . . . . *http://www.ross.com/jobs.html*
RoweCom . . . . *http://www.rowe.com/currentjobs.html*
RSA Data Security, Inc. . . . . *http://www.rsa.com/rsa/OpenJobs.html*
Rubbermaid, Inc. . . . . *http://www.rubbermaid.com/corporate/hr/*
RWD Technologies, Inc. *http://www.rwd.com/rwd8.htm*
Ryder System, Inc. . . . . *http://www.ryder.inter.net/html/employment.html*
S-COM Computer Systems Engineers, Ltd. (UK) *http://www.scom.com:80/*
S-MOS Systems . . . . *http://www.smos.com/jobs.html*
S3 Incorporated *http://www.s3.com/corporate/jobs/*
SafetyNet . . . . *http://www.safe.net/*
Sage Solutions, Inc. *http://www.sagesoln.com/employ.htm*
Salomon Brothers . . . . *http://www.salomon.com/careerop.htm*
Salomon Brothers International Limited (UK) . . . . *http://www.sbil.co.uk/Career/intro.html*
Samsung Electronics . . . . *http://www.samsung.co.kr/Recruit/Foreign/index.html*
San Francisco Symphony . . . . *http://www.hooked.net/sfsymphony/admin/stf-menu.html*
Sanders–Lockheed Martin Company . . . . *http://www.sanders.com/HR/Sanders_Jobs.html*
Sandia National Laboratories . . . . *http://www.sandia.gov/Human_Resources/dep3535.html*
SanDisk Corporation . . . . *http://www.sandisk.com/sd/hr/hr.htm*
Santa Cruz Operation–SCO . . . . *http://www.sco.com/Company/Jobs/jobs.html*
Santa Cruz Operation–SCO Visionware (UK) . . . *http://www.visionware.co.uk/wanted/wanted.html*
SAP . . . . *http://www.sap.com/discsap/career/career.htm*
SAS Institute, Inc. . . . . *http://www.sas.com/jobs/intro.html*
Saudi Aramco . . . . *http://www.careermosaic.com/cm/aramco/*
SBC Communications, Inc. *http://www.sbc.com:80/swbell/credits/jobs/opportunity.html*
SBE, Inc. . . . . *http://www.sbei.com/hr/employ.htm*
SBT Accounting Systems . . . . *http://www.sbtcorp.com/sbtlib/jobboard.html*
Scala, Inc. . . . . *http://www.scala.com/employment.html*
Scan-Graphics, Inc. . . . . *http://www.scangraphics.com/scang/employ.htm*
Schering Health Care UK Ltd (UK) . . . . *http://www.schering.co.uk/*
Schlumberger . . . . *http://www.slb.com/recr/*
Schneider National . . . . *http://www.schneiderjobs.com/netscape/index.html*
Science Applications International Corporation (SAIC) . . . . . *http://www.saic.com/career/index.html*
Scientific-Atlanta . . . . *http://www.sciatl.com/D/b/index.html*
Scopus Technology . . . . *http://www.scopus.com/employment/default.html*
Scottish Enterprise . . . . *http://www.scotent.co.uk/html/sen/recruit/recruit.htm*
Seagate Software Information
    Management Group . . . . *http://www.nsmg.seagatesoftware.com/jobpostings.html*
    . . . . *http://www.img.seagatesoftware.com/general/career.htm*
Seagate Technology, Inc. . . . . *http://www.seagate.com/corp/hr/hrtop.shtml*
Seanet . . . . *http://www.seanet.com/about/employment.html*
SEARS Termite & Pest Control, Inc. . . . . *http://www.searspest.com/searspest/positions.htm*
SEEQ Technologies, Inc. *http://www.seeq.com/webjob.shtml*
Seer Technologies, Inc. . . . . *http://www.seer.com/hrpage/empopps.htm*
Segue Software, Inc. . . . . *http://www.segue.com/intro.htm#jobs*

SEMATECH . . . . *http://www.sematech.org/public/jobs/jobpage.htm*
SENSE8 Corporation *http://www.sense8.com/company/employment.html*
Sensoray Company, Inc. . . . . *http://www.teleport.com/~sray/jobpage:html*
Sentex Systems, Inc. . . . . *http://www.sentexsystems.com/jobs.html*
Sequent Computer Systems, Inc. . . . . *http://www.sequent.com/cgi-bin/org/cgi-jrf*
ServiceSoft Corporation . . . . *http://www.servicesoft.com/jobopps.htm*
Sharp Electronics Corporation *http://www.sharp-usa.com/careers/c01.html*
Sherpa Corporation . . . . *http://www.sherpa.com/overview/hr.html*
Shiva Corporation . . . . *http://www.shiva.com/corp/hr/index.html*
SHL Systemhouse, Inc. *http://www.shl.com:80/500.html*
Shoals Marine laboratory *http://128.253.50.135/Shoals/jobs.html*
Shomiti Systems . . . . *http://www.shomiti.com/jobs.html*
Shore.Net . . . . *http://www.shore.net/jobs/*
Shure Brothers, Inc. . . . . *http://www.shure.com/employment/employment.html*
Siemens . . . . *http://www.siemens.com/usa/employment.html*
Sierra On-line . . . . *http://www.sierra.com/news/recruiting*
Sigma Chemical Company *http://www.sigma.sial.com/sigma/tpcint12.htm*
Silicon Graphics, Inc. . . . . *http://www.sgi.com/Overview/#jobs*
Silicon Reef, Inc. . . . . *http://blacksun.reef.com/opps/reefopps.html*
Silicon Studio . . . . *http://www.sgi.com/Staffing/Jobs/index.html*
Silicon Systems, Inc. *http://www.ssi1.com/employment/employment.html*
Silvaco International . . . . *http://www.silvaco.com/cgi-bin/jobs/listIndex*
Simba Technologies *http://www.pageahead.com/company/jobs2.html*
Simpact Associates, Inc. . . . . *http://www.simpact.com/career.html*
Simware . . . . *http://www.simware.com/brains/*
Singapore Technologies (Singapore) . . . . *http://www.st.com.sg/career.htm#jobs*
Skidaway Institute of Oceanography . . . . *http://minnow.skio.peachnet.edu/job.html*
Skywire, Corp. . . . . *http://www.skywire.com/employ_2.htm*
SMART Corporation . . . . *http://www.smartdb.com/jobs.html*
Sofcom . . . . *http://www.sofcom.com.au/Employment.html*
SoftArc, Inc. . . . . *http://www.softarc.com/fcjobs.htm*
SoftAware, Inc. . . . . *http://www.softaware.com/employment.html*
SOFTBANK Exposition and Conference Co., Inc. . . . . *http://www.sbexpos.com/sbexpos/*
human_resources/index.html
SoftDesk . . . . *http://www.softdesk.com/softcare.htm*
Softimage, Inc. . . . . *http://www.microsoft.com/Softimage/About/Jobs/*
SoftQuad, Inc. . . . . *http://www.sq.com/jobs/jobs.html*
Software AG of North America, Inc. . . . . *http://www.sagus.com/hr/joblist.html*
Software Artistry, Inc. . . . . *http://www.softart.com/jobs/employment.stm*
Software Publishing Corporation . . . . *http://www.spco.com/SPC/SPCHR/HTM*
Software Spectrum *http://192.152.152.10/prd.i/pgen/ssi/OL/fyi.html*
Solomon Software . . . . *http://www.solomon.com/employ.htm*
Soma Group, Inc. <The> . . . . *http://www.ultranet.com/~soma/jobs.html*
Sonic Systems, Inc. . . . . *http://www.sonicsys.com/job.html*
Sorrento Corporation <The> . . . . *http://www.sorrento.net/employ.html*
Southern Life (South Africa) . . . . *http://www.southernlife.co.za/sla/jobs/sljobhp.htm*
Southwest Business Corporation . . . . *http://www.swbc.com/hmnres.html*
Southwest Research Institute, Inc. *http://www.swri.edu/5news/person/joblist/titles.htm*
Southwestern Bell Corporation . . . . *http://www.sbc.com/swbell/credits/jobs/opportunity.html*
Southwestern Bell Technology Resources . . . . *http://www.tri.sbc.com/employment.html*
SpaceCom Systems . . . . *http://www.uvsg.com/jobs/netjobs.htm*
SpaceWorks, Inc. . . . . *http://www.spaceworks.com/wantads.htm*
SPECOM Technologies Corporation . . . . *http://www.specom.com/employ.htm*
Spectrian . . . . *http://www.spectrian.com/joblist.htm*
Specular International, Ltd. . . . . *http://www.specular.com/profile/hiring.html*

SpeedSim, Inc. . . . . *http://www.speedsim.com/company/jobs/jobs.htm*
Spider Technologies . . . . *http://www.w3spider.com/cgi-bin/zipforum?read:jobs*
Sprint Corporation . . . . *http://www.sprint.com/lowrez/sprint/jobs.html*
SprintLink . . . . *http://www.sprintlink.net/SPLK/career.html*
Spry, Inc. . . . . *http://www.compuserve.com/inside/careers/spry/index.html*
SPSS, Inc. . . . . *http://www.spss.com/UsJobs/*
Spyglass, Inc. . . . . *http://www.spyglass.com/company/jobs.htm*
SSDS, Inc. . . . . *http://www.ssds.com/jobs.html*
SSE, Inc. . . . . *http://www.sse-inc.com/Jobs_Frame.htm*
SSGI Medical Systems . . . . *http://www.prowess.com/Jobs/jobs.html*
Stac Electronics . . . . *http://www.stac.com/Homepages/Employmt/joblist.html*
Standard Microsystems Corporation . . . . *http://www.smc.com/hr/joblist.html*
Stanford Telecom (STel) . . . . *http://www.stel.com/stel/ads/ads.htm*
Stardust Technologies . . . . *http://www.stardust.com/corp/employme.html*
Starfish Software . . . . *http://www.starfishsoftware.com/news/employ.html*
Starlight Networks . . . . *http://www.starlight.com/starlight/html/careers.html*
StarNet . . . . *http://www.starnetinc.com/noframes/SNn_Jobs.shtml*
StarSight Telecast, Inc. . . . . *http://www.starsight.com/jobs.html*
StarWave Corporation . . . . *http://www.starwave.com/text/starwave/jobs/*
State of the Art, Inc. . . . . *http://www.stateoftheart.com/employ/employ.html*
Sterling Payot Company . . . . *http://www.spcom.com/job/job.html*
Sterling Software . . . . *http://www.sterling.com/employment/*
Storage Dimensions . . . . *http://www.storagedimensions.com/company/career.html*
Storage Technology Corporation *http://www.stortek.com/StorageTek/stkjob1.html*
StormCloud Development Corporation *http://perdix.ndev.com/ndc2/newsinfo/jobs.ht*
Strata, Inc. *http://www.strata3d.com/strata/employ.html*
StrataCom, Inc. *http://www.stratacom.com/corporate2/employment/s8.html*
                                                         http://www.cisco.com/jobs/
Stratus Computer, Inc. . . . . *http://www.stratus.com/hr/*
Stream International, Inc. . . . . *http://www.stream.com/about/index.dyn*
Structural Dynamics Research Corporation . . . . *http://www.sdrc.com/nav/company/jobs/*
Stylus Innovation . . . . *http://www.stylus.com/jobs.htm*
Summagraphics Corporation . . . . *http://www.calcomp.com/summagraphics/jobs/jobs.htm*
Sun Microsystems . . . . *http://www.sun.com/corporateoverview/*
                                        CorporateEmployment/LISTINGDIR/
Sun Microsystems (JavaSoft) . . . . *http://java.sun.com/aboutJavaSoft/jobs*
Sunquest Information Systems . . . . *http://www.sunquest.com/employment/*
Super Highway Consulting . . . . *http://www.stpt.com/shc/hire.html*
Superscape VR plc. . . . . *http://www.superscape.com/aboutus/vacancy/jbos.htm*
SVEC Computer Corporation . . . . *http://www.svec.com/graphics/corporate/*
                                        CareerOpportunities.htm
Swan Technologies Corporation . . . . *http://www.zdsdirect.com/company/jobs.htm*
Sybase, Inc. . . . . *http://www.sybase.com/careers/careeropps/*
Symantec Corporation . . . . *http://www.careermosaic.com/cm/symantec/*
Symbios Logic . . . . *http://www.symbios.com/employ/job_post.htm*
Symbol Technologies *http://www.symbol.com/ST000103.HTM*
Synectics, Inc. . . . . *http://www.synectics.com/viewjobs.html*
Synergy Semiconductor . . . . *http://www.synergysemi.com/employ/employ.html*
Synon, Inc. *http://www.synon.com/public/hr/careerops.html*
Synopsys, Inc. . . . . *http://www.synopsys.com/abtsynop/employment/employ.html*
System Management ARTS . . . . *http://www.smarts.com/careers.html*
Systems & Computer Technology Corporation (SCT) . . . . *http://www.sctcorp.com/hrhome.html*
Systems & Networks (Alta Group) . . . . *http://www.sysnet.com/jobs/employ.html*
Systems Partners . . . . *http://www.syspart.com/public_html/fulltime.html*
Systems Techniques, Inc. . . . . *http://www.systecinc.com/jobs/jobs.htm*

SystemSoft Corporation . . . . *http://www.systemsoft.com/*
Taligent, Inc. . . . . *http://www.taligent.com/*
Tandem Computers, Inc. *http://www.careermosaic.com/cm/tandem/tm3.html*
Tangram Enterprise Solutions . . . . *http://www.tesi.com/employ.htm*
TASC, Inc. . . . . *http://www.tasc.com/employ/employ.html*
TCSI Corporation . . . . *http://www.tcsi.com/Working/*
TDK Systems . . . . *http://www.tdksystems.com/*
TechGnosis International (Intersolv) . . . . *http://www.techgnosis.com/hr-req/index.htm*
Technology Service Corporation . . . . *http://www.tsc.com/employment/ads.html*
Technomatrix Technologies, Inc. . . . . *http://www.valisys.com/jobs/jobs.html*
Technomatrix Technologies, Ltd. . . . . *http://www.tecnomatix.com/pages/jobs.html*
Tee-Comm Electronics (Canada) . . . . *http://www.teecomm.com/jobs.html*
Tekelec . . . . *http://www.tekelec.com/corporate/resources.html*
Teknowledge Corporation . . . . *http://www.teknowledge.com/company/job_posting.html*
Tektronix, Inc. . . . . *http://www.tek.com/Tektronix/Careers/*
Telco Systems . . . . *http://www.telco.com/jobs.htm*
Telebit Corporation *http://www.telebit.com/CompanY/hr1.html*
Telegen Corporation . . . . *http://www.telegen.com/*
Teleport Internet Services . . . . *http://www.tasoft.com/teleport/jobs.shtml*
Telescan Incorporated . . . . *http://www.telescan.com/employ.htm*
Telewest Communications (UK) . . . . *http://www.telewest.co.uk/jobs/*
Telexis . . . . *http://www.appsil.com/*
Tellabs, Inc. . . . . *http://www.tellabs.com/about/career.html*
Telogy Networks . . . . *http://www.telogy.com/employ/tnemploy.htm*
Telos Corporation . . . . *http://www.telos.com/corpinfo/employment/employ.html*
TelTech . . . . *http://www.teltechinc.com/recs.htm*
Teltronics, Inc. . . . . *http://www.teltronics.com/job.html*
Template Graphics Software, Inc. *http://www.tgs.com/Staff/jobs.htm*
Template Software . . . . *http://www.template.com/jobs.html*
Tera Computer Company . . . . *http://www.tera.com/tera/opportunities.htm*
Teradyne . . . . *http://teradyne.com/hr/tocindex.html*
Terayon Corporation *http://www.terayon.com/index5.html*
Terisa Systems *http://dengue.terisa.com:80/jobs/*
Tesco Stores, Ltd. (UK) . . . . *http://www.Tesco.co.uk/*
Texas Instruments . . . . *http://www.ti.com/cgi-bin/recruit/jobbrws.cgi*
Texas Microsystems, Inc. *http://www.texmicro.com/employment.html*
TGV Software, Inc. . . . . *http://www.tgv.com/company_information/open-positions.html*
Thermo LabSystems, Inc. *http://www.labsystems.com/jobs.htm*
Thinking Machines Corporation . . . . *http://www.think.com/html/about/employ.htm*
Third Party Solutions, Inc. . . . . *http://www.tpsol.com/jobs.html*
Thomson Publishing . . . . *http://www.thomson.com/tcom/ry.html*
Thomson Software Products . . . . *http://www.thomsoft.com/Company/jobs.html*
ThrustMaster . . . . *http://www.thrustmaster.com/job-ops.htm*
TIBCO . . . . *http://www.tibco.com/*
TMSSequoia, Inc. . . . . *http://www.tmsinc.com/corpinfo/jobs.html*
TopLog Limited (UK) . . . . *http://www.tploguk.co.uk/jobs.htm*
Toys 'R Us *http://www.careermosaic.com:80/cm/toysrus/toys4.html*
Trane Company <The> . . . . *http://www.trane.com/about/jobs.html*
Transaction Information Systems, Inc. *http://www.tisny.com/index10.html*
Transarc Corporation *http://www.transarc.com:80/afs/transarc.com/*
public/www/Public/Recruiting/index.html
Transtech . . . . *http://www.trans-tech.com/transtech/emp.html*
TranSwitch Corporation . . . . *http://www.transwitch.com/employ.html*
Traveling Software, Inc. . . . . *http://www.travsoft.com/company/emplopp.htm*
Trendtec *http://www.trendtec.com/employ1.html*

Tribase Systems, Inc. . . . . *http://www.trisys.com/jobs.html*
Tribune . . . . *http://www.tribune.com/employment/index.html*
Tricord Systems . . . . *http://www.tricord.com/cgi-bin/hr*
Trilobyte, Inc. . . . . *http://www.tbyte.com/digs/opps.htm*
Triology Consulting Services . . . . *http://www.occ.com/occ/member/cptrilog.html*
TriTeal Corporation . . . . *http://www.triteal.com/company_news/*
True Software, Inc. . . . . *http://www.truesoft.com/jobs.html*
TrueVision . . . . *http://www.truevision.com/main*
Trusted Information Systems, Inc. . . . . *http://www.tis.com/docs/TIS/*
TRW, Inc. . . . . *http://www.trw.com/seg/recruitment/index.html*
TRW Space & Electronics Group . . . . *http://www.trw.com/seg/recruitment/index.html*
Tumbleweed Software . . . . *http://www.twcorp.com/jobs.htm*
TwinStar Semiconductor, Inc. . . . . *http://www.careermosaic.com:80/cm/twin_star/tw2.html*
U.S. Long Distance . . . . *http://oldwww.usld.com/users/usld_hr/jobline.html*
U.S. Navy . . . . *http://www.navyjobs.com/*
Ultra Clean Technology *http://www2.uctnow.com/uctnow/uctjobs.html*
Ultradata Corporation . . . . *http://www.ultradata.com/hr/index.htm*
Ungermann-Bass (UB) Networks, Inc. . . . . *http://www2.ub.com/weblink.nsf/?OpenDatabase*
Unidata, Inc. . . . . *http://www.unidata.com/*
Unify Corporation . . . . *http://www.unify.com/overview.html#EMP*
Unigraphics (EDS Division) *http://www.eds.com/jobnet/opportun/ejc10019.shtml*
Unison Software, Inc. *http://www.unison.com/marketin/26de-31a.html*
Unisys . . . . *http://www.unisys.com/Jobs/*
United Nations . . . . *http://www.undcp.org/unlinks.html*
United States Cellular Corporation . . . . *http://www.uscc.com/job.htm*
United Technologies Automotive . . . . *http://www.uta.com/jobs/jobs.html*
United Technologies Corp . . . . *http://www.utc.com/workingatutc.html*
Unitil Corporation . . . . *http://www.unitil.com/new/workhere.html*
US Robotics *http://www.usr.com/aboutus/104.html*
US WEST . . . . *http://www.careermosaic.com/cm/uswest/*
USAir . . . . *http://www.usair.com/ci_job.htm*
USoft . . . . *http://www.usoft.com/company/jobs/home.htm*
Utopia, Inc. . . . . *http://www.utopia.com/jobs/index.html*
UTRC Employment Postings . . . . *http://utrcwww.utc.com/UTRC/Jobs/Jobs.html*
UUNET . . . . *http://www.uu.net/jobs.html*
UUNET PIPEX (UK) . . . . *http://www.uunet.pipex.com/company/employment/*
Vanguard Group, Inc. <The> . . . . *http://www.vanguard.com/employ/6_0.html*
Vanstar Corporation . . . . *http://www.vanstar.com/careers.html*
Vantive Corporation . . . . *http://www.vantive.com/jobs/jobs.htm*
Varian Associates, Inc. . . . . *http://www.varian.com/jobs.html*
Varitel . . . . *http://www.varitel-eds.com/jobs.html*
VDOnet Corp. . . . . *http://www.vdo.net/info/recruit/*
Veda, Inc. . . . . *http://www.mv.com/users/wsjor/vedainc/veda-emp.html*
Venable, Baetjer, Howard & Civiletti . . . . *http://venable.com/govern/position.htm*
VeriFone . . . . *http://www.verifone.com/jobs/*
VeriSign, Inc. . . . . *http://www.verisign.com/about/jobs.html*
Veritas Software, Inc. . . . . *http://www.veritas.com/People/Jobs/index.html*
Verity, Inc. . . . . *http://www.verity.com/JOBS/*
Verlink Corporation . . . . *http://www.verilink.com/byrum/jobs/jobhome.htm*
Vermeer Technologies . . . . *http://www.vermeer.com/employment.html*
Versar, Inc. . . . . *http://www.versar.com/position/careerop.htm*
Vertex Pharmaceuticals, Inc. . . . . *http://www.vpharm.com/job_info/jobopen.html*
Viasat . . . . *http://www.viasat.cerfnet.com/employ.htm*
VIASOFT, Inc. *http://www.viasoft.com/hr/emp1.htm*
Video Server, Inc. . . . . *http://www.helpwanted.com/compay/videoserver/vshp.htm*

Videonics, Inc. . . . . *http://www.videonics.com/Employment.html*

Viewlogic Systems, Inc. . . . . *http://www.viewlogic.com/about/jobs.html*

Virtual i-O, Inc. . . . . *http://www.vio.com/vio/about/jobs.html*

Visigenic Software, Inc. . . . . *http://www.visigenic.com/misc/recruit.html*

Visionary Design Systems . . . . *http://www.vds.net/about-VDS/company_info/job-openings.html*

Visioner Communications, Inc. . . . . *http://www.visioneer.com/cwebc.cgi?Fm_uRH?WsgJIS4JNdp6/*
pKFAGKJQW309PZWOGB11Q8K17

Visual Components . . . . *http://www.visualcomp.com/corp/jobs.htm*

Visual Numerics, Inc. . . . . *http://www.vni.com/jobs.html*

Vivid Studios . . . . *http://www.vivid.com/vividians/jobs.html*

Vividus Corporation . . . . *http://www.vividus.com/jobs.html*

Vivo Software, Inc. . . . . *http://www.vivo.com/company/joboppor.htm*

VLSI Technology . . . . *http://www.vlsi.com/vlsi/company/*
employmentinformation/jobs.qry?graphics=noframes

Vodafone Group (UK) *http://www.vodafone.co.uk/n3/staff/staff.html*

Voxware . . . . *http://www.voxware.com/*

VXR Corporation . . . . *http://www.virtuocity.com/employ/employvxr.html*

W3 Consortium *http://www.w3.org/pub/WWW/Consortium/Recruitment/*

Wabash National Corporation . . . . *http://www.nlci.com/wabash/emplymnt.htm*

Wal-Mart Stores . . . . *http://www.wal-mart.com/home/index.shtml*
http://www.wal-mart.com/cgi-bin/htmldisp?ci:5

Walgreens Company *http://www.walgreens.com/rect/rect1.html*

Walker Interactive Systems . . . . *http://www.walker.com/walker/career/*

Walker Richer & Quinn, Inc. *http://www.wrq.com/employ/job1.htm*

Waterloo Maple, Inc. . . . . *http://www.maplesoft.com/company/documents/employment.html*

Wave System Corp . . . . *http://www.wavesys.com/index.shtml*

Wavetek, Inc. . . . . *http://www.wavetek.com/jobs/wtjobs.html*

Wayne Memorial Hospital . . . . *http://www.wmh.org/*

Web Developer Magazine . . . . *http://www.webdeveloper.com/wdjobs.html*

Webflow, Inc. . . . . *http://www.webflow.com/jobs.html*

Weidenhammer Systems Corporation . . . . *http://www.hammer.net/jobs/*

Well . . . . *http://www.well.com/jobs.html*

Wells Fargo . . . . *http://wellsfargo.com/jobs/*

Werner Enterprises . . . . *http://www.werner.com/employ.html*

Western Digital . . . . *http://www.wdc.com/employment/*

Whirlpool Corporation . . . . *http://www.whirlpool.com/html/corp/career/*

Whistle Communications . . . . *http://www.whistle.com/employ.html*

White Pine Software, Inc. . . . . *http://www.wpine.com/jobs.html*

Whittman-Hart, Inc. *http://www.whittman-hart.com/carops.html*

Wickes Lumber . . . . *http://www.wickes.com/about/position/index.htm*

Wildfire Communications, Inc. . . . . *http://www.utopia.com/companies/wildfire/jobs.html*

Williams Electronics Games, Inc. . . . . *http://www.pinball.wms.com/employment.html*

Willows Software Corporation . . . . *http://oralce.willows.com/Company/employment.htm*

Wind River Systems . . . . *http://www.wrs.com/wremplop.html*

Wingra Technologies, Inc. . . . . *http://www.wingra.com/jobs*

WK Information Systems Ltd. . . . . *http://www.caseware.com/employ.htm*

Wolf Communications—WorldCom . . . . . *http://www.worldcom.com/private/HR.nsf?OpenDatabase*

Wolfram Research, Inc. . . . . *http://www.wri.com/wolfram/employment.html*

Wollongang Group, Inc. *http://www.attachmate.com/corpinfo/cooljob/cooljob1.htm*

Wonderware Corporation . . . . *http://www.jobinfo.com/wonderware/*

Woodward-Clyde . . . . *http://www.wcc.com/employ.htm*

WorkGroup Technology Corporation, Inc. . . . . *http://www.workgroup.com/jobs.html*

Worldtalk Corporation . . . . *http://www.worldtalk.com/html/employment/jobs.html*

X Consortium *http://www.x.org:80/xjobs/*

XcelleNet, Inc. *http://www1ipi.net/xcellenet/about/index.htm*

XCOM Corporation	http://www.xcom.com/xcom/frames/toc/job.htm
Xerox Coproration	http://www.careermosaic.com/cm/xerox/
Xicor, Inc.	http://www.xicor.com/xicor/menulink/link9.htm
Xilinx, Inc.	http://www.xilinx.com/hr/jobs.htm
Xing Technology Corporation	http://www.xingtech.com/about_xing/jobs.html
Xionics Document Technologies, Inc.	http://www.xionics.com/corporate/employment/
XOMA Corporation	http://www.xoma.com/job/Jobs.html
Xpedite Systems, Inc.	http://www.xpedite.com/jobs.htm
Xronos, Inc.	http://www.xronos.com/pages/opportunities.html
Xylan Corporation	http://www.xylan.com/hr/xylanjob.html
Xylogics, Inc.	http://www.xylogics.com/hr/opportun.htm
Xyplex, Inc.	http://www.xyplex.com/jobs/jobs.html
Xyvision, Inc.	http://www.xyvision.com/CORPORATE/jobs.html
Yahoo	http://www.yahoo.com/docs/hr/
Yellowstone Treatment Centers	http://www.mcn.net./~yellowstone/indexe.html
Your Software Solutions (YSS)	http://helpwanted.com/
ZeitNet	http://www.zeitnet.com/employ/employ.html
Zenith Data Systems	http://www.zdsdirect.com/company/jobs.htm
Zilog, Inc.	http://www.zilog.com/jobs.html
Zitel Corporation	http://www.zitel.com/httdocs/jobsmain.html
Zoom Telephonics, Inc.	http://www.zoomtel.com/jobs.html
Zycad Corporation	http://www.zycad.com:80/jobs/
Zygo Corporation	http://www.zygo.com/employment/openings.htm
ZyXEL, Inc.	http://www.zyxel.com/html/jobs.html

In addition to the search engines discussed in Chapter 10, there are indexes of commercial organizations that can help you find the Internet addresses for thousands of companies. Here are the URLs for a few of them:

- NetSearch
  http://www.ais.net:80/

- Open Market Commercial Sites Index
  http://www.directory.net/

- Thomas Register of American Manufacturers
  http://www.thomasregister.com/

■ *Résumé Databases and Job Banks*

A résumé database is a file of résumés stored electronically on a computer. Employers pay a fee to search the résumé databases on the Internet when they need to fill a particular position. Résumé databases are similar to the ones that are maintained by companies that use applicant tracking systems (scanned résumés, faxed résumés, and e-mailed résumés combined into one database). The difference is that Internet résumé databases are available to any company who will pay the service to access the database, while the other is more proprietary (used only by the one company who owns the database).

Many times, a job bank (like help wanted ads, a place where job openings are posted) also allows you to post your résumé into their résumé database. You will notice in the lists of career-related Internet sites at the end of this chapter that there are times when you can both search for job openings and post your résumé.

So, what types of companies are posting their job openings in these job banks? About 45 percent of them are in the computer, scientific, or technical industries, which means that the job openings they are posting tend to be very technically oriented. As late as 1995, almost all job postings online fell into this category. Today, however, an increasing number of job openings are being posted for middle to upper management positions (45 percent at this writing), with the remaining 10 percent for all other types of positions. These percentages will change daily until all professions are represented. No matter where you fall in this continuum, you will not lose anything by posting your résumé online or searching the lists of available jobs, so don't hesitate to try.

One very important fact to keep in mind, however, is that many large companies will not post their job openings in a multitude of job banks but will, instead, pay only for a hyperlink to their own home page where they will both accept résumés and list job openings. That means, if you are in E-Span or OCC or CareerPath or Monster Board, you must hyperlink to the company profile section and then click on the company name to get to their home page. MCI is one good example of this. Rather than pay 10 or 12 different services to post their job openings (and have to keep each one up to date), they simply update their home page daily with current job openings and pay for a hyperlink from the major sites. Don't neglect this important resource, especially if you are targeting specific companies.

Many professional associations now offer résumé databases and job banks as membership benefits, either through a presence on the Internet, in news-groups, or through bulletin board services. Check your association's newsletter or other correspondence to get their URL or access phone number. The Scholarly Societies Project of the University of Waterloo, Canada, has created a Gopher that provides links to Gophers and other servers of scholarly societies. Access the site at *http://www.lib.uwaterloo.ca/society/overview.html.*

Some of these sites are listed at the end of this chapter under specific industry classifications, but the following list of associations with a presence on the Internet will get you started. Again, if you would like to hyperlink to these sites without typing in the URLs, simply access this list through my home page at *http://members.aol.com/criscito* and click on the association you would like to visit.

Academic Physician and Scientist Association
    of American Medical Colleges (AAMC) . . . . *gopher://aps.acad-psy-sci.com/*
Academy of Advertising . . . . *http://www.utexas.edu/coc/adv/AAA/*
AFL-CIO . . . . *http://www.aflcio.org/*
Air and Waste Management Association . . . . *http://www.awma.org/employment.html*
Air Traffic Controllers Association . . . . *http://www.natca.org/*
Air Transport Association . . . . *http://www.air-transport.org/*
American Association for Blacks in Energy *http://xerxes.nas.edu:70/1/cwse/AABE.html*
American Association for the Advancement of Science . . . . *http://www.aaas.org*
                                                                   http://www.edoc.com/sgcn/Lineads.html
American Association of Black Women
    Entrepreneurs *http://xerxes.nas.edu:70/1/cwse/AABWE.html*

American Association of Finance and Accounting (AAFA) . . . . *http://www.aafa.com/*
American Astronomical Society *http://www.aas.org:80/JobRegister/aasjobs.html*
American Chemical Society . . . . *http://www.acs.org/memgen/employmt/pdb/acsmenu.htm*
http://www.acs.org/
American Communication Association . . . *http://www.uark.edu/depts/comminfo/www/grants.html*
American Council on International Personnel (ACIP) . . . . *http://www.ahrm.org/acip/acip.htm*
American Crystallography Association . . . . *http://www.sdsc.edu/*
American Dairy Science Association . . . . *http://orion.animal.uiuc.edu:80/~adsa/1995/position.html*
American Education Research Association . . . . *http://tikkun.ed.asu.edu/~jobs/joblinks.html*
American Evaluation Association . . . . *http://www.theriver.com/public/aea*
American Heart Association . . . . *http://www.amhrt.org/jobs/index.html*
American Indian Council of Architects
    and Engineers *http://xerxes.nas.edu:70/1/cwse/AICAE.html*
American Indian Science and Engineering Society *http://bioc02.uthscsa.edu/aisesnet.html*
American Industrial Hygiene Association . . . . *http://www.aiha.org/es.html*
American Library Association . . . . *http://www.ala.org/alanow/alanow_home.html*
American Marketing Association . . . . *http://www.ama.org*
American Mathematical Society . . . . *http://www.ams.org/committee/profession/*
American Medical Association . . . . *http://www.ama-assn.org*
American Physical Society . . . . *http://aps.org/jobs/index.html*
American Physiological Association *gopher://oac.hsc.uth.tmc.edu:3300/11/employ*
American Phytopathological Society . . . . *http://www.scisoc.org/career.htm*
American Psychological Society (APS) . . . . *http://www.hanover.edu/psych/APS/aps.html*
American Society for Engineering Education . . . . *http://www.asee.org/asee/publications/*
prism/classifieds/
American Society for Gravitational and Space Biology . . *http://www.indstate.edu/asgsb/index.html*
American Society for Histocompatibility
    and Immunogenetics . . . . *http://www.swmed.edu/home_pages/ASHI/jobs/jobs.htm*
American Society for Horticultural Science *http://www.ashs.org/hortop20.html*
American Society for Mass Spectrometry . . . . *http://www.asms.org/employ.html*
American Society for Quality Control . . . . *http://www.asqc.org/*
American Society of Agricultural Engineers (ASAE) . . . . *http://asae.org/resource/*
http://www.asae.org:80/jobs
American Society of Animal Science . . . . *http://www.asas.org/*
American Society of Ichthyologists
    and Herpetologists . . . . *http://www.utexas.edu/depts/asih/pubs/pubs.html*
American Society of Mechanical Engineers ASMENET . . . . . . *http://www.asme.org/jobs/index.html*
American Society of Plant Physiologists
    (Midwest Section) *http://baby.indstate.edu:80/mwaspp/gradposi.html*
American Statistical Association . . . . *http://www.amstat.org/opportunities/*
http://www.amstat.org/
Architects Institute of America . . . . *http://www.aia.org/*
Association for Computing Machinery . . . . *http://www.acm.org/member_services/career/*
Association for Education in Journalism . . . . *http://www.aejmc.sc.edu/online/home.html*
Association for Education of Young Children . . . . *http://www.america-tomorrow.com/naeyc/*
Association for Higher Education . . . . *http://www.aahe.org/*
Association for Puerto Ricans in Science
    and Engineering *http://xerxes.nas.edu:70/1/cwse/ASPIRA.html*
Association of Advertising Agencies . . . . *http://www.commercepark.com/AAAA/*
Association of American Geographers (AAG) . . . . *http://www.aag.org/jobs.html*
Association of Broadcasters . . . . *http://www.nab.org/*
Association of College Admissions Counselors . . . . *http://www.nacac.com/*
Association of Commonwealth Universities . . . . *http://www.niss.ac.uk/news/acu/acu.html*
Association of Computing Machinery . . . . *http://www.acm.org/*
Association of Developmental Disabilities Council . . . . *http://www.igc.apc.org/NADDC/#NADDC*

Association of Energy Services Professionals . . . . http://www.dnai.com/AESP/jobs.html
Association of Graduate Career Advisory Services (UK) . . . . http://agcas.csu.man.ac.uk/
Association of Independent Insurers . . . . http://www.naii.org/
Association of Muslim Scientists and Engineers http://xerxes.nas.edu:70/1/cwse/AMSE.html
Association of Realtors . . . . http://www.realtor.com/
Association of Science . . . . http://www.nas.edu/
Associations for Architects—The Drawing Board . . . . http://www.dwg.com/associat.htm
Associations Online Directory . . . . http://www.asaenet.org/Gateway/OnlineAssocDir.html#Gs
Astronomical Society . . . . http://www.aas.org/
Athletic Trainers Association . . . . http://www.nata.org/
Audio Engineering Society . . . . http://www.cudenver.edu/aes/career/info.html
Biophysical Society . . . . http://biosci.cbs.umn.edu/biophys/employ.html
Booksellers Association . . . . http://www.bookweb.org/aba/
British Crystallographic Association . . . . http://www.cryst.bbk.ac.uk/BCA/jobs.html
Canadian Association of Career Educators and Employers . . . . . http://www.cacee.com/workweb/
Canadian Bankers Association . . . . http://www.cba.ca/
Careers Service Unit (CSU)—the UK equivalent to the National
        Association of Colleges and Employers (NACE) . . . . http://www.prospects.csu.man.ac.uk/
CEO Club . . . . http://www.ceo-clubs.org/index.html
Certified General Accountants' Association
        of Manitoba (Canada) . . . . http://sulla.cyberstore.ca/Provincial/Manitoba/employ.htm
Chaosgruppe—Association for
        Non-linear Dynamics . . . . http://www.nonlin.tu-muenchen.de/chaos/Jobs/jobs.html
College and University Personnel Association . . . . http://www.ahrm.org/cupa/cupa.htm
Colorado Advanced Technology Institute . . . . http://www.csn.net/pvb/catiempl.html
Compendium of Women's Resources http://www.mit.edu:8001/people/
                                                                sorokin/women/index.html
Council on Foundations . . . . http://www.cof.org/
Directory Publishing Association . . . . http://www.auto-graphics.com/ndpa/ndpahome.htm
Education Association . . . . http://www.nea.org/
Education Research Association . . . . http://tikkun.ed.asu.edu/aera/home.html
Electronic Industries Association . . . . http://www.eia.org/
Employee Assistance Professionals Association . . . . http://www.ahrm.org/eapa/eapa.htm
Employee Benefit Research Institute . . . . http://www.ebri.org
Employee Relocation Council . . . . http://www.erc.org/
Employment Management Association . . . . http://www.ahrm.org/ema/ema.htm
Environmental Associations . . . . http://www.envirobiz.com/
Equipment Leasing Association OnLine . . . . http://www.elaonline.com
European Astronomical Society . . . . telnet://STARJOBS@rlstar.bnsc.rl.ac.uk
European Society of Vascular Surgery . . . . http://www.et.aarhus.ih.dk/~esvs/jobs.html
Federation of International Trade Association . . . . http://www.webhead.com/FITA/home.html
Federation of Paralegal Association . . . . http://www.paralegals.org/
First Pointers for a Women's Guide to the Internet . . . . http://mevard.www.media.mit.edu/
                                                                people/mevard/women.html
Gender Issues in Computer Networking . . . . http://www.careermosaic.com/
Global Environmental Management Initiative . . . . http://www.gemi.org/
Graphic Artists Guild . . . . http://www.gag.org/
History of Science Society . . . . http://weber.u.washington.edu/~hssexec/hss_jobs.html
Human Resources Systems Professionals . . . . http://www.ahrm.org/hrsp/hrsp.htm
IEEE Computer Society . . . . http://www.computer.org/pubs/computer/career/career.htm
Index of Native American Resources on the Internet . . . . http://hanksville.phast.umass.edu/
                                                                misc/NAresources.html
Industrial Hygiene Association . . . . http://www.aiha.org/
Information Technology Association http://206.65.84.24/index.html
Information Technology Talent Association, LLC . . . . http://www.it-ta.com/

Institute for Electric & Electrical Engineers . . . . *http://www.ieee.org/*
Institute of Chemical Engineers . . . . *http://www.che.ufl.edu/WWW-CHE/aiche/*
Insurance Associations . . . . *http://connectyou.com/ins/ap.htm*
International Association of Business Communications . . . . . *http://www.iabc.com//homepage.htm*
International Environmental Information Network . . . . *http://www.envirobiz.com/*
International Interactive Communications Society (IICS) . . . . *http://www.iicsny.org/jobs/*
International Personnel Management Association . . . . *http://www.ahrm.org/ipma/ipma.htm*
International Teleproduction Society . . . . *http://www.itsnet.org/jobs.html*
Internet Professional Association (IPA) . . . . *http://www.ipa.com/*
JOM Minerals, Metals, and Materials Society . . . . *http://www.tms.org/pubs/journals/*
JOM/classifieds.html
Kansas Careers for Women . . . . *http://www-personal.ksu.edu/~dangle/*
Labor Policy Association . . . . *http://www.lpa.org/lpa/index.html*
Lasers and Electro Optics Society (LEOS) . . . . . *http://msrc.wvu.edu/leos/LEOSprof/LEOSprof.html*
Law Organizations . . . . *http://www.txlaw.com/associa.html*
League of Cities . . . . *http://www.cais.com/nlc/*
Library Association . . . . *http://www.ala.org/*
Los Angeles Urban League *http://www.careermosaic.com/cm/ul/ul1.html*
Marketing Science Institute . . . . *http://cism.bus.utexas.edu/ravi/marketing_science.html*
Materials Research Society . . . . *http://dns.mrs.org/awards/fellowship.html*
Mathematical Association of America . . . . *http://www.maa.org/pubs/focus/employ.html*
Medical Library Association . . . . *http://www.kumc.edu/MLA/career.html*
Minority Online Information Service . . . . *http://web.fie.com/web/mol/*
National Academy of Sciences, National Academy of
Engineering, Institute of Medicine, and National
Research Council Home Page . . . . *http://www.nas.edu/*
National Alumni Placement Association . . . . *http://www.career.com*
National Association for Equal Opportunity
in Higher Education *http://xerxes.nas.edu:70/1/cwse/NAFEO.html*
National Association for Minorities in
Engineering Program Administrators *http://xerxes.nas.edu:70/1/cwse/NAMEPA.html*
National Association of Black Consulting Engineers *http://xerxes.nas.edu:70/1/*
cwse/NABCE.html
National Association of Colleges and Employers—NACE . . . . *http://www.jobweb.org*
National Association of Purchasing Management . . . . *http://catalog.com/napmsv/jobs.htm*
National Chicano Council on Higher Education *http://xerxes.nas.edu:70/1/cwse/NCCHE.html*
National Council of Negro Women *http://xerxes.nas.edu:70/1/cwse/NCNW.html*
National Employee Services and Recreation Association . . . *http://www.ahrm.org/nesra/nesra.htm*
National Foreign Trade Council, Inc. *http://www.ahrm.org/nftc/nftc.htm*
National Homeworkers Association . . . . *http://www.homeworkers.com/*
National Multimedia Association of America . . . . *http://www.nmaa.org/nmaa/jobbank.htm*
National Network of Minority Women in Science *http://xerxes.nas.edu:70/1/cwse/MWIS.html*
National Organization for the Professional Advancement of
Black Chemists and Chemical Engineers . . . *http://xerxes.nas.edu:70/1/cwse/NOBCChE.html*
National Puerto Rican Coalition, Inc. *http://xerxes.nas.edu:70/1/cwse/NPRC.html*
National Society of Black Engineers . . . . *http://www.nsbe.org*
National Society of Professional Engineering HP . . . . *http://www.nspe.org*
National Standards Institute . . . . *http://www.ansi.org/home.html*
National Urban League . . . . *http://www.nul.org/*
Network Professionals Associations . . . . *http://www.npanet.org/*
New Market Forum . . . . *http://www.newmarket-forum.com/*
Newspaper Association of America . . . . *http://www.naa.org/*
Optical Society of America, Optics Net . . . . *http://www.osa.org/*
Organizations Encouraging Women in Science and Engineering . . . . . . *http://www.nas.edu/cwse/*
Physical Society . . . . *http://aps.org/*

Physical Therapy Association . . . . *http://apta.edoc.com/apta/*
Poultry Science Association *http://gallus.tamu.edu/1h/psa/psaplacement.html*
Precision Machined Products Association . . . . *http://www.pmpa.org/car/career.htm*
Press Club . . . . *http://town.hall.org/places/npc/*
Professional and Student Journalism Organizations . . . . *http://www.journalism.sfsu.edu/*
 www/orgs/orgs.htm
Public Health Association . . . . *http://www.apha.org/*
Public Transit Association . . . . *http://www.apta.com/*
Public Works Association . . . . *http://www.tfs.net/apwa/*
Royal Society of Chemistry (UK) *http://chemistry.rsc.org/rsc/jobs3.htm*
Saludos Web: Hispanic Careers, Employment and Culture . . . . . . *http://www.hooked.net/saludos/*
Scholarly Society Project via the University
 of Waterloo, Canada . . . . *http://www.lib.uwaterloo.ca/society/*
Society for Cinema Studies . . . . *http://www.sa.ua.edu/TCF/teach/employ/scsjob.htm*
Society for Civil Engineers . . . . *http://www.asce.org/*
Society for Experimental Mechanics . . . . *http://www.sem.bethel.ct.us/sem/jobs/jobs.html*
Society for Human Resource Management . . . . *http://www.ahrm.org/shrm/shrm.htm*
Society for Human Resources Professionals . . . . *http://www.shrm.org/*
Society for Industrial and Applied Mathematics (SIAM) . . *http://www.siam.org/profops/profops.htm*
Society for Technical Communications . . . . *http://stc.org/*
Society of Competitive Intelligence Professionals (SCIP) . . . . *http://www.scip.org/*
Society of Hispanic Professional Engineers *http://xerxes.nas.edu:70/1/cwse/SHPE.html*
Society of Mechanical Engineers . . . . *http://www.asme.org/index.html*
Society of Mexican American Engineers
 and Scientists *http://xerxes.nas.edu:70/1/cwse/MAES.html*
Society of Professional Journalists . . . . *http://town.hall.org/places/spj/*
Society of Women Engineers . . . . *http://www.swe.org*
Software Publishers Association . . . . *http://www.spa.org/*
Southeastern Software Association (SSA) . . . . *http://www.sesoft.org/news/joblink.html*
Special Libraries Association (SLA) . . . . *http://www.indiana.edu/~slajob/*
Victoria Freenet Association *gopher://freenet.victoria.bc.ca/11/business*
Women Homepage *http://www.mit.edu:8001/people/*
 sorokin/women/index.html
Women in Computer Science and
 Electrical Engineering . . . . *http://www.cs.berkeley.edu/*
Women in Computer Science and Engineering . . *http://www.ai.mit.edu/people/ellens/gender.html*
Writers Union . . . . *http://www.nwu.org/nwu/*
Yahoo's Listing of Professional Associations . . . . *http://www.yahoo.com/Economy/*
 Organizations/Professional/

■ Career-related Internet Sites

There are thousands of sites on the Internet where you can either post your résumé or search for job openings. All of the URLs listed here were current at the time this book was published, but the Internet is ever changing, so be prepared for some dead sites. Remember that you can try to delete all of the Internet address after the *.com* and attempt to reach the home page. Then you can hyperlink deeper into the site. If that doesn't work, it is also possible to visit the following meta-sites to find lists of career-related Internet addresses:

- ■ Best Bets from the Net
 http://asa.ugl.lib.umich.edu/chdocs/employment/

- Career Net – Career Resource Center
  http://www.careers.org

- Career Paradise
  http://www.emory.edu/CAREER/

- The Catapult
  http://www.jobweb.org

- Jobs and Career Information
  gopher://main.morris.org/11gopher_root%3a%5b_jobs%5d

- Jobs and Employment
  gopher://academic.cc.colorado.edu/11%5b_library._data.jobs%5d

- ProType, Ltd.
  http://members.aol.com/criscito

- RiceInfo
  http://riceinfo.rice.edu/Internet/subject.html

- The Riley Guide
  http://www.jobtrak.com/jobguide/

- RPI Career Resources
  http://www.rpi.edu/dept/cdc/

Most of the firms that are searching the Internet for potential employees are the nation's largest companies with offices in multiple locations throughout the United States and the world. However, as the résumé databases and job banks become bigger and represent more geographically diverse talent, small and medium companies will begin to use these resources first before paying thousands of dollars to advertise job openings in local and national newspapers.

❑ *The Big Ten*

The sources listed in the rest of this chapter are divided by industry or type. However, this first section lists what I call "The Big Ten." These sites have either been around for a while or are so large that they are worth checking out first. They tend to have more jobs listed, represent more companies, and have larger résumé databases, which attract even more companies.

Adams JobBank Online . . . . *http://www.adamsonline.com*
Telephone . . . . (617) 767-8100

This site is brought to you by Adams Media Corporation, the publisher of the JobBank books. Posting your résumé is as simple as creating an e-mail message. Their form allows you to type (or cut and paste) your cover letter into the message screen and then attach your ASCII text résumé file. There is no need to fill in tedious boxes of information. Current job openings in the job bank are divided into industry categories and are accessed through hypertext links. Jobs can be sorted by employer. Also available at the Adams site are conferences; company profiles; a section for college students, women, and minorities; a talent bank; and a resource for ordering the Adams career books.

America's Job Bank . . . . *http://www.ajb.dni.us/*

A service of the United States Department of Labor and more than 1,800 state Employment Service offices, America's Job Bank has more job listings than any other site on the Internet—at this writing, about 250,000 jobs with 1,000 jobs being added every day. About 5 percent of the jobs listed are in government and the rest are in the private sector. There is no charge to either the employers who list their job vacancies or to job seekers, because each state's Employment Service program is funded through unemployment insurance taxes paid by employers. Jobs can be searched by job title, job order number, or specific code from either the Occupational Employment Survey, Dictionary of Occupational Titles, or the military. There is a résumé database at this site called America's Talent Bank.

CareerMosaic J.O.B.S. . . . . *http://www.careermosaic.com*

E-mail for comments . . . . *feedback@pa.hodes.com*

CareerMosaic was created by Bernard Hodes Advertising, Inc., and is one of the easiest résumé databases and job bank sites to use. Résumés remain in the database for 90 days and must be reposted after that time period. This isn't a difficult chore, however, since CareerMosaic allows you to cut and paste your ASCII text file résumé directly into their form without filling in little boxes. When you search the job database, results are presented in a single line format with hyperlinks to detailed job descriptions, allowing a "quick and dirty" perusal. Listings are sorted by date posted, which makes it easy to focus on the newest additions. The site tends to move quickly and its searches are very flexible. Besides the J.O.B.S. database (which, by the way, stands for Job Opportunities By Search), there is a Usenet page called *jobs.offered* that allows you to perform full-text searches of jobs listed in regional and occupational newsgroups in the United States and abroad. This site is continuously indexed and saves you from having to subscribe to each newsgroup separately. As with most of the large job banks, CareerMosaic has an employer profile section where you can link directly to hundreds of potential employers. In addition to job resources, check out the online job fairs, career resource center, college connection, and the human resource professional plaza.

CareerPath . . . . *http://www.careerpath.com*

E-mail for questions or comments . . . . *cpwebmaster@careerpath.com*

CareerPath is a compilation of more than 100,000 classified job advertisements from some of the country's largest metropolitan newspapers, including the *Los Angeles Times*, *The New York Times*, the *Boston Globe*, the *Chicago Tribune*, and other newspapers owned by Times Mirror. It posts more than 250,000 new jobs on the Internet every month and is updated daily by participating newspapers. You can search the database by newspaper, job category, and keyword. At this writing, CareerPath's users conducted nearly 3½ million searches every month. There is no résumé database, but this is a very useful site if you are looking for a job in a major metropolitan area of the country.

E-Span . . . . *http://www.espan.com*

Through CompuServe . . . . *GO ESPAN*

E-mail your ASCII résumé directly . . . . *resume@espan3.espan.com*

Founded in 1991, E-Span is a pioneer in online employment recruiting. The majority of résumés in their database represent job seekers who are well-educated (76 percent have a BA/BS degree or higher), mostly male (60 percent), and in their prime career years (52 percent between 20 and 40). E-Span is accessible at no charge to job seekers and is searchable by category or geography. Employers pay to advertise their openings (more than 18,000 at this writing) and can search the résumé database 24 hours a day. Only those companies that advertise can search the résumé database. E-Span includes position descriptions from thousands of U.S. and international companies representing virtually every industry, including AT&T, CompuServe, Quaker Oats, Lotus, Disney, American Express, IBM, Ciber National, Federated Systems Group, ITT Corporation, Keane, Medi-Span, and Signet Bank. Ads are updated twice a week and are organized by category (medicine, engineering, education, finance, government, pharmaceuticals, manufacturing, computer programming, management, sales, business systems, and human resources). Job seekers can input their résumés directly at the Internet site into an electronic form or simply e-mail their résumé to the address shown above. In addition to a résumé database and job bank, you will also find in-depth career counseling sections, including NAS, the nation's largest HR communications company, and company profiles. There are even hyperlinks to articles by experts in job hunting and to the Occupational Outlook Handbook, salary guides, interviewing strategies, motivational support, and advice on creating résumés. The Career Companion provides links to more than 4,000 sites, including 800 newspapers, many of which post their employment classifieds online. E-Span also offers a Career Mail service that automatically e-mails job listings that match your search criteria on a weekly basis.

JOBTRAK . . . . *http://www.jobtrak.com*

E-mail for questions . . . . *www@jobtrak.com*

JOBTRAK has partnered with more than 400 college and university career centers to provide their students and alumni with job listings and a résumé database. In order to access the job bank and enter your résumé from a particular campus, you must contact the college career center for a password. Most career centers allow pathway access from on-campus computers, which doesn't require a password. JOBTRAK is provided free of charge to schools, and employers pay a nominal fee. There is no charge to the job seeker. More than 2,100 new job openings are posted each day, and more than 200,000 employers use JOBTRAK to target college graduates or students. This is a particularly good site for finding an internship or part-time student opportunity, although it is not limited to these types of positions. You may enter your résumé into JOBTRAK's résumé database by typing it directly online or cutting and pasting the information into the online form. When you search the job bank, there is a box at the bottom of most listings where you can enter your résumé number so it will be forwarded directly to the employer. Your résumé remains in the résumé database for 90 days, but this time can be extended by simply updating or reposting your résumé at any time.

JobWeb . . . . *http://www.jobweb.org*

JobWeb is a product of the National Association of Colleges and Employers (NACE), a nonprofit professional association of more than 1,700 colleges and universities and in excess of 1,400 employer organizations. It is an excellent place to search for jobs aimed at college graduates and experienced professionals. It has direct links to internships and co-op opportunities and federal government jobs. There is a great deal of content at this site for researching cutting-edge employment topics, including legal issues in employment, job search techniques, hiring practices, and trends. The *JobPlace* discussion forum and bulletin board area are great ways to ask questions of the nation's top college career service and company human resources professionals. NACE took over the *Catapult* from Williams and Mary College, which is a general resource for career-related sites on the Internet.

MedSearch America . . . . *http:/www.medsearch.com*

E-mail your ASCII résumé directly . . . . *office@medsearch.com*

MedSearch America is your connection to health care employers with openings around the corner or around the globe. This site also offers career direction, industry analysis, and much more. You can post your résumé at no charge for thousands of employers and recruiters to see, and you can search thousands of job postings for positions that you find interesting. You can input your résumé into their résumé entry form for free or pay $30 and send it via e-mail to the address listed above. Do not send your résumé as an e-mail attachment. The résumé must be part of the e-mail message itself. Complete instructions for submitting your résumé via either method are given at the site. Your résumé is kept in the résumé database for four months, but you can update or remove your online résumé at any time. Many of the jobs in the database have direct response links where you can send inquiries directly to the recruiter who placed the ad.

Monster Board . . . . *http://www.monster.com*

E-mail your ASCII résumé directly . . . . *resumes@monster.com*

Owned by TMP Worldwide, the Monster Board is an interactive service listing more than 55,000 job opportunities. You can limit your job searches by industry, discipline, location, title, or company. You may enter your résumé at their site by filling out a form or e-mail it to the address above; however, the only way to get your résumé into *Resume City* is to fill out their form. Many sites on the Internet lack a help feature for when you experience problems, but not the Monster Board. You can hyperlink to their help section where you will find a page with complete instructions for common problems people experience when entering their résumés online. The site has hyperlinks to employer profiles and places where you can conduct extensive research on employers worldwide. The *Corporate Sphere* is a place where recruiters, hiring managers, and human resource professionals can find Monster Board products, rates, and success stories. In fact, if you want to get psyched up for your online job search, the success stories can give you a lot of hope. The Monster Board also has special "communities" for entrepreneurs and franchisees, health care professionals, CEOs and executives, human resource professionals, and entry-level job seekers. When you hyperlink to *Career Safari*, you will find special shortcuts to databases that allow you to search for job opportunities in Australia, the United Kingdom, and Quebec, a direct link to MedSearch for health care employees, and special categories just for entry-level opportunities and human resource careers. The *Cool Works* hyperlink from this site has information about jobs in national parks, resorts, cruise ships, camps, and ski resorts, and for volunteers and owners of recreational vehicles.

Online Career Center . . . . *http://www.occ.com*

Through America Online . . . . *GO CAREERS*

E-mail your ASCII résumé directly . . . . *occ-resumes@occ.com*

Online Career Center (OCC) has a large presence in America Online's GO CAREERS and is accessible through all of the commercial online services in addition to direct access through the Internet, Usenet, Gopher, and Telnet. You can search for jobs by state, city, or industry. In addition to jobs, OCC provides company profiles, a recruiting center, and a résumé database. You can e-mail your résumé at no charge directly to the address above in ASCII text format, or there are special instructions for sending HTML résumés. You may also enter your résumé online into the OCC Internet database. Regardless of how you send the résumé, it is kept in the database for 90 days and must be re-entered when the time expires. To change or update your résumé, you simply re-enter it and the previous one will be deleted. You can remove your résumé by sending an e-mail message to *occ100@occ.com*.

❏ *All the Rest*

These sites, as well as all of the others listed in this book, are kept up to date at my home page on the Internet *(http://members.aol.com/criscito)* on a regular basis. By accessing this page, you can hyperlink to the sites without typing in URLs. We are constantly looking for new Internet locations that post jobs, accept résumés, and provide career advice. If you discover a particularly interesting one, feel free to send me an e-mail message at *criscito@aol.com* and I will add it to the hyperlinks.

All Industries

100 Hot Jobs *http://www.100hot.com/jobs/*

1st Steps: Employment and Recruiting News . . . . *http://www.interbiznet.com/hunt/*

24 Hours, Recorded Job Lines for the
     San Francisco Bay Area . . . . *http://www.webcom.com/~rmd/index_body.html*

4Work *http://4work.com*

A+ On-Line Résumés *http://www.hway.net:80/olresume*

AAA Résumé . . . . *http://www.infi.net/~resume/upload.html*

Access Career and Job Resources . . . . *http://www.hawk.igs.net/jobresources*

Acorn Career Counseling . . . . *http://www1.mhv.net:80/~acorn/Acorn.html*

Adams Job Bank Online . . . . *http://www.adamsonline.com*

ADEPT Job Search . . . . *http://www.adeptinc.com/openjobs/jobcateg.htm*

AdOne Classified Network(10) . . . . *http://www.adone.com*

AdSearch . . . . *http://www.adsearch.com*

Advanced Staffing . . . . *http://www.adstaff.com*

AdvanceTech . . . . *http://www.swcp.com/~mharris*

AK Jobnet, Austin Knight Company . . . . *http://www.ak.com.au/akjobnet.html*

Alabama Jobs . . . . *http://www.the-matrix.com/ph/ph.html*

Alaska—Anchorage Daily News . . . . *http://www.adn.com/*

Alaskan Jobs . . . . *http://www.state.ak.us/local/akpages/ADMIN/rbtitl.htm*

American Council on International Personnel . . . . *http://ahrm.org/acip/acip.htm*

American Employment Weekly . . . . *http://branch.com/aew*

America's Help Wanted . . . . *http://jobquest.com/*

America's Job Bank . . . . *http://www.ajb.dni.us/*

APK Net, Ltd. *http://www.apk.net:80/main.html*

Appointments Section—Jobs & Careers <The> . . . . *http://taps.com*

Archives of the French Jobs Newsgroups *http://www.loria.fr:80/news/fr.jobs.d.html*
                                                      http://www.loria.fr:80/news/fr.jobs.offres.html

Arizona Careers Online . . . . *http://amsquare.com/america/arizona.html*

Asia-Net or AsiaNet, JapanNet . . . . *http://www.asia-net.com*

Asian Career Web . . . . *http://www.rici.com/acw/*

ASPIRE . . . . *http://www.indiana.edu/~intlcent/aspire/*

Association of Commonwealth Universities . . . . . . *http://www.niss.ac.uk/noticeboard/acu/acu.html*

Association of Graduate Career Advisory Services (UK) . . . . *http://agcas.csu.man.ac.uk/*

Atlanta Web Guide . . . . *http://www.webguide.com/*

AUSNet . . . . *http://www.world.net/cgi-bin/ausnet_jobs*

Austin, Texas Job Listings . . . . *http://www.ci.austin.tx.us/*

Australian Résumé Server . . . . *http://www.herenow.com.au/*

Bankey Temporary Services . . . . *http://gwabbs.com/~bankey/tempagency.htm*

Bark, Foehr und Partner GmbH,
     Personalberatung (Germany) . . . . *http://ourworld.compuserve.com/homepages/barkjobs/*

Bay Area Job Location Finder . . . . *http://none.coolware.com/jobs/location.html*

Bay Area Jobs . . . . *http://www.sonic.net/~allan/ba_jobs.html*

Best Bets from the Net: Job Search *http://www.lib.umich.edu:80/chdocs/employment/*

Best Jobs in the USA Today . . . . *http://www.bestjobsusa.com/top.htm*

BFSI Internet Marketing . . . . *http://www.bfservs.com/states.html*

Boldface Jobs . . . . *http://www.boldfacejobs.com/*

Boston Area Career Opportunities . . . . *http://www.winterwyman.com/*

Boston Economy . . . . *http://www.std.com/NE/boseconomy.html*

Boston Globe's Help Wanted . . . . *http://www.boston.com/helpwanted/boshelw.htm*
                                               http://www.boston.com

Boston Job Bank . . . . *http://www.bostonjobs.com*

Bullseye Job Shop . . . . *http://interoz.com*

Byron Employment—Australia . . . . *http://www.byron.com.au/employment_australia/*

California Career and Employment Center . . . . *http://www.webcom.com/~career/*

California Polytechnic State University—Summer Jobs *gopher://gopher.calpoly.edu/11/campus_info/*
campus_serv_and_fac/career_services

Canada Employment Centre . . . . *http://ein.ccia.st-thomas.on.ca/agencies/cec/index.html*

Canada Employment Centre in Nanaimo . . . . *http://www.island.net/~hrcnan/emp.html*

Canadian Résumé Centre . . . . *http://netaccess.on.ca/~resume/*

Career Action Center . . . . *http://www.careeraction.org*

Career Advice . . . . *http://www.review.com/career/career_homepage.html*

Career Advisory Service (UK) . . . . *http://www.aston.ac.uk/~haxbype/cas-home.html*

Career and Labour Market Information . . . . *http://www.etc.bc.ca/provdocs/careers/home.html*

Career and Placement Services (CaPS) . . . . *gopher://chinchaga.ucs.ualberta.ca/*

Career and Résumé Management for the 21st Century! *http://crm21.com*

Career Atlas for the Road . . . . *http://www.isdn.net/nis/*

Career Blazers . . . . *http://www.compu-link.com*

Career Center (from the Internet Professional) . . . . *http://www.netline.com/Career/career.html*

Career Center for Workforce Diversity, Equal
    Opportunity Publications, Inc. (EOP) . . . . *http://www.eop.com*

Career Centre—Canada . . . . *http://qb.island.net/~careers/*

Career Connections . . . . *http://www.career.com/*

Career-Connector . . . . *http://www.wons.com/cc/*

Career Counseling—LITE . . . . *http://www.execpc.com/~cclite/*

Career Dynamics Inc. . . . . *http://www.webspan.com/*

Career Exchange . . . . *http://www.careerexchange.com/*

Career Fairs <The> *http://www.cweb.com/employersandorgs/lendmangrp/home1.htm*

Career Information System . . . . *http://career-info.uoregon.edu/whoweaare.html*

Career Magazine . . . . *http://www.careermag.com*

Career Management International . . . . *http://www.cmi-lmi.com/*

Career Mapper . . . . *http://www.careermapper.com/*

Career Mentor . . . . *http://www.opendoor.com/*

Career Opportunities in Singapore . . . . *http://www.singapore-careers.com*

Career Paths . . . . *http://www.etc.bc.ca/~szukiwsk/yes/Career/p1.html*

Career Quest (Japan) . . . . *http://www.venture-web.or.jp/axiom/axiom_english/index.html*

Career Resource Home Page . . . . *http://www.rip.edu/dept/cdc/homepage.html*

Career Shop . . . . *http://www.careershop.com/*

Career Talk . . . . *http://www.careertalk.com*

Career Toolbox . . . . *http://careertoolbox.com/*

Career Transitions . . . . *http://www.bfservs.com*

Career Way . . . . *http://Internet-plaza.net/streets/career.html*

CareerBuilder . . . . *http://careerbuilder.com/*

CareerChina, Career China . . . . *http://www.globalvillager.com/villager/CC.html*

CareerCity Jobs . . . . *http://www.careercity.com/jobs/*

CareerLynx–USA . . . . *http://gold.lsn.com*

CareerMart . . . . *http://www.careermart.com*

CareerMosaic . . . . *http://www.careermosaic.com*

CareerNet, Career Resource Center *http://www.careers.org:80/catg/02jobs-05.htm*

CareerPath . . . . *http://www.careerpath.com*

Careers On-Line . . . . *http://www.disserv.stu.umn.edu*

Careers Online (Australia) . . . . *http://www.ideaf.com/jobs/pps.htm*
http://www.careersonline.com.au/

CareerSearch—Jobs Online . . . . *http://www.greatinfo.com/business_cntr/career.html*

CareerSite . . . . *http://www.careersite.com*

CareerSurf . . . . *http://careersurf.com*

CareerWeb, Landmark Communications . . . . *http://www.cweb.com*

Case Western Reserve University—
    Part-time/Summer Job List . . . . *http://www.cwru.edu/CWRU/Admin/cpp/summer.html*

Catapult, Career Service Professionals Homepage . . . *http://www.jobweb.org/catapult/catapult.htm*
http://www.wm.edu/catapult/catapult.html

Chattanooga Free-Press . . . . *http://www.chatpub.com*

Chicago Tribune Career Finder . . . . *http://www.chicago.tribune.com/home.html*

Chicano/Latino Electronic Network (CLENet) *gopher://latino.sscnet.ucla.edu/11/*
The%20News%20Center/Job%20Announcements
gopher://latino.sscnet.ucla.edu:70/11/Employment%20Center/Job%20Announcements/

City of Morgantown Jobs . . . . *http://www.dmssoft.com/city/jobs.htm*

City of Oklahoma City, Oklahoma . . . . *http://www.ionet.net/~okcpio/index.html*

CityLink *http://www.NeoSoft.com:80/citylink/*

CityNet . . . . *http://www.city.net/*

Classifieds on the Gate . . . . *http://www.sfgate.com/classifieds*

Clearinghouse for Subject-Oriented Internet . . . . *http://www.lib.umich.edu/chhome.html*
Resource Guides *gopher://una.hh.lib.umich.edu/inetdirs/*

CLNET . . . . *http://latino.sscnet.ucla.edu/*

College Grad Job Hunter . . . . *http://www.collegegrad.com*

College of St. Catherine—Internships *gopher://gopher.stkate.edu/11/dept/career/intshp*

Colorado–New Mexico Job Listings . . . . *http://www.dirs.com/employ/colnm*

Colorado, State of . . . . *http://www.state.co.us/*

Colton Information Technology . . . . *http://www.coltonexec.com*

Commercial Sites Index from Open Market . . . . *http://www.directory.net/*

Community Workplace . . . . *http://galaxy.einet.net/galaxy/Community/Workplace.html*

Coolware Classifieds . . . . *http://www.coolware.com/jobs/jobs/html*

CoolWorks Job Bulletin Board . . . . *http://www.coolworks.com/showme/*

Cornell University—Internships and Summer Jobs . . . . *http://student-jobs.ses.cornell.edu/jobs/*

Corporate Staffing Center, Inc. . . . . *http://www.corporate-staffing.com/csc/hunt/html*

CyberDyne CS Ltd. *http://www.demon.co.uk/cyberdyne/cyber.html*

Dallas Morning News . . . . *http://www.pic.net/tdmn/tdmn.html*

Dawson & Dawson Consultants . . . . *http://www.dawson-dawson.com*

DC's Résumé Net . . . . *http://www.resume.net/*

DC's Site for On-Line Résumés . . . . *http://www.intr.net/*

De Carrierebank (Netherlands) . . . . *http://www.carrierebank.nl*

Decisive Quest . . . . *http://www.decisivequest.com*

Definitive Internet Career Guide <The> . . *http://phoenix.placement.oakland.edu/career/internet.htm*

DejaNews . . . . *http://www.dejanews.com/*

Department of Employment *http://161.7.163.2/*

Department of Employment (Idaho) . . . . *http://www.doe.state.id.us/*

Department of Employment (Wyoming) . . . . *http://wyjobs.state.wy.us/*

Department of Employment and Training (Rhode Island) . . . . *http://www.det.state.ri.us/*

Department of Employment, New Jersey's Job Search . . . . *http://nj.jobsearch.org/*

Department of Employment Relations (Wisconsin) *http://badger.state.wi.us:70/1/*

Department of Employment Security (Utah) . . . . *http://udesb.state.ut.us/*

Department of Employment Security (Tennessee)*http://www.state.tn.us/other/empsec/tdeshome.htm*

Department of Industry, Labor and Human Relations,
Wisconsin Employment Bureau . . . . *http://badger.state.wi.us/agencies/dilhr/*

Department of Labor (U.S.) . . . . *http://www.dol.gov/*

Department of Labor (Louisiana) . . . . *http://www.state.la.us/*

Department of Library Services: Sailor . . . . *http://sailor.lib.md.us/*

Development Dimensions International . . . . *http://ddiworld.com/index.html*

Direct Marketing World Job Center . . . . *http://www.dmworld.com*
http://mainsail.com/jobs.html

Directory of Electronic Journals, Newsletters, and Academic . . . . *gopher://arl.cni.org*
Discussions Lists (Association of Research Libraries) select *Scholarly Communication*

Disability Services Careers On-Line . . . . *http://www.disserv.stu.umn.edu/TC/Grants/COL/*

Diverse Employment Industries . . . . *http://www.cfonline.com/cli/jobs/diverse/diverse.htm*

Drake University—Summer Jobs . . . . *http://www.drake.edu/stulife/carsum.html*
Drexel University—Résumés . . . . *http://cmc.www.drexel.edu/*
Dun and Bradstreet on Finding a Job . . . . *http://www.dbisna.com/dbis/jobs/vjobhunt.htm*
Eclectic International Executive Search . . . . *http://www.cyber.nl/eclectic/*
Education & Career Center <The> . . . . *http://www.petersons.com*
Electronic Job Match International . . . . *http://www.ejs@tnc.com/*
Emory University/Career Paradise . . . . *http://www.emory.edu/*
EMPLOI @ . . . . *http://www.login.net/emploi-a/public_html/*
Employease Benefits Network . . . . *http://www.eease.com/novaindex.html*
Employment and Business Opportunities Online . . . . *http://www.ebom.com/*
Employment Channel . . . . *http://www.employ.com*
Employment Counseling Services, Inc. *http://amsquare.com/america/amerway/ajob4u/*
Employment Depot . . . . *http://www.employmentdepot.com/*
Employment Edge . . . . *http://sensemedia.net/employment.edge*
Employment Network—People Bank *http://194.73.171.131/pbank/owa/pbk06w00.main*
Employment Online . . . . *http://www.nando.net/classads/employment/*
Employment Opportunities in Australia . . . . *http://employment.com.au/index.html*
Employment Opportunities in New York City . . . . *http://www.panix.com/clay/nyc/*
Employment Post . . . . *http://world.net/emp-post/welcome.html*
Engine Room (UK and Europe) <The>, iWEB . . . . *http://www.iweb.co.uk/iwsearch.html*
Entry-Level Job Seeker Assistant <The> . . . . *http://members.aol.com/dylander/jobhome.html*
EPage Classifieds . . . . *http://www.ep.com*
E.R. States & Associates . . . . *http://www.ceo-online.com/erstates*
Eurojobs On-line Belgium . . . . *http://www.belganet.be/belganet/jobs/*
ExeCon . . . . *http://www.execonweb.com*
Exec-U-Net . . . . *http://www.execunet.com*
Executive Taskforce . . . . *http://exectask.co.nz/*
Experience on Demand . . . . *http://www.experienceondemand.com/*
Fairfax JobMarket (Australia) . . . . *http://www.market.fairfax.com.au/bin/*
iaquery?NS-use-frames=0&NS-search-pat=/Fairfax/jobs/NS-query.pat
Finding and Getting a Job . . . . *http://edie.cprost.sfu.ca/~gophers/find.html*
Focus International Career Services . . . . *http://www.unige.ch/focus/*
FOREM—Work Information System (Belgium) . . . . *http://www.forem.be/*
Forty Plus . . . . *http://www.hal-pc.org/~sid/40plus.html*
Fournier Transformation (Visual FoxPro Yellow Pages) . . . . *http://www.transformation.com/*
Freenets and Bulletin Boards via Eastern Kentucky University *gopher://acs.eku.edu:70*
select *Explore the Internet*
Freenets via the University of Colorado, Boulder . . . . *gopher://gopher.Colorado.EDU/*
select *Other Gophers (by subject)*
Future Access Employment Guide *http://futureaccess.com:80/employ.html*
Future Resource Systems, Inc. . . . . *http://www.webb.com/future*
Galaxy at Trade Wave <The> . . . . *http://galaxy.einet.net/galaxy.html*
Get a Job! . . . . *http://www.getajob.com*
GetNet International—Employment . . . . *http://www.getnet.com/endeavor/*
Getting Past Go: A Survival Guide for College   *http://www.lattanze.loyola.edu:80/mongen/home.html*
Global Job Services . . . . *http://www.indirect.com/www/dtomczyk/*
Global Marketing Strategies . . . . *http://www.ioa.com/home/kelbell/*
Global Net's Latin American Career Center
    (Bolsa de Trabajo Global Net) . . . . *http://www.bolsadetrabajo.com*
GLOBEnet—Canada . . . . *http://www.theglobeandmail.com/*
GO2: Guardian OnLine Jobs . . . . *http://www.guardian.co.uk/jobs/jobs.html*
Good Works . . . . *http://www.essential.org/goodworks/*
Gordon Library Home Page,
    Worcester Polytechnic Institute . . . . *http://www.WPI.EDU/Academics/IMS/Library/*
GraduNet (UK) . . . . *http://www.gradunet.co.uk/*

GrapeVine, Grapevine Network . . . . *http://job.index.com/*
Greater Columbus Freenet . . . . *gopher://gizmo.freenet.columbus.oh.us*
Grinwis & Partners (Netherlands) . . . . *http://www.iway.nl/grinwis/*
Guide to Working Overseas . . . . *http://www.magi.com/~issi/*
Haskins & Roache . . . . . *http://ourworld.compuserve.com/homepages/James_Haskins/haskins.htm*
HeadHunt Korea . . . . *http://www.headhunt.co.kr*
H.E.A.R.T.—Career Connection's
     On-Line Information System . . . . *http://www.career.com/PUB/searchmenu.html*
HEC Group . . . . *http://hec-group.com*
Hiring Assistant and Placements Program . . . . *http://www.sonic.net/~richw/zjobapps.html#top*
Hiring Employers . . . . *http://phoenix.placement.oakland.edu/career/career.htm*
H.L. Yoh . . . . *http://www.hlyoh.com/*
Hong Kong Jobs . . . . *http://www.hkjobs.com*
Hongkong Standard . . . . *http://www.hkstandard.com/online/job/hksjob.htm*
Hoover's Online . . . . *http://www.hoovers.com/*
Houston Chronicle Interactive, Houston Chronicle . . . . *http://classifieds.astranet.com/*
                                                                           HCI/bin/nclassy.x/hciBHM06
Houston Employment Opportunities . . . . *http://www.wt.net/cgi/bb/bbb.pl?hccom_job*
HR Headquarters . . . . *http://www.hrhq.com/*
Human Element Network . . . . *http://mindlink.net/vci/thehp.htm*
Human Resource Store <The> . . . . *http://www.mcs.com/~jmruh*
Human Resources Development Canada—Metro Toronto . . *http://www.the-wire.com/hrdc/jobs.html*
Huntington Group's Career Network <The>, CareerWeb . . . . *http://sgx.com/cw/*
Hytelnet . . . . *http://galaxy.einet.net/hytelnet/HYTELNET.html*
Ian Martin Limited . . . . *http://www.iml.com*
Idaho Department of Employment, Idaho Jobs . . . . *http://www.doe.state.id.us/occmain.htm*
IDL Solutions . . . . *http://www.idl.com/*
Impact Online . . . . *http://www.impactonline.org/*
Index of Delaware Web Sites from Delaware
     Technical and Community College . . . . *http://www.dtcc.edu/delaware/*
Index of Native American Resources on the Internet . . . . . *http://www.hanksville.phast.umass.edu/*
                                                                           misc.NAresources.html
Indiana Jobs . . . . *http://www.inetdirect.net/*
Indiana University School of Public and
     Environmental Affairs—Internships . . . . *http://www.indiana.edu/~speacare/intern.html*
InfoLink HIRE . . . . *http://cystop.com/home-links.htm*
Information Network of Kansas . . . . *http://www.ink.org*
InJersey . . . . *http://www.injersey.com*
InstaMatch Resume Database . . . . *http://www.instamatch.com*
IntelliMatch . . . . *http://www.intellimatch.com*
Inter-Links Employment Resources . . . . *http://www.nova.edu/Inter-Links/employment.html*
International Internship Directory . . . . *gopher://gopher.clemson.edu/*
International Job Centers . . . . *http://members.tripod.com/~IJC/index.html*
Internet Career Connection (Help Wanted USA) . . . . *http://iccweb.com*
Internet Career Exchange *http://www2.softechcorp.com/ice/ice.htm*
Internet Employment Network . . . . *gopher://gopher.careers.com/*
Internet Guide to Women's Resources . . . . *http://mevard.www.media.mit.edu/*
                                                                           people/mevvard/women.html
Internet Job Information Center . . . . *http://tvp.com/vpjic.html*
Internet Job Locator <The> . . . . *http://www.joblocator.com/jobs/*
Internet Mall <The> . . . . *http://www.internet-mall.com/*
Internet Professional Association (IPA) . . . . *http://www.ipa.com/*
Internet Vacature Overzicht (Netherlands) . . . . *http://www.iway.nl/intervac/*
Iowa Jobs Information from the Department
     of Employment Services (DES) . . . . *http://www.state.ia.us/jobs/index.html*

Irish Job Vacancies Page <The> . . . . *http://www.exp.ie/*
IS World Net . . . . *http://www.pitt.edu/~malhotra/isworld/postavai.htm*
It's My Future . . . . *http://www.myfuture.com/*
J. Boragine & Associates . . . . *http://www.jboragine.com/*
Jaeger's Interactive Career Center . . . . *http://www.jaegerinc.com*
James Duncan & Associates (UK) . . . . *http://www.jda-uk.co.uk/*
JIS Home Page . . . . *http://www.esc.state.nc.us/jis/index.html*
Job Accommodation Network . . . . *http://janweb.icdi.wvu.edu/*
Job Connection <The> . . . . *http://www.jobconnection.com/*
Job Hotlines for Washington . . . . . *http://www.gspa.washington.edu/Career/hotlines_welcome.html*
Job Hunt: On-Line Job Meta.List . . . . *http://www.job-hunt.org*
Job-Net <The> (Italy) . . . . *http://www.webcom.com/~jobnet/*
Job Net Work: Employment Made Simple <The> . . . . *http://www.conquest-prod.com/*
jobnetwrk/main.html#return
Job Search *http://www.ventura.com/jsearch/jshome1.html*
Job Search and Employment Opportunities:
  Best Bets from the Net . . . . *http://asa.ugl.lib.umich.edu/chdocs/employment/*
Job Search Techniques . . . . *http://www.jobtrak.com/jobsearch_docs/index.html*
Job Searching in Africa *http://www.sas.upenn.edu/African_Studies/Home_Page/menu_job_srch.html*
Job SearchUK . . . . *http://WWW.JOBSEARCH.CO.UK/*
Job Tailor Employment Online Service *http://www.205.181.25.27*
Job Vacancies Outside of Academe . . . . *http://chronicle.merit.edu/*
JOB – DIRECT (Austria) . . . . *http://www.job-direct.co.at/job-direct/*
JobBank USA . . . . *http://www.jobbankusa.com*
JobCenter . . . . *http://www.jobcenter.com/*
JobFind . . . . *http://www.dlcwest.com/~comdata/jobfind.htm*
JobIndex . . . . *http://www.danielsen.com/jobs/*
JobLynx–Connect With Your Next Career . . . . *http://joblynx.com*
JobNet . . . . *http://www.westga.edu/~coop/*
JOBNET (Hong Kong) . . . . *http://kwuntong.hk.super.net/~websol/jobnet.htm*
JobNet (Netherlands) . . . . *http://www.jobnet.nl/*
JobNet & OnLine Opportunities . . . . *http://www.jobnet.com*
JobNet-SanDiego . . . . *http://www.jobopportunities.com/*
JobPoint Connection . . . . *http://www.jobpoint.com/jpc*
Jobs & Adverts Online GmbH (in German) . . . . *http://www.jobs.adverts.de/*
Jobs & Career (Belgium) . . . . *http://www.jobs-career.be/*
Jobs & Careers Online . . . . *http://www.servonet.com/jobs*
Jobs and Career Information . . . . *gopher://main.morris.org/*
Jobs Links . . . . *http://cip.physik.uni-wuerzburg.de/job.html*
Jobs Online . . . . *http://JobsOnLine.com/*
Jobs Online (France) [In French only] . . . . *http://www.cegos.fr/*
JOBS: Vakatures op het Internet . . . . *http://www.jobs.nl/*
Jobsite UK . . . . *http://www.jobsite.co.uk/*
JobSmart: Résumé Help . . . . *http://jobsmart.org/tools/resume/*
JobSmart Salary Surveys . . . . *http://jobsmart.org/tools/salary/index.htm*
JobTrak . . . . *http://www.jobtrak.com*
JobTree . . . . *http://peace.netnation.com/joblink/*
JobWeb, Job Choices Guides . . . . *http://www.jobweb.org/*
JobWire . . . . *http://www.jobweb.org/jobwire.htm*
JobZone (Netherlands) . . . . *http://valley.interact.nl/jz/*
JP Resources . . . . *http://www.webscope.com/jp/*
JWT Works . . . . *http://www.jwtworks.com/*
K3 & Company *http://www.k3k3k3.com/aactest.html*
Kaiser Nationwide . . . . *http://www.jobpoint.com/jpc*
Kansas City Star . . . . *http://www.kansascity.com/*

Kelly Technical Services . . . . *http://www.io.com/~kellysrv/*
Kennison & Associates, Inc. . . . . *http://www.kennison.com/*
KLA Instruments Corporation Employment . . . . *http://www.kla.ccom/in-yahoo.htm*
Korean Employment Connection . . . . *http://www.korean.com/employment.html*
KQED, Inc.: Public Broadcasting
      for Northern California . . . . *http://www.kqed.org/fromKQED/HR/menu.html*
Kratec Company . . . . *http://www.motor-city.com/kratec/*
Krislyn Corporation . . . . *http://www.krislyn.com/sites/empl.htm*
L.W. Foote Company . . . . *http://www.wolfenet.com/~brightn/*
Le Recrutement (France) *http://gplc.u-bourgogne.fr:8080/Recrut/Welcome.html*
Le Web Cafe Career . . . . *http://lewebcafe.com/pages/career.htm*
Lee Hecht Harrison . . . . *http://www.careerlhh.com*
Lendmam Groupe <The> . . . . *http://www.lendman.com/employers.htm*
Lendman's Recruiting Resources Gateway . . . . *http://www.lendman.com*
Little Employment Group, Inc. <The> . . . . *http://www.netaccess.on.ca/~leg/*
Little Nickel Employment Website *http://www2.littlenickel.com/lnwa/info/employment*
Livelihood Center . . . . *http://www.ingress.com/nyworks*
Logan Group, Inc. <The> . . . . *http://access.advr.com/~logan/loganttl.htm*
Los Angeles Times . . . . *http://www.latimes.com/*
Man at Work (Italy) . . . . *http://www.vol.it/man_@_work*
Management Recruiters International of LA/Encino . . . . *http://www.mri-la.com*
Manpower . . . . *http://www.manpower.com/*
Marksman InterStaff (Israel) . . . . *http://www.marksman.co.il/*
Marlborough Group (Ireland) <The> . . . . *http://ireland.iol.ie/resource/margroup/*
MAS-JOBS . . . . *http://www.mas-jobs.com/*
Maui News <The> . . . . *http://www.maui.net/*
MBA Employment Connection Association . . . . *http://www.MBAnetwork.com/meca*
McGregor Boyall Associates (UK) . . . . *http://www.mcgregor-boyall.co.uk/*
MetroPages Worcester . . . . *http://www.metropages.com*
Metroworld . . . . *http://www.metroworld.com*
Mildura's Employment Opportunities (Australia) . . . . *http://www.mildura.net.au/employ/*
Milwaukee Journal . . . . *http://www.adquest.com/menu.htm*
Minnesota Department of Economic Security, ... *http://mn.jobsearch.org*
     Minnesota Job Bank . . . . *http://mn.jobsearch.org/ajb/mn.htm*
Mississippi Careers Online . . . . *http://www.webcom.com/whipcomm/mscareer*
Monroe Systems . . . . *http://www.monroe.co.uk/monroe/*
Monster Board <The> . . . . *http://www.monster.com/mb/client/ui/bios/mbbios.htm*
                                     http://www.monster.com/mb/client/ui/mb60home.htm
Monster Board Australia <The> . . . . *http://www.armstrongs.com.au/*
Montana Job Service . . . . *http://jsd_server.dli.mt.gov/*
Morgan & Banks Limited . . . . *http://www.morganbanks.com.au*
Mt. Holyoke College—Internships *gopher://gopher.mtholyoke.edu:2772/11/mhc/internship/*
Multi-Avantages, Inc. . . . . *http://www.avantage.com/*
Nando Times . . . . *http://www.nando.net*
Nate's Job Pate *http://www.monash.edu.au/alst6/com/nate/WWW/jobs.html*
National Alumni Placement Association . . . . *http://www.career.com*
National Information Services and Systems (UK) *http://www.niss.ac.uk/noticeboard/jobs/index.html*
National Urban League <The> . . . . *http:www.nul.org/*
NationJob Online Jobs Database . . . . *http://www.nationjob.com*
NBJ's Job Journal, The Nashville Business Journal *http://www.newschannel5.com/nbj.html*
Nebraska Department of Personnel . . . . *http://www.state.ne.us/personnel/per.html*
Net-Happenings Archive *http://www.mid.net:80/NET/*
Net-Temps . . . . *http://www.Net-Temps.com/*
Net-Work (Canada) . . . . *http://www.onsetmag.com/jobmarket*
NetJobs *http://www.netjobs.com:8000/*

Netlink *http://netlink.wlu.edu:1020/*
NetWork Employment Agency . . . . *http://www.zoom.com/network/*
Network Recruitment Inc. . . . . *http://amsquare.com/america/network.html*
Networking on the Network by Phil Agre,
        UCSD Department of Communication . . . *http://communication.ucsd.edu/pagre/network.html*
NetworkWorld Fusion . . . . *http://www.nwfusion.com*
New Boston Select (UK) . . . . *http://www.selectgroup.com/newboston/*
New Jersey Jobs . . . . *http://www.njjobs.com/*
New York State Department of Labor,
        NYSDOL—Employment Opportunities . . . . *http://www.labor.state.ny.us/*
New York Times . . . . *http://www.nytimes.com*
Norfolk Virginian-Pilot . . . . *http://www.pilotonline.com/*
North Carolina Career & Employment Resource Center . . . . . . *http://www.webcom.com/~nccareer/*
North Carolina Employment Security Commission (NCESC),
        North Carolina Job Service . . . . *http://www.esc.state.nc.us/*
North Carolina Information Server . . . . *http://www.sips.state.nc.us/*
North Carolina, State of . . . . *http://www.osp.state.nc.us/OSP/jobs/*
Northern Virginia Career Center . . . . *http://amsquare.com/america/virginia.html*
NYC Headhunters' Mall . . . . *http://jobs-nyc.com*
Occupational Resources . . . . *http://pegasus.adnc.com/~occupational/*
Olivier Recruitment Group *http://www.employment.com.au/olivier/olivier2.html*
OneWorld Jobs (UK) . . . . *http://www.oneworld.org/jobs/index.html*
Online Career Center (Canada) . . . . *http://www.etc.bc.ca/provdocs/careers/first_page.html*
Online Employment Service . . . . *http://www.spie.org:80/web/employment/employ_home.html*
on-TRAC America . . . . *http://www.on-trac.com*
Oregon Employment Department . . . . *http://www.emp.state.or.us/EMPLSVCS/*
Pacific Coast Recruiting . . . . *http://www.pacificsearch.com/*
Palo Alto Weekly . . . . *http://www.service.com/PAW/home.html*
Passport Access . . . . *http://www.passportaccess.com*
Pemberton & Associates . . . . *http://www.biddeford.com/pemberton/*
Pennsylvania Careers Online . . . . *http://amsquare.com/america/pacareer.html*
Personal Services . . . . *http://www.presidio-jobs.com/*
Personalberatung Geest (Germany) . . . . *http://members.aol.com/pbgeest/index.htm*
Personnel Select . . . . *http://www.pselect.com*
Personnel Services Group <The> . . . . *http://www.ctn.on.ca/psg/*
Peterson's Education Center: Careers & Jobs . . . . *http://www.petersons.com/career/*
Philadelphia Online Classifieds . . . . *http://www.phillynews.com/ads*
P.J. Scout—Job Scout by Nation Job Bank . . . . *http://www.nationjob.com/pjscout*
Placement Solutions . . . . *http://www.execpc.com/~msshort/index.html*
Potpourri Classifieds . . . . *http://www.netview.com/pp/employ*
Premier Staff . . . . *http://www.webscope.com/premier/info.html*
Premier Staffing . . . . *http://www.premier-staff.com*
Price Jamieson . . . . *http://www.pricejam.com*
Princeton College Review . . . . *http://www.review.com/index.html-ssi*
Princeton1Info.com *http://www.princeton1info.com*
Profiles (Belgium) . . . . *http://www.nomad.be/profiles/*
Prosper Wales (UK) . . . . *http://prosper.swan.ac.uk/bin/web/*
Purdue University—Internet Sites for
        Job Seekers and Employers . . . . *http://www.purdue.edu/UPS/Student/jobsites.htm*
Purdue University SSINFO Gopher *gopher://oasis.cc.purdue.edu:2525/11/employ-info*
Pursuitnet Jobs, PursuitNet . . . . *http://www.tiac.net/users/jobs/index.html*
Quay Partners International . . . . *http://www.quaypartners.com/*
RAI: The Executive Search Firm . . . . *http://www.raijobs.com/*
Re-Employment 2000 . . . . *http://www.inetbiz.com/re-employment2000/*
RECRUIT GUIDE on the NET (Japan) . . . . *http://job.rnet.or.jp/RG/index-j-s.html*

Recruit PLC (UK)	http://www.newdawn.co.uk/recruit/
Recruiters Network	http://www.xs4all.nl~avotek
Recruiters Online Network	http://www.onramp.net/ron
	http://www.ipa.com
RecruitEx	http://www.recruitex.com/launch96/11home.htm
Recruiting-Links	http://www.recruiting-links.com
Recruiting Services, Inc.	http://www.careerex.com/rsi/index.html
Red Guide to Temp Agencies <The>	http://www.best.com/~ezy/redguide.html
Rensselaer Career Development Center, Optical Science Center—University of Arizona	http://www.rpi.edu/dept/cdc
Resources for Asia	http://www.asia-inc.com/aid/index.html
Resucom, Résumé Canada (Canada)	http://www.bconnex.net/~resume/frame3.htm
Résumé Hut <The>	http://www.islandnet.com/penlan
RésuméNet	http://www.resumenet.com
Résumé Reservoir	http://www.resume.il.com
Résumés on the Web	http://www.resweb.com
RésuméWeb	http://www.netclub.com/resume/resume.htm
RGA International's Job Listings	http://www.rga-joblink.com/docs/joblist.html
RH-Online (Brazil)	http://www.bhvirtual.com/rhol/
RIDET, Rhode Island Department of Employment and Training	http://det2.det.state.ri.us/
Roanoke Times Online	http://www.roanoke.com/index.html
Russian and East European Institute Employment Opportunities, Indiana University	http://www.indiana.edu/~reeiweb/indemp.html
RWH	http://www.figment.net/rwh/
Saludos Web: Careers, Employment & Culture	http://www.wenet.net/saludos/
	http://www.hooked.net/saludos/index.html
San Francisco Bay Area Web Guide	http://www.hyperion.com/ba/sfbay.html
San Francisco Chronicle and Examiner, Classified Gateway	http://www.sfgate.com/classifieds/sunday/Job-Opportunities.shtml
San Jose Mercury	http://www.sjmercury.com/class
Sanford Rose Associates	http://www.sanfordrose.com/
Scholarly Societies Project <The>	http://www.lib.uwaterloo.ca/society
SciComp Job List	http://scicomp.math.uni-augsburg.de/scicomp/gsci/jobs/jobs.html
Seattle Times	http://www.seatimes.com/classified/
SelectCandidate Career Network	http://www.eagleview.com
Seniors On-Line Job Bank	http://www.seniorsnet.com/jobbank.htm
SenseMedia Job Board	http://sensemedia.net/getajob/
SiamJOB (Thailand)	http://www.siam.net/jobs/
Skill Search	http://www.internet-is.com/skillsearch/index.html
SkillBANK	http://www.lapis.com/skillbank/
Snelling Personnel Services	http://www.snelling.com/cgi-bin/home.pl
Solutions for the Human Resources Manager	http://www.in.net/careers
South Australian Department for Employment, Training and Further Education	http://dino.tafe.sa.edu.au/
South Carolina Job Opportunities	http://www.state.sc.us/jobopps.html
South Dakota Bureau of Personnel Job Openings	http://www.state.sd.us/state/executive/bop/
South Dakota's Job Bank—Job Search	http://sd.jobsearch.org/
Southern Utah Job Listing	http://www.sci.dixie.edu/JobService/JobService.html
Spectra International, Inc.	http://www.indirect.com/www/spectra/
Spectrum Concepts Consulting	http://www.sconcepts.com/
SPTimes	http://www.sptimes.com
St. Louis Area Companies on the Net	http://www.st-louis.mo.us/st-louis/companies.html
St. Thomas CEC Job Opportunities Page	http://ein.ccia.st-thomas.on.ca/agencies/cec/jobs/jobbank.html
Stanford Linear Accelerator Center, Stanford, CA	http://www.slac.stanford.edu:5080/

```
                                                          emp/emp-opp/emp-opp.html
Stanley, Barber & Associates  . . . . . . . . . . . . . . . . . . . . . . . . . . . . . . . . http://www.stanleyb.com
Starting Point: Professional . . . . . . . . . . . . . . . . . . . . . . . . . . . . . http://www.stpt.com/profe.html
STEPS GmbH Personalberatung (Germany) . . . . . . . . . . . . . . . . . . . . . . . http://www.steps.de/
Steven Douglas Associates  . . . . . . . . . . . . . . . . . . . . . . . . http://www.web-site1.com/sdassoc/
Student Search System  . . . . . . . . . . . . . . . . . . . . . . . . . . http://www.studentsearch.com
Summer Jobs, Summer Jobs World Wide  . . . . . . . . . . . . . . . . . . http://www.summerjobs.com/
Sunday Paper <The>  . . . . . . . . . . . . . . . . . . . . . . . . . . . http://www.sundaypaper.com
Syracuse Sunday Herald American, Syracuse Online  . . . . . . . . . . . . http://www.syracuse.com
Tacoma News Tribune  . . . . . . . . . . . . . . . . . . . . . . . . . . . . . http://www.tribnet.com
TED, The Training and Employment Database,
        Massachusetts Department of Employment and Training  . . . . . . . . . . http://ma.jobsearch.org
TenKey Interactive  . . . . . . . . . . . . . . . . . . . . . . . . . . . . http://www.careershop.com
Texas Employment Commission . . . . . . . . . . . . . . . . . . . . . . http://www.twc.state.tx.us/
Texas Marketplace . . . . . . . . . . . . . . . . . . . . . . . . . . . . . . http://www.texas-one.org
TKO Personnel, Inc. . . . . . . . . . . . . . . . . . . . . . . . . . . . . . . http://www.tkointl.com
Top Jobs on the Net . . . . . . . . . . . . . . . . . . . . . . http://www.topjobs.co.uk/intel/intel.htm
Tradewave Galaxy  . . . . . . . . . . . . . . . . . . . . . . . . . . . http://galaxy.tradewave.com/
University of California, Berkeley, Work Study Home Page . . . . . . . . . http://workstudy.Berkeley.edu
University of Minnesota—Internships . . . . . . . . . . . . . . . . . . . . . gopher://next1.mrs.umn.edu/
                                        11/Student%20Services/Career%20Center/Internships/
University of Penn Career Services . . . . . . . . . . . . . . . . . . . . . . http://www.upenn.edu/CPPS
University of Virginia—Externships . . . . . . . . . . . . . . http://www.virginia.edu/~career/exinfo.html
University of Virginia—Internship Services . . . . . . . . . . . . . . http://www.virginia.edu/~career/
Utah Department of Employment Security—Job Service . . . . . . . . . http://udesb.state.ut.us/jobs/
Van Zoelen Recruitment . . . . . . . . . . . . . . . . . . . . . . . . . http://www.vz-recruitment.nl
Vermont Department of Employment and Training . . . . . . . . http://www.state.vt.us/det/dethp.htm
Virginian Pilot Online . . . . . . . . . . . . . . . . . . . . . . . . . . . http://www.infi.net/~pilot/
Virtual Job Fair . . . . . . . . . . . . . . . . . . . . . . . . . . . . http://www.careerexpop.com
Virtual Press <The> . . . . . . . . . . . . . . . . . . . . http://www.aloha.com/~william/jnews.html
VirtualResume . . . . . . . . . . . . . . . . . . . . . . . . . . http://www.virtualresume.com/vitae
Wang & Li Asia Resources . . . . . . . . . . . . . . . . . . . . . . . . . . http://www.wang-li.com
Washington Employment Web Pages . . . . . . . . . . . . http://members.aol.com/gwattier/washjob.htm
Washington Post . . . . . . . . . . . . . . . . . . . . . . . . . . http://www.washingtonpost.com
West Bend Community Career Network  . . . . . . . . . . . . . . . . . . . . . http://156.46.110.2/
Whitehouse Fellowships . . . http://www.whitehouse.gov/WH/WH_Fellows/html/fellows1-plain.html
Whole Internet Catalogue . . . . . . . . . . . . . . . . . . . . . . . . . . . http://www.gnn.com
Wide World Web Employment Office . . . . . . . . . . http://www.harbornet.com/biz/office/annex.html
WinWay Corporation . . . . . . . . . . . . . . . . . . . . . . . . . . . . http://www.winway.com
Wisconsin JobNet, Department of Industry,
        Labor, and Human Relations . . . . . . . . . . . . . . . . . . http://danenet.wicip.org/jets/
WITI Campus . . . . . . . . . . . . . . . . . . . . . . . . . . . . . . . . http://www.witi.com
Women in Technology Directory . . . . . . . . . . . . . . . . . . . . . . http://www.sdsu.edu/wit
WorkWeb . . . . . . . . . . . . . . . . . . . . . . . . . . . . . . . . http://www.work-web.com/
World.Hire . . . . . . . . . . . . . . . . . . . . . . . . . . . . . . . http://www.world.hire.com
World Job Seekers . . . . . . . . . . . . . . . . http://cban.worldgate.edmonton.ab.ca.resume/index.html
World Wide Job Seekers . . . . . . . . . . . . . . . . . . . . . http://www.cban.com/resume/
World Wide Résumé/Talent Bank . . . . . . . . . . . . http://www.webcom.com/~career/hwusa.html
Wyoming Personnel Management Division . gopher://ferret.state.wy.us/11/wgov/eb/osd/adm/ead
Yahoo's Listings of Employment Information . . . http://www.yahoo.com/business/employment/jobs
```

Academia

```
Academic Chemistry Employment Clearinghouse . . . http://hackberry.chem.niu.edu:70/1/ChemJob
Academic Employment Network . . . . . . . . . . . . . . . . . . . . . . http:///www.academploy.com/
Academic Internet Services . . . . . . . . . . . . . . . . . . . . . . . . http://www.mousetrap.com:80/ais/
```

Academic Physician and Scientist, Association of American
     Medical Colleges (AAMC) Job Listings . . . . *gopher://aps.acad-psy-sci.com/*
Academic Position Network (APN) . . . . *http://www.umn.edu/apn/*
Academic Positions in Science . . . . *http://www.anu.edu.au/psychology/Academia/science.htm*
Academy of Management . . . . *http://www.usi.edu/aom/placemnt.htm*
Advanced Technology Information Network *http://caticsuf.csufresno.edu:70/1/atinet*
Agricultural Job Listings in British Columbia . . . . . . *http://qb.island.net/~awpb/emop/startag.html*
American Communication Association
     (Grants and Fellowships) . . . . *http://www.uark.edu/depts/comminfo/www/grants.html*
American Dairy Science Association . . . . *http://orion.animal.uiuc.edu:80/~adsa/1995/position.html*
American Education Research Association
     Jobs Corner at ASU . . . . *http://tikkun.ed.asu.edu/~jobs/joblinks.html*
American Evaluation Association . . . . *http://www.theriver.com/public/aea/*
American Indian Science & Engineering Society (AISESnet) . *http://bioc02.uthscsa.edu/aisesnet.html*
American Institute of Architects . . . . *http://www.aia.org/career.htm*
                                              http://www.aia.org/
American Marketing Association . . . . *http://www.ama.org*
American Mathematical Society . . . . *http://www.ams.org/committee/profession/employ.html*
American Physical Society <The> . . . . *http://aps.org/*
                                          http://aps.org/jobs/index.html
American Psychological Society (APS)
     Observer Job Listings . . . . *http://www.hanover.edu/psych/APS/aps.html*
American Society for Engineering Education (ASEE) . . . . *http://www.asee.org/nein/pd/*
                  http://www.asee.org/asee/publications/prism/classifieds/
American Society of Animal Science . . . . *http://www.asas.org/*
American Society of Ichthyologists and Herpetologists . . . . *http://www.utexas.edu/depts/*
                                            asih/pubs/pubs.html
American Statistical Association . . . . *http://www.amstat.org/opportunities/*
                                          http://www.amstat.org/
Ann Arbor Campus . . . . *http://www.med.umich.edu/~mchrd/jobs/*
Architecture and Land Architecture Jobs (CLRNet) *http://www.clr.toronto.edu/VIRTUALLIB/jobs.html*
Army High Performance Computing (HPC) Research Center . . . . *http://www.arc.umn.edu/*
ArtJob *gopher://gopher.tmn.com/11/Artswire/artjob*
Askew School Job Placement Services . . . . *http://www.fpac.fsu/spap/job_intern/jobs/*
Askew School of Public Administration and Policy . . . . . *http://www.fsu.edu/spap/job_intern/jobs/*
                                 http://www.fsu.edu:80/~spap/job/job/html
Association for Education in Journalism
     and Mass Communication . . . . *http://www.aejmc.sc.edu/online/home.html*
Association of Midwest College Biology Teachers . . . . *http://papa.indstate.edu/*
Bermuda Biological Station for Research . . . . *http://www.bbsr.edu/*
Brookings Institution <The> . . . . *http://www.brook.edu/pa/int_fel/intern.htm*
                            http://www.brook.edu/pa/int_fel/fellow.htm
BUBL Employment Bulletin Board *gopher://ukoln.bath.ac.uk:7070/11/Academic/Employment*
California State University Employment Board . . . . *http://csueb.sfsu.edu/csueb.html*
Career Index . . . . *http://www.beloit.edu/*
Catholic University of America <The> . . . . *http://www.cua.edu/*
Computer Science Jobs in Academia . *http://www.cs.brandeis.edu:80/~zippy/academic-cs-jobs.html*
Cornell University . . . . *http://www.cornell.edu/Admin/JOBOPS/JOBOPS.html*
Council for the Support and Advancement of
     Education (CASE) Job Classifieds *gopher://gopher.case.org:70/11/currents*
Crystallography *http://www.unige.ch/crystal/w3v1c/job-index.html*
                                http://www.unige.ch/crystal/job-index.html
CSU the Higher Education Careers Service Unit (UK) . . . . *http://buzzard.csu.man.ac.uk/*
Data Lake (UK) . . . . *http://www.westlake.co.uk/*

Department of Instructional Technologies,
San Francisco State University . . . . *http://www.itec.sfsu.edu/*
Department of Mathematics—University of Toronto . . . . *http://www.math.toronto.edu/jobs/*
Directory (Australia) <The> *http://www.thedirectory.aone.net.au/page8.htm*
Directory: Global Academic Recruiters <The> . . . . *http://www.thedirectory.aone.net.au/*
Easynet Job-Centre (The Virtual Job Centre) . . . . *http://www.cyberiacafe.net/jobs/*
Economists (Europe) . . . . *http://maynard.ww.tu-berlin.de/e-joe/*
Editor and Publisher Interactive . . . . *http://www.mediainfo.com/ephome/class/classhtm/class.htm*
Educatie Emancipatie Gehandicapte Arbeidskrachten . . . . *http://www.eega.nl/*
Education Jobs Page . . . . *http://www.nationjob.com/education*
EduNetCom: Education Employment . . . . *http://www.ccnet.com/~pstrader/*
EE-Link: The Environmental Education Web Server . . . *http://www.nceet.snre.umich.edu/jobs.html*
gopher://nceet.snre.umich.edu/11/networking/
Employment Opportunities . . . . *http://education.indiana.edu/ist/students/jobs/joblink.html*
Employment Opportunities in Water Resources . . . . *http://www.uwin.siu.edu/announce/jobs/*
Engineering Specific Career Advisory
Problem-Solving Environment <The> . . . . *http://fairway.ecn.purdue.edu/ESCAPE/*
ERIC Clearinghouse on Assessment and Evaluation . . . . *gopher://vmsgopher.cua.edu/*
11gopher_root_eric_ae%3a%5bjobs%5d
European Bioinformatics Institute Career Connection . . . . . . *http://www.ebi.ac.uk/htbin/biojobs.pl*
Faculty Positions in Computer Science . . . . *http://www.cs.cmu.edu/afs/*
cs.cmu.edu/user/burks/www/faculty.html
Fellowship Office . . . . *http://fellowships.nas.edu/index.html*
Florida State University . . . . *http://www.fsu.edu/Jobs.html*
Foothill-De Anza Community College District . . . *http://www.fhda.edu/district/hr/employment.html*
Foreign Language Listings *http://condor.stcloud.msus.edu:20020/careerannounce.html*
Georgia State University Career Services,
Job Opportunity Bulletin *http://www.gsu.edu/dept/admin/plc/homepg4.html*
Grants & Fellowships . . . . . . *http://www.sas.upenn.edu/African_Studies/Grants/menu_Grants.html*
GrantsWeb . . . . *http://web.fie.com/cws/sra/resource.htm*
Herpetology Job Listings *http://xtal200.harvard.edu:8000/herp/general/jobs/jobs.html*
History of Science Society . . . . *http://weber.u.washington.edu/~hssexec/hss_jobs.html*
Hospital.Net . . . . *http://hospital.net*
Institute of Molecular Biology (Germany)—Department of Structural
Biology & Crystallography—IMB Jena . . . . . *http://www.imb-jena.de/www_sbx/sbxjobs.html*
Instructional Technology Jobs,
Indiana University, Bloomington . *http://education.indiana.edu/ist/students/jobs/joblink.html*
International Academic Job Market . . . . *http://www.camrev.com.au/share/jobs.html*
International Agribusiness Internship Center . . . . *http://www.usu.edu/*
Internships U.S.A. . . . . *http://www.collegegrad.com/internships*
Job Listing at tamu.edu . . . . *http://ageninfo.tamu.edu/jobs.html*
Job Listings in Academia . . . . *http://volvo.gslis.utexas.edu/~acadres/jla.html*
Job Opportunities (in U.S. and Europe) . . . . *http://www.sas.upenn.edu/*
African_Studies/Jobs_US/menu_Jobs_US.html
Job Opportunities in Entomology . . . . . *http://www.colostate.edu/Depts/Entomology/jobs/jobs.html*
Job Search Materials for Engineers . . . . *http://www.englib.cornell.edu/*
JOM, The Minerals, Metals, and
Materials Society Journal . . . . *http://www.tms.org/pubs/journals/JOM/classifieds.html*
Kaplan . . . . *http://www.kaplan.com/*
Lasers and Electro Optics Society (LEOS) . . . . . *http://msrc.wvu.edu/leos/LEOSprof/LEOSprof.html*
Mathematical Association of America . . . . *http://www.maa.org/pubs/focus/employ.html*
Mathematics Job Market . . . . *http://www.cs.dartmouth.edu/~gdavis/policy/jobmarket.html*
National Academy of Sciences, National Research Council,
Institute of Medicine . . . . *http://www.nas.edu/*
National Association for College Admission Counseling . . . . *http://www.nacac.com/*
Naval Research Library's Job Link . . . . . . *http://infoweb.nrl.navy.mil/catalogs_and_databases/job/*

NISS (National Information Services .... *http://www.niss.ac.uk/noticeboard/index.html#jobs*
   and Systems) Noticeboard   *http://www.niss.ac.uk/news/index*
Nursing Career Opportunities *gopher://umabnet.ab.umd.edu/11/*
O-Hayo Sensei .... *http://www.ohayosensei.com/~ohayo/*
Ohio State University *gopher://gopher.acs.ohio-state.edu/11/Opportunities/Job%20Listings*
                                          gopher://gopher.acs.ohio-state.edu/11/Opportunities/
Physics Job Announcements by Thread, NASA .... *http://XXX.lanl.gov/Announce/Jobs/*
Positions in Bioscience and Medicine, Hum-Molgen Bioscience and Medicine
   (Germany) .... *http://www.informatik.uni-rostock.de/HUM-MOLGEN/anno/position.html*
ProEd World Wide Clearinghouse .... *http://www.proed.com/ch/*
Professional Information for Mathematicians .... *http://www.ams.org/committee/profession/*
Russian and East European Institute Employment
   Opportunities, Indiana University .... *http://www.indiana.edu/~reeiweb/indemp.html*
Science Global Career Network, Science JobNet, American
   Association for the Advancement of Science .... *http://www.aaas.org*
                          http://www.science-mag.aaas.org:888/science/scripts/recruit/search
                                  http://science-mag.aaas.org/science/
                                http://www.edoc.com/sgcn/Lineads.html
                 http://www.sciencemag.org/science/feature/classified/search.shtml
Scientist (Electronic Journal) *gopher://ds.internic.net/1/pub/the-scientist*
                                  ftp://ds.internic.net/pub/the-scientist
TeleJob .... *http://ezinfo.ethz.ch/ETH/TELEJOB/tjb_home_e.html*
TESLJB-L, Teaching English as a Foreign Language *gopher://CUNYVM.CUNY.EDU/11/*
                            Subject%20Specific%20Gophers/teslfl/Teaching%20English
                        %20as%20a%20Foreign%20Language%20-%20The%20Profession
Times Higher Education Supplement InterView .... *http://www.timeshigher.newsint.co.uk/*
                    http://www.timeshigher.newsint.co.uk/INTERVIEW/interview.html
                    http://www.timeshigher.newsint.co.uk/mainmenu.html
University of Colorado, Boulder .... *gopher://gopher.Colorado.EDU/*
                                select *Other Gophers by Subject*
                    select *Employment Opportunities and Resume Postings*
University of Florida Department of Statistics .... *http://www.stat.ufl.edu/vlib/jobs*
U.S. Dept of Agriculture—Cooperative Extension *gopher://sulaco.oes.orst.edu/11/ext/jobs*
Utah Department of Employment Security—Job Service .... *http://udesb.state.ut.us/jobs/*
Victoria Freenet Association (Employment Resources) .. *gopher://freenet.victoria.bc.ca/11/business*
Women in Higher Education Career Page .... *http://www.itis.com/wihe/*
Wyoming Employment Resources, Wyoming Job Bank .... *http://wyjobs.state.wy.us/*

Accounting/Taxes

AAFA—The American Association of Finance and Accounting .... *http://www.aafa.com/*
Advanced Marketing .... *http://www.amgi.com/*
Banking Related Jobs .... *http://www.cob.ohio-state.edu/~fin/osujobs.htm*
Baywatch Personnel (New Zealand) .... *http://ourworld.compuserve.com/*
                                    homepages/pages/baywatch.htm
Bizlinks (Singapore) .... *http://sunflower.singnet.com.sg/~g6615000/*
Certified General Accountants' Association
   of Manitoba (Canada) .... *http://sulla.cyberstore.ca/Provincial/Manitoba/employ.htm*
Childs, Smith & Associates .... *http://www.accounting-jobs.com/*
Dana-Farber Cancer Institute *gopher://farber2.dfci.harvard.edu/11/.bulletin/.hr/.positions*
David Aplin and Associates (Canada) .... *http://www.tgx.com/aplin/*
Dynamic HR Solutions .... *http://www.dynamichr.com*
EagleView .... *http://www.eagleview.com*
Employment Edge *http://www.employmentedge.com:80/employment.edge/*
Employment Opportunities in India ... *http://www.webpage.com/hindu/960210/10/10hdline.html*

Financial Job Opportunities
    (Business Job Finder) . . . . *http://www.cob.ohio-state.edu/dept/fin/osujobs.htm*
Hamilton Jones & Koller (Australia) . . . . *http://www.hjk.com.au/*
Harcourt and Associates . . . . *http://www.comcept.ab.ca/harcourt/*
Harrison Willis Group (UK) *http://194.128.198.201/hwgroup/main.html*
Infonet's Classifieds . . . . *http://www.infonetwww.com/clfdjo.htm*
Internal Revenue Service . . . . *http://www.irs.ustreas.gov/prod/*
Job Access Limited (Hong Kong) . . . . *http://www.hk.net/~jal/*
Job Banker <The> . . . . *http://www.nmaa.org/jobbank.htm*
Jobs in Finance for MBAs *http://www.cob.ohio-state.edu:80/dept/fin/osujob.htm*
Kunin Associates . . . . *http://www.gate.net/~kassoc/index.html?*
Ohio State University *gopher://gopher.acs.ohio-state.edu/11/Opportunities/Job%20Listings*
                                        gopher://gopher.acs.ohio-state.edu/11/Opportunities/
Reed Personnel Services, Reed Computing . . . . *http://www.reed.co.uk/*
RJ Pascale & Company . . . . *http://www.ct-jobs.com/pascale/*
Staffing Options & Solutions . . . . *http://iypn.com/staffing*
Staffing Services Online . . . . *http://www.staffingservices.com/*
VJ Enterprises . . . . *http://www.vjenterprises.com*

Administration
(Includes academic, business, education, and medical administration)
Academic Physician and Scientist, Association of
    American Medical Colleges (AAMC) Job Listings . . . . *gopher://aps.acad-psy-sci.com/*
Alliance Management Resources *http://www.amsquare.com/america/medpro1.html*
American Society for Engineering Education (ASEE) . . . . *http://www.asee.org/nein/pd/*
                                   http://www.asee.org/asee/publications/prism/classifieds/
ArtJob *gopher://gopher.tmn.com/11/Artswire/artjob*
ASA Information Services . . . . *http://www.eskimo.com/~pageless/asa/*
Askew School Job Placement Services . . . . *http://www.fpac.fsu/spap/job_intern/jobs/*
Askew School of Public Administration and Policy . . . . *http://www.fsu.edu/spap/job_intern/jobs/*
                                   http://www.fsu.edu:80/~spap/job/job/html
BBN Networking, Inc. . . . . *http://www.bbn.com/bbnjobs/jobsrch.htm*
Belcan Information Services . . . . *http://www.belcan.com/infoserv.htm*
Bernard Haldane Associates . . . . *http://www.intex.net/careers/index.html*
BIO-ONLINE . . . . *http://www.bio.com/hr/hr_index.html*
Bizlinks (Singapore) . . . . *http://sunflower.singnet.com.sg/~g6615000/*
Bolsa de Trabajo de Pixelnet (Mexico) [in Spanish] *http://www.pixel.com.mx:80/Curriculums/*
California State University Employment Board . . . . *http://csueb.sfsu.edu/csueb.html*
Canadian Association of Career Educators and Employers (CACEE) *http://www.cacee.com/workweb/*
Career Quest . . . . *http://www.careerquest.com/*
Career Source . . . . *http://www.netusa.com/jobs.htm*
Chronicle of Higher Education, Academe this Week . . . . . *http://chronicle.merit.edu/.ads/.links.html*
Council for the Support and Advancement of Education
    (CASE) Job Classifieds *gopher://gopher.case.org:70/11/currents*
EDNET—Job Net for Educators *http://pages.prodigy.com/CA/luca52a/bagley.html*
Education Gazette (New Zealand) . *http://www.learningmedia.co.nz/egissues/eglatest/eg_conts.htm*
Education Jobs Page . . . . *http://www.nationjob.com/education*
Elk Grove Unified School District *http://www.egusd.k12.ca.us/webdocs/claspost.htm*
Executive BioSearch . . . . *http://www.scientificjobs.com/*
Florida State University . . . . *http://www.fsu.edu/Jobs.html*
Fogarty and Associates . . . . *http://www.fogarty.com/*
Foothill-De Anza Community College District . . . *http://www.fhda.edu/district/hr/employment.html*
Georgia Tech Career Services . . . . *http://www.gatech.edu/career*
HealthLine Management, Inc. (HMI) . . . . *http://www.hmistl.com/*
Hunterskil (UK), Hunterskil Howard (UK) *http://194.128.198.201/hhplc/*

IndustryNet, Industry Net Career Opportunities . . . . *http://www.industry.net/c/mn/_co*
IUPUI Integrated Technologies *gopher://INDYCMS.IUPUI.EDU/11/*
IUPUI%20Information%20Sources/Staff%20Job%20Openings
J. B. Groner Executive Search, Inc. . . . . *http://www.execjobsearch.com/*
Job Listings in Academia . . . . *http://volvo.gslis.utexas.edu/~acadres/jla.html*
M. David Lowe Professional Service . . . . *http://www.mdlowe.com/*
National Educators Employment Review . . . . *http://www.netgrafx.com/neer/default.htm*
National Institute of Health (NIH)
        Senior Job Opportunities *http://helix.nih.gov:8001/jobs/*
National Network for HealthCare Professionals . . . . *http://www.treknet.net/hcroaz*
National Science Foundation, New Hampshire
        and Maine Careers Online *gopher://stis.nsf.gov/11/NSF/vacancies*
Networking Jobs in North California . . . . *http://www.pcpersonnel.com/*
Nursing Career Opportunities *gopher://umabnet.ab.umd.edu/11/*
Software AG Community . . . . *http://www.nauticom.net/users/sferrell/sagjobs.html*
Staffing Services Online . . . . *http://www.staffingservices.com/*
University of Minnesota's College of Education
        Job Search Bulletin Board *gopher://rodent.cis.umn.edu:11119/*
VJ Enterprises . . . . *http://www.vjenterprises.com*

Aerospace
(Includes aeronautics, astronautics, aviation, airlines, etc.)
Airline Employee Placement Service . . . . *http://www.aeps.com/aeps/aepshm.html*
Airline Employment Assistance Corps. *http://www2.csn.net/AEAC/*
American Institute of Aeronautics
        and Astronautics . . . . *http://www.lmsc.lockheed.com/aiaa/sf/career.html*
Aviation/Aerospace Jobs Page . . . . *http://www.nationjob.com/aviation*
Aviation Connection . . . . *http://www.flying.net/ac/employme.htm*
Corporate Aviation Résumé Exchange <The> . . . . *http://scendtek.com/care/*
employment.net.au (Australia) . . . . *http://www.employment.net.au/*
Executive Recruitment Services (UK) . . . . *http://www.ers.co.uk/ers/*
NASA Ames Research Center . . . . *http://huminfo.arc.nasa.gov/NASAvacancy.html*
NetWorld MarketPlace Career Opportunities . . . . *http://www.networldmkt.com/networld/career.htm*
Royal Air Force (UK) . . . . *http://www.open.gov.uk/raf/rafhome.htm*

Agriculture
(Includes agribusiness, dairy, fisheries, forestry, horticulture, natural resources, wildlife, etc.)
Advanced Technology Information Network *http://caticsuf.csufresno.edu:70/1/atinet*
Agricultural Job Listings *http://caticsuf.csufresno.edu:70/1/atinet/agjobs*
Agricultural Job Listings in British Columbia . . . . . . *http://qb.island.net/~awpb/emop/startag.html*
American Dairy Science Association . . . . *http://orion.animal.uiuc.edu:80/~adsa/1995/position.html*
American Society for Horticultural Science <The> *http://www.ashs.org/hortop20.html*
American Society for Mass Spectrometry <The> . . . . *http://www.asms.org/employ.html*
American Society of Agricultural Engineers (ASAE) <The> . . . . *http://asae.org/resource/*
http://www.asae.org:80/jobs
American Society of Animal Science . . . . *http://www.asas.org/*
Association Bernard Gregory (France) . . . . *http://www-com.grenet.fr/abg/*
Automated Vacancy Announcement System (AVADS) . *http://info.er.usgs.gov/doi/avads/index.html*
Biological Control and Sciences Jobs . . . . *http://www.aphis.usda.gov/*
Biotech Career Center . . . . *http://www.gene.com/ae/AB/CC/index.html*
Department of the Interior Automated
        Vacancy Announcement System (AVADS) . . . . *http://www.usgs.gov/doi/avads/index.html*
Federal Funded Research in the US . . . . *http://medoc.gdb.org/best/fed-fund.html*
Forest Products Job Board *gopher://mercury.forestry.umn.edu:70/11/fp/job*

Georgia State University Career Services,
        Job Opportunity Bulletin *http://www.gsu.edu/dept/admin/plc/homepg4.html*
GIS Jobs Clearinghouse, University of Minnesota,
        Forestry, Remote Sensing Lab . . . . *http://www.gis.umn.edu/rsgisinfo/jobs.html*
Institute of Molecular Agrobiology (Singapore) . . . . . . *http://www.nus.sg/NUSinfo/Appoint/IMA.html*
International Agribusiness Internship Center . . . . *http://www.usu.edu/*
International Fund for Agricultural Development (Italy) . . *http://www.unicc.org/ifad/vac395en.html*
Job Board *http://wfscnet.tamu.edu:80/jobs.html*
Jobs in Horticulture . . . . *http://www.aksi.net/agquest/*
Manzey Associates, Inc. . . . . *http://www.manzey.com*
Poultry Science Association *http://gallus.tamu.edu/1h/psa/psaplacement.html*
U.S. Dept of Agriculture—Cooperative
        Extension Job Vacancies *gopher://sulaco.oes.orst.edu/11/ext/jobs*
U.S. Fish & Wildlife Service . . . . *http://www.fws.gov/*
                                                                http://www.fws.gov/employmt.html
Wildlife & Fisheries Employment . . . . *http://wfscnet.tamu.edu/jobs.html*

Archaeology
Archaeological Fieldwork Server . . . . *http://durendal.cit.cornell.edu/*

Architecture
American Institute of Architects . . . . *http://www.aia.org/career.htm*
                                                                http://www.aia.org/
Architecture and Land Architecture Jobs (CLRNet) *http://www.clr.toronto.edu/VIRTUALLIB/jobs.html*
Architecture Resources: Berkley *gopher://infolib.lib.berkeley.edu/11/eres/resdbs/land*
Bolsa de Trabajo de Pixelnet (Mexico) [in Spanish] *http://www.pixel.com.mx:80/Curriculums/*
Construction Site's Guide to Jobs <The> . . . . *http://www.emap.com/construct/jobs.htm*
Online Design . . . . *http://www.thesphere.com/OnLine/*

Art
(Includes drawing, painting, photography, graphics, illustration, computers, typography)
3DSite *http://www.lightside.com/3dsite/cgi/offers/index.html*
Academy of Advertising . . . . *http://www.utexas.edu/coc/adv/AAA/*
American Institute of Architects . . . . *http://www.aia.org/career.htm*
                                                                http://www.aia.org/
Artisan, your freelance network . . . . *http://www.artisan-inc.com*
ArtJob *gopher://gopher.tmn.com/11/Artswire/artjob*
Arts Deadlines List <The> . . . . *http://www.ircam.fr/divers/arts-deadlines.html*
Arts Wire Current . . . . *http://www.tmn.com/Artswire/*
ArtsNet . . . . *http://artsnet.heinz.cmu.edu/career/career.html*
CGI Job Offers . . . . *http://www.lightside.com/~dani/cgi/offers/index.html*
Cinenet Communications . . . . *http://www.cinenet.net/*
Computer Graphics (Insight Studios) . . . . *http://emporium.turnpike.net/I/INSIGHT/jobs.htm*
Editor and Publisher Interactive . . . . *http://www.mediainfo.com/ephome/class/classhtm/class.htm*
Engineering/Manufacturing Jobs Page . . . . *http://www.nationjob.com/engineering*
Entertainment Recruiting Network . . . . *http://www.showbizjobs.com/middle.htm*
Extreme Résumé Drop . . . . *http://www.mainquad.com/theQuad/wich/introPages/lo/erd.html*
Fashion Exchange . . . . *http://fashionexch.com/*
Freelance Access . . . . *http://www.freelanceaccess.com/*
Graphic Arts Marketing Associates . . . . *http://members.aol.com/GRaphicama*
GWeb, An Electronic Trade Journal for Computer Animators . . . . *http://www.gweb.org/*
International Home Workers Association <The> . . . . *http://www.homeworkers.com/*
International Teleproduction Society . . . . *http://www.itsnet.org/jobs.html*
J. Arthur Group . . . . *http://www.jarthurgroup.com/*
OASYS . . . . *http://www.oasysnet.com/home.html*

PhotoForum's Photo/Imaging Jobs . . . . *http://www.rit.edu/~andpph/jobs.html*
VideoPro Classifieds *http://www.txdirect.net:80/videopro/adv.htm*

Atmospheric Science
(Includes astronomy, climatology, gravitational and space biology, meteorology, observatories, space research, etc.)

American Astronomical Society *http://www.aas.org:80/JobRegister/aasjobs.html*
http://www.aas.org/
American Society for Gravitational and Space Biology . . *http://www.indstate.edu/asgsb/index.html*
Astronomical Observatory Jobs *http://www.pd.astro.it:80/Jobs/*
BioSpace Career Center . . . . *http://www.biospace.com/g/synd/career*
Canadian Institute of Theoretical Astronomy . . . . *http://www.cita.utoronto.ca/CITA/jobs.html*
ESO—European Southern Observatory (Germany) . . . . . . *http://www.eso.org/announcements.html*
NASA Ames Research Center . . . . *http://huminfo.arc.nasa.gov/NASAvacancy.html*

Audio
Audio Engineering Society . . . . *http://www.cudenver.edu/aes/*
CERL Sound Group . . . . *http://datura.cerl.uiuc.edu/netStuff/jobs/jobs.html*

Banking
Banking Related Jobs . . . . *http://www.cob.ohio-state.edu/~fin/osujobs.htm*

Biological Sciences
(Includes aquatic science, bioengineering, bioinformatics, biomedical, biology, biotechnology, ecology, entomology, gravitational biology, herpetology, histopathology, ichthyology, limnology, marine biology, natural sciences, oceanography, water resources, marine, molecular, phyto- pathology, plant physiology, radiation biology, research, space biology, spectrometry, etc.)

Air and Waste Management Association . . . . *http://www.awma.org/employment.html*
American Institute of Physics . . . . *http://www.aip.org/aip/careers/careers.html*
American Physical Society <The> . . . . *http://aps.org/jobs/index.html*
American Physiological Association *gopher://oac.hsc.uth.tmc.edu:3300/11/employ*
American Phytopathological Society . . . . *http://www.scisoc.org/career.htm*
American Society for Gravitational and Space Biology . . *http://www.indstate.edu/asgsb/index.html*
American Society for Histocompatibility and Immunogenetics . . . . *http://www.swmed.edu/*
home_pages/ASHI/jobs/jobs.htm
American Society for Horticultural Science <The> *http://www.ashs.org/hortop20.html*
American Society for Mass Spectrometry <The> . . . . *http://www.asms.org/employ.html*
American Society of Ichthyologists and Herpetologists . . . . *http://www.utexas.edu/depts/*
asih/pubs/pubs.html
American Society of Limnology and Oceanography . . . . *http://www.ngdc.noaa.gov/paleo/aslo/*
American Society of Plant Physiologists (Midwest Section) *http://baby.indstate.edu:80/*
mwaspp/gradposi.html
Association of Midwest College Biology Teachers . . . . *http://papa.indstate.edu/*
Bermuda Biological Station for Research . . . . *http://www.bbsr.edu/*
BIO-ONLINE . . . . *http://www.bio.com/hr/hr_index.html*
Biodata Navigator Job Board . . . . *http://www.biodata.com/biodata/bd_jobs.html*
Biological Control and Sciences Jobs . . . . *http://www.aphis.usda.gov/*
BioNet (BioSci) Employment Opportunities *http://www.bio.net:80/hypermail/EMPLOYMENT/*
BIONET Employment . . . . *http://www.bio.net*
Biophysical Society . . . . *http://biosci.cbs.umn.edu/biophys/employ.html*
Biosciences Job Listings and Career Services . . . . *http://golgi.harvard.edu/biopages/jobs.html*
BioSource . . . . *http://www.biosource-tech.com/*
BioSpace Career Center . . . . *http://www.biospace.com/g/synd/career*
Biotech Career Center . . . . *http://www.gene.com/ae/AB/CC/index.html*
Cell—Journal of Biological Sciences . . . . *http://www.cell.com/cell/posi/*

Employment Opportunities in Water Resources . . . . *http://www.uwin.siu.edu/announce/jobs/*
European Bioinformatics Institute Career Connection . . . . . . *http://www.ebi.ac.uk/htbin/biojobs.pl*
European Molecular Biology Laboratory,
       Heidelberg, Germany . . . . *http://www.embl-heidelberg.de/ExternalInfo/jobs/*
Executive BioSearch . . . . *http://www.scientificjobs.com/*
FASEB Careers Online . . . . *http://www.faseb.org/careers/*
Fitzroy Undergraduate Research in Biology . . . . *http://firstmarket.com/fitzroy/*
Franklin Search Group . . . . *http://www.medmarket.com/tenants/fsg/*
Herpetology Job Listings *http://xtal200.harvard.edu:8000/herp/general/jobs/jobs.html*
Institute of Molecular Agrobiology (Singapore) . . . . . . *http://www.nus.sg/NUSinfo/Appoint/IMA.html*
Institute of Molecular Biology (Germany), Department of Structural
       Biology & Crystallography—IMB Jena . . . . . *http://www.imb-jena.de/www_sbx/sbxjobs.html*
Job Board *http://wfscnet.tamu.edu:80/jobs.html*
Job Opportunities in Entomology . . . . . *http://www.colostate.edu/Depts/Entomology/jobs/jobs.html*
National Skin Centre (Singapore) . . . . *http://biomed.nus.sg/nsc/vacancy.html*
NATO's SACLANT Undersea Research Centre (Italy) *http://www.saclantc.nato.int:80/staff/*
Nature's International Science Jobs *http://www.nature.com/Nature2/*
       serve?SID=7502384&CAT=Classified&PG=Jobs/jobshome.html
NetWorld MarketPlace Career Opportunities . . . . *http://www.networldmkt.com/networld/career.htm*
Pharmacy Week Jobs Listing, PharmInfoNet . . . . *http://pharminfo.com/pharmmall/*
       PharmWeek/pharmweek.html
Positions in Bioscience and Medicine, Hum-Molgen Bioscience and Medicine
       (Germany) . . . . *http://www.informatik.uni-rostock.de/HUM-MOLGEN/anno/position.html*
Radiation Biology Job Board . . . . *http://www.science.ubc.ca/departments/physics/radbio/jobs.html*
Virginia Coast Reserve Information System
       (VCRIS) (Job Listings) . . . . *http://atlantic.evsc.virginia.edu/*
       gopher://atlantic.evsc.Virginia.EDU/11/Opportunities
Woods Hole Oceanographic Institution *gopher://pearl.whoi.edu/11/education-employment*

Broadcasting

(Includes radio, television, engineering, graphics, videographer, video production, etc.)
Academy of Advertising . . . . *http://www.utexas.edu/coc/adv/AAA/*
Airwaves Job Services . . . . *http://www.airwaves.com/*
Broadcast Employment Services . . . . *http://www.tvjobs.com/index_a.htm*
Broadcasters Training Network . . . . *http://www.learn-by-doing.com*
Corporation for Public Broadcasting (CPB) Job Line . . . . *http://www.cpb.org/jobline/index.html*
International Teleproduction Society . . . . *http://www.itsnet.org/jobs.html*
National Association of Broadcasters . . . . *http://www.nab.org/*
TV JobNet . . . . *http://www.tvjobnet.com/*
UTV—T.V. Job Classifieds . . . . *http://tvnet.kspace.com/jobs/*
VideoPro Classifieds *http://www.txdirect.net:80/videopro/adv.htm*

Business

(Includes administration, clerical, competitive intelligence, management, secretarial, systems, etc.)
Academy of Management . . . . *http://www.usi.edu/aom/placemnt.htm*
Adia . . . . *http://www.adia.com*
Andersen Consulting . . . . *http://www.ac.com/main.html*
Arvon, LLC . . . . *http://www.arvon.com/*
Bizlinks (Singapore) . . . . *http://sunflower.singnet.com.sg/~g6615000/*
Bridge Information Technology Inc. (Canada Net Pages) . . . . *http://www.visions.com/*
Communication Arts: Business and Career . . . . *http://www.commarts.com/bin/ca/bc_jl_o*
Corporate Recruiters Ltd. (Canada) . . . . *http://WWW.PIE.VANCOUVER.BC.CA/pie/*
       business/personne/corp_rec/corp_rec.htm
Dana-Farber Cancer Institute *gopher://farber2.dfci.harvard.edu/11/.bulletin/.hr/.positions*

EDGAR Development Project, NYU Stern School of Business . . . . *http://edgar.stern.nyu.edu*
Europages—The European Business Directory . . . . *http://www.europages.com/*
Federal Funded Research in the US . . . . *http://medoc.gdb.org/best/fed-fund.html*
FEDnet—Foundation for Enterprise Development . . . . *http://www.fed.org/*
Financial Job Opportunities
      (Business Job Finder) . . . . *http://www.cob.ohio-state.edu/dept/fin/osujobs.htm*
Institute for Operations Research
      and Management Science (INFORMS) . . . . *http://www.informs.org/JPS/index.html*
International Home Workers Association <The> . . . . *http://www.homeworkers.com/*
Job Seekers Edging the Competition . . . . *http://bcn.boulder.co.us/business/*
K3 & Company *http://www.k3k3k3.com/aactest.html*
M. David Lowe Professional Service . . . . *http://www.mdlowe.com/*
Management Recruiters International . . . . *http://www.mrinet.com/*
MBA Job Net, MBA Search! . . . . *http://www.mbasearch.com/index.htm*
Office Specialists . . . . *http://www.officespec.com*
OzJobs (ACP OnLine) . . . . *http://columbia.digiweb.com/~aep1/cgi-bin/jobidx.cgi*
Plaxel . . . . *http://www.gol.com/plaxel/*
Resources for Asia . . . . *http://www.asia-inc.com/aid/index.html*
Roevin Management Services, Ltd. *http://194.128.198.201/roevin/*
Sanford Rose Associates . . . . *http://www.sanfordrose.com/*
Society of Competitive Intelligence Professionals (SCIP) . . . . *http://www.scip.org/*
Staffing Services Online . . . . *http://www.staffingservices.com/*
TeleJob . . . . *http://ezinfo.ethz.ch/ETH/TELEJOB/tjb_home_e.html*
University of Florida Department of Statistics . . . . *http://www.stat.ufl.edu/vlib/jobs*

Career Counseling/Human Resources

Advocate Career Services . . . . *http://www.amsquare.com/america/advocate.html*
AS ASISTENT d.o.o. (Slovenia) . . . . *http://www.c-and-c.si/asas/inang.html*
Asia Pacific Management Forum . . . . *http://www.mcb.co.uk/apmforum/nethome.htm*
Association of Graduate Career Advisory Services (UK) . . . . *http://agcas.csu.man.ac.uk/*
Benefit Associates . . . . *http://www.benefitassociates.com/*
Bernard Haldane Associates . . . . *http://www.intex.net/careers/index.html*
California School-to-Career Information System . . . . *http://wwwstc.cahwnet.gov/*
Canada Employment Centre in Nanaimo . . . . *http://www.island.net/~hrcnan/emp.html*
CANDO—The Career Advisory Network
      on Disability Opportunities (UK) . . *http://www.comp.lancs.ac.uk/uni-services/careers/cando/*
Career Advice . . . . *http://www.review.com/career/career_homepage.html*
Career and Labour Market Information . . . . *http://www.etc.bc.ca/provdocs/careers/home.html*
Career and Résumé Management for the 21st Century! *http://crm21.com*
Career Atlas for the Road . . . . *http://www.isdn.net/nis/*
Career Blazers Learning Centre (Canada) . . . . *http://cblazers.ns.ca/*
Career Counseling—LITE . . . . *http://www.execpc.com/~cclite/*
Career Data Resources . . . . *http://amsquare.com/america/cdr.html*
Career Fairs <The> *http://www.cweb.com/employersandorgs/lendmangrp/home1.htm*
Career Information System . . . . *http://career-info.uoregon.edu/whoweaare.html*
Career Managemnet International . . . . *http://www.cmi-lmi.com/*
Career.net (UK) . . . . *http://www.atlas.co.uk/mbacareer/*
de Recat & Associates . . . . *http://www.derecat.com/*
Department of Education and Employment (UK) . . . . . *http://www.open.gov.uk/dfee/dfeehome.htm*
Development Dimensions International . . . . *http://ddiworld.com/index.html*
Dynamic HR Solutions . . . . *http://www.dynamichr.com*
Eduplus Management Group Inc. . . . . *http://www.eduplus.ca/*
Employee Services Inc. . . . . *http://www.cris.com/~Esinc/*
Employment Detective . . . . *http://netside.com/~ccofcola/adpages/employdt.html*
Environmental Careers Organization <The> . . . . *http://www.eco.org*

Getting a Job . . . . *http://www.americanexpress.com/student/moneypit/getjob/getajob.html*
HR Headquarters . . . . *http://www.hrhq.com/*
HR World . . . . *http://www.hrworld.com*
HRCOMM . . . . *http://ccnet.com/hrcomm/*
HRNEWS Job Openings . . . . *http://www.shrm.org/jobs/*
J.B. Groner Executive Search, Inc. . . . . *http://www.execjobsearch.com/*
Networking on the Network by Phil Agre,
    UCSD Department of Communication . . . *http://communication.ucsd.edu/pagre/network.html*
ProEd World Wide Clearinghouse . . . . *http://www.proed.com/ch/*
Society for Human Resource Management—NJ State Council . . . . *http://www.njshrm.com/hr/*
                                               http://www.shrm.org/
Training and Development Job Mart,
    T&D Business Showcase . . . . *http://www.tcm.com/trdev/jobs/jobs.htm*
TrainingNet . . . . *http://www.trainingnet.com/*

Chemistry

(Includes analytical, biochemistry, dietetic research, electrochemical finishing, engineering, inorganic, organic, physical, plastics/rubber, polymers, spectrometry, etc.)

Academic Chemistry Employment Clearinghouse . . . *http://hackberry.chem.niu.edu:70/1/ChemJob*
American Association of Cereal Chemists . . . . *http://wwwnt.scisoc.org/aacc/career/*
American Chemical Society . . . . *http://www.acs.org/memgen/employmt/pdb/acsmenu.htm*
American Institute of Chemical Engineers . . . . *http://www.aiche.org/employment/*
                                          http://www.che.ufl.edu/WWW-CHE/aiche/
American Society for Mass Spectrometry <The> . . . . *http://www.asms.org/employ.html*
Biophysical Society . . . . *http://biosci.cbs.umn.edu/biophys/employ.html*
Biosciences Job Listings and Career Services . . . . *http://golgi.harvard.edu/biopages/jobs.html*
BioSource . . . . *http://www.biosource-tech.com/*
Chemtech, Ltd . . . . *http://www.interaccess.com/ctld/*
Cirrus Links for Chemistry-Related Postions . . . . *http://rainier.chem.plu.edu/chem_careers.html*
finishing.com's Help-Wanted . . . . *http://www.finishing.com/Directory/wanted.html*
Franklin Search Group . . . . *http://www.medmarket.com/tenants/fsg/*
IEEE, University of Massachusetts Student Branch . . . . *http://www.ecs.umass.edu/*
Pharmacy Week Jobs Listing, PharmInfoNet . . . . *http://pharminfo.com/pharmmall/*
                                        PharmWeek/pharmweek.html
Poly-Links-Job Bank . . . . *http://www.polymers.com/polylink/jobank.html*
PolySort Classifieds . . . . *http://www.polysort.com/classifieds/help_wanted.htm*
Royal Society of Chemistry (UK) *http://chemistry.rsc.org/rsc/jobs3.htm*
YSN Jobs Page (Young Scientists Network),
    Jobs Listings Archive . . . . *http://www.physics.uiuc.edu/ysn/*

Communication

American Communication Association
    (Grants and Fellowships) . . . . *http://www.uark.edu/depts/comminfo/www/grants.html*
Ardent Group, Inc. <The> . . . . *http://www.ardentgrp.com/*
Camelot Consultants Limited (UK) . . . . *http://www.eclipse.co.uk/camelot/*
Communication Arts: Business and Career . . . . *http://www.commarts.com/bin/ca/bc_jl_o*
Communications Engineering Employment Network . . *http://www.destek.net/ejdort/ce_emply.html*
International Interactive Communications Society
    (IICS), New York Chapter . . . . *http://www.iicsny.org/jobs/*
ISOCOR . . . . *http://www.isocor.com/*
Society for Technical Communication . . . . *http://stc.org/*
Synergistech Communications . . . . *http://www.synergistech.com*

Computer Science

(Includes animation, AS/400, client/server applications, communications, consulting, data processing, data management, engineering, graphic design, hardware, information processing, information technology, modeling, multimedia, networks, programming, research, simulation, software, systems integration, technical support, etc.)

3DSite *http://www.lightside.com/3dsite/cgi/offers/index.html*

Absolutely Australian . . . . *http://www.netm.com/mall/infoprod/absol/bus.htm*

Advanced Technology Employment Consultants . . . . *http://home.eznet.net/~atec*

Allen Davis & Associates Software Jobs Home Page . . . . *http://www.softwarejobs.com*

Apple Recruitment (UK) . . . . *http://www.u-net.com/~applerec/*

Ardent Group, Inc. <The> . . . . *http://www.ardentgrp.com/*

Ardex Executive Search <The> . . . . *http://www.andex.com/*

Argonne National Laboratory, Mathematics
     and Computer Science Division . . . . *http://www.mcs.anl.gov/Divisional/positions.html*

Artificial Intelligence Applications Institute . . . . *http://www.aiai.ed.ac.uk/aiai/jobs/*

Artificial Intelligence Jobs Repository . . . . *http://www.cs.cmu.edu/Groups/AI/html/other/jobs.html*

ASA Information Services . . . . *http://www.eskimo.com/~pageless/asa/*

ASA Solutions . . . . *http://www.asasol.com*

Association for Computing Machinery . . . . , ... *http://www.acm.org/member_services/career/*

Association of Midwest College Biology Teachers . . . . *http://papa.indstate.edu/*

Australian Computer Professionals . . . . *http://www.ozjobs.com*

Australian Computer Professionals Jobs Online . . . . *http://www.digiweb.com/~aep1/*

Baber's Employment Directory . . . . *http://www.baber.com/em-plt.htm*

Baywatch Personnel (New Zealand) . . . . *http://ourworld.compuserve.com/*
                                                                   homepages/pages/baywatch.htm

BBN Networking, Inc. . . . . *http://www.bbn.com/bbnjobs/jobsrch.htm*

BCL International (UK) . . . . *http://www.bcl.com/*

Beardsley Group <The> . . . . *http://www.beardsleygroup.com/*

Belcan Information Services . . . . *http://www.belcan.com/infoserv.htm*

Biodata Navigator Job Board . . . . *http://www.biodata.com/biodata/bd_jobs.html*

BlackHawk Information Services . . . . *http://www.blackhawkis.com*

Bogue Company . . . . *http://www.bogueco.com*

Bolton Group <The> . . . . *http://www.webcreations.com/bolton/*

Brannon and Tully Consulting Services . . . . *http://www.brannontully.com*

Brei & Associates, Inc. Jobs Database . . . . *http://www.netins.net/showcase/rdbrei/*

British Crystallographic Association . . . . *http://www.cryst.bbk.ac.uk/BCA/jobs.html*

Cambridge Group . . . . *http://cambridgegroup.com/C/cambridge*

Canadian Computing Careers, ProNet Search–Canada . . . . *http://bisinc.com/pronet/ccc/*

Cape Connections Software . . . . *http://www.vital.co.za/ccs*

Career Blazers Learning Centre (Canada) . . . . *http://cblazers.ns.ca/*

Career Command Center . . . . *http://www.CareerCommandCenter.com/ccc.html*

Career Source . . . . *http://www.netusa.com/jobs.htm*

Center for Applied Large-Scale Computing *http://quasar.poly.edu:80/CALC/jobs.html*

Cerberus Computing Corporation . . . . *http://www.cerb.com*

CERL Sound Group . . . . *http://datura.cerl.uiuc.edu/netStuff/jobs/jobs.html*

Certes Computing Ltd. (UK) . . . . *http://www.certes.co.uk/docs/home.htm*

CFD (Computational Fluid Dynamics) Online . . . . *http://www.tfd.chalmers.se/CFD_Online/cfd-job/*

CGI Job Offers . . . . *http://www.lightside.com/~dani/cgi/offers/index.html*

Chancellor & Chancellor . . . . *http://www.chancellor.com*

Chemtech, Ltd . . . . *http://www.interaccess.com/ctld/*

Chicago Mosaic . . . . *http://www.ci.chi.il.us*

C.I. Software Associates . . . . *http://www.cisoftware.com*

Cinenet Communications . . . . *http://www.cinenet.net/*

Cochran Consulting . . . . *http://www.cochranctg.com*

Collaborative Computational Projects (UK) *http://www.dl.ac.uk/CCP/CCP5/vacancies.html*

CompuData . . . . *http://www.gncs.com/cdi/*

Computer Consulting Group . . . . *http://www.cconsulting.com/positions.html*

Computer Graphics (Insight Studios) . . . . *http://emporium.turnpike.net/I/INSIGHT/jobs.htm*

Computer Management Consultants . . . . *http://www.jobbankusa.com/cmc/*

Computer Personnel . . . . *http://cpi-seattle.com/*

Computer Resellers Weekly . . . . *http://www.techweb.cmp.com/crn/career/career.html*

Computer Resources Group . . . . *http://www.crgusa.com/*

Computer Science Employment Resources at Carnegie
      Mellon University . . . . . . *http://www.cs.cmu.edu/afs/cs/cmu.edu/Web/Library/tips/jobs.html*

Computer Staffing Provider <The> . . . . *http://www.atr.com/*

ComputerWeek Jobs Online . . . . *http://www.jobs.co.za/*

Computing and Technology Companies Online . . . . . . *http://www.cmpcmm.com/cc/companies.html*

Computing Careers Online . . . . *http://www.isgjobs.com*

Computing/IT Jobs WorldWide . . . . *http://www.Britain.EU.net/vendor/jobs/main.html*

Contract Jobs . . . . *http://www.contract-jobs.com*

CSUS Student/Alumni Employment Opportunities *gopher://gopher.csus.edu/11/employment*

CV Direct Services Ltd. . . . . *http://www.cvdirect.co.uk/*

Daley Consulting & Search and Daley Technical Search . . . . *http://www.dpsearch.com/*

Dallas ComputerJobs Store . *http://www.computerjobs.com/scripts/dbml.exe?template=/index.dbm*

Data Careers . . . . *http://www.vnu.com/datanews/careers/careers_eng.html*

Data Processing Career Centers . . . . *http://www.careercenter.com/*

Data Processing Independent Consultant's Exchange (DICE) . . . . *http://www.dice.com*

DataMasters . . . . *http://www.datamasters.com*

David Aplin and Associates (Canada) . . . . *http://www.tgx.com/aplin/*

Development Systems . . . . *http://www.webcreations.com/dsi/*

DP Independent Consultants Exchange *http://www.dice.dlinc.com:8181/*

Duncan and Ryan Associates (New Zealand) *http://www.jobnetnz.co.nz/Agencies/Duncan-Ryan.html*

DXI Corporation, Atlanta, GA . . . . *http://isotropic.com/dxicorp/dxihome.html*

EagleView . . . . *http://www.eagleview.com*

EDP Contract Services . . . . *http://edpcs.com/*

European Centre for Research and Advanced Training
      in Scientific Computation (CERFACS) . . . . *http://www.cerfacs.fr/admin/vacteams.html*

Excellence in Consulting . . . . *http://www.exic.com/eichome.html*

Faculty Positions in Computer Science . . . . *http://www.cs.cmu.edu/afs/cs.cmu.edu/*
                                                                   user/burks/www/faculty.html

FDSI's Job Center . . . . *http://www.fdsi-cons.com/*

Flavell Divett International (UK) . . . . *http://www.mistral.co.uk/fdi/*

Florida Sentinal . . . . *http://www.chicago.tribune.com/career/sentinel_ads.html*

Forbes Ltd. (UK) *http://194.128.198.201/forbes/*

Forum Personnel, Inc. . . . . *http://www.brainlink.com/*

Freelance Access . . . . *http://www.freelanceaccess.com/*

GeoSearch . . . . *http://www.geosearch.com/*

Hallahan & Associates . . . . *http://www.hallahan.com*

Help Wanted.Com, YSS Inc. *http://www.helpwanted.com/career.html*

HKA CompuSearch . . . . *http://www.hkacompusearch.com*

Howard Systems International . . . . *http://www.howardsystems.com*

Hummer Winblad Venture Partners . . . . *http://www.humwin.com*

IEEE Computer Society . . . . *http://www.computer.org/pubs/computer/career/career.htm*

India Connect's Job Classified . . . . *http://www.indiaconnect.com/classadv/svacant.htm*

Informatics Search Group . . . . *http://www.isgjobs.com*

Information Professional Resource . . . . *http://www.nrv.net/~ipr/*

Information Science and
      Telecommunications Placement . . . . *http://www2.lis.pitt.edu/~sochats/placement.html*

InfoServ Technologies . . . . *http://members.aol.com/tampacs/infoserv.htm*

InfoTech–Placement Services Group . . . . *http://www.itweb.com/infotec/index.html*

Institut fur Arbeitswirtschaft und
    Organisation, Germany . . . . *http://www.iao.fhg.de/Public/hiwi/OVERVIEW-en.html*
Instructional Technology Jobs,
    Indiana University, Bloomington . *http://education.indiana.edu/ist/students/jobs/joblink.html*
Integrated Computer Solutions . . . . *http://www.ics.com/Jobs/*
Intellimatch On-Line Career Services . . . . *http://www.intellimatch.com/intellimatch/*
Interactive Recruitment Limited (UK) *http://194.128.198.201/inter-active/*
International Interactive Communications Society
    (IICS), New York Chapter . . . . *http://www.iicsny.org/jobs/*
International Teleproduction Society . . . . *http://www.itsnet.org/jobs.html*
Interskill Services S.A. . . . . *http://www.interskill.ch/*
INTERTECH Computer Consultants (UK) . . . . *http://www.intertech.co.uk/*
Irish and Associates . . . . *http://www.frontiernet.net/~wairish*
ISOCOR . . . . *http://www.isocor.com/*
I.T. Staffing (Canada) . . . . *http://www.itstaff.com/*
ITTA Connection . . . . *http://www.it-ta.com*
ITTA Recruiter Services . . . . *http://www.it-ta.com/rcselect.htm*
J. Arthur Group . . . . *http://www.jarthurgroup.com/*
J. B. Groner Executive Search, Inc. . . . . *http://www.execjobsearch.com/*
J. D. Heinz & Associates . . . . *http://www.staffing.net/misnet.htm*
J. Robert Scott, Executive Search . . . . *http://j-robert-scott.com/*
JKL Enterprises, Inc . . . . *http://www.jklenterprises.com*
Job.net from Computer Contractor *http://www.vnu.co.uk/:81/ip_user/owa/register.main?c_mag_id=*
JobNet NZ <The> . . . . *http://www.jobnetnz.co.nz/*
Jobs Northwest . . . . *http://www.jobsnorthwest.com/*
JobServe (UK) . . . . *http://www.jobserve.com/*
JobSmart . . . . *http://jobsmart.org/*
Jobware . . . . *http://www.jobware.de/*
JWEvans & Company . . . . *http://www.jwevans.com*
Kelly Luxford (New Zealand) . . . . *http://www.jobnetnz.co.nz/Agencies/Kelly-Luxford.html*
KENDA Systems, Inc. . . . . *http://www.kenda.com/*
Kendall & Davis—Data Processing Professionals *http://www.fwi.com:80/kd-resources/*
KGB Resources (UK) *http://194.128.198.201/kgb/main.html*
Kinetic Agency Services . . . . *http://www.interlog.com/~kas/*
Kingsford-Smith Partnership Ltd (UK) . . . . *http://www.kingsford-smith.co.uk/kingsford-smith*
Kratec Company . . . . *http://www.motor-city.com/kratec/*
Lester Associates Job Bureau . . . . *http://www.ozemail.com.au:80/~lesters/*
Lynx . . . . *http://www.lynxinc.com*
MacTemps . . . . *http://www.mactemps.com/*
Management Recruiters of North Canton . . . . *http://www.mrnc.com/*
Management Recruiters of Silicon Valley . . . . *http://www.mrisanjose.com/*
Marr Group <The> . . . . *http://www.marrgroup.com*
Mathcor . . . . *http://ourworld.compuserve.com/homepages/Mathcor*
Matrix Resources, Inc. . . . . *http://www.matrixres.com/*
McBride and Associates Computer Placement Professionals . . . *http://www.pacificrim.net/~andrew/*
McCormick Search–Executive Search and Recruitment . . . . *http://www.xnet.com/~itopport*
McCoy Ltd. . . . . *http://www.netview.com/mccoy/*
                                                               http://www.mccoy.com/index.html
Medianet (UK) . . . . *http://www.pavilion.co.uk/medianet/jobs/jobs.htm*
MHC Consulting Services Ltd (UK) . . . . *http://www.lds.co.uk/mhc/*
MicroTemps . . . . *http://microtemps.com/*
Midwest Computer Consultants Ltd (UK) . . . . *http://www.mwcc.com/*
Mindsource Software . . . . *http://www.mindsrc.com/reqs_body.html*
Modeling, Simulation and Training Employment Postings . . . . *http://itsc.sc.ist.ucf.edu/jobs.htm*

MultiMedia Wire Classifieds . . . . *http://www.phillips.com/mmwire*
http://www.mmwire.com:80/classifieds.html
Nano Solutions Associates . . . . *http://www.nanosolutions.com*
National Computer Board (Singapore) . . . . *http://www.ncb.gov.sg/ncb/recruit.html*
National Multimedia Association of America . . . . *http://www.nmaa.org/nmaa/jobbank.htm*
National Writer's Union JobHotline . . . . *http:www.nwu.org/nwu/hotline/*
Naval Research Library's Job Link . . . . . . *http://infoweb.nrl.navy.mil/catalogs_and_databases/job/*
NCSA, The National Center for
    Supercomputer Applications *http://www.ncsa.uiuc.edu/General/Jobs/00Jobs.html*
Net Contractor (UK) . . . . *http://www.demon.co.uk/syntaxis/contract/home.html*
Net-Globe's Job Data Base . . . . *http://mail.travel-net.com/*
NISS (National Information Services . . . . *http://www.niss.ac.uk/noticeboard/index.html#jobs*
    and Systems) Noticeboard   *http://www.niss.ac.uk/news/index*
Olsten Information Technology Staffing *http://olsten.boulder.net:80/olstenskills.html*
Online Consultants . . . . *http://www.idsonline.com/online/*
Online Design . . . . *http://www.thesphere.com/OnLine/*
OptoLink . . . . *http://www.spie.org/web/employment/employ_home.html*
OzJobs (ACP OnLine) . . . . *http://columbia.digiweb.com/~aep1/cgi-bin/jobidx.cgi*
Patricia Pocock and Associates . . . . *http://homepage.interaccess.com/~ppocock2/PPA.html*
Portfolio . . . . *http://www.portfolio.skill.com/*
Post a Job . . . . *http://www.postajob.com*
Price Jamieson . . . . *http://www.pricejam.com*
Prime Recruitment (UK) . . . . *http://www.tcp.co.uk/~primerec/*
Prism Group (Recruiting) <The> . . . . *http://www.theprismgroup.com*
Professional Computer Consultants Group Ltd. . . . . *http://infoweb.magi.com/~procom/*
Professionals <The> . . . . *http://www.theprofessionals.com*
Professionals On Line/Employment and Recruitment . . *http://www.wordsimages.com/emp_rec.htm*
ProNet Search . . . . *http://bisinc.com/pronet/*
ProQuest . . . . *http://www.onramp.net/proquest*
Prospectus Computer (UK) . . . . *http://www.prospectus.co.uk/prospectus/*
Provident Search Group . . . . *http://www.dpjobs.com/*
QCC Associates' Job Search Page . . . . *http://www.cnj.digex.net/~qcc/*
Quest Systems . . . . *http://www.questsyst.com*
Reed Personnel Services . . . . *http://www.reed.co.uk/*
Richard Wheeler Associates (UK) . . . . *http://www.hiway.co.uk/rwa/*
Rimpac Systems (UK) *http://194.128.198.201/rimpac/*
RJ Pascale & Company . . . . *http://www.ct-jobs.com/pascale/*
Rollins Search Group . . . . *http://www.rollinssearch.com/*
Roy Talman & Associates . . . . *http://www.roy-talman.com/*
RS/6000® *http://www.s6000.com/job.html*
Saber Consultants . . . . *http://www.saberedge.com/*
Sally Silver Incorporated . . . . *http://www.sallysilver.com/*
Schulenburg & Associates . . . . *http://www.vnet.net/neil*
SciComp Job List . . . . *http://scicomp.math.uni-augsburg.de/scicomp/gsci/jobs/jobs.html*
Setka Computer Consulting . . . . *http://www.setka.com/*
SIAM News Professional Opportunities *gopher://gopher.siam.org/11/siamnews/profops*
Silicon Alley Connections, LLC . . . . *http://www.salley.com*
Singapore Online . . . . *http://www.singapore.com/jobs.htm*
Skandinavisk Computer Rekruttering . . . . *http://www.scrwest.dk/indexuk.htm*
SnellingSearch . . . . *http://www.snellingsearch.com*
Softskill . . . . *http://www.indigo.ie/softskill*
Software AG Community . . . . *http://www.nauticom.net/users/sferrell/sagjobs.html*
Software Consulting Services . . . . *http://nscs.fast.net/jobs.html*
Software Jobs Homepage . . . . *http://clever.net/swjobs/*
Software Personnel . . . . *http://www.jobserve.com/sp*

Source One Data Processing *http://www.career1.com*
Source Services . . . . *http://www.primenet.com/~sors/*
South Oregon *http://www2.vertexgroup.com/soredi/*
Southeastern Software Association (SSA) . . . . *http://www.sesoft.org/news/joblink.html*
Span Consultancy <The> . . . . *http://www.span-consultancy.co.uk/contact.html*
Spiderline . . . . *http://www.spiderline.com*
Staffing Options & Solutions . . . . *http://iypn.com/staffing*
Stanford Associates (UK) *http://194.128.198.201/stanford/*
Sykes Enterprises . . . . *http://www.sykes.com*
Synergistech Communications . . . . *http://www.synergistech.com*
Syntax Consultancy Limited (UK) . . . . *http://www.syntaxco.co.uk/xmas/syntaxco.htm*
Systems Network . . . . *http://www.SystemsNet.com/*
Tech Search Jobsight . . . . *http://www.jobsight.com/*
Tech Specialists . . . . *http://www.techspec.com*
Technical Employment Consultants . . . . *http://www.tech-employ-consult.com/*
TKO Personnel . . . . *http://www.tkointl.com*
Top Jobs on the Net . . . . *http://www.topjobs.co.uk/intel/intel.htm*
Training and Development Job Mart,
    T&D Business Showcase . . . . *http://www.tcm.com/trdev/jobs/jobs.htm*
TSG Professional Services, Inc. . . . . *http://www.tsgpro.com/*
Westech Career Expos . . . . *http://www.vjf.com/pub/westech/*
Winter, Wyman, and Co. Employment InfoCenter . . . *http://www.winterwyman.com/wwcsjobs.htm*
Women in Computer Science & Engineering . . . . *http://www.ai.mit.edu/people/ellens/gender.html*
Zeitech . . . . *http://www.zeitech.com*

Construction

Building Industry Exchange . . . . *http://www.building.org*
CollegePro Painters . . . . *http://wanda.pond.com/mall/collegepro/intern.html*
                                        http://wanda.phl.pond.com/mall/collegepro/
Construction Site's Guide to Jobs <The> . . . . *http://www.emap.com/construct/jobs.htm*
Engineering News Record . . . . *http://www.enr.com/find/onnet.htm*
Hotflash Jobs . . . . *http://iquest.com/~ntes/jobslist.html*
IEEE, University of Massachusetts Student Branch . . . . *http://www.ecs.umass.edu/*
Ketner & Associates . . . . *http://www.ketner.com*
Right of Way . . . . *http://www.rightofway.com/*

Consulting

Andersen Consulting . . . . *http://www.ac.com/main.html*
ANSA Job Opportunities . . . . *http://www.ansa.co.uk/APM/job-ad.html*
Application Resources, Inc. . . . . *http://www.appres.com/ari/*
Asia Pacific Management Forum . . . . *http://www.mcb.co.uk/apmforum/nethome.htm*
Australian Computer Professionals Jobs Online . . . . *http://www.digiweb.com/~aep1/*
AUX Technology, Inc. . . . . *http://kiwi.futuris.net/aux/*
Banking Related Jobs . . . . *http://www.cob.ohio-state.edu/~fin/osujobs.htm*
Believe and Succeed . . . . *http://www.ens.net/*
Careers in Management Consulting . . *http://www.cob.ohio-state.edu:80/dept/fin/jobs/consult.htm*
Computer Consulting Group . . . . *http://www.cconsulting.com/positions.html*
Computer Resources Group . . . . *http://www.crgusa.com/*
Dallas Computer Jobs Store . *http://www.computerjobs.com/scripts/dbml.exe?template=/index.dbm*
Data Careers . . . . *http://www.nnu.com/datanews/careers/careers_eng.html*
Donnington Associates (UK) . . . . *http://www.i-way.co.uk/donnington/*
Eclectic International Executive Search . . . . *http://www.cyber.nl/eclectic/sap/welcome.html*
EgoSearch (Belgium) . . . . *http://www.interpac.be/egosearch/welcome.html*
Energys Technical Services Ltd (UK) . . . . *http://www.energys.co.uk/energys/*
Environmental Careers Organization <The> . . . . *http://www.eco.org*

Eurolink Group PLC (UK) . . . . *http://www.eurolinkgroup.plc.uk/*
Financial Job Opportunities
    (Business Job Finder) . . . . *http://www.cob.ohio-state.edu/dept/fin/osujobs.htm*
Information Technology Talent Association, LLC . . . . *http://www.it-ta.com/*
INTERTECH Computer Consultants (UK) . . . . *http://www.intertech.co.uk/*
JKL Enterprises, Inc . . . . *http://www.jklenterprises.com*
Ketner & Associates . . . . *http://www.ketner.com*
National Computer Board (Singapore) . . . . *http://www.ncb.gov.sg/ncb/recruit.html*
OptoLink . . . . *http://www.spie.org/web/employment/employ_home.html*
Professional Computer Consultants Group Ltd. . . . . *http://infoweb.magi.com/~procom/*
Professionals On Line/Employment and Recruitment . . *http://www.wordsimages.com/emp_rec.htm*
Profil d.o.o. (Slovenia) . . . . *http://www.profil.si/profile.html*
QCC Associates' Job Search Page . . . . *http://www.cnj.digex.net/~qcc/*
Seamless Web's Legal Job Center <The> . . . . *http://www.seamless.com/jobs/*
Software Contractors' Guild <The> . . . . *http://www.scguild.com/*
Span Consultancy <The> . . . . *http://www.span-consultancy.co.uk/contact.html*
Transaction Information Systems . . . . *http://www.tisny.com/jobs/jobs.htm*
WDVL: Jobs for Web Developers <The> . . . . *http://www.stars.com/jobs/*
Winter, Wyman, and Co. Employment InfoCenter . . . *http://www.winterwyman.com/wwcsjobs.htm*
World Wide Web Consortium *http://www10.w3.org/hypertext/WWW/*
                                         Consortium/Recruitment/Overview.html

Contracting

1-800-NETWORK *http://www.1800network.com/*
Adderley Group <The> . . . . *http://www.adderley.com/*
Andersen Contracting (Australia) . . . . *http://www.swcontracting.com.au/body.htm*
Application Resources, Inc. . . . . *http://www.appres.com/ari/*
ASC Connections LTD. . . . . *http://www.itjobsearch.com/asc/*
Bankey Temporary Services . . . . *http://gwabbs.com/~bankey/tempagency.htm*
BCL International (UK) . . . . *http://www.bcl.com/*
Computer Contracting on the Internet, ETX
    Melbourne, Australia . . . . *http://www.ozemail.com.au/~contract/etx.html*
Contract Jobs . . . . *http://www.contract-jobs.com*
Daley Consulting & Search and Daley Technical Search . . . . *http://www.dpsearch.com/*
DataMasters . . . . *http://www.datamasters.com*
David Aplin and Associates (Canada) . . . . *http://www.tgx.com/aplin/*
Doughty Group Ltd (New Zealand) <The> . . . . . . *http://www.jobnetnz.co.nz/Agencies/doughty.html*
Duncan and Ryan Associates (New Zealand) *http://www.jobnetnz.co.nz/Agencies/Duncan-Ryan.html*
DXI Corporation, Atlanta, GA . . . . *http://isotropic.com/dxicorp/dxihome.html*
EDP Contract Services . . . . *http://edpcs.com/*
Education Gazette (New Zealand) . *http://www.learningmedia.co.nz/egissues/eglatest/eg_conts.htm*
Engine Room (UK and Europe) <The>, iWEB . . . . *http://www.iweb.co.uk/iwsearch.html*
Eurolink Group PLC (UK) . . . . *http://www.eurolinkgroup.plc.uk/*
Executive Recruitment Services (UK) . . . . *http://www.ers.co.uk/ers/*
Expertel Consultants Ltd (UK) . . . . *http://www.pncl.co.uk/expertel/*
Flavell Divett International (UK) . . . . *http://www.mistral.co.uk/fdi/*
Hotflash Jobs . . . . *http://iquest.com/~ntes/jobslist.html*
Intrinsica Systems (UK) . . . . *http://www.intrinsica.co.uk/*
J. Edgar & Associates Inc. . . . . *http://www.the-wire.com/careers/*
JKL Enterprises, Inc . . . . *http://www.jklenterprises.com*
Job.net from Computer Contractor *http://www.vnu.co.uk/:81/ip_user/owa/register.main?c_mag_id=*
Lockheed Martin Energy Systems . . . . *http://www.ornl.gov/mmes-www/MMESemployment.html*
                                  http://www.ornl.gov/employment.html
MicroTemps . . . . *http://microtemps.com/*
Mindsource Software . . . . *http://www.mindsrc.com/reqs_body.html*
Net Contractor (UK) . . . . *http://www.demon.co.uk/syntaxis/contract/home.html*

Object People (Australia) . . . . *http://www.ozemail.com.au/objectpeople/view.html*
Sally Silver Incorporated . . . . *http://www.sallysilver.com/*
Software Contractors' Guild <The> . . . . *http://www.scguild.com/*
Winter, Wyman, and Co. Employment InfoCenter . . . *http://www.winterwyman.com/wwcsjobs.htm*

Disabled

CANDO—The Career Advisory Network on
      Disability Opportunities (UK) . . . . *http://www.comp.lancs.ac.uk/uni-services/careers/cando/*
Career Center for Workforce Diversity,
      Equal Opportunity Publications, Inc. (EOP) . . . . *http://www.eop.com*
Careers On-Line . . . . *http://www.disserv.stu.umn.edu*
City of Morgantown Jobs . . . . *http://www.dmssoft.com/city/jobs.htm*
Disability Services Careers On-Line . . . . *http://www.disserv.stu.umn.edu/TC/Grants/COL/*
Employment and Training Agencies . . . . *http://bcn.boulder.co.us/employment/agencies.html*
Hiring Assistant and Placements Program . . . . *http://www.sonic.net/~richw/zjobapps.html#top*
Job Accommodation Network . . . . *http://janweb.icdi.wvu.edu/*

Diversity

(Includes American Indian affairs, Asian, African-American, cultural studies, Hispanic, over 40, senior citizens, etc.)

American Chemical Society . . . . *http://www.acs.org/memgen/employmt/pdb/acsmenu.htm*
American Communication Association
      (Grants and Fellowships) . . . . *http://www.uark.edu/depts/comminfo/www/grants.html*
American Indian Science & Engineering Society (AISESnet) . *http://bioc02.uthscsa.edu/aisesnet.html*
Automated Vacancy Announcement System (AVADS) . *http://info.er.usgs.gov/doi/avads/index.html*
Biosciences Job Listings and Career Services . . . . *http://golgi.harvard.edu/biopages/jobs.html*
Career Center for Workforce Diversity,
      Equal Opportunity Publications, Inc. (EOP) . . . . *http://www.eop.com*
Career Development Network <The> . . . . *http://www.webscope.com/webscope/*
Chicano/Latino Electronic Network (CLENet) *gopher://latino.sscnet.ucla.edu/11/*
                               The%20News%20Center/Job%20Announcements
                               gopher://latino.sscnet.ucla.edu:70/11/
                               Employment%20Center/Job%20Announcements/
CLNET . . . . *http://latino.sscnet.ucla.edu/*
Department of the Interior Automated Vacancy
      Announcement System (AVADS) . . . . *http://www.usgs.gov/doi/avads/index.html*
Diverse Employment Industries . . . . *http://www.cfonline.com/cli/jobs/diverse/diverse.htm*
Education Jobs Page . . . . *http://www.nationjob.com/education*
Employment and Training Agencies . . . . *http://bcn.boulder.co.us/employment/agencies.html*
Employment Opportunities in Women's Studies and Feminism   *gopher://gopher.inform.umd.edu:70/*
                               11/EdRes/Topic/WomensStudies/Employment
Entertainment Recruiting Network . . . . *http://www.showbizjobs.com/middle.htm*
EOP's Career Center for Workforce Diversity . . . . *http://www.eop.com/*
Forty Plus . . . . *http://www.hal-pc.org/~sid/40plus.html*
Global Net's Latin American Career Center
      (Bolsa de Trabajo Global Net) . . . . *http://www.bolsadetrabajo.com*
Grants & Fellowships . . . . . . *http://www.sas.upenn.edu/African_Studies/Grants/menu_Grants.html*
GrantsWeb . . . . *http://web.fie.com/cws/sra/resource.htm*
Index of Native American Resources on the Internet . . . . . *http://www.hanksville.phast.umass.edu/*
                                        misc.NAresources.html
Internship Director . . . . *http://www.snpa.org/snpa/web/home.html*
Los Angeles Urban League . . . . *http://www.careermosaic.com/cm/ul/ull.html*
Manitoba Senior Citizens Employment Opportunities . . . . *http://www.mbnet.mb.ca/crm/*
                               other/genmb/msch/msch10.html
Minority Online Information Service <The> . . . . *http://web.fie.com/web/mol/*

188

National Diversity Journalism Job Bank . . . . *http://www.newsjobs.com*
National Institute of Health (NIH)
    Senior Job Opportunities *http://helix.nih.gov:8001/jobs/*
National Society of Black Engineers . . . . *http://www.nsbe.org*
Russian and East European Institute Employment
    Opportunities, Indiana University . . . . *http://www.indiana.edu/~reeiweb/indemp.html*
Saludos Web: Careers, Employment & Culture *http://www.hooked.net:80/saludos/index.html*
                                              http://www.wenet.net/saludos/
Seniors On-Line Job Bank . . . . *http://www.seniorsnet.com/jobbank.htm*
TKO Personnel, Inc. . . . . *http://www.tkointl.com*
Wang & Li Asia Resources . . . . *http://www.wang-li.com*
Women in Technology . . . . *http://www-personal.ksu.edu/~dangle*

Domestic

APPLE PIE, USA, Nannies . . . . *http://www.nanny.com/*
Au Pair in Europe . . . . *http://netaccess.on.ca/aupair/*
Au Pairs Job Match . . . . *http://www.aupairs.co.uk/*
Nanny Jobs, USA . . . . *http://www.parentsplace.com/shopping/nanny/jobs*

Economics

Avotek Publishing, International Headhunters Guide . . . . *http://www.universal.nl/jobhunt/*

Education

(Includes administration, assessment, counseling, early childhood development, evaluation, media specialists, research, teaching K-12, testing, etc.)
Academic Employment Network . . . . *http:///www.academploy.com/*
Agricultural Job Listings *http://caticsuf.csufresno.edu:70/1/atinet/agjobs*
American Educational Research Association . . . . *http://tikkun.ed.asu.edu/aera/home.html*
American Evaluation Association . . . . *http://www.theriver.com/public/aea/*
Association for Institutional Research . . . . *http://ike.engr.washington.edu/general/air.html*
Canadian Association of Career Educators and Employers . . . . . *http://www.cacee.com/workweb/*
Career Blazers Learning Centre (Canada) . . . . *http://cblazers.ns.ca/*
Career Corner . . . . *http://www.isminc.com/mm.html*
Catholic University of America <The> . . . . *http://www.cua.edu/*
CAUSE Job Posting Service . . . . *http://cause-www.colorado.edu/pd/jobpost/jobpost.html*
Center for Education and Work . . . . *http://www.cew.wisc.edu/*
Chronicle of Higher Education, Academe This Week . . . . *http://chronicle.merit.edu/.ads/.links.html*
Council for the Support and Advancement of
    Education (CASE) Job Classifieds *gopher://gopher.case.org:70/11/currents*
Department of Education and Employment (UK) . . . . . *http://www.open.gov.uk/dfee/dfeehome.htm*
EDNET—Job Net for Educators *http://pages.prodigy.com/CA/luca52a/bagley.html*
EDphysician . . . . *http://www.edphysician.com/*
Educatie Emancipatie Gehandicapte Arbeidskrachten . . . . *http://www.eega.nl/*
Education & Career Center <The> . . . . *http://www.petersons.com*
Education Gazette (New Zealand) . . . . *http://www.learningmedia.co.nz/*
                                       egissues/eglatest/eg_conts.htm
Education Jobs Page . . . . *http://www.nationjob.com/education*
EduNetCom: Education Employment . . . . *http://www.ccnet.com/~pstrader/*
Eduplus Management Group Inc. . . . . *http://www.eduplus.ca/*
EE-Link: The Environmental Education Web Server . . . *http://www.nceet.snre.umich.edu/jobs.html*
                                  gopher://nceet.snre.umich.edu/11/networking/
Elk Grove Unified School District *http://www.egusd.k12.ca.us/webdocs/claspost.htm*
Employment Opportunities in Women's *gopher://gopher.inform.umd.edu:70/11/*
    Studies and Feminism   *EdRes/Topic/WomensStudies/Employment*

ERIC Clearinghouse on Assessment and Evaluation . . . . *gopher://vmsgopher.cua.edu/*
11gopher_root_eric_ae%3a%5bjobs%5d

Federal Information Exchange (FEDIX) . . . . *http://web.fie.com/htdoc/fed/*
all/any/any/menu/any/index.htm

FinanceNet . . . . *http://www.financenet.gov/wwwlib5.htm#employ*

Florida School-to-Work . . . . *http://fcn.state.fl.us/flstw*

Foreign Language Listings *http://condor.stcloud.msus.edu:20020/careerannounce.html*

Georgia State University Career Services,
    Job Opportunity Bulletin *http://www.gsu.edu/dept/admin/plc/homepg4.html*

International Academic Job Market . . . . *http://www.camrev.com.au/share/jobs.html*

JobWeb's Database of U.S. School Districts . . . . *http://www.jobweb.org/sdistric.htm*

Kaplan . . . . *http://www.kaplan.com/*

Marin County Office of Education *http://www.marin.k12.ca.us/job.html*

Mayo Clinic Online Career Center . . . . *http://www.mayo.edu/career/career.html*

National Educators Employment Review . . . . *http://www.netgrafx.com/neer/default.htm*

Pasco County Schools Jobs *http://www.pasco.k12.fl.us/PascoJobs.html*

Project Connect . . . . *http://careers.soemadison.wisc.edu/projcon.htm*

San Francisco Unified School District *http://nisus.sfusd.k12.ca.us/*

Santa Clara County Office of Education *http://www.sccoe.k12.ca.us/eo.html*

Syracuse University, NY . . . *http://www.syr.edu/WWW-Syr/HumanResources/JobOppsatSU/index.html*
gopher://cwis.syr.edu/11/employment

TESLJB-L, Teaching English As a Foreign Language *gopher://CUNYVM.CUNY.EDU/11/*
Subject%20Specific%20Gophers/teslfl/Teaching%20English
%20as%20a%20Foreign%20Language%20-%20The%20Profession

Texas Education Agency . . . . *http://www.tea.texas.gov*

TrainingNet . . . . *http://www.trainingnet.com/*

University of Colorado, Boulder . . . . *gopher://gopher.Colorado.EDU/*
select *Other Gophers by Subject*
select *Employment Opportunities and Resume Postings*

University of Minnesota's College of Education
    Job Search Bulletin Board *gopher://rodent.cis.umn.edu:11119/*

Usjobnet K-12 . . . . *http://www.usjobnet.com/*

Web Dog's Job Hunt . . . . *http://www.itec.sfsu.edu/jobs/*

Women in Higher Education Career Page . . . . *http://www.itis.com/wihe/*

Electrical

IEEE, Institute of Electrical and Electronic
    Engineers Job Bank . . . . *http://www.ieee.org/jobs.html*

IEEE, University of Massachusetts Student Branch . . . . *http://www.ecs.umass.edu/*

Institution of Electrical Engineers *http://www.iee.org.uk:80/*

Technical Employment Consultants . . . . *http://www.tech-employ-consult.com/*

Energy

Ames Laboratory . . . . *http://www.ameslab.gov/Job.html*

Association of Energy Services Professionals . . . . *http://www.dnai.com/AESP/jobs.html*

Department of Energy (DOE) *http://www.em.doe.gov/emnet1i.html*

National Institute for Nuclear Physics and
    High-Energy Physics (Netherlands) . . . . *http://www.nikhef.nl/*

YSN Jobs Page (Young Scientists Network),
    Jobs Listings Archive . . . . *http://www.physics.uiuc.edu/ysn/*

Engineering
(Includes ceramics, computers, construction, contracting, electrical, electronics, government, mapping, mechanical, technical writing, trouble shooting, etc.)

1st St. NW . . . . *http://www.fsnw.com/*

ACM Sigmod's On-line Career Center . . . . *http://www.acm.org/cacm/careerops/*

Advanced Technology Employment Consultants . . . . *http://home.eznet.net/~atec*
Africa Online: Jobs . . . . *http://www.AfricaOnline.com/AfricaOnline/classifieds.html*
American Ceramic Society's Ceramic Futures <The> *http://www.acers.org/mem/futures/futures.stm*
American Chemical Society . . . . *http://www.acs.org/memgen/employmt/pdb/acsmenu.htm*
American Indian Science & Engineering Society (AISESnet) . *http://bioc02.uthscsa.edu/aisesnet.html*
American Institute of Chemical Engineers . . . . *http://www.aiche.org/employment/*
 http://www.che.ufl.edu/WWW-CHE/aiche/
American Society for Engineering Education (ASEE) . . . . *http://www.asee.org/nein/pd/*
 http://www.asee.org/asee/publications/prism/classifieds/
American Society of Agricultural Engineers (ASAE) <The> . . . . *http://asae.org/resource/*
 http://www.asae.org:80/jobs
American Society of Civil Engineers . . . . *http://www.asce.org/*
American Society of Mechanical Engineers ASMENET . . . . *http://www.asme.org/index.html*
Apple Recruitment (UK) . . . . *http://www.u-net.com/~applerec/*
Argonne National Laboratory, Mathematics and
 Computer Science Division . . . . *http://www.mcs.anl.gov/Divisional/positions.html*
Audio Engineering Society . . . . *http://www.cudenver.edu/aes/*
Australian Computer Professionals Jobs Online . . . . *http://www.digiweb.com/~aep1/*
AUX Technology, Inc. . . . . *http://kiwi.futuris.net/aux/*
Avotek Publishing, International Headhunters Guide . . . . *http://www.universal.nl/jobhunt/*
AVR . . . . *http://www.mkt-place.com/laavrinc/avrpl.html*
Beardsley Group <The> . . . . *http://www.beardsleygroup.com/*
Belcan Information Services . . . . *http://www.belcan.com/infoserv.htm*
Bizlinks (Singapore) . . . . *http://sunflower.singnet.com.sg/~g6615000/*
Bolsa de Trabajo de Pixelnet (Mexico) [in Spanish] *http://www.pixel.com.mx:80/Curriculums/*
Bolton Group <The> . . . . *http://www.webcreations.com/bolton/*
Brei & Associates, Inc. Jobs Database . . . . *http://www.netins.net/showcase/rdbrei/*
Buzz Buzz @ads: Banen aangeboden (Netherlands) . . . . *http://valley.interact.nl/@ds/*
 banen-aanbod/home.html
Career Match *http://www.fleethouse.com/career/cm-pg1.htm*
Catalyst Corporation . . . . *http://www.catalystcorp.com*
Chancellor & Chancellor . . . . *http://www.chancellor.com*
Communications Engineering Employment Network . . *http://www.destek.net/ejdort/ce_emply.html*
Computer Science Employment Resources at Carnegie
 Mellon University . . . . . . *http://www.cs.cmu.edu/afs/cs/cmu.edu/Web/Library/tips/jobs.html*
Construction Site's Guide to Jobs <The> . . . . *http://www.emap.com/construct/jobs.htm*
Contract Employment Weekly, Jobs Online . . . . *http://www.ceweekly.wa.com/*
 http://www.ceweekly.com/
 gopher://gopher.ceweekly.wa.com/1
CSUS Student/Alumni Employment Opportunities *gopher://gopher.csus.edu/11/employment*
Data Careers . . . . *http://www.vnu.com/datanews/careers/careers_eng.html*
Donnington Associates (UK) . . . . *http://www.i-way.co.uk/donnington/*
DXI Corporation, Atlanta, GA . . . . *http://isotropic.com/dxicorp/dxihome.html*
Dynamic HR Solutions . . . . *http://www.dynamichr.com*
Electronic Industries Association . . . . *http://www.eia.org/norm.htm*
Employment Edge *http://www.employmentedge.com:80/employment.edge/*
ENews . . . . *http://www.sumnet.com/enews*
Engineering Job Source <The> . . . . *http://www.wwnet.com/~engineer/*
Engineering/Manufacturing Jobs Page . . . . *http://www.nationjob.com/engineering*
Engineering News Record . . . . *http://www.enr.com/find/onnet.htm*
Engineering Specific Career Advisory
 Problem-Solving Environment <The> . . . . *http://fairway.ecn.purdue.edu/ESCAPE/*
Executive Search Consultants . . . . *http://www.escinc.com/eschome.html*
Expertel Consultants Ltd (UK) . . . . *http://www.pncl.co.uk/expertel/*
Extreme Résumé Drop . . . . *http://www.mainquad.com/theQuad/wich/introPages/lo/erd.html*
Fermi National Accelerator Laboratory . . . . *http://www.fnal.gov/employ.html*

finishing.com's Help-Wanted . . . . http://www.finishing.com/Directory/wanted.html

Florida Sentinal . . . . http://www.chicago.tribune.com/career/sentinel_ads.html

Foreign Language Listings http://condor.stcloud.msus.edu:20020/careerannounce.html

Georgia State University Career Services,
       Job Opportunity Bulletin http://www.gsu.edu/dept/admin/plc/homepg4.html

Help Wanted.Com, YSS Inc. . . . . http://www.helpwanted.com/career.html

Hotflash Jobs . . . . http://iquest.com/~ntes/jobslist.html

Houston Advanced Research Center . . . . http://www.harc.edu/jobs.html

IBA reSearch . . . . http://web.wingsbbs.com/ibaresearch/

IEEE Computer Society . . . . http://www.computer.org/pubs/computer/career/career.htm

IEEE, Institute of Electrical and Electronic
       Engineers Job Bank . . . . http://www.ieee.org/jobs.html

IEEE, University of Massachusetts Student Branch . . . . http://www.ecs.umass.edu/

IndustryNet Career Opportunities . . . . http://www.industry.net/c/mn/_co

Institution of Electrical Engineers http://www.iee.org.uk:80/

Integrated Computer Solutions . . . . http://www.ics.com/Jobs/

Interpac Belgium . . . . http://www.interpac.be/jobs.html

IPC Technologies . . . . http://www.ipctech.com/employment.htm

J. Edgar & Associates Inc. . . . . http://www.the-wire.com/careers/

Jay Tracey Associates http://amsquare.com/america/search1.html

Job Search Materials for Engineers . . . . http://www.englib.cornell.edu/

Lockheed Martin Energy Systems . . . . . . http://www.ornl.gov/mmes-www/MMESemployment.html

                                               http://www.ornl.gov/employment.html

Mathcor . . . . http://ourworld.compuserve.com/homepages/Mathcor

Mindsource Software . . . . http://www.mindsrc.com/reqs_body.html

National Computer Board (Singapore) . . . . http://www.ncb.gov.sg/ncb/recruit.html

National Society of Black Engineers . . . . http://www.nsbe.org

National Society of Professional Engineering HP . . . . http://www.nspe.org

National Technical Employment Services . . . . http://iquest.com/~ntes/

Network Operations Worldwide (Belgium) . . . . http://www.belgium.eu.net/company/jobs/jobs.html

Networking Jobs in North California . . . . http://www.pcpersonnel.com/

NetWorld MarketPlace Career Opportunities . . . . http://www.networldmkt.com/networld/career.htm

Oak Ridge National Laboratory . . . . http://www.ornl.gov

Online Design . . . . http://www.thesphere.com/OnLine/

Optical Society of America, Optics Net . . . . http://www.osa.org/

OPTICS.ORG, SPIE Employment . . . . http://optics.org/employment/

OptoLink . . . . http://www.spie.org/web/employment/employ_home.html

Prime Recruitment (UK) . . . . http://www.tcp.co.uk/~primerec/

Right of Way . . . . http://www.rightofway.com/

Sally Silver Incorporated . . . . http://www.sallysilver.com/

Science Global Career Network, Science JobNet, ... http://www.aaas.org

      American Association for the Advancement of Science   http://science-mag.aaas.org/science/

                          http://www.science-mag.aaas.org:888/science/scripts/recruit/search

                                   http://www.edoc.com/sgcn/Lineads.html

                 http://www.sciencemag.org/science/feature/classified/search.shtml

Singapore Online . . . . http://www.singapore.com/jobs.htm

Society for Experimental Mechanics . . . . http://www.sem.bethel.ct.us/sem/jobs/jobs.html

Society of Hispanic Professional Engineers http://xerxes.nas.edu:70/1/cwse/SHPE.html

Society of Mexican American Engineers and Scientists   http://xerxes.nas.edu:70/1/cwse/MAES.html

Society of Women Engineers . . . . http://www.swe.org

TechWeb/TechCareers/TechHunter . . . . http://www.techweb.com/default.html.body?

                             http://techweb.com/careers/careers.html.body?

Westech Career Expos, WESTECH Career EXPO . . . . http://www.vjf.com/pub/westech/

Women in Computer Science & Engineering . . . . http://www.ai.mit.edu/people/ellens/gender.html

World Wide Web Consortium http://www10.w3.org/hypertext/WWW/

                                       Consortium/Recruitment/Overview.html

Entertainment
(Includes acting, choral, cinema, dance, film, music, orchestra, theater, etc.)

Arts Wire Current . . . . *http://www.tmn.com/Artswire/*
ArtsNet . . . . *http://artsnet.heinz.cmu.edu/career/career.html*
Broadcast Employment Services . . . . *http://www.tvjobs.com/index_a.htm*
CERL Sound Group . . . . *http://datura.cerl.uiuc.edu/netStuff/jobs/jobs.html*
Cinenet Communications . . . . *http://www.cinenet.net/*
Entertainment Recruiting Network . . . . *http://www.showbizjobs.com/middle.htm*
Film, TV, & Commercial Employment Network <The> . . . . *http://www.employnow.com*
MultiMedia Wire Classifieds . . . . *http://www.phillips.com/mmwire*
http://www.mmwire.com:80/classifieds.html
Music Exchange . . . . *http://scsn.net/~musex/*
Online Design . . . . *http://www.thesphere.com/OnLine/*
Society for Cinema Studies . . . . *http://www.sa.ua.edu/TCF/teach/employ/scsjob.htm*
Talent Network . . . . *http://www.talentnet.com/*
Talentworks . . . . *http://www.talentworks.com*
TV JobNet . . . . *http://www.tvjobnet.com/*
UTV—T.V. Job Classifieds . . . . *http://tvnet.kspace.com/jobs/*
Virtual Headbook . . . . *http://www.xmission.com:80/~wintrnx/vh/virtual.html*

Environment

Air and Waste Management Association . . . . *http://www.awma.org/employment.html*
American Industrial Hygiene Association . . . . *http://www.aiha.org/es.html*
Association of Energy Services Professionals . . . . *http://www.dnai.com/AESP/jobs.html*
Bermuda Biological Station for Research . . . . *http://www.bbsr.edu/*
BioSource . . . . *http://www.biosource-tech.com/*
Department of Energy (DOE) *http://www.em.doe.gov/emnet1i.html*
Department of the Interior Automated
Vacancy Announcement System (AVADS) . . . . *http://www.usgs.gov/doi/avads/index.html*
EarthWatch . . . . *http://www.earthwatch.org/t/Temployment.html*
EE-Link: The Environmental Education Web Server . . . *http://www.nceet.snre.umich.edu/jobs.html*
gopher://nceet.snre.umich.edu/11/networking/
Envirobiz—International Environmental Information Network . . . . *http://www.envirobiz.com/*
Environmental Careers Organization <The> . . . . *http://www.eco.org*
Environmental Protection Agency . . . . *http://www.epa.gov/epahome/Jobs.html*
finishing.com's Help-Wanted . . . . *http://www.finishing.com/Directory/wanted.html*
GeoSearch . . . . *http://www.geosearch.com/*
Global Environmental Management Initiative (GEMI) . . . . *http://www.gemi.org/*
Virginia Coast Reserve Information System (VCRIS) . . . . *http://atlantic.evsc.virginia.edu/*
gopher://atlantic.evsc.Virginia.EDU/11/Opportunities

Fashion
Internet Fashion Exchange . . . . *http://www.fashionexch.com/*
Models Online . . . . *http://www.models-online.com*

Finance

100 Careers in Wall Street . . . . *http://www.globalvillager.com/*
AAFA—The American Association of Finance and Accounting . . . . *http://www.aafa.com/*
Avotek Publishing, International Headhunters Guide . . . . *http://www.universal.nl/jobhunt/*
Banking Related Jobs . . . . *http://www.cob.ohio-state.edu/~fin/osujobs.htm*
BBN Networking, Inc. . . . . *http://www.bbn.com/bbnjobs/jobsrch.htm*
Bridge Information Technology Inc. (Canada Net Pages) . . . . *http://www.visions.com/*
Coopers and Lybrand (Australia) . . . . *http://www.colybrand.com.au/*
Dynamic HR Solutions . . . . *http://www.dynamichr.com*
Easynet Job-Centre (The Virtual Job Centre) . . . . *http://www.cyberiacafe.net/jobs/*
EDGAR at the SEC . . . . *http://www.sec.gov*
EDGAR Development Project, NYU Stern School of Business . . . . *http://edgar.stern.nyu.edu*

Employment News . . . . *http://www.ftn.net/*
Employment Opportunities in India . . . *http://www.webpage.com/hindu/960210/10/10hdline.html*
employment.net.au (Australia) . . . . *http://www.employment.net.au/*
Equipment Leasing Association OnLine . . . . *http://www.elaonline.com*
Executive Access . . . . *http://www.hk.net/~eal/index.html*
FinanceNet . . . . *http://www.financenet.gov/wwwlib5.htm#employ*
Financial Job Opportunities (Business Job Finder) . . . . *http://www.cob.ohio-state.edu/*
dept/fin/osujobs.htm

Gemini Personnel Ltd. . . . . *http://www.glink.net.hk:80/~gemini/*
Hamilton Jones & Koller (Australia) . . . . *http://www.hjk.com.au/*
Harrison Willis Group (UK) *http://194.128.198.201/hwgroup/main.html*
HEL—Human Enterprises Limited . . . . *http://www.demon.co.uk/hument/*
Hummer Winblad Venture Partners . . . . *http://www.humwin.com*
Information Center <The> . . . . *http://greatinfo.com/*
Institute of Fiscal Studies (UK) *http://www1.ifs.org.uk/ifsinfo/jobs/index.htm*
Insurance Career Center *http://www.connectyou.com:80/talent/*
Interactive Recruitment Limited (UK) *http://194.128.198.201/inter-active/*
J. Robert Scott, Executive Search . . . . *http://j-robert-scott.com/*
Jacobson Associates . . . . *http://www.jacobson-associates.com/*
Job Access Limited (Hong Kong) . . . . *http://www.hk.net/~jal/*
Job Banker <The> . . . . *http://www.nmaa.org/jobbank.htm*
Job Seekers Edging the Competition . . . . *http://bcn.boulder.co.us/business/*
Jobs in Consulting . . . . *http://www.cob.ohio-state.edu/dept/fin/*
Jobs in Finance for MBAs *http://www.cob.ohio-state.edu:80/dept/fin/osujob.htm*
Kunin Associates . . . . *http://www.gate.net/~kassoc/index.html?*
Reed Personnel Services, Reed Computing . . . . *http://www.reed.co.uk/*
Rollins Search Group . . . . *http://www.rollinssearch.com/*
Source Services . . . . *http://www.primenet.com/~sors/*

Food Service/Hospitality
(Includes bartenders, beverage industry, concierge, cooks, hotel clerks, supermarkets, waitpersons, etc.)
Food and Drug Packaging . . . . *http://www.fdp.com*
Hospitality Net, Hospitality Industry Job Exchange . . . . *http://www.hospitalitynet.nl/job/home.htm*
Hotel Jobs . . . . *http://www.webcom.com/jaeg/welcome.html*
Net-Globe's Job Data Base . . . . *http://mail.travel-net.com/*
Supermarket News . . . . *http://www.supermarketnews.com*

Geography
(Includes geographic information systems, mapping, remote sensing, physical sciences, etc.)
Association of American Geographers (AAG) <The> . . . . *http://www.aag.org/jobs.html*
GeoSearch . . . . *http://www.geosearch.com/*
GeoWeb for GIS/GPS/RS . . . . *http://www.ggrweb.com*
GIS Jobs Clearinghouse, University of Minnesota,
   Forestry, Remote Sensing Lab . . . . *http://www.gis.umn.edu/rsgisinfo/jobs.html*
Right of Way . . . . *http://www.rightofway.com/*

Geology
(Includes crystallography, geophysics, minerals/metals, mining, paleontology, petroleum, seismology, spectrometry, etc.)
American Crystallography Association . . . . *http://www.sdsc.edu/ACA/*
Automated Vacancy Announcement System (AVADS) . *http://info.er.usgs.gov/doi/avads/index.html*
British Crystallographic Association . . . . *http://www.cryst.bbk.ac.uk/BCA/jobs.html*
Crystallography *http://www.unige.ch/crystal/w3v1c/job-index.html*
http://www.unige.ch/crystal/job-index.html

Department of the Interior Automated
    Vacancy Announcement System (AVADS) . . . . *http://www.usgs.gov/doi/avads/index.html*
Geology Job Listings . . . . *http://diamond.ge.ic.ac.uk/careers/*
GeoScience Careers *http://www.science.uwaterloo.ca/earth/geoscience/table1.html*
GeoWeb for GlS/GPS/RS . . . . *http://www.ggrweb.com*
GIS Jobs Clearinghouse, University of Minnesota,
    Forestry, Remote Sensing Lab . . . . *http://www.gis.umn.edu/rsgisinfo/jobs.html*
Houston Advanced Research Center . . . . *http://www.harc.edu/jobs.html*
Info-Mine . . . . *http://www.info-mine.com/*
JOM, The Minerals, Metals, and Materials
    Society Journal . . . . *http://www.tms.org/pubs/journals/JOM/classifieds.html*
Selection, Recruiting of Latvian Seamen . . . . *http://www.unitree.lv/~sms/*

Government

(Includes federal, state, local, foreign, civil service, Department of Energy, Department of Interior, Internal Revenue Service, Military, NASA, NIH, NSF, OSHA, Park Service, etc.)

ABAG Globe . . . . *http://www.abag.ca.gov/bayarea/commerce/globe/globe.html*
Advocate Career Services . . . . *http://www.amsquare.com/america/advocate.html*
Alaskan Jobs . . . . *http://www.state.ak.us/local/akpages/ADMIN/rbtitl.htm*
American Industrial Hygiene Association . . . . *http://www.aiha.org/es.html*
Ames Laboratory . . . . *http://www.ameslab.gov/Job.html*
Army High Performance Computing (HPC) Research Center . . . . *http://www.arc.umn.edu/*
Askew School Job Placement Services . . . . *http://www.fpac.fsu/spap/job_intern/jobs/*
Askew School of Public Administration and Policy . . . . . *http://www.fsu.edu/spap/job_intern/jobs/*
                                                            http://www.fsu.edu:80/~spap/job/job/html
Attorney Job Listings, Department of Justice *gopher://justice2.usdoj.gov/1*
Attorney Job Network . . . . *http://www.jurisjob.com*
Austin, Texas Job Listings . . . . *http://www.ci.austin.tx.us/*
Australian Defence Forces . . . . *http://www.adfa.oz.au/DOD/recruit/recruit.htm*
Automated Vacancy Announcement System (AVADS) . *http://info.er.usgs.gov/doi/avads/index.html*
California Civil Service Employment Information . . . . *http://www.spb.ca.gov/*
California State Government . . . . *http://www.ca.gov/*
CITE Job Bank *gopher://esusda.gov/11/data/archive/cite-jobs-mg*
City and County of San Francisco . . . . *http://www.well.com/user/ctywatch/joblstng.html*
City of Cambridge, Massachusetts . . . . *http://www.ci.cambridge.ma.us/jobs/city_jobs.html*
City of Morgantown Jobs . . . . *http://www.dmssoft.com/city/jobs.htm*
City of Mountain View, California . . . . *http://www.abag.ca.gov/abag/*
                                                            local_gov/city/mt_view/mves/mves.html
City of Rochester, Minnesota . . . . *http://www.isl.net/city/joblink.html*
City of Roseville, Minnesota . . . . *http://www.ci.roseville.mn.us/admin/jobs.htm*
City of Saint Paul, Minnesota . . . . *http://www.stpaul.gov/jobopenings/*
City of Vancouver, Canada . . . . *http://www.city.vancouver.bc.ca/jobs/jobspage.html*
Civil Engineering and Public Works Career Paths *http://www.fileshop.com:80/apwa/civil.html*
Clark County, Nevada Personnel Department . . . . . . *http://www.sundaypaper.com/www/hwlv.htm*
Colorado Department of Labor and Employment . . . . *http://www.state.co.us/gov_dir/*
                                                            labor_dir/employment_services_le.html
Defense Nuclear Facilities Safety Board *gopher://nic.sura.net:7070/11/vacancy*
Department of Education and Employment (UK) . . . . . *http://www.open.gov.uk/dfee/dfeehome.htm*
Department of Employment *http://161.7.163.2/*
Department of Employment (Idaho) . . . . *http://www.doe.state.id.us/*
Department of Employment (Wyoming) . . . . *http://wyjobs.state.wy.us/*
Department of Employment and Training (Rhode Island) . . . . *http://www.det.state.ri.us/*
Department of Employment, Massachusetts Job Search . . . . *http://ma.jobsearch.org/*
Department of Employment, New Jersey Job Search . . . . *http://nj.jobsearch.org/*
Department of Employment Relations (Wisconsin) *http://badger.state.wi.us:70/1/*

Department of Employment Security (Utah) . . . . *http://udesb.state.ut.us/*

Department of Employment Security (Tennessee)*http://www.state.tn.us/other/empsec/tdeshome.htm*

Department of Energy (DOE) *http://www.em.doe.gov/emnet1i.html*

Department of Industry, Labor and Human Relations,
      Wisconsin Employment Bureau . . . . *http://badger.state.wi.us/agencies/dilhr/*

Department of Labor . . . . *http://www.dol.gov/*

Department of Labor (Louisiana) . . . . *http://www.state.la.us/*

Department of the Interior Automated
      Vacancy Announcement System (AVADS) . . . . *http://www.usgs.gov/doi/avads/index.html*

DigiBook . . . . *http://www.cybercomm.net/~digibook*

Electronic Industries Association . . . . *http://www.eia.org/norm.htm*

Employment and Business Information . . . . *http://www.pan.ci.seattle.wa.us/*

Employment and Training Agencies . . . . *http://bcn.boulder.co.us/employment/agencies.html*

Employment Centre (Bermuda Government
      Careers Opportunities) . . . . *http://www.bermudasun.org/bdasun/employment.html*

Employment Development Department . . . . *http://wwwedd.cahwnet.gov/*

Employment Opportunities in Water Resources . . . . *http://www.uwin.siu.edu/announce/jobs/*

Envirobiz—International Environmental Information Network . . . . *http://www.envirobiz.com/*

Environmental Protection Agency . . . . *http://www.epa.gov/epahome/Jobs.html*

European Bioinformatics Institute Career Connection . . . . . . *http://www.ebi.ac.uk/htbin/biojobs.pl*

Expertel Consultants Ltd (UK) . . . . *http://www.pncl.co.uk/expertel/*

Extreme Résumé Drop . . . . *http://www.mainquad.com/theQuad/wich/introPages/lo/erd.html*

Federal Funded Research in the US . . . . *http://medoc.gdb.org/best/fed-fund.html*

Federal Information Exchange (FEDIX) . . . . *http://web.fie.com/htdoc/fed/*
                                       all/any/any/menu/any/index.htm

Federal Jobs Central . . . . *http://www.fedjobs.com/*

Federal Jobs Database from NACE . . . . *http://www.jobweb.org/fedjobsr.htm*

Fermi National Accelerator Laboratory . . . . *http://www.fnal.gov/employ.html*

FinanceNet . . . . *http://www.financenet.gov/wwwlib5.htm#employ*

Forest Products Job Board *gopher://mercury.forestry.umn.edu:70/11/fp/job*

Forsyth County, Winston-Salem . . . . *http://www.co.forsyth.nc.us/*

Georgia, State of . . . . *http://www.State.Ga.US/SMS/*

Greater Columbus Freenet . . . . *gopher://gizmo.freenet.columbus.oh.us*

Hawaii, State of . . . . *http://www.aloha.net/~edpso/*

Hennepin County (Minnesota) . . . . *http://www.co.hennepin.mn.us/wjobs.html*

Idaho and Montana Online Employment . . . . *http://amsquare.com/america/*

Indiana State Department of Personnel . . . . *http://www.state.in.us/acin/personnel/index.html*

Internal Revenue Service . . . . *http://www.irs.ustreas.gov/prod/*

Iowa Jobs Information from the
      Department of Employment Services (DES) . . . . *http://www.state.ia.us/jobs/index.html*

Job Board *http://wfscnet.tamu.edu:80/jobs.html*

Job Hotlines for Washington . . . . . *http://www.gspa.washington.edu/Career/hotlines_welcome.html*

Jobs and Career Information . . . . *gopher://main.morris.org/*

Kentucky Opportunities in State Government . . *http://www.state.ky.us/nasire/STemployment.html*

Kentucky StateSearch . . . . *http://www.state.ky.us/nasire/NASIREhome.html*

Lasers and Electro Optics Society (LEOS) . . . . . *http://msrc.wvu.edu/leos/LEOSprof/LEOSprof.html*

Lockheed Martin Energy Systems . . . . *http://www.ornl.gov/mmes-www/MMESemployment.html*
                                    http://www.ornl.gov/employment.html

MAGNet's Massachusetts Access to
      Government Information Server . . . . *http://www.magnet.state.ma.us/refshelf.htm#jobs*

Maine, State of . . . . *http://www.state.me.us/bhr/career/career.htm*

Manitoba Advantage . . . . *http://www.gov.mb.ca*

Massachusetts Internet Job Bank,
      Department of Employment and Training . . . . *http://www.magnet.state.ma.us/*

Metropolitan Government of Nashville and Davidson County . . . . *http://janis.nashville.org/*
http://www.nashville.org/job_opportunities.html
Missouri Merit System Job Opportunities . . . . *http://www.state.mo.us/oa/pers/jobopps.htm*
NASA Ames Research Center . . . . *http://huminfo.arc.nasa.gov/NASAvacancy.html*
National Science Foundation,
New Hampshire and Maine Careers Online *gopher://stis.nsf.gov/11/NSF/vacancies*
Naval Research Library's Job Link . . . . . . *http://infoweb.nrl.navy.mil/catalogs_and_databases/job/*
NavyJobs . . . . *http://www.navyjobs.com/*
New Hampshire, State of . . . . *http://www.state.nh.us/*
New York State Department of Labor . . . . *http://www.labor.state.ny.us/job.search.html*
Employment Opportunities *http://www.labor.state.ny.us/dol.htm*
North Carolina, State of . . . . *http://www.osp.state.nc.us./OSP/jobs/*
Oak Ridge National Laboratory . . . . *http://www.ornl.gov*
Ohio State Government Jobs . . . . *http://www.state.oh.us/*
http://www.odn.ohio.gov/hr/emprec.html
Oregon Job Listings *gopher://gopher.state.or.us.11/.d9.dir*
http://www.dashr.state.or.us/jobs/jobhead.html
http://www.state.or.us/
Pennsylvania, Commonwealth of . . . . *http://www.auditorgen.state.pa.us/jobs/*
Ramsey County (Minnesota) . . . . *http://www.co.ramsey.mn.us/Pers/hrjobs.htm*
RIDET, Rhode Island Department of Employment and Training *http://det2.det.state.ri.us/*
Royal Air Force (UK) . . . . *http://www.open.gov.uk/raf/rafhome.htm*
Royal Navy (UK) *http://www.royal-navy.mod.uk/home1.htm*
Social Work and Social Services Jobs . *http://www.gwbssw.wustl.edu/~gwbhome/jobs/swjobs.html*
South Australian Department for Employment,
Training and Further Education . . . . *http://dino.tafe.sa.edu.au/*
South Carolina Job Opportunities . . . . *http://www.state.sc.us/jobopps.html*
South Dakota Bureau of Personnel Job Openings . . . . *http://www.state.sd.us/state/executive/bop/*
State and Local Government on the NET . . . . *http://www.piperinfo.com/piper/state/states.html*
State of Ohio . . . . *http://www.ohio.gov*
gopher://gizmo.freenet.columbus.oh.us:70/11/governmentcenter/stateofohio
Texas Employment Commission . . . . *http://www.twc.state.tx.us/*
Texas State Government . . . . *http://www.texas.gov/*
U.S. Dept of Agriculture—Cooperative
Extension Job Vacancies *gopher://sulaco.oes.orst.edu/11/ext/jobs*
U.S. Fish & Wildlife Service . . . . *http://www.fws.gov/employmt.html*
Utah Department of Employment Security—Job Service . . . . *http://udesb.state.ut.us/jobs/*
Victoria Freenet Association (Employment Resources) . . *gopher://freenet.victoria.bc.ca/11/business*
Virginia, Commonwealth of . . . . *http://va.jobsearch.org/*
Washington (Metro) (DC) Council of Governments . *http://www.mwcog.org/mwcog/geninfo/jobs.html*
Washington State Department of Personnel . . . . *http://www.wa.gov/dop/home.html*
Washington State Information Exchange . . . . *http://olympus.dis.wa.gov*
Wisconsin, State of . . . . *http://www.state.wi.us/*
Wyoming Employment Resources, Wyoming Job Bank . . . . *http://wyjobs.state.wy.us/*

History

History of Science Society . . . . *http://weber.u.washington.edu/~hssexec/hss_jobs.html*

Industrial

(Includes ceramics, competitive intelligence, industrial hygiene, manufacturing, metalurgy, precision machinery, quality improvement, etc.)

Advanced Technology Employment Consultants . . . . *http://home.eznet.net/~atec*
Airline Employment Assistance Corps. *http://www2.csn.net/AEAC/*
American Ceramic Society's Ceramic Futures <The> *http://www.acers.org/mem/futures/futures.stm*

American Industrial Hygiene Association . . . . *http://www.aiha.org/es.html*
http://www.aiha.org/
American Society for Quality Control . . . . *http://www.asqc.org/*
American Society of Mechanical Engineers ASMENET . . . . . . *http://www.asme.org/jobs/index.html*
http://www.asme.org/index.html
Army High Performance Computing (HPC) Research Center . . . . *http://www.arc.umn.edu/*
Arvon, LLC . . . . *http://www.arvon.com/*
Association for Computing Machinery . . . . *http://www.acm.org/member_services/career/*
Automated Graphic Systems . . . . *http://www.ags.com/employment/employment.htm*
Bolsa de Trabajo de Pixelnet (Mexico) [in Spanish] *http://www.pixel.com.mx:80/Curriculums/*
Career Development Network <The> . . . . *http://www.webscope.com/webscope/*
Career Quest . . . . *http://www.careerquest.com/*
Electronic Industries Association . . . . *http://www.eia.org/norm.htm*
ENews . . . . *http://www.sumnet.com/enews*
Engineering/Manufacturing Jobs Page . . . . *http://www.nationjob.com/engineering*
European Bioinformatics Institute Career Connection . . . . . . *http://www.ebi.ac.uk/htbin/biojobs.pl*
Florida Sentinal . . . . *http://www.chicago.tribune.com/career/sentinel_ads.html*
Food and Drug Packaging . . . . *http://www.fdp.com*
GeoWeb for GIS/GPS/RS . . . . *http://www.ggrweb.com*
Gintic Institute of Manufacturing Technology (Singapore) *http://www.gintic.ntu.ac.sg:8000/jobs.html*
Hotflash Jobs . . . . *http://iquest.com/~ntes/jobslist.html*
Industry Canada . . . . *http://info.ic.gc.ca/ic-data/ic-eng.html*
IndustryNet, Industry Net Career Opportunities . . . . *http://www.industry.net/c/mn/_co*
Institute of Molecular Biology (Germany), Department of Structural Biology
& Crystallography – IMB Jena . . . . *http://www.imb-jena.de/www_sbx/sbxjobs.html*
Interpac Belgium (Belgium) . . . . *http://www.interpac.be/jobs.html*
InterView . . . . *http://www.sbu.ac.uk/home/career.html*
JOM, The Minerals, Metals, and Materials Society Journal
JOM Classifieds . . . . *http://www.tms.org/pubs/journals/JOM/classifieds.html*
Lasers and Electro Optics Society (LEOS) . . . . . *http://msrc.wvu.edu/leos/LEOSprof/LEOSprof.html*
National Network for HealthCare Professionals . . . . *http://www.treknet.net/hcroaz*
NetWorld MarketPlace Career Opportunities . . . . *http://www.networldmkt.com/networld/career.htm*
Poly-Links-Job Bank . . . . *http://www.polymers.com/polylink/jobank.html*
http://www.polymers.com/
PolySort Classifieds . . . . *http://www.polysort.com*
http://www.polysort.com/classifieds/help_wanted.htm
Precision Machined Products Association . . . . *http://www.pmpa.org/car/career.htm*
Society of Competitive Intelligence Professionals (SCIP) . . . . *http://www.scip.org/*
Staffing Services Online . . . . *http://www.staffingservices.com/*
Technical Employment Consultants . . . . *http://www.tech-employ-consult.com/*

International—Africa

Africa Online: Jobs . . . . *http://www.AfricaOnline.com/AfricaOnline/classifieds.html*
ComputerWeek Jobs Online (South Africa) . . . . *http://www.jobs.co.za/*
Job Searching in Africa . . . . *http://www.sas.upenn.edu/African_Studies/*
Home_Page/menu_job_srch.html

International—Asia

Asia Pacific Management Forum . . . . *http://www.mcb.co.uk/apmforum/nethome.htm*
Asia-Net or AsiaNet, JapanNet . . . . *http://www.asia-net.com*
Asian Career Web . . . . *http://www.rici.com/acw/*
ASPIRE . . . . *http://www.indiana.edu/~intlcent/aspire/*
Bizlinks (Singapore) . . . . *http://sunflower.singnet.com.sg/~g6615000/*
Career Opportunities in Singapore . . . . *http://www.singapore-careers.com*
Career Quest (Japan) . . . . *http://www.venture-web.or.jp/axiom/axiom_english/index.html*
CareerChina, Career China . . . . *http://www.globalvillager.com/villager/CC.html*

198

CareerMosaic (Asia) . . . . *http://www.careerasia.com/*
CareerNET (Hong Kong) . . . . *http://www.hk.super.net/~salesnet/career/home.htm*
EML–BNB Group . . . . *http://mmserve.com/eml-bnb*
Employment Opportunities in India . . . *http://www.webpage.com/hindu/960210/10/10hdline.html*
Executive Access . . . . *http://www.hk.net/~eal/index.html*
Gemini Personnel Ltd. . . . . *http://www.glink.net.hk:80/~gemini/*
Gintic Institute of Manufacturing Technology *http://www.gintic.ntu.ac.sg:8000/jobs.html*
Global Technical Recruitment *http://ourworld.compuserve.com:80/homepages/*
global_technical_recruit/
HeadHunt Korea . . . . *http://www.headhunt.co.kr*
Hong Kong Jobs . . . . *http://www.hkjobs.com*
Hong Kong Standard . . . . *http://www.hkstandard.com/online/job/hksjob.htm*
India Connect's Job Classified . . . . *http://www.indiaconnect.com/classadv/svacant.htm*
Information Technology Institute (Singapore) . . . . *http://www.iti.gov.sg/iti_info/job/job.html*
Institute of Molecular Agrobiology (Singapore) . . . . . . *http://www.nus.sg/NUSinfo/Appoint/IMA.html*
Job Access Limited (Hong Kong) . . . . *http://www.hk.net/~jal/*
JOBNET (Hong Kong) . . . . *http://kwuntong.hk.super.net/~websol/jobnet.htm*
KLA Instruments Corporation Employment . . . . *http://www.kla.ccom/in-yahoo.htm*
Korean Employment Connection . . . . *http://www.korean.com/employment.html*
Morgan & Banks Limited . . . . *http://www.morganbanks.com.au*
National Computer Board (Singapore) . . . . *http://www.ncb.gov.sg/ncb/recruit.html*
National Skin Centre (Singapore) . . . . *http://biomed.nus.sg/nsc/vacancy.html*
O-Hayo Sensei . . . . *http://www.ohayosensei.com/~ohayo/*
Recruit Guide on the Net (Japan) . . . . *http://job.rnet.or.jp/RG/index-j-s.html*
Resources for Asia . . . . *http://www.asia-inc.com/aid/index.html*
SenseMedia Job Board . . . . *http://sensemedia.net/getajob/*
SIAM News Professional Opportunities *gopher://gopher.siam.org/11/siamnews/profops*
SiamJOB (Thailand) . . . . *http://www.siam.net/jobs/*
Singapore Online . . . . *http://www.singapore.com/jobs.htm*
TKO Personnel, Inc. . . . . *http://www.tkointl.com*
Wang & Li Asia Resources . . . . *http://www.wang-li.com*

International—Australia, New Zealand

Academic Positions in Science . . . . *http://www.anu.edu.au/psychology/Academia/science.htm*
ACP On-line, Australian Computer Professionals . . . . *http://www.ozjobs.com/*
AK Jobnet, Austin Knight Company . . . . *http://www.ak.com.au/akjobnet.html*
Andersen Contracting (Australia) . . . . *http://www.swcontracting.com.au/body.htm*
Armstrongs' Employment Database (Australia) . . . *http://www.armstrongs.com.au/employment.html*
AUSNet . . . . *http://www.world.net/cgi-bin/ausnet_jobs*
Australian Academy of Science Scientific
Exchanges and Fellowships . . . . *http://www.asap.unimelb.edu.au/aas/foreigne/contscix.htm*
Australian Computer Professionals . . . . *http://www.ozjobs.com*
Australian Computer Professionals Jobs Online . . . . *http://www.digiweb.com/~aep1/*
Australian Defence Forces . . . . *http://www.adfa.oz.au/DOD/recruit/recruit.htm*
Australian IT Job Recruitment Pty Ltd . . . . *http://www.ozemail.com.au/~jobtic/*
Australian Mathematical Society . . . . *http://solution.maths.unsw.edu.au/*
htdocs.ams/People/Jobs/jobs.html
Australian Résumé Server . . . . *http://www.herenow.com.au/*
Baywatch Personnel (New Zealand) . . . . *http://ourworld.compuserve.com/*
homepages/pages/baywatch.htm
Byron Employment—Australia . . . . *http://www.byron.com.au/employment_australia/*
Careers Online (Australia) . . . . *http://www.ideaf.com/jobs/pps.htm*
http://www.careersonline.com.au/
CompuForce (New Zealand) . . . . *http://compuforce.com/*
Computer Age Classifieds (Australia) *http://www.theage.com.au:80/class/*

Computer Contracting on the Internet,
    ETX—Melbourne, Australia . . . . *http://www.ozemail.com.au/~contract/etx.html*
Coopers and Lybrand (Australia) . . . . *http://www.colybrand.com.au/*
Directory (Australia) <The> *http://www.thedirectory.aone.net.au/page8.htm*
Directory: Global Academic Recruiters <The> . . . . *http://www.thedirectory.aone.net.au/*
Doughty Group Ltd (New Zealand) <The> . . . . . . *http://www.jobnetnz.co.nz/Agencies/doughty.html*
Duncan and Ryan Associates (New Zealand) *http://www.jobnetnz.co.nz/Agencies/Duncan-Ryan.html*
Education Gazette (New Zealand) . *http://www.learningmedia.co.nz/egissues/eglatest/eg_conts.htm*
employment.net.au (Australia) . . . . *http://www.employment.net.au/*
Employment Opportunities in Australia . . . . *http://employment.com.au/index.html*
Executive Taskforce . . . . *http://exectask.co.nz/*
Fairfax JobMarket (Australia) . . . . . . *http://www.market.fairfax.com.au/bin/iaquery?NS-use-frames*
                                    =0&NS-search-pat=/Fairfax/jobs/NS-query.pat
Global Technical Recruitment *http://ourworld.compuserve.com:80/homepages/*
                                                    global_technical_recruit/
Hamilton Jones & Koller (Australia) . . . . *http://www.hjk.com.au/*
Infotech . . . . *http://www.infotech.co.nz*
International Academic Job Market . . . . *http://www.camrev.com.au/share/jobs.html*
JobNet NZ <The> . . . . *http://www.jobnetnz.co.nz/*
Kelly Luxford (New Zealand) . . . . *http://www.jobnetnz.co.nz/Agencies/Kelly-Luxford.html*
Mildura's Employment Opportunities (Australia) . . . . *http://www.mildura.net.au/employ/*
Monster Board Australia <The> . . . . *http://www.armstrongs.com.au/*
Morgan & Banks Limited . . . . *http://www.morganbanks.com.au*
Nate's Job Pate *http://www.monash.edu.au/alst6/com/nate/WWW/jobs.html*
Object People (Australia) . . . . *http://www.ozemail.com.au/objectpeople/view.html*
Olivier Recruitment Group *http://www.employment.com.au/olivier/olivier2.html*
OzJobs (ACP OnLine) . . . . *http://columbia.digiweb.com/~aep1/cgi-bin/jobidx.cgi*
Professionals On Line/Employment and Recruitment . . *http://www.wordsimages.com/emp_rec.htm*
South Australian Department for Employment,
    Training and Further Education . . . . *http://dino.tafe.sa.edu.au/*

International—Canada

Adia . . . . *http://www.adia.com*
Agricultural Job Listings in British Columbia . . . . . . *http://qb.island.net/~awpb/emop/startag.html*
American Society for Quality Control . . . . *http://www.asqc.org/*
Architecture and Land Architecture Jobs (CLRNet) *http://www.clr.toronto.edu/VIRTUALLIB/jobs.html*
Bridge Information Technology Inc. (Canada Net Pages) . . . . *http://www.visions.com/*
Canada Employment Centre . . . . *http://ein.ccia.st-thomas.on.ca/agencies/cec/index.html*
Canada Employment Centre in Nanaimo . . . . *http://www.island.net/~hrcnan/emp.html*
Canadian Association of Career Educators and Employers . . . . . *http://www.cacee.com/workweb/*
Canadian Computing Careers, ProNet Search—Canada . . . . *http://bisinc.com/pronet/ccc/*
Canadian Institute of Theoretical Astronomy . . . . *http://www.cita.utoronto.ca/CITA/jobs.html*
Canadian Résumé Centre . . . . *http://netaccess.on.ca/~resume/*
Career and Placement Services (CaPS) . . . . *gopher://chinchaga.ucs.ualberta.ca/*
Career Blazers Learning Centre (Canada) . . . . *http://cblazers.ns.ca/*
Career Centre—Canada . . . . *http://qb.island.net/~careers/*
Career Internetworking . . . . *http://www.careerkey.com/careerky.htm*
Career Paths . . . . *http://www.etc.bc.ca/~szukiwsk/yes/Career/p1.html*
CAUSE Job Posting Service . . . . *http://cause-www.colorado.edu/pd/jobpost/jobpost.html*
Certified General Accountants' Association
    of Manitoba (Canada) . . . . *http://sulla.cyberstore.ca/Provincial/Manitoba/employ.htm*
City of Vancouver, Canada . . . . *http://www.city.vancouver.bc.ca/jobs/jobspage.html*
Computer Management Consultants . . . . *http://www.jobbankusa.com/cmc/*
Computer-Tech Consultants (Canada) . . *http://www.islandnet.com/~ctc10000/www/ctc10000.html*

Corporate Recruiter's Ltd. (Canada) . . . . *http://WWW.PIE.VANCOUVER.BC.CA/pie/*
business/personne/corp_rec/corp_rec.htm
David Aplin and Associates (Canada) . . . . *http://www.tgx.com/aplin/*
Department of Mathematics—University of Toronto . . . . *http://www.math.toronto.edu/jobs/*
Eduplus Management Group Inc. . . . . *http://www.eduplus.ca/*
Electronic Job Match International . . . . *http://www.ejs@tnc.com/*
Electronic Labor Exchange (Canada) . . . . *http://ele.ingenia.com/*
GLOBEnet—Canada . . . . *http://www.theglobeandmail.com/*
Harcourt and Associates . . . . *http://www.comcept.ab.ca/harcourt/*
Health Search Canada . . . . *http://healthsearch.ca/*
H.E.C. Career Center . . . . *http://www.hec-group.com*
Human Resources Development Canada
   Metro Toronto HRDC Job Board . . . . *http://www.the-wire.com/hrdc/jobs.html*
Industry Canada . . . . *http://info.ic.gc.ca/ic-data/ic-eng.html*
Informatics Search Group . . . . *http://www.isgjobs.com*
I.T. Staffing (Canada) . . . . *http://www.itstaff.com/*
Little Employment Group, Inc. <The> . . . . *http://www.netaccess.on.ca/~leg/*
Manitoba Advantage . . . . *http://www.gov.mb.ca*
Manitoba Senior Citizens Employment Opportunities . . . . *http://www.mbnet.mb.ca/crm/*
other/genmb/msch/msch10.html
Net-Work (Canada) . . . . *http://www.onsetmag.com/jobmarket*
Online Career Center (Canada) . . . . *http://www.etc.bc.ca/provdocs/careers/first_page.html*

Personnel Services Group <The> . . . . *http://www.ctn.on.ca/psg/*
Resucom, Résumé Canada (Canada) . . . . *http://www.bconnex.net/~resume/frame3.htm*
SecurSEARCH (Canada) . . . . *http://www.acs.ca/job.htm*
St. Thomas CEC Job Opportunities Page . . . . *http://ein.ccia.st-thomas.on.ca/*
agencies/cec/jobs/jobbank.html
Victoria Freenet Association (Employment Resources) . . *gopher://freenet.victoria.bc.ca/11/business*
World Job Seekers . . . . *http://cban.worldgate.edmonton.ab.ca.resume/index.html*

International—Caribbean

Bermuda Biological Station for Research . . . . *http://www.bbsr.edu/*
Employment Centre (Bermuda Government
   Careers Opportunities) . . . . *http://www.bermudasun.org/bdasun/employment.html*

International—Eastern European

AS ASISTENT d.o.o. (Slovenia) . . . . *http://www.c-and-c.si/asas/inang.html*
Profil d.o.o. (Slovenia) . . . . *http://www.profil.si/profile.html*
Russian and East European Institute Employment Opportunities,
   Indiana University . . . . *http://www.indiana.edu/~reeiweb/indemp.html*

International—Europe

AAFA—The American Association of Finance and Accounting . . . . *http://www.aafa.com/*
Abraxas plc (UK) . . . . *http://www.abraxas.co.uk/*
ANSA Job Opportunities (UK) . . . . *http://www.ansa.co.uk/APM/job-ad.html*
Apple Recruitment (UK) . . . . *http://www.u-net.com/~applerec/*
Appointments Section–Jobs & Careers <The> . . . . *http://taps.com*
Archives of the French Jobs Newsgroups *http://www.loria.fr:80/news/fr.jobs.d.html*
http://www.loria.fr:80/news/fr.jobs.offres.html
Artificial Intelligence Applications Institute (UK) . . . . *http://www.aiai.ed.ac.uk/aiai/jobs/*
Association Bernard Gregory (France) . . . . *http://www-com.grenet.fr/abg/*
Association of Commonwealth Universities (UK) . . *http://www.niss.ac.uk/noticeboard/acu/acu.html*
Association of Graduate Career Advisory Services (UK) . . . . *http://agcas.csu.man.ac.uk/*
Au Pair in Europe . . . . *http://netaccess.on.ca/aupair/*

Avotek Publishing, International Headhunters Guide (Netherlands) *http://www.universal.nl/jobhunt/*

Baber's Employment Directory . . . . *http://www.baber.com/em-plt.htm*

Bark, Foehr und Partner GmbH,
       Personalberatung (Germany) . . . . *http://ourworld.compuserve.com/homepages/barkjobs/*

BCL International (UK) . . . . *http://www.bcl.com/*

British Crystallographic Association (UK) . . . . *http://www.cryst.bbk.ac.uk/BCA/jobs.html*

BUBL Employment Bulletin Board (UK)   *gopher://ukoln.bath.ac.uk:7070/11/Academic/Employment*

Buzz Buzz @ads: Banen aangeboden (Netherlands) . . . . *http://valley.interact.nl/@ds/*
                                               banen-aanbod/home.html

Camelot Consultants Limited (UK) . . . . *http://www.eclipse.co.uk/camelot/*

CANDO—The Career Advisory Network on
       Disability Opportunities (UK) . . . . *http://www.comp.lancs.ac.uk/uni-services/careers/cando/*

Career Advisory Service (UK) . . . . *http://www.aston.ac.uk/~haxbype/cas-home.html*

CareerMart . . . . *http://www.careermart.com*

Career.net (UK) . . . . *http://www.atlas.co.uk/mbacareer/*

Central Services Unit (UK) . . . . *http://www.prospects.csu.man.ac.uk/*

CERC Jobs Database (Belgium) *http://gis.linkline.be/jmh/gb/index1.htm*

CERN The European Laboratory for Particle
       Physics (Switzerland) . . . . *http://www.cern.ch/CERN/Divisions/PE/HRS/Recruitment/*

Certes Computing Ltd. (UK) . . . . *http://www.certes.co.uk/docs/home.htm*

Chaosgruppe—Association for Non-Linear Dynamics . . . . *http://www.nonlin.tu-muenchen.de/*
                                               chaos/Jobs/jobs.html

CIMTT Job-Boerse, CIMTT Chemnitz (Germany)   *http://ziu_4.mb2.tu-chemnitz.de/CIM/jobs/info.html*

CitiElite Management and Recruitment Consultants (UK) . . . . *http://www.citielite.co.uk/*

Collaborative Computational Projects (UK) *http://www.dl.ac.uk/CCP/CCP5/vacancies.html*

ComputAppoint (UK) . . . . *http://www.rednet.co.uk/homepages/computap/*

Computer Help (UK) . . . . *http://ourworld.compuserve.com/homepages/tblake_computerhelp/*

Compuvac Personnel Services Limited (UK) . . . . *http://www.compuvac.com/*

Construction Site's Guide to Jobs <The> . . . . *http://www.emap.com/construct/jobs.htm*

CSU the Higher Education Careers Service Unit (UK) . . . . *http://buzzard.csu.man.ac.uk/*

CV + (Belgium) . . . . *http://www.metaphor.be/cvplus/*

CyberCONTRACTS (UK) . . . . *http://www.cybernation.co.uk/~cybercon/index.htm*

CyberDyne CS Ltd. (UK) . . . . *http://www.demon.co.uk/cyberdyne/cyber.html*

D & P International Limited (UK) . . . . *http://www.pavilion.co.uk/dandp/*

Data Lake (UK) . . . . *http://www.westlake.co.uk/*

De Carrierebank (Netherlands) . . . . *http://www.carrierebank.nl*

De Intermediair Online (Netherlands) . . . . *http://www.vnu.com/intermediair/homepage.html*

Department of Education and Employment (UK) . . . . . *http://www.open.gov.uk/dfee/dfeehome.htm*

Donnington Associates (UK) . . . . *http://www.i-way.co.uk/donnington/*

DPP International Ltd (UK) *http://194.128.198.201/dpp/*

Eclectic International Executive Search . . . . *http://www.cyber.nl/eclectic/sap/welcome.html*

Economists (Europe) . . . . *http://maynard.ww.tu-berlin.de/e-joe/*

Educatie Emancipatie Gehandicapte Arbeidskrachten (Netherlands) . . . . *http://www.eega.nl/*

EgoSearch (Belgium) . . . . *http://www.interpac.be/egosearch/welcome.html*

Elan Computing (UK) . . . . *http://www.elan.co.uk/*

Elite Permanent and Contract Recruitment Agency (UK) . . . . *http://www.elite-cs.co.uk/elite/*

EMPLOI @ . . . . *http://www.login.net/emploi-a/public_html/*

Employment Network—People Bank *http://194.73.171.131/pbank/owa/pbk06w00.main*

Energys Technical Services Ltd (UK) . . . . *http://www.energys.co.uk/energys/*

Engine Room (UK and Europe), iWEB . . . . *http://www.iweb.co.uk/iwsearch.html*

ESO—European Southern Observatory (Germany) . . . . . *http://www.eso.org/announcements.html*

Eurojobs On-line Belgium . . . . *http://www.belganet.be/belganet/jobs/*

Eurolink Group PLC (UK) . . . . *http://www.eurolinkgroup.plc.uk/*

Europages—The European Business Directory . . . . *http://www.europages.com/*

European Bioinformatics Institute Career Connection (UK) . . *http://www.ebi.ac.uk/htbin/biojobs.pl*

European Centre for Research and Advanced Training
     in Scientific Computation (CERFACS) . . . . *http://www.cerfacs.fr/admin/vacteams.html*
European Molecular Biology Laboratory,
     Heidelberg, Germany . . . . *http://www.embl-heidelberg.de/ExternalInfo/jobs/*
European Society of Vascular Surgery (Denmark) . . . . *http://www.et.aarhus.ih.dk/~esvs/jobs.html*
Executive Recruitment Services (UK) . . . . *http://www.ers.co.uk/ers/*
Expertel Consultants Ltd (UK) . . . . *http://www.pncl.co.uk/expertel/*
Flavell Divett International (UK) . . . . *http://www.mistral.co.uk/fdi/*
Focus International Career Services (Switzerland) . . . . *http://www.unige.ch/focus/*
Forbes Ltd. (UK) *http://194.128.198.201/forbes/*
FOREM—Work Information System (Belgium) . . . . *http://www.forem.be/*
GIS Jobs Clearinghouse, University of Minnesota,
     Forestry, Remote Sensing Lab . . . . *http://www.gis.umn.edu/rsgisinfo/jobs.html*
GraduNet (UK) . . . . *http://www.gradunet.co.uk/*
Grinwis & Partners (Netherlands) . . . . *http://www.iway.nl/grinwis/*
Harrison Willis Group (UK) *http://194.128.198.201/hwgroup/main.html*
HEL—Human Enterprises Limited (UK) . . . . *http://www.demon.co.uk/hument/*
Hobsons Publishing PLC (UK) . . . . *http://www.hobsons.co.uk/*
Hospitality Net, Hospitality Industry
     Job Exchange (Netherlands) . . . . *http://www.hospitalitynet.nl/job/home.htm*
Hunterskil Howard (UK) *http://194.128.198.201/hhplc/*
IBNIX Recruitment (UK) . . . . *http://www.ibnix.co.uk/*
Institut fur Arbeitswirtschaft und
     Organisation (Germany) . . . . *http://www.iao.fhg.de/Public/hiwi/OVERVIEW-en.html*
Institute of Fiscal Studies (UK) *http://www1.ifs.org.uk/ifsinfo/jobs/index.htm*
Institute of Molecular Biology (Germany), Department of Structural Biology
     & Crystallography—IMB Jena . . . . *http://www.imb-jena.de/www_sbx/sbxjobs.html*
Institution of Electrical Engineers (UK) *http://www.iee.org.uk:80/*
Interactive Recruitment Limited (UK) *http://194.128.198.201/inter-active/*
International Committee of the Red Cross (Switzerland) *http://www.icrc.ch/icrcnews/37e6.htm*
International Fund for Agricultural Development (Italy) . . *http://www.unicc.org/ifad/vac395en.html*
International Telecommunications Union (Switzerland) . . *http://www.itu.ch/itudoc/gs/vacancy.html*
Internet Vacature Overzicht (Netherlands) . . . . *http://www.iway.nl/intervac/*
Interpac Belgium (Belgium) . . . . *http://www.interpac.be/jobs.html*
INTERTECH Computer Consultants (UK) . . . . *http://www.intertech.co.uk/*
InterView (UK) . . . . *http://www.sbu.ac.uk/home/career.html*
Intrinsica Systems (UK) . . . . *http://www.intrinsica.co.uk/*
Irish Job Vacancies Page <The> . . . . *http://www.exp.ie/*
IT Jobs . . . . *http://www.internet-solutions.com/itjobs.htm*
IT Link Ltd (UK) . . . . *http://www.itlink.co.uk/*
ITJobSearch (UK) . . . . *http://www.itjobsearch.com/*
James Duncan & Associates (UK) . . . . *http://www.jda-uk.co.uk/*
Jenrick-CPI Nederland (Netherlands) . . . . *http://www.jenrick.nl/*
Jobs Links (Germany) . . . . *http://cip.physik.uni-wuerzburg.de/job.html*
JOB—DIRECT (Austria) . . . . *http://www.job-direct.co.at/job-direct/*
Job-Net <The> (Italy) . . . . *http://www.webcom.com/~jobnet/*
Job Opportunities (in U.S. and Europe) . . . . *http://www.sas.upenn.edu/*
     African_Studies/Jobs_US/menu_Jobs_US.html
Job SearchUK . . . . *http://WWW.JOBSEARCH.CO.UK/*
JobNet (Netherlands) . . . . *http://www.jobnet.nl/*
Job.net from Computer Contractor (UK) . . . . *http://www.vnu.co.uk/:81/ip_user/*
     owa/register.main?c_mag_id=
Jobs & Adverts Online GmbH (in German) . . . . *http://www.jobs.adverts.de/*
Jobs & Career (Belgium) . . . . *http://www.jobs-career.be/*
Jobs Offered (UK) . . . . *http://www.futurenet.co.uk/Ads/jobs.html*

Jobs Online (France) [in French only] .... http://www.cegos.fr/
JOBS: Vakatures op het Internet .... http://www.jobs.nl/
JobServe (UK) .... http://www.jobserve.com/
Jobsite UK .... http://www.jobsite.co.uk/
Jobware (Germany) .... http://www.jobware.de/
JobZone (Netherlands) .... http://valley.interact.nl/jz/
KGB Resources (UK) http://194.128.198.201/kgb/main.html
Kingsford-Smith Partnership Ltd (UK) .... http://www.kingsford-smith.co.uk/kingsford-smith
Le Recrutement (France) http://gplc.u-bourgogne.fr:8080/Recrut/Welcome.html
Man at Work (Italy) .... http://www.vol.it/man_@_work
Marlborough Group (Ireland) <The> .... http://ireland.iol.ie/resource/margroup/
Masterclass (UK) http://194.128.198.201/masterclass/
McGregor Boyall Associates (UK) .... http://www.mcgregor-boyall.co.uk/
Medianet (UK) .... http://www.pavilion.co.uk/medianet/jobs/jobs.htm
MediStaff–A division of Worldwide Staffing .... http://www.medistaff.com
MHC Consulting Services Ltd (UK) .... http://www.lds.co.uk/mhc/
Michael Page On-Line Career Brochure .... http://taps.com/broch/Michael_Page/salesmkt.htm
Midwest Computer Consultants Ltd (UK) .... http://www.mwcc.com/
Morgan & Banks Limited .... http://www.morganbanks.com.au
National Information Services and Systems (UK) http://www.niss.ac.uk/noticeboard/jobs/index.html
National Institute for Nuclear Physics and
     High-Energy Physics (Netherlands) .... http://www.nikhef.nl/
NATO's SACLANT Undersea Research Centre (Italy) http://www.saclantc.nato.int:80/staff/
Net Contractor (UK) .... http://www.demon.co.uk/syntaxis/contract/home.html
Netherlands Organization of Scientific Research (Netherlands) ...... http://www.nwo.nl/vacatures
Network Operations Worldwide (Belgium) .... http://www.belgium.eu.net/company/jobs/jobs.html
New Boston Select (UK) .... http://www.selectgroup.com/newboston/
NISS (National Information Services .... http://www.niss.ac.uk/noticeboard/index.html#jobs
     and Systems) Noticeboard (UK)   http://www.niss.ac.uk/news/index
OneWorld Jobs (UK) .... http://www.oneworld.org/jobs/index.html
Orient Pacific Century (UK) http://www.mcb.co.uk/apmforum/opc/opc2.htm
Personalberatung Geest (Germany) .... http://members.aol.com/pbgeest/index.htm
Physics Job Vacanicies (UK) .... http://www.physics.ox.ac.uk/jobs-index.html
Physics Jobs On-Line (Sweden) .... http://www.tp.umu.se/TIPTOP/FORUM/JOBS/
Physics World Jobs Online .... http://www.iop.org/cgi.bin/Jobs/main
Positions in Bioscience and Medicine, Hum-Molgen Bioscience and Medicine
     (Germany) .... http://www.informatik.uni-rostock.de/HUM-MOLGEN/anno/position.html
Price Jamieson (UK) .... http://www.pricejam.com
Prime Recruitment (UK) .... http://www.tcp.co.uk/~primerec/
Profiles (Belgium) .... http://www.nomad.be/profiles/
Prospective Management Overseas (Belgium) .... http://www.pmo.be/home.htm
Prospectus Computer (UK) .... http://www.prospectus.co.uk/prospectus/
Prosper Wales (UK) .... http://prosper.swan.ac.uk/bin/web/
Quantum Consultancy Services (UK) .... http://www.quantum-cs.co.uk/
Recruit PLC (UK) .... http://www.newdawn.co.uk/recruit/
Recruiters Network (Netherlands) .... http://www.xs4all.nl~avotek
Reed Personnel Services, Reed Computing (UK) .... http://www.reed.co.uk/
Richard Wheeler Associates (UK) .... http://www.hiway.co.uk/rwa/
Rimpac Systems (UK) http://194.128.198.201/rimpac/
Royal Air Force (UK) .... http://www.open.gov.uk/raf/rafhome.htm
Royal Navy (UK) http://www.royal-navy.mod.uk/home1.htm
Royal Society of Chemistry (UK) http://chemistry.rsc.org/rsc/jobs3.htm
SciComp Job List (Germany) .... http://scicomp.math.uni-augsburg.de/scicomp/gsci/jobs/jobs.html
Skandinavisk Computer Rekruttering .... http://www.scrwest.dk/indexuk.htm
Span Consultancy <The> (UK) .... http://www.span-consultancy.co.uk/contact.html

Stanford Associates (UK) *http://194.128.198.201/stanford/*
STEPS GmbH Personalberatung (Germany) . . . . *http://www.steps.de/*
Summer Jobs, Summer Jobs World Wide . . . . *http://www.summerjobs.com/*
Syntax Consultancy Limited (UK) . . . . *http://www.syntaxco.co.uk/xmas/syntaxco.htm*
TeleJob (Switzerland) . . . . *http://ezinfo.ethz.ch/ETH/TELEJOB/tjb_home_e.html*
Times Higher Education Supplement InterView (UK) . . . . *http://www.timeshigher.newsint.co.uk/*
http://www.timeshigher.newsint.co.uk/mainmenu.html
http://www.timeshigher.newsint.co.uk/INTERVIEW/interview.html
Top Jobs on the Net (UK) . . . . *http://www.topjobs.co.uk/intel/intel.htm*
Welcome to the UKdirectory . . . . *http://www.ukdirectory.com/employ/employ.htm*

International—Latin America

Bolsa de Trabajo de Pixelnet (Mexico) [in Spanish] *http://www.pixel.com.mx:80/Curriculums/*
Global Net's Latin American Career Center
    (Bolsa de Trabajo Global Net) . . . . *http://www.bolsadetrabajo.com*
RH-Online (Brazil) . . . . *http://www.bhvirtual.com/rhol/*

International—Middle East

Computer Jobs in Israel (CJI) . . . . *http://www.jr.co.il/cji*
Eclectic International Executive Search . . . . *http://www.cyber.nl/eclectic/*
Marksman InterStaff (Israel) . . . . *http://www.marksman.co.il/*

International—Other

100 Hot Jobs *http://www.100hot.com/jobs/*
4Work *http://4work.com*
A+ On-Line Résumés *http://www.hway.net:80/olresume*
Academic Position Network (APN) . . . . *http://www.umn.edu/apn/*
ACM Sigmod's On-line Career Center . . . . *http://www.acm.org/cacm/careerops/*
Aleph—The Global Translation Alliance . . . . *http://www.aleph.com*
Andersen Consulting . . . . *http://www.ac.com/main.html*
Archaeological Fieldwork Server . . . . *http://durendal.cit.cornell.edu/*
Au Pairs Job Match . . . . *http://www.aupairs.co.uk/*
BFSI Internet Marketing . . . . *http://www.bfservs.com/states.html*
Brei & Associates, Inc., Jobs Database . . . . *http://www.netins.net/showcase/rdbrei/*
CanMed Consultants Inc. . . . . *http://www.canmed.com/*
Career Quest . . . . *http://www.careerquest.com/*
Career Résumés . . . . *http://branch.com/cr/cr.html*
CareerSearch—Jobs Online . . . . *http://www.greatinfo.com/business_cntr/career.html*
Commonwealth Jobsearch, Commonwealth Job Search . . . . . *http://www.corpinfohub.com/cjs.htm*
Computing/IT Jobs WorldWide . . . . *http://www.Britain.EU.net/vendor/jobs/main.html*
Cumbria Careers Ltd. . . . . *http://www.u-net.com/~c-career/*
Development Dimensions International . . . . *http://ddiworld.com/index.html*
Easynet Job-Centre (The Virtual Job Centre) . . . . *http://www.cyberiacafe.net/jobs/*
EDP Contract Services . . . . *http://edpcs.com/*
Experience On Demand . . . . *http://www.experienceondemand.com/*
Fenwick Partners . . . . *http://www.fenwickpartners.com/*
Fitzroy Undergraduate Research in Biology . . . . *http://firstmarket.com/fitzroy/*
Foreign Language Listings *http://condor.stcloud.msus.edu:20020/careerannounce.html*
Fournier Transformation (Visual FoxPro Yellow Pages) . . . . *http://www.transformation.com/*
Future Med . . . . *http://ourworld.compuserve.com/homepages/futuremed/main.htm*
Global Job Services . . . . *http://www.indirect.com/www/dtomczyk/*
Global Marketing Strategies . . . . *http://www.ioa.com/home/kelbell/*
Global Medical Search . . . . *http://www.moran.com/gms*
Guide to Working Overseas . . . . *http://www.magi.com/~issi/*

H.E.A.R.T.—Career Connection's On-Line
     Information System .... *http://www.career.com/PUB/searchmenu.html*
IEEE, Institute of Electrical and Electronic Engineers Job Bank .... *http://www.ieee.org/jobs.html*
International Agribusiness Internship Center .... *http://www.usu.edu/*
International Interactive Communications Society (IICS) .... *http://www.iicsny.org/jobs/*
International Internship Directory .... *gopher://gopher.clemson.edu/*
International Medical Placement, Ltd. .... *http://www.niagara.com/*
International Service Agencies .... *http://www.charity.org/*
International Teleproduction Society .... *http://www.itsnet.org/jobs.html*
Internet Job Information Center .... *http://tvp.com/vpjic.html*
Internet-Solutions.Com .... *http://www.internet-solutions.com/*
Interskill Services S.A. .... *http://www.interskill.ch/*
Job Listings in Academia .... *http://volvo.gslis.utexas.edu/~acadres/jla.html*
Job Square .... *http://www.euro.net/InfoCraft/*
JobIndex .... *http://www.danielsen.com/jobs/*
JobTree .... *http://peace.netnation.com/joblink/*
Management Recruiters International .... *http://www.mrinet.com/*
Management Recruiters International of LA/Encino .... *http://www.mri-la.com*
Models Online .... http://www.models-online.com
Nature's International Science Jobs *http://www.nature.com/Nature2/*
     serve?SID=7502384&CAT=Classified&PG=Jobs/jobshome.html
Net-Globe's Job Data Base .... *http://mail.travel-net.com/*
NetWorld MarketPlace Career Opportunities .... *http://www.networldmkt.com/networld/career.htm*
Optical Society of America, Optics Net .... *http://www.osa.org/*
Physics Job Announcements by Thread, NASA .... *http://XXX.lanl.gov/Announce/Jobs/*
Plaxel .... *http://www.gol.com/plaxel/*
Quay Partners International .... *http://www.quaypartners.com/*
Résumé Hut <The> .... *http://www.islandnet.com/penlan*
     http://www.islandnet.com/penlancareers/
RGA International's Job Listings .... *http://www.rga-joblink.com/docs/joblist.html*
RWH .... *http://www.figment.net/rwh/*
Selection, Recruiting of Latvian Seamen .... *http://www.unitree.lv/~sms/*
Spectra International, Inc. .... *http://www.indirect.com/www/spectra/*
Talentworks .... *http://www.talentworks.com*
TrainingNet .... *http://www.trainingnet.com/*
Whole Internet Catalogue .... *http://www.gnn.com*
World Wide Web Employment Office .... *http://www.harbornet.com/*
     http://www.harbornet.com/biz/office/annex.html

Journalism

Arts Deadlines List <The> .... *http://www.ircam.fr/divers/arts-deadlines.html*
Asia Pacific Management Forum .... *http://www.mcb.co.uk/apmforum/nethome.htm*
Association for Education in Journalism
    and Mass Communication .... *http://www.aejmc.sc.edu/online/home.html*
Editor and Publisher Interactive .... *http://www.mediainfo.com/*
Internship Director .... *http://www.snpa.org/snpa/web/home.html*
J-JOBS DIGEST: Journalism Jobs and Internships .... *gopher://blick.journ.latech.edu*
Job Openings in Newspaper New Media (and Related Fields) .... *http://www.mediainfo.com/*
National Diversity Journalism Job Bank .... *http://www.newsjobs.com*
National Writer's Union JobHotline .... *http:www.nwu.org/nwu/hotline/*
NewsLink (AJR NewsLink) .... *http://www.newslink.org*
Newspaper Association of America .... *http://www.naa.org/*
Professional and Student
    Journalism Organizations .... *http://www.journalism.sfsu.edu/www/orgs/orgs.htm*
Society of Professional Journalists .... *http://town.hall.org/places/spj/*

Language/Translation

Aleph—The Global Translation Alliance . . . . *http://www.aleph.com*
AS ASISTENT d.o.o. (Slovenia) . . . . *http://www.c-and-c.si/asas/inang.html*
Asia-Net or AsiaNet, JapanNet . . . . *http://www.asia-net.com*
Asian Career Web . . . . *http://www.rici.com/acw/*
Elk Grove Unified School District *http://www.egusd.k12.ca.us/webdocs/claspost.htm*
Foreign Language Listings *http://condor.stcloud.msus.edu:20020/careerannounce.html*
International Fund for Agricultural Development (Italy) . . *http://www.unicc.org/ifad/vac395en.html*
International Telecommunications Union (Switzerland) . . *http://www.itu.ch/itudoc/gs/vacancy.html*
Russian and East European Institute Employment Opportunities,
     Indiana University . . . . *http://www.indiana.edu/~reeiweb/indemp.html*
Southeastern Conference on Linguistics (SECOL) . . . . *http://www.msstate.edu/Org/SECOL/*
TESLJB-L, Teaching English as a Foreign Language *gopher://CUNYVM.CUNY.EDU/11/*
                    Subject%20Specific%20Gophers/teslfl/Teaching%20English
                    %20as%20a%20Foreign%20Language%20-%20The%20Profession
TKO Personnel, Inc. . . . . *http://www.tkointl.com*
Wang & Li Asia Resources . . . . *http://www.wang-li.com*

Law

(Includes attorneys, criminal justice, enforcement, consulting, government, legal assistants, secretaries, paralegals, etc.)

Attorney Job Listings, Department of Justice *gopher://justice2.usdoj.gov/1*
Attorney Job Network . . . . *http://www.jurisjob.com*
Career Center . . . . *http://www.paralegals.org/Center/home.html*
Clausman Legal Staffing . . . . *http://www.clausman.com*
EagleVisions National Directory of Emergency Services . . . . *http://www.policejobs.com*
Eustis Police Department . . . . *http://www.sundial.net/~galaxy/emp.html*
FCF . . . . *http://www.gnatnet.net/~fcfjobs*
Hallahan & Associates . . . . *http://www.hallahan.com*
Hamilton Jones & Koller (Australia) . . . . *http://www.hjk.com.au/*
Harrison Willis Group (UK) *http://194.128.198.201/hwgroup/main.html*
Hennepin County (Minnesota) . . . . *http://www.co.hennepin.mn.us/wjobs.html*
Law Employment Center . . . . *http://www.lawjobs.com/*
Law Mall Résumé Listings . . . . *http://www.lawmall.com/resumes/resumes.html*
Legal Classifieds . . . . *http://www.ljextra.com/classifieds/*
National Federation of Paralegal Associations . . . . *http://www.paralegals.org/*
Seamless Web's Legal Job Center <The> . . . . *http://www.seamless.com/jobs/*
WorldNet Communications Corporation . . . . *http://www.legnetwork.com*

Library Science

American Library Association . . . . *http://www.ala.org/alanow/alanow_home.html*
BUBL Employment Bulletin Board *gopher://ukoln.bath.ac.uk:7070/11/Academic/Employment*
CAUSE Job Posting Service . . . . *http://cause-www.colorado.edu/pd/jobpost/jobpost.html*
College and Research Libraries Jobs *gopher://gopher.uic.edu/11/library/crl/crljobs*
Colorado State Library JOBLINE *gopher://gopher.jefferson.lib.co.us:71/11/jobline*
Elk Grove Unified School District *http://www.egusd.k12.ca.us/webdocs/claspost.htm*
History of Science Society . . . . *http://weber.u.washington.edu/~hssexec/hss_jobs.html*
Jobline, School of Library Science
     and Instructional Technology . . . . *http://www.scsu-cs.ctstateu.edu/library/jobline.html*
JobSearch: The GSLIS Job Placement Database . . . . *http://alexia.lis.uiuc.edu/gslis/research/*
Library Jobs and Library Employment: Navigating the
     Electronic Web *gopher://una.hh.lib.umich.edu:70/00/inetdirsstacks/jobs%3Afenner*
National Association of Broadcasters . . . . *http://www.nab.org/*
Southern Connecticut State University Library . . . . *http://www.scsu-cs.ctstateu.edu/*
                                        library/careerpage.html
Special Libraries Association (SLA) . . . . *http://www.indiana.edu/~slajob/*

Management

A Virtual Job Fair . . . . *http://www.careerexpo.com/*
Academy of Management . . . . *http://www.usi.edu/aom/placemnt.htm*
Advanced Technology Information Network *http://caticsuf.csufresno.edu:70/1/atinet*
Aegis Group . . . . *http://aegis-group.com*
Agricultural Job Listings *http://caticsuf.csufresno.edu:70/1/atinet/agjobs*
Airline Employee Placement Service . . . . *http://www.aeps.com/aeps/aepshm.html*
Alliance Management Resources *http://www.amsquare.com/america/medpro1.html*
American Marketing Association . . . . *http://www.ama.org*
America's Employers: The Job Seekers "Home" . . . . *http://www.americasemployers.com*
Anchor Group <The> . . . . *http://www.espan.com/spot/anchor/anchor.html*
Andersen Consulting . . . . *http://www.ac.com/main.html*
Apple Recruitment (UK) . . . . *http://www.u-net.com/~applerec/*
Ardex Executive Search <The> . . . . *http://www.andex.com/*
Asia Pacific Management Forum . . . . *http://www.mcb.co.uk/apmforum/nethome.htm*
Association of Energy Services Professionals . . . . *http://www.dnai.com/AESP/jobs.html*
Australian Computer Professionals Jobs Online . . . . *http://www.digiweb.com/~aep1/*
AUX Technology, Inc. . . . . *http://kiwi.futuris.net/aux/*
Banking Related Jobs . . . . *http://www.cob.ohio-state.edu/~fin/osujobs.htm*
Bernard Haldane Associates . . . . *http://www.intex.net/careers/index.html*
Bolton Group <The> . . . . *http://www.webcreations.com/bolton/*
Cambridge Group . . . . *http://cambridgegroup.com/C/cambridge*
Career Internetworking . . . . *http://www.careerkey.com/careerky.htm*
Career Quest . . . . *http://www.careerquest.com/*
Careers in Management Consulting . . *http://www.cob.ohio-state.edu:80/dept/fin/jobs/consult.htm*
Department of Energy (DOE) *http://www.em.doe.gov/emnet1i.html*
Donnington Associates (UK) . . . . *http://www.i-way.co.uk/donnington/*
EarthWatch . . . . *http://www.earthwatch.org/t/Temployment.html*
Eclectic International Executive Search . . . . *http://www.cyber.nl/eclectic/sap/welcome.html*
EDP Staffing Services, Inc. . . . . *http://www.edpstaffing.com/index.html*
EgoSearch (Belgium) . . . . *http://www.interpac.be/egosearch/welcome.html*
EML–BNB Group . . . . *http://mmserve.com/eml-bnb*
Employment Edge *http://www.employmentedge.com:80/employment.edge/*
Engine Room (UK and Europe) <The>, iWEB . . . . *http://www.iweb.co.uk/iwsearch.html*
Excellence in Consulting . . . . *http://www.exic.com/eichome.html*
Exec-U-Net . . . . *http://www.execunet.com*
Executive Access . . . . *http://www.hk.net/~eal/index.html*
Executive BioSearch . . . . *http://www.scientificjobs.com/*
Executive Search Consultants . . . . *http://www.escinc.com/eschome.html*
Executive Taskforce . . . . *http://exectask.co.nz/*
FDSI's Job Center . . . . *http://www.fdsi-cons.com/*
Fenwick Partners . . . . *http://www.fenwickpartners.com/*
FinanceNet . . . . *http://www.financenet.gov/wwwlib5.htm#employ*
Financial Job Opportunities
    (Business Job Finder) . . . . *http://www.cob.ohio-state.edu/dept/fin/osujobs.htm*
finishing.com's Help-Wanted . . . . *http://www.finishing.com/Directory/wanted.html*
Fogarty and Associates . . . . *http://www.fogarty.com/*
Hamilton Jones & Koller (Australia) . . . . *http://www.hjk.com.au/*
Harrison Willis Group (UK) *http://194.128.198.201/hwgroup/main.html*
HealthLine Management, Inc. (HMI) . . . . *http://www.hmistl.com/*
Help Wanted.Com, YSS Inc. . . . . *http://www.helpwanted.com/career.html*
History of Science Society . . . . *http://weber.u.washington.edu/~hssexec/hss_jobs.html*
Hummer Winblad Venture Partners . . . . *http://www.humwin.com*
Industry Canada . . . . *http://info.ic.gc.ca/ic-data/ic-eng.html*
Institute for Operations Research and
    Management Science (INFORMS) . . . . *http://www.informs.org/JPS/index.html*

208

Intellimatch On-Line Career Services . . . . *http://www.intellimatch.com/intellimatch/*
International Interactive Communications Society
    (IICS), New York Chapter . . . . *http://www.iicsny.org/jobs/*
Interpac Belgium . . . . *http://www.interpac.be/jobs.html*
Jay Tracey Associates *http://amsquare.com/america/search1.html*
Ketner & Associates . . . . *http://www.ketner.com*
Kingsford-Smith Partnership Ltd (UK) . . . . *http://www.kingsford-smith.co.uk/kingsford-smith*
Management Recruiters International . . . . *http://www.mrinet.com/*
Management Recruiters International of LA/Encino . . . . *http://www.mri-la.com*
Management Recruiters of North Canton . . . . *http://www.mrnc.com/*
Management Recruiters of Portland . . . . *http://www.mrportland.com/*
Management Recruiters of Silicon Valley . . . . *http://www.mrisanjose.com/*
Management Recruiters of St. Lucie . . . . *http://www.imageplaza.com*
MIT Sloan School of Management . . . . *http://web.mit.edu/cdo/www/*
                                                  http://web.mit.edu/sloan/www
National Association of Purchasing Management—
    Silicon Valley, Inc. . . . . *http://catalog.com/napmsv/jobs.htm*
National Computer Board (Singapore) . . . . *http://www.ncb.gov.sg/ncb/recruit.html*
National Institute for Nuclear Physics and
    High-Energy Physics (Netherlands) . . . . *http://www.nikhef.nl/*
National Network for HealthCare Professionals . . . . *http://www.treknet.net/hcroaz*
NCSA, National Center for Supercomputer Applications . . . . *http://www.ncsa.uiuc.edu/*
                                                  General/Jobs/00Jobs.html
Network Operations Worldwide (Belgium) . . . . . *http://www.belgium.eu.net/company/jobs/jobs.html*
NetWorld MarketPlace Career Opportunities . . . . *http://www.networldmkt.com/networld/career.htm*
Nonprofit/Fundraising JobNet, Philanthropy
    Journal of North Carolina <The> . . . . . . *http://www.philanthropy-journal.org/jobnet/jobs.htm*
Olsten Information Technology Staffing *http://olsten.boulder.net:80/olstenskills.html*
Orient Pacific Century *http://www.mcb.co.uk/apmforum/opc/opc2.htm*
Proactive Executive Search . . . . *http://www.icon-stl.net/~proact*
ProEd World Wide Clearinghouse . . . . *http://www.proed.com/ch/*
Professionals <The> . . . . *http://www.theprofessionals.com*
Profil d.o.o. (Slovenia) . . . . *http://www.profil.si/profile.html*
Prospective Management Overseas (Belgium) . . . . *http://www.pmo.be/home.htm*
REAL JOBS . . . . *http://www.real-jobs.com/*
Roevin Management Services, Ltd. *http://194.128.198.201/roevin/*
Sanford Rose Associates . . . . *http://www.sanfordrose.com/*
Schulenburg & Associates . . . . *http://www.vnet.net/neil*
Shawn's Internet Résumé Center . . . . *http://www.inpursuit.com/sirc/seeker.html*
VJ Enterprises . . . . *http://www.vjenterprises.com*
Washington (Metro) (DC) Council of Governments . *http://www.mwcog.org/mwcog/geninfo/jobs.html*
WDVL: Jobs for Web Developers <The> . . . . *http://www.stars.com/jobs/*
World Wide Web Consortium *http://www10.w3.org/hypertext/WWW/*
                                              Consortium/Recruitment/Overview.html

Marketing/Sales/Advertising

Agricultural Job Listings *http://caticsuf.csufresno.edu:70/1/atinet/agjobs*
American Marketing Association . . . . *http://www.ama.org*
American Society for Horticultural Science <The> *http://www.ashs.org/hortop20.html*
Avotek Publishing, International Headhunters Guide . . . . *http://www.universal.nl/jobhunt/*
BBN Networking, Inc. . . . . *http://www.bbn.com/bbnjobs/jobsrch.htm*
Beardsley Group <The> . . . . *http://www.beardsleygroup.com/*
Career Match *http://www.fleethouse.com/career/cm-pg1.htm*
CareerNET (Hong Kong) . . . . *http://www.hk.super.net/~salesnet/career/home.htm*
Computer Resellers Weekly . . . . *http://www.techweb.cmp.com/crn/career/career.html*
Data Careers . . . . *http://www.vnu.com/datanews/careers/careers_eng.html*

209

David Aplin and Associates (Canada) . . . . *http://www.tgx.com/aplin/*
Direct Marketing World Job Center . . . . *http://www.dmworld.com*
http://mainsail.com/jobs.html
http://mainsail.com/cgi/perl/5.001/;erl.exe/job10.ini*0?/httpd/htdocs/cgi/job10/job10.pl
Donnington Associates (UK) . . . . *http://www.i-way.co.uk/donnington/*
EarthWatch . . . . *http://www.earthwatch.org/t/Temployment.html*
EgoSearch (Belgium) . . . . *http://www.interpac.be/egosearch/welcome.html*
Employment Opportunities in India . . . *http://www.webpage.com/hindu/960210/10/10hdline.html*
Equipment Leasing Association OnLine . . . . *http://www.elaonline.com*
Executive Access . . . . *http://www.hk.net/~eal/index.html*
Executive Search Consultants . . . . *http://www.escinc.com/eschome.html*
Fashion Exchange . . . . *http://fashionexch.com/*
Graphic Arts Marketing Associates . . . . *http://members.aol.com/GRaphicama*
Harcourt and Associates . . . . *http://www.comcept.ab.ca/harcourt/*
HealthLine Management, Inc. (HMI) . . . . *http://www.hmistl.com/*
Help Wanted.Com, YSS Inc. . . . . *http://www.helpwanted.com/career.html*
IndustryNet, Industry Net Career Opportunities . . . . *http://www.industry.net/c/mn/_co*
Infonet's Classifieds . . . . *http://www.infonetwww.com/clfdjo.htm*
Intellimatch On-Line Career Services . . . . *http://www.intellimatch.com/intellimatch/*
International Interactive Communications Society, New York Chapter . *http://www.iicsny.org/jobs/*
International Teleproduction Society . . . . *http://www.itsnet.org/jobs.html*
Internet Fashion Exchange . . . . *http://www.fashionexch.com/*
ISOCOR . . . . *http://www.isocor.com/*
J. Edgar & Associates Inc. . . . . *http://www.the-wire.com/careers/*
J. Robert Scott, Executive Search . . . . *http://j-robert-scott.com/*
Marketing Science Institute . . . . *http://cism.bus.utexas.edu/ravi/marketing_science.html*
Masterclass (UK) *http://194.128.198.201/masterclass/*
Michael Page On-Line Career Brochure . . . . *http://taps.com/broch/Michael_Page/salesmkt.htm*
National Association of Purchasing Management—
   Silicon Valley, Inc. *http://catalog.com/napmsv/jobs.htm*
Network Operations Worldwide (Belgium) . . . . *http://www.belgium.eu.net/company/jobs/jobs.html*
OASYS . . . . *http://www.oasysnet.com/home.html*
P.O.P. Jobs . . . . *http://www.popjobs.com*
Price Jamieson . . . . *http://www.pricejam.com*
Proactive Executive Search . . . . *http://www.icon-stl.net/~proact*
REAL JOBS . . . . *http://www.real-jobs.com/*
TechWeb/TechCareers/TechHunter . . . . *http://www.techweb.com/default.html.body?*
http://techweb.com/careers/careers.html.body?

Mathematics/Statistics

American Evaluation Association . . . . *http://www.theriver.com/public/aea/*
American Mathematical Society . . . . *http://www.ams.org/committee/profession/employ.html*
American Statistical Association . . . . *http://www.amstat.org/opportunities/*
Argonne National Laboratory, Mathematics
   and Computer Science Division . . . . *http://www.mcs.anl.gov/Divisional/positions.html*
Australian Mathematical Society . . . . *http://solution.maths.unsw.edu.au/*
htdocs.ams/People/Jobs/jobs.html
Careers in Mathematics . . . . *http://www.math.purdue.edu/~rcp/Careers.html*
Department of Mathematics—University of Toronto . . . . *http://www.math.toronto.edu/jobs/*
ERIC Clearinghouse on Assessment and Evaluation . . . . *gopher://vmsgopher.cua.edu/*
11gopher root eric ae%3a%5bjobs%5d
Faculty Positions in Computer Science . . . . *http://www.cs.cmu.edu/afs/*
cs.cmu.edu/user/burks/www/faculty.html
Jobs in Mathematics . . . . *http://www.cs.dartmouth.edu/~gdavis/policy/jobmarket.html*
Mathcor . . . . *http://ourworld.compuserve.com/homepages/Mathcor*
Mathematical Association of America <The> . . . . *http://www.maa.org/pubs/focus/employ.html*

Mathematics Job Market . . . . *http://www.cs.dartmouth.edu/~gdavis/policy/jobmarket.html*
Professional Information for Mathematicians . . . . *http://www.ams.org/committee/profession/*
SIAM News Professional Opportunities *gopher://gopher.siam.org/11/siamnews/profops*
Society for Industrial and Applied Mathematics (SIAM) . . *http://www.siam.org/profops/profops.htm*
University of Florida Department of Statistics . . . . *http://www.stat.ufl.edu/vlib/jobs*

MBA Careers
Career.net (UK) . . . . *http://www.atlas.co.uk/mbacareer/*
Hobsons Publishing PLC (UK) . . . . *http://www.hobsons.co.uk/*
MBA Employment Connection Association . . . . *http://www.MBAnetwork.com/meca*
MBA Job Net, MBA Search! . . . . *http://www.mbasearch.com/index.htm*

Medicine
(Includes all specialties, administration, clinical, dentistry, health care, histocompatibility, histopathology, immunogenetics, industrial hygiene, MRI, nursing, nutrition, pharmacology, physicians, physical therapy, records, research, sales, spin imaging, sports medicine, veterinary, etc.)

Academic Physician and Scientist Association of
     American Medical Colleges (AAMC) Job Listings . . . . *gopher://aps.acad-psy-sci.com/*
Aegis Group . . . . *http://aegis-group.com*
Alliance Management Resources *http://www.amsquare.com/america/medpro1.html*
American Heart Association . . . . *http://www.amhrt.org/jobs/index.html*
American Industrial Hygiene Association . . . . *http://www.aiha.org/es.html*
American Medical Association, JAMA . . . . *http://www.ama-assn.org*
American Society for Histocompatibility
     and Immunogenetics . . . . *http://www.swmed.edu/home_pages/ASHI/jobs/jobs.htm*
American Society for Mass Spectrometry <The> . . . . *http://www.asms.org/employ.html*
APTA Home Page . . . . *http://www.edoc.com/apta/*
Bay State . . . . *http://www.inter-mall.com/service/allied/baystate*
Best Jobs in the USA Today . . . . *http://www.bestjobsusa.com/top.htm*
BIO-ONLINE . . . . *http://www.bio.com/hr/hr_index.html*
Biodata Navigator Job Board . . . . *http://www.biodata.com/biodata/bd_jobs.html*
Biophysical Society . . . . *http://biosci.cbs.umn.edu/biophys/employ.html*
Biosciences Job Listings and Career Services . . . . *http://golgi.harvard.edu/biopages/jobs.html*
Biotech Career Center . . . . *http://www.gene.com/ae/AB/CC/index.html*
Cambridge Group . . . . *http://cambridgegroup.com/C/cambridge*
CanMed Consultants Inc. . . . . *http://www.canmed.com/*
Career Match *http://www.fleethouse.com/career/cm-pg1.htm*
Careers in Health and Community Service . . . . *http://www.csuchico.edu/hcsv/hcsvcar.html*
CDC & ATSDR Employment Opportunities . . . . *http://www.cdc.gov/hrmo/hrmo.html*
Children's Hospital of Alabama,
     Division of Pediatric Surgery . . . . *http://pedsurg.surgery.uab.edu/jobs.htm*
CompHealth . . . . *http://www.comphealth.co*
Dana-Farber Cancer Institute *gopher://farber2.dfci.harvard.edu/11/.bulletin/.hr/.positions*
Department of Labor, Occupational
     Safety and Health Administration (OSHA) . . . . *http://www.osha.gov/*
DOC on the Web . . . . *http://www.webdoc.com/homepage.html*
Double Dutch Enterprises . . . . *http://www.hia.net/pdesmidt/Physicaltherapy.htm*
Dynamic HR Solutions . . . . *http://www.dynamichr.com*
EDphysician . . . . *http://www.edphysician.com/*
Emory University/Career Paradise . . . . *http://www.emory.edu/*
Engineering/Manufacturing Jobs Page . . . . *http://www.nationjob.com/engineering*
Erickson & Associates . . . . *http://www.nursesearch.com*
European Society of Vascular Surgery . . . . *http://www.et.aarhus.ih.dk/~esvs/jobs.html*
Executive BioSearch . . . . *http://www.scientificjobs.com/*

Executive Search Consultants . . . . *http://www.escinc.com/eschome.html*

FASEB Careers Online . . . . *http://www.faseb.org/careers/*

Fogarty and Associates . . . . *http://www.fogarty.com/*

Franklin Search Group . . . . *http://www.medmarket.com/tenants/fsg/*

Future Med . . . . *http://ourworld.compuserve.com/homepages/futuremed/main.htm*

Global Environmental Management Initiative (GEMI) . . . . *http://www.gemi.org/*

Global Medical Search . . . . *http://www.moran.com/gms*

Harcourt and Associates . . . . *http://www.comcept.ab.ca/harcourt/*

Health Search Canada . . . . *http://healthsearch.ca/*

Healthcare Consultants Pharmacy Staffing . . . . *http://rxrelief.com*

HealthCare International, L.L.C. . . . . *http://www.HealthCare-Int.com/career_ops.html*

HealthLine Management, Inc. (HMI) . . . . *http://www.hmistl.com/*

HealthStaf Medical Services . . . . *http://www.healthstaf.com*

Hennepin County (Minnesota) . . . . *http://www.co.hennepin.mn.us/wjobs.html*

Hospital.Net . . . . *http://hospital.net*

Hospital Web . . . . *http://neuro-www.mgh.harvard.edu/hospitalweb.nclk*

Institution of Electrical Engineers *http://www.iee.org.uk:80/*

International Committee of the Red Cross (Switzerland) *http://www.icrc.ch/icrcnews/37e6.htm*

International Medical Placement, Ltd. . . . . *http://www.niagara.com/*

International Service Agencies . . . . *http://www.charity.org/*

J. Robert Scott, Executive Search . . . . *http://j-robert-scott.com/*

JobLink—Mental Health Net *http://www.cmhc.com/wwwboard/bb2.htm*

Matrix Medical Resources . . . . *http://www.jrwaters.com/matrix/*

Mayo Clinic Online Career Center . . . . *http://www.mayo.edu/career/career.html*

Med Nexus . . . . *http://www.mednexus.com*

Medconnect's Interactive Jobs Line . . . . *http://www.medconnect.com/home-job.htm*

Medical Library Association . . . . *http://www.kumc.edu/MLA/career.html*

Medical Therapy Jobs *gopher://gopher.gate.net/11/*

Medical Transcription Resources—
　　　Health Information Management (HIM) . . . . *http://www.wwma.com/*

Medicine Wheel <The> . . . . *http://www.ids.net/medwheel/career.html*

MediStaff–A division of Worldwide Staffing . . . . *http://www.medistaff.com*

MEDJOB . . . . *http://www.MEDJOB.com/*

MedMarket . . . . *http://www.medmarket.com/employ/empall.html*

MedSearch . . . . *http://www.medsearch.com*

MedWeb . . . . *http://www.jen.emory.edu/medweb/medweb.jobs.html*

National Academy of Sciences, National Research Council,
　　　Institute of Medicine . . . . *http://www.nas.edu/*

National Athletic Trainers' Association <The> . . . . *http://www.nata.org/*

National Institute of Health (NIH) Senior Job Opportunities *http://helix.nih.gov:8001/jobs/*

National Network for HealthCare Professionals . . . . *http://www.treknet.net/hcroaz*

National Physician Job Listing Directory . . . . *http://www.njnet.com/~embbs/job/jobs.html*

National Skin Centre (Singapore) . . . . *http://biomed.nus.sg/nsc/vacancy.html*

New England Journal of Medicine . . . . *http://www.nejm.org/*

Nuclear Medical Resonance (NMR) Resources *gopher://micro.ifas.ufl.edu:70/*
　　　　　　　　　　　　　　　　　　　　　　　1m/NMR_Information_Server/NMR_Positions

Nursing Career Opportunities *gopher://umabnet.ab.umd.edu/11/*

Pharmacy Week Jobs Listing, PharmInfoNet . . . . *http://pharminfo.com/pharmmall/*
　　　　　　　　　　　　　　　　　　　　　　　PharmWeek/pharmweek.html

Physician Recruiting & Employment—Panther Enterprises . . . . . *http://www.seanet.com/~panther/*

Physician RecruitNet . . . . *http://www.physiciannet.com/*

Physician Search Consultants . . . . *http://www.drsearch.com*

Physicians Employment . . . . *http://www.physemp.com*
　　　　　　　　　　　　　　　　　http://www.fairfield.com/physemp/index.html

Pinnacle Health Group . . . . *http://www.phg.com*

Positions in Bioscience and Medicine, Hum-Molgen Bioscience and Medicine

(Germany) . . . . *http://www.informatik.uni-rostock.de/HUM-MOLGEN/anno/position.html*

Poultry Science Association *http://gallus.tamu.edu/1h/psa/psaplacement.html*

Pro Med National Staffing of Wichita Falls . . . . *http://www.wf.net/~promed*

Radiation Biology Job Board . . . . *http://www.science.ubc.ca/departments/physics/radbio/jobs.html*

Radiology Jobs . . . . *http://www.rad.washington.edu/Positions.html*

RPh on the Go USA . . . . *http://www.interaccess.com/rph*

Sports Medicine Online . . . . *http://www.sports-med.com/*

Therapy Resource Network . . . . *http://www.access.digex.net/~david/pt.html*

TSG Professional Services, Inc. . . . . *http://www.tsgpro.com/*

Mental Health

Academic Positions in Science . . . . *http://www.anu.edu.au/psychology/Academia/science.htm*

American Evaluation Association . . . . *http://www.theriver.com/public/aea/*

American Psychological Society (APS)

Observer Job Listings . . . . *http://www.hanover.edu/psych/APS/aps.html*

Education Jobs Page . . . . *http://www.nationjob.com/education*

Employee Services Inc. . . . . *http://www.cris.com/~Esinc/*

Employment and Training Agencies . . . . *http://bcn.boulder.co.us/employment/agencies.html*

Hennepin County (Minnesota) . . . . *http://www.co.hennepin.mn.us/wjobs.html*

Hospital Web . . . . *http://neuro-www.mgh.harvard.edu/hospitalweb.nclk*

JobLink—Mental Health Net *http://www.cmhc.com/wwwboard/bb2.htm*

University of Minnesota's College of Education

Job Search Bulletin Board *gopher://rodent.cis.umn.edu:11119/*

Nonprofit

4Work *http://4work.com*

Careers in Health and Community Service . . . . *http://www.csuchico.edu/hcsv/hcsvcar.html*

Christian Mission Opportunity Database . . . . *http://www.netaccess.on.ca/*
fingertip/gallery/oppor/oppor.htm

Employment Opportunities in Water Resources . . . . *http://www.uwin.siu.edu/announce/jobs/*

Environmental Careers Organization <The> . . . . *http://www.eco.org*

Fundaising and Nonprofit Organizations . . . . *http://www.philanthropy-journal.org*

Good Works . . . . *http://www.essential.org/goodworks/*

Impact Online . . . . *http://www.impactonline.org/*

International Committee of the Red Cross (Switzerland) *http://www.icrc.ch/icrcnews/37e6.htm*

International Service Agencies . . . . *http://www.charity.org/*

Internet Non-Profit Center: Home to Donors and Volunteers . . . . *http://www.nonprofits.org/*

J.B. Groner Executive Search, Inc. . . . . *http://www.execjobsearch.com/*

Job Board *http://wfscnet.tamu.edu:80/jobs.html*

Nonprofit/Fundraising JobNet, Philanthropy

Journal of North Carolina <The> . . . . . . *http://www.philanthropy-journal.org/jobnet/jobs.htm*

TESLJB-L, Teaching English As a Foreign Language *gopher://CUNYVM.CUNY.EDU/11/*
Subject%20Specific%20Gophers/teslfl/Teaching%20English
%20as%20a%20Foreign%20Language%20-%20The%20Profession

VISTA Web . . . . *http://libertynet.org/~zelson/section1.html*

Occupational Safety

Defense Nuclear Facilities Safety Board *gopher://nic.sura.net:7070/11/vacancy*

Department of Labor, Occupational Safety and Health Admistration (OSHA) . *http://www.osha.gov/*

Optics

Lasers and Electro Optics Society (LEOS) . . . . . *http://msrc.wvu.edu/leos/LEOSprof/LEOSprof.html*

Optical Society of America, Optics Net . . . . *http://www.osa.org/*

OPTICS.ORG, SPIE Employment . . . . *http://optics.org/employment/*

OptoLink . . . . *http://www.spie.org/web/employment/employ_home.html*
Rensselaer Career Development Center, Optical Science
    Center, University of Arizona . . . . *http://www.rpi.edu/dept/cdc*

Other Specialized Industries
(Includes ceramics, computational fluid dynamics, delivery, enterprise, insurance, real estate, security, truck drivers, etc.)

1-800-DRIVERS Interactive JobLine *http://rwa.metronetworks.com/800drivers.html*
American Ceramic Society's Ceramic Futures . . . . . *http://www.acers.org/mem/futures/futures.stm*
ARI Summit Search Specialists . . . . *http://www.phoenix.net/~summit*
Automated Graphic Systems . . . . *http://www.ags.com/employment/employment.htm*
CFD (Computational Fluid Dynamics) Online . . . . *http://www.tfd.chalmers.se/CFD_Online/cfd-job/*
EagleVisions National Directory of Emergency Services . . . . *http://www.policejobs.com*
FEDnet—Foundation for Enterprise Development . . . . *http://www.fed.org/*
Food and Drug Packaging . . . . *http://www.fdp.com*
Hornberger Management Company . . . . *http://www.building.org/sponsors/hmc/*
Infonet's Classifieds . . . . *http://www.infonetwww.com/clfdjo.htm*
Information Center <The> . . . . *http://greatinfo.com/*
REAL JOBS . . . . *http://www.real-jobs.com/*
Realtor.com . . . . *http://www.realtor.com/*
SecurSEARCH (Canada) . . . . *http://www.acs.ca/job.htm*
Selection, Recruiting of Latvian Seamen . . . . *http://www.unitree.lv/~sms/*
Truck Drivers Job Directory . . . . *http://www.bcl.net/~padgett/truckers.cgi*

Physics
(Includes atomic, laboratory, nonlinear dynamics, nuclear, particle, plasma, reactor engineering, research, spin imaging, etc.)

AIPJOBS, The American Institute of Physics
    Employment Opportunities Database *http://www.aip.org:80/aip/careers/careers.html*
American Institute of Physics . . . . *http://www.aip.org/aip/careers/careers.html*
American Physical Society <The> . . . . *http://aps.org/jobs/index.html*
Ames Laboratory . . . . *http://www.ameslab.gov/Job.html*
Astronomical Observatory Jobs *http://www.pd.astro.it:80/Jobs/*
Biophysical Society . . . . *http://biosci.cbs.umn.edu/biophys/employ.html*
CERN The European Laboratory for
    Particle Physics (Switzerland) . . . . *http://www.cern.ch/CERN/Divisions/PE/HRS/Recruitment/*
Chaosgruppe—Association for Nonlinear Dynamics . . . . *http://www.nonlin.tu-muenchen.de/*
                                                                        chaos/Jobs/jobs.html
Defense Nuclear Facilities Safety Board *gopher://nic.sura.net:7070/11/vacancy*
Fermi National Accelerator Laboratory . . . . *http://www.fnal.gov/employ.html*
Houston Advanced Research Center . . . . *http://www.harc.edu/jobs.html*
Jobs in Atomic and Plasma Physics . . . . *http://plasma-gate.weizmann.ac.il/*
Mathcor . . . . *http://ourworld.compuserve.com/homepages/Mathcor*
National Institute for Nuclear Physics and
    High-Energy Physics (Netherlands) . . . . *http://www.nikhef.nl/*
Physics Careers Bulletin Board . . . . *http://www.aip.org/aip/careers/careers.html*
Physics Job Announcements by thread, NASA . . . . *http://XXX.lanl.gov/Announce/Jobs/*
Physics Job Vacancies . . . . *http://www.physics.ox.ac.uk/jobs-index.html*
Physics Jobs On-Line . . . . *http://www.tp.umu.se/TIPTOP/FORUM/JOBS/*
Physics World Jobs Online . . . . *http://www.iop.org/cgi.bin/Jobs/main*
Radiation Biology Job Board . . . . *http://www.science.ubc.ca/departments/physics/radbio/jobs.html*
Radiology Jobs . . . . *http://www.rad.washington.edu/Positions.html*
YSN Jobs Page (Young Scientists Network),
    Jobs Listings Archive . . . . *http://www.physics.uiuc.edu/ysn/*

Publishing/Printing

Arts Deadlines List <The> . . . . *http://www.ircam.fr/divers/arts-deadlines.html*
Automated Graphic Systems . . . . *http://www.ags.com/employment/employment.htm*
Editor and Publisher Interactive . . . . *http://www.mediainfo.com/*
Employment Opportunities . . . . *http://education.indiana.edu/ist/students/jobs/joblink.html*
EPPA . . . . *http://rampages.onramp.net/~eppa*
Hobsons Publishing PLC (UK) . . . . *http://www.hobsons.co.uk/*
Internship Director . . . . *http://www.snpa.org/snpa/web/home.html*
J. Arthur Group . . . . *http://www.jarthurgroup.com/*
National Diversity Journalism Job Bank . . . . *http://www.newsjobs.com*
National Writer's Union JobHotline . . . . *http:www.nwu.org/nwu/hotline/*
P.O.P. Jobs . . . . *http://www.popjobs.com*

Recreation/Sports

National Athletic Trainers' Association <The> . . . . *http://www.nata.org/*
Online Sports Career Center *http://www.onlinesports.com:80/pages/CareerCenter.html*

Research

Academic Chemistry Employment Clearinghouse . . . *http://hackberry.chem.niu.edu:70/1/ChemJob*
Academic Physician and Scientist, Association of
    American Medical Colleges (AAMC) Job Listings . . . . *gopher://aps.acad-psy-sci.com/*
Advanced Technology Information Network *http://caticsuf.csufresno.edu:70/1/atinet*
Agricultural Job Listings *http://caticsuf.csufresno.edu:70/1/atinet/agjobs*
Air and Waste Management Association . . . . *http://www.awma.org/employment.html*
American Association of Cereal Chemists . . . . *http://wwwnt.scisoc.org/aacc/career/*
American Dairy Science Association . . . . *http://orion.animal.uiuc.edu:80/~adsa/1995/position.html*
American Education Research Association—
    Jobs Corner at ASU . . . . *http://tikkun.ed.asu.edu/~jobs/joblinks.html*
American Educational Research Association . . . . *http://tikkun.ed.asu.edu/aera/home.html*
American Heart Association . . . . *http://www.amhrt.org/jobs/index.html*
American Institute of Physics . . . . *http://www.aip.org/aip/careers/careers.html*
American Marketing Association . . . . *http://www.ama.org*
American Society for Gravitational and
    Space Biology . . . . *http://www.indstate.edu/asgsb/index.html*
American Society for Histocompatibility and
    Immunogenetics . . . . *http://www.swmed.edu/home_pages/ASHI/jobs/jobs.htm*
American Society for Mass Spectrometry <The> . . . . *http://www.asms.org/employ.html*
American Society of Animal Science . . . . *http://www.asas.org/*
American Society of Ichthyologists and
    Herpetologists . . . . *http://www.utexas.edu/depts/asih/pubs/pubs.html*
American Statistical Association . . . . *http://www.amstat.org/opportunities/*
Ames Laboratory . . . . *http://www.ameslab.gov/Job.html*
ANSA Job Opportunities . . . . *http://www.ansa.co.uk/APM/job-ad.html*
Archaeological Fieldwork Server . . . . *http://durendal.cit.cornell.edu/*
Argonne National Laboratory, Mathematics and
    Computer Science Division . . . . *http://www.mcs.anl.gov/Divisional/positions.html*
Army High Performance Computing (HPC) Research Center . . . . *http://www.arc.umn.edu/*
AS ASISTENT d.o.o. (Slovenia) . . . . *http://www.c-and-c.si/asas/inang.html*
Asia Pacific Management Forum . . . . *http://www.mcb.co.uk/apmforum/nethome.htm*
Association for Institutional Research . . . . *http://ike.engr.washington.edu/general/air.html*
Astronomical Observatory Jobs *http://www.pd.astro.it:80/Jobs/*
Bermuda Biological Station for Research . . . . *http://www.bbsr.edu/*
Biosciences Job Listings and Career Services . . . . *http://golgi.harvard.edu/biopages/jobs.html*
BioSpace Career Center . . . . *http://www.biospace.com/g/synd/career*
Biotech Career Center . . . . *http://www.gene.com/ae/AB/CC/index.html*

Canadian Institute of Theoretical Astronomy . . . . *http://www.cita.utoronto.ca/CITA/jobs.html*
Catholic University of America <The> . . . . *http://www.cua.edu/*
CDC & ATSDR Employment Opportunities . . . . *http://www.cdc.gov/hrmo/hrmo.html*
CERN The European Laboratory for
      Particle Physics (Switzerland) . . . . *http://www.cern.ch/CERN/Divisions/PE/HRS/Recruitment/*
Collaborative Computational Projects (UK) *http://www.dl.ac.uk/CCP/CCP5/vacancies.html*
College and Research Libraries Jobs *gopher://gopher.uic.edu/11/library/crl/crljobs*
Crystallography *http://www.unige.ch/crystal/w3v1c/job-index.html*
                                  http://www.unige.ch/crystal/job-index.html
Dana-Farber Cancer Institute *gopher://farber2.dfci.harvard.edu/11/.bulletin/.hr/.positions*
Directory: Global Academic Recruiters <The> . . . . *http://www.thedirectory.aone.net.au/*
Directory of Electronic Journals, Newsletters, and Academic . . . . *gopher://arl.cni.org*
        Discussions Lists (Association of Research Libraries)   select *Scholarly Communication*
Envirobiz—International Environmental Information Network . . . . *http://www.envirobiz.com/*
Environmental Careers Organization <The> . . . . *http://www.eco.org*
Environmental Protection Agency . . . . *http://www.epa.gov/epahome/Jobs.html*
ERIC Clearinghouse on Assessment and Evaluation . . . . *gopher://vmsgopher.cua.edu/*
                                  11gopher_root_eric_ae%3a%5bjobs%5d
ESO—European Southern Observatory (Germany) . . . . . . *http://www.eso.org/announcements.html*
European Centre for Research and Advanced Training in
      Scientific Computation (CERFACS) . . . . *http://www.cerfacs.fr/admin/vacteams.html*
European Molecular Biology Laboratory,
      Heidelberg, Germany . . . . *http://www.embl-heidelberg.de/ExternalInfo/jobs/*
FASEB Careers Online . . . . *http://www.faseb.org/careers/*
Federal Funded Research in the US . . . . *http://medoc.gdb.org/best/fed-fund.html*
Federal Information Exchange (FEDIX) . . . . *http://web.fie.com/htdoc/fed/all/*
                                    any/any/menu/any/index.htm
Fellowship Office . . . . *http://fellowships.nas.edu/index.html*
finishing.com's Help-Wanted . . . . *http://www.finishing.com/Directory/wanted.html*
Fitzroy Undergraduate Research in Biology . . . . *http://firstmarket.com/fitzroy/*
Gintic Institute of Manufacturing Technology (Singapore) *http://www.gintic.ntu.ac.sg:8000/jobs.html*
Herpetology Job Listings *http://xtal200.harvard.edu:8000/herp/general/jobs/jobs.html*
Houston Advanced Research Center . . . . *http://www.harc.edu/jobs.html*
Institute of Fiscal Studies (UK) *http://www1.ifs.org.uk/ifsinfo/jobs/index.htm*
Institute of Molecular Agrobiology (Singapore) . . . . . . *http://www.nus.sg/NUSinfo/Appoint/IMA.html*
Institute of Molecular Biology (Germany), Department of Structural Biology
      & Crystallography—IMB Jena . . . . *http://www.imb-jena.de/www_sbx/sbxjobs.html*
IUPUI Integrated Technologies . . . . *gopher://INDYCMS.IUPUI.EDU/*
                      11/IUPUI%20Information%20Sources/Staff%20Job%20Openings
Job Opportunities in Entomology . . . . . *http://www.colostate.edu/Depts/Entomology/jobs/jobs.html*
Jobs and Career Information . . . . *gopher://main.morris.org/*
Jobs in Atomic and Plasma Physics . . . . *http://plasma-gate.weizmann.ac.il/*
JOM, The Minerals, Metals, and Materials Society Journal
      JOM Classifieds . . . . *http://www.tms.org/pubs/journals/JOM/classifieds.html*
Materials Research Society . . . . *http://dns.mrs.org/awards/fellowship.html*
Mayo Clinic Online Career Center . . . . *http://www.mayo.edu/career/career.html*
MedSearch . . . . *http://www.medsearch.com*
NASA Ames Research Center . . . . *http://huminfo.arc.nasa.gov/NASAvacancy.html*
National Academy of Sciences, National Research Council,
      Institute of Medicine . . . . *http://www.nas.edu/*
National Association of Broadcasters . . . . *http://www.nab.org/*
National Institute of Health (NIH) Senior Job Opportunities *http://helix.nih.gov:8001/jobs/*
National Network for HealthCare Professionals . . . . *http://www.treknet.net/hcroaz*
National Science Foundation, New Hampshire
      and Maine Careers Online *gopher://stis.nsf.gov/11/NSF/vacancies*
National Skin Centre (Singapore) . . . . *http://biomed.nus.sg/nsc/vacancy.html*

NATO's SACLANT Undersea Research Centre (Italy) *http://www.saclantc.nato.int:80/staff/*
Naval Research Library's Job Link . . . . . . *http://infoweb.nrl.navy.mil/catalogs_and_databases/job/*
NCSA, The National Center for
     Supercomputer Applications *http://www.ncsa.uiuc.edu/General/Jobs/00Jobs.html*
Netherlands Organization of Scientific Research . . . . *http://www.nwo.nl/vacatures*
Operations Research Jobs . . . . *http://mat.gsia.cmu.edu/jobs.html*
Physics Job Announcements by thread, NASA . . . . *http://XXX.lanl.gov/Announce/Jobs/*
PolySort Classifieds . . . . *http://www.polysort.com*
                                        http://www.polysort.com/classifieds/help_wanted.htm
RSI Résumé and Job Information . . . . *http://rsi.cee.org/jobs.html*
Sally Silver Incorporated . . . . *http://www.sallysilver.com/*
Science Global Career Network, Science JobNet, ... *http://www.aaas.org*
    American Association for the Advancement of Science   *http://science-mag.aaas.org/science/*
                    http://www.science-mag.aaas.org:888/science/scripts/recruit/search
                            http://www.edoc.com/sgcn/Lineads.html
              http://www.sciencemag.org/science/feature/classified/search.shtml
Scientist (Electronic Journal) <The> *gopher://ds.internic.net/1/pub/the-scientist*
                              ftp://ds.internic.net/pub/the-scientist
Singapore Online . . . . *http://www.singapore.com/jobs.htm*
Society for Experimental Mechanics . . . . *http://www.sem.bethel.ct.us/sem/jobs/jobs.html*
Times Higher Education Supplement . . . . . . *http://www.timeshigher.newsint.co.uk/mainmenu.html*
    InterView   *http://www.timeshigher.newsint.co.uk/INTERVIEW/interview.html*
UTRC, United Technologies Research Center . . . . . . *http://utrcwww.utc.com/UTRC/Jobs/Jobs.html*
Virginia Coast Reserve Information System . . . . *http://atlantic.evsc.virginia.edu/*
    (VCRIS) (Job Listings)   *gopher://atlantic.evsc.Virginia.EDU/11/Opportunities*
YSN Jobs Page (Young Scientists Network),
    Jobs Listings Archive . . . . *http://www.physics.uiuc.edu/ysn/*

Science (see also biology, chemistry, computer, physics)
(Includes oceanography, optics, physiology, research, zoology, etc.)

Academic Physician and Scientist, Association of
    American Medical Colleges (AAMC) Job Listings . . . . *gopher://aps.acad-psy-sci.com/*
Academic Positions in Science . . . . *http://www.anu.edu.au/psychology/Academia/science.htm*
Africa Online: Jobs . . . . *http://www.AfricaOnline.com/AfricaOnline/classifieds.html*
American Indian Science & Engineering
    Society (AISESnet) *http://bioc02.uthscsa.edu/aisesnet.html*
Association Bernard Gregory (France) . . . . *http://www-com.grenet.fr/abg/*
Australian Academy of Science Scientific
    Exchanges and Fellowships . . . . *http://www.asap.unimelb.edu.au/aas/foreigne/contscix.htm*
Biological Control and Sciences Jobs . . . . *http://www.aphis.usda.gov/*
Career Match *http://www.fleethouse.com/career/cm-pg1.htm*
Directory: Global Academic Recruiters <The> . . . . *http://www.thedirectory.aone.net.au/*
employment.net.au (Australia) . . . . *http://www.employment.net.au/*
Energys Technical Services Ltd (UK) . . . . *http://www.energys.co.uk/energys/*
European Centre for Research and Advanced Training in
    Scientific Computation (CERFACS) . . . . *http://www.cerfacs.fr/admin/vacteams.html*
GeoSearch . . . . *http://www.geosearch.com/*
History of Science Society . . . . *http://weber.u.washington.edu/~hssexec/hss_jobs.html*
Industry Canada . . . . *http://info.ic.gc.ca/ic-data/ic-eng.html*
Marketing Science Institute . . . . *http://cism.bus.utexas.edu/ravi/marketing_science.html*
National Academy of Sciences, National Research Council,
    Institute of Medicine . . . . *http://www.nas.edu/*
National Institute of Health (NIH)
    Senior Job Opportunities *http://helix.nih.gov:8001/jobs/*

National Science Foundation, New Hampshire
and Maine Careers Online *gopher://stis.nsf.gov/11/NSF/vacancies*
NATO's SACLANT Undersea Research Centre (Italy) *http://www.saclantc.nato.int:80/staff/*
Naval Research Library's Job Link . . . . . . *http://infoweb.nrl.navy.mil/catalogs_and_databases/job/*
Netherlands Organization of Scientific Research . . . . *http://www.nwo.nl/vacatures*
Oak Ridge National Laboratory . . . . *http://www.ornl.gov*
RSI Résumé and Job Information . . . . *http://rsi.cee.org/jobs.html*
Science Classifieds . . . . *http://recruit.sciencemag.org/*
Science Global Career Network, Science JobNet, ... *http://www.aaas.org*
American Association for the Advancement of Science *http://science-mag.aaas.org/science/*
http://www.science-mag.aaas.org:888/science/scripts/recruit/search
http://www.edoc.com/sgcn/Lineads.html
http://www.sciencemag.org/science/feature/classified/search.shtml
Scientist (Electronic Journal) *gopher://ds.internic.net/1/pub/the-scientist*
ftp://ds.internic.net/pub/the-scientist
SIAM News Professional Opportunities *gopher://gopher.siam.org/11/siamnews/profops*
Society for Advancement of Chicanos and
Native Americans in Science (SACNAS) *http://xerxes.nas.edu:70/1/cwse/SACNAS.html*
http://vflylab.calstatela.edu/sacnas/www/Otherhtml/Employment/jobs.html
Society of Mexican American Engineers and Scientists *http://xerxes.nas.edu:70/1/cwse/MAES.html*
U.S. Dept of Agriculture—Cooperative Extension
Job Vacancies *gopher://sulaco.oes.orst.edu/11/ext/jobs*
WITI Campus . . . . *http://www.witi.com*
YSN Jobs Page (Young Scientists Network),
Jobs Listings Archive . . . . *http://www.physics.uiuc.edu/ysn/*

Student Services
(Includes fellowships, internships, summer jobs, co-ops, etc.)
Academy of Advertising . . . . *http://www.utexas.edu/coc/adv/AAA/*
Africa Online: Jobs . . . . *http://www.AfricaOnline.com/AfricaOnline/classifieds.html*
American Chemical Society . . . . *http://www.acs.org/memgen/employmt/pdb/acsmenu.htm*
American Communication Association
(Grants and Fellowships) . . . . *http://www.uark.edu/depts/comminfo/www/grants.html*
American Institute of Architects . . . . *http://www.aia.org/career.htm*
American Mathematical Society . . . . *http://www.ams.org/committee/profession/employ.html*
American Physical Society <The> . . . . *http://aps.org/jobs/index.html*
American Psychological Society (APS)
Observer Job Listings . . . . *http://www.hanover.edu/psych/APS/aps.html*
American Society for Horticultural Science <The> *http://www.ashs.org/hortop20.html*
American Society of Plant Physiologists
(Midwest Section) *http://baby.indstate.edu:80/mwaspp/gradposi.html*
Argonne National Laboratory, Mathematics and
Computer Science Division . . . . *http://www.mcs.anl.gov/Divisional/positions.html*
Artificial Intelligence Jobs Repository . . . . *http://www.cs.cmu.edu/Groups/AI/html/other/jobs.html*
ArtJob *gopher://gopher.tmn.com/11/Artswire/artjob*
Arts Deadlines List <The> . . . . *http://www.ircam.fr/divers/arts-deadlines.html*
Askew School of Public Administration and Policy . . . . . *http://www.fsu.edu:80/~spap/job/job/html*
ASPIRE . . . . *http://www.indiana.edu/~intlcent/aspire/*
Association for Computing Machinery . . . . *http://www.acm.org/member_services/career/*
Association of Graduate Career Advisory Services (UK) . . . . *http://agcas.csu.man.ac.uk/*
Attorney Job Listings, Department of Justice *gopher://justice2.usdoj.gov/1*
Attorney Job Network . . . . *http://www.jurisjob.com*
Audio Engineering Society . . . . *http://www.cudenver.edu/aes/*
Australian Academy of Science Scientific
Exchanges and Fellowships . . . . *http://www.asap.unimelb.edu.au/aas/foreigne/contscix.htm*

Bermuda Biological Station for Research . . . . *http://www.bbsr.edu/*

Brookings Institution <The> . . . . *http://www.brook.edu/pa/int_fel/intern.htm*
http://www.brook.edu/pa/int_fel/fellow.htm

California School-to-Career Information System . . . . *http://wwwstc.cahwnet.gov/*

Canadian Association of Career Educators and Employers . . . . . *http://www.cacee.com/workweb/*

Canadian Institute of Theoretical Astronomy . . . . *http://www.cita.utoronto.ca/CITA/jobs.html*

CANDO—The Career Advisory Network on
       Disability Opportunities (UK) . . . . . *http://www.comp.lancs.ac.uk/uni-services/careers/cando/*

Career Advisory Service (UK) . . . . *http://www.aston.ac.uk/~haxbype/cas-home.html*

Career and Placement Services (CaPS) . . . . *gopher://chinchaga.ucs.ualberta.ca/*

Career Index . . . . *http://www.beloit.edu/*

Catholic University of America <The> . . . . *http://www.cua.edu/*

College of St. Catherine—Internships *gopher://gopher.stkate.edu/11/dept/career/intshp*

Dana-Farber Cancer Institute *gopher://farber2.dfci.harvard.edu/11/.bulletin/.hr/.positions*

Data Lake (UK) . . . . *http://www.westlake.co.uk/*

Definitive Internet Career Guide <The> . . *http://phoenix.placement.oakland.edu/career/internet.htm*

Department of Mathematics—University of Toronto . . . . *http://www.math.toronto.edu/jobs/*

Directory (Australia) <The> *http://www.thedirectory.aone.net.au/page8.htm*

Drake University—Summer Jobs . . . . *http://www.drake.edu/stulife/carsum.html*

Drexel University—Résumés . . . . *http://cmc.www.drexel.edu/*

EarthWatch . . . . *http://www.earthwatch.org/t/Temployment.html*

EE-Link: The Environmental Education Web Server . . . *http://www.nceet.snre.umich.edu/jobs.html*
gopher://nceet.snre.umich.edu/11/networking/

Emory University/Career Paradise . . . . *http://www.emory.edu/*

Employment Opportunities . . . . *http://education.indiana.edu/ist/students/jobs/joblink.html*

Employment Opportunities in Water Resources . . . . *http://www.uwin.siu.edu/announce/jobs/*

Extreme Résumé Drop . . . . *http://www.mainquad.com/theQuad/wich/introPages/lo/erd.html*

Federal Jobs Database from NACE . . . . *http://www.jobweb.org/fedjobsr.htm*

Fitzroy Undergraduate Research in Biology . . . . *http://firstmarket.com/fitzroy/*

Fundraising and Nonprofit Organizations . . . . *http://www.philanthropy-journal.org*

Georgia State University Career Services
       Job Opportunity Bulletin *http://www.gsu.edu/dept/admin/plc/homepg4.html*

Georgia Tech Career Services . . . . *http://www.gatech.edu/career*

Getting a Job . . . . *http://www.americanexpress.com/student/moneypit/getjob/getajob.html*

GraduNet (UK) . . . . *http://www.gradunet.co.uk/*

Grants & Fellowships . . . . . . *http://www.sas.upenn.edu/African_Studies/Grants/menu_Grants.html*

Herpetology Job Listings *http://xtal200.harvard.edu:8000/herp/general/jobs/jobs.html*

IEEE, University of Massachusetts Student Branch . . . . *http://www.ecs.umass.edu/*

Information Science and Telecommunications Placement *http://www2.lis.pitt.edu/*
~sochats/placement.html

Institut fur Arbeitswirtschaft und Organisation, Germany . . . . *http://www.iao.fhg.de/Public/*
hiwi/OVERVIEW-en.html

Institute of Molecular Agrobiology (Singapore) . . . . . . *http://www.nus.sg/NUSinfo/Appoint/IMA.html*

Institute of Molecular Biology (Germany), Department of Structural
       Biology & Crystallography—IMB Jena . . . . . *http://www.imb-jena.de/www_sbx/sbxjobs.html*

International Agribusiness Internship Center . . . . *http://www.usu.edu/*

International Internship Directory . . . . *gopher://gopher.clemson.edu/*

International Telecommunications Union (Switzerland) . . *http://www.itu.ch/itudoc/gs/vacancy.html*

Internship Director . . . . *http://www.snpa.org/snpa/web/home.html*

InterView . . . . *http://www.sbu.ac.uk/home/career.html*

Job Board *http://wfscnet.tamu.edu:80/jobs.html*

Job Listing at tamu.edu, Job Opportunities, JOBS . . . . *http://ageninfo.tamu.edu/jobs.html*

Job Searching in Africa . . . . *http://www.sas.upenn.edu/African_Studies/*
Home_Page/menu_job_srch.html

National Academy of Sciences, National Research Council,
    Institute of Medicine . . . . *http://www.nas.edu/*
National Association for College Admission Counseling . . . . *http://www.nacac.com/*
National Diversity Journalism Job Bank . . . . *http://www.newsjobs.com*
National Technology Transfer Center's Job Index . . . . *http://iridium.nttc.edu/*
NATO's SACLANT Undersea Research Centre (Italy) *http://www.saclantc.nato.int:80/staff/*
Peterson's Education Center: Careers & Jobs . . . . *http://www.petersons.com/career/*
Physics Job Announcements by thread, NASA . . . . *http://XXX.lanl.gov/Announce/Jobs/*
Purdue University SSINFO Gopher *gopher://oasis.cc.purdue.edu:2525/11/employ-info*
Russian and East European Institute Employment Opportunities,
    Indiana University . . . . *http://www.indiana.edu/~reeiweb/indemp.html*
StudentCenter LLC . . . . *http://www.studentcenter.com*
Washington (Metro) (DC) Council of Governments . *http://www.mwcog.org/mwcog/geninfo/jobs.html*
Whitehouse Fellowships . . . *http://www.whitehouse.gov/WH/WH_Fellows/html/fellows1-plain.html*

Technology

1-800-NETWORK *http://www.1800network.com/*
100 Careers in Wall Street . . . . *http://www.globalvillager.com/*
1st St. NW . . . . *http://www.fsnw.com/*
1st Steps: Employment and Recruiting News . . . . *http://www.interbiznet.com/hunt/*
A Virtual Job Fair . . . . *http://www.careerexpo.com/*
Able Associates, Inc. . . . . *http://www.ablesearch.com/*
About Work . . . . *http://www.aboutwork.com/*
Abraxas plc (UK) . . . . *http://www.abraxas.co.uk/*
Academic Internet Services *http://www.mousetrap.com:80/ais/*
Academic Positions in Science . . . . *http://www.anu.edu.au/psychology/Academia/science.htm*
Academy of Advertising . . . . *http://www.utexas.edu/coc/adv/AAA/*
ACM Sigmod's On-line Career Center . . . . *http://www.acm.org/cacm/careerops/*
ACP On-line, Australian Computer Professionals . . . . *http://www.ozjobs.com/*
Ada Project <The> . . . . *http://www.cs.yale.edu/HTML/YALE/CS/HyPlans/tap/tap.html*
Adderley Group <The> . . . . *http://www.adderley.com/*
ADSWeb . . . . *http://walden.mo.net/~devino/ads.htm*
Advance HTC . . . . *http://www.advancehtc.com*
Advanced Technical Resources *http://www.atr1.com/*
Advanced Technology Information Network *http://caticsuf.csufresno.edu:70/1/atinet*
Africa Online: Jobs . . . . *http://www.AfricaOnline.com/AfricaOnline/classifieds.html*
Allen Davis & Associates Software Jobs Home Page . . . . *http://www.softwarejobs.com*
American Crystallography Association . . . . *http://www.sdsc.edu/ACA/*
American Evaluation Association . . . . *http://www.theriver.com/public/aea/*
American Society for Histocompatibility and
    Immunogenetics . . . . *http://www.swmed.edu/home_pages/ASHI/jobs/jobs.htm*
American Society of Plant Physiologists
    (Midwest Section) *http://baby.indstate.edu:80/mwaspp/gradposi.html*
Anchor Group <The> . . . . *http://www.espan.com/spot/anchor/anchor.html*
Andersen Consulting . . . . *http://www.ac.com/main.html*
Andersen Contracting (Australia) . . . . *http://www.swcontracting.com.au/body.htm*
ANSA Job Opportunities . . . . *http://www.ansa.co.uk/APM/job-ad.html*
Apple Recruitment (UK) . . . . *http://www.u-net.com/~applerec/*
Application Resources, Inc. . . . . *http://www.appres.com/ari/*
Architecture and Land Architecture Jobs (CLRNet) *http://www.clr.toronto.edu/VIRTUALLIB/jobs.html*
Ardent Group, Inc. <The> . . . . *http://www.ardentgrp.com/*
Ardex Executive Search <The> . . . . *http://www.andex.com/*
Army High Performance Computing (HPC)
    Research Center . . . . *http://www.arc.umn.edu/*
Artificial Intelligence Applications Institute . . . . *http://www.aiai.ed.ac.uk/aiai/jobs/*

Artificial Intelligence Jobs Repository . . . . *http://www.cs.cmu.edu/Groups/AI/html/other/jobs.html*
Arvon, LLC . . . . *http://www.arvon.com/*
ASA Information Services . . . . *http://www.eskimo.com/~pageless/asa/*
ASC Connections LTD. . . . . *http://www.itjobsearch.com/asc/*
Asia-Net or AsiaNet, JapanNet . . . . *http://www.asia-net.com*
Askew School Job Placement Services . . . . *http://www.fpac.fsu/spap/job_intern/jobs/*
Association for Women in Computing . . . . *http://www.halcyon.com/monih/awc.html*
Association of Midwest College Biology Teachers . . . . *http://papa.indstate.edu/*
Atlanta's Computerjobs Store . . . . *http://www.computerjobs.com*
Atlanta's CyberJobs *http://155.229.44.6/jobs/*
Audio Engineering Society . . . . *http://www.cudenver.edu/aes/*
Australian Computer Professionals Jobs Online . . . . *http://www.digiweb.com/~aep1/*
Australian IT Job Recruitment Pty Ltd . . . . *http://www.ozemail.com.au/~jobtic/*
AUX Technology, Inc. . . . . *http://kiwi.futuris.net/aux/*
Axis Technologies . . . . *http://axis.micron.net/*
Aztech Computer Recruitment *http://194.128.198.201/aztech/*
Baywatch Personnel (New Zealand) . . . . *http://ourworld.compuserve.com/*
homepages/pages/baywatch.htm
BBN Networking, Inc. . . . . *http://www.bbn.com/bbnjobs/jobsrch.htm*
Beardsley Group <The> . . . . *http://www.beardsleygroup.com/*
Belcan Information Services . . . . *http://www.belcan.com/infoserv.htm*
Believe and Succeed . . . . *http://www.ens.net/*
Bernard Haldane Associates . . . . *http://www.intex.net/careers/index.html*
BIO-ONLINE . . . . *http://www.bio.com/hr/hr_index.html*
Biophysical Society . . . . *http://biosci.cbs.umn.edu/biophys/employ.html*
BioSource . . . . *http://www.biosource-tech.com/*
Biotech Career Center . . . . *http://www.gene.com/ae/AB/CC/index.html*
Bizlinks (Singapore) . . . . *http://sunflower.singnet.com.sg/~g6615000/*
BlackHawk Information Services . . . . *http://www.blackhawkis.com*
Bolsa de Trabajo de Pixelnet (Mexico) [in Spanish] *http://www.pixel.com.mx:80/Curriculums/*
Bolton Group <The> . . . . *http://www.webcreations.com/bolton/*
Brannon and Tully Consulting Services . . . . *http://www.brannontully.com*
Brei & Associates, Inc. Jobs Database . . . . *http://www.netins.net/showcase/rdbrei/*
Bridge Information Technology Inc. (Canada Net Pages) . . . . *http://www.visions.com/*
British Crystallographic Association . . . . *http://www.cryst.bbk.ac.uk/BCA/jobs.html*
Buzz Buzz @ads: Banen aangeboden (Netherlands) . . . . *http://valley.interact.nl/@ds/*
banen-aanbod/home.html
Camelot Consultants Limited (UK) . . . . *http://www.eclipse.co.uk/camelot/*
Career Blazers Learning Centre (Canada) . . . . *http://cblazers.ns.ca/*
Career Command Center . . . . *http://www.CareerCommandCenter.com/ccc.html*
Career Internetworking . . . . *http://www.careerkey.com/careerky.htm*
Career Match *http://www.fleethouse.com/career/cm-pg1.htm*
Career Network . . . . *http://phoenix.placement.oakland.edu*
Career Opportunities in Singapore . . . . *http://www.singapore-careers.com*
Career Quest . . . . *http://www.careerquest.com/*
Career Source . . . . *http://www.netusa.com/jobs.htm*
CareerLine . . . . *http://www.careerline.com*
CareerMosaic (Asia) . . . . *http://www.careerasia.com/*
CAUSE Job Posting Service . . . . *http://cause-www.colorado.edu/pd/jobpost/jobpost.html*
Center for Applied Large-Scale Computing *http://quasar.poly.edu:80/CALC/jobs.html*
CERL Sound Group . . . . *http://datura.cerl.uiuc.edu/netStuff/jobs/jobs.html*
Chicago Mosaic . . . . *http://www.ci.chi.il.us*
Chicago Software Newspaper . . . . *http://www.chisoft.com*
CitySites Production . . . . *http://www.stonesearch.com*
CompuSource, Inc . . . . *http://www.biddeford.com/compusource/*

ComputAppoint (UK) . . . . *http://www.rednet.co.uk/homepages/computap/*
Computemp . . . . *http://www.computemp.com/*
Computer Age Classifieds (Australia) *http://www.theage.com.au:80/class/*
Computer Contracting on the Internet,
     ETX—Melbourne, Australia . . . . *http://www.ozemail.com.au/~contract/etx.html*
Computer Help (UK) . . . . *http://ourworld.compuserve.com/homepages/tblake_computerhelp/*
Computer Science Jobs in Academia . *http://www.cs.brandeis.edu:80/~zippy/academic-cs-jobs.html*
Computer-Tech Consultants (Canada) . . *http://www.islandnet.com/~ctc10000/www/ctc10000.html*
ComputerWorld . . . . *http://www.computerworld.com*
Computing and Technology Companies Online . . . . . . *http://www.cmpcmm.com/cc/companies.html*
Computing/IT Jobs WorldWide . . . . *http://www.Britain.EU.net/vendor/jobs/main.html*
Compuvac Personnel Services Limited (UK) . . . . *http://www.compuvac.com/*
Consulting Companies on the Web *http://www.phoenix.oakland.edu:80/career/consult.htm*
Contract Employment Weekly, Jobs Online . . . . *http://www.ceweekly.wa.com/*
                                                        http://www.ceweekly.com/
                                         gopher://gopher.ceweekly.wa.com/1
CTG . . . . *http://www.ctg.com*
CTS Network Services . . . . *http://www.cts.com/*
CyberCONTRACTS (UK) . . . . *http://www.cybernation.co.uk/~cybercon/index.htm*
CybeRésumé Associates LLC . . . . *http://tkweb.com/resume/*
CybeRezumes . . . . *http://www.seanet.com/HTML/Vendors/raj/cyberez.html*
                                    http://seanet.com/HTML/Vendors/raj/job.html
Cyberspace Jobs . . . . *http://www.best.com:80/~lianne/*
D & P International Limited (UK) . . . . *http://www.pavilion.co.uk/dandp/*
Daley Consulting & Search and Daley Technical Search . . . . *http://www.dpsearch.com/*
Dallas ComputerJobs Store . *http://www.computerjobs.com/scripts/dbml.exe?template=/index.dbm*
Data Careers . . . . *http://www.vnu.com/datanews/careers/careers_eng.html*
Data Processing Independent Consultant's Exchange (DICE) . . . . *http://www.dice.com*
DataMasters . . . . *http://www.datamasters.com*
DataWay Resources . . . . *http://www.csn.net/dataway/*
David Aplin and Associates (Canada) . . . . *http://www.tgx.com/aplin/*
DEI Staffing . . . . *http://www.calldei.com/*
Department of Energy (DOE) *http://www.em.doe.gov/emnet1i.html*
Department of Instructional Technologies,
     San Francisco State University . . . . *http://www.itec.sfsu.edu/*
DesignSphere Online . . . . *http://www.dsphere.net/jobs.html*
Donnington Associates (UK) . . . . *http://www.i-way.co.uk/donnington/*
Doughty Group Ltd (New Zealand) <The> . . . . . . *http://www.jobnetnz.co.nz/Agencies/doughty.html*
DP Independent Consultants Exchange *http://www.dice.dlinc.com:8181/*
DPP International Ltd (UK) *http://194.128.198.201/dpp/*
Duncan and Ryan Associates (New Zealand) *http://www.jobnetnz.co.nz/Agencies/Duncan-Ryan.html*
DXI Corporation, Atlanta, GA . . . . *http://isotropic.com/dxicorp/dxihome.html*
EagleView . . . . *http://www.eagleview.com*
EarthWatch . . . . *http://www.earthwatch.org/t/Temployment.html*
Easynet Job-Centre (The Virtual Job Centre) . . . . *http://www.cyberiacafe.net/jobs/*
Eclectic International Executive Search . . . . *http://www.cyber.nl/eclectic/sap/welcome.html*
EDP Contract Services . . . . *http://edpcs.com/*
EDP Staffing Services, Inc. . . . . *http://www.edpstaffing.com/index.html*
Eduplus Management Group Inc. . . . . *http://www.eduplus.ca/*
EgoSearch (Belgium) . . . . *http://www.interpac.be/egosearch/welcome.html*
Elan Computing (UK) . . . . *http://www.elan.co.uk/*
Electronic Labor Exchange (Canada) . . . . *http://ele.ingenia.com/*
Elite Permanent and Contract Recruitment Agency (UK) . . . . *http://www.elite-cs.co.uk/elite/*
Employment and Training Agencies . . . . *http://bcn.boulder.co.us/employment/agencies.html*
Employment Edge *http://www.employmentedge.com:80/employment.edge/*

Employment News . . . . *http://www.ftn.net/*
Employment Opportunities . . . . *http://education.indiana.edu/ist/students/jobs/joblink.html*
Employment Opportunities in India . . . *http://www.webpage.com/hindu/960210/10/10hdline.html*
Energys Technical Services Ltd (UK) . . . . *http://www.energys.co.uk/energys/*
ENews . . . . *http://www.sumnet.com/enews*
Engine Room (UK and Europe) <The>, iWEB . . . . *http://www.iweb.co.uk/iwsearch.html*
Engineering Job Source <The> . . . . *http://www.wwnet.com/~engineer/*
Engineering/Manufacturing Jobs Page . . . . *http://www.nationjob.com/engineering*
Envirobiz—International Environmental Information Network . . . . *http://www.envirobiz.com/*
Eurolink Group PLC (UK) . . . . *http://www.eurolinkgroup.plc.uk/*
European Bioinformatics Institute Career Connection . . . . . . *http://www.ebi.ac.uk/htbin/biojobs.pl*
European Molecular Biology Laboratory,
 Heidelberg, Germany . . . . *http://www.embl-heidelberg.de/ExternalInfo/jobs/*
Excellence in Consulting . . . . *http://www.exic.com/eichome.html*
Executive Recruitment Services (UK) . . . . *http://www.ers.co.uk/ers/*
Executive Search Consultants . . . . *http://www.escinc.com/eschome.html*
Expertel Consultants Ltd (UK) . . . . *http://www.pncl.co.uk/expertel/*
Extreme Résumé Drop . . . . *http://www.mainquad.com/theQuad/wich/introPages/lo/erd.html*
Faculty Positions in Computer Science . . . . *http://www.cs.cmu.edu/*
 afs/cs.cmu.edu/user/burks/www/faculty.html
FDSI's Job Center . . . . *http://www.fdsi-cons.com/*
Federal Funded Research in the US . . . . *http://medoc.gdb.org/best/fed-fund.html*
FEDnet—Foundation for Enterprise Development . . . . *http://www.fed.org/*
Fenwick Partners . . . . *http://www.fenwickpartners.com/*
Flavell Divett International (UK) . . . . *http://www.mistral.co.uk/fdi/*
Florida Sentinal . . . . *http://www.chicago.tribune.com/career/sentinel_ads.html*
Forbes Ltd. (UK) *http://194.128.198.201/forbes/*
Foreign Language Listings *http://condor.stcloud.msus.edu:20020/careerannounce.html*
Franklin Search Group . . . . *http://www.medmarket.com/tenants/fsg/*
Gemini Personnel Ltd. . . . . *http://www.glink.net.hk:80/~gemini/*
Georgia Job Bank . . . . *http://www.mindspring.com/~exchange/jobbank/ga/jobs.html*
Georgia Tech Career Services . . . . *http://www.gatech.edu/career*
GeoWeb for GIS/GPS/RS . . . . *http://www.ggrweb.com*
Get a Job! . . . . *http://www.getajob.com*
Gintic Institute of Manufacturing Technology
 (Singapore) *http://www.gintic.ntu.ac.sg:8000/jobs.html*
GIS Jobs Clearinghouse, University of Minnesota,
 Forestry, Remote Sensing Lab . . . . *http://www.gis.umn.edu/rsgisinfo/jobs.html*
Global Technical Recruitment *http://ourworld.compuserve.com:80/homepages/*
 global_technical_recruit/
Hamilton Jones & Koller (Australia) . . . . *http://www.hjk.com.au/*
Harrison Willis Group (UK) *http://194.128.198.201/hwgroup/main.html*
HEL—Human Enterprises Limited . . . . *http://www.demon.co.uk/hument/*
HIGH Technology Careers Magazine . . . . *http://www.hightechcareers.com/*
HiTechCareers, HiTech Careers . . . . *http://www.hitechcareer.com/hitech*
Hotflash Jobs . . . . *http://iquest.com/~ntes/jobslist.html*
HotJobs . . . . *http://www.hotjobs.com*
Houston Advanced Research Center . . . . *http://www.harc.edu/jobs.html*
Hunterskil Howard (UK) *http://194.128.198.201/hhplc/*
Huntington Group's Career Network <The>, CareerWeb . . . . *http://sgx.com/cw/*
IBA reSearch . . . . *http://web.wingsbbs.com/ibaresearch/*
IBNIX Recruitment (UK) . . . . *http://www.ibnix.co.uk/*
IEEE Computer Society . . . . *http://www.computer.org/pubs/computer/career/career.htm*
India Connect's Job Classified . . . . *http://www.indiaconnect.com/classadv/svacant.htm*
Industry Canada . . . . *http://info.ic.gc.ca/ic-data/ic-eng.html*

IndustryNet Career Opportunities . . . . *http://www.industry.net/c/mn/_co*
INFONET . . . . *http://www.info.net/*
Infonet's Classifieds . . . . *http://www.infonetwww.com/clfdjo.htm*
Informatics Search Group . . . . *http://www.isgjobs.com*
Information Science and Telecommunications
      Placement . . . . *http://www2.lis.pitt.edu/~sochats/placement.html*
Information Technology Institute . . . . *http://www.iti.gov.sg/iti_info/job/job.html*
Information Technology Talent Association, LLC . . . . *http://www.it-ta.com/*
Infotech . . . . *http://www.infotech.co.nz*
InfoTech–Placement Services Group . . . . *http://www.itweb.com/infotec/index.html*
Institut fur Arbeitswirtschaft und
      Organisation, Germany . . . . *http://www.iao.fhg.de/Public/hiwi/OVERVIEW-en.html*
Institute for Operations Research and
      Management Science (INFORMS) . . . . *http://www.informs.org/JPS/index.html*
Institution of Electrical Engineers *http://www.iee.org.uk:80/*
Instructional Technology Jobs, Indiana
      University, Bloomington . . . . *http://education.indiana.edu/ist/students/jobs/joblink.html*
Integral Technologies, Inc. . . . . . , ... *http://www.integralIT.com*
Integrated Computer Solutions . . . . *http://www.ics.com/Jobs/*
Integrity Center, Inc. <The> . . . . *http://www.integctr.com/*
Intellimatch On-Line Career Services . . . . *http://www.intellimatch.com/intellimatch/*
International Interactive Communications Society, New York Chapter . *http://www.iicsny.org/jobs/*
International Telecommunications Union (Switzerland) . . *http://www.itu.ch/itudoc/gs/vacancy.html*
Internet-Solutions.Com . . . . *http://www.internet-solutions.com/*
Interpac Belgium (Belgium) . . . . *http://www.interpac.be/jobs.html*
Interskill Services S.A. . . . . *http://www.interskill.ch/*
Intrinsica Systems (UK) . . . . *http://www.intrinsica.co.uk/*
IPC Technologies . . . . *http://www.ipctech.com/employment.htm*
IT Jobs . . . . *http://www.internet-solutions.com/itjobs.htm*
IT Link Ltd (UK) . . . . *http://www.itlink.co.uk/*
I.T. Staffing (Canada) . . . . *http://www.itstaff.com/*
ITJobSearch (UK) . . . . *http://www.itjobsearch.com/*
ITTA Recruiter Services . . . . *http://www.it-ta.com/rcselect.htm*
IUPUI Integrated Technologies *gopher://INDYCMS.IUPUI.EDU/11/*
      IUPUI%20Information%20Sources/Staff%20Job%20Openings
J. Arthur Group . . . . *http://www.jarthurgroup.com/*
J. Edgar & Associates Inc. . . . . *http://www.the-wire.com/careers/*
Jay Tracey Associates *http://amsquare.com/america/search1.html*
Jenrick-CPI Nederland (Netherlands) . . . . *http://www.jenrick.nl/*
Jim Sease's Home Page . . . . *http://www.sease.com/*
Job Access Limited (Hong Kong) . . . . *http://www.hk.net/~jal/*
Job.net from Computer Contractor *http://www.vnu.co.uk/:81/ip_user/owa/register.main?c_mag_id=*
Job Search Materials for Engineers . . . . *http://www.englib.cornell.edu/*
Job Square . . . . *http://www.euro.net/InfoCraft/*
Jobs for WWW Developers . . . . *http://www.charm.net/*
Katron . . . . *http://www.occ.com/katron/*
Kingsford-Smith Partnership Ltd (UK) . . . . *http://www.kingsford-smith.co.uk/kingsford-smith*
Lockheed Martin Energy Systems . . . . *http://www.ornl.gov/mmes-www/MMESemployment.html*
      http://www.ornl.gov/employment.html
Management Recruiters International . . . . *http://www.mrinet.com/*
Medianet (UK) . . . . *http://www.pavilion.co.uk/medianet/jobs/jobs.htm*
MultiMedia Wire Classifieds . . . . *http://www.phillips.com/mmwire*
      http://www.mmwire.com/classifieds.html
      http://www.mmwire.com:80/classifieds.html

Modeling, Simulation and Training
    Employment Postings . . . . *http://itsc.sc.ist.ucf.edu/jobs.htm*
National Association of Broadcasters . . . . *http://www.nab.org/*
National Association of Purchasing
    Management—Silicon Valley, Inc. . . . . *http://catalog.com/napmsv/jobs.htm*
National Computer Board (Singapore) . . . . *http://www.ncb.gov.sg/ncb/recruit.html*
National Institute for Nuclear Physics and
    High-Energy Physics (Netherlands) . . . . *http://www.nikhef.nl/*
National Multimedia Association of America . . . . *http://www.nmaa.org/nmaa/jobbank.htm*
National Technical Employment Services . . . . *http://iquest.com/~ntes/*
National Technology Transfer Center's Job Index . . . . *http://iridium.nttc.edu/*
National Writer's Union JobHotline . . . . *http:www.nwu.org/nwu/hotline/*
NCSA, The National Center for Supercomputer
    Applications *http://www.ncsa.uiuc.edu/General/Jobs/00Jobs.html*
Network Operations Worldwide (Belgium) . . . . . *http://www.belgium.eu.net/company/jobs/jobs.html*
Network Professional Association (NPA) . . . . *http://www.npanet.org/home/index.htm*
Networking Jobs in North California . . . . *http://www.pcpersonnel.com/*
New Dimensions in Technology, Inc. . . . . *http://www.ndt.com/users/ndt/index.html*
O-Hayo Sensei . . . . *http://www.ohayosensei.com/~ohayo/*
Olsten Information Technology Staffing *http://olsten.boulder.net:80/olstenskills.html*
Omaha CareerLink . . . . *http://www.omaha.org/careerlink.html*
                                              http://www.synergy.net/CareerLink/Select.html
OptoLink . . . . *http://www.spie.org/web/employment/employ_home.html*
OzJobs (ACP OnLine) . . . . *http://columbia.digiweb.com/~aep1/cgi-bin/jobidx.cgi*
Paul-Tittle *http://www.careermosaic.com:80/cm/pta/pta1.html*
PhotoForum's Photo/Imaging Jobs . . . . *http://www.rit.edu/~andpph/jobs.html*
Post A Job . . . . *http://www.postajob.com*
Prime Recruitment (UK) . . . . *http://www.tcp.co.uk/~primerec/*
Professionals On Line/Employment and Recruitment . . *http://www.wordsimages.com/emp_rec.htm*
Prospective Management Overseas (Belgium) . . . . *http://www.pmo.be/home.htm*
Reed Personnel Services, Reed Computing . . . . *http://www.reed.co.uk/*
Richard Wheeler Associates (UK) . . . . *http://www.hiway.co.uk/rwa/*
Roevin Management Services, Ltd. *http://194.128.198.201/roevin/*
Saber Consultants . . . . *http://www.saberedge.com/*
Sally Silver Incorporated . . . . *http://www.sallysilver.com/*
Schulenburg & Associates . . . . *http://www.vnet.net/neil*
Senior Design Corporation . . . . *http://www.cts.com/browse/sdc/*
Shawn's Internet Résumé Center . . . . *http://www.inpursuit.com/sirc/seeker.html*
SIAM News Professional Opportunities *gopher://gopher.siam.org/11/siamnews/profops*
Silicon Alley Connections, LLC . . . . *http://www.salley.com*
Singapore Online . . . . *http://www.singapore.com/jobs.htm*
SK Writers . . . . *http://www.skwriters.com/*
Society for Technical Communication . . . . *http://stc.org/*
Staffing Services Online . . . . *http://www.staffingservices.com/*
Synergistech Communications . . . . *http://www.synergistech.com*
Systems Network . . . . *http://www.SystemsNet.com/*
TalentScout . . . . *http://www.sjmercury.com/talentscout/*
Tech Specialists . . . . *http://www.techspec.com*
Technology Registry . . . . *http://techreg.com*
TechWeb/TechCareers/TechHunter . . . . *http://www.techweb.com/default.html.body?*
                                        http://techweb.com/careers/careers.html.body?
TeleJob . . . . *http://ezinfo.ethz.ch/ETH/TELEJOB/tjb_home_e.html*
TKO Personnel, Inc. . . . . *http://www.tkointl.com*
Top Jobs on the Net . . . . *http://www.topjobs.co.uk/intel/intel.htm*
Transaction Information Systems . . . . *http://www.tisny.com/jobs/jobs.htm*

UTRC, United Technologies Research Center . . . . . . *http://utrcwww.utc.com/UTRC/Jobs/Jobs.html*
VideoPro Classifieds *http://www.txdirect.net:80/videopro/adv.htm*
VJ Enterprises . . . . *http://www.vjenterprises.com*
Washington State Information Exchange . . . . *http://olympus.dis.wa.gov*
WDVL: Jobs for Web Developers <The> . . . . *http://www.stars.com/jobs/*
Web Dog's Job Hunt . . . . *http://www.itec.sfsu.edu/jobs/*
Westech Career Expos, WESTECH Career EXPO . . . . *http://www.vjf.com/pub/westech/*
Winter, Wyman, and Co. Employment InfoCenter . . . *http://www.winterwyman.com/wwcsjobs.htm*
WITI Campus . . . . *http://www.witi.com*
Women in Computer Science & Engineering . . . . *http://www.ai.mit.edu/people/ellens/gender.html*
Women in Technology . . . . *http://www-personal.ksu.edu/~dangle*
Women in Technology Directory . . . . *http://www.sdsu.edu/wit*
World Wide Web Consortium *http://www10.w3.org/hypertext/WWW/*
Consortium/Recruitment/Overview.html

Telecommunications

Advantage Technical Services . . . . *http://www.advantagets.com*
ANSA Job Opportunities . . . . *http://www.ansa.co.uk/APM/job-ad.html*
AUX Technology, Inc. . . . . *http://kiwi.futuris.net/aux/*
Bogue Company . . . . *http://www.bogueco.com*
Bolton Group <The> . . . . *http://www.webcreations.com/bolton/*
DSR–Diversity Search and Recruitment . . . . *http://www.telecomsearch.com/*
Elan Computing (UK) . . . . *http://www.elan.co.uk/*
Electronic Industries Association . . . . *http://www.eia.org/norm.htm*
Hallahan & Associates . . . . *http://www.hallahan.com*
Industry Canada . . . . *http://info.ic.gc.ca/ic-data/ic-eng.html*
Information Science and
   Telecommunications Placement . . . . *http://www2.lis.pitt.edu/~sochats/placement.html*
International Telecommunications Union (Switzerland) . . *http://www.itu.ch/itudoc/gs/vacancy.html*
J. Robert Scott, Executive Search . . . . *http://j-robert-scott.com/*
Paul-Tittle *http://www.careermosaic.com:80/cm/pta/pta1.html*
SnellingSearch . . . . *http://www.snellingsearch.com*
Tech Specialists . . . . *http://www.techspec.com*

Telecommuting

Infonet's Classifieds . . . . *http://www.infonetwww.com/clfdjo.htm*
International Home Workers Association <The> . . . . *http://www.homeworkers.com/*
Telecommuting Jobs . . . . *http://www.tjobs.com*

Women

Ada Project <The> . . . . *http://www.cs.yale.edu/HTML/YALE/CS/HyPlans/tap/tap.html*
Advancing Women . . . . *http://www.advancingwomen.com*
Africa Online: Jobs . . . . *http://www.AfricaOnline.com/AfricaOnline/classifieds.html*
Career Center for Workforce Diversity, Equal
   Opportunity Publications, Inc. (EOP) . . . . *http://www.eop.com*
Career Management International . . . . *http://www.cmi-lmi.com/*
Employment Opportunities in Women's Studies and Feminism   *gopher://gopher.inform.umd.edu:70/*
11/EdRes/Topic/WomensStudies/Employment
EOP's Career Center for Workforce Diversity . . . . *http://www.eop.com/*
Society of Women Engineers . . . . *http://www.swe.org*
WITI Campus . . . . *http://www.witi.com*
Women in Computer Science & Engineering . . . . *http://www.ai.mit.edu/people/ellens/gender.html*
Women in Higher Education Career Page . . . . *http://www.itis.com/wihe/*
Women in Technology . . . . *http://www-personal.ksu.edu/~dangle*
Women in Technology Directory . . . . *http://www.sdsu.edu/wit*

Writing Arts

Apple Recruitment (UK) . . . . *http://www.u-net.com/~applerec/*

Arts Wire Current . . . . *http://www.tmn.com/Artswire/*

Belcan Information Services . . . . *http://www.belcan.com/infoserv.htm*

Bridge Information Technology Inc. (Canada Net Pages) . . . . *http://www.visions.com/*

Buzz Buzz @ads: Banen aangeboden (Netherlands) . . . . *http://valley.interact.nl/@ds/*
banen-aanbod/home.html

Data Processing Independent Consultant's Exchange (DICE) . . . . *http://www.dice.com*

DXI Corporation, Atlanta, GA . . . . *http://isotropic.com/dxicorp/dxihome.html*

Instructional Technology Jobs, Indiana
University, Bloomington . . . . *http://education.indiana.edu/ist/students/jobs/joblink.html*

Internship Director . . . . *http://www.snpa.org/snpa/web/home.html*

J. Arthur Group . . . . *http://www.jarthurgroup.com/*

J-JOBS DIGEST: Journalism Jobs and Internships . . . . *gopher://blick.journ.latech.edu*

National Writer's Union JobHotline . . . . *http:www.nwu.org/nwu/hotline/*

SK Writers . . . . *http://www.skwriters.com/*

7 Online Services and Your Job Search

A commercial online service provides more than just access to the Internet, which is the primary purpose of an Internet service provider. Commercial online services provide "content," meaning that, in addition to Internet access, they offer discussion forums, databases of information, magazines, access to online shopping malls, e-mail accounts, home page space, and special interest information areas. They also provide the ability to interact with others to exchange ideas, share experiences, and ask/answer questions in real time.

The cost of these services varies widely, but all of the major services offer free trial periods, followed by monthly fees ranging from $9.95 and up for five hours of online time to $19.95 for unlimited access. The software is free and, if you haven't already received several sets of disks a year in your junk mail, you simply need to call a toll-free number to order your disks (or CD-ROM). The software is easy to install and requires little expertise to use.

After you install the software, you need to obtain a local access number that corresponds to the speed of your modem (9,600, 14,400, 28,800, etc.). One of the nice things about commercial online services is that you can gain access through local phone numbers all across the country and around the world. This means you can get your e-mail from almost anywhere without paying long distance. If you travel a lot, this can be a real savings.

Once you dial into your account, you are ready to surf the computers of the service itself or to use its Internet gateway to surf the Web instead. Because the software is so seamless, it is difficult to tell when you are using one or the other, but it doesn't make any difference in your cost. You are just a mouse click away from many service options with commercial online services.

It would take a book of its own to list all of the different forums and service options available from the commercial online services, but following are some of the more relevant areas that will help you in your job search. New services and databases are added every day and some of the lesser used ones will disappear, so be certain to check the indexes of your service for the most current listings.

■ *America Online*

8619 Westwood Center Drive
Vienna, Virginia 22182-2285
Toll Free: (800) 827-6364
Phone: (703) 448-8700
Fax: (703) 883-1509
Internet: *http://www.aol.com*

America Online (AOL) was started in 1985 by Steve Case and now serves more than 7 million members. AOL provides you with access to a broad range of information, communication, education, entertainment, and transactional services. The Internet gateway allows access to the World Wide Web, e-mail, newsgroups, databases, and file transfer protocols. AOL will host, at no extra charge, up to two megabytes of home pages for each of its subscribers, accessible at *http://members.aol.com.* There are new services added almost daily, and AOL is very user friendly. You can find help in written form by clicking an icon or you can chat live with technical support representatives through the Member Services site.

For a first-time user, AOL is simple to install, and local access numbers are available in more than 700 cities across the United States and Canada. Costs vary depending on the type of plan you choose. The best deal is unlimited access for $19.95 per month.

The CAREER site on AOL is a rich source of information for job seekers. Not only does it offer the Online Career Center's database of résumé and job openings, but there are many resources for career guidance for everything from interviewing to cover letters. Under this category, you will find the Occupational Profiles Database, Career Focus 2000 Directory, career counseling, career analysis, career resources library, federal career opportunities, Hoover's Handbook, employment agency database, the Executive Desk Register of Publicly Held Corporations, résumé templates, cover letter library, and the list goes on. E-Span's JobSearch, Help Wanted–USA, and the World Wide Résumé Talent Bank can all be found on AOL. James Gonyea, president of Gonyea and Associates, Inc., plays a leading role in most of the career sites at America Online.

AOL has an area that features the employer profiles and job-seeking tools published by Plunkett Research, Ltd. The Almanac of American Employers, Plunkett's Health Care Industry Almanac, and Plunkett's InfoTech Industry Almanac have been combined to create a powerful resource for job seekers. The company profiles are especially useful since they provide salary and benefits outlines as well as overviews of each company's culture.

The "Employment Agency Database" menu takes you to the executive search firms area. Here you will find information on more than 4,000 recruiters who might be able to help you find a job.

Because of its partnerships with Bertelsmann AG in Europe, AOL Canada, and Mitsui & Company in Japan, America Online has a true international flavor.

■ *CompuServe*

500 Arlington Centre Boulevard
P.O. Box 20212
Columbus, Ohio 43220
Toll Free: (800) 848-8199
Fax: (614) 457-0348
Internet: *http://www.compuserve.com*

CompuServe is a commercial online service owned by H&R Block. With more than 4 million users in an excess of 150 countries, CompuServe is the most business oriented of the major online services. As a subscriber, you can research reference materials, shop in the online mall, interact with manufacturers of computer and software products, carry on discussions in more than a thousand forums, and download all types of software. If you go to INDEX, you can download a list of all the services available on CompuServe.

CompuServe's job-related "content" includes a Career Management Forum that helps to ensure long-term employability. The Sysop is Michael Rowe, marketing director of E-Span, a jobs database available on CompuServe as well as the Internet. Martin Yate, author of *Beat the Odds* and the *Knock 'em Dead* series, has a presence in this forum. He holds regular live conferences to give advice in the BEAT THE ODDS forum message section. Use this and other live conferences in the CAREERS forum to make connections with employers, human resource experts, recruiters, and fellow job seekers who may one day be potential contacts in your network.

CompuServe members have access to exclusive files in the library about how to approach their careers. There are articles on how to find jobs through networking, what not to say in an interview, how to upload your résumé to a résumé database, how to use keywords, and even the U.S. Department of Labor's job-market forecasts. You will also find an extensive database of newspapers, magazines, journals, and other research sources to help you prepare for an interview. Check out CompuServe's Value Line financial statements, Standard & Poor's company information, and Investext investment analyst research reports to give you even more information power. Some of the more career-related periodicals available on CompuServe include: *Occupational Outlook Quarterly Magazine* (Go: MDP), *Labor Today Magazine* (Go: MDP), *Careers and the Workplace* (Go: INFOUSA).

Besides E-Span, there are two other libraries on CompuServe that allow members to upload their résumés. One is called "Regional Talent" and the other is called "Relocatable Talent" for those willing to move to a new area. You can also access the JOURNALISM forum for job listings and free-lance opportunities. Go

CLASSIFIEDS and you will find the Classified Service for Employment and Education, and in IQUEST is a Career Placement Registry Database.

CompuServe subscribers can post up to five megabytes of home pages for free at *http://ourworld.compuserve.com*. Download CompuServe's Home Page Wizard and you won't even have to learn HTML coding. The program will walk you through creating each element of your home page and then help you save it in a format that is ready to upload to your Web site.

■ *Delphi*

1030 Massachusetts Avenue
Cambridge, Massachusetts 02138
Toll Free: (800) 544-4005
Phone: (617) 441-4500
Fax: (508) 558-2944
Internet: *http://www.delphi.com*
E-mail: *service@delphi.com*

Delphi was one of the first online services to offer full Internet access. It began its services more than 15 years ago as the world's first online encyclopedia. It evolved over the years into a meeting place for hundreds of people with like interests. With more than 220 local access numbers, it offers unlimited access for as low as $16.96 per month if you make an annual commitment, although the price can be as much as $23.95 for the same service on a month-by-month basis.

Besides the full range of value-added services common to such services, Delphi offers JOB COMPLEX in the CUSTOM FORUMS section with mail and conferencing options, interviewing exercises, an Internet Gopher, employment database, job offerings, résumés, and so on. In the BUSINESS FORUM through GROUPS & CLUBS, you will find classified advertisements and employment opportunities in addition to information on business opportunities, résumés, career consultations, and other valuable information.

Delphi will host up to 10 megabytes of personal Web pages free. The Web pages are accessible at *http://people.delphi.com*.

■ *GEnie*

General Electric Network for Information Exchange
401 North Washington Street
Rockville, Maryland 20850
Toll Free: (800) 638-9636
Internet: *http://www.genie.com*
E-mail: *info@genie.com*

GEnie is owned by General Electric and is well-known for its specialized career categories, such as Judge and Lawyers Corner, Engineers on GEnie, and Health Care Providers, on its Peer-to-Peer Network. These specialized discussion areas allow you to expand your networking contacts and industry knowledge. The

RoundTables (discussion forums) provide general business and employment information, live conferences, and advice, especially the Workplace RoundTable and Home Office/Small Business RoundTable, which are places for like-minded people to gather and exchange news and ideas.

Journalist Sandar Pesmen hosts a question and answer column covering career and employment issues. Dr. Job is a career advice column where subscribers can ask questions and get answers from "Dr. Job." Like the other major services, GEnie has access to the job postings and résumé database of E-Span's JobSearch. It also offers a résumé directory, business resource directory, the Thomas Register, Dun & Bradstreet company profiles, and occupational exploration and profiling.

This service tends to be a little more expensive than the rest. For nine hours of standard connect time, the monthly subscription cost as of this writing was $23.95. There are premium charges for many of their services, including travel services, news clipping service, and many of the database research services.

■ *Microsoft Network*

One Microsoft Way
Redmond, Washington 98052-6399
(800) 386-5550 (U.S. & Canada)
(800) 952-1110 (French Canadian)
Internet: *http://www.microsoft.com*

Microsoft Network is owned by Microsoft and the software to access MSN is built into every copy of Windows 95. Microsoft's commitment to producing innovative products that meet the evolving needs of its customers has led to the creation of the Internet Explorer, the closest competition to the Netscape browser software to date.

In addition to the standard reference sources available on most commercial online services, MSN offers the Mainstream Career Center with databases and information about companies and careers. You will also find a free service called FirePower designed for people facing downsizing, firing, retirement, layoff, and so on. Use the FirePower Career Forum to develop job hunting strategies and to improve your résumé.

To order a free trial subscription, call 1-800-328-2427. The standard monthly plan costs $4.95 for three hours of access per month. Each additional hour is $2.50. The same three hours per month can be purchased with the annual plan for $49.95. The frequent user plan is $19.95 per month with 20 hours of online time. Each additional hour is $2.00.

■ *Prodigy*

445 Hamilton Avenue
White Plains, New York 10601
Toll Free: (800) 776-3449
E-mail (Prodigy Internet): *piservice_help@prodigy.com*
E-mail (Prodigy Classic): *webmaster@prodigy.com*
Newsgroup: *prodigynet.help.service*
Internet: *http://www.prodigy.net*

Prodigy was formed as a partnership between Sears and IBM in 1984. The online service was launched in the United States in 1988 and was available nationally by 1990. Today it has more than one million subscribers who chat in real time, send e-mail messages, check live newswire feeds, and enjoy more than 500 other features, including personal Web pages, medical information, games, music, interest groups, and more than 1,000 bulletin boards. In 1996, Prodigy merged with International Wireless, a leading telephone and technology company. Because of its subsidiary, Africa Online, Prodigy is a good source for international information *(http://www.AfricaOnline.com)*.

Prodigy's CAREERS bulletin boards provide information on relocating, finding jobs, changing careers, consulting, and specific information related to various industries. The CLASSIFIEDS forum lists jobs, but Prodigy doesn't provide as many career-related interest areas of some of the other online services.

Prodigy offers a dedicated Internet connection (Prodigy Internet) that is totally separate from its classic commercial online service. Prodigy Internet offers full Internet access, including IRC rooms, newgroups, Telnet, and ftp. Although it is creating a version that uses the Microsoft Explorer browser, its current browser of choice is Netscape. Unlike a dedicated Internet service provider, however, Prodigy Internet has its own content. In fact, programmers are in the process of taking most of the Prodigy Classic service content over to the Internet site for use by its subscribers.

8 Using a BBS in Your Job Search

This chapter will introduce you to the concept of a Bulletin Board Service (BBS) and show you how to access the more than 60,000 local bulletin boards in the United States and 100,000 worldwide. Many BBSs offer résumé databases and/or job postings, but even when they don't, you can use them to develop networking contacts within your industry.

■ What Is a Bulletin Board Service?

Ward Christensen started the first bulletin board service in 1978 as a means of exchanging messages and files between computer users more quickly than through conventional printed information and ground transportation. Instead of waiting days to receive information, files could be accessed through the telephone lines and downloaded in a matter of minutes. Most BBSs today continue to offer file transfers and special interest groups (SIGs) that are focused on a single subject or industry of interest to a select group of individuals.

Anyone with a computer, modem, phone line, and specialized bulletin board system software can host a bulletin board service. A system operator (or SysOp, pronounced "siss-op") is the person responsible for creating the system, installing the files, managing the messages, and answering user questions.

■ How to Find a BBS That Meets Your Needs

Call your local bulletin board services and talk with them about what they offer. But, where do you find a local BBS? Your telephone book, newspapers, or local computer publications are your best sources for BBS listings. In Colorado Springs, for instance, you will find the weekly *Peak Computing Magazine* free at most grocery stores. In the back is a list of bulletin board services, including:

DataBass Connection
719-570-7291
14,000
classified advertising and résumé database

There are even lists of bulletin boards on commercial online services. For instance, at America Online, you will find complete lists of bulletin board services for every part of the country, sorted by region, then by state, and then by area code. Access the list through *BBS CORNER*. In the same forum is a database of frequently asked questions about BBSs that is especially useful, as well as full copies of *Boardwatch Magazine*, the nation's most informational and popular magazine about BBSs.

The *Computer Shopper* magazine publishes a list of bulletin boards, but because the list has grown so large, it only publishes half of the list one month and half the next. You must purchase two consecutive copies of the magazine in order to get a listing of all bulletin boards. There are several other magazines that include numbers for BBSs, including *Online Access*, *BBS Magazine*, and *Computer User Magazine*, which you will find at your local bookstore or newsstand.

On the Internet, you can find a list of bulletin boards at the following site:

- Freenets and Bulletin Boards, Eastern Kentucky University
  gopher://acs.eku.edu:70/
  Select: *Explore the Internet*
  Select: *FreeNets* or *Bulletin Boards*

Once you have logged onto a bulletin board service, you will often find lists of access numbers for related BBSs, although you may have to search a bit to find them.

■ *How to Access a BBS*

Besides a computer, modem, and phone line, you will need a special communications software package in order to access a bulletin board service. Unfortunately, not all of this software works in exactly the same way and some packages are more difficult to configure than others. Once configured, any of the major communications software packages (like ProComm or Delrina's Wincomm Pro) will allow you to access a bulletin board service. All you need to do is to tell your software which modem settings you need and what phone number to dial. For most bulletin boards, the settings are:

- No parity
- 8 data bits
- 1 stop bit
- Full duplex
- Set your terminal emulation at either ANSI or VT 100

Remember, unless you live in the home town of the BBS, you will incur long distance phone charges for most bulletin boards, although you can Telnet to some of them. In order to Telnet to a BBS, you must first discover the host name or the

Internet protocol (IP) address of the service. You can do that by first logging onto the system with your modem long distance and asking the SysOp for the information. Then log off and Telnet back through your Internet service provider.

Before you dial a BBS, set your modem to a timeout delay of 60 seconds or more. It takes a little longer to logon to a BBS than other types of online services. When you connect with a BBS, don't press any keys until you get a screen from the BBS. If you press enter before the initial screen is loaded, you will probably see garbage on your screen. Once you have logged onto the BBS, you will usually be asked to fill out a questionnaire about yourself first. Most boards keep this information confidential.

■ *Career-related Bulletin Board Services*

Even though many bulletin board services offer space for posting your résumé, this may not be your best use of a BBS. As I advise with multimedia résumés and home pages, as long as it is free—or nearly so—you won't lose anything by posting your résumé to a BBS, but the chances of a recruiter searching a local bulletin board service for résumés every few days is rather remote. Instead, use the BBS to find out about the local job market, search for job openings, find out who's hiring and what kinds of people they are looking for, salary levels, taxes, cost of living, and answers to the multitude of questions that arise when you are considering a move to a new city. Use the chat rooms to increase your networking contacts and to exchange ideas. In other words, use bulletin board services as an add-on to your job search repertoire, not as your primary tool.

Access America . . . . (918) 747-2542
Tulsa, Oklahoma: Job-related Usenet newsgroups and FIDONet echoes of jobs. Internet e-mail and résumé uploads.

Ad Connection . . . . (804) 978-3927
Charlottesville, Virginia: Classified ads and federal government job listings.

Advanced R&D's Pipeline . . . . (407) 894-0580
Orlando, Florida: Job listings in Midwest and Southeast regions. Résumé uploads.

Aerospace Test Technologies . . . . (908) 741-9460
New Jersey: Employment opportunities for aerospace test technologists, computer technicians, engineers and programmers, and draftsmen.

American Building Design Exchange . . . . (617) 665-0448
Massachusetts: Building design and construction.

Analysts International Corporation . . . . (214) 263-9161
Dallas, Texas: Computer job listings for contract positions in the Dallas-Fort Worth area. Operated by AIC.

Automated Library Information eXchange (ALIX) . . . . (202) 707-4885
Washington, D.C.: Current federal library job openings, hotlines and federal government hotlines and BBS operated by the Federal Library and Information Center Committee.

Automation Insight . . . . (201) 335-7202
New Jersey: Process control, instrumentation, and automation.

AVADS-BBS (DOI) . . . . (800) 368-3321
United States: U.S. Department of the Interior job announcements. The Automated
Vacancy Announcement Information Center provides information on job vacancies at the
Department of the Interior.

AXCESS—Emergency Medicine Online System . . . . (412) 363-7510
Pennsylvania: Emergency medicine job opportunities for physicians.

Bizopps Connection . . . . (310) 677-7034
California: Business and franchise opportunities, venture capital sources, and money-
making opportunities.

Bust Out BBS . . . . (510) 888-1443
Hayward, California: Job listings and information nationwide. Fee required.

CAPACCESS Career Center . . . . (202) 785-1523
Washington, D.C.: Computer and noncomputer job information from the National Science
Foundation, National Institute of Health, Public Health Service, Department of the
Interior, Department of Defense, and U.S. Department of Agriculture. Operated by the
National Capital Area Public Access Network, Inc.

Career Board . . . . (214) 931-5792
Texas: Job listings primarily in the Southwest but also nationally.

Career Connection . . . . (214) 247-0675
Texas: National job listings in administration, data processing, engineering, manufacturing, and sales/marketing, among others.

Career Connection . . . . (414) 258-0164
Wauwatosa, Wisconsin: Employment opportunities nationwide.

Career Connections . . . . (415) 903-5815, (415) 903-5840, (415) 917-2129
Los Altos, California: Worldwide job listings.

Career Decisions . . . . (909) 864-8287
California: Jobs, recruiters, résumé service, profiles, book reviews, and other career-
related information.

Career-Link . . . . (714) 952-1431
California: Résumé database accessed by Southern California employers.

Career Link, Inc. . . . . (602) 973-2002
Phoenix, Arizona: International job database. Must call (800) 453-3350 for information
to access BBS. Fee required for full access.

Career Systems Online . . . . (413) 592-9208
Chicopee, Massachusetts: Job listings and résumé uploads for primarily MIS and software
engineers nationwide.

Careers BBS . . . . (305) 828-5697
Florida: Local and national areas for reading and posting employment classifieds. Online forums, national echo conferences, Netmail access. FIDONet: 100:1260/100

Careers First, Inc. . . . . (609) 786-2666, (609) 786-2667, (215) 676-5528
Cinnaminson, New Jersey: Job listings for computer and miscellaneous positions, updated weekly. Résumé uploads and job-hunting tips.

Careers Online . . . . (508) 879-4700
Framingham, Massachusetts: *Computer World* newspaper's BBS with listings of data processing jobs nationwide. Online résumé board.

Careers Online . . . . (408) 248-7029
California: Job listings and résumé fax service.

Census Personnel Board . . . . (800) 451-6128, (301) 763-4574
Washington, D.C.: Job listings for Suitland, Maryland only. Operated by the U.S. Department of Commerce, Bureau of the Census.

Chicago Syslink . . . . (708) 795-4442, (708) 495-4485, (708) 795-4456
Berwyn, Illinois: Help Wanted USA job listings, Internet e-mail. Fee required. FIDONet: 1:115/622.

City of Fort Worth Information Center . . . . (817) 871-8612
Fort Worth, Texas: Job listings in various areas and miscellaneous information for the Fort Worth area. Operated by the City of Fort Worth Public Information Center.

Classacomputerfields . . . . (800) 753-4223

Classifieds BBS . . . . (415) 665-7918
California: Help wanted advertisements.

CloneBd . . . . (805) 527-8704
California: Employment information.

Club House . . . . (908) 276-2581
New Jersey: Classified advertisements.

Comp-U-Sell . . . . (801) 944-8786
Utah: Classified advertisements.

Computer Careers . . . . (704) 554-1102
Charlotte, North Carolina: Specialized in data processing jobs nationwide. Operated by EDPO Professionals, Inc.

Computer Department EIC . . . . (310) 421-6089
California: Computer consulting.

Computer Job . . . . (817) 268-2193
Bedford, Texas: Job listings for experienced computer professionals in Texas only. Operated by Data Processing Careers, Inc.

Computer Plumber . . . . (319) 337-6723
Iowa: A listing of engineering-related bulletin board services.

Computerworld Careers Online . . . . (508) 879-4700

Condell Online . . . . (803) 686-3465
Hilton Head, South Carolina: Job listings in the title insurance industry. Free access to "Employment Exchange" section for nonmembers. Résumé uploads.

Construction Hotline . . . . (209) 982-1297
California: Northern California construction jobs. Computer-related jobs. Architectural/engineering jobs.

Contractors Exchange . . . . (415) 334-7393
San Francisco, California: Construction-type contractor jobs. Few data processing jobs.

Corpus Christi On-Line . . . . (512) 850-8255
Corpus Christi, Texas: Computer and noncomputer job listings for Corpus Christi, San Antonio, national, international job markets, and job lists from Internet newsgroups. Fee required.

Data Dimension PCBoard . . . . (404) 921-1186
Georgia: Local job listings and résumé writing.

Department of Labor . . . . (202) 219-4784
Washington, D.C.: Jobs with the Department of Labor. Download jobs from every city listed in the JOBS Library.

Delight the Customer . . . . (517) 797-3740, (616) 662-0393
Hudsonville, Michigan: Job listings for manager level and above customer service, training and help desk professionals. Fee required.

Detroit Service Center . . . . (313) 226-4423
Detroit, Michigan: Federal job listings and information for the Detroit region. Operated by the U.S. Office of Personnel Management.

D.I.C.E. National Network: Contract and permanent data processing jobs nationwide. Job postings from over 80 agencies.
Boston, Massachusetts . . . . (617) 266-1080
Chicago, Illinois . . . . (708) 782-0960
Dallas, Texas . . . . (214) 782-0960
Des Moines, Iowa . . . . (515) 280-3423
Newark, New Jersey . . . . (201) 242-4166
Sunnyvale, California . . . . (408) 737-9339

Digital X-Connect . . . . (214) 517-8443, (214) 517-8315
Plano, Texas: Home of the JOBNet echo. Hundreds of job listings and information in 16 message bases. Also, BBS listing of all BBSs that carry the JOBNet echo nationwide.

Doc's Place . . . . (309) 682-6560
Illinois: Employment opportunities in the medical technical area.

DP Careers . . . . (817) 268-2193
Texas: Job listings for Texas only.

DP Job Works . . . . (813) 495-1801
Florida: Data processing/MIS jobs nationwide.

DP Job Works . . . . (219) 436-9702
Fort Wayne, Indiana: Data processing/management information system/information system (DP/MIS/IS) national job listings in downloadable files, updated weekly. Résumé uploads.

DP NETwork (Toner Corporation) . . . . (415) 788-7101, (415) 788-8663
San Francisco, California: Data processing jobs for San Francisco and Sacramento areas and nationwide. Updated daily.

ECCO* . . . . (415) 331-7227
California: National permanent and contract job listings.

ECCO* . . . . (312) 404-8685
Chicago, Illinois: Computer contract and permanent jobs for Chicago and Illinois areas only. Free Internet e-mail.

ECCO* . . . . (212) 580-4510
New York City, New York: Computer and related contract and permanent jobs for most of the East Coast.

EDP Professionals . . . . (704) 554-1102
North Carolina: Data processing search and placement services.

Elf's Den . . . . (212) 402-1382
New York: Technical and administrative positions in radiologic sciences, EMT, and general medical fields.

Employer's Network . . . . (206) 475-0665, (206) 471-7575
Tacoma, Washington: Internet, federal, and local (Pierce County) job listings, résumé programs, and database.

Employment Board . . . . (619) 689-1348, (619) 993-9319
San Diego, California: Employment information for the San Diego area. JOBS-Now echo.

Employment Connection . . . . (508) 537-1862
Leominster, Massachusetts: Job listings in all areas (mostly East Coast).

Employment Line . . . . (219) 485-3551
Indiana: Job listings and résumé database.

Employment Line . . . . (508) 865-7928
Sutton, Massachusetts: Job listings in all areas (mostly East Coast). Must submit résumé. Fee for full registration.

Enginet . . . . (513) 858-2688
Fairfield, Ohio: Referral service for engineers. Internet e-mail and Usenet job newsgroups.

Environet . . . . (415) 512-9108, (415) 512-9120
California: Job openings with Greenpeace. Most jobs in United States.

Exec-PC . . . . (414) 789-4210
Wisconsin: E-Span JobSearch access. Job listings in all areas.

Executive Connection . . . . (214) 306-3393
Dallas, Texas: Local and national job listings. Career, employment, and business management.

Federal Job Network . . . . (703) 715-1016
Virginia: Subscription-based. Federal job openings, both national and abroad.

Federal Job Opportunities Board . . . . (912) 757-3100

Federal Jobline . . . . (818) 575-6521
Los Angeles, California: Federal job listings and information for Western region from the Federal Job Information Center operated by the Office of Personnel Management (OPM).

FedWorld . . . . (703) 321-8020
Springfield, Virginia: Federal government job listings worldwide. Also has gateway to 100+ other government BBSs. Operated by the National Technical Information Service.

FirstStep . . . . (404) 642-0665
Atlanta, Georgia: Job listings for approximately 100 occupations. Internet e-mail and Usenet newsgroups. Résumé uploads. Fee required.

FJOB . . . . (912) 757-3100, (912) 471-3771
Macon, Georgia: Federal job listings and information for the United States. Federal Job Information Center operated by Office of Personnel Management.

FORTUNE Consultants of Or . . . . (407) 875-1028
Maitland, Florida: Job listings and résumé uploads.

Georgia Online . . . . (404) 591-0777
Atlanta, Georgia: Job listings, résumé database, Help Wanted USA services, Internet e-mail and Usenet newsgroups. Operated by Foster Employment Services. Fee required.

Global Trade Net . . . . (415) 668-0422
California: Job listings. International trade. Bid and sell areas. Help for starting new businesses.

Grapevine Job Network . . . . (404) 924-8414
Georgia: High-tech jobs, job hotlines, job seekers helping one another find jobs. Software.

hi-TEC BBS . . . . (512) 475-4893
Austin, Texas: Governor's Job Bank. Information on job-placement services, unemployment compensation, and employment law. Job listings from various Texas state agencies. Also accessible via Window on State Government BBS.

Horseman's BBS . . . . (517) 596-3233
Michigan: For horse lovers or business people in the horse industry. Extensive classified ad section.

HRCOMM . . . . (510) 944-5011
Pleasant Hill, California: Online network exclusively for human resource professionals containing products and services, skills registry, résumé uploads, job postings, and more.

Index Systems TBBS . . . . (404) 924-8414, (404) 924-8472
Atlanta, Georgia: Job networking, high tech job listings, job hotlines, job seeker software. Fee for expanded access.

I-NET BBS . . . . (301) 564-6749
Maryland: Résumé database.

INFO-Line . . . . (908) 922-4742
Oakhurst, New Jersey: Pharmaceutical job listings. Résumé uploads.

Infodata . . . . (404) 621-0804
Georgia: Classified ad service.

InfoMat . . . . (714) 492-8727
San Clemente, California: Echoes JOBNet, Laran Communications, Rime and Intelec job forums. Job opportunity and franchise information.

J-Connection: Data processing job listings, skill registration, downloadable job files.
Atlanta, Georgia . . . . (404) 662-5500
Clearwater, Florida . . . . (813) 791-0101
Washington, D.C., Metro . . . . (703) 379-0553

Job and Opportunity Link . . . . (708) 690-9860
Winfield, Illinois: Home of JOB-LINK and RÉSUMÉ-LINK. Jobs listings are downloadable.

Job Bank . . . . (315) 449-1838
Jamesville, New York: DP/MIS/IS contract and permanent job listings. Résumé uploads. Operated by Information Systems Staffing, Inc. (ISSI).

Job Bulletin Board . . . . (214) 612-9925
Plano, Texas: Job listings for data processing. Résumé uploads.

Job Search Board . . . . (416) 588-3821
Canada: Job and résumé postings. Home of Trans-Canada jobs conference. Small fee.

Job Trac . . . . (214) 349-0527
Dallas, Texas: Job listings, résumé uploads, and job forums in the Dallas-Fort Worth area.

JOBBS . . . . (504) 851-0274
Louisiana: Nationwide job listings.

JOBBS . . . . (404) 992-8937
Roswell, Georgia: Job listings, all areas and positions. Listings for recruiting firms and companies. Operated by Alpha Systems, Inc.

JOBS-BBS . . . . (503) 281-6808
Portland, Oregon: Thousands of job openings nationwide. Home of the moderator of the JOBS-NOW echo. Updated three to four times daily, Monday through Friday, and five to six times daily, Saturday and Sunday.

Jobs in America . . . . (619) 462-5627
California: Nationwide help wanted ads. Help Wanted-USA job listings.

Kasta, James and Associates . . . . (612) 536-0533
Edina, Minnesota: Job listings for management information system and engineering in the Twin Cities metro area.

Lee Johnson International . . . . (510) 787-3191
Crockett, California: Search firm specializing in employer-paid recruiting and placement of software engineering professionals.

Legal Genius . . . . (610) 695-9689
Philadelphia, Pennsylvania: Legal files, law school outlines, message areas, and résumé bank.

Logikal Career Connection . . . . (708) 420-0424
Illinois: Specializing in data processing professionals who are either employees or contractors. Downloadable software required.

Look Smart . . . . (510) 794-7381
Fremont, California: Indexes of business directories, reports, and salary surveys.

Matrix Resources . . . . (214) 239-5627
Dallas, Texas: Computer job listings for permanent and contract positions. Résumé uploads.

Multi-Tech Support . . . . (305) 596-6841
Florida: Job postings in the medical field and biomedicine.

Mushin BBS . . . . (619) 452-8137
San Diego, California: Job listings for the San Diego area.

Music Network USA . . . . (310) 312-8753
California: Musicians referral service.

NABE—National Association of Business Economists . . . . (216) 464-1757
Ohio: Résumé database for members of the association. Résumés are coded.

National Software Employment . . . . (800) 860-7860
Burlington, Vermont: In excess of 15,000 job listings from more than 17 U.S. cities. Fee required.

National Technical Search . . . . (413) 549-8136
Amherst, Massachusetts: National job listings, forums, and career guides. Updated every Monday. Operated by Allen Davis & Associates.

Nationserv Network . . . . (812) 426-9968
Indiana: Job Service. Résumé database and job listings. Fee required.

Nebraska Online . . . . (800) 392-7932
Omaha, Nebraska: Job listings and state-related information for State of Nebraska.

Network . . . . (301) 681-5331
Maryland: Job and applicant posts, employment-related information, conferences. All industries.

Network World Online . . . . (508) 620-1178
Framingham, Massachusetts: Job listings and information and advice on issues related to career and job. Operated by *Network World* magazine.

NFB Net . . . . (410) 752-5011
Baltimore, Maryland: Information and training materials to assist the blind for job seekers and employers. Sponsored by the National Federation for the Blind.

Olai . . . . (703) 450-1790
Virginia: Job listings, mostly for the Maryland, Virginia, and Washington, D.C. area.

Online Career Fair . . . . (603) 726-3344
New Hampshire: Job openings with direct access. Password: newjob.

Online Info Service . . . . (206) 253-5213
Vancouver, Washington: Job listings from FIDONet, ESN (Enterprise System Network), and Usenet. Also has job broker profiles.

Online Job Service of America . . . . (813) 237-8257
Florida: Job listings and résumé database.

Online Opportunities . . . . (610) 873-7170
Philadelphia, Pennsylvania: Help Wanted USA echo. Carries career information, programs, voice job hotlines, etc. Philadelphia résumé database is free and marketed only in the Philadelphia tri-state area.

Online Opportunities . . . . (215) 873-7170

OPM Atlanta . . . . (404) 730-2370
Atlanta, Georgia: Online job search facility and downloadable files for Federal Job Information Center Atlanta (all regions).

OPEM Express . . . . (214) 767-0565
Texas: A BBS for federal personnel agencies run by the Office of Personnel Management.

OPM FEDJOBS . . . . (201) 645-3887
New Jersey: Federal government job information and employment applications.

OPM FEDJOBS . . . . (610) 580-2216
Philadelphia, Pennsylvania: Open federal government jobs and training schedules for all the United States. Updated daily. PC PURSUITable. Operated by the U.S. Office of Personnel Management.

OPM Mainstreet . . . . (202) 606-4800
Washington, D.C.: Variety of information for government employees operated by the Office of Personnel Management. Available to all. Has gateway to other federal job information centers.

Opportunity . . . . (804) 588-4031
Virginia: Job openings in the federal, state, local, and private sectors. Résumé database.

Opportunity Network . . . . (415) 673-4080
California: Technical jobs and candidates. Résumé writing suggestions, conferences. Free résumé database.

Opportunity Network . . . . (404) 578-0544
Atlanta, Georgia: High-tech jobs.

ouT therE . . . . (408) 263-2248
San Jose, California: Contract and permanent job listings for San Francisco Bay Area. Updated every two days.

Pacific Rim . . . . (619) 278-7361
San Diego, California: Job listings from Usenet newsgroups and FIDONet. Internet e-mail access. Fee required.

PC CompoNet . . . . (213) 943-0367
California: Job opportunities.

PCAD User Group . . . . (714) 625-2679
California: Job postings for those interested in circuit board design.

PenCycle . . . . (215) 892-9940
Pennsylvania: Job listings for environmental specialists.

Praedo . . . . (609) 953-0769
New Jersey: Federal job listings and listings for senior executive and CEOs. Tips on résumé writing.

Project Enable . . . . (304) 759-0727
Cross Lanes, West Virginia: Job information and help guides for people with disabilities. Sponsored by the President's Committee on Employment of People with Disabilities.

PWTG . . . . (302) 328-0381
Delaware. Job opportunities, résumé database, contracts. Run by Alternatives PLUS, Inc.

Radiocomm . . . . (708) 518-8336
Park Ridge, Illinois: Network for people in the radio broadcasting field. Job info and industry news. Fee required.

Résumé Data Services . . . . (515) 288-4067
Des Moines, Iowa: Résumé database for Des Moines employers. Small fee required.

Résumé Exchange . . . . (602) 947-4283
Arizona: Résumé database.

Résumé File . . . . (805) 581-6210
Simi Valley, California: Nationwide job listings with job hunting information and tips.
Small Business Administration and federal government job information.

RHost . . . . (404) 392-9164
Atlanta, Georgia: Job listings in all areas, updated daily. Operated by Robert Half of
Atlanta.

SAK Consulting BBS . . . . (703) 715-1016
Reston, Virginia: Federal job listings (national and international), specialized searches.
Fee required.

San Antonio On-Line . . . . (210) 520-8015
San Antonio, Texas: Computer and noncomputer job listings for Corpus Christi, San
Antonio, national, international job markets, and job lists from Internet newsgroups. Fee
required.

Search . . . . (206) 253-5213
Washington: Profile database of high-tech companies. Data processing job listings.

Small Business Administration (SBA) . . . . (800) 697-4636
United States: Small Business Administration BBS.

Society for Technical Communications . . . . (703) 522-3299
Washington, D.C.: Technical writers only. Job service and freelance registry available only
to verified STC members.

Systems Personnel . . . . (413) 592-9208
Massachusetts: Job listings for experienced MIS/software engineers.

TAG Online Career Bank . . . . (215) 969-3845
Pennsylvania: Job listings for the United States and Japan. Résumé database,
employment assistance, conferences, and more.

Tech Pro . . . . (619) 755-7357
San Diego, California: San Diego technology jobs.

Techtips BBS . . . . (615) 662-5712
Nashville, Tennessee: Biomedical/imaging service forum with job-related files. National
job-related echoes, Internet e-mail, and newsgroups. Fee required.

Texas Education Agency . . . . (512) 475-3689
Austin, Texas: Texas state government job listings in Austin. Operated by the Texas
Education Agency Human Resources Division.

Traders Connection . . . . (317) 359-5199
Indiana: Classified job openings from various newspapers.

Transnet, Inc. . . . . (217) 384-5101
Illinois: Résumé database for translators. Fee required.

Triangle Fraternity . . . . (317) 872-4305
Indiana: Employment listings for alumni. Limited to students of engineering, physical sciences, and architecture.

Turning Point . . . . (512) 219-7848, (512) 703-4400
Austin, Texas: Job listings from Usenet newsgroups and Internet e-mail. Fee required. FIDONet: 1:382/106.

U.S. Department of Labor . . . . (212) 219-4784
Washington, D.C.: Federal job opportunities nationwide. Downloadable.

Unicom Info Service . . . . (614) 538-9250, (614) 538-0548, (614) 538-0549
Columbus, Ohio: Information exchange for entrepreneurs, managers, and business professionals. Trade leads and other business information. Usenet newsgroups and Internet e-mail. Fee required for expanded access.

Vanguard Chronicle Network . . . . (305) 524-4411
Florida: Hospital positions in nursing, administration and other. Business employment, community and health information. Résumé uploads. Requires special downloadable software.

VIEWlogic Personnel Dept. . . . . (508) 480-8769
Marlboro, Massachusetts: VIEWlogic Systems, Inc., human resource and employment opportunities with career opening for California and Massachusetts, résumé uploads, benefits information, and HR contact information.

Virginia Employment Commission . . . . (804) 371-6521
Charlottesville, Virginia: The Virginia Employment Commission is an ALEX system that contains military, federal, state, international, and regional job listings. Auxiliary aides and services are available to individuals with disabilities.

Wall Résumé Exchange . . . . (601) 825-2820
Mississippi: Job openings and résumé database for all disciplines.

Walt Disney Imagineering . . . . (800) 959-3725
Florida: Disney Applicant Information System (DAISY) for scientists and engineers. Résumé database.

WASNET—Washington Area Service Network . . . . (202) 606-1113
Voice phone . . . . (202) 606-1848
Washington: Federal job information and recruitment-related matters. Must call voice number first and leave name plus a password of up to eight characters.

Window on State Government BBS . . . . (800) 227-8392
Austin, Texas (for Texas only): Contains information and provides a gateway to other state
BBSs such as Hi-TEC BBS (Texas Employment Commission) and TEC-HR BBS (Texas
Education Agency). Operated by the Texas State Comptroller's office.

9 Creating a Home Page for Your Résumé

■ Why Create a Home Page for Your Résumé?

Imagine a musician playing her latest composition from the Internet or a teacher incorporating a video of his teaching style or a poet reading clips from her poetry on the screen or an entertainer demonstrating his latest dance steps. The creative juices are flowing! Multimedia résumés are the perfect place to showcase skills that are better seen (or heard) in all their glory.

As discussed in Chapter 1, if you are a computer programmer, home page developer, graphics designer, artist, sculptor, actor, model, animator, cartoonist, or anyone who would benefit by the photographs, graphics, animation, sound, color, or movement inherent in a multimedia résumé, then a multimedia résumé could be to your benefit. For most people, however, a home page on the Internet is not a necessity. Most recruiters and hiring managers looking for ordinary employees don't have the time to surf the Net looking for home pages.

Having said that, it never hurts to try, especially if you can get free server space for your home page on a commercial online service or with your Internet service provider. You never know when your résumé will be the one that happens to get read by the casual surfer. Your multimedia résumé becomes just another networking tool to add to your repertoire.

■ How to Create a Home Page

There are simple ways to create a home page, but first you need to understand Hypertext Markup Language. HTML is an uncompli- cated computer programming language used to format documents for display on the World Wide Web. When displayed using a WWW browser, documents created with HTML look like they were typeset. In other words, they look pretty.

HTML is built from tags that tell a computer the text size, font, style, graphics placement, links to other Web pages, and so on. As an example, if you want to make a headline large, you would put a tag at the beginning of the line of text that reads <h1> and a tag at the end of the line to turn it off, </h1>. The slash turns off the code. Your actual line would look something like this:

```
<h1>This Is My First Headline</h1>
```

<h1> produces the biggest headlines, <h2> makes a slightly smaller one, and so on through <h6>. Once you turn on any style using a tag, you must remember to turn it off with a slash in order to return to normal text. As you can see, you are working in plain vanilla ASCII text, but your Web browser sees the codes and turns the text, graphics, and sounds into something beautiful on your computer monitor.

One of the easiest ways to create your home page is to use an HTML editor that automatically converts your formatting codes into HTML tags. Many of the editors are free through commercial online services. For instance, America Online provides you with its Personal Publisher program, which guides you step-by-step through the creation of a home page. CompuServe has its Home Page Wizard, which is free for the downloading. Even WordPerfect for Windows and Microsoft Word can convert your word processing files into home pages, complete with HTML codes and ready to be uploaded to your Web site.

It would take an entire book to list all of the tags possible in HTML, which is outside the scope of this text. It is much better to direct you to several excellent resources that are available on the Internet free of charge. You simply need to navigate to the site and print the documents that interest you.

- HTML quick reference guide and comprehensive listing of HTML codes
  http://www.cc.ukans.edu/info/HTML_quick.html

- Composing good HTML
  http://www.cs.cmu.edu/afs/cs.cmu.edu/Web/People/tilt/cgh/

- W3C's style guide to online hypertext
  http://www.w3.org/hypertext/WWW/Provider/Style/Introduction.html

- Official HTML specifications
  http://www.w3.org/hypertext/WWW/MarkUp/MarkUp.html

- How to write HTML files
  http://www.ucc.ie/info/net/htmldoc.html

- Introduction to HTML
  http://members.aol.com/htmlguru/about_html.html

- Home page development tools
  http://mosaic.mcom.com/home/manual_docs/graphics.html

- Do's and don'ts of web design
  http://millkern.com/do-dont.html

- HTML document style guide
  http://www.che.ufl.edu/help/style1/index.html

- Index of many online style guides
  http://www.stars.com/Vlib/Providers/Style.html

- Netscape's pointers on creating net sites
  http://home.netscape.com/assist/net_sites/index.html

- Frequently asked questions about graphics and desktop publishing.
  http://www.teleport.com

- Yale style manual
  http://info.med.yale.edu/caim/StyleManual_Top.HTML

- Web 66 CookBook
  http://web66.coled.umn.edu/Cookbook

- Tables on the Web
  http://www.ncsa.uiuc.edu:80/SDG/Software/Mosaic/Tables/

- Background images
  http://www.ncsa.uiuc.edu/SDG/Software/WinMosaic/Backgrnd/

- Java scripts for perking up your Web site
  http://java.sun.com/

CompuServe and Paul M. Allen of PMA Technology Group offer some good advice on formatting your home page in their Tip Sheet on Design Dos and Don'ts (*http://www.compuserve.com/index/tipsheet.html*). Here are some of their tips:

1. Remember when desktop publishing first surfaced and people loaded up their documents with 20 different fonts just because they could? That is called "design bloat," and the opportunity to repeat those excesses and even magnify them lies wide open before you as you embark on your first attempts at a World Wide Web home page. Of course, the best way to get an idea of what you want to do with your personal digital space is to first visit a lot of other people's Web homes. Spend some time visiting the pages of your friends, business associates, online compadres, and the bigger commercial sites. Follow your interests and then, when creating your page(s), your instincts. Everybody has a little creativity inside them—just try not to overdo it.

2. When using headlines, stick to the smaller sizes. The three largest headline sizes display a lot larger on a Mosaic viewer than in Netscape or Internet Explorer.

3. Don't use italics too often. They can be *very hard to read* when used in regular text, and nearly impossible to decipher at smaller font sizes. ***Boldfacing italicized type,*** or simply **boldfacing** instead, will help legibility.

4. Use centering liberally. You don't have many formatting tools available to you on the Web, and this is a good one.

5. Replace the standard gray background to give your page a more contemporary look. White is a safe choice, although that color will give horizontal rules on the page a "tail" on the left side. Other background colors are more difficult to work with since they have a noticeable impact on other page elements (especially transparent GIF images).

6. Don't use textured backgrounds that are too busy. Like italics, most make the text harder to read.

7. Changing link colors? If you're bothering to alter the colors of visited and unvisited links, at least sync them up with colors occurring in images you've used on the page. And keep link colors consistent across multiple pages.

8. Web surfers really appreciate knowing whether the information they are perusing is fresh stuff or moldy bread. Somewhere on your home page, let users know when the page was last updated.

9. Your opening graphic should display fully on the user's screen without scrolling. That means nothing larger than 640 × 480 pixels. Always assume that a user's browser will be on its default settings at its smallest size vertically.

10. Always ALT! Some browsers display small windows where yet-to-be-downloaded images will be laid out on the page. ALT information, which is easily entered using CompuServe's Home Page Wizard and describes the image's contents, gives Web surfers something to look at while your pictures trickle down the pipe.

11. Keep graphics as simple and small as possible. Remember that computer screens are low in resolution compared to the quality of a print magazine, so things that might work in that medium won't translate to the Web where 256 colors are the standard. Most modern computers can actually display millions of colors, but their users often don't run them at higher resolutions. After you have uploaded your page, log on with a browser and time how long it takes for an opening graphic or the entire page to load. If it's too long, make adjustments to get the size of your graphics (or the number of graphics on the page) down. If you are logging on at 28.8 kbps, double the time and think about what someone coming into your page on a 14.4 modem is going through. If you have something that might take several minutes to transfer, it had better be worth the time the user spends waiting to see it.

12. Make hot buttons look hot. If you are using images as hotlinks and are removing the colored border that identifies them as links (using the HTML image command BORDER=0), do something to distinguish them from images on the page that aren't clickable links. The user shouldn't have to try to figure out what's hot and what's not.

13. Be cognizant of color. If you are scanning personal images for use on your page, plan to spend a lot of time fine-tuning them. Make sure all images

on the same page share a common palette. If you use a custom palette, it should include the 16 colors that Windows uses. If the image isn't transparent, putting some type of border around it will usually give the page it is on a more finished look.

14. Lower the resolution on scanned graphics, too. Windows machines can't display anything higher than 96 dpi (dots per inch), so saving graphics at 150 or 300 dpi is overkill and will make them too large to download anyway.

15. Wrap text around images that are less than half as wide as the display area. The text may not wrap in all browsers, but at least you have added the feature for those who can take advantage of it.

16. Crop! Nothing is worse than a 200K graphic that contains 25K of information. Use a graphic-manipulation program not only to improve color and contrast, but also to edit out parts of a picture that don't relate anything useful.

17. Got dithering? If you have dithered colors (a washed-out, grainy look to graphics) when you test your page on a Netscape browser, you are using colors that Netscape doesn't recognize. Adjust your palette to the Netscape values for the offending colors. You can download the table listing acceptable color values from Netscape's Web site *(http://www. netscape.com)*.

18. GIF versus JPEG? Save your images as JPEGs when they are continuous tone (i.e., photographs). JPEG files will compress to a smaller size and generally look better than GIFs of the same image. GIF should be used only for line-art images such as screen shots and logos created in a paint program.

19. Don't use "under construction" graphics. Just go with what you have. Web pages, if you haven't noticed, are *always* under construction.

20. No moving experiences, please. Scrolling text, marquees, and some animated GIFs chew up just enough processor time to make interacting with a page annoying. And blinking text is widely regarded on the Net as "just plain evil."

21. Get "back," man. If your site is composed of multiple pages (HTML documents), include links on every page that return users to the master page with its table of contents. Such "orphan" pages can be confusing if a Web surfer bypasses your home page and hits one of your secondary pages directly.

22. Break it up. As you might guess, a very small percentage of people ever bother to scroll an unfamiliar page to see what's further down, unless it contains information they really need. Put all of your navigation functions and gee-whiz information on the top part of the page, and move long passages of text across multiple pages so readers feel as though they are getting somewhere.

23. It's the browser! Whether your page is viewed in Netscape or Internet Explorer or some flavor of Mosaic ultimately determines what it will look like. If you are using Netscape-only HTML commands (like centering, text

wrap around images, and backgrounds), some viewers will ignore them. Try viewing your page in various browsers to get a feel for what happens, and then adjust your design to achieve the best compromise. If you use a 17-inch or larger monitor, also test your design on a computer with a standard 14-inch screen just to be certain.

24. And, last but not least, fine tune the thing to death. A word or two more or less in a key location will change the way the copy lays out on the screen, and a little more or less height (maybe 2 or 3 pixels) on a graphic image can frequently clean things up considerably. It's the little things that count.

Many people don't realize that they can actually download the HTML files that create the pages they view on the Internet. Spend some time reviewing the résumés other job hunters have posted online and see how yours measures up. When you are at a site that you think is well designed, click on your file menu in Windows and select "Save As."

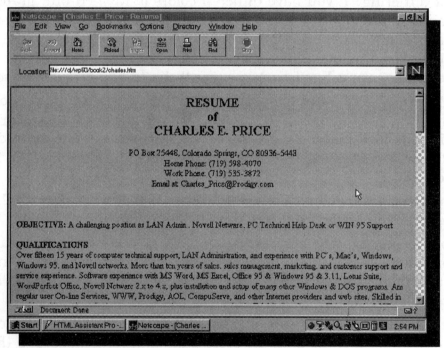

Make a note of the path name where the file has been saved, log off your Internet service provider, exit from your browser, and start your text editor (Notepad in Windows or an HTML editor). Open the file you saved and look at the codes.

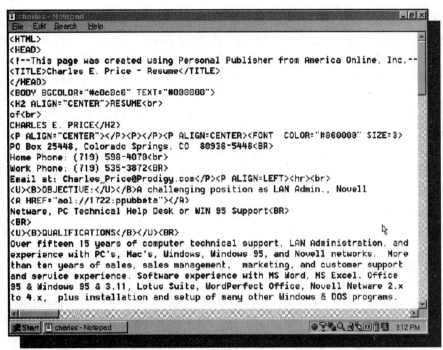

Screen shot of Microsoft Notepad reprinted with permission from Microsoft Corporation.

You can change the text portion of the document to reflect your information, leaving the codes intact, and then view the resulting file with your browser software (you can start your browser software without logging onto the Internet and tell it to load the file you are creating). This allows you to see your file as others will see it on the Internet.

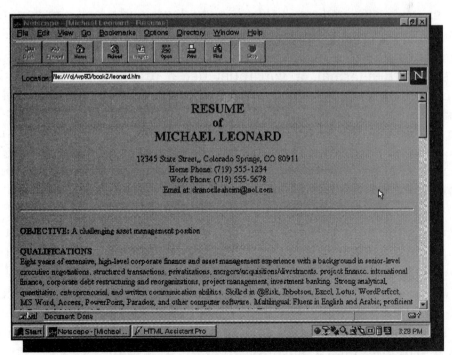

The last thing you need to consider is adding a counter to your home page. A counter will allow you to keep track of how many people are passing through your site. Granted, it doesn't tell you who was there, but it is nice to know that someone has seen your home page besides you and your mom. Hit counters are not written in HTML. They are a CGI script that is dependent on your Internet service provider's computer, so you will need to contact your ISP in order to get directions for adding a counter to your home page. To make one a part of your site, you use a tag similar to an image tag that directs the browser to go to the counter every time someone hits your page. The counter itself is a GIF image that is updated every time the page is chosen. The code in America Online looks something like: *<img src="/cgi-bin/counter?criscito">*

■ Adding Multimedia to Your Résumé

Adding your photograph or other graphic images to your home page is a simple matter of typing in an HTML tag that sends the browser in search of either a GIF or JPEG image file. You can create these graphic files in a couple of ways, but first you need to understand what these files are. GIF (Graphics Interchange Format) files and JPEG (Joint Photographics Experts Group) are both common image file formats used in Web pages. They are just different ways of storing graphics information on a computer.

JPEG images are generally better suited for photographic images since they can support millions of colors. If you scan your photograph, it will look better and take up less disk space in JPEG format than in GIF format. GIF images are best used for line art, like logos, and are limited to 256 colors. Both types of files are relatively small in size and won't take long to download when someone views your home page. Most Web browsers can display both GIF and JPEG images.

To create these graphic files, you must first have a scanner that will save your files in either format or you must use a drawing program to create the graphic images you want to place on your home page and then save them in the appropriate format. Since most people are not comfortable creating their own graphics or don't have the equipment to scan their photograph, this is the time to hire someone to help you. Turn to your phone directory's Yellow Pages and find a graphic artist or graphics service bureau that can create these files for you. Just make sure they know you need GIF or JPEG files on disk in addition to a hard copy printout of the scanned image or other graphics.

If you are the do-it-yourself type, your local Kinko's photocopy and printing store *(http://www.kinkos.com/)* will usually have a computer hooked to a scanner that you can use for a fee, and they may even show you how to use it!

If you have a roll of film with your photograph (or any other picture) on it, there is another way to get a JPEG file. Kodak, Floppy Shots, and Seattle FilmWorks will process your film and place the picture on a disk for you. The disk includes a Windows-based software program that allows you to view, edit, and print the images. In larger cities, many photofinishing stores also offer this service. You can find two of the mail order companies on the Internet at the following addresses:

- *http://www.kodak.com/ciHome/imageMagic/pictureDisk/*
- *http://www.floppyshots.com/*

There are also resources on the Internet that are loaded with free graphics and sound files that you may use on your home page:

- *http://www.yahoo.com/Computers_and_Internet/Internet/World_Wide_Web/Programming/Icons/*
- *http://www.octagamm.com/boutique/mainball.htm*
- *http://www.clark.net/pub/evins/Icons/*
- *http://www.iconbazaar.com*
- *http://www.rainfrog.com/webart/*
- *http://www.clever.net/gld*
- *http://www.cbil.vcu.edu:8080/gifs/bullet.html*
- *http://www.mccannas.com/*
- *http://www.geocities.com/Heartland/1448/main.htm*
- *http://www.geocities.com/Heartland/1448/iconz_links.htm*
- *http://www.yahoo.com/Computers_and_Internet/Internet/World_Wide_Web/Page_Design_and_Layout/Backgrounds/*
- *http://www.aimnet.com/~bosman/TextureStation_Lobby.htm*
- *http://www.netscape.com/assist/net_sites/bg/backgrounds.html*
- *http://www.sonic.net/~lberlin/new/3dnscape.html*
- *http://www.ecn.net.au/~iain/htextures/*
- *http://www.netcreations.com/patternland/index.html*
- *http://www.execpc.com/~jeffo/webdes/bckgrnd2.html*
- *http://wuarchive.wustl.edu/multimedia/images/*
- *http://www.eit.com/web/gopher.icons/gopher.html*
- *http://www.n-vision.com/*
- *http://www.barrysclipart.com*
- *http://www.acy.digex.net/~infomart/clipart/*
- *http://www.teleport.com/~eidos/dtpij/clipart.html*
- *http://www.caboodles.com*
- *http://www.jpl.nasa.gov/archive/images.html*
- *http://www.life.uiuc.edu/Entomology/insectgifs.html*
- *http://www.northcoast.com/savetz/pd/pd.html*
- *http://www.yahoo.com/Computers_and_Internet/Multimedia/Pictures/*
- *http://www.yahoo.com/Computers_and_Internet/Graphics/*
- *http://www.yahoo.com/Arts/Computer_Generated/*
- *http://www.pbrc.hawaii.edu/~kunkel/*

- *http://www.yahoo.com/Computers_and_Internet/Multimedia/Sound/*
- *http://www.excite.com/Subject/Computing/Internet/Net_Video_And_Audio/ s-index.h.html*
- *http://www.tvtrecords.com/tvbytes*

Don't forget the huge stock of graphics and sound clips that are stored in the libraries and forums of your commercial online service. CompuServe has an entire forum devoted just to graphics (GO GRAPHICS), and almost every forum library has a stash of graphics files (from animals to the world).

Once you have the files on disk, the HTML tags that you would place in your document in order to call down a graphic image (say your photograph centered on the page) would look something like this:

<CENTER><IMG SRC="photo.jpg"></CENTER>

Adding sound files, animation, and movies to your Web page gets a little more complicated. The resources mentioned above should give you some guidance, but keep in mind that audio and video take up a lot of disk space and there may be only a limited amount of free server space available through your ISP or commercial online service. For some premade animated GIF files, check out these sites:

- *http://www.yahoo.com/Computers_and_Internet/Graphics/Computer_ Animation/Animated_GIFs/Collections/*
- *http://www.webpromotion.com/stock.html*
- *http://www.geocities.com/SoHo/1085/*
- *http://web2.airmail.net/nicktg/moving/index.html*

■ Where and How to Upload Your Home Page

Once you have created your home page, you can view it with your browser to make sure it looks good without being connected to the Internet. After you have saved your HTML documents to your hard disk (usually in a separate directory where you can find them easily), load your Web browser. You don't have to be logged on to do this. Select "Open File" or "Open Local" from the "File" menu of the Web browser and open the HTML file that you saved earlier. Your Web page will appear, complete with graphics and formatting. If you don't like what you see, you can switch back and forth between your browser and your HTML editor as you make changes, save them, and reload the image until you are satisfied with the results.

When your page is perfect, you can logon to your commercial online service (AOL, CompuServe, etc.) or your Internet service provider and upload your home page. That means copying your files to your provider's computer. You can't just leave the files on your computer, since your computer is probably not connected to the Internet 24 hours a day to allow access by anyone wishing to see your home page. The Internet Business Directory offers a résumé section where individuals can place their multimedia résumé at no charge. Check *http:// ibd.ar.com/Resume* for current policies and upload procedures.

Since my home pages are at America Online, I will talk you through uploading your home page on that service. Not all ISPs offer free space and every service will have a different process for uploading a home page, so you will need to check the frequently asked questions, which most services post online, in order to get full instructions for uploading your home page. Uploading your home page to AOL is a simple matter of copying your files into "MyPlace."

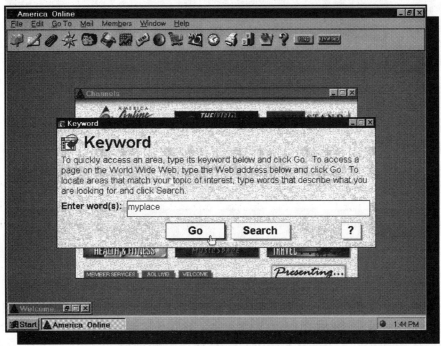

If this is your first time to use your ftp space, you should GO MYPLACE and read the frequently asked questions.

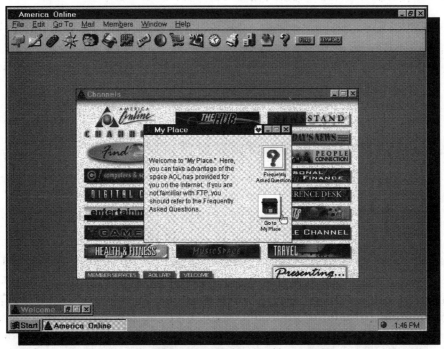

After you have read the FAQs, press the UPLOAD button and follow the prompts to upload your files.

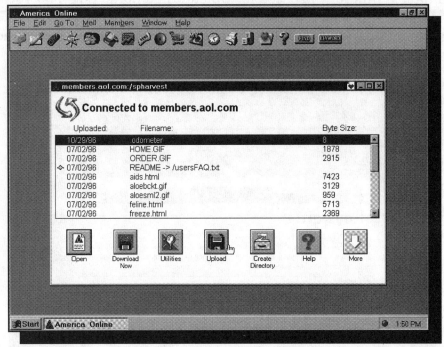

Select ASCII (text mode) for your HTML files and BINARY mode for any graphic image files. When you type in the file names, make sure you use the same case you used in your HTML document. In other words, if you typed in all capital letters in your HTML document, the file name you type in AOL must also be in all capital letters. Be sure that your HTML files all end with the file extension .html or .htm (index.html or index.htm) and that all of your graphic images end with the appropriate file extensions (.gif or .jpg).

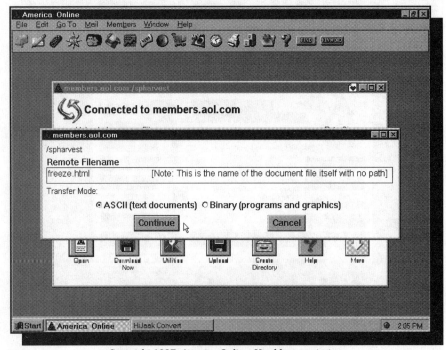

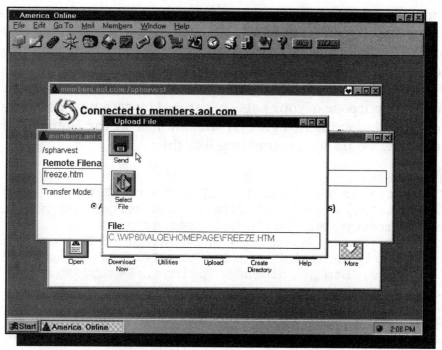

When you are finished, you can close all of the ftp windows and run your Web browser to check your home page. Your URL would look something like this:

http://members.aol.com/criscito/index.htm

■ *Getting the Word Out*

Now that you have a home page for your résumé on the Internet, you have to get the word out to potential employers and networking contacts. Besides putting the address of the home page (its URL) on your business cards and every piece of correspondence and paper résumé you send out, you need to tell the search engines on the Internet where you are located. Not long ago, that meant going to each search engine separately and typing in some basic information about your home page. Today, there are several Web announcement services that allow you to fill in the information once and submit it to a variety of search engines and directories. If you type "Web Announcement" at Yahoo or any other search engine, you will get a long list of Web announcement services, but here are a few of the better known sites that can help you list your Web address on search engines:

- *http://www.submit-it.com*

- *http://www.netcreations.com/postmaster/*

- *http://www.iTools.com/promote-it/promote-it.html*

- *http://www.mmgco.com/top100.html*

- *http://www.yahoo.com/Computers_and_Internet/Internet/World_Wide_Web/Announcement_Services/*

Search engines send out "spiders" that gather data on Web pages automatically. When these spiders reach your home page for the first time, they read the first few lines of text in the document and use those words to index your page. To better control how these spiders index your page, use a META tag in your HTML coding. A META tag contains descriptive information about your page but the information doesn't show up on the Web page itself when human beings view it. The tag is only visible to search-engine spiders and should contain the keywords that describe the purpose of your page, separated by commas. For instance, if you viewed your HTML document in an HTML editor or in the Notepad of Windows, the first few lines would look something like this:

```
<HTML> <HEAD>
<TITLE>Patricia K. Criscito, CPS, CPRW</TITLE>
<META NAME="keywords" CONTENT="résumé writer, author, entrepre-
neur, senior management, national speaker">
 <META NAME="description" CONTENT="Author of Barron's <i>Résumés
in Cyberspace</i> and <i>Designing the Perfect Résumé,</i> Presi-
dent of ProType, Ltd., Colorado Springs, Résumé Writer, National
Speaker.">
```

Once the search engine's spider has accessed this home page and captured the lines, someone searching for a résumé writer would see the following search results:

Patricia K. Criscito, CPS, CPRW
Author of Barron's *Résumés in Cyberspace* and *Designing the Perfect Résumé*, President of ProType, Ltd., Colorado Springs, Résumé Writer, National Speaker. *http://members.aol.com/criscito/index.html*

Another way to get the word out is to add a link to your online résumé at *http://galaxy.einet.net/galaxy/Community/Workplace.html.*

As discussed in Chapter 6, newsgroups are a great way to network and sometimes post your résumé. Once you have a home page for your résumé on the Internet, you can add its URL to your signature line every time you upload an article to a newsgroup. It is a discrete way of advertising to everyone who reads your comments that you have a home page. Don't forget to include your e-mail address so people can contact you.

The Norm by Michael Jantze reprinted with special permission of King Features Syndicate.

10 Into the Future

■ *The Electronic Revolution Isn't Over Yet*

The Internet of today is simply the beginning. The environment is changing so rapidly that tomorrow's Internet will be like the difference between black and white televisions of the 1960s and the surround sound, big-picture sets of today, only it won't take 30 years to get there. The future of the Internet includes faster computers, digital phone lines, cable modems, lightning-quick data transfer rates, wallet-sized PCs, more use of sound and video, the ability to share applications in real time, Intranets accessible by only specific groups of people (within companies, schools, or organizations), and the list goes on.

■ *How to Keep Up with the Times*

Using the Internet in your job search is not just for active job seekers. Today's new reality is that jobs are not forever. The U.S. Bureau of Labor Statistics has determined that you can count on changing jobs from four to 20 times during your career! The only constant in today's job market is change. You need to be prepared. The Internet is the perfect place to research the current job market . . . and all from the safety of your home, school, library, cybercafe, or friend's computer.

Keep your electronic résumé posted even when you are working at a job you love. You never know when the company you work for will fall on hard times or decide to restructure like so many companies are doing today. Three million corporate layoffs were announced between 1989 and the end of 1995. An additional 170,000 jobs were eliminated in the first quarter of 1996—74 percent more than in the first quarter of 1995. Yours could be one of them, so be prepared for change.

Integrate networking into your career strategy. According to Richard Bolles, one of the country's top job-market experts and author of *What Color Is Your Parachute?*, up to 80 percent of all available jobs are not advertised in the classifieds. That means your best bet for finding a job is through networking. Touch base with everyone you know, and the higher up the ladder, the better. Most employers fill jobs by hiring from within their companies. If they can't hire from within, they go to friends or business associates and ask if they know anyone who would be qualified for the positions. That's why developing and tapping into relationships with key people is more important than ever in job hunting.

Write a list of the names and addresses of at least 100 people you know. Make a note beside each name of how this person can help you get a job. Then send either a letter or an e-mail message to each one, letting them know you are looking for a job. You would be surprised at how many people you know. Add to your list every day, and call everyone at least one time during your job search. Always remember to thank these people for anything they do to help you make contacts.

■ *Strategies for Finding New Online Resources*

Search engines are your key to finding new resources on the Internet. The Web is a huge, messy, disorganized place. There are millions of pages of information floating around in cyberspace, and the number is growing every day. You need search engines to find information in this vast maze of data just like you need a map to find your way in an unfamiliar city.

There are more than 200 of these search engines available on the Web, but you only need a few. Therefore, only the most popular ones are listed here. To find more search engines on the Internet, check out the meta-sites at:

- *http://cuiwww.unige.ch/meta-index.html*
- *http://www.albany.net/allinone/*
- *http://home.mcom.com/home/internet-search.html*
- *http://home.mcom.com/escapes/search/global_search.html*

To reach a search engine, type its address in the space provided by your browser for URLs and press enter. When you reach the site, it is a simple matter to type in the words for which you would like to search. If you are looking for a general topic, like "résumé," you type that word in the search box and ask the search engine to find pages with that word. Be prepared for more than three-quarters of a million hits!

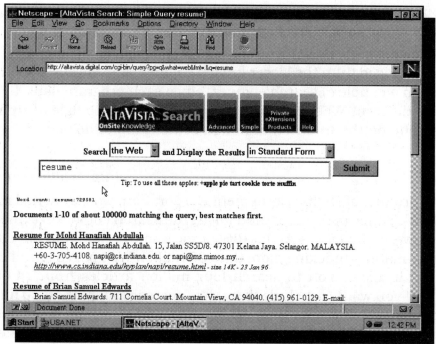

Reproduced with the permission of Digital Equipment Corporation.
AltaVista and the AltaVista logo are trademarks of Digital Equipment Corporation.

To narrow your search, you might type in two words, like "résumé AND engineer." The search engine will find pages with both of those words, but not necessarily in that order. The AND is Boolean logic. You can also use the word OR to find pages with either word, which actually widens your search instead of narrowing it. Use NOT to eliminate items you don't want included in a search. Words can be nested in brackets to create phrases. For instance, "[software OR industrial] AND engineer" will retrieve records that contain the words *software* or *industrial* somewhere in the record but also contain the word *engineer*. Adding a WITH operator instead of AND will ensure that the word *engineer* is always preceded immediately by either *software* or *industrial*, i.e., software engineer or industrial engineer.

There is a difference between a search engine and a directory, too. Search engines (sometimes called "spiders" or "crawlers") constantly visit Web sites on the Internet in order to create searchable catalogs of Web pages. A directory, on the other hand, is created by a human being. Sites are submitted and then assigned to a category. Many search engine sites also have directories.

Once you have the search results in front of you, what do you do with them? By clicking on the hypertext (highlighted words or pictures) that you think relate to your subject, the search engine will take you directly to the home page of that site. If you discover that the site isn't what you thought it would be, then click the "Back" button on your browser to return to the search results and try another until you have found what you are seeking.

Search engines use a very sophisticated logic and something called relevance numbers to determine which pages are the most relevant to your query. Therefore, the pages that appear at the top of the list are the most likely to meet your needs. Some search engines will display only a limited number of hits at a time in order to save time, but that can still be 20 or more pages of URLs. It is much better to narrow your query as much as possible with your keyword search than to scroll through page after page of irrelevant search results.

The following search engines are some of the best on the Internet. They have more sites cataloged than the lesser known engines. It is always a good idea to try your search in a couple of search engines, since each program uses different logic and indexes different Web sites. It is impossible for any single search engine to index *every* site on the Internet, although some claim to do so.

AltaVista . . . . *http://altavista.digital.com*

AltaVista, a product of Digital Equipment Corporation, was launched in 1995 and partnered with Yahoo (a directory and not a true search engine) in June 1996. The system is powered by DEC's Alpha RISC processor. It claims to have the largest Web index available—indexing more than 35 million Web pages found on 275,600 servers—and it allows you to search four million articles from 14,000 Usenet newsgroups if you want to include them. It is accessed more than 20 million times per weekday. AltaVista uses plus and minus signs to limit searches but also recognizes quotation marks (which tie two words together) and capital letters. This search engine has an advanced query option that allows you to use Boolean terms. It also lets you choose which word is the most important and to limit your search by date.

Deja News . . . . *http://www.dejanews.com*

Deja News is a search engine just for newsgroups. Since its inception in May of 1995, it has the largest collection of Usenet news available anywhere. While most Usenet search engines will carry at the most one month of news, Deja News typically gives you access to newsgroups that go back to March of 1995 (at this writing, 53 million articles). Their ultimate goal is to index almost all of the Usenet since it began in 1979. In searching the database, you can filter your search by word, newsgroup, author, posting date, subject, and topic threads. You can even get author profiles and statistics on articles originating from a single e-mail address. The documents retrieved by your search are weighted so that recent articles are given precedence over older ones, since late-breaking news is often more important than older news.

ERIC . . . . *http://ericir.syr.edu/About/*

ERIC (Educational Research Information Catalog) is a federally funded, national information system headquartered at Syracuse University. You can search ERIC's database for abstracts of more than 850,000 documents and journal articles on education research and practice; however, at the present time, full-text documents can only be found in libraries, through a journal's publisher, or from article reprint services such as The UMI/InfoStore (1-800-248-0360) or the Institute for Scientific Information (1-800-523-1850). ERIC does have plans to become a full-text database at sometime in the future.

Excite NetSearch . . . . *http://www.excite.com*

Excite (formerly known at Architext) is a multi-purpose search engine founded in 1993 by six Stanford University graduates who were tired of making keyword searches. In July 1996, Excite purchased the Magellan search engine and directory from McKinley, making it even more powerful. Excite uses "concept-based" search technology to summarize information on 50 million Web pages. As with most major search engines, Excite has a catalog of reviewed sites called Excite NetDirectory. Excite's editors surf the Net to find new listings for this directory, which you access through Excite's home page address above. The search and directory functions are complemented by 60,000 reviews of Web sites (Excite.Review), which helps you find the best, most relevant sites. In addition, Excite City.Net allows you to search information about events in 3,000 major cities worldwide and even look at maps for most of those destinations. Excite has identified 5 million popular URLs, which it updates weekly; the remaining 45 million sites are updated every couple of weeks. The only drawback to Excite is its lack of advanced search options for the serious researcher.

HotBot . . . . *http://www.hotbot.com/*

Launched in May 1996 by HotWired, HotBot is powered by the University of California at Berkeley's Inktomi search engine. It is the first site to use multi-machine parallel computing for Internet searching. HotBot has a searchable index of the full text of more than 54 million documents, which it updates weekly.

InfoSeek . . . . *http://www.infoseek.com*

InfoSeek lets you refine your search in ways similar to Yahoo and Lycos. It searches more than 4 million Web pages, Usenet newsgroups, ftp sites, and Gopher sites. Integrated into the same URL listed above is a directory service with rated sites. In addition to its search and directory features, InfoSeek offers a free personalized news service *(http://personal.infoseek.com)*, which creates an individually tailored Web site with news from Reuters, Business Wire, PR Newswire, Quote.com, and Usenet newsgroups.

Lycos . . . . *http://www.lycos.com*

Lycos is operated by Carnegie-Mellon University and indexes more than 68 million sites on the Internet. It has been around since late 1994, which makes it one of the oldest search engines. Lycos includes not only Web pages but also Gopher and ftp sites, and you can search for text, graphics, sounds, and video. You can use Boolean logic to narrow your search in Lycos, although it does not support NOT. Instead, use a minus sign in front of a word to eliminate it from the search. For instance, if you wanted to search for information on recruiters, but not the ones located in Chicago, your query would look like this: *recruiter -Chicago.* A period (.) after a keyword indicates you want an exact match, while a dollar sign ($) after a partial word (bank$) will give you "bankers" and "banking." Lycos also operates a directory called A2Z *(http://a2z.lycos.com)*, which lists picks from the most popular Web sites. Also included in Lycos are PeopleFind (for locating e-mail addresses), Road Map (maps to millions of U.S. street addresses), Top News (breaking headlines on the Web), Sound Catalog (audio files), Picture Catalog (photographs, graphics, and movies), and City Guide (virtual tours of 400 metropolitan areas).

OpenText . . . . *http://www.opentext.com/*

Owned by the Open Text Corporation, OpenText has been around since early 1995. It indexes more than 21 billion words and phrases from 1.5 million URLs, including every word on every page. The Open Text Index is updated continually, and more than 50,000 Web pages are added or updated daily. You can search for a single word, groups of words, phrases, URLs, titles, or narrow your search with AND, OR, BUT, NOT, NEAR, or FOLLOWED BY.

WebCrawler . . . . *http://www.webcrawler.com*

WebCrawler is one of the most popular search engines on the Internet, although it has the fewest URLs cataloged of any of the engines. It indexes only 500,000 sites, which it updates daily. Its graphical interface is user friendly and you can get help at any time by pressing the help button at WebCrawler's home page. Although it supports Boolean logic, this search engine is designed to speak ordinary language. WebCrawler is owned by America Online and has its own associated directory (GNN Select) with sites reviewed by its editors.

Yahoo . . . . *http://www.yahoo.com*

Created in 1994, Yahoo is technically not a search engine but a directory, which is actually to your advantage. Since a directory is created by humans who assign sites to an appropriate category, they often provide better results than search engines. If you don't find what you are looking for in this directory, Yahoo will forward your search to your choice of search engine by clicking on a hyperlink. AltaVista is Yahoo's preferred search engine, but all of the major engines are listed. Yahoo also includes a personalized information service called My Yahoo!

In addition to the major sites above, here are addresses for some of the other popular search engines:

- AccuFind . . . . *http://accufind.com*
- AIRS II . . . . *http://www.arachnae.com*
- Allinone . . . . *http://www.albany.net/allinone/*
- The Clearinghouse . . . . *http://www.clearinghouse.net/*
- DisInformation . . . . *http://www.disinfo.com/*
- Electric Library *http://www2.elibrary.com/id/2525/search.cgi*
- The Galaxy at TradeWave . . . . *http://galaxy.einet.net/galaxy.html*
- IBM InfoMarket (fee-based) . . . . *http://www.informarket.ibm.com/*
- Inter-Links . . . . *http://www.nova.edu/Inter-Links/web/wwwsearch.html*
- C/NET Search.Com . . . . *http://www.search.com/*

- Starting Point . . . . *http://www.stpt.com*
- W3catalog *http://cuiwww.unige.ch/cgi-bin/w3catalog*

❑ *Gophers*

Gophers are basically interconnected tables of contents for the Internet. The search is menu oriented, which means there are no pretty graphics to slow down your search, just text. This is the basic difference between Gopher searches and World Wide Web search engines like Yahoo, AltaVista, WebCrawler, and so on, which are graphics oriented. They organize Internet resources into hierarchies of menus with plain English names. When you use Gopher, you see a menu that spans the Internet. When you move deeper and deeper into the menus, you are tunneling in Gopherspace. The best Gopher resources are quickly found under "Main Categories." Using Gopher, you can access library catalogs, files, and WAIS databases. If you get lost in Gopherspace, all you need to do is type the letter "u" to take you back a page at a time to the main menu. When you are finished, simply type "q" for "quit."

Gopher was originally created at the University of Minnesota (where the Golden Gopher is the university's mascot) as a better way to find and access files on the Internet, but there are now thousands of Gopher servers all over the world. Almost all browsers will have a Gopher option, so you don't have to know your nearest Gopher site. Once you are connected to a Gopher site, you have access to all Gophers. If you know the exact address of a Gopher site, you can type its address in the space provided by your browser for the URL. A Gopher address looks something like this: *gopher://ericer.syr.edu.*

In 1994, David Riggins oversaw the creation of the Gopher Jewels Project, which collected all the Gopher menus from many of the leading Gopher sites and then classified each menu item by subject. To get to the Gopher Jewels, choose Gopher from your browser and type in *cwis.usc.edu.* Choose "Other Gophers and Information Resources" and then "Gopher Jewels." This mother site is duplicated at the following mirror sites, which might be closer to your location:

- *http://galaxy.einet.net/gopher/gopher.html*
- *http://galaxy.einet.net/GJ/index.html*
- *gopher://cwis.usc.edu/11/Other_Gophers_and_Information_Resources/ Gophers_by_Subject/Gopher_Jewels*
- *gopher://info.monash.edu.au/11/Other/sources/Gopher_Jewels*
- *gopher://gopher.technion.ac.il/11/Other_gophers/Gopher-Jewels*

Veronica . . . . *gopher://liberty.uc.wlu.edu*
gopher://gopher.scs.unr.edu:70

Veronica (Very Easy Rodent-Oriented Net Index of Computerized Archives) is an addition to Gopher that will help you find Gopher files. It will search for words in all Gopher directories anywhere in the world. You simply type in key words in the text box and press enter. Within seconds, Veronica will display a list of Gopher

271

menus containing the words you want. By clicking on any of these items, Veronica takes you directly to that resource. You can search Veronica using the connector words AND, NOT, OR, and wildcards to narrow your search. Use Veronica to search "The Mother Gopher" at *gopher://gopher.micro.umn.edu:70*. This is the central registry for the Gopher network and is arranged geographically.

Jughead . . . . *gopher://liberty.uc.wlu.edu*
gopher://marvel.loc.gov

Jughead (Jonzy's Universal Gopher Heirarchy Excavation and Display) will search for words in the directory of the Gopher server to which you are connected. It is basically a utility program that searches the local Gopher site, which means it is only searching a small area of Gopherspace at a time.

Archie . . . . *gopher://liberty.uc.wlu.edu*

Archie (from the word *archive*) was developed at McGill University School of Computer Science in Montreal, Canada. Archie is a tool that will search the directories of titles in ftp archives, but it will not give you the document itself. Using ftp, Internet users can copy programs, texts, pictures, and even movies to their own computers. Archie keeps a running catalog of what files are stored on which ftp servers. You can also Telnet to Archie at the following URLs: *archie.sura. net, archie.unl.edu, archie.rutgers.edu, archie.ans.net.*

WAIS . . . . *gopher://liberty.uc.wlu.edu*

WAIS (Wide Area Information Searching, pronounced "ways") was originally designed to help corporate executives find information stored in large databases. Apple Computer, Dow Jones & Co., Thinking Machines Corporation, and KPMG Peat Marwick formed a consortium in 1991 to create the WAIS project, but today WAIS has expanded into a huge information resource with more than 450 major databases available over the Internet. Most browsers come equipped with a WAIS button, so you don't need to Telnet to a WAIS site. However, if yours does not, you will need to Telnet to a site with WAIS capabilities. Unlike Gopher and Archie, which tell you where a file *is*, WAIS searches based on what is *in* a file. It looks for keywords and phrases that are in the contents of documents rather than only in document titles. Instead of using Boolean logic, WAIS answers natural language questions like, "Tell me about the Internet." WAIS would respond to such a question by giving you a list of databases, text articles, and graphics that mention the Internet, all ranked by relevance. The article that WAIS thought would be the most likely to answer your question would be first. WAIS is not always easy to use, so I recommend that you go to the *comp.infosystems.wais* newsgroup for more information before using this search engine.

Job hunting with search engines is a little like going to the library to find a specific book and then getting lost in the attic among the stacks. You set out with a goal in mind but stumble across dozens of other avenues to explore. Many of these destinations offer more information than you expected and lead to even other avenues until you finally find yourself far away from where you started but richer in possible sites to post your résumé or look for jobs.

For more information about Web search engines and how to use them, check out these sites:

- *http://sunsite.berkeley.edu/Help/searchdetails.html*
- *http://www.bubl.bath.ac.uk/BUBL/IWinship.html*

■ *Using Search Engines to Research Potential Employers*

Using the search engines just described (or the company list beginning on page 123), you can find a wealth of information on company home pages on the Internet and in online newspapers, magazines, and databases, including annual reports, press releases, company histories, product lines, number of employees, ownership, and other information that will be invaluable during your interview. A number of companies even allow their employees to create home pages where you can learn a lot about a company's culture. You can send e-mail messages back and forth to these same employees and develop networking contacts within the company.

The Public Register's Annual Report Service (PRARS) makes annual reports from 3,000 companies available free of charge via the Internet. Visit its home page at *http://wwwprars.com* or call 1-800-426-6825 to request an annual report. Orders are processed within 24 hours and take about a week to arrive.

A Nexus search on CompuServe will allow you to access more than 50 journals simultaneously. Imagine going to an interview armed with the latest sales figures and product development ideas from all the trade-press and magazine articles published in the last two years. This kind of electronic research will give you a definite competitive advantage in the job market.

University archives are another incredibly rich source of information about almost any topic. They can be accessed via the Internet just like the company information above. Simply search by university name or topic, and you will find everything from information databases to student theses on almost any subject imaginable. While searching for information on McCormick seasonings, I recently ran across a term paper in a university archive that covered the company's history in great detail. This kind of information will strengthen your performance during an interview and help you decide whether or not a particular company is your kind of place. It is very impressive at an interview to know what a company's competitors are doing, so don't limit your search to the company itself. Try searching by industry, for example, pharmaceutical, and not just by Merck or Eli Lily.

How do you access this information? You simply type in the keywords for your search (a company name or topic) and send the search engine to do its job. You may have to narrow your search if you end up with 300,000 hits, but the first few pages of the search results should be sufficient to get you started.

You can also use these Internet search engines, and CD-ROM databases at your local library, to assemble a list of potential employers and executive recruiters to contact. The learning curve for some of these databases can be steep, and there is usually a fee associated with using them, so you might want to consider hiring an online research service to do the search for you. There are some 300 firms nationwide who conduct employment research, and about 15 of them offer online research capabilities, according to Kenneth J. Cole, publisher of the *Executive Search Research Directory* in Panama City Beach, Florida.

To locate a researcher, check your library for Mr. Cole's book or the *Directory of Independent Researchers* published by the Research Roundtable in New York. Local recruiting firms may have these resources or know of someone in your community who offers these services. Once you locate a service, it is always a good idea to check with the Better Business Bureau and to ask for references from former clients. This is a new industry and most firms have been in business for less than five years.

Ask about fees up front. Research fees range from $62 an hour to $135 an hour. You shouldn't have to spend more than $100 to $200 for custom lists of companies and recruiters, but some researchers have minimum fees of $500.

■ *Colleges and Your Electronic Job Search*

If you are presently a student at a college or university, your career service center is the first place to start your electronic job search. They have wonderful resources for helping you write and design your electronic résumé. They also have reference books that can guide you in all aspects of your job search, not just the electronic kind.

Many of these schools maintain a résumé database of all their students that can be accessed by companies worldwide. Sometimes they use *1st Place!* software where you input your résumé onto a disk and submit it to the career center, and other times they scan your résumé into a résumé database much like the companies they service.

Career service centers are connected with many employers who list entry-level job openings and internships available to students of that particular school. Take advantage of those internships and other work experiences long before your graduation. Join student chapters of professional associations, like the American Marketing Association, American Geological Association, and so on. They will produce marketable keywords that will help your electronic résumé pop to the top in a keyword search.

Many larger companies have special sites on their Internet home pages just for students. For instance, Microsoft has a hyperlink under "Employment Opportunities" at *http://www.microsoft.com* where students can peruse full-time and internship opportunities targeted specifically for them. MCI does the same at *http://www.mci.com.*

Sometimes colleges offer reciprocal services to students of other schools, but the only way to find out is to make a telephone call to the career center of the school nearest you. Alumni associations are another good place to start. There is an Internet site at *http://www.rpi.edu/dept/cdc/alumni* that is an excellent source for hyperlinks to hundreds of college alumni services. Check there first to see what type of support your alma mater provides. Colleges and universities often offer their alumni the same services as current students, while others limit free services to a year after graduation. Again, check your school just to make sure.

The career center may have a home page or a hyperlink from the university's main home page where you can find lists of the career resources available from your particular school. In addition, most major universities and colleges post their own job openings on the school's Gopher site or home page. If you can't find your school listed below, then it may be listed with Online Career Center (OCC) at *http://www.occ.com/occ/CollegePlacement.html*. If you wish to check multiple sites without typing in the URL each time, this list is reproduced and kept up to date with hyperlinks on my home page on the Internet at: *http://members.aol. com/criscito*.

Abilene Christian University . . . . *http://www.acu.edu/help/careers/*
Allegheny College . . . . *http://www.alleg.edu/Admin/CareerServices/*
Anglia Polytechnic University, U.K. . . . . *http://www.anglia.ac.uk/stu_services/ecgs.htm*
Arizona State University . . . . *http://www.asu.edu/career/*
Arkansas State University, Jonesboro . . . . *http://www.astate.edu*
Babson College . . . . *http://www.Babson.edu/ocs*
Ball State University . . . . *http://www.bsu.edu/careers/home.html*
Bates College . . . . *http://www.bates.edu/AdminOffices/Career.Services/index.html*
Binghamton University . . . . *http://cdc_cyberscope.adm.binghamton.edu/*
Biola University . . . . *http://www.biola.edu/admin/career/*
Bloomsburg University . . . . *http://www.bloomu.edu/departments/cardev/pages/CDCmmf.html*
Boise State University . . . . *http://www.idbsu.edu/career/wwwcctr.html*
Boston College . . . . *http://www.bc.edu/bc_org/svp/carct/Career.html*
Boston University School of Management . . . . *http://management.bu.edu/service/career/career.htm*
Bowling Green State University . . . . *http://www.bgsu.edu/offices/careers/*
Bradley University . . . . *http://www.bradley.edu/scc/*
Brandeis University
    Hiatt Career Development Center . . . . *http://www.brandeis.edu/hiatt/hiatt_home.html*
Bridgewater College . . . . *http://www.bridgewater.edu/departments/career/career.html*
Brooklyn College . . . . *http://www.brooklyn.cuny.edu/bc/depthome/career/pccsmain.html*
Brown University . . . . . . *http://www.brown.edu/Student_Services/Career_Planning/homepage.html*
Bucknell University . . . . *http://www.bucknell.edu/departments/career_dev*
Butler University . . . . *http://www.butler.edu/~harding/sacs.html*
California Institute of Technology . . . . *http://www.cco.caltech.edu/~gatti/cdc.html*
California Polytechnic State University . . . . *http://www.calpoly.edu/~cservice/*
California State University at Chico *http://www.csuchico.edu/plc/welcome2.html*
California State University at Fullerton *http://www2.fullerton.edu/vpss/cdcstuff/cdchome.html*
Canisius College . . . . *http://www.canisius.edu/canhp/canadmin/career/career.html*
Carleton College *http://www.carleton.edu:80/campus/career/*
Case Western Reserve University . . . . *http://www.cwru.edu/CWRU/Admin/cpp/cpp.html*
Chadron State College . . . . *http://www.csc.edu/career-services/career-default.html*
Champlain College . . . . *http://www.champlain.edu/deptcareer/*
Chapman University . . . . *http://www.chapman.edu/cdc/index.html*
City University, U.K. . . . . *http://www.city.ac.uk/~sm321/careers.html*
Colby College . . . . *http://www.colby.edu/career.serv/index.html*
Colgate University *http://149.43.25.250/ccs.html*
College of William and Mary . . . . *http://www.wm.edu/csrv/career/index.html*
College of William and Mary, Career Services . . . . *http://www.wm.edu/csrv/career/career.html*
Coventry University, U.K. *http://www.gold.net/users/ac29/empwww2.htm*
Dartmouth College . . . . *http://www.dartmouth.edu/pages/csrc/*
DeVry Institute, Phoenix . . . . *http://www.devry-phx.edu/careersv/*
Drake University . . . . *http://www.drake.edu/stulife/careerctr.html*
Duke University . . . . *http://careernet.stuaff.duke.edu/*

East Carolina University . . . . *http://ecuvax.cis.ecu.edu/studlife/career/index.htm*
Eastern Oregon State College . . . . *http://www.eosc.osshe.edu/career/crhome.html*
Eastern Washington University *http://146.187.208.175/*
Emory University . . . . *http://www.emory.edu/CAREER/index.html*
Emporia State University . . . . *http://www.emporia.edu/S/www/cdceps/career.htm*
Florida State University . . . . *http://www.fsu.edu:80/~career/*
Florida State University School of Law . . . . . *http://law.fsu.edu/placement/placement.html*
Fort Hays State University . . . . *http://www.fhsu.edu/htmlpages/services/career/welcome.htm*
Franklin & Marshall College . . . . *http://www.fandm.edu/Departments/*
CareerServices/CareerServices.html
George Mason University . . . . *http://www.gmu.edu/departments/cdc/studalum.htm*
Georgia State University . . . . *http://www.gsu.edu/dept/admin/plc/homepg.html*
Goldey-Beacom College . . . . *http://goldey.gbc.edu/career/career.html*
Goucher College . . . . *http://www.goucher.edu/cdo*
Hamline University . . . . *http://www.hamline.edu/admin/mwilbour/index.html*
Hampshire College . . . . *http://www.hampshire.edu/Hampshire/oo/html/CORChome.html*
Hanover College . . . . *http://www.hanover.edu/career_center/career.html*
Hartwick College . . . . *http://www.hartwick.edu/tcpd/*
Harvard Graduate School of Education . . . . *http://hugse1.harvard.edu/~cso/cso.html*
Hendrix College . . . . *http://www.hendrix.edu/studev/careercenter.html*
Hood College . . . . *http://www.hood.edu/cfscnter/cfshome.htm*
Hope College . . . . *http://www.hope.edu/career/index.html*
Idaho State University . . . . *http://www.isu.edu/departments/employ/studempl.htm*
Indiana State University . . . . *http://career.indstate.edu/*
Indiana University . . . . *http://www.indiana.edu/~speacare/index.html*
Indiana University at Bloomington . . . . *http://www.indiana.edu:80/~career/*
Indiana University of Pennsylvania . . . . *http://www.iup.edu/career/*
Indiana University, Purdue University, Indianapolis . . . *http://www.iupui.edu/it/career/career.html*
Iowa State University . . . . *http://www.public.iastate.edu/~career_info/*
James Madison University . . . . *http://www.jmu.edu/career*
John Marshall Law School . . . . *http://www.jmls.edu/programs/careers.html*
Johns Hopkins University . . . . *http://www.scs.jhu.edu/~clpc/index.htm*
Kansas State University . . . . *http://www.ksu.ksu.edu/ces/ces.html*
Keene State College . . . . *http://www.keene.edu/CareerServices/CShome.html*
Knox College *http://www.knox.edu/knox%20web/*
career_services/career_servicesbroch.html
Lafayette College . . . . *http://www.lafayette.edu/~rothmj/*
Lake Forest College . . . . *http://www.lfc.edu/www/who/career/cdchome.html*
Lancaster University, U.K. . . . . *http://www.comp.lancs.ac.uk/uni-services/careers/careers.html*
Lebanon Valley College . . . . *http://www.lvc.edu/www/career/index.html*
Lehigh University *http://nss1.CC.Lehigh.EDU:80/CSINF*
Lewis and Clark College . . . . *http://www.lclark.edu/~career/*
Linfield College . . . . *http://www.linfield.edu/occls/Career.html*
Lock Haven University of Pennsylvania . . . . *http://www.lhup.edu/career_services/home.htm*
Long Island University, C.W. Post Campus . . . *http://www.liunet.edu/cwis/cwp/pep/pep_start.html*
Louisiana State University . . . . *http://www.lsu.edu/guests/stuserv/*
public_html/career-services/homepage.html
Loyola College in Maryland . . . . *http://www.loyola.edu/dept/career-dev*
Macalester College . . . . *http://www.macalstr.edu/~cdc/*
Mankato State University . . . . *http://www.mankato.msus.edu/dept/cdc/HP.html*
Marquette University . . . . *http://www.mu.edu/dept/csc/index.html*
Metropolitan State College of Denver . . . . *http://www.mscd.edu/~waltd/Welcome.html*
Miami University . . . . *http://www.muohio.edu/careers/*
Middlebury College . . . . *http://www.middlebury.edu/~cpp/*
Milwaukee Area Technical College . . . . *http://www.milwaukee.tec.wi.us*
Montana State University . . . . *http://www.montana.edu/wwwcp*
Montclair State University . . . . *http://www.montclair.edu/Pages/*
CareerServices/Career.html
New Mexico State University . . . . *http://www.nmsu.edu/Resources_References/*
PCS/pcsmainmenu.html
New York University . . . . *http://www.nyu.edu/careerservices*

Newcastle University, U.K. .... http://kalonji.ncl.ac.uk/careers/careers.html
North Carolina State University .... http://www.acs.ncsu.edu/CareerPlan/
North Carolina State University's
      Online Career Resources http://www2.acs.ncsu.edu/creerpln/library.htm
North Harris Montgomery Community College .... http://www.nhmccd.cc.tx.us/groups/jtpa/
Northeastern University .... http://www.dac.neu.edu/Units/Coop/CareerServices
Northern Kentucky University .... http://www.nku.edu/~cdc
Northwestern University .... http://www.nwu.edu/student/ucareer.html
Notre Dame .... http://www.nd.edu/~ndcps/
Oakland University .... http://phoenix.placement.oakland.edu
Oberlin College .... http://www.oberlin.edu/~careerdv/OCCS.HomePage.html
Ohio Northern University .... http://www.onu.edu/Admin-offices/studaffairs/cpc/
Ohio University .... http://cscwww.cats.ohiou.edu/~carserv/careerservhome.html
Old Dominion University .... http://www.odu.edu/~cmc/cmchome.htm
Oregon Institute of Technology ... http://www.oit.osshe.edu/student_life/services/career/index.htm
Polytechnic University .... http://rama.poly.edu/htdocs/carserv/index.html
Portland State University ..... http://www.pdx.edu/cgi-bin/lsdir/gopher-data/campusinfo/career/
Randolph-Macon College .... http://www.rmc.edu/administration/career_counseling
Randolph-Macon Woman's College .... http://www.rmwc.edu/
Rensselaer Polytechnic Institute .... http://www.rpi.edu/dept/cdc/
Rice University .... http://riceinfo.rice.edu/projects/careers/
Rutgers University .... http://info.rutgers.edu/Services/Career/
Rutgers University, Camden Campus .... http://camden-www.rutgers.edu/CPP/cpp.html
Rutgers University, Newark Campus .... http://newark.rutgers.edu/~lynneo/NCAScdc.html
San Diego State University .... http://www.sa.sdsu.edu/career/cs_homepage.html
San Francisco State University .... http://careercenter.sfsu.edu/
San Jose State University .... http://www.sjsu.edu/depts/career/career.html
Seattle Pacific University .... http://www.spu.edu/depts/cdc/
Shippensburg University .... http://www.ship.edu/~pubinfo/CDC.html
Sonoma State University .... http://www.sonoma.edu/SAS/crc/
Southern Illinois University at Edwardsville .... http://www.careers.siue.edu/
St. Cloud State University .... http://www.stcloud.msus.edu/~careersv/
Stanford University .... http://www-leland.stanford.edu/dept/CPPC
State University of New York College at Oswego .... http://www.oswego.edu/other_campus/
                                          student.svcs/career_svcs/
State University of New York at Buffalo, School of Management ... http://www.mgt.buffalo.edu/crc/
State University of New York at Buffalo .... http://wings.buffalo.edu/hh/employment
State University of New York at Stony Brook .... http://www.sunysb.edu/career/
State University of West Georgia, School of Business .... http://www.westga.edu/~busn/
Stetson University .... http://www.stetson.edu/~career/
Syracuse University, Center for Career Services .... http://web.syr.edu/~clreutli/career/
Texas A&M University .... http://aggienet.tamu.edu/cctr
Texas Woman's University .... http://www.twu.edu/o-cs/
The Ohio State University, Fisher College of Business ..... http://www.cob.ohio-state.edu/careers/
The Ohio State University, College of Engineering ...... http://career.eng.ohio-state.edu/index.htm
The University of Akron .... http://www.uakron.edu/placement
Tuck School of Business, Dartmouth College .... http://www.dartmouth.edu/tuck/career/
Tulane University Law School .... http://www.law.tulane.edu/cs/cs.htm
Union College .... http://www.union.edu/career/CDC/CDC.html
Union University .... http://www.uu.edu/union/student/studaff/career/
University of Arizona .... http://w3.arizona.edu/~career/carscvs.html
University of Arkansas at Little Rock .... http://www.uark.edu/depts/coopinfo/
University of Baltimore .... http://www.ubalt.edu/www/sserv/cswel.html
University of Birmingham, U.K. .... http://www.bham.ac.uk/careers/
University of California, Berkeley .... http://www.uga.berkeley.edu/wsp/
University of California Career and Life Planning Center .... http://www.uci.edu/~career/
University of California, Irvine .... http://www.uci.edu/~career/
University of California, Los Angeles .... http://www.saonet.ucla.edu/career
University of California, Riverside http://career333.ucr.edu/
University of California, San Diego .... http://www.ucsd.edu/data/campus/department/
                                          administrative/personnel/csc.fixed/career.htm

University of Colorado at Denver . . . . *http://www.cudenver.edu/public/career/ccenter.html*
University of Colorado at Boulder . . . . *http://stripe.colorado.edu/~rai/carserv/*
University of Delaware . . . . *http://www.udel.edu/richard/CSC/career.html*
University of Dundee, U.K. . . . . *http://gotwo.dundee.ac.uk/*
University of Greenwich, U.K. . . . . *http://www.gre.ac.uk/central/studsrv/careers(.htm*
University of Hawaii at Manoa *http://www2.hawaii.edu/career*
University of Houston . . . . *http://cppcnov.career.uh.edu/*
University of Houston Law Center . . . . *http://www.law.uh.edu/LawCenter/Career/*
University of Illinois at Champaign . . . . *http://www.cso.uiuc.edu/careers/careers.top.html*
University of Illinois at Champaign
    Biological Sciences . . . . *http://www.life.uiuc.edu/biotech/placement.html*
University of Kansas . . . . *http://www.ukans.edu/~upc*
University of Lethbridge, Canada . . . . *http://www.uleth.ca/~man_www00*
University of Maine . . . . *http://cardinal.umeais.maine.edu/~career/Welcome.html*
University of Maine at Farmington . . . . *http://www.umf.maine.edu/~chd*
University of Manitoba, Canada . . . . *http://www.umanitoba.ca/counselling/crc.html*
University of Maryland at College Park . . . . *http://www.umcp.umd.edu/CareerCenter*
University of Memphis . . . . *http://www.people.memphis.edu/~univplace*
University of Miami Office of Student Employment . . . . *http://www.miami.edu/stuemp*
University of Miami School of Business . . . . *http://www.bus.miami.edu/plcmt/*
University of Minnesota at Duluth . . . . *http://www.d.umn.edu/careers/*
University of Minnesota
    Employee Career Enrichment Program . . . . *http://www.umn.edu/ohr/ecep/ecep.html*
University of Mississippi . . . . *http://www.olemiss.edu/depts/career_services/*
University of Missouri, Columbia . . . . *http://www.phlab.missouri.edu/~cppcwww/*
University of Missouri, Rolla . . . . *http://www.umr.edu/~career*
University of Montana . . . . *http://www.umt.edu*
University of Nebraska, Kearney . . . . *http://www.unk.edu/departments/*
                                       student_services/career_services/
University of Nebraska, Lincoln . . . . *http://www.unl.edu/careers/csc.html*
University of New Hampshire . . . . *http://www.unh.edu/career-services/index.html*
University of North Carolina at Chapel Hill . . . . *http://www.unc.edu/depts/career/*
University of North Carolina at Greensboro *http://www.uncg.edu:80/student.affairs/careers/*
University of North Dakota, Cooperative Education . . . . . . *http://www.und.nodak.edu/dept/co-op/*
University of North Dakota, Career Services . . . . *http://www.und.nodak.edu/dept/career/*
University of Oregon . . . . *http://uocareer.uoregon.edu/*
University of Pennsylvania *http://www.upenn.edu:80/CPPS/*
University of Phoenix . . . . *http://www.uophx.edu*
University of Pittsburgh . . . . *http://www.placement.pitt.edu/*
University of Richmond . . . . *http://www.urich.edu/~career/*
University of San Francisco . . . . *http://www.usfca.edu/usf/career/*
University of Scranton . . . . *http://werewolf.uofs.edu/academic/ocs-page.html*
University of Sheffield, U.K. . . . . *http://www.shef.ac.uk/uni/services/cas/*
University of South Carolina . . . . *http://web.csd.sc.edu/career*
University of South Florida, Tampa . . . . *http://www.rmit.usf.edu/enroll/crc.htm*
University of Southern California Law Center . . . . *http://www.usc.edu/dept/law-lib/*
                                       careers/careers.html
University of Southern California Career Center . . . . *http://www.usc.edu/dept/cdc/*
University of Southern Maine . . . . *http://macweb.acs.usm.maine.edu/csce/*
University of Staffordshire, U.K. . . . . *http://www.staffs.ac.uk/sands/care/careers.html*
University of Tasmania, Australia . . . . *http://info.utas.edu.au/docs/careers/*
University of Technology, Sydney, Australia . . . . *http://www.uts.edu.au/div/cas/*
University of Tennessee, Knoxville . . . . *http://funnelweb.utcc.utk.edu/~career/career.html*
University of Texas at Austin,
    College of Communication . . . . *http://www.utexas.edu/coc/career/*
University of Texas at Austin,
    College of Engineering . . . . *http://www.utexas.edu/coe/student/ecac/*
University of Texas at El Paso . . . . *http://www.utep.edu/~careers*
University of Texas School of Law . . . . *http://www.law.utexas.edu/school/services/career.html*
University of Toronto, Canada . . . . *http://www.utoronto.ca/career/*
University of Virginia . . . . *http://minerva.acc.virginia.edu/~career/home.html*

278

University of Wales, Cardiff, U.K. . . . . *http://info.cf.ac.uk/cgi-bin/info2www?menu|student/*
careers/main.men|UWCC+Careers+Service|This
University of Washington . . . . *http://weber.u.washington.edu/~careers*
University of Waterloo, Canada *http://www.adm.uwaterloo.ca:80/*
infocecs/CRC/Career_Resource_Centre.html
University of Western Ontario, Canada . . . . *http://www.uwo.ca/ses/*
University of Wisconsin, Green Bay . . . . *http://www.uwgb.edu/~placoffc/index.html*
University of Wisconsin, La Crosse . . . . *http://www.uwlax.edu/StuServ/CarServ/uwlink.html*
University of Wisconsin
Madison School of Business . . . . *http://www.wisc.edu/bschool/career.html*
Utah State University . . . . *http://www.usu.edu/~career*
Vanderbilt University . . . . *http://www.vanderbilt.edu/career/*
Vassar College . . . . *http://webcentral.vassar.edu/*
CareerDevelopment/CareerDevHomepage.html
Virginia Commonwealth University . . . . *http://www.vcu.edu/safweb/careers/ucchome.html*
Virginia Tech . . . . *http://www.career.vt.edu/*
Wake Forest University . . . . *http://www.mba.wfu.edu/WFUMBA/Placement/placement.html*
Washington and Lee University . . . . *http://www.wlu.edu/~career/home.html*
Washington State University *http://www.careers.wsu.edu/csweb/cs-home2.html*
Washington University at St. Louis . . . . *http://www.wustl.edu/careers/*
Washington University at St. Louis . . . . *http://www.gwbssw.wustl.edu/*
George Warren Brown School of Social Work . . . . *~gwbhome/services/career/career.html*
Wesleyan University . . . . *http://www.alumni.wesleyan.edu/cpc.html*
West Virginia University in Morgantown . . . . *http://www.wvu.edu/~careersc/*
Western Baptist College . . . . *http://www.wbc.edu*
Whitman College . . . . *http://www.whitman.edu/Departments/Career/homepage.html*
Worcester Polytechnic Institute . . . . *http://www.wpi.edu/Admin/Depts/CDC/*
Yale University Undergraduate Career Services . . . . *http://www.cis.yale.edu/career/*

To locate online information about universities and colleges in general, including the addresses for their home pages, check the following resources:

American Universities . . . . *http://www.clas.ufl.edu/CLAS/american-universities.html*
Career Assistance Center *http://www.careermosaic.com/cm/cc/cc3.html*
Career Resource Home Page . . . . *http://www.rpi.edu/dept/cdc/homepage.html*
Catapult Career Offices Home Pages . . . . *http://www.jobweb.org/catapult/home/*
College and University Home Pages *http://www.mit.edu:8001/people/cdemello/univ.html*
CollegeConnection *http://www.careermosaic.com/cm/cc/cc1.html*
CollegeNET . . . . *http://www.collegenet.com/*
Find a Job *http://www.careermosaic.com/cm/cc/cc2.html*
Index of Career Centers at Various Universities . . . . *http://www.rpi.edu/dept/cdc/carserv/*
Internet College Exchange (ICX) . . . . *http://www.usmall.com/college/*
Peterson's Education Center . . . . *http://www.petersons.com/*
ResumeCM *http://www.careermosaic.com/cm/cm40.html*
U.S. Universities and Community Colleges . . . . *http://www.utexas.edu/world/univ/*

Glossary:
The Terms You
Need to Know

Antivirus: A computer software program that detects viruses and destroys them (see *virus)*.

Applicant tracking system: A means of storing, finding, and retrieving information about a candidate in a computer database.

ARPAnet: A network created by the Advanced Research Projects Agency to study how to make computer networks secure in the event of nuclear war.

Article: An electronic message sent to a newsgroup or mailing list for distribution to all list members.

ASCII: American Standard Code for Information Interchange—a plain text file, stripped of all formatting codes. This generic file format is created when you save a file in a word processing or text editing program with special "save as" commands. The Notepad program in Microsoft Windows saves all of its files as ASCII text by default. ASCII (or text) files can be read by any word processor or text editing program.

Baud: The measure of how fast a computer modem can transfer data via a telephone line. Speeds range from 2400 baud (slow) to 56,000 (fast and getting faster).

BBS: Bulletin Board Service—usually a local computer system where individuals or companies can dial in and exchange information, programs, data, files, or carry on live conversations. Each BBS generally caters to some specific interest.

Boolean logic: A form of algebra fundamental to computer operations developed in the mid-1800s by English mathematician George Boole and having to do with logical, true/false values. Boolean operators (AND, NOT, OR) are often used as qualifiers in database searches.

Browser: A computer program used to find, retrieve, display, and move information on the Internet. Netscape, Microsoft Internet Explorer, Netcruiser, and Mosaic are some examples.

Byte: The amount of space required to store a single character on a disk.

CD-ROM: Similar to a music compact disk, CD-ROMs can store large volumes of data for access by computers. They are read only, meaning you cannot save information onto a CD-ROM but can run programs or read information directly from the disk. There are WORM (write once, read many) drives that allow your computer to write to a CD-ROM, but they tend to be costly and offer slower access speeds.

Client: A program that requests services from another computer, called the server.

Commercial online service: A company that allows you to dial in via modem to access their computer servers. Examples are CompuServe, America Online, Prodigy, GEnie, Delphi, etc.

Cyberspace: A term that refers to a place where people can communicate through the use of computers and computer network services. A term coined by William Gibson in his novel, *Necromancer.*

Database: A collection of electronically stored information structured in such a way that it can be sorted by fields, either alphabetically or numerically. In this book, it refers to a collection of résumés or jobs that can be searched by keywords.

Digest: A collection of mailing list articles.

Domain name: A multi-part name that identifies an Internet computer. Each component of the name refers to a computer, network, or organization.

DOS: Disk Operating System—a program that runs a PC. The original version is from Microsoft, hence the name MS-DOS.

Download: The process of transferring information from another computer to your computer. If you want to retrieve a file from the Internet, BBS, or a commercial online service, you download the file from the remote computer to your own computer.

Electronic résumé: A résumé that is in an electronic format ready for transfer in cyberspace, via the Internet or e-mail. The computer file is in a generic ASCII text format, either created by you or generated by a scanner from your paper résumé.

E-mail: Electronic mail—an electronic message sent from one computer to another via the Internet or commercial online service.

Encryption: The encoding of information to prevent someone from reading the information.

FAQ: Frequently Asked Questions—a document that covers basic information from a Usenet newsgroup, mailing list, or Internet site.

Forum: A chat room on a commercial online service where you can carry on live conversations with people of similar interests.

ftp: File transfer protocol—a means of sending computer files from one computer to another. The file does not have to be an ASCII text file. Entering "anonymous" as your logon and your e-mail address as your password allows you to use resources that the site has made accessible to the public.

Gateway: A computer that handles moving data from one network to another. Normally used to refer to communications between two different kinds of networks.

GIF: Graphic Interchange Format—the most common format for graphics on the Web.

Home page: The first page of an Internet site.

HTML: Hypertext Markup Language—a simple programming language used to format documents for display on the World Wide Web. It is this language that makes a home page appear "pretty" when your browser views it on your computer screen.

http: Hypertext transfer protocol—one of the behind-the-scenes protocols that computers on the Internet use to exchange information. When you see an URL that begins with http://, you know that the address points to a Web page.

Hyperlink: The part of the Web page that links you to another file. They are either images or words in a different color from the other items on the page.

Hypermedia: The ability to display a range of different media, accessible through hyperlinks. A Web page, for example, may contain photographs or drawings, formatted text, and links to audio and video sources. Distributed hypermedia simply means that these resources are distributed all over the world.

Hypertext: Highlighted text or picture on a Web page that provides a link between pages or sites, allowing you to move through information at random.

Information superhighway: An electronic communications network that will link homes, businesses, computers, televisions, and telephones into an integrated information network. The Internet is the beginning of the information superhighway, and interactive television and cable modems are the next step toward combining the various mediums.

Internet: The world's largest network of connected computers, linking government, military, businesses, organizations, educational institutions, and private individuals.

ISDN: Integrated Services Digital Network—a digital telephone service.

Job bank: A database of job openings on a computer, like the classified advertisements in a newspaper, that can be searched by keywords, job titles, geographic location, company, and so on.

JPEG: Joint Photographics Expert Group—a common graphic image file format that supports millions of colors. Better suited for photographs than the GIF format.

kbps: Kilobits per second—a measure of a modem's data transfer rate (for example, 28.8 kpbs equals 28,800 bits per second).

List owner: One or more people who are in charge of a mailing list.

Logoff: The process of disconnecting from a computer network.

Logon: The process required to dial in and identify yourself to a network's host computer. It usually requires dialing a certain number and typing in your user name and password. Login has the same meaning.

Mailing list: A collection of people with similar interests who are connected via e-mail where they receive the messages automatically.

Modem: A piece of computer hardware that connects your computer to a phone line, allowing you to communicate with another computer. *Modem* stands for *modulate–demodulate*, which is the converting of digital signals from your computer to the analog signals of your telephone line and then back into digital signals at the other end of the line.

Multimedia: A computer file that contains more than one media: text, graphics, video, animation, and/or sound.

Netiquette: The etiquette of using the Internet.

Network: More than one computer connected together for the purpose of sharing data.

Newsgroup: An electronic discussion or information group distributed by the Usenet.

OCR: Optical Character Recognition—a special kind of computer software that can examine, via a scanner, the dots of ink on a printed page and determine by their shapes which letters they represent. This information is then converted into binary form that a computer can read in a text editor or word processor.

Offline: Disconnected from a computer network so you are unable to access information or transmit data. The opposite of online.

Online: Connected to a computer network and able to access information or transmit data. The opposite of offline.

Password: A combination of letters and/or numbers that you choose to access your commercial online service, bulletin board service, or Internet service provider. Don't use your first name, last name, initials, phone number, or anything else that can be easily guessed. Keep this password a secret. Anyone who knows your password and user name can access your accounts and any credit card information you have provided to those accounts.

Post: The act of leaving your information (like a résumé) on another computer. Can be uploading a file or typing your information into an electronic form at an Internet site and then clicking a button to send.

Protocol: SLIP (Serial Line Internet Protocol) and PPP (Point-to-Point Protocol) give you access to the World Wide Web and let you use graphical Internet tools. When information is sent over the Internet, it is divided into smaller pieces in transit and reassembled at a final destination. Protocols allow computers to exchange these packets with the Internet. These protocols work behind the scenes of your browser with little input from the user.

Queue: To wait in line.

Résumé database: A collection of résumés on a computer that can be searched using keywords. Your electronic résumé will end up in a database like this. A hiring manager can type in keywords to call up résumés that match job requisitions.

Router: A computer that determines which path Internet traffic will take to reach its destination.

Scanner: A computer peripheral (piece of hardware attached to a computer) that uses light-sensing equipment to scan paper and then translate the pattern of light and dark (or color) into a digital signal that can be manipulated by computer software.

Server: A computer that provides a resource on the Internet. Client programs access servers to obtain data.

Shareware: Computer programs that you can try before purchasing. Although some shareware programs are free, most request that you pay the author a fee if you decide to keep and use the program.

Site: Also called Web site. The entire contents of a location on the Internet, including all of its multiple pages.

Surfing: Accessing the Internet and indiscriminately window shopping, wandering from site to site with no real plan.

SysOp: System Operator—the person responsible for managing a forum on a commercial online service or bulletin board system.

TCP/IP: Transmission Control Protocol/Internet Protocol—a set of protocols that standardizes the transmission of data over the Internet. TCP/IP stack programs (like the Trumpet Winsock) talk to the Internet behind the scenes while you run Internet tools such as Netscape, Mosaic, or Eudora.

Telnet: An Internet protocol that allows you to logon to a remote computer.

Terminal emulation: Communicating with a remote computer in which your PC acts as a terminal connected to it.

Text file: A generic file that can be read by any word processor or e-mail program.

Upload: The process of transmitting information from your computer to someone else's computer. The opposite of download.

URL: Universal Resource Locator—the address of an Internet site, for example: *http://www.careerpath.com.* An URL is a road map to help you get to a particular Internet site.

Usenet: Users network—thousands of computers that are organized under a set of groupings known as newsgroups.

Virus: A computer program that is intended to cause damage to your computer files if it is allowed to enter. Viruses are not spread by simple e-mail messages but may reside in any files you download. Commercial antivirus programs are a must for any computer with an Internet connection.

Web: World Wide Web (WWW)—a graphically oriented overlay on the Internet that may contain text, graphics, video, sound, and other data. The original Internet was text only. The World Wide Web was developed as a part of the Internet to allow the use of graphics and sound.

Appendix: Alphabetical Listing of URLs

The primary purpose of this list is to take the industry sites mentioned in Chapter 6 and present them alphabetically in a single list. This list also includes all of the other Internet sites mentioned in the book except the mailing lists, Telnet sites, company home pages, and college career centers since they are arranged alphabetically in the text of the book. Please reference the appropriate chapters for these listings.

1-800-DRIVERS Interactive JobLine
http://rwa.metronetworks.com/800drivers.html

1-800-NETWORK
http://www.1800network.com/

100 Careers in Wall Street
http://www.globalvillager.com/

100 Hot Jobs
http://www.100hot.com/jobs/

1st Impressions Résumés & Career Strategies
http://www.1st-Imp.com

1st St. NW
http://www.fsnw.com/

1st Steps: Employment and Recruiting News
http://www.interbiznet.com/hunt/

24-Hours, Recorded Job Lines for the San Francisco Bay Area
http://www.webcom.com/~rmd/index_body.html

3DSite
http://www.lightside.com/3dsite/cgi/offers/index.html

4Work
http://4work.com

A Virtual Job Fair
http://www.careerexpo.com/

A+ On-Line Résumés
http://www.hway.net:80/olresume
http://ol-resume.com

A2Z
http://a2z.lycos.com

AAA Résumé
http://www.infi.net/~resume/upload.html

AAFA The American Association of Finance and Accounting
http://www.aafa.com/

ABAG Globe
http://www.abag.ca.gov/bayarea/commerce/globe/globe.html

Able Associates, Inc.
http://www.ablesearch.com/

About Work
http://www.aboutwork.com/

Abraxas plc (UK)
http://www.abraxas.co.uk/

Absolutely Australian
http://www.netm.com/mall/infoprod/absol/bus.htm

Academic Chemistry Employment Clearinghouse
http://hackberry.chem.niu.edu:70/1/ChemJob

Academic Employment Network
http:///www.academploy.com/

Academic Internet Services
http://www.mousetrap.com:80/ais/

Academic Physician and Scientist, Association of American Medical Colleges (AAMC) Job Listings
gopher://aps.acad-psy-sci.com/

Academic Position Network (APN)
http://www.umn.edu/apn/

Academic Positions in Science
http://www.anu.edu.au/psychology/Academia/science.htm

Academy of Advertising
http://www.utexas.edu/coc/adv/AAA/

Academy of Management
http://www.usi.edu/aom/placemnt.htm

Access Career and Job Resources
http://www.hawk.igs.net/jobresources

AccuFind
http://accufind.com

ACM Sigmod's On-line Career Center
http://www.acm.org/cacm/careerops/

Acorn Career Counseling
http://www1.mhv.net:80/~acorn/Acorn.html

ACP On-line, Australian Computer Professionals
http://www.ozjobs.com/

Ada Project <The>
http://www.cs.yale.edu/HTML/YALE/CS/HyPlans/tap/tap.html

Adams Job Bank Online
http://www.adamsonline.com

Adderley Group <The>
http://www.adderley.com/

ADEPT Job Search
http://www.adeptinc.com/openjobs/jobcateg.htm

Adia
http://www.adia.com

AdOne Classified Network(10)
http://www.adone.com

AdSearch
http://www.adsearch.com

ADSWeb
http://walden.mo.net/~devino/ads.htm

Advance HTC
http://www.advancehtc.com

Advanced Marketing
http://www.amgi.com/

Advanced Staffing
http://www.adstaff.com

Advanced Technical Resources
http://www.atr1.com/

Advanced Technology Employment Consultants
http://home.eznet.net/~atec

Advanced Technology Information Network
http://caticsuf.csufresno.edu:70/1/atinet

AdvanceTech
http://www.swcp.com/~mharris

Advancing Women
http://www.advancingwomen.com

Advantage Technical Services
http://www.advantagets.com

Advocate Career Services
http://www.amsquare.com/america/advocate.html

Aegis Group
http://aegis-group.com

Affordable Résumé and Interview Skills Service
http://www.aaow.com/john_schwartz

Africa Online: Jobs
http://www.AfricaOnline.com/AfricaOnline/classifieds.html

AfricaOnline
http://www.AfricaOnline.com

Agricultural Job Listings
http://caticsuf.csufresno.edu:70/1/atinet/agjobs

Agricultural Job Listings in British Columbia
http://qb.island.net/~awpb/emop/startag.html

AIPJOBS, The American Institute of Physics Employment Opportunities Database
http://www.aip.org:80/aip/careers/careers.html

Air and Waste Management Association
http://www.awma.org/employment.html

Airline Employee Placement Service
http://www.aeps.com/aeps/aepshm.html

Airline Employment Assistance Corps.
http://www2.csn.net/AEAC/

AIRS II
http://www.arachnae.com

Airwaves Job Services
http://www.airwaves.com/

AK Jobnet, Austin Knight Company
http://www.ak.com.au/akjobnet.html

Alabama Jobs
http://www.the-matrix.com/ph/ph.html

Alaska Anchorage Daily News
http://www.adn.com/

Alaskan Jobs
http://www.state.ak.us/local/akpages/ADMIN/rbtitl.htm

Aleph The Global Translation Alliance
http://www.aleph.com

Allen Davis & Associates Software Jobs Home Page
http://www.softwarejobs.com

Alliance Management Resources
http://www.amsquare.com/america/medpro1.html

Allinone
http://www.albany.net/allinone/

AltaVista
http://www.altavista.digital.com

Alumni Services
http://www.rpi.edu/dept/cdc/alumni

America Online
http://www.aol.com

America Online Subscriber Web Pages
http://members.aol.com

America's Employers: The Job Seekers "Home"
http://www.americasemployers.com

America's Help Wanted
http://jobquest.com/

America's Job Bank
http://www.ajb.dni.us/

American Association of Cereal Chemists
http://wwwnt.scisoc.org/aacc/career/

American Astronomical Society
http://www.aas.org/
http://www.aas.org:80/JobRegister/aasjobs.html

American Ceramic Society's Ceramic Futures
http://www.acers.org/mem/futures/futures.stm

American Chemical Society
http://www.acs.org/memgen/employmt/pdb/acsmenu.htm

American Communication Association (Grants and Fellowships)
http://www.uark.edu/depts/comminfo/www/grants.html

American Council on International Personnel
http://ahrm.org/acip/acip.htm

American Crystallography Association
http://www.sdsc.edu/ACA/

American Dairy Science Association
http://orion.animal.uiuc.edu:80/~adsa/1995/position.html

American Education Research Association Jobs Corner at ASU
http://tikkun.ed.asu.edu/~jobs/joblinks.html

American Employment Weekly
http://branch.com/aew

American Evaluation Association
http://www.theriver.com/public/aea/

American Heart Association
http://www.amhrt.org/jobs/index.html

American Indian Science & Engineering Society (AISESnet)
http://bioc02.uthscsa.edu/aisesnet.html

American Industrial Hygiene Association
http://www.aiha.org/es.html

American Institute of Aeronautics and Astronautics
http://www.lmsc.lockheed.com/aiaa/sf/career.html

American Institute of Architects
http://www.aia.org/career.htm http://www.aia.org/

American Institute of Chemical Engineers
http://www.aiche.org/employment/
http://www.che.ufl.edu/WWW-CHE/aiche/

American Institute of Physics
http://www.aip.org/aip/careers/careers.html

American Library Association
http://www.ala.org/alanow/alanow_home.html

American Marketing Association
http://www.ama.org

American Mathematical Society
http://www.ams.org/committee/profession/employ.html

American Medical Association, JAMA
http://www.ama-assn.org

American Physical Society <The>
http://aps.org/jobs/index.html

American Physiological Association
gopher://oac.hsc.uth.tmc.edu:3300/11/employ

American Phytopathological Society
http://www.scisoc.org/career.htm

American Psychological Society (APS) Observer Job Listings
http://www.hanover.edu/psych/APS/aps.html

American Society for Engineering Education (ASEE)
http://www.asee.org/asee/publications/prism/classifieds/
http://www.asee.org/nein/pd/

American Society for Gravitational and Space Biology
http://www.indstate.edu/asgsb/index.html

American Society for Histocompatibility and Immunogenetics
http://www.swmed.edu/home_pages/ASHI/jobs/jobs.htm

American Society for Horticultural Science <The>
http://www.ashs.org/hortop20.html

American Society for Mass Spectrometry <The>
http://www.asms.org/employ.html

American Society for Quality Control
http://www.asqc.org/

American Society of Agricultural Engineers (ASAE)
http://www.asae.org:80/jobs
http://asae.org/resource/

American Society of Animal Science
http://www.asas.org/

American Society of Civil Engineers
http://www.asce.org/

American Society of Ichthyologists and Herpetologists
http://www.utexas.edu/depts/asih/pubs/pubs.html

American Society of Limnology and Oceanography
http://www.ngdc.noaa.gov/paleo/aslo/

American Society of Mechanical Engineers ASMENET
http://www.asme.org/jobs/index.html
http://www.asme.org/index.html

American Society of Plant Physiologists (Midwest Section)
http://baby.indstate.edu:80/mwaspp/gradposi.html

American Statistical Association
http://www.amstat.org/opportunities/

America's Job Bank
http://www.ajb.dni.us/

Ames Laboratory
http://www.ameslab.gov/Job.html

Anchor Group <The>
http://www.espan.com/spot/anchor/anchor.html

Andersen Consulting
http://www.ac.com/main.html

Andersen Contracting (Australia)
http://www.swcontracting.com.au/body.htm

Animated GIF Files
http://www.yahoo.com/Computers_and_Internet/Graphics/
Computer_ Animation/Animated_GIFs/Collections/
http://www.webpromotion.com/stock.html
http://www.geocities.com/SoHo/1085/
http://web2.airmail.net/nicktg/moving/index.html

Ann Arbor Campus
http://www.med.umich.edu/~mchrd/jobs/

ANSA Job Opportunities
http://www.ansa.co.uk/APM/job-ad.html

APK Net, Ltd.
http://www.apk.net:80/main.html

Apple Recruitment (UK)
http://www.u-net.com/~applerec/

APPLE PIE, USA, Nannies
http://www.nanny.com/

Application Resources, Inc.
http://www.appres.com/ari/

Appointments Section—Jobs & Careers <The>
http://taps.com

APTA Home Page
http://www.edoc.com/apta/

Archaeological Fieldwork Server
http://durendal.cit.cornell.edu/

Archie
gopher://liberty.uc.wlu.edu

Architecture and Land Architecture Jobs (CLRNet)
http://www.clr.toronto.edu/VIRTUALLIB/jobs.html

Architecture Resources: Berkley
gopher://infolib.lib.berkeley.edu/11/eres/resdbs/land

Archives of the French Jobs Newsgroups
http://www.loria.fr:80/news/fr.jobs.offres.html
http://www.loria.fr:80/news/fr.jobs.d.html

Ardent Group, Inc. <The>
http://www.ardentgrp.com/

Ardex Executive Search <The>
http://www.andex.com/

Argonne National Laboratory, Mathematics and Computer Science
Division
http://www.mcs.anl.gov/Divisional/positions.html

ARI Summit Search Specialists
http://www.phoenix.net/~summit

Arizona Careers Online
http://amsquare.com/america/arizona.html

Armstrong's Employment Database (Australia)
http://www.armstrongs.com.au/employment.html

Army High Performance Computing (HPC) Research Center
http://www.arc.umn.edu/

Artificial Intelligence Applications Institute
http://www.aiai.ed.ac.uk/aiai/jobs/

Artificial Intelligence Jobs Repository
http://www.cs.cmu.edu/Groups/AI/html/other/jobs.html

Artisan, your freelance network
http://www.artisan-inc.com

ArtJob
gopher://gopher.tmn.com/11/Artswire/artjob

Arts Deadlines List <The>
http://www.ircam.fr/divers/arts-deadlines.html

Arts Wire Current
http://www.tmn.com/Artswire/

ArtsNet
http://artsnet.heinz.cmu.edu/career/career.html

Arvon, LLC
http://www.arvon.com/

AS ASISTENT d.o.o. (Slovenia)
http://www.c-and-c.si/asas/inang.html

ASA Information Services
http://www.eskimo.com/~pageless/asa/

ASA Solutions
http://www.asasol.com

ASC Connections LTD.
http://www.itjobsearch.com/asc/

Asia-Net or AsiaNet, JapanNet
http://www.asia-net.com

Asia Pacific Management Forum
http://www.mcb.co.uk/apmforum/nethome.htm

Asian Career Web
http://www.rici.com/acw/

Askew School Job Placement Services
http://www.fpac.fsu/spap/job_intern/jobs/

Askew School of Public Administration and Policy
http://www.fsu.edu:80/~spap/job/job/html
http://www.fsu.edu/spap/job_intern/jobs/

ASPIRE
http://www.indiana.edu/~intlcent/aspire/

Association Bernard Gregory (France)
http://www-com.grenet.fr/abg/

Association for Computing Machinery
http://www.acm.org/member_services/career/

Association for Education in Journalism and Mass Communication
http://www.aejmc.sc.edu/online/home.html

Association for Institutional Research
http://ike.engr.washington.edu/general/air.html

Association for Women in Computing
http://www.halcyon.com/monih/awc.html

Association of American Geographers (AAG) <The>
http://www.aag.org/jobs.html

Association of Commonwealth Universities
http://www.niss.ac.uk/noticeboard/acu/acu.html

Association of Energy Services Professionals
http://www.dnai.com/AESP/jobs.html

Association of Graduate Career Advisory Services (UK)
http://agcas.csu.man.ac.uk/

Association of Midwest College Biology Teachers
http://papa.indstate.edu/

Astronomical Observatory Jobs
http://www.pd.astro.it:80/Jobs/

Atlanta Web Guide
http://www.webguide.com/

Atlanta's Computerjobs Store
http://www.computerjobs.com

Atlanta's CyberJobs
http://155.229.44.6/jobs/

Attorney Job Listings, Department of Justice
gopher://justice2.usdoj.gov/1

Attorney Job Network
http://www.jurisjob.com

Au Pair in Europe
http://netaccess.on.ca/aupair/

Au Pairs Job Match
http://www.aupairs.co.uk/

Audio Engineering Society
http://www.cudenver.edu/aes/

AUSNet
http://www.world.net/cgi-bin/ausnet_jobs

Austin, Texas Job Listings
http://www.ci.austin.tx.us/

Australian Academy of Science, Scientific Exchanges and Fellowships
http://www.asap.unimelb.edu.au/aas/foreigne/contscix.htm

Australian Computer Professionals
http://www.ozjobs.com

Australian Computer Professionals Jobs Online
http://www.digiweb.com/~aep1/

Australian Defence Forces
http://www.adfa.oz.au/DOD/recruit/recruit.htm

Australian IT Job Recruitment Pty Ltd
http://www.ozemail.com.au/~jobtic/

Australian Mathematical Society
http://solution.maths.unsw.edu.au/htdocs.ams/People/Jobs/jobs.html

Australian Résumé Server
http://www.herenow.com.au/

Automated Graphic Systems
http://www.ags.com/employment/employment.htm

Automated Vacancy Announcement System (AVADS)
http://info.er.usgs.gov/doi/avads/index.html

AUX Technology, Inc.
http://kiwi.futuris.net/aux/

Aviation/Aerospace Jobs Page
http://www.nationjob.com/aviation

Aviation Connection
http://www.flying.net/ac/employme.htm

Avotek Publishing, International Headhunters Guide
http://www.universal.nl/jobhunt/

AVR
http://www.mkt-place.com/laavrinc/avrpl.html

Awebs Newsgroups Archive
http://awebs.com/news_archive

Axis Technologies
http://axis.micron.net/

Aztech Computer Recruitment
http://194.128.198.201/aztech/

Baber's Employment Directory
http://www.baber.com/em-plt.htm

Bakos Résumé Service
http://www.branch.com/

Bankey Temporary Services
http://gwabbs.com/~bankey/tempagency.htm

Banking Related Jobs
http://www.cob.ohio-state.edu/~fin/osujobs.htm

Bark, Foehr und Partner GmbH, Personalberatung (Germany)
http://ourworld.compuserve.com/homepages/barkjobs/

Bay Area Job Location Finder
http://none.coolware.com/jobs/location.html

Bay Area Jobs
http://www.sonic.net/~allan/ba_jobs.html

Bay State
http://www.inter-mall.com/service/allied/baystate

Baywatch Personnel (New Zealand)
http://ourworld.compuserve.com/homepages/pages/baywatch.htm

BBN Networking, Inc.
http://www.bbn.com/bbnjobs/jobsrch.htm

BCL International (UK)
http://www.bcl.com/

Beardsley Group <The>
http://www.beardsleygroup.com/

Belcan Information Services
http://www.belcan.com/infoserv.htm

Believe and Succeed
http://www.ens.net/

Benefit Associates
http://www.benefitassociates.com/

Bermuda Biological Station for Research
http://www.bbsr.edu/

Bernard Haldane Associates
http://www.intex.net/careers/index.html

Best Bets from the Net
http://asa.ugl.lib.umich.edu/chdocs/employment/

Best Bets from the Net: Job Search
http://www.lib.umich.edu:80/chdocs/employment/

Best Jobs in the USA Today
http://www.bestjobsusa.com/top.htm

BFSI Internet Marketing
http://www.bfservs.com/states.html

BIO-ONLINE
http://www.bio.com/hr/hr_index.html

Biodata Navigator Job Board
http://www.biodata.com/biodata/bd_jobs.html

Biological Control and Sciences Jobs
http://www.aphis.usda.gov/

BioNet (BioSci) Employment Opportunities
http://www.bio.net:80/hypermail/EMPLOYMENT/

Biophysical Society
http://biosci.cbs.umn.edu/biophys/employ.html

Biosciences Job Listings and Career Services
http://golgi.harvard.edu/biopages/jobs.html

BioSource
http://www.biosource-tech.com/

BioSpace Career Center
http://www.biospace.com/g/synd/career

Biotech Career Center
http://www.gene.com/ae/AB/CC/index.html

Bizlinks (Singapore)
http://sunflower.singnet.com.sg/~g6615000/

BlackHawk Information Services
http://www.blackhawkis.com

Bogue Company
http://www.bogueco.com

Boldface Jobs
http://www.boldfacejobs.com/

Bolsa de Trabajo de Pixelnet (Mexico) [in Spanish]
http://www.pixel.com.mx:80/Curriculums/

Bolton Group <The>
http://www.webcreations.com/bolton/

Boston Area Career Opportunities
http://www.winterwyman.com/

Boston Economy
http://www.std.com/NE/boseconomy.html

Boston Globe's Help Wanted
http://www.boston.com/helpwanted/boshelw.htm
http://www.boston.com

Boston Job Bank
http://www.bostonjobs.com

Brannon and Tully Consulting Services
http://www.brannontully.com

Brei & Associates, Inc. Jobs Database
http://www.netins.net/showcase/rdbrei/

Bridge Information Technology Inc. (Canada Net Pages)
http://www.visions.com/

British Crystallographic Association
http://www.cryst.bbk.ac.uk/BCA/jobs.html

Broadcast Employment Services
http://www.tvjobs.com/index_a.htm

Broadcasters Training Network
http://www.learn-by-doing.com

Brookings Institution <The>
http://www.brook.edu/pa/int_fel/fellow.htm

BUBL Employment Bulletin Board
gopher://ukoln.bath.ac.uk:7070/11/Academic/Employment

Building Industry Exchange
http://www.building.org

Bullseye Job Shop
http://interoz.com

Businesses on the Internet with Location Maps
http://www.onvillage.com/

Buzz Buzz @ads: Banen aangeboden (Netherlands)
http://valley.interact.nl/@ds/banen-aanbod/home.html

Byron Employment Australia
http://www.byron.com.au/employment_australia/

C/NET Search.Com
http://www.search.com/

C.I. Software Associates
http://www.cisoftware.com

California Career and Employment Center
http://www.webcom.com/~career/

California Civil Service Employment Information
http://www.spb.ca.gov/

California Polytechnic State University Summer Jobs
gopher://gopher.calpoly.edu/11/campus_info/campus_serv_a nd_fac/career_services

California School-to-Career Information System
http://wwwstc.cahwnet.gov/

California State Government
http://www.ca.gov/

California State University Employment Board
http://csueb.sfsu.edu/csueb.html

Cambridge Group
http://cambridgegroup.com/C/cambridge

Camelot Consultants Limited (UK)
http://www.eclipse.co.uk/camelot/

Canada Employment Centre
http://ein.ccia.st-thomas.on.ca/agencies/cec/index.html

Canada Employment Centre in Nanaimo
http://www.island.net/~hrcnan/emp.html

Canadian Association of Career Educators and Employers (CACEE)
http://www.cacee.com/workweb/

Canadian Computing Careers, ProNet Search Canada
http://bisinc.com/pronet/ccc/

Canadian Institute of Theoretical Astronomy
http://www.cita.utoronto.ca/CITA/jobs.html

Canadian Résumé Centre
http://netaccess.on.ca/~resume/

CANDO Career Advisory Network on Disability Opportunities
http://www.comp.lancs.ac.uk/uni-services/careers/cando/

CanMed Consultants Inc.
http://www.canmed.com/

Cape Connections Software
http://www.vital.co.za/ccs

Career Action Center
http://www.careeraction.org

Career Advice
http://www.review.com/career/career_homepage.html

Career Advisory Service (UK)
http://www.aston.ac.uk/~haxbype/cas-home.html

Career and Labour Market Information
http://www.etc.bc.ca/provdocs/careers/home.html

Career and Placement Services (CaPS)
gopher://chinchaga.ucs.ualberta.ca/

Career and Résumé Management for the 21st Century!
http://crm21.com

Career Atlas for the Road
http://www.isdn.net/nis/

Career Blazers
http://www.compu-link.com

Career Blazers Learning Centre (Canada)
http://cblazers.ns.ca/

Career Center
http://www.paralegals.org/Center/home.html

Career Center (from the Internet Professional)
http://www.netline.com/Career/career.html

Career Center for Workforce Diversity, Equal Opportunity Publications, Inc. (EOP)
http://www.eop.com

Career Centre Canada
http://qb.island.net/~careers/

Career Command Center
http://www.CareerCommandCenter.com/ccc.html

Career Connections
http://www.career.com/

Career-Connector
http://www.wons.com/cc/

Career Corner
http://www.isminc.com/mm.html

Career Counseling LITE
http://www.execpc.com/~cclite/

Career Data Resources
http://amsquare.com/america/cdr.html

Career Development Network <The>
http://www.webscope.com/webscope/

Career Dynamics Inc.
http://www.webspan.com/

Career Exchange
http://www.careerexchange.com/

Career Fairs <The>
http://www.cweb.com/employersandorgs/lendmangrp/home1. htm

Career Index
http://www.beloit.edu/

Career Information System
http://career-info.uoregon.edu/whoweaare.html

Career Internetworking
http://www.careerkey.com/careerky.htm

Career Magazine
http://www.careermag.com

Career Management International
http://www.cmi-lmi.com/

Career Mapper
http://www.careermapper.com/

Career Marketing-Résumé Service
http://www.careermarketing.com

Career Match
http://www.fleethouse.com/career/cm-pg1.htm

Career Mentor
http://www.opendoor.com/

Career Network
http://phoenix.placement.oakland.edu

Career Net–Career Resource Center
http://www.careers.org

Career Opportunities in Singapore
http://www.singapore-careers.com

Career Paradise
http://www.emory.edu/CAREER/

Career Paths
http://www.etc.bc.ca/~szukiwsk/yes/Career/p1.html

Career Quest
http://www.careerquest.com/

Career Quest (Japan)
http://www.venture-web.or.jp/axiom/axiom_english/index.html

Career Resource Home Page
http://www.rip.edu/dept/cdc/homepage.html

Career Résumés
http://branch.com/cr/cr.html

Career Shop
http://www.careershop.com/

Career Source
http://www.netusa.com/jobs.htm

Career Talk
http://www.careertalk.com

Career Toolbox
http://careertoolbox.com/

Career Transitions
http://www.bfservs.com
http://www.bfservs.com:80/bfserv.html

Career Way
http://Internet-plaza.net/streets/career.html

Career.net (UK)
http://www.atlas.co.uk/mbacareer/

CareerBuilder
http://careerbuilder.com/

CareerChina, Career China
http://www.globalvillager.com/villager/CC.html

CareerCity Jobs
http://www.careercity.com/jobs/

CareerLine
http://www.careerline.com

CareerLynx USA
http://gold.lsn.com

CareerMart
http://www.careermart.com

CareerMosaic
http://www.careermosaic.com

CareerMosaic (Asia)
http://www.careerasia.com/

CareerNet, Career Resource Center
http://www.careers.org:80/catg/02jobs-05.htm

CareerNET (Hong Kong)
http://www.hk.super.net/~salesnet/career/home.htm

CareerPath
http://www.careerpath.com

CareerPro
http://www.career-pro.com/
http://www.catalog.com/tsw/geturjob/index.htm

Careers in Health and Community Service
http://www.csuchico.edu/hcsv/hcsvcar.html

Careers in Management Consulting
http://www.cob.ohio-state.edu:80/dept/fin/jobs/consult.htm

Careers in Mathematics
http://www.math.purdue.edu/~rcp/Careers.html

Careers On-Line
http://www.disserv.stu.umn.edu

Careers Online (Australia)
http://www.careersonline.com.au/
http://www.ideaf.com/jobs/pps.htm

CareerSearch Jobs Online
http://www.greatinfo.com/business_cntr/career.html

CareerSite
http://www.careersite.com

CareerSurf
http://careersurf.com

CareerWeb, Landmark Communications
http://www.cweb.com

Case Western Reserve University Part-time/Summer Job List
http://www.cwru.edu/CWRU/Admin/cpp/summer.html

Catalyst Corporation
http://www.catalystcorp.com

Catapult
http://www.jobweb.org

Catholic University of America <The>
http://www.cua.edu/

CAUSE Job Posting Service
http://cause-www.colorado.edu/pd/jobpost/jobpost.html

CDC & ATSDR Employment Opportunities
http://www.cdc.gov/hrmo/hrmo.html

Cell Journal of Biological Sciences
http://www.cell.com/cell/posi/

Center for Applied Large-Scale Computing
http://quasar.poly.edu:80/CALC/jobs.html

Center for Education and Work
http://www.cew.wisc.edu/

Central Services Unit (UK)
http://www.prospects.csu.man.ac.uk/

Cerberus Computing Corporation
http://www.cerb.com

CERC Jobs Database (Belgium)
http://gis.linkline.be/jmh/gb/index1.htm

CERL Sound Group
http://datura.cerl.uiuc.edu/netStuff/jobs/jobs.html

CERN The European Laboratory for Particle Physics (Switzerland)
http://www.cern.ch/CERN/Divisions/PE/HRS/Recruitment/

Certes Computing Ltd. (UK)
http://www.certes.co.uk/docs/home.htm

Certified General Accountants' Association of Manitoba (Canada)
http://sulla.cyberstore.ca/Provincial/Manitoba/employ.htm

CFD (Computational Fluid Dynamics) Online
http://www.tfd.chalmers.se/CFD_Online/cfd-job/

CGI Job Offers
http://www.lightside.com/~dani/cgi/offers/index.html

Chancellor & Chancellor
http://www.chancellor.com

Chaosgruppe Association for Non-Linear Dynamics
http://www.nonlin.tu-muenchen.de/chaos/Jobs/jobs.html

Chattanooga Free-Press
http://www.chatpub.com

Chemtech, Ltd
http://www.interaccess.com/ctld/

Chicago Mosaic
http://www.ci.chi.il.us

Chicago Software Newspaper
http://www.chisoft.com

Chicago Tribune Career Finder
http://www.chicago.tribune.com/home.html

Chicano/Latino Electronic Network (CLENet)
gopher://latino.sscnet.ucla.edu:70/11/Employment%20Center/
Job%20Announcements/

Children's Hospital of Alabama, Division of Pediatric Surgery
http://pedsurg.surgery.uab.edu/jobs.htm

Childs, Smith & Associates
http://www.accounting-jobs.com/

Christian Mission Opportunity Database
http://www.netaccess.on.ca/fingertip/gallery/oppor/oppor.htm

Chronicle of Higher Education, Academe this Week
http://chronicle.merit.edu/.ads/.links.html

CIMTT Job-Boerse, CIMTT Chemnitz (Germany)
http://ziu_4.mb2.tu-chemnitz.de/CIM/jobs/info.html

Cinenet Communications
http://www.cinenet.net/

Cirrus Links for Chemistry-Related Positions
http://rainier.chem.plu.edu/chem_careers.html

CITE Job Bank
gopher://esusda.gov/11/data/archive/cite-jobs-mg

CitiElite Management and Recruitment Consultants (UK)
http://www.citielite.co.uk/

City and County of San Francisco
http://www.well.com/user/ctywatch/joblstng.html

City of Cambridge, Massachusetts
http://www.ci.cambridge.ma.us/jobs/city_jobs.html

City of Morgantown Jobs
http://www.dmssoft.com/city/jobs.htm

City of Mountain View, California
http://www.abag.ca.gov/abag/local_gov/city/mt_view/mves/
mves.html

City of Oklahoma City, Oklahoma
http://www.ionet.net/~okcpio/index.html

City of Rochester, Minnesota
http://www.isl.net/city/joblink.html

City of Roseville, Minnesota
http://www.ci.roseville.mn.us/admin/jobs.htm

City of Saint Paul, Minnesota
http://www.stpaul.gov/jobopenings/

City of Vancouver, Canada
http://www.city.vancouver.bc.ca/jobs/jobspage.html

CityLink
http://www.NeoSoft.com:80/citylink/

CityNet
http://www.city.net/

CitySites Production
http://www.stonesearch.com

Civil Engineering and Public Works Career Paths
http://www.tileshop.com:80/apwa/civil.html

Clark County, Nevada Personnel Department
http://www.sundaypaper.com/www/hwlv.htm

Classifieds on the Gate
http://www.sfgate.com/classifieds

Clausman Legal Staffing
http://www.clausman.com

Clearinghouse
http://www.clearinghouse.net/

Clearinghouse for Subject-Oriented Internet Resource Guides
http://www.lib.umich.edu/chhome.html

CLNET
http://latino.sscnet.ucla.edu/

Cochran Consulting
http://www.cochranctg.com

Cole Employment Services
http://www.shopperusa.com/employment.html

Collaborative Computational Projects (UK)
http://www.dl.ac.uk/CCP/CCP5/vacancies.html

College and Research Libraries Jobs
gopher://gopher.uic.edu/11/library/crl/crljobs

College Grad Job Hunter
http://www.collegegrad.com

College of St. Catherine Internships
gopher://gopher.stkate.edu/11/dept/career/intshp

CollegePro Painters
http://wanda.phl.pond.com/mall/collegepro/
http://wanda.pond.com/mall/collegepro/intern.html

Colorado Department of Labor and Employment
http://www.state.co.us/gov_dir/labor_dir/employment_services
_le.html

Colorado New Mexico Job Listings
http://www.dirs.com/employ/colnm

Colorado State Library JOBLINE
gopher://gopher.jefferson.lib.co.us:71/11/jobline

Colorado, State of
http://www.state.co.us/

Colton Information Technology
http://www.coltonexec.com

Commercial Sites Index from Open Market
http://www.directory.net/

Commonwealth Jobsearch, Commonwealth Job Search
http://www.corpinfohub.com/cjs.htm

Communication Arts: Business and Career
http://www.commarts.com/bin/ca/bc_jl_o

Communications Engineering Employment Network
http://www.destek.net/ejdort/ce_emply.html

Community Workplace
http://galaxy.einet.net/galaxy/Community/Workplace.html

Companies that Use the Internet for Recruiting
http://www.occ.com/occ/occMemberJobs.html

CompHealth
http://www.comphealth.co

CompuData
http://www.gncs.com/cdi/

CompuForce (New Zealand)
http://compuforce.com/

CompuServe
http://www.compuserve.com

CompuServe Subscriber Web Pages
http://ourworld.compuserve.com

CompuSource, Inc
http://www.biddeford.com/compusource/

ComputAppoint (UK)
http://www.rednet.co.uk/homepages/computap/

Computemp
http://www.computemp.com/

Computer Age Classifieds (Australia)
http://www.theage.com.au:80/class/

Computer Consulting Group
http://www.cconsulting.com/positions.html

Computer Contracting on the Internet, ETX Melbourne, Australia
http://www.ozemail.com.au/~contract/etx.html

Computer Graphics (Insight Studios)
http://emporium.turnpike.net/I/INSIGHT/jobs.htm

Computer Help (UK)
http://ourworld.compuserve.com/homepages/tblake_computer help/

Computer Jobs in Israel (CJI)
http://www.jr.co.il/cji

Computer Management Consultants
http://www.jobbankusa.com/cmc/

Computer Personnel
http://cpi-seattle.com/

Computer Resellers Weekly
http://www.techweb.cmp.com/crn/career/career.html

Computer Resources Group
http://www.crgusa.com/

Computer Science Employment Resources at Carnegie Mellon University
http://www.cs.cmu.edu/afs/cs/cmu.edu/Web/Library/tips/jobs.html

Computer Science Jobs in Academia
http://www.cs.brandeis.edu:80/~zippy/academic-cs-jobs.html

Computer Staffing Provider <The>
http://www.atr.com/

Computer-Tech Consultants (Canada)
http://www.islandnet.com/~ctc10000/www/ctc10000.html

ComputerWeek Jobs Online
http://www.jobs.co.za/

ComputerWorld
http://www.computerworld.com

Computing and Technology Companies Online
http://www.cmpcmm.com/cc/companies.html

Computing Careers Online
http://www.isgjobs.com

Computing/IT Jobs WorldWide
http://www.Britain.EU.net/vendor/jobs/main.html

Compuvac Personnel Services Limited (UK)
http://www.compuvac.com/

Construction Site's Guide to Jobs <The>
http://www.emap.com/construct/jobs.htm

Consulting Companies on the Web
http://www.phoenix.oakland.edu:80/career/consult.htm

Contract Employment Weekly, Jobs Online
gopher://gopher.ceweekly.wa.com/1
http://www.ceweekly.com/
http://www.ceweekly.wa.com/

Contract Jobs
http://www.contract-jobs.com

Coolware Classifieds
http://www.coolware.com/jobs/jobs/html

CoolWorks Job Bulletin Board
http://www.coolworks.com/showme/

Coopers and Lybrand (Australia)
http://www.colybrand.com.au/

Cornell University
http://www.cornell.edu/Admin/JOBOPS/JOBOPS.html

Cornell University Internships and Summer Jobs
http://student-jobs.ses.cornell.edu/jobs/

Corporate Aviation Résumé Exchange <The>
http://scendtek.com/care/

Corporate Recruiter's Ltd. (Canada)
http://WWW.PIE.VANCOUVER.BC.CA/pie/business/personne /corp_rec/corp_rec.htm

Corporate Staffing Center, Inc.
http://www.corporate-staffing.com/csc/hunt/html

Corporation for Public Broadcasting (CPB) Job Line
http://www.cpb.org/jobline/index.html

Council for the Support and Advancement of Education (CASE) Job Classifieds
gopher://gopher.case.org:70/11/currents

Criscito, Pat
http://members.aol.com/criscito

Crystallography
http://www.unige.ch/crystal/job-index.html
http://www.unige.ch/crystal/w3v1c/job-index.html

CSU the Higher Education Careers Service Unit (UK)
http://buzzard.csu.man.ac.uk/

CSUS Student/Alumni Employment Opportunities
gopher://gopher.csus.edu/11/employment

CTG
http://www.ctg.com

CTS Network Services
http://www.cts.com/

Cumbria Careers Ltd.
http://www.u-net.com/~c-career/

CV + (Belgium)
http://www.metaphor.be/cvplus/

CV Direct Services Ltd.
http://www.cvdirect.co.uk/

CyberCONTRACTS (UK)
http://www.cybernation.co.uk/~cybercon/index.htm

CyberDyne CS Ltd.
http://www.demon.co.uk/cyberdyne/cyber.html

CybeRésumé Associates LLC
http://tkweb.com/resume/
http://seanet.com/HTML/Vendors/raj/job.html

CybeRezumes
http://www.seanet.com/HTML/Vendors/raj/cyberez.html

Cyberspace Jobs
http://www.best.com:80/~lianne/

D & P International Limited (UK)
http://www.pavilion.co.uk/dandp/

Daley Consulting & Search and Daley Technical Search
http://www.dpsearch.com/

Dallas ComputerJobs Store
*http://www.computerjobs.com/scripts/dbml.exe?template=/
index.dbm*

Dallas Morning News
http://www.pic.net/tdmn/tdmn.html

Dana-Farber Cancer Institute
gopher://farber2.dfci.harvard.edu/11/.bulletin/.hr/.positions

Data Careers
http://www.vnu.com/datanews/careers/careers_eng.html

Data Lake (UK)
http://www.westlake.co.uk/

Data Processing Career Centers
http://www.careercenter.com/

Data Processing Independent Consultant's Exchange (DICE)
http://www.dice.com

DataMasters
http://www.datamasters.com

DataWay Resources
http://www.csn.net/dataway/

David Aplin and Associates (Canada)
http://www.tgx.com/aplin/

Dawson & Dawson Consultants
http://www.dawson-dawson.com

DC's Résumé Net
http://www.resume.net/

DC's Site for On-Line Résumés
http://www.intr.net/

de Recat & Associates
http://www.derecat.com/

De Carrierebank (Netherlands)
http://www.carrierebank.nl

De Intermediair Online (Netherlands)
http://www.vnu.com/intermediair/homepage.html

Decisive Quest
http://www.decisivequest.com

Defense Nuclear Facilities Safety Board
gopher://nic.sura.net:7070/11/vacancy

Definitive Internet Career Guide <The>
http://phoenix.placement.oakland.edu/career/internet.htm

DEI Staffing
http://www.calldei.com/

Deja News
http://www.dejanews.com

Delphi
http://www.delphi.com

Delphi Subscriber Web Pages
http://people.delphi.com

Department of Education and Employment (UK)
http://www.open.gov.uk/dfee/dfeehome.htm

Department of Employment
http://161.7.163.2/

Department of Employment, Idaho
http://www.doe.state.id.us/

Department of Employment, Massachusetts Job Search
http://ma.jobsearch.org/

Department of Employment, New Jersey Job Search
http://nj.jobsearch.org/

Department of Employment, Wyoming
http://wyjobs.state.wy.us/

Department of Employment and Training, Rhode Island
http://www.det.state.ri.us/

Department of Employment Relations, Wisconsin
http://badger.state.wi.us:70/1/

Department of Employment Security, Utah
http://udesb.state.ut.us/

Department of Employment Security, Tennessee
http://www.state.tn.us/other/empsec/tdeshome.htm

Department of Energy (DOE)
http://www.em.doe.gov/emnet1i.html

Department of Industry, Labor and Human Relations, Wisconsin
Employment Bureau
http://badger.state.wi.us/agencies/dilhr/

Department of Instructional Technologies, San Francisco State
University
http://www.itec.sfsu.edu/

Department of Labor
http://www.dol.gov/

Department of Labor (Louisiana)
http://www.state.la.us/

Department of Labor, Occupational Safety and Health
Administration (OSHA)
http://www.osha.gov/

Department of Library Services: Sailor
http://sailor.lib.md.us/

Department of Mathematics University of Toronto
http://www.math.toronto.edu/jobs/

Department of the Interior Automated Vacancy Announcement
System (AVADS)
http://www.usgs.gov/doi/avads/index.html

DesignSphere Online
http://www.dsphere.net/jobs.html

Development Dimensions International
http://ddiworld.com/index.html

Development Systems
http://www.webcreations.com/dsi/

DigiBook
http://www.cybercomm.net/~digibook

Direct Marketing World Job Center
*http://mainsail.com/cgi/perl/5.001/;erl.exe/job10.ini*0?/httpd/ht
docs/cgi/job10/job10.pl*
http://www.dmworld.com http://mainsail.com/jobs.html

Directory (Australia) <The>
http://www.thedirectory.aone.net.au/page8.htm

Directory: Global Academic Recruiters <The>
http://www.thedirectory.aone.net.au/

Directory of Electronic Journals, Newsletters, and Academic
Discussions Lists (Association of Research Libraries)
gopher://arl.cni.org, select Scholarly Communication

Disability Services Careers On-Line
http://www.disserv.stu.umn.edu/TC/Grants/COL/

DisInformation
http://www.disinfo.com/

Diverse Employment Industries
http://www.cfonline.com/cli/jobs/diverse/diverse.htm

DOC on the Web
http://www.webdoc.com/homepage.html

Donnington Associates (UK)
http://www.i-way.co.uk/donnington/

Double Dutch Enterprises
http://www.hia.net/pdesmidt/Physicaltherapy.htm

Doughty Group Ltd (New Zealand) <The>
http://www.jobnetnz.co.nz/Agencies/doughty.html

Do's and Don'ts of Web Design
http://millkern.com/do-dont.html

DP Independent Consultants Exchange
http://www.dice.dlinc.com:8181/

DPP International Ltd (UK)
http://194.128.198.201/dpp/

Drake University Summer Jos
http://www.drake.edu/stulife/carsum.html

Drexel University Résumés
http://cmc.www.drexel.edu/

DSR Diversity Search and Recruitment
http://www.telecomsearch.com/

Dun and Bradstreet on Finding a Job
http://www.dbisna.com/dbis/jobs/vjobhunt.htm

Duncan and Ryan Associates (New Zealand)
http://www.jobnetnz.co.nz/Agencies/Duncan-Ryan.html

DXI Corporation, Atlanta, GA
http://isotropic.com/dxicorp/dxihome.html

Dynamic HR Solutions
http://www.dynamichr.com

E-mail Addresses
http://www.cis.ohio-state.edu/hypertext/faq/usenet/finding-addresses/faq.html
http://kaml1.csi.uottawa.ca:3000/how-to-email.html
ftp://ftp.qucis.queensu.ca/pub/dalamb/college-email/college.html
http://www.qucis.queensu.ca/FAQs/email/college.html
http://www.whowhere.com/
http://www.four11.com/
http://www.bigbook.com/

E.R. States & Associates
http://www.ceo-online.com/erstates

E-Span
http://www.espan.com

EagleView
http://www.eagleview.com

EagleVisions National Directory of Emergency Services
http://www.policejobs.com

EarthWatch
http://www.earthwatch.org/t/Temployment.html

Easynet Job-Centre (The Virtual Job Centre)
http://www.cyberiacafe.net/jobs/

Eclectic International Executive Search
http://www.cyber.nl/eclectic/

Economists (Europe)
http://maynard.ww.tu-berlin.de/e-joe/

EDGAR at the SEC
http://www.sec.gov

EDGAR Development Project, NYU Stern School of Business
http://edgar.stern.nyu.edu

Editor and Publisher Interactive
http://www.mediainfo.com/ephome/class/classhtm/class.htm

EDNET Job Net for Educators
http://pages.prodigy.com/CA/luca52a/bagley.html

EDP Contract Services
http://edpcs.com/

EDP Staffing Services, Inc.
http://www.edpstaffing.com/index.html

EDphysician
http://www.edphysician.com/

Educatie Emancipatie Gehandicapte Arbeidskrachten
http://www.eega.nl/

Education & Career Center <The>
http://www.petersons.com

Education Gazette (New Zealand)
http://www.learningmedia.co.nz/egissues/eglatest/eg_conts.htm

Education Jobs Page
http://www.nationjob.com/education

EduNetCom: Education Employment
http://www.ccnet.com/~pstrader/

Eduplus Management Group Inc.
http://www.eduplus.ca/

EE-Link: The Environmental Education Web Server
http://www.nceet.snre.umich.edu/jobs.html
gopher://nceet.snre.umich.edu/11/networking/

EgoSearch (Belgium)
http://www.interpac.be/egosearch/welcome.html

Elan Computing (UK)
http://www.elan.co.uk/

Electric Library
http://www2.elibrary.com/id/2525/search.cgi

Electronic Industries Association
http://www.eia.org/norm.htm

Electronic Job Match International
http://www.ejs@tnc.com/

Electronic Labor Exchange (Canada)
http://ele.ingenia.com/

Elite Permanent and Contract Recruitment Agency (UK)
http://www.elite-cs.co.uk/elite/

Elk Grove Unified School District
http://www.egusd.k12.ca.us/webdocs/claspost.htm

EML BNB Group
http://mmserve.com/eml-bnb

Emory University/Career Paradise
http://www.emory.edu/

EMPLOI @
http://www.login.net/emploi-a/public_html/

Employease Benefits Network
http://www.eease.com/novaindex.html

Employee Services Inc.
http://www.cris.com/~Esinc/

Employment and Business Information
http://www.pan.ci.seattle.wa.us/

Employment and Business Opportunities Online
http://www.ebom.com/

Employment and Training Agencies
http://bcn.boulder.co.us/employment/agencies.html

Employment Centre (Bermuda Government Careers Opportunities)
http://www.bermudasun.org/bdasun/employment.html

Employment Channel
http://www.employ.com

Employment Counseling Services, Inc.
http://amsquare.com/america/amerway/ajob4u/

Employment Depot
http://www.employmentdepot.com/

Employment Detective
http://netside.com/~ccofcola/adpages/employdt.html

Employment Development Department
http://wwwedd.cahwnet.gov/

Employment Edge
http://sensemedia.net/employment.edge

Employment Network People Bank
http://194.73.171.131/pbank/owa/pbk06w00.main

Employment News
http://www.ftn.net/

Employment Online
http://www.nando.net/classads/employment/

Employment Opportunities
http://education.indiana.edu/ist/students/jobs/joblink.html

Employment Opportunities in Australia
http://employment.com.au/index.html

Employment Opportunities in India
http://www.webpage.com/hindu/960210/10/10hdline.html

Employment Opportunities in New York City
http://www.panix.com/clay/nyc/

Employment Opportunities in Water Resources
http://www.uwin.siu.edu/announce/jobs/

Employment Opportunities in Women's Studies and Feminism
gopher://gopher.inform.umd.edu:70/11/EdRes/Topic/Womens Studies/Employment

Employment Post
http://world.net/emp-post/welcome.html

employment.net.au (Australia)
http://www.employment.net.au/

Energys Technical Services Ltd (UK)
http://www.energys.co.uk/energys/

ENews
http://www.sumnet.com/enews

Engine Room (UK and Europe) <The>, iWEB
http://www.iweb.co.uk/iwsearch.html

Engineering Job Source <The>
http://www.wwnet.com/~engineer/

Engineering/Manufacturing Jobs Page
http://www.nationjob.com/engineering

Engineering News Record
http://www.enr.com/find/onnet.htm

Engineering Specific Career Advisory Problem-Solving Environment <The>
http://fairway.ecn.purdue.edu/ESCAPE/

Entertainment Recruiting Network
http://www.showbizjobs.com/middle.htm

Entry-Level Job Seeker Assistant <The>
http://members.aol.com/dylander/jobhome.html

Envirobiz International Environmental Information Network
http://www.envirobiz.com/

Environmental Careers Organization <The>
http://www.eco.org

Environmental Protection Agency
http://www.epa.gov/epahome/Jobs.html

EOP's Career Center for Workforce Diversity
http://www.eop.com/

EPage Classifieds
http://www.ep.com

EPPA
http://rampages.onramp.net/~eppa

Equipment Leasing Association OnLine
http://www.elaonline.com

eRésumés & Resources
http://www.resumelink.com

ERIC
http://ericir.syr.edu/About/

ERIC Clearinghouse on Assessment and Evaluation
gopher://vmsgopher.cua.edu/11gopher_root_eric_ae%3a%5b jobs%5d

Erickson & Associates
http://www.nursesearch.com

ESO European Southern Observatory (Germany)
http://www.eso.org/announcements.html

Eurojobs On-line Belgium
http://www.belganet.be/belganet/jobs/

Eurolink Group PLC (UK)
http://www.eurolinkgroup.plc.uk/

Europages—The European Business Directory
http://www.europages.com/

European Bioinformatics Institute Career Connection
http://www.ebi.ac.uk/htbin/biojobs.pl

European Centre for Research and Advanced Training in Scientific Computation (CERFACS)
http://www.cerfacs.fr/admin/vacteams.html

European Molecular Biology Laboratory, Heidelberg, Germany
http://www.embl-heidelberg.de/ExternalInfo/jobs/

European Society of Vascular Surgery
http://www.et.aarhus.ih.dk/~esvs/jobs.html

Eustis Police Department
http://www.sundial.net/~galaxy/emp.html

Excellence in Consulting
http://www.exic.com/eichome.html

Excite
http://www.excite.com

Exec-U-Net
http://www.execunet.com

ExeCon
http://www.execonweb.com

Executive Access
http://www.hk.net/~eal/index.html

Executive BioSearch
http://www.scientificjobs.com/

Executive Recruitment Services (UK)
http://www.ers.co.uk/ers/

Executive Search Consultants
http://www.escinc.com/eschome.html

Executive Taskforce
http://exectask.co.nz/

Experience On Demand
http://www.experienceondemand.com/

Expertel Consultants Ltd (UK)
http://www.pncl.co.uk/expertel/

Extreme Résumé Drop
http://www.mainquad.com/theQuad/wich/introPages/lo/erd.html

Faculty Positions in Computer Science
http://www.cs.cmu.edu/afs/cs.cmu.edu/user/burks/www/faculty.html

Fairfax JobMarket (Australia)
http://www.market.fairfax.com.au/bin/iaquery?NS-use-frames=0&NS-search-pat=/Fairfax/jobs/NS-query.pat

FASEB Careers Online
http://www.faseb.org/careers/

Fashion Exchange
http://fashionexch.com/

FCF
http://www.gnatnet.net/~fcfjobs

FDSI's Job Center
http://www.fdsi-cons.com/

Federal Funded Research in the US
http://medoc.gdb.org/best/fed-fund.html

Federal Information Exchange (FEDIX)
http://web.fie.com/htdoc/fed/all/any/any/menu/any/index.htm

Federal Jobs Central
http://www.fedjobs.com/

Federal Jobs Database from NACE
http://www.jobweb.org/fedjobsr.htm

FEDnet Foundation for Enterprise Development
http://www.fed.org/

Fellowship Office
http://fellowships.nas.edu/index.html

Fenwick Partners
http://www.fenwickpartners.com/

Fermi National Accelerator Laboratory
http://www.fnal.gov/employ.html

Film, TV, & Commercial Employment Network <The>
http://www.employnow.com

FinanceNet
http://www.financenet.gov/wwwlib5.htm#employ

Financial Job Opportunities (Business Job Finder)
http://www.cob.ohio-state.edu/dept/fin/osujobs.htm

Finding and Getting a Job
http://edie.cprost.sfu.ca/~gophers/find.html

finishing.com's Help-Wanted
http://www.finishing.com/Directory/wanted.html

Fitzroy Undergraduate Research in Biology
http://firstmarket.com/fitzroy/

Flavell Divett International (UK)
http://www.mistral.co.uk/fdi/

Florida School-to-Work
http://fcn.state.fl.us/flstw

Florida Sentinal
http://www.chicago.tribune.com/career/sentinel_ads.html

Florida State University
http://www.fsu.edu/Jobs.html

Focus International Career Services
http://www.unige.ch/focus/

Fogarty and Associates
http://www.fogarty.com/

Food and Drug Packaging
http://www.fdp.com

Foothill-De Anza Community College District
http://www.fhda.edu/district/hr/employment.html

Forbes Ltd. (UK)
http://194.128.198.201/forbes/

Foreign Language Listings
http://condor.stcloud.msus.edu:20020/careerannounce.html

FOREM Work Information System (Belgium)
http://www.forem.be/

Forest Products Job Board
gopher://mercury.forestry.umn.edu:70/11/fp/job

Forsyth County, Winston-Salem
http://www.co.forsyth.nc.us/

Forty Plus
http://www.hal-pc.org/~sid/40plus.html

Forum Personnel, Inc.
http://www.brainlink.com/

Fournier Transformation (Visual FoxPro Yellow Pages)
http://www.transformation.com/

Franklin Search Group
http://www.medmarket.com/tenants/fsg/

Freelance Access
http://www.freelanceaccess.com/

Freenets and Bulletin Boards
gopher://acs.eku.edu:70/, Select: *Explore the Internet*, Select: *FreeNets* or *Bulletin Boards*

Freenets via the University of Colorado, Boulder
gopher://gopher.Colorado.EDU/
Gophers (by subject)

Fundraising and Nonprofit Organizations
http://www.philanthropy-journal.org

Future Access Employment Guide
http://futureaccess.com:80/employ.html

Future Med
http://ourworld.compuserve.com/homepages/futuremed/main.htm

Future Resource Systems, Inc.
http://www.webb.com/future

Galaxy at TradeWave
http://galaxy.einet.net/galaxy.html

Gemini Personnel Ltd.
http://www.glink.net.hk:80/~gemini/

GEnie
http://www.genie.com

Geology Job Listings
http://diamond.ge.ic.ac.uk/careers/

Georgia Job Bank, Georgia JobBank
http://www.mindspring.com/~exchange/jobbank/ga/jobs.html

Georgia, State of
http://www.State.Ga.US/SMS/

Georgia State University Career Services, Job Opportunity Bulletin
http://www.gsu.edu/dept/admin/plc/homepg4.html

Georgia Tech Career Services
http://www.gatech.edu/career

GeoScience Careers
http://www.science.uwaterloo.ca/earth/geoscience/table1.html

GeoSearch
http://www.geosearch.com/

GeoWeb for GIS/GPS/RS
http://www.ggrweb.com

Get a Job!
http://www.getajob.com

Get to Work
http://global.net.au/~sasman/

GetNet International Employment
http://www.getnet.com/endeavor/

Getting a Job
http://www.americanexpress.com/student/moneypit/getjob/get ajob.html

Getting Past Go: A Survival Guide for College
http://www.lattanze.loyola.edu:80/mongen/home.html

Gintic Institute of Manufacturing Technology
http://www.gintic.ntu.ac.sg:8000/jobs.html

GIS Jobs Clearinghouse, University of Minnesota, Forestry, Remote Sensing Lab
http://www.gis.umn.edu/rsgisinfo/jobs.html

Global Environmental Management Initiative (GEMI)
http://www.gemi.org/

Global Job Services
http://www.indirect.com/www/dtomczyk/

Global Marketing Strategies
http://www.ioa.com/home/kelbell/

Global Medical Search
http://www.moran.com/gms

Global Net's Latin American Career Center (Bolsa de Trabajo Global Net)
http://www.bolsadetrabajo.com

Global Technical Recruitment
http://ourworld.compuserve.com:80/homepages/global_technical _recruit/

Global White Pages
http://www.bigfoot.com/

GLOBEnet Canada
http://www.theglobeandmail.com/

GO2: Guardian OnLine Jobs
http://www.guardian.co.uk/jobs/jobs.html

Good Works
http://www.essential.org/goodworks/

Gopher Jewels Mirror Sites
http://galaxy.einet.net/gopher/gopher.html
http://galaxy.einet.net/GJ/index.html
gopher://cwis.usc.edu/11/Other_Gophers_and_Information_ Resources/ Gophers_by_Subject/Gopher_Jewels
gopher://info.monash.edu.au/11/Other/sources/Gopher_Jewels
gopher://gopher.technion.ac.il/11/Other_gophers/Gopher-Jewels

Gordon Library Home Page, Worcester Polytechnic Institute
http://www.WPI.EDU/Academics/IMS/Library/

GraduNet (UK)
http://www.gradunet.co.uk/

Grants & Fellowships
http://www.sas.upenn.edu/African_Studies/Grants/menu_ Grants.html

GrantsWeb
http://web.fie.com/cws/sra/resource.htm

GrapeVine, Grapevine Network
http://job.index.com/

Graphic and Sound Files for Web Pages
http://www.yahoo.com/Computers_and_Internet/Internet/World _Wide_ Web/Programming/Icons/
http://www.octagamm.com/boutique/mainball.htm
http://www.clark.net/pub/evins/Icons/
http://www.iconbazaar.com
http://www.rainfrog.com/webart/
http://www.clever.net/gld
http://www.cbil.vcu.edu:8080/gifs/bullet.html
http://www.mccannas.com/
http://www.geocities.com/Heartland/1448/main.htm
http://www.geocities.com/Heartland/1448/iconz_links.htm
http://www.yahoo.com/Computers_and_Internet/Internet/World _Wide_ Web/Page_Design_and_Layout/Backgrounds/
http://www.aimnet.com/~bosman/TextureStation_Lobby.htm
http://www.netscape.com/assist/net_sites/bg/backgrounds.html
http://www.sonic.net/~lberlin/new/3dnscape.html
http://www.ecn.net.au/~iain/htextures/
http://www.netcreations.com/patternland/index.html
http://www.execpc.com/~jeffo/webdes/bckgrnd2.html
http://wuarchive.wustl.edu/multimedia/images/
http://www.eit.com/web/gopher.icons/gopher.html
http://www.n-vision.com/
http://www.barrysclipart.com
http://www.acy.digex.net/~infomart/clipart/
http://www.teleport.com/~eidos/dtpij/clipart.html
http://www.caboodles.com
http://www.jpl.nasa.gov/archive/images.html
http://www.life.uiuc.edu/Entomology/insectgifs.html
http://www.northcoast.com/savetz/pd/pd.html
http://www.yahoo.com/Computers_and_Internet/Multimedia/ Pictures/
http://www.yahoo.com/Computers_and_Internet/Graphics/
http://www.yahoo.com/Arts/Computer_Generated/
http://www.pbrc.hawaii.edu/~kunkel/
http://www.yahoo.com/Computers_and_Internet/Multimedia/ Sound/
http://www.excite.com/Subject/Computing/Internet/Net_Video _And_Audio/ s-index.h.html
http://www.tvtrecords.com/tvbytes

Graphic Arts Marketing Associates
http://members.aol.com/GRaphicama

Graphics and Desktop Publishing
http://www.teleport.com

Greater Columbus Freenet
gopher://gizmo.freenet.columbus.oh.us

Grinwis & Partners (Netherlands)
http://www.iway.nl/grinwis/

Guide to Working Overseas
http://www.magi.com/~issi/

GWeb, An Electronic Trade Journal For Computer Animators
http://www.gweb.org/

H.E.A.R.T. Career Connection's On-Line Information System
http://www.career.com/PUB/searchmenu.html

H.E.C. Career Center
http://www.hec-group.com

H.L. Yoh
http://www.hlyoh.com/

Hallahan & Associates
http://www.hallahan.com

Hamilton Jones & Koller (Australia)
http://www.hjk.com.au/

Harcourt and Associates
http://www.comcept.ab.ca/harcourt/

Harrison Willis Group (UK)
http://194.128.198.201/hwgroup/main.html

Haskins & Roache
http://ourworld.compuserve.com/homepages/James_Haskins/haskins.htm

Hawaii, State of
http://www.aloha.net/~edpso/

HeadHunt Korea
http://www.headhunt.co.kr

Health Search Canada
http://healthsearch.ca/

Healthcare Consultants Pharmacy Staffing
http://rxrelief.com

HealthCare International, L.L.C.
http://www.HealthCare-Int.com/career_ops.html

HealthLine Management, Inc. (HMI)
http://www.hmistl.com/

HealthStaf Medical Services
http://www.healthstaf.com

HEC Group
http://hec-group.com

HEL Human Enterprises Limited
http://www.demon.co.uk/hument/

Help Wanted.Com, YSS Inc.
http://www.helpwanted.com/career.html

Hennepin County (Minnesota)
http://www.co.hennepin.mn.us/wjobs.html

Herpetology Job Listings
http://xtal200.harvard.edu:8000/herp/general/jobs/jobs.html

HIGH Technology Careers Magazine
http://www.hightechcareers.com/

Hiring Assistant and Placements Program
http://www.sonic.net/~richw/zjobapps.html#top

Hiring Employers
http://phoenix.placement.oakland.edu/career/career.htm

History of Science Society
http://weber.u.washington.edu/~hssexec/hss_jobs.html

HiTechCareers, HiTech Careers
http://www.hitechcareer.com/hitech

HKA CompuSearch
http://www.hkacompusearch.com

Hobsons Publishing PLC (UK)
http://www.hobsons.co.uk/

Home Page Background Images
http://www.ncsa.uiuc.edu/SDG/Software/WinMosaic/Backgrnd/

Home Page Development Tools
http://mosaic.mcom.com/home/manual_docs/graphics.html

Hong Kong Jobs
http://www.hkjobs.com

Hong Kong Standard
http://www.hkstandard.com/online/job/hksjob.htm

Hoover's Online
http://www.hoovers.com/

Hornberger Management Company
http://www.building.org/sponsors/hmc/

Hospital Web
http://neuro-www.mgh.harvard.edu/hospitalweb.nclk

Hospitality Net, Hospitality Industry Job Exchange
http://www.hospitalitynet.nl/job/home.htm

HotBot
http://www.hotbot.com/

Hotel Jobs
http://www.webcom.com/jaeg/welcome.html

Hotflash Jobs
http://iquest.com/~ntes/jobslist.html

HotJobs
http://www.hotjobs.com

Houston Advanced Research Center
http://www.harc.edu/jobs.html

Houston Chronicle Interactive, Houston Chronicle
http://classifieds.astranet.com/HCI/bin/nclassy.x/hciBHM06

Houston Employment Opportunities
http://www.wt.net/cgi/bb/bbb.pl?hccom_job

Howard Systems International
http://www.howardsystems.com

HR Headquarters
http://www.hrhq.com/

HR World
http://www.hrworld.com

HRCOMM
http://ccnet.com/hrcomm/

HRNEWS Job Openings
http://www.shrm.org/jobs/

HTML Document Style Guide
http://www.che.ufl.edu/help/style1/index.html

HTML Files—How to Write
http://www.ucc.ie/info/net/htmldoc.html

HTML Information
http://www.infoseek.com/Home?page=Home.html&sv=N2

HTML Pointers from Netscape
http://home.netscape.com/assist/net_sites/index.html

HTML Quick Reference Guide and Codes
http://www.cc.ukans.edu/info/HTML_quick.html

HTML Specifications
http://www.w3.org/hypertext/WWW/MarkUp/MarkUp.html

HTML Style Guide Index
http://www.stars.com/Vlib/Providers/Style.html

HTML Tip Sheet on Design Dos and Don'ts
http://www.compuserve.com/index/tipsheet.html

HTML—Composing
  http://www.cs.cmu.edu/afs/cs.cmu.edu/Web/People/tilt/cgh/

HTML—Introduction
  http://members.aol.com/htmlguru/about_html.html

HTML—W3C's Style Guide to Online Hypertext
  http://www.w3.org/hypertext/WWW/Provider/Style/Introduction
  .html

HTML—Yale Style Manual
  http://info.med.yale.edu/caim/StyleManual_Top.HTML

Human Element Network
  http://mindlink.net/vci/thehp.htm

Human Resource Store <The>
  http://www.mcs.com/~jmruh

Human Resources Development Canada Metro Toronto HRDC Job
Board
  http://www.the-wire.com/hrdc/jobs.html

Hummer Winblad Venture Partners
  http://www.humwin.com

Hunterskil (UK), Hunterskil Howard (UK)
  http://194.128.198.201/hhplc/

Huntington Group's Career Network <The>, CareerWeb
  http://sgx.com/cw/

Hytelnet, HYTELNET
  http://galaxy.einet.net/hytelnet/HYTELNET.html

I.T. Staffing (Canada)
  http://www.itstaff.com/

Ian Martin Limited
  http://www.iml.com

IBA reSearch
  http://web.wingsbbs.com/ibaresearch/

IBM InfoMarket
  http://www.informarket.ibm.com/

IBNIX Recruitment (UK)
  http://www.ibnix.co.uk/

Idaho and Montana Online Employment
  http://amsquare.com/america/

Idaho Department of Employment, Idaho Jobs
  http://www.doe.state.id.us/occmain.htm

IDL Solutions
  http://www.idl.com/

IEEE Computer Society
  http://www.computer.org/pubs/computer/career/career.htm

IEEE, Institute of Electrical and Electronic Engineers Job Bank
  http://www.ieee.org/jobs.html

IEEE, University of Massachusetts Student Branch
  http://www.ecs.umass.edu/

Impact Online
  http://www.impactonline.org/

Index of Delaware Web Sites from Delaware Technical and
Community College
  http://www.dtcc.edu/delaware/

Index of Native American Resources on the Internet
  http://www.hanksville.phast.umass.edu/misc.NAresources.html

India Connect's Job Classified
  http://www.indiaconnect.com/classadv/svacant.htm

Indiana Jobs
  http://www.inetdirect.net/

Indiana State Department of Personnel
  http://www.state.in.us/acin/personnel/index.html

Indiana University School of Public and Environmental Affairs
Internships
  http://www.indiana.edu/~speacare/intern.html

Industry Canada
  http://info.ic.gc.ca/ic-data/ic-eng.html

IndustryNet, Industry Net Career Opportunities
  http://www.industry.net/c/mn/_co

Info-Mine
  http://www.info-mine.com/

InfoLink HIRE
  http://cystop.com/home-links.htm

INFONET
  http://www.info.net/

Infonet's Classifieds
  http://www.infonetwww.com/clfdjo.htm

Informatics Search Group
  http://www.isgjobs.com

Information Center <The>
  http://greatinfo.com/

Information Network of Kansas
  http://www.ink.org

Information Professional Resource
  http://www.nrv.net/~ipr/

Information Science and Telecommunications Placement
  http://www2.lis.pitt.edu/~sochats/placement.html

Information Technology Institute
  http://www.iti.gov.sg/iti_info/job/job.html

Information Technology Talent Association, LLC
  http://www.it-ta.com/

InfoSeek
  http://www.infoseek.com

InfoServ Technologies
  http://members.aol.com/tampacs/infoserv.htm

Infotech
  http://www.infotech.co.nz

InfoTech Placement Services Group
  http://www.itweb.com/infotec/index.html

InJersey
  http://www.injersey.com

InstaMatch Résumé Database
  http://www.instamatch.com

Institut fur Arbeitswirtschaft und Organisation (Germany)
  http://www.iao.fhg.de/Public/hiwi/OVERVIEW-en.html

Institute for Operations Research and Management Science
(INFORMS)
  http://www.informs.org/JPS/index.html

Institute of Fiscal Studies, UK
  http://www1.ifs.org.uk/ifsinfo/jobs/index.htm

Institute of Molecular Agrobiology (Singapore)
  http://www.nus.sg/NUSinfo/Appoint/IMA.html

Institute of Molecular Biology (Germany), Department of Structural
Biology & Crystallography IMB Jena
  http://www.imb-jena.de/www_sbx/sbxjobs.html

Institution of Electrical Engineers
  http://www.iee.org.uk:80/

Instructional Technology Jobs, Indiana University, Bloomington
http://education.indiana.edu/ist/students/jobs/joblink.html

Insurance Career Center
http://www.connectyou.com:80/talent/

Integral Technologies, Inc.
http://www.integralIT.com

Integrated Computer Solutions
http://www.ics.com/Jobs/

Integrity Center, Inc. <The>
http://www.integctr.com/

Intellimatch On-Line Career Services
http://www.intellimatch.com/intellimatch/

Inter-Links Employment Resources
http://www.nova.edu/Inter-Links/employment.html

Interactive Recruitment Limited (UK)
http://194.128.198.201/inter-active/

Internal Revenue Service
http://www.irs.ustreas.gov/prod/

International Academic Job Market
http://www.camrev.com.au/share/jobs.html

International Agribusiness Internship Center
http://www.usu.edu/

International Committee of the Red Cross (Switzerland)
http://www.icrc.ch/icrcnews/37e6.htm

International Fund for Agricultural Development (Italy)
http://www.unicc.org/ifad/vac395en.html

International Home Workers Association <The>
http://www.homeworkers.com/

International Interactive Communications Society (IICS), New York Chapter
http://www.iicsny.org/jobs/

International Internship Directory
gopher://gopher.clemson.edu/

International Job Centers
http://members.tripod.com/~IJC/index.html

International Medical Placement, Ltd.
http://www.niagara.com/

International Service Agencies
http://www.charity.org/

International Telecommunications Union (Switzerland)
http://www.itu.ch/itudoc/gs/vacancy.html

International Teleproduction Society
http://www.itsnet.org/jobs.html

Internet Business Directory, Résumé Section
http://ibd.ar.com/Resume

Internet Career Connection (Help Wanted USA)
http://iccweb.com

Internet Career Exchange
http://www2.softechcorp.com/ice/ice.htm

Internet Employment Network
gopher://gopher.careers.com/

Internet Fashion Exchange
http://www.fashionexch.com/

Internet Guide to Women's Resources
http://mevard.www.media.mit.edu/people/mevvard/women.html

Internet Job Information Center
http://tvp.com/vpjic.html

Internet Job Locator <The>
http://www.joblocator.com/jobs/

Internet Mall <The>
http://www.internet-mall.com/

Internet Non-Profit Center: Home to Donors and Volunteers
http://www.nonprofits.org/

Internet Professional Association (IPA)
http://www.ipa.com/

Internet Service Providers
http://www.yahoo.com/Business_and_Economy/Companies/Internet_Service_Providers/Internet_Access_Providers/
http://thelist/iworld.com/

Internet-Solutions.Com
http://www.internet-solutions.com/

Internet Vacature Overzicht (Netherlands)
http://www.iway.nl/intervac/

Internship Director
http://www.snpa.org/snpa/web/home.html

Internships U.S.A.
http://www.collegegrad.com/internships

Interpac Belgium
http://www.interpac.be/jobs.html

Interskill Services S.A.
http://www.interskill.ch/

INTERTECH Computer Consultants (UK)
http://www.intertech.co.uk/

InterView
http://www.sbu.ac.uk/home/career.html

Intrinsica Systems (UK)
http://www.intrinsica.co.uk/

Iowa Jobs Information from the Department of Employment Services (DES)
http://www.state.ia.us/jobs/index.html

IPC Technologies
http://www.ipctech.com/employment.htm

Irish and Associates
http://www.frontiernet.net/~wairish

Irish Job Vacancies Page <The>
http://www.exp.ie/

IS World Net
http://www.pitt.edu/~malhotra/isworld/postavai.htm

ISOCOR
http://www.isocor.com/

IT Jobs
http://www.internet-solutions.com/itjobs.htm

IT Link Ltd (UK)
http://www.itlink.co.uk/

It's My Future
http://www.myfuture.com/

ITJobSearch (UK)
http://www.itjobsearch.com/

ITTA Recruiter Services
http://www.it-ta.com/rcselect.htm

IUPUI Integrated Technologies
gopher://INDYCMS.IUPUI.EDU/11/IUPUI%20Information%20Sources/Staff%20Job%20Openings

J-JOBS DIGEST: Journalism Jobs and Internships
gopher://blick.journ.latech.edu

J. Arthur Group
http://www.jarthurgroup.com/

J. B. Groner Executive Search, Inc.
http://www.execjobsearch.com/

J. Boragine & Associates
http://www.jboragine.com/

J. D. Heinz & Associates
http://www.staffing.net/misnet.htm

J. Edgar & Associates Inc.
http://www.the-wire.com/careers/

J. Robert Scott, Executive Search
http://j-robert-scott.com/

Jacobson Associates
http://www.jacobson-associates.com/

Jaeger's Interactive Career Center
http://www.jaegerinc.com

James Duncan & Associates (UK)
http://www.jda-uk.co.uk/

Java Scripts
http://java.sun.com/

Jay Tracey Associates
http://amsquare.com/america/search1.html

Jenrick-CPI Nederland (Netherlands)
http://www.jenrick.nl/

Jim Sease's Home Page
http://www.sease.com/

JIS Home Page
http://www.esc.state.nc.us/jis/index.html

JKL Enterprises, Inc
http://www.jklenterprises.com

Job Access Limited (Hong Kong)
http://www.hk.net/~jal/

Job Accommodation Network
http://janweb.icdi.wvu.edu/

Job Banker <The>
http://www.nmaa.org/jobbank.htm

Job Board
http://wfscnet.tamu.edu:80/jobs.html

Job Connection <The>
http://www.jobconnection.com/

JOB DIRECT (Austria)
http://www.job-direct.co.at/job-direct/

Job Hotlines for Washington
http://www.gspa.washington.edu/Career/hotlines_welcome.html

Job Hunt: On-Line Job Meta.List
http://www.job-hunt.org

Job Listing at tamu.edu, Job Opportunities, JOBS
http://ageninfo.tamu.edu/jobs.html

Job Listings in Academia
http://volvo.gslis.utexas.edu/~acadres/jla.html

Job-Net <The> (Italy)
http://www.webcom.com/~jobnet/

Job Net Work: Employment Made Simple <The>
http://www.conquest-prod.com/jobnetwrk/main.html#return

Job Openings in Newspaper New Media (and Related Fields)
http://www.mediainfo.com/

Job Opportunities (in U.S. and Europe)
http://www.sas.upenn.edu/African_Studies/Jobs_US/menu_Jobs_US.html

Job Opportunities in Entomology
http://www.colostate.edu/Depts/Entomology/jobs/jobs.html

Job Search
http://www.ventura.com/jsearch/jshome1.html

Job Search and Employment Opportunities: Best Bets from the Net
http://asa.ugl.lib.umich.edu/chdocs/employment/

Job Search Materials for Engineers
http://www.englib.cornell.edu/

Job Search Techniques
http://www.jobtrak.com/jobsearch_docs/index.html

Job Searching in Africa
http://www.sas.upenn.edu/African_Studies/Home_Page/menu_job_srch.html

Job SearchUK
http://WWW.JOBSEARCH.CO.UK/

Job Seekers Edging the Competition
http://bcn.boulder.co.us/business/

Job Square
http://www.euro.net/InfoCraft/

Job Tailor, JOBTAILOR Employment Online Service
http://www.205.181.25.27

Job Vacancies Outside of Academe
http://chronicle.merit.edu/

Job.net from Computer Contractor
http://www.vnu.co.uk/:81/ip_user/owa/register.main?c_mag_id=

JobBank USA
http://www.jobbankusa.com

JobCenter
http://www.jobcenter.com/

JobFind
http://www.dlcwest.com/~comdata/jobfind.htm

JobIndex
http://www.danielsen.com/jobs/

Jobline, School of Library Science and Instructional Technology
http://www.scsu-cs.ctstateu.edu/library/jobline.html

JobLink Mental Health Net
http://www.cmhc.com/wwwboard/bb2.htm

JobLynx Connect With Your Next Career
http://joblynx.com

JobNet
http://www.westga.edu/~coop/

JobNet (Netherlands)
http://www.jobnet.nl/

JobNet & OnLine Opportunities
http://www.jobnet.com

JobNet NZ <The>
http://www.jobnetnz.co.nz/

JobNet-SanDiego
http://www.jobopportunities.com/

JOBNET (Hong Kong)
http://kwuntong.hk.super.net/~websol/jobnet.htm

JobPoint Connection
http://www.jobpoint.com/jpc

Jobs & Adverts Online GmbH (in German)
http://www.jobs.adverts.de/

Jobs & Career (Belgium)
http://www.jobs-career.be/

Jobs & Careers Online
http://www.servonet.com/jobs

Jobs and Career Information
gopher://main.morris.org/11gopher_root%3a%5b_jobs%5d

Jobs and Employment
gopher://academic.cc.colorado.edu/11%5b_library._data.jobs %5d

Jobs for WWW Developers
http://www.charm.net/

Jobs in Atomic and Plasma Physics
http://plasma-gate.weizmann.ac.il/

Jobs in Consulting
http://www.cob.ohio-state.edu/dept/fin/

Jobs in Finance for MBAs
http://www.cob.ohio-state.edu:80/dept/fin/osujob.htm

Jobs in Mathematics
http://www.cs.dartmouth.edu/~gdavis/policy/jobmarket.html

Jobs In Horticulture
http://www.aksi.net/agquest/

Jobs Links
http://cip.physik.uni-wuerzburg.de/job.html

Jobs Northwest
http://www.jobsnorthwest.com/

Jobs Offered (UK)
http://www.futurenet.co.uk/Ads/jobs.html

Jobs Online
http://JobsOnLine.com/

Jobs Online (France) (in French only)
http://www.cegos.fr/

JOBS: Vakatures op het Internet
http://www.jobs.nl/

JobSearch: The GSLIS Job Placement Database
http://alexia.lis.uiuc.edu/gslis/research/

JobServe (UK)
http://www.jobserve.com/

Jobsite UK
http://www.jobsite.co.uk/

JobSmart: Résumé Help
http://jobsmart.org/tools/resume/

JobSmart Salary Surveys
http://jobsmart.org/tools/salary/index.htm

JobTrak
http://www.jobtrak.com

JobTree
http://peace.netnation.com/joblink/

Jobware
http://www.jobware.de/

JobWeb
http://www.jobweb.org

JobWeb, Job Choices Guides
http://www.jobweb.org/

JobWeb's Database of U.S. School Districts
http://www.jobweb.org/sdistric.htm

JobWire
http://www.jobweb.org/jobwire.htm

JobZone (Netherlands)
http://valley.interact.nl/jz/

JOM Classifieds
http://www.tms.org/pubs/journals/JOM/classifieds.html

JP Resources
http://www.webscope.com/jp/

Jughead
gopher://liberty.uc.wlu.edu
gopher://marvel.loc.gov

JWEvans & Company
http://www.jwevans.com

JWT Works
http://www.jwtworks.com/

K&F Résumés and Professional Services
http://wyp.net/us/20003740

K3 & Company
http://www.k3k3k3.com/aactest.html

Kaiser Nationwide
http://www.jobpoint.com/jpc

Kansas City Star
http://www.kansascity.com/

Kaplan
http://www.kaplan.com/

Katron
http://www.occ.com/katron/

Kelly Luxford (New Zealand)
http://www.jobnetnz.co.nz/Agencies/Kelly-Luxford.html

Kelly Technical Services
http://www.io.com/~kellysrv/

KENDA Systems, Inc.
http://www.kenda.com/

Kendall & Davis Data Processing Professionals
http://www.fwi.com:80/kd-resources/

Kennison & Associates, Inc.
http://www.kennison.com/

Kentucky Opportunities in State Government
http://www.state.ky.us/nasire/STemployment.html

Kentucky StateSearch
http://www.state.ky.us/nasire/NASIREhome.html

Ketner & Associates
http://www.ketner.com

Keyword Résumé and Fax Service
http://ourworld.compuserve.com/homepages/DeckerServices

KGB Resources (UK)
http://194.128.198.201/kgb/main.html

Kinetic Agency Services
http://www.interlog.com/~kas/

Kingsford-Smith Partnership Ltd (UK)
http://www.kingsford-smith.co.uk/kingsford-smith

Kinko's
http://www.kinkos.com/

KLA Instruments Corporation Employment
http://www.kla.ccom/in-yahoo.htm

Korean Employment Connection
http://www.korean.com/employment.html

KQED, Inc.: Public Broadcasting for Northern California
http://www.kqed.org/fromKQED/HR/menu.html

Kratec Company
http://www.motor-city.com/kratec/

Krislyn Corporation
http://www.krislyn.com/sites/empl.htm

Kunin Associates
http://www.gate.net/~kassoc/index.html?

L.W. Foote Company
http://www.wolfenet.com/~brightn/

Lasers and Electro Optics Society (LEOS)
http://msrc.wvu.edu/leos/LEOSprof/LEOSprof.html

Last Files From the News
http://www.cnam.fr/Images/Usenet/

Law Employment Center
http://www.lawjobs.com/

Law Mall Résumé Listings
http://www.lawmall.com/resumes/resumes.html

Le Recrutement (France)
http://gplc.u-bourgogne.fr:8080/Recrut/Welcome.html

Le Web Cafe Career
http://lewebcafe.com/pages/career.htm

Lee Hecht Harrison
http://www.careerlhh.com

Legal Classifieds
http://www.ljextra.com/classifieds/

Lendmam Groupe <The>
http://www.lendman.com/employers.htm

Lester Associates Job Bureau
http://www.ozemail.com.au:80/~lesters/

Library Jobs and Library Employment: Navigating the Electronic Web
gopher://una.hh.lib.umich.edu:70/00/inetdirsstacks/jobs%3Afenner

Liszt: Directory of E-mail Discussion Groups
http://www.liszt.com

Little Employment Group, Inc. <The>
http://www.netaccess.on.ca/~leg/

Little Nickel Employment Website
http://www2.littlenickel.com/lnwa/info/employment

Livelihood Center
http://www.ingress.com/nyworks

Lockheed Martin Energy Systems
http://www.ornl.gov/mmes-www/MMESemployment.html
http://www.ornl.gov/employment.html

Logan Group, Inc. <The>
http://access.advr.com/~logan/loganttl.htm

Los Angeles Times
http://www.latimes.com/

Los Angeles Urban League
http://www.careermosaic.com/cm/ul/ull.html

Lycos
http://www.lycos.com

Lynx
http://www.lynxinc.com

M. David Lowe Professional Service
http://www.mdlowe.com/

MacTemps
http://www.mactemps.com/

MAGNet's Massachusetts Access to Government Information Server
http://www.magnet.state.ma.us/refshelf.htm#jobs

Mailing List Archive
http://scwww.ucs.indiana.edu/mlarchive/

Maine, State of
http://www.state.me.us/bhr/career/career.htm

Man at Work (Italy)
http://www.vol.it/man_@_work

Management Recruiters International
http://www.mrinet.com/

Management Recruiters International of LA/Encino
http://www.mri-la.com

Management Recruiters of North Canton
http://www.mrnc.com/

Management Recruiters of Portland
http://www.mrportland.com/

Management Recruiters of Silicon Valley
http://www.mrisanjose.com/

Management Recruiters of St. Lucie
http://www.imageplaza.com

Manitoba Advantage
http://www.gov.mb.ca

Manitoba Senior Citizens Employment Opportunities
http://www.mbnet.mb.ca/crm/other/genmb/msch/msch10.html

Manpower
http://www.manpower.com/

Manzey Associates, Inc.
http://www.manzey.com

Marin County Office of Education
http://www.marin.k12.ca.us/job.html

Market Yourself Services
http://www.webcom.com/nccareer/market/mymain.html

Marketing Science Institute
http://cism.bus.utexas.edu/ravi/marketing_science.html

Marksman InterStaff (Israel)
http://www.marksman.co.il/

Marlborough Group (Ireland) <The>
http://ireland.iol.ie/resource/margroup/

Marr Group <The>
http://www.marrgroup.com

MAS-JOBS
http://www.mas-jobs.com/

Massachusetts Internet Job Bank, Department of Employment and Training
http://www.magnet.state.ma.us/

Masterclass (UK)
http://194.128.198.201/masterclass/

Materials Research Society
http://dns.mrs.org/awards/fellowship.html

Mathcor
http://ourworld.compuserve.com/homepages/Mathcor

Mathematical Association of America
http://www.maa.org/pubs/focus/employ.html

Mathematics Job Market
http://www.cs.dartmouth.edu/~gdavis/policy/jobmarket.html

Matrix Medical Resources
http://www.jrwaters.com/matrix/

Matrix Resources, Inc.
http://www.matrixres.com/

Maui News <The>
http://www.maui.net/

Mayo Clinic Online Career Center
http://www.mayo.edu/career/career.html

MBA Employment Connection Association
http://www.MBAnetwork.com/meca

MBA Job Net, MBA Search!
http://www.mbasearch.com/index.htm

McBride and Associates Computer Placement Professionals
http://www.pacificrim.net/~andrew/

McCormick Search Executive Search and Recruitment
http://www.xnet.com/~itopport

McCoy Ltd.
http://www.mccoy.com/index.html
http://www.netview.com/mccoy/

McGregor Boyall Associates (UK)
http://www.mcgregor-boyall.co.uk/

Med Nexus
http://www.mednexus.com

Medconnect's Interactive Jobs Line
http://www.medconnect.com/home-job.htm

Medianet (UK)
http://www.pavilion.co.uk/medianet/jobs/jobs.htm

Medical Library Association
http://www.kumc.edu/MLA/career.html

Medical Therapy Jobs
gopher://gopher.gate.net/11/

Medical Transcription Resources Health Information Management (HIM)
http://www.wwma.com/

Medicine Wheel <The>
http://www.ids.net/medwheel/career.html

MediStaff, A division of Worldwide Staffing
http://www.medistaff.com

MEDJOB
http://www.MEDJOB.com/

MedMarket
http://www.medmarket.com/employ/empall.html

MedSearch
http://www.medsearch.com

MedWeb
http://www.jen.emory.edu/medweb/medweb.jobs.html

MetroPages Worcester
http://www.metropages.com

Metropolitan Government of Nashville and Davidson County
http://www.nashville.org/job_opportunities.html

Metroworld
http://www.metroworld.com

MHC Consulting Services Ltd (UK)
http://www.lds.co.uk/mhc/

Michael Page On-Line Career Brochure
http://taps.com/broch/Michael_Page/salesmkt.htm

Microsoft Network
http://www.microsoft.com

MicroTemps
http://microtemps.com/

Midwest Computer Consultants Ltd (UK)
http://www.mwcc.com/

Mildura's Employment Opportunities (Australia)
http://www.mildura.net.au/employ/

Milwaukee Journal
http://www.adquest.com/menu.htm

Mindsource Software
http://www.mindsrc.com/reqs_body.html

Minnesota Department of Economic Security, Minnesota Job Bank
http://mn.jobsearch.org/ajb/mn.htm

Minority Online Information Service <The>
http://web.fie.com/web/mol/

Mississippi Careers Online
http://www.webcom.com/whipcomm/mscareer

Missouri, State of, Merit System Job Opportunities
http://www.state.mo.us/oa/pers/jobopps.htm

MIT Sloan School of Management
http://web.mit.edu/cdo/www/

Modeling, Simulation and Training Employment Postings
http://itsc.sc.ist.ucf.edu/jobs.htm

Models Online
http://www.models-online.com

Monroe Systems
http://www.monroe.co.uk/monroe/

Monster Board
http://www.monster.com

Monster Board Australia <The>
http://www.armstrongs.com.au/

Montana Job Service
http://jsd_server.dli.mt.gov/

Morgan & Banks Limited
http://www.morganbanks.com.au

Mother Gopher
gopher://gopher.micro.umn.edu:70

Mt. Holyoke College Internships
gopher://gopher.mtholyoke.edu:2772/11/mhc/internship/

Multi-Avantages, Inc.
http://www.avantage.com/

MultiMedia Wire Classifieds
http://www.mmwire.com:80/classifieds.html
http://www.phillips.com/mmwire

Music Exchange
http://scsn.net/~musex/

Myth Breakers Résumé Service
http://www.mythbreakers.com/resumes.htm

Nando Times
http://www.nando.net

Nanny Jobs, USA
http://www.parentsplace.com/shopping/nanny/jobs

Nano Solutions Associates
http://www.nanosolutions.com

NASA Ames Research Center
http://huminfo.arc.nasa.gov/NASAvacancy.html

Nate's Job Pate
http://www.monash.edu.au/alst6/com/nate/WWW/jobs.html

National Academy of Sciences, National Research Council, Institute of Medicine
http://www.nas.edu/

National Alumni Placement Association
http://www.career.com

National Association for College Admission Counseling
http://www.nacac.com/

National Association of Broadcasters
http://www.nab.org/

National Association of Purchasing Management Silicon Valley, Inc.
http://catalog.com/napmsv/jobs.htm

National Athletic Trainers' Association <The>
http://www.nata.org/

National Computer Board (Singapore)
http://www.ncb.gov.sg/ncb/recruit.html

National Diversity Journalism Job Bank
http://www.newsjobs.com

National Educators Employment Review
http://www.netgrafx.com/neer/default.htm

National Federation of Paralegal Associations
http://www.paralegals.org/

National Information Services and Systems (UK)
http://www.niss.ac.uk/noticeboard/jobs/index.html

National Institute for Nuclear Physics and High-Energy Physics (Netherlands)
http://www.nikhef.nl/

National Institute of Health (NIH) Senior Job Opportunities
http://helix.nih.gov:8001/jobs/

National Multimedia Association of America
http://www.nmaa.org/nmaa/jobbank.htm

National Network for HealthCare Professionals
http://www.treknet.net/hcroaz

National Physician Job Listing Directory
http://www.njnet.com/~embbs/job/jobs.html

National Science Foundation, New Hampshire and Maine Careers Online
gopher://stis.nsf.gov/11/NSF/vacancies

National Skin Centre (Singapore)
http://biomed.nus.sg/nsc/vacancy.html

National Society of Black Engineers
http://www.nsbe.org

National Society of Professional Engineering HP
http://www.nspe.org

National Technical Employment Services
http://iquest.com/~ntes/

National Technology Transfer Center's Job Index
http://iridium.nttc.edu/

National Urban League <The>
http:www.nul.org/

National Writer's Union JobHotline
http:www.nwu.org/nwu/hotline/

NationJob Online Jobs Database
http://www.nationjob.com

NATO's SACLANT Undersea Research Centre (Italy)
http://www.saclantc.nato.int:80/staff/

Nature's International Science Jobs
http://www.nature.com/Nature2/serve?SID=7502384&CAT=Classified&PG=Jobs/jobshome.html

Naval Research Library's Job Link
http://infoweb.nrl.navy.mil/catalogs_and_databases/job/

NavyJobs
http://www.navyjobs.com/

NBJ's Job Journal, The Nashville Business Journal
http://www.newschannel5.com/nbj.html

NCSA, National Center for Supercomputer Applications
http://www.ncsa.uiuc.edu/General/Jobs/00Jobs.html

Nebraska Department of Personnel
http://www.state.ne.us/personnel/per.html

Net Contractor (UK)
http://www.demon.co.uk/syntaxis/contract/home.html

Net-Globe's Job Data Base
http://mail.travel-net.com/

Net-Happenings Archive
http://www.mid.net:80/NET/

Net-Temps
http://www.Net-Temps.com/

Net-Work (Canada)
http://www.onsetmag.com/jobmarket

Netherlands Organization of Scientific Research
http://www.nwo.nl/vacatures

NetJobs
http://www.netjobs.com:8000/

Netlink
http://netlink.wlu.edu:1020/

Netscape
http://www.netscape.com

NetSearch
http://www.ais.net:80/

Network Operations Worldwide (Belgium)
http://www.belgium.eu.net/company/jobs/jobs.html

Network Professional Association (NPA)
http://www.npanet.org/home/index.htm

Network Recruitment Inc.
http://amsquare.com/america/network.html

NetWork Employment Agency
http://www.zoom.com/network/

Networking Jobs in North California
http://www.pcpersonnel.com/

Networking on the Network by Phil Agre, UCSD Department of Communication
http://communication.ucsd.edu/paqre/network.html

NetworkWorld Fusion
http://www.nwfusion.com

NetWorld MarketPlace Career Opportunities
http://www.networldmkt.com/networld/career.htm

New Boston Select (UK)
http://www.selectgroup.com/newboston/

New Dimensions in Technology, Inc.
http://www.ndt.com/users/ndt/index.html

New England Journal of Medicine
http://www.nejm.org/

New Hampshire, State of
http://www.state.nh.us/

New Jersey Jobs
http://www.njjobs.com/

New York State Department of Labor Employment Opportunities
http://www.labor.state.ny.us/dol.htm
http://www.labor.state.ny.us/job.search.html

New York Times
http://www.nytimes.com

NewsLink (AJR NewsLink)
http://www.newslink.org

Newspaper Association of America
http://www.naa.org/

NewsWatcher for Macintosh
ftp.acns.nwu.edu (/pub/newswatcher)

NISS (National Information Services and Systems) Noticeboard
http://www.niss.ac.uk/noticeboard/index.html#jobs

Nonprofit/Fundraising JobNet, Philanthropy Journal of North Carolina <The>
http://www.philanthropy-journal.org/jobnet/jobs.htm

Norfolk Virginian-Pilot
http://www.pilotonline.com/

North American Business Concepts
http://www.digimark.net/NoAm/

North Carolina Career & Employment Resource Center
http://www.webcom.com/~nccareer/

North Carolina Employment Security Commission (NCESC), North Carolina Job Service
http://www.esc.state.nc.us/

North Carolina Information Server
http://www.sips.state.nc.us/

North Carolina, State of
http://www.osp.state.nc.us./OSP/jobs/

Northern Virginia Career Center
http://amsquare.com/america/virginia.html

NPAC Oracle 7
http://asknpac.npac.syr.edu

Nuclear Medical Resonance (NMR) Resources
gopher://micro.ifas.ufl.edu:70/1m/NMR_Information_Server/NMR_Positions

Nursing Career Opportunities
gopher://umabnet.ab.umd.edu/11/

NYC Headhunters' Mall
http://jobs-nyc.com

O-Hayo Sensei
http://www.ohayosensei.com/~ohayo/

Oak Ridge National Laboratory
http://www.ornl.gov

OASYS
http://www.oasysnet.com/home.html

Object People (Australia)
http://www.ozemail.com.au/objectpeople/view.html

Occupational Resources
http://pegasus.adnc.com/~occupational/

Office Specialists
http://www.officespec.com

Ohio State Government Jobs
http://www.odn.ohio.gov/hr/emprec.html
http://www.state.oh.us/

Ohio State University
gopher://gopher.acs.ohio-state.edu/11/Opportunities/
gopher://gopher.acs.ohio-state.edu/11/Opportunities/Job%20Listings

Olivier Recruitment Group
http://www.employment.com.au/olivier/olivier2.html

Olsten Information Technology Staffing
http://olsten.boulder.net:80/olstenskills.html

Omaha CareerLink
http://www.synergy.net/CareerLink/Select.html
http://www.omaha.org/careerlink.html

on-TRAC America
http://www.on-trac.com

One-Way Résumé
http://www2.connectnet.com/users/blorincz

OneWorld Jobs (UK)
http://www.oneworld.org/jobs/index.html

Online Career Center
http://www.occ.com

Online Career Center (Canada)
http://www.etc.bc.ca/provdocs/careers/first_page.html

Online Consultants
http://www.idsonline.com/online/

Online Design
http://www.thesphere.com/OnLine/

Online Employment Service
http://www.spie.org:80/web/employment/employ_home.html

Online Sports Career Center
http://www.onlinesports.com:80/pages/CareerCenter.html

Open Market Commercial Sites Index
http://www.directory.net/

OpenText
http://www.opentext.com/

Operations Research Jobs
http://mat.gsia.cmu.edu/jobs.html

Optical Society of America, Optics Net
http://www.osa.org/

OPTICS.ORG, SPIE Employment
http://optics.org/employment/

OptoLink
http://www.spie.org/web/employment/employ_home.html

Oregon Employment Department
http://www.emp.state.or.us/EMPLSVCS/

Oregon, State of, Job Listings
http://www.state.or.us/
http://www.dashr.state.or.us/jobs/jobhead.html
gopher://gopher.state.or.us.11/.d9.dir

Orient Pacific Century
http://www.mcb.co.uk/apmforum/opc/opc2.htm

OWL—Online Writing Lab, Purdue University
http://owl.trc.purdue.edu/

OzJobs (ACP OnLine)
http://columbia.digiweb.com/~aep1/cgi-bin/jobidx.cgi

P.J. Scout Job Scout by Nation Job Bank
http://www.nationjob.com/pjscout

P.O.P. Jobs
http://www.popjobs.com

Pacific Coast Recruiting
http://www.pacificsearch.com/

Palo Alto Weekly
http://www.service.com/PAW/home.html

Paper Works
http://www.websrus.com/theworks/index.html

Pasco County Schools Jobs
http://www.pasco.k12.fl.us/PascoJobs.html

Passport Access
http://www.passportaccess.com

Patricia Pocock and Associates
http://homepage.interaccess.com/~ppocock2/PPA.html

Paul-Tittle
http://www.careermosaic.com:80/cm/pta/pta1.html

Pemberton & Associates
http://www.biddeford.com/pemberton/

Pennsylvania Careers Online
http://amsquare.com/america/pacareer.html

Pennsylvania, Commonwealth of
http://www.auditorgen.state.pa.us/jobs/

Personal Services
http://www.presidio-jobs.com/

Personalberatung Geest (Germany)
http://members.aol.com/pbgeest/index.htm

Personalized News Service
http://personal.infoseek.com

Personnel Select
http://www.pselect.com

Personnel Services Group <The>
http://www.ctn.on.ca/psg/

Peterson's Education Center: Careers & Jobs
http://www.petersons.com/career/

Pharmacy Week Jobs Listing, PharmInfoNet
http://pharminfo.com/pharmmall/PharmWeek/pharmweek.html

Philadelphia Online Classifieds
http://www.phillynews.com/ads

Photofinishing Stores
http://www.kodak.com/ciHome/imageMagic/pictureDisk/
http://www.floppyshots.com/

PhotoForum's Photo/Imaging Jobs
http://www.rit.edu/~andpph/jobs.html

Physician Recruiting & Employment Panther Enterprises
http://www.seanet.com/~panther/

Physician RecruitNet
http://www.physiciannet.com/

Physician Search Consultants
http://www.drsearch.com

Physicians Employment
http://www.fairfield.com/physemp/index.html
http://www.physemp.com

Physics Careers Bulletin Board
http://www.aip.org/aip/careers/careers.html

Physics Job Announcements by thread, NASA
http://XXX.lanl.gov/Announce/Jobs/

Physics Job Vacancies
http://www.physics.ox.ac.uk/jobs-index.html

Physics Jobs On-Line
http://www.tp.umu.se/TIPTOP/FORUM/JOBS/

Physics World Jobs Online
http://www.iop.org/cgi.bin/Jobs/main

Pinnacle Health Group
http://www.phg.com

Placement Solutions
http://www.execpc.com/~msshort/index.html

Plaxel
http://www.gol.com/plaxel/

Poly-Links-Job Bank
http://www.polymers.com/
http://www.polymers.com/polylink/jobank.html

PolySort Classifieds
http://www.polysort.com/classifieds/help_wanted.htm

Portfolio
http://www.portfolio.skill.com/

Positions in Bioscience and Medicine, Hum-Molgen Bioscience and Medicine (Germany)
http://www.informatik.uni-rostock.de/HUM-MOLGEN/anno/position.html

Post A Job
http://www.postajob.com

Potpourri Classified's
http://www.netview.com/pp/employ

Poultry Science Association
http://gallus.tamu.edu/1h/psa/psaplacement.html

Precision Machined Products Association
http://www.pmpa.org/car/career.htm

Premier Staff
http://www.webscope.com/premier/info.html

Premier Staffing
http://www.premier-staff.com

Price Jamieson
http://www.pricejam.com

Prime Recruitment (UK)
http://www.tcp.co.uk/~primerec/

Princeton College Review
http://www.review.com/index.html-ssi

Princeton1Info.com
http://www.princeton1info.com

Prism Group (Recruiting) <The>
http://www.theprismgroup.com

Pro Med National Staffing of Wichita Falls
http://www.wf.net/~promed

Proactive Executive Search
http://www.icon-stl.net/~proact

Prodigy
http://www.prodigy.net

ProEd World Wide Clearinghouse
http://www.proed.com/ch/

Professional and Student Journalism Organizations
http://www.journalism.sfsu.edu/www/orgs/orgs.htm

Professional Association of Résumé Writers Membership List
http://PARW.com

Professional Computer Consultants Group Ltd.
http://infoweb.magi.com/~procom/

Professional Information for Mathematicians
http://www.ams.org/committee/profession/

Professionals <The>
http://www.theprofessionals.com

Professionals On Line/Employment and Recruitment
http://www.wordsimages.com/emp_rec.htm

Profil d.o.o. (Slovenia)
http://www.profil.si/profile.html

Profiles (Belgium)
http://www.nomad.be/profiles/

Project Connect
http://careers.soemadison.wisc.edu/projcon.htm

ProNet Search
http://bisinc.com/pronet/

ProQuest
http://www.onramp.net/proquest

Prospective Management Overseas (Belgium)
http://www.pmo.be/home.htm

Prospectus Computer (UK)
http://www.prospectus.co.uk/prospectus/

Prosper Wales, PROSPER WALES (UK)
http://prosper.swan.ac.uk/bin/web/

ProType, Ltd.
http://members.aol.com/criscito

Provident Search Group
http://www.dpjobs.com/

Public Register's Annual Report Service (PRARS)
http://wwwprars.com

Publicly Accessible Mailing Lists (PAML)
http://www.neosoft.com/internet/paml/

Purdue University Internet Sites for Job Seekers and Employers
http://www.purdue.edu/UPS/Student/jobsites.htm

Purdue University SSINFO Gopher
gopher://oasis.cc.purdue.edu:2525/11/employ-info

Pursuitnet Jobs, PursuitNet
http://www.tiac.net/users/jobs/index.html

QCC Associates' Job Search Page
http://www.cnj.digex.net/~qcc/

Quantum Consultancy Services (UK)
http://www.quantum-cs.co.uk/

Quay Partners International
http://www.quaypartners.com/

Quest Systems
http://www.questsyst.com

R&R Associates
http://pages.prodigy.com/proposal/resume.htm

Radiation Biology Job Board
http://www.science.ubc.ca/departments/physics/radbio/jobs.html

Radiology Jobs
http://www.rad.washington.edu/Positions.html

RAI: The Executive Search Firm
http://www.raijobs.com/

Ramsey County (Minnesota)
http://www.co.ramsey.mn.us/Pers/hrjobs.htm

Re-Employment 2000
http://www.inetbiz.com/re-employment2000/

REAL JOBS
http://www.real-jobs.com/

Realtor.com
http://www.realtor.com/

Recruit Guide on the Net (Japan)
http://job.rnet.or.jp/RG/index-j-s.html

Recruit PLC (UK)
http://www.newdawn.co.uk/recruit/

Recruiters
http://www.onramp.net/ron/

Recruiters Network
http://www.xs4all.nl~avotek

Recruiters Online Network
http://www.onramp.net/ron http://www.ipa.com

RecruitEx
http://www.recruitex.com/launch96/11home.htm

Recruiting-Links
http://www.recruiting-links.com

Recruiting Services, Inc.
http://www.careerex.com/rsi/index.html

Red Guide to Temp Agencies <The>
http://www.best.com/~ezy/redguide.html

Reed Personnel Services
http://www.reed.co.uk/

Reference.Com
http://www.reference.com

Rensselaer Career Development Center, Optical Science Center, University of Arizona
http://www.rpi.edu/dept/cdc

Resources for Asia
http://www.asia-inc.com/aid/index.html

Resucom, Résumé Canada (Canada)
http://www.bconnex.net/~resume/frame3.htm

Résumé Hut <The>
http://www.islandnet.com/penlan

Résumé Reservoir
http://www.resume.i1.com

Résumé Maker
http://www.iguide.com/work_mny/resume/rmaker.htm

Résumé Management—21st Century
http://amsquare.com/america/amerway/res21ndx.html

Résumé Publishing Company
http://www.csn.net

Résumé Solution
http://tribeca.ios.com/~Dave2

RésuméPosters
http://wons.com/resumeposters/index.html

Résumés in a Flash
http://www.northcoast.com/unlimited/services_listing/resflash/resflash.html

Résumés on the Web
http://www.resweb.com

RésuméWeb
http://www.netclub.com/resume/resume.htm

RésuméXPRESS!
http://ResumeXPRESS.com

Résumé'Net
http://www.resumenet.com/main.html

RGA International's Job Listings
http://www.rga-joblink.com/docs/joblist.html

RH-Online (Brazil)
http://www.bhvirtual.com/rhol/

RiceInfo
http://riceinfo.rice.edu/Internet/subject.html

Richard Wheeler Associates (UK)
http://www.hiway.co.uk/rwa/

RIDET, Rhode Island Department of Employment and Training
http://det2.det.state.ri.us/

Right of Way
http://www.rightofway.com/

Riley Guide
http://www.jobtrak.com/jobguide/

Rimpac Systems (UK)
http://194.128.198.201/rimpac/

RJ Pascale & Company
http://www.ct-jobs.com/pascale/

Roanoke Times Online
http://www.roanoke.com/index.html

Roevin Management Services, Ltd.
http://194.128.198.201/roevin/

Rollins Search Group
http://www.rollinssearch.com/

Roy Talman & Associates
http://www.roy-talman.com/

Royal Air Force (UK)
http://www.open.gov.uk/raf/rafhome.htm

Royal Navy (UK)
http://www.royal-navy.mod.uk/home1.htm

Royal Society of Chemistry (UK)
http://chemistry.rsc.org/rsc/jobs3.htm

RPh on the Go USA
http://www.interaccess.com/rph

RPI Career Resources
http://www.rpi.edu/dept/cdc/

RS/6000 ; Jobs
http://www.s6000.com/job.html

RSI Résumé and Job Information
http://rsi.cee.org/jobs.html

Russian and East European Institute Employment Opportunities, Indiana University
http://www.indiana.edu/~reeiweb/indemp.html

RWH
http://www.figment.net/rwh/

Saber Consultants
http://www.saberedge.com/

Sally Silver Incorporated
http://www.sallysilver.com/

Saludos Web: Careers, Employment & Culture
http://www.hooked.net:80/saludos/index.html
http://www.wenet.net/saludos/

San Francisco Bay Area Web Guide
http://www.hyperion.com/ba/sfbay.html

San Francisco Chronicle and Examiner, Classified Gateway
http://www.sfgate.com/classifieds/sunday/Job-Opportunities.html

San Francisco Unified School District
http://nisus.sfusd.k12.ca.us/

San Jose Mercury
http://www.sjmercury.com/class

Sanford Rose Associates
http://www.sanfordrose.com/

Santa Clara County Office of Education
http://www.sccoe.k12.ca.us/eo.html

Scholarly Societies Project
http://www.lib.uwaterloo.ca/society/overview.html

Schulenburg & Associates
http://www.vnet.net/neil

SciComp Job List
http://scicomp.math.uni-augsburg.de/scicomp/gsci/jobs/jobs.html

Science Classifieds
http://recruit.sciencemag.org/

Science Global Career Network, Science JobNet, American Association for the Advancement of Science
http://www.science-mag.aaas.org:888/science/scripts/recruit/search
http://www.aaas.org
http://science-mag.aaas.org/science/
http://www.sciencemag.org/science/feature/classified/search.html
http://www.edoc.com/sgcn/Lineads.html

Scientist (Electronic Journal)
ftp://ds.internic.net/pub/the-scientist
gopher://ds.internic.net/1/pub/the-scientist

Seamless Web's Legal Job Center <The>
http://www.seamless.com/jobs/

Search Engines Indexes
http://sunsite.berkeley.edu/Help/searchdetails.html
http://www.bubl.bath.ac.uk/BUBL/IWinship.html
http://cuiwww.unige.ch/meta-index.html
http://www.albany.net/allinone/
http://home.mcom.com/home/internet-search.html
http://home.mcom.com/escapes/search/global_search.html

Seattle Times
http://www.seatimes.com/classified/

SecurSEARCH (Canada)
http://www.acs.ca/job.htm

SelectCandidate Career Network
http://www.eagleview.com

Selection, recruiting of Latvian seamon
http://www.unitree.lv/~sms/

Senior Design Corporation
http://www.cts.com/browse/sdc/

Seniors On-Line Job Bank
http://www.seniorsnet.com/jobbank.htm

SenseMedia Job Board
http://sensemedia.net/getajob/

Setka Computer Consulting
http://www.setka.com/

Shawn's Internet Résumé Center
http://www.inpursuit.com/sirc/seeker.html

SIAM News Professional Opportunities
gopher://gopher.siam.org/11/siamnews/profops

SiamJOB (Thailand)
http://www.siam.net/jobs/

SIFT—Stanford Information Filtering Tool
http://hotpage.stanford.edu/

Silicon Alley Connections, LLC
http://www.salley.com

Singapore Online
http://www.singapore.com/jobs.htm

SK Writers
http://www.skwriters.com/

Skandinavisk Computer Rekruttering
http://www.scrwest.dk/indexuk.htm

Skill Search
http://www.internet-is.com/skillsearch/index.html

SkillBANK
http://www.lapis.com/skillbank/

Snelling Personnel Services
http://www.snelling.com/cgi-bin/home.pl

SnellingSearch
http://www.snellingsearch.com

Social Work and Social Services Jobs
http://www.gwbssw.wustl.edu/~gwbhome/jobs/swjobs.html

Society for Advancement of Chicanos and Native Americans in Science (SACNAS)
http://vflylab.calstatela.edu/sacnas/www/Otherhtml/Employment/jobs.html
http://xerxes.nas.edu:70/1/cwse/SACNAS.html

Society for Cinema Studies
http://www.sa.ua.edu/TCF/teach/employ/scsjob.htm

Society for Experimental Mechanics
http://www.sem.bethel.ct.us/sem/jobs/jobs.html

Society for Human Resource Management NJ State Council
http://www.njshrm.com/hr/
http://www.shrm.org/

Society for Industrial and Applied Mathematics (SIAM)
http://www.siam.org/profops/profops.htm

Society for Technical Communication
http://stc.org/

Society of Competitive Intelligence Professionals (SCIP)
http://www.scip.org/

Society of Hispanic Professional Engineers
http://xerxes.nas.edu:70/1/cwse/SHPE.html

Society of Mexican American Engineers and Scientists
http://xerxes.nas.edu:70/1/cwse/MAES.html

Society of Professional Journalists
http://town.hall.org/places/spj/

Society of Women Engineers
http://www.swe.org

Softskill
http://www.indigo.ie/softskill

Software AG Community
http://www.nauticom.net/users/sferrell/sagjobs.html

Software Consulting Services
http://nscs.fast.net/jobs.html

Software Contractors' Guild <The>
http://www.scguild.com/

Software Jobs Homepage
http://clever.net/swjobs/

Software Personnel
http://www.jobserve.com/sp

Solutions for the Human Resources Manager
http://www.in.net/careers

Source One Data Processing
http://www.career1.com

Source Services
http://www.primenet.com/~sors/

South Australian Department for Employment, Training and Further Education
http://dino.tafe.sa.edu.au/

South Carolina Job Opportunities
http://www.state.sc.us/jobopps.html

South Dakota Bureau of Personnel Job Openings
http://www.state.sd.us/state/executive/bop/

South Dakota's Job Bank Job Search, South Dakota Job Service
http://sd.jobsearch.org/

South Oregon
http://www2.vertexgroup.com/soredi/

Southeastern Conference on Linguistics (SECOL)
http://www.msstate.edu/Org/SECOL/

Southeastern Software Association (SSA)
http://www.sesoft.org/news/joblink.html

Southern Connecticut State University Library
http://www.scsu-cs.ctstateu.edu/library/careerpage.html

Southern Utah Job Listing
http://www.sci.dixie.edu/JobService/JobService.html

Span Consultancy <The>
http://www.span-consultancy.co.uk/contact.html

Special Libraries Association (SLA)
http://www.indiana.edu/~slajob/

Spectra International, Inc.
http://www.indirect.com/www/spectra/

Spectrum Concepts Consulting
http://www.sconcepts.com/

Spiderline
http://www.spiderline.com

Sports Medicine Online
http://www.sports-med.com/

SPTimes
http://www.sptimes.com

St. Louis Area Companies on the Net
http://www.st-louis.mo.us/st-louis/companies.html

St. Thomas CEC Job Opportunities Page
http://ein.ccia.st-thomas.on.ca/agencies/cec/jobs/jobbank.html

Staffing Options & Solutions
http://iypn.com/staffing

Staffing Services Online
http://www.staffingservices.com/

Stanford Associates (UK)
http://194.128.198.201/stanford/

Stanford Linear Accelerator Center, Stanford, CA
http://www.slac.stanford.edu:5080/emp/emp-opp/emp-opp.html

Stanley, Barber & Associates
http://www.stanleyb.com

Starting Point
http://www.stpt.com

Starting Point: Professional
http://www.stpt.com/profe.html

State and Local Government on the NET
http://www.piperinfo.com/piper/state/states.html

State of Ohio
gopher://gizmo.freenet.columbus.oh.us:70/11/governmentcenter/
stateofohio
http://www.ohio.gov

STEPS GmbH Personalberatung (Germany)
http://www.steps.de/

Steven Douglas Associates
http://www.web-site1.com/sdassoc/

Student Search System
http://www.studentsearch.com

StudentCenter LLC
http://www.studentcenter.com

Summer Jobs, Summer Jobs World Wide
http://www.summerjobs.com/

Sunday Paper <The>
http://www.sundaypaper.com

Sunrise Press
http://www.garlic.com/vplex/sunrise

Superior Résumés
http://www.mindtrust.com

Supermarket News
http://www.supermarketnews.com

Sykes Enterprises
http://www.sykes.com

Synergistech Communications
http://www.synergistech.com

Syntax Consultancy Limited (UK)
http://www.syntaxco.co.uk/xmas/syntaxco.htm

Syracuse Sunday Herald American, Syracuse Online
http://www.syracuse.com

Syracuse University, NY
http://www.syr.edu/WWW-Syr/HumanResources/JobOppsatS
U/index.html
gopher://cwis.syr.edu/11/employment

Systems Network
http://www.SystemsNet.com/

Tables on the Web
http://www.ncsa.uiuc.edu:80/SDG/Software/Mosaic/Tables/

Tacoma News Tribune
http://www.tribnet.com

Talent Network
http://www.talentnet.com/

TalentScout
http://www.sjmercury.com/talentscout/

Talentworks
http://www.talentworks.com

Tech Search Jobsight
http://www.jobsight.com/

Tech Specialists
http://www.techspec.com

Technical Employment Consultants
http://www.tech-employ-consult.com/

Technology Registry
http://techreg.com

TechWeb/TechCareers/TechHunter
http://techweb.com/careers/careers.html.body?
http://www.techweb.com/default.html.body?

TED, The Training and Employment Database, Massachusetts
Department of Employment and Training
http://ma.jobsearch.org

Telecommuting Jobs
http://www.tjobs.com

TeleJob
http://ezinfo.ethz.ch/ETH/TELEJOB/tjb_home_e.html

Telnet Sites
http://www.magna.com.au/bdgtti/bdg_92.html#SEC95
http://www.nova.edu/Inter-Links/start.html
http://galaxy.einet.net/hytelnet/HYTELNET.html
http://library.usask.ca/hytelnet/
gopher://marvel.loc.gov/ (Select: Internet Resources and then
HYTELNET)

TenKey Interactive
http://www.careershop.com

TESLJB-L, Teaching English as a Foreign Language
gopher://CUNYVM.CUNY.EDU/11/Subject%20Specific%20G
ophers/teslfl/Teaching%20English%20as%20a%20Foreign%2
0Language%20%20The%20Profession

Texas Education Agency
http://www.tea.texas.gov

Texas Employment Commission
http://www.twc.state.tx.us/

Texas Marketplace
http://www.texas-one.org

Texas State Government
http://www.texas.gov/

Therapy Resource Network
http://www.access.digex.net/~david/pt.html

Thomas Register of American Manufacturers
http://www.thomasregister.com/

Times Higher Education Supplement InterView
http://www.timeshigher.newsint.co.uk/mainmenu.html

TKO Personnel, Inc.
http://www.tkointl.com

Top Jobs on the Net
http://www.topjobs.co.uk/intel/intel.htm

Tradewave Galaxy
http://galaxy.tradewave.com/

Training and Development Job Mart, T&D Business Showcase
http://www.tcm.com/trdev/jobs/jobs.htm

TrainingNet
http://www.trainingnet.com/

Transaction Information Systems
http://www.tisny.com/jobs/jobs.htm

Truck Drivers Job Directory
http://www.bcl.net/~padgett/truckers.cgi

Trumpet for DOS
ftp://oak.oakland.edu

TSG Professional Services, Inc.
http://www.tsgpro.com/

TV JobNet
http://www.tvjobnet.com/

U.S. Dept of Agriculture Cooperative Extension
gopher://sulaco.oes.orst.edu/11/ext/jobs

U.S. Fish & Wildlife Service
http://www.fws.gov/employmt.html

University of California, Berkeley, Work Study Home Page
http://workstudy.Berkeley.edu

University of Colorado, Boulder
gopher://gopher.Colorado.EDU/
select Other Gophers by Subject—select Employment Opportunities and Résumé Postings

University of Florida Department of Statistics
http://www.stat.ufl.edu/vlib/jobs

University of Minnesota Internships
gopher://next1.mrs.umn.edu/11/Student%20Services/Career%20Center/Internships/

University of Minnesota's College of Education Job Search Bulletin Board
gopher://rodent.cis.umn.edu:11119/

University of Penn Career Services
http://www.upenn.edu/CPPS

University of Virginia Externships
http://www.virginia.edu/~career/exinfo.html

University of Virginia Internship Services
http://www.virginia.edu/~career/

Usenet FAQs
http://www.cis.ohio-state.edu/hypertext/faq/usenet/FAQ-List.html

Usenet Newsstand
http://CriticalMass.com/Concord

Usjobnet K-12
http://www.usjobnet.com/

Utah Department of Employment Security Job Service
http://udesb.state.ut.us/jobs/

UTRC, United Technologies Research Center
http://utrcwww.utc.com/UTRC/Jobs/Jobs.html

UTV T.V. Job Classifieds
http://tvnet.kspace.com/jobs/

Van Zoelen Recruitment
http://www.vz-recruitment.nl

Vermont Department of Employment and Training
http://www.state.vt.us/det/dethp.htm

Veronica
gopher://liberty.uc.wlu.edu

Victoria Freenet Association (Employment Resources)
gopher://freenet.victoria.bc.ca/11/business

VideoPro Classifieds
http://www.txdirect.net:80/videopro/adv.htm

Virginia Coast Reserve Information System (VCRIS) (Job Listings)
http://atlantic.evsc.virginia.edu/
gopher://atlantic.evsc.Virginia.EDU/11/Opportunities

Virginia, Commonwealth of
http://va.jobsearch.org/

Virginian Pilot Online
http://www.infi.net/~pilot/

Virtual Headbook
http://www.xmission.com:80/~wintrnx/vh/virtual.html

Virtual Job Fair
http://www.careerexpop.com

Virtual Press <The>
http://www.aloha.com/~william/jnews.html

VirtualRésumé
http://www.virtualresume.com/vitae

VISTA Web
http://libertynet.org/~zelson/section1.html

VJ Enterprises
http://www.vjenterprises.com

W3catalog
http://cuiwww.unige.ch/cgi-bin/w3catalog

WAIS
gopher://liberty.uc.wlu.edu

Wang & Li Asia Resources
http://www.wang-li.com

Washington (Metro) (DC) Council of Governments
http://www.mwcog.org/mwcog/geninfo/jobs.html

Washington Employment Web Pages
http://members.aol.com/gwattier/washjob.htm

Washington Post
http://www.washingtonpost.com

Washington State Department of Personnel
http://www.wa.gov/dop/home.html

Washington State Information Exchange
http://olympus.dis.wa.gov

WDVL: Jobs for Web Developers <The>
http://www.stars.com/jobs/

Web 66 CookBook
http://web66.coled.umn.edu/Cookbook

Web Announcement Services
http://www.submit-it.com
http://www.netcreations.com/postmaster/
http://www.iTools.com/promote-it/promote-it.html
http://www.mmgco.com/top100.html
http://galaxy.einet.net/galaxy/Community/Workplace.html
http://www.yahoo.com/Computers_and_Internet/Internet/World_Wide_Web/Announcement_Services/

Web Dog's Job Hunt
http://www.itec.sfsu.edu/jobs/

WebCrawler
http://www.webcrawler.com

Welcome to the UKdirectory
http://www.ukdirectory.com/employ/employ.htm

West Bend Community Career Network
http://156.46.110.2/

Westech Career Expos, WESTECH Career EXPO
http://www.vjf.com/pub/westech/

Whitehouse Fellowships
http://www.whitehouse.gov/WH/WH_Fellows/html/fellows1-plain.html

Whole Internet Catalogue
http://www.gnn.com

Wide World Web Employment Office
http://www.harbornet.com/biz/office/annex.html

Wildlife & Fisheries Employment
http://wfscnet.tamu.edu/jobs.html

Winning Résumés
http://pages.prodigy.com/FL/mike3/mike5.html

Winter, Wyman, and Co. Employment InfoCenter
http://www.winterwyman.com/wwcsjobs.htm

WinWay Corporation
http://www.winway.com

Wisconsin JobNet, Department of Industry, Labor, and Human Relations
http://danenet.wicip.org/jets/

Wisconsin, State of
http://www.state.wi.us/

WITI Campus
http://www.witi.com

Women in Computer Science & Engineering
http://www.ai.mit.edu/people/ellens/gender.html

Women in Higher Education Career Page
http://www.itis.com/wihe/

Women in Technology
http://www-personal.ksu.edu/~dangle

Women in Technology Directory
http://www.sdsu.edu/wit

Woods Hole Oceanographic Institution
gopher://pearl.whoi.edu/11/education-employment

WorkWeb
http://www.work-web.com/

World Job Seekers
http://cban.worldgate.edmonton.ab.ca.resume/index.html

World Wide Job Seekers
http://www.cban.com/resume/

World Wide Résumé/Talent Bank
http://www.webcom.com/~career/hwusa.html

World Wide Web Consortium
http://www10.w3.org/hypertext/WWW/

World.Hire
http://www.world.hire.com

WorldNet Communications Corporation
http://www.legnetwork.com

Wyoming Employment Resources, Wyoming Job Bank
http://wyjobs.state.wy.us/

Wyoming Personnel Management Division
gopher://ferret.state.wy.us/11/wgov/eb/osd/adm/ead

Yahoo
http://www.yahoo.com

Yahoo's Listings of Employment Information
http://www.yahoo.com/business/employment/jobs

Yellow Pages
http://www.whowhere.com/
http://superpages.gte.net/
http://yp.uswest.com

YSN Jobs Page (Young Scientists Network), Jobs Listings Archive
http://www.physics.uiuc.edu/ysn/

Zeitech
http://www.zeitech.com

Index

A

Abbreviations, 15
Accomplishments, 14
Account Executive
    sample résumé, 56, 61
Account Representative
    sample résumé, 69
Achievements, 83
Acronyms, 15
Actor
    home page, 251
Adams JobBank Online, 157
Address, 50
Advertising Account Executive
    sample résumé, 61
Affiliations, 16
AltaVista, 268
Alumni associations, 274
America Online, 230, 236
Animator
    home page, 251
Annual reports
    company, 273
Antivirus, 281
Applicant tracking system, 31, 37, 40,
    42, 98, 122, 151, 281, 285
Archie, 272
ARPAnet, 99, 281
Article, 281
Artist
    home page, 251
ASCII text file, 3, 20, 21, 28, 82, 83, 98,
    286
Assembler III
    sample résumé, 57
Asset Specialist
    sample résumé, 85
Assistant Manager
    sample résumé, 61, 89
Assistant Project Manager
    sample résumé, 71
Assistant to the Deputy Chief of Staff for
    Logistics
    sample résumé, 70
Assistant to the Program Manager
    sample résumé, 24

Associate Director of Sales
    sample résumé, 64
Associate General Manager
    sample résumé, 59
Associations, 152–156, 274
Atmospheric Propagation Engineer
    sample résumé, 23
Attorney
    sample résumé, 26

B

Backbone, 100
Baud, 281
BBS (see bulletin board service)
Binary files, 37, 97
Bookmarks, 102
Boolean logic, 267, 281
Boxes, 53
Browser, 101, 282
Bulletin board service
    definition of, 235, 281
    how to find, 235
    lists of, 237–249
Bullets, 53, 82
Business Manager
    keywords, 32
    sample résumé, 8
Business Operations Specialist
    keywords, 33
Byte, 282

C

Cable modems, 80
Camps, 161
Captain/Firefighter
    sample résumé, 63
Career analysis, 230
Career counseling, 159, 230
Career resources library, 230
Career service centers, 274–279
CareerMosaic, 158
CareerPath, 158
Cartoonist
    home page, 251
CD-ROM, 282
CEOs, 161

Certifications, 16
Certified Banyan Engineer
    sample résumé, 24
Charge Nurse
    sample résumé, 66
Chief Engineer, Electrical Power and
    Communications System
    sample résumé, 23
Chief, Computer Hardware Services Division
    sion
    sample résumé, 24
Chief, Computer Network Control Center
    sample résumé, 23
Clean Room Facilitator
    sample résumé, 57
Client, 282
Clinical Speech-Language Pathologist
    sample résumé, 67
College
    resources, 274
College career center, 159
College connection, 158
Columns, 53
Commercial online service, 80, 229, 282
Company
    Fortune 1000, 42–47
    high tech, 42
    home pages, 121–151
    Internet sites, 123
    job postings, 151
    profiles, 17, 121, 161, 230, 233
    research, 273
    that scan résumés, 10
CompuServe, 231
Computer, 79
Computer Electronics
    sample résumé, 68
Confidentiality, 78
Consultant
    sample résumé, 24, 70
Contract Flight Instructor
    sample résumé, 70
Contracts Manager
    sample résumé, 71
Cook
    sample résumé, 7
Corporate Finance
    sample résumé, 85
Corporate Instructor
    sample résumé, 6
Counter
    home page, 258

Cover letter, 38, 230
Creativity, 5, 251
Critical Care Nurse
    sample résumé, 66
Cruise ships, 161
Customer Service
    sample résumé, 7
Cyberspace, 99, 282

D

Database, 282
Dates, 13
Deja News, 113, 268
Delphi, 232
Deputy Base Commander
    sample résumé, 70
Digest, 282
Director of Sales
    sample résumé, 64
Director of Supply
    sample résumé, 70
Directory, 267
Discrimination, 4
Distributed hypermedia, 101
Domains, 73, 74, 282
    newsgroups, 105
DOS, 282
Dot leaders, 53
Download, 282
Driver/Engineer
    sample résumé, 63

E

E-mail, 39, 73, 80, 90, 94, 283
    addresses, 73, 76, 77, 81, 82
    confidentiality, 78
    returned, 77
E-mailable résumé, 73
    advantages of, 3
    definition of, 3
E-Span, 159, 230, 231, 233
Education, 12
    college, 12
    continuing, 12
    high school, 12
    technical school, 12
Electrical Engineer
    sample résumé, 23
Electronic form, 38
Electronic résumé, 282

advantages of, 10
kinds of, 2
purpose of, 1
Electronic Technician
sample résumé, 60
Electronics Specialist
sample résumé, 68
Em-dashes, 82
En-dashes, 82
Encryption, 283
Engineers, 232
Entrepreneur
sample résumé, 59
Entrepreneurs, 161
Entry-level jobs, 161, 274
ERIC (Educational Research Information
Catalog), 268
Excite, 269
Executives, 161

F

FAQs, 107, 283
Faxed résumés, 2, 39
Field Engineer
sample résumé, 25
Field Supervisor/Crew Chief
sample résumé, 63
Figure Skating Professional
sample résumé, 64
File transfer protocol, 97, 283
Film
conversion to graphic file, 258
Financial Advisor
sample résumé, 71
Financial Analyst
keywords, 32
Fine Arts Major
sample résumé, 7
Fire Chief
sample résumé, 63
Fire Code Inspector
sample résumé, 63
Firefighter
sample résumé, 63
Floor Supervisor
sample résumé, 71
Folding, 55
Fonts, 38, 49–52
home page, 253
Forecasts, 231

Foreign accents, 53
Fortune 1000 companies, 42–47
Forum, 283
Franchisee, 161
Frequently asked questions, 107
ftp, 97, 283

G

Gateway, 100, 283
General Manager
sample résumé, 59
GEnie, 232
GIF files, 258, 283
Gophers, 271–273
Graphics Designer
home page, 251

H

Head Figure Skating Coach
sample résumé, 65
Headlines
HTML, 252
Health care profession, 160, 161, 232
Help Wanted—USA, 230
Home page, 4, 251, 283
background, 254
color, 254
company, 121–151
counter, 258
disadvantages of, 4
design, 253
fonts, 253
graphics, 254, 255, 258–260
headlines, 253
hot buttons, 254
italics, 253
link colors, 254
links, 255
META tag, 264
multimedia, 4, 251, 258, 284
newsgroups, 264
photograph, 258
search engines, 263
sound files, 259, 260
testing, 260
uploading, 260
URL, 263
Hoover's Handbook, 230
HotBot, 269
Hotel Professional
sample résumé, 64

HTML, 251, 252, 283
http, 283
Human resource profession, 158, 161
Hyperlink, 283
Hypermedia, 283
Hypertext, 98, 101, 283
Hypertext Markup Language, 251, 252,
   283

I

Independent Systems Consultant
   sample résumé, 24
Information superhighway, 99, 283
InfoSeek, 269
Interests, 16
International Marketing Specialist
   sample résumé, 89
Internet, 99, 100, 284
   future of, 265
Internet service provider, 80
Internships, 160, 274
Interview, 231, 232
ISDN, 79, 284
Italics, 53

J

Job banks, 121, 151–227, 284
Job descriptions, 13
Job fairs, 158
JobBank, 157
JOBTRAK, 159
JobWeb, 160
JPEG, 258, 284
Jughead, 272
Juris Doctor
   sample résumé, 26

K

kbps, 284
Keyword summary, 17
Keywords, 31, 40
   definition of, 15
   sources for, 13, 16
Kiosk, 39

L

Lawyers, 232
Licenses, 16
Line lengths, 83

Lines
   horizontal, 53
   vertical, 53
Logoff, 284
Logon, 284
Lurking, 106
Lycos, 269

M

Mailer-Daemon, 77
Mailing list, 114–119, 284
   list of, 116–119
   owner, 284
   subscribe, 114
   unsubscribe, 116
Management
   sample résumé, 8
Management Consultant
   sample résumé, 8
Manager
   sample résumé, 64
Manager in Training
   sample résumé, 61
Market Intelligence Manager
   sample résumé, 88
Marketing Coordinator
   sample résumé, 69
Marketing Intern
   sample résumé, 61
Material Controller
   sample résumé, 57
Material Handler
   sample résumé, 57
Mathematical symbols, 82
MedSearch America, 160
META tag, 263
Microsoft Network, 233
Microsoft Word, 21, 82, 84
Misspellings, 52
Model, fashion
   home page, 251
Modem, 79, 284
Monster Board, 160
MS-DOS text (see ASCII text file)
Multimedia résumé (see also home page)
   definition of, 4, 284

N

Name, 49, 50
National Sales Representative
   sample résumé, 60

Native word processing format, 82
Netiquette, 106, 284
Network, computer, 77, 284
    sample résumé, 73
Networking, 106, 231, 266, 273
Newsgroups, 104, 264, 268, 284, 286
    finding, 108
    job-related, 108
Newspapers, 158
NSFnet, 100

O

Objective, 11
Office Manager
    sample résumé, 8
Offline, 285
Online, 285
Online Career Center, 161, 230
OpenText, 270
Operations Manager
    sample résumé, 6
Optical character recognition, 37, 38,
    285
Oversight Asset Specialist
    sample résumé, 85
Owner/Manager
    sample résumé, 56

P

Page length, 54
Paper, 54
    11×17, 55
Parks, 161
Partner
    sample résumé, 27
Password, 285
Photocopies, 55
Photograph, 4, 258
Plant Manager/Production Manager
    sample résumé, 56
Post, 285
Power verbs, 28
Prodigy, 234
Professional associations, 152–156, 274
Profile, 17
    company, 121, 161, 230, 233
Program Manager for Computer Informa-
    tion Systems
    sample résumé, 24
Programmer, 5

Project Manager
    sample résumé, 70
Project Manager Human Resources
    keywords, 33
Project Specialist
    sample résumé, 86
Protocol, 285
Public Speaker
    sample résumé, 58

Q

Qualifications summary, 17, 83
Quality Assurance Inspector
    sample résumé, 57
Queue, 285
Quotes, 82

R

Ranch Hand
    sample résumé, 71
Real Estate Consultant
    sample résumé, 8
Receptionist
    sample résumé, 7, 61
Recreational vehicles, 161
Recruiters, 42, 108, 161, 274
References, 22
Regional Account Manager
    sample résumé, 69
Relevance numbers, 267
Researchers, 274
Resorts, 161
Resources, 252
Restaurant Manager
    sample résumé, 59
Résumé
    design, 5, 49
    length, 31
    posting, 119
    purpose of, 1
    updating, 22
    writing, 11–18
Résumé database (applicant tracking
    system), 31, 37, 40, 42, 98, 122,
    151, 161, 281, 285
Router, 285

S

Sales Manager
    sample résumé, 64

Sales Professional
    sample résumé, 60
Sales Representative
    sample résumé, 56, 61, 88
Sales/Marketing Assistant
    sample résumé, 69
Scannable résumé, 37–42
    definition of, 2
    designing, 49–55
    samples of, 56–71
Scanner, 285
Sculptor
    home page, 251
Search
    concept, 31
    keyword, 31
Search engines, 113, 266–274
    Boolean logic, 267
    listing a home page with, 263
Secretary III
    keywords, 33
Senior Accountant
    keywords, 32
Senior Asset Specialist
    sample résumé, 85
Senior Software Engineer, 34
Senior Staff Information Systems and
        Technology Analyst
    sample résumé, 24
Server, 285
Shareware, 286
Site, 286
Ski resorts, 161
Societies, 152–156, 274
Soft skills
    keywords, 15
Sole Proprietor
    sample résumé, 60
Spamming, 107, 114
Special Markets Manager
    sample résumé, 69
Speech-Language Pathologist
    sample résumé, 67
Spell check, 94
Staff Attorney
    sample résumé, 27
Staff Nurse
    sample résumé, 66
Staff Supply Officer
    sample résumé, 70
Staple, 55

Students, 274
Supply Squadron Commander
    sample résumé, 70
Surfing, 286
SysOp, 286
Systems Administrator
    sample résumé, 60

T
Tags, HTML, 252
TCP/IP, 99, 286
Teacher
    sample résumé, 6
Telecommunications Sales and Marketing
    sample résumé, 69
Telephone line, 79
Telnet, 103, 286
Terminal emulation, 286
Text File (see ASCII text file)
Type style (see fonts)
Typesetting, 18

U
U.S. Air Force
    sample résumé, 70
Underlines, 53
Universal resource locator, 77
University resources, 274–279
Upload, 286
URL, 286
Usenet (see newsgroups)
User name, 73

V
Veronica, 271
Video, 4
Virus, 94, 286
Volunteers, 161

W
WAIS (Wide Area Information Searching),
        272
Walt Disney Management Development
        Program
    sample résumé, 59
WebCrawler, 270
White pages, 81
White space, 53, 82

Windows Notepad, 94
WordPerfect, 21, 82, 83
Workers' Compensation Attorney
    sample résumé, 26
World Wide Résumé Talent Bank, 230
World Wide Web, 99, 101, 286
    private, 102

Y

Yahoo, 270
Yellow Pages, 82

Z

Zoning Inspector
    sample résumé, 63

No One Can Build
Your Writing Skills Better
Than We Can...